# The Growing and Finishing Pig:
# Improving Efficiency

# The Growing and Finishing Pig: Improving Efficiency

*Peter R. English, Vernon R. Fowler,*
*Seaton Baxter, Bill Smith*

FARMING PRESS

*First published 1988*
*Reprinted with alterations 1996*

A catalogue record for this book is available from the British Library
ISBN 0-85236-138-6


**Published by Farming Press**
**Miller Freeman Professional Ltd**
**Wharfedale Road, Ipswich IP1 4LG, United Kingdom**


*Distributed in North America*
*by Diamond Farm Enterprises,*
*Box 537, Alexandria Bay, NY 13607, USA*


Cover design by Mark Beesley
Phototypeset by MHL Typesetting Ltd, Coventry
Printed and bound in Great Britain by Butler & Tanner Ltd, Frome & London

# Contents

# Colour Plates

These are grouped in a section between text pages 240 and 241.

# Text Plates

# Acknowledgements

In a book of this kind it is impossible for the authors to do justice to the inestimable contribution of all those who have contributed to the facts and ideas presented. These include basic and applied scientists in research institutes, universities and commercial companies, pig industry advisers and teachers, veterinarians and, indeed, pig farmers, their managers and their stockmen. To the people in all these sectors with whom we have communicated and whose work we have read we owe an immense debt of thanks.

At a local level we would like to acknowledge the encouragement and help we have had in this work from our colleagues in Aberdeen including Professor Arthur Jones, Professor James Greenhalgh, Dr Malcom Fuller, Mr Gethyn Burgess, Mr Donald Macdonald, Dr Morley Hutchinson, Mr Nigel Feilden, Dr Jim Bruce, Mr Jamie Robertson, Mr Alan Robertson, Mr Bill Robinson, Dr Sandra Edwards, Mr Pinder Gill, Dr Tony Petchey, Dr Mike Baxter, Dr Larry Bark and Mr Keith Hunt. We owe a considerable debt of thanks to pig producers with whom we have integrated closely and who have provided a great deal of stimulus for this work. These include Arthur Simmers of J.A. Simmers & Sons, Forbes Davidson, John Argo, Bob Ritchie, Andrew MacCartney, Douglas Cargill, Jim Gilbert, Chris Shepherd, Sandy Ingram, Gordon McKen, Ian Davidson, Jim Duncan and countless others in the North-East of Scotland, in Britain generally and in many countries overseas who are too numerous to mention individually.

Among other professional colleagues who have been of considerable assistance in the preparation of this book are Dr Tom Hanrahan of the Agricultural Research Institute in Eire and Dr Jeff Owen of the University of Reading. To our very many undergraduate and postgraduate students from both local and from many overseas environments who, by their enquiring minds, by their research and by their interest and enthusiasm have provided us over the years with a great source of motivation and information, we owe a very great deal.

We are most grateful to the many individuals and organisations who supplied photographs for inclusion in the book. The considerable support work provided by Mr Owen MacPherson, Mr Mike Birnie, Mr Steve Kinnaird and Miss Susan Andrews in the Aberdeen School of Agriculture, who helped with the preparation of photographs and in so many other ways, was greatly appreciated. Mrs Morag (Mo) Wilson was responsible for drawing the cover illustration and most of the diagrams. She responded to pressing deadlines in her usual convivial and cooperative way and for this and also for her artistry we are extremely grateful. Penultimately, Mrs Joey Parker, whose great patience never ran out in the prolonged and laborious work of typing the first drafts and whose cooperative spirit, competence and good humour were often much more than we deserved, is due an immense debt of thanks. Finally, to our wives and families who are so often taken for granted and who had to put up with us being posted missing on many occasions, particularly in the last 6 months of feverish activity, we would like to accord much gratitude and admiration for their extreme patience and cheerfulness in the face of considerable provocation!

# Preface

Ever since the publication of the earlier book on 'The Sow: Improving her efficiency' there have been numerous requests for an equivalent book on the subject of the growing and finishing pig. The pressure has come from pig producers, their managers and stockmen, breeders, feed companies, teachers, pig industry consultants and students alike. On the assumption that the demand was real, and encouraged by the publisher, we stepped into the alleged breach and accepted the challenge. It was immediately apparent that the scale of the undertaking was much greater than that for the book on the sow, and that there was a much greater array of material to condense into a readable book. The output of the breeding animal is, at the end of the day, fairly simply evaluated; it is sound, healthy piglets and these can be counted by any numerate person. The output of the growing pig is much more complex, compounded as it is by different markets, grading systems and, indeed, by fads and fashions.

The purpose of the book is to provide the student of pig production, including the technically minded farmer, manager and stockman, with a grasp of the subject at several levels. Although it is not a specialist book in genetics or in nutrition, every effort has been made to present the important technical and scientific issues and support these by reference to relevant scientific work. Although we apologise to our scientific colleagues for having distilled their distinguished work into such a tiny container of passing references, we hope they will bear with us. Our defence is that we only hoped to be able to transmit the flavour and the merest sample of the substance, in the hope that it would satisfy the lesser appetite for detail of the generalists, whilst pointing the specialist, with his greater appetite for detail, in the right direction. There are many books for the specialist but, in our view, few which attempt to encompass the major part of the growing-pig industry in one volume.

The virtue of the multiple authorship is that in addition to our own fields of expertise, we have known and worked with each other for many years. The Aberdeen area in the North-East of Scotland is unique in that there is close proximity and scientific interchange between the University Department of Agriculture, the North of Scotland College of Agriculture, the Centre for Rural Building (previously the Scottish Farm Buildings Investigation Unit), the Rowett Research Institute and the Veterinary Investigation Centre of the Scottish Agricultural Colleges. Although such an array is a formidable force, the undoubted catalyst is the remarkable contact which we have with pioneer farmers in Scotland. Their energy and desire to succeed in difficult circumstances have put pressure on us all to strive harder to make our science more relevant to farmers' needs and indeed to those of the whole pig industry. This thrust, however, is also tempered by our concern for the related but different problems of countries which are still developing their industrial and rural base. It has been our privilege and delight to welcome to Aberdeen students from such countries to undertake research for Master or Doctorate Degrees or to participate in our one year MSc Courses in Pig Production and Animal Nutrition — and also to travel extensively in those countries from which our students have come. The biological problems in pig production between countries may be similar but the technical solutions may be very different.

We hope that this book will be of value to all engaged in pig production, whether academics or practical people with an interest in the technology, and whether from developed pig industries or from new ones.

There is no doubt in our minds that the versatile pig can play a key role in food production in the simple world of peasant economies or in the sophisticated world of high-tech meat production. We hope that our readers will not only respect the pig for its biological and economic attributes, but also as a noble mammal with certain needs which extend beyond just feed and water to the pre-eminent considerations of basic welfare and well-being as a sensitively husbanded animal in our care.

PETER R. ENGLISH
VERNON FOWLER
SEATON BAXTER
BILL SMITH

# The Growing and Finishing Pig:
# Improving Efficiency

undertake research for Master or Doctorate Degrees or to participate in our one year MSc Courses in Pig Production, Animal Production and Animal Nutrition – and also to travel extensively in those countries from which our students have come. The biological problems in pig production between countries may be similar but the technical solutions may be very different.

We hope that this book will be of value to all engaged in pig production, whether academics or practical people with an interest in the technology, and whether from developed pig industries or from new ones.

There is no doubt in our minds that the versatile pig can play a key role in food production in the simple world of peasant economies or in the sophisticated world of high-tech meat production. We hope that our readers will not only respect the pig for its biological and economic attributes, but also as a noble mammal with certain needs which extend beyond just feed and water to the pre-eminent considerations of basic welfare and well-being as a sensitively husbanded animal in our care.


PETER R. ENGLISH
VERNON FOWLER
SEATON BAXTER
BILL SMITH

*Chapter 1*

# Pigmeat Production and Consumption

Domesticated pigs are derived in varying proportions from the wild species *Sus scrofa*, the wild boar of temperate Europe and northern Asia, and *Sus vitatus*, the pot-bellied small black pig of sub-tropical and tropical South-East Asia.

Pigs are kept solely for meat production, while cattle (meat, milk and draft), sheep (meat and wool) and poultry (meat and eggs) can be used for two or more purposes. Domesticated pigs are kept throughout the world under widely varying climatic conditions; they are to be found in very small herds forming an integral part of the rural economy of peasants and in huge herds under intensive, 'industrialised' conditions; their diet may consist in whole or in part of grazing, forages, roots, organic wastes of animal or vegetable origin or concentrates based on cereals and highly digestible protein sources of vegetable or animal origin; pigmeat may be consumed in fresh or cured form or may be processed into a very wide variety of interesting and attractive manufactured products. In other words, the pig is a very versatile and adaptable animal and its meat is highly prized either as a staple source of dietary protein or as a dish for the gastronomic connoisseur.

## THE RELATIVE IMPORTANCE OF PIGMEAT

The importance of pigmeat in world meat supplies derived from the main animals farmed for this purpose is illustrated in Table 1.1, where it can be seen that the

**TABLE 1.1   World production of meat from the most important farm livestock species**

| Species | Production of meat ('000 metric tonnes) |
|---|---|
| Cattle and buffalo | 52,739 |
| Sheep and goats | 9,872 |
| Pigs | 73,891 |
| Horse | 530 |
| Poultry | 46,021 |

(Source: FAO Production Yearbook, 1993)

1

pig is well ahead of cattle and buffalo as the main source of world meat supplies. The most dense populations of pigs are to be found in Europe (including the USSR) and China. This is illustrated in Figure 1.1 and Table 1.2.

\* m indicates millions

FIGURE 1.1   Pig population in different areas of the world (Source: FAO Production Yearbook, 1993).

A measure of the relative importance of pig production in different countries can be gauged from the number of pigs per member of the human population and this is illustrated in Table 1.3.

It can be seen that, per unit of human population, Denmark has by far the highest density of pigs with the aggregate value for Europe and China also being relatively high.

## CONSUMPTION OF PIGMEAT AND OTHER MEATS

Consumption of pigmeat and other meats per head of population for some selected countries is shown in Table 1.4.

Meat consumption is higher in the richer, industrialised nations than in underdeveloped countries. Pigmeat constitutes the highest proportion of total meat consumption in Europe, particularly Eastern Europe, followed by parts of Asia, China and North America.

**TABLE 1.2    Pig population in different countries (thousands)**

| North/Central America | | | |
|---|---|---|---|
| USA | 59,815 | Bulgaria | 2,680 |
| Mexico | 16,832 | Portugal | 2,547 |
| Canada | 10,572 | Sweden | 2,390 |
| Guatemala | 850 | Switzerland | 1,692 |
| Nicaragua | 530 | Finland | 1,309 |
| Honduras | 596 | Greece | 1,040 |
| El Salvador | 325 | Ireland | 1,423 |
| Costa Rica | 224 | Norway | 745 |
| Panama | 287 | **Africa** | |
| **South America** | | Cameroon | 1,434 |
| Brazil | 31,050 | Ghana | 450 |
| Argentina | 2,200 | Madagascar | 1,495 |
| Venezuela | 2,100 | Malawi | 240 |
| Colombia | 2,635 | Nigeria | 6,660 |
| Peru | 2,400 | South Africa | 1,499 |
| Paraguay | 2,915 | Tanzania | 335 |
| Chile | 1,288 | Uganda | 900 |
| Uruguay | 223 | Zaire | 1,130 |
| **Europe** | | Zambia | 293 |
| Ukraine | 16,175 | Zimbabwe | 270 |
| Germany | 26,466 | **Asia** | |
| Poland | 18,860 | China | 393,965 |
| Rumania | 9,852 | Japan | 10,783 |
| Netherlands | 13,709 | India | 10,547 |
| France | 12,564 | Philippines | 7,954 |
| Spain | 18,000 | Thailand | 4,800 |
| Denmark | 10,870 | Taiwan | 3,850 |
| Italy | 8,307 | Korea (Rep. of) | 5,928 |
| Hungary | 5,364 | Singapore | 150 |
| UK | 7,869 | Malaysia | 2,983 |
| Yugoslavia, FR | 4,092 | Hong Kong | 104 |
| Czech Rep. | 4,599 | **Australasia/Oceania** | |
| Belgium + Luxembourg | 6,963 | Australia | 2,646 |
| Austria | 3,720 | New Zealand | 430 |

(Source: FAO Production Yearbook, 1993)

## TRENDS IN CONSUMPTION OF PIGMEAT RELATIVE TO OTHER MEATS IN THE UNITED KINGDOM

In the last few decades, meat consumption in the United Kingdom has been fairly static, although some meats have become less popular and others more so (see Table 1.5 and Figure 1.2). Thus, consumption of beef, bacon and particularly lamb has declined. Pork consumption has increased steadily while poultry meat has shown the most rapid increase in popularity.

## FACTORS LIKELY TO INFLUENCE THE FUTURE DEMAND FOR PIGMEAT AND OTHER MEATS

As discussed above, recent trends have indicated a fairly static demand for meat in the United Kingdom with certain meats, including bacon and ham, becoming less

**TABLE 1.3   Pig numbers per member of the human population in different countries**

|  | Population (millions) | | Pigs per capita |
|  | Human | Pig | |
| --- | --- | --- | --- |
| World | 5,572 | 871 | 0.16 |
| Europe | 505 | 170 | 0.34 |
| United Kingdom | 58.1 | 7.9 | 0.14 |
| Germany | 80.7 | 26.5 | 0.33 |
| Poland | 38.5 | 22.1 | 0.57 |
| Denmark | 5.2 | 10.9 | 2.10 |
| North and Central America | 442 | 93.3 | 0.21 |
| South America | 310 | 49.7 | 0.16 |
| USSR | 292 | 75.4 | 0.26 |
| China | 1,206 | 394 | 0.33 |

(Source: FAO Production Yearbook, 1993)

**TABLE 1.4   Meat consumption per capita in selected countries in 1993**

| Country | All meat (kg) | Pigmeat (kg) | Pigmeat as proportion of total meat (%) |
| --- | --- | --- | --- |
| Argentina | 95.3 | 6.4 | 6.7 |
| Australia | 102.8 | 18.5 | 18.0 |
| Brazil | 55.8 | 7.7 | 13.8 |
| Canada | 90.7 | 27.5 | 30.3 |
| Colombia | 38.6 | 4.0 | 10.4 |
| EU | 86.3 | 42.0 | 48.7 |
| Hungary | 56.0 | 30.0 | 53.4 |
| Japan | 41.6 | 16.6 | 39.9 |
| Poland | 58.4 | 38.0 | 65.1 |
| South Africa | 47.0 | 3.1 | 6.6 |
| Sweden | 57.7 | 32.5 | 56.3 |
| UK | 62.3 | 20.9 | 33.5 |
| USA | 118.0 | 30.6 | 25.9 |
| Uruguay | 102.6 | 7.4 | 7.2 |

(Source: FAO Production Yearbook, 1994)

**TABLE 1.5    Meat consumption in the United Kingdom**

| | 1938 | 1963 | *Kilogrammes per head per annum* 1965 | 1970 | 1975 | 1980 | 1986 | 1994 |
|---|---|---|---|---|---|---|---|---|
| Beef & veal | 24.7 | 23.8 | 19.8 | 22.5 | 23.5 | 20.9 | 19.4 | 15.9 |
| Mutton & lamb | 11.3 | 10.5 | 10.3 | 9.8 | 8.5 | 7.5 | 6.4 | 5.9 |
| Pork | 5.5 | 9.9 | 11.6 | 11.1 | 10.4 | 12.6 | 12.8 | 13.7 |
| Bacon & ham | 11.9 | 11.3 | 11.6 | 11.4 | 8.9 | 9.0 | 8.1 | 7.1 |
| Poultry | 2.3 | 6.6 | 7.4 | 10.8 | 11.5 | 13.4 | 17.2 | 20.3 |
| Total pigmeat | 17.4 | 21.2 | 23.1 | 22.5 | 19.3 | 21.6 | 20.9 | 20.8 |
| Total meat | 55.7 | 62.1 | 60.6 | 65.6 | 62.8 | 63.4 | 63.9 | 62.9 |

(Sources: Meat and Livestock Commission, 1987 and FAO Production Yearbook, 1994)

popular, while other meats, which include fresh pork, are becoming more popular. It is important to try to determine the factors underlying these trends so that attempts can be made to influence them for the benefit of the pig industry.

Among the factors likely to influence the future demand for a particular meat are price, quality and acceptability, range and attractiveness of products available, efficiency of sales promotion and marketing and aspects of ethics and welfare associated with the production systems of a particular meat-producing farm animal. Recently, it has become clear that the implications for human health of particular meats have become significant.

Plate 1.1   Pigmeat is consumed in greater quantity on a global scale than any other meat. In the United Kingdom in recent years, consumption of bacon and ham has declined while that of fresh pigmeat or pork has been increasing. (Courtesy of the Meat and Livestock Commission)

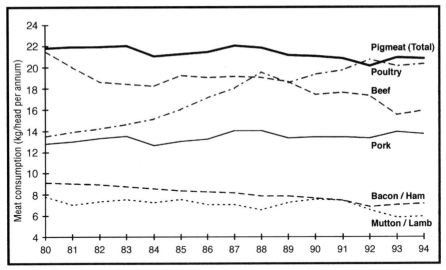

FIGURE 1.2   Trends in consumption of various meats in the United Kingdom 1980–1994 (Source: Meat and Livestock Commission, 1995)

## HEALTH

Recent concerns regarding the possible association between the consumption of saturated fats and coronary heart disease have resulted in discrimination against meat with substantial amounts of visible fat. Fortunately, the development of much leaner strains of pigs, the use of entire males and improved processing techniques have vastly improved the image of pork and bacon. It is also of relevance to point out that pig fat has fewer saturated fatty acids than the fat of beef or lamb and is therefore less implicated in the alleged health risks.

Indeed, it is interesting to point out that in two major countries, Japan and China, both of which have a high consumption of pork, the incidence of coronary heart disease is amongst the lowest in the world.

## COMPETITION FROM OTHER MEATS

Regarding the effect of relative price on the demand for different meats, it is of interest to examine the price trends for different fresh meats in the United Kingdom (see Figure 1.3).

It can be seen that, since 1985, prices of beef and lamb have increased considerably more than those of pork and chicken and these changes have undoubtedly influenced the increased demand for chicken and pork in recent years.

While the reduction in bacon consumption over the last two decades may have been influenced by its relatively high price, a major factor involved in this trend has been the change in eating habits from the traditional 'British breakfast' of bacon and eggs to one based on breakfast cereals alone.

In addition to the price element, other factors may have contributed to the in-

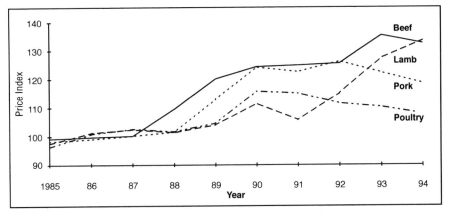

FIGURE 1.3   Indices of retail prices for different meats in the United Kingdom (January 1987 = 100) (Source: Meat and Livestock Commission, 1995)

creased consumption of chicken and pork in recent years. These may include presentation at point of sale, aspects related to ease and quickness of cooking, lower fat levels, tenderness, a greater variety and attractiveness of manufactured products and more efficient marketing.

Future prospects for pigmeat from the viewpoint of both the producer and consumer would appear to be reasonably bright in the United Kingdom. There has been no effective price support for pigmeat in recent years in the United Kingdom while support systems have been in operation for both beef and lamb. In the future, however, such price support is likely to decline which may result in lamb and beef becoming relatively more scarce and expensive. In addition, the generous support in recent years for cereal production within the EU will not increase further and this is likely to result in a small reduction in cereal prices in real terms. With pig and poultry producers being more dependent on cereals than those producing meat from ruminants, this likely change will also be of greater relative benefit to pig and poultry production.

## COMPETITION FROM MEAT SUBSTITUTES

Probably a lesser threat to future demand for meat comes from meat analogues based on textured vegetable protein or single cell protein. Vegetable protein has been used as a meat extender in the catering sector, particularly in the provision of school meals. In general, meat analogues to date have not been a commercial success, probably because their degree of consumer acceptability relative to their cost has not been sufficient to divert people from their normal consumption of real meat. There is no doubt that these meat analogues will be improved and will become more acceptable in relation to their cost; however, it is up to producers and processors of meat from farm animals likewise to improve their efficiency of production and the attractiveness of their product in relation to its cost so as to maintain their competitive advantage over meat analogues.

## TRADE IN PIGMEAT

The EU is more than self-sufficient in pigmeat, although certain individual member countries are not; the United Kingdom, for instance, is only 45 per cent self-sufficient in bacon supplies, with Denmark and the Netherlands making up the main deficit in the form of exports.

Details of the main international trade in pigmeat are presented in Table 1.6. World trade in pigmeat represents only some 3 per cent of production. The largest importers of pigmeat are Japan, the United States, Hong Kong and the Russian Federation, while the largest exporters are the EU, Canada, Taiwan, the United States and China. In addition, of course, there is considerable trade within the EU countries, with Denmark, the Netherlands and Belgium/Luxembourg being the major exporters while Germany, Italy, France and Britain are the main importers.

Competition for the available markets for pigmeat is keen and major importers such as Japan are very demanding in terms of quality and consistency of product. It is in these respects that Denmark, the major exporter of pigmeat, excels. This has helped Denmark to obtain and retain major export markets for pigmeat in the United Kingdom, Japan and Central and South America.

Expansion of the market for pigmeat in the United Kingdom or any other country is dependent on increased domestic consumption of pigmeat and/or on winning increased export orders. The attainment of these objectives is dependent on efficient production, processing and marketing of high-quality pigmeat and an attractive range of manufactured convenience products at a competitive price.

While the level of total meat consumption in western industrialised countries is unlikely to increase, the downward trends in consumption of beef and lamb and the upward trends in that of pigmeat and chicken are likely to continue. In addition, as standards of living increase in underdeveloped countries, meat consumption is likely to rise and pigmeat is likely to feature in this increased demand except in those countries where religious beliefs inhibit it.

**TABLE 1.6   Main importers and exporters of pigmeat, 1993**

| Importers | | Exporters | |
|---|---|---|---|
| Country | '000 tonnes | Country | '000 tonnes |
| Japan | 652 | EU | 713 |
| United States | 336 | Canada | 301 |
| Hong Kong | 208 | Taiwan | 283 |
| Russian Federation | 63 | United States | 197 |
| Poland | 44 | China | 150 |
| EU | 26 | Germany | 132 |
| Sweden | 19 | Rumania | 62 |
| Hungary | 17 | Hungary | 45 |
|  |  | Sweden | 17 |
|  |  | Poland | 7 |

(Source: USDA, 1994)

## Preparing for the Future

Meat and Livestock Commission forecasts to the year 2000 for the United Kingdom indicate that current levels of meat consumption will be maintained even though beef and lamb consumption is forecast to decline. This decline will be compensated for by forecast increases in poultry and pork consumption, albeit at reduced real retail prices.

While forecasts also indicate that the cost of feeding stuffs, especially cereals, will not rise so quickly as meat prices, the only sure way to prepare for the future is to strive for increased efficiency of production of pigmeat. Paradoxically, there are some who argue that we have gone too far along the road to increased efficiency of production and that we should call a halt in this quest and put our emphasis on more nebulous objectives. However, no country, industry sector or individual farmer can afford to reduce the quest for higher efficiency of production provided always that high standards of animal comfort, contentment and welfare are maintained, that good working conditions are provided for stockmen, that pollution is effectively controlled and that the emphasis is always placed on producing a consistent, high-quality end-product. If an individual country gives up such a quest for higher efficiency it will be overtaken by its competitors; if pig producers lapse, those producing poultry meat will forge ahead; and if an individual farmer starts to free-wheel he will be left behind by his neighbours.

## What This Book Sets Out To Achieve

This book examines the basic factors which control the efficiency of the pig from weaning to slaughter. These basic factors are as follows:

### 1. Genotype

To achieve a high level of efficiency in the production of pigmeat, the pig must have adequate potential to keep healthy, grow quickly, convert its food efficiently and, at the appropriate slaughter weight, produce the type of carcass and meat which is required by the meat processor and which is most attractive to the consumer. Thus, *it must be bred correctly so as to have the optimum combination of genes*. For these reasons we have gone to some lengths in this book to identify genetically determined attributes which make the greatest contribution to economic efficiency.

### 2. Nutrients

The pig's potential for growth, of lean tissue in particular, cannot be fully expressed without the requisite building bricks in terms of nutrients being supplied in the correct proportions and in appropriate quantities. Thus, *a succession of optimal diets must be formulated to meet the pig's changing nutrient requirements as it grows and matures*. It is not possible to achieve this end without going into some technical detail identifying the reason for particular nutrient requirements, giving some attention to aspects of the growth process and describing chemical attributes of dietary constituents and the economic framework which determines diet construction.

### 3.  Social, Physical and Climatic Environment

To ensure that housing and penning arrangements are optimal for pigs at a given stage of development, they must be provided with an equable temperature and adequate supply of fresh air without draughts; their group size and stocking density must not be excessive; they must have adequate feeding space to ensure that even the smallest and most timid pig in the group can obtain its full ration; they must be able to obtain their full liquid requirements easily; the arrangements for defecation and urination must be such that they can keep their lying area clean and dry (except in hotter parts of the world where wallows are used) and they must be able to lie in comfort. Thus, *housing, penning and climatic control must be such that pigs are comfortable at all times with the most vulnerable pig in the pen being adequately catered for.*

Whilst it is easy to make generalisations about the pig's requirements in these respects, modern scientific pig production must go much further than this. We do not apologise, therefore, for giving tables of technical data which enable the stockman to accurately define the necessary environments and to equip houses to achieve these desirable objectives.

### 4.  Health

Growing pigs may be unhealthy because of:

(a)  genetic or congenital problems
(b)  problems derived from the sow or developed in the pre-weaning period
(c)  infections from other pigs
(d)  infection transmitted from outside sources via wind, water, feed or personnel
(e)  insults imposed by inadequate diet or by any deficiency in penning, climatic or physical environment, housing, management or stockmanship

*Prevention of disease is better than cure: One must set out to ensure healthy pigs in the first instance and maintain this desirable state by minimising risks of infection and by ensuring adequate nutrition, housing, management and stockmanship.*

The chapters relating to health are not intended to displace the advice and care of the qualified veterinarian. They should, however, help the producer to have an enhanced awareness of the importance of health in his herd and of the implications of all husbandry procedures for good health status. These chapters should assist the producer in identifying health-related problems and enable him to discuss these in an informed partnership with his veterinarian.

### 5.  Management and Stockmanship

Essentially pig production is a business; it operates at three levels which can be described as stockmanship, management and entrepreneurial skill. Often these are incorporated in a single person but it is important to recognise the distinctions between them and the importance of each. It is impossible to be a stockman by merely looking at computer outputs because the stockman, by definition, must understand the behaviour and the psychology of his stock and react promptly and sensitively to meet their needs. *Stockmanship is the lynch-pin in ensuring efficient production in that it is the controlling influence over all the other vital components of production.* Management is primarily about providing and making the best use of existing resources and ensuring a well-regulated production system. Management plays the key role in integrating the separate components of production so that the overall efficiency of the production unit can be optimised. The entrepreneurial aspect of pig production is mainly concerned with judgements about what is technically possible within the unit in relation to the cost of funding the operation. Many units fail because of over-optimism about their technical potential without an adequate understanding of the value of different capital resources.

Later chapters therefore discuss the interaction of these components in the pig production business and aim to synthesise them into efficient production systems through the various stages from weaning to marketing. It must be remembered too that pig production does not finish with the despatch of the animals from the farm gate. The entrepreneur must satisfy his market and this involves an understanding of carcass and meat quality, which are dealt with in some detail.

Before proceeding to discuss the components of efficient production of pigmeat, criteria for measuring efficiency must be established. These form the basis of the next chapter.

*Chapter 2*

# Measures of Efficiency in Pigmeat Production and the Major Controlling Factors

Efficiency of any system is measured as output per unit of input either in biological or physical parameters or in financial terms. We cannot set out to improve the efficiency of any system until we define the basis of our efficiency measures. The purpose of this chapter, therefore, is to define the main components of the inputs and outputs of a pig enterprise to allow us to discuss different aspects of efficiency. One of the most obvious measures of efficiency to the pig farmer is the cost of producing one kilogram of pigmeat, and the amazing fact is that, within a single country, such costs can be twice as high on some farms as on others.

## OUTPUT FROM THE PIG ENTERPRISE

We need a simple definition of the output from the pig enterprise. We can identify this as the basic product, lean meat. It is, of course, obvious that associated with lean meat we get many other carcass components, and these are shown in Table 2.1.

The composition of the carcass of such a pig can also be expressed in terms of protein, fat, minerals and water (see Table 2.2). We see that the major constituent

**TABLE 2.1   Typical composition of a genetically improved pig of 100 kg liveweight**

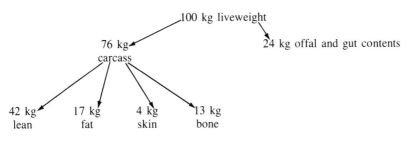

13

**TABLE 2.2  Composition of a 76 kg carcass**

| Carcass components | Weight of tissue (kg) | Protein (kg) | Lipid (kg) | Carbohydrate (kg) | Water (kg) | Ash (kg) |
|---|---|---|---|---|---|---|
| Lean | 42 | 8.4 | 1.3 | 0.5 | 31.53 | 0.27 |
| Fat | 17 | 0.95 | 11.9 | | 4.12 | 0.03 |
| Skin | 4 | 0.69 | 0.91 | | 2.4 | |
| Bone | 13 | 1.12 | 5.5 | | 4.48 | 1.9 |
| Total (kg) | 76 | 11.16 | 19.61 | 0.5 | 42.53 | 2.20 |
| Per cent | 100 | 14.69 | 25.80 | 0.66 | 55.96 | 2.89 |

of the pig carcass is water. However, from the consumer's viewpoint, the important component is edible lean meat. Lean meat (or dissected muscle) contains only some 2 to 4 per cent of fat within the muscle which is usually described as *intramuscular fat*; lean meat presented to the consumer will normally have, in addition, some fat between the muscles, i.e. *intermuscular fat*, and possibly some subcutaneous fat on one side. Many consumers believe that this additional fat is necessary to ensure succulence and flavour and to assist the cooking process. However, the amount of fat required to achieve this is a subject of considerable debate and we can greatly simplify our discussion of efficiency by regarding the desirable product of the pig production process as being lean meat.

## MAJOR INPUT FACTORS IN A PIG ENTERPRISE

A large number of input factors are involved individually and collectively in producing pigmeat, the major ones being stock, feed, buildings, climatic environment (e.g. heating and supply of fresh air), capital, management and labour. Comments on the importance of some of these inputs and on the factors which influence their cost will be made at this stage.

### 1.  Stock

Pigs can come into the pigmeat production enterprise (or 'feeding' enterprise) from the sow herd as early as 3 weeks of age (approximately 5 kg liveweight). In terms of the total cost of production of a pig weighing 100 kg, the cost attributable to this young animal is some 25 per cent of the total and this cost clearly has a big influence on the profitability of the growing pig operation. The cost or value of the stock will normally be based on their genetic potential in terms of desirable performance traits (e.g. growth, feed conversion efficiency, carcass and meat quality) and their health.

### 2.  Feed

Feed constitutes up to 70 to 80 per cent of the cost of raising pigs from weaning to slaughter and is the most critical element of all the cost items. The major nutrients and those incurring the highest total cost in pig feeding are energy, protein and essential amino acids. The pig requires small amounts of minerals and vitamins in the diet, and the cost of these is low (approximately 4 per cent of total diet cost). Two of the important factors which influence feed requirements are as follows:

- Maintenance requirements for energy, protein and other nutrients. For pigs on normal intakes of a suitable diet, about 33 per cent of all food consumed will be required merely to keep normal body processes functioning. The slower the growth of the pig, the higher the proportion of the total food consumed that will be used for maintenance. Thus, fast growth will reduce the amount of food required for maintenance.
- Lean and fatty tissue growth. 15 MJ DE (megajoules of digestible energy) are required per kg of lean tissue growth, while 50 MJ DE are required per kg of fatty tissue. Thus, it takes over three times more energy to produce fatty than lean tissue.

## 3.  Buildings

Buildings for growing pigs range from very primitive shelters to sophisticated, controlled environment structures. The latter, at 1988 prices in the United Kingdom, may cost £80 per pig place to build. Such a building written off after 10 years incurs, at a 13 per cent interest charge, a cost of approximately £15 per pig place per year. This charge is equivalent to a cost of about 4p per pig place per day or approximately 28p per pig place per week. Thus, the slower pigs grow and the longer they have to be housed, the higher the building overhead charge they will incur. However, in relative terms, especially to feed costs, building costs per pig are small and are normally less than 10 per cent of the total costs.

## 4.  Climatic Environment

A pig's climatic requirements are simple. It requires a warm, dry bed and a steady supply of fresh air without draughts. The pig is comfortable if kept within its thermoneutral zone (see Chapter 8), which lies between the upper critical temperature (UCT) and the lower critical temperature (LCT). For example, a pig of 10 kg liveweight, penned with equivalent pigs and eating a conventional diet to appetite, will be comfortable within the temperature of 19°C (LCT) and 26°C (UCT). For each 1°C below LCT, a pig of 10 kg liveweight will require an extra 5 g of food daily to compensate. On the other hand, for each 1°C above the UCT, the feed intake of a 50 kg pig will be reduced by about 5 per cent and its liveweight gain will be reduced by 7.5 per cent as a result. A slight draught (air speed of 0.4 m/sec) has the same effect on the pig as a 1°C drop in temperature. If the lying area of the pig pen is wet, this effectively increases the LCT by 3°C. It can quite easily be demonstrated that a poor environment can increase the costs of production by as much as 15 per cent based on feed conversion efficiency alone quite apart from the costs incurred by increased morbidity.

## 5.  Living and Feeding Space

If pigs are too crowded, if there is an excessive number per pen or if feeding space is inadequate, one effect will be a reduction in food intake. Over the liveweight range of 5 to 100 kg and at an average daily intake of feed of 1.5 kg and of energy of 20 MJ DE, a 5 per cent reduction in daily feed intake (i.e. 1 MJ DE) will reduce daily liveweight gain, carcass weight gain and lean meat gain by 50 g, 36 g and 20 g respectively and increase days to slaughter by 13 days.

## 6. Capital

A major resource and often a limiting one in pig production is capital. It is convenient to consider capital as having two elements, namely fixed capital, which is the money tied up in buildings, equipment, stock, etc., and working capital, which is required for the costs of feed, labour and other recurring inputs. It is of the utmost importance that a proper cash flow exercise is undertaken regularly taking account of the realised biological efficiency of the pigs and of the real costs associated with each aspect of the enterprise. Extreme care is necessary in the way capital is invested in separate components of production in relation to optimising cash flow and returns on investment. Whilst one may suppose that profitability is the ultimate index of success, diagnosing why profitability is low may require a range of other indices of efficiency and the following section is intended to show which ones may be of value.

## SUITABLE MEASURES OF EFFICIENCY

The foregoing major input factors of stock, feed, buildings, climatic environment, pen and feeding space per pig have important influences on both the amount and value of pigmeat produced per unit of time and the cost of pigmeat production. In order to ensure that the margin between the value of pigmeat produced and production costs are maximised, it is essential to develop simple and effective measures of efficiency so that pigmeat production objectives are clear. A possible set of simple, basic objectives is as follows:

1.  To maximise daily growth of
       liveweight
       and/or carcass
       and/or edible meat
     ˙and/or lean tissue
2.  To minimise production costs consistent with objective 1
3.  By achieving objectives 1 and 2, to maximise the margin between the value of pigmeat or edible meat or lean tissue produced per day and the costs incurred.

Much support and little criticism can be levelled at these very simple objectives. Maximising growth of pig carcass and edible tissue or lean meat helps to minimise maintenance requirements and housing overhead costs and helps to reduce stocking density when total pig space is limited as is usually the case in commercial practice. The only possible disadvantage of setting out to maximise carcass gain throughout the growth period is the risk of excessive fat deposition towards the end of the period of growth. This is more likely to be a problem in genotypes which are relatively unimproved in terms of lean tissue growth. Moreover, it may be possible to avoid this problem in the future by slaughtering at an earlier stage those animals which tend to deposit more fat during the later stages of growth.

Associated with this tendency to deposit more fat in the later period of growth may be a slight deterioration in feed conversion efficiency (see Figure 2.1). It can be seen that in the case of the genotype on which this work was based and over the liveweight range of 40 to 100 kg, feed conversion efficiency was maximised around 86 per cent of appetite. The extent of deterioration in FCR with maximum food intake was very small and it is likely that this would be almost non-existent for genotypes which have been further improved in terms of lean tissue growth rate. Thus, in most situations, setting out to maximise the rate of lean tissue growth will at the same time result in the feed conversion efficiency also being maximised. Thus, for improved genotypes, except in cases where carcass grading based on backfat thickness is very stringent, there would appear to be little justification for deviating from the simple objective of maximising carcass lean meat gain throughout the entire growth period. Basic to the achievement of this objective is the twin objective of maximising intake of optimal diets throughout the growth period.

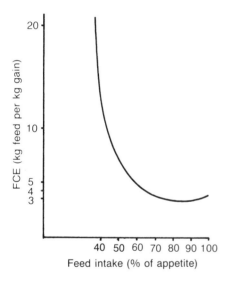

FIGURE 2.1   The effect of level of feeding on food conversion efficiency (Source: Fowler, 1968).

Many factors in commercial practice tend to impose serious constraints on these twin objectives of maximising intake of balanced diets and of maximising growth of lean tissue. These constraints and their control are dealt with in detail in separate chapters of this book. However, to provide some early indication of these constraints and their effects, the major ones will now be outlined briefly. The effects of these will be discussed against a background of current performance in commercial pig herds in the United Kingdom and of performance levels which are theoretically possible. These performance levels for growth and food conversion efficiency are outlined in Table 2.3.

## CURRENT PERFORMANCE LEVELS IN UNITED KINGDOM PIG HERDS RELATIVE TO WHAT IS THEORETICALLY POSSIBLE

It can be seen in Table 2.3 that, relative to what is achievable, even the best herds in Britain (top 10 per cent) could be improved by in excess of 20 per cent in both liveweight gain and feed conversion efficiency.

**TABLE 2.3   Theoretically possible and current performance levels in United Kingdom pig herds over the growth period 5 to 90 kg liveweight**

|  | Theoretically possible* | MLC recorded herd data† | | |
|---|---|---|---|---|
|  |  | Average | Top 1/3 | Top 10% |
| FCR (kg food per kg liveweight gain) | 2.0 | 2.56 | 2.38 | 2.29 |
| Liveweight gain/day (g) | 900 | 545 | 556 | 576 |
| Carcass gain/day (g) | 685 |  |  |  |
| Lean tissue growth/day (g) | 380 |  |  |  |

* Based on the series of most cost effective diets outlined in Chapter 10.
† (From: Meat and Livestock Commission *Yearbook*, 1994)

## THE CONSTRAINTS ON ACHIEVING HIGH PERFORMANCE LEVELS IN TERMS OF FCR, LIVEWEIGHT GAIN AND LEAN TISSUE GROWTH

Some examples of the major constraints to achieving high performance levels will now be presented.

### 1.   Genotype

It is obvious from Table 2.4 that the best genotypes are vastly superior not only in terms of liveweight gain, food conversion efficiency, carcass lean percentage and

**TABLE 2.4   Comparison of the best, average and worst genotypes in the CPE tests[1] over the 20 to 95 kg liveweight range (on ad lib. feeding)**

|  | Best genotype | Average of all genotypes | Worst genotype |
|---|---|---|---|
| Food intake/day (kg) | 2.09 | 2.16 | 2.20 |
| FCR (kg food per kg liveweight gain) | 2.45 | 2.59 | 2.87 |
| Liveweight gain/day g) | 858 | 842 | 774 |
| Lean tissue growth/day (g) | 400 | 365 | 315 |
| LTFC (kg food per kg lean tissue) | 5.28 | 6.12 | 7.28 |
| Lean in carcass (per cent) | 58.2 | 55.2 | 51.6 |
| $P_2$ backfat (mm) | 10.7 | 12.5 | 15.4 |

[1]CPE test = Commercial Product Evaluations of the genotypes of the major UK breeding companies carried out by the Meat and Livestock Commission from 1986–1989. In this table, 'Best' and 'Worst' herds are classified on the basis of LTFC.
(Source: MLC 1990)

absence of fat, but also in lean tissue growth (LTG) and lean tissue food conversion efficiency (LTFC). The last two measures are the major determinants of profitability on the pig farm.

## 2. Health

Muirhead (1986) has estimated the effects of various diseases on food conversion efficiency and days taken to reach 90 kg liveweight and his data are presented in Table 2.5. As expected, the adverse effects in terms of both feed conversion efficiency and growth are greater when a disease is introduced to the herd for the first time (acute disease). However, the continuing effects of endemic disease can also be considerable, even after a degree of immunity has been developed in response to the initial infection. The considerable effects of the various diseases indicated in Table 2.5 do not take into account the further considerable losses resulting from mortality, especially after a disease is first introduced to a herd; neither does it consider the cost of drugs and veterinary expenses.

**TABLE 2.5   Effects of the major infectious diseases on food conversion efficiency and growth rates on a herd basis (pigs slaughtered at 90 kg liveweight)**

| DISEASE | ACUTE | | ENDEMIC | |
| --- | --- | --- | --- | --- |
| | Reduced FCE | Increased days to 90 kg | Reduced FCE | Increased days to 90 kg |
| TGE | 0.1 | 4−10 | 0−0.05 | 0−3 |
| Epidemic diarrhoea | 0.1 | 4−10 | 0 | ? |
| Aujeszky's disease | 0.1−0.2 | ? | 0.1−0.3 | 6−14 |
| Parvovirus | − | − | − | − |
| Enzootic pneumonia | 0.2−0.4 | 10−21 | 0.05−0.3 | 3−21 |
| Haemophilus pneumonia | 0.1−0.4 | 7−30 | 0.1−0.3 | 4−15 |
| Atrophic rhinitis | 0.1−0.2 | 4−15 | 0.1−0.2 | 4−15 |
| Swine dysentery | 0.05−0.2 | 15−20 | 0.05−0.1 | 4−8 |
| Streptococcal meningitis | 0.05 | 1−3 | 0.05 | 0 |
| Mange | 0.1−0.3 | 7−18 | 0.05−0.1 | 3−8 |
| Internal parasites | 0.1 | 7−18 | 0.1 | 3−6 |

Note 1.   A deterioration in FCE of 0.1 is equivalent to a 3 per cent increase in feed costs.
    2.   Each extra day taken to grow from birth to slaughter at 90 kg liveweight is equivalent to reducing daily liveweight gain by 4 g.
(From: Muirhead, 1986)

## 3. Diet

After the energy requirement has been satisfied, lysine is the most critical nutrient and the one most likely to be deficient in United Kingdom diets. It has a critical effect on pig performance and profitability as indicated in Table 2.6.

**TABLE 2.6  Comparison of dietary regimes (5 to 90 kg liveweight)**

|  | Diets with adequate ideal protein | Diets 10% deficient in lysine | % difference |
|---|---|---|---|
| FCR (kg food per kg liveweight gain) | 2.25 | 2.43 | 8 |
| Liveweight gain per day (g) | 660 | 605 | 8 |
| Lean tissue growth per day (g) | 300 | 270 | 10 |

## 4. Food Restriction

Food restriction will reduce carcass fatness but, as is obvious from Table 2.7, restricting pigs to 70 per cent of their potential reduces liveweight gain by over 25 per cent and increases the need for pig places by over 40 per cent during the finishing stages.

**TABLE 2.7  Varying degrees of feed restriction from appetite (55 to 90 kg liveweight)**

|  | To appetite | 90% | 70% |
|---|---|---|---|
| FCR (kg food per kg liveweight gain) | 3.0 | 2.94 | 3.09 |
| Liveweight gain per day (g) | 800 | 736 | 592 |
| Lean tissue growth per day (g) | 270 | 250 | 200 |

## 5. Number of Pigs per Pen

Pens are often stocked more heavily than desirable. This may result after a greater degree of food restriction is imposed during the finishing stages in an attempt to reduce carcass fatness. Such overstocking can also follow a reduction in liveweight gain associated with a disease outbreak. Small increases in the number of pigs per pen from the planned stocking, such as the increase from 16 to 18 illustrated in Table 2.8, can have an important adverse influence on both liveweight gain and food conversion efficiency.

**TABLE 2.8  Effect of increasing number of pigs per pen from the planned number of 16 (growth stage 30 to 82 kg liveweight)**

|  | Pigs per pen | |
|---|---|---|
|  | 16 | 18 |
| Floor space per pig (m²) | 0.64 | 0.57 |
| FCR (kg food per kg liveweight gain) | 3.15 | 3.23 |
| Liveweight gain per day (g) | 686 | 649 |

(From: Hanrahan, 1980)

## 6.   Lying Space per Pig

If pigs have inadequate space in the pen, not only are they subjected to strain, but food intake, at least of some pigs, is depressed and poorer average liveweight gain and feed conversion efficiency results. Improvements in floor space allowances per pig have the desirable effects illustrated in Table 2.9 and, likewise, reductions in space allowance depress pig performance.

**TABLE 2.9   Responses to increased provision of floor space for growing and finishing pigs**

| Stage | Liveweight range (kg) | Basic floor space allowance per pig (m²) | Improvement per 0.1 m² increase in floor space per pig (%) | | |
|---|---|---|---|---|---|
| | | | Daily gain | Feed intake | Food to gain ratio |
| Growing | 27–53 | 0.3 | 5.2 | 3.2 | 1.6 |
| Finishing | 44–92 | 0.7 | 2.6 | 2.3 | 0.4 |

(From: Kornegay and Notter, 1984)

## 7.   Feeding Space per Pig

On both ab lib. and restricted feeding, adequate feeding space is essential. Where this is sub-optimal as in the case of the lower space allowance (3 cm per pig) in Table 2.10, important reductions in feed intake and liveweight gain and deterioration of feed conversion efficiency will result. In this situation, it is often the least assertive pigs that suffer and their inferior performances depress the average results for the group.

**TABLE 2.10   Comparison of feeding space allowance on ad lib. feeding over the liveweight range of 7 to 18 kg**

| | Feeding space per pig (cm) | | Advantage of 6.0 over 3.0 cm (%) |
|---|---|---|---|
| | 6.0 | 3.0 | |
| Feed intake (g/day) | 586 | 572 | 2.4 |
| Liveweight gain (g/day) | 322 | 304 | 5.9 |
| Feed to gain ratio (kg feed per kg gain) | 1.83 | 1.89 | 3.2 |

(From: Lindemann, Kornegay, Meldrum, Schurig and Gwazdauskas, 1984)

## 8.   Efficiency of Ad Lib. Feeders

Feed wastage can be considerable from ad lib. feeders that are poorly designed or leaking. Proper management of ad lib. feeders is also essential in terms of adjusting the flow rate of feed from hopper to the trough section, while allowing pigs to clear up all the feed once weekly before refilling helps to avoid the build-up of stale feed and minimises wastage. Hanrahan in Ireland estimated that this simple practice improved the efficiency of food use of growing-finishing pigs by 4 per cent.

## 9.  Environmental Temperature

Between 20 and 100 kg liveweight, for each 1°C pigs are kept below their lower critical temperature (LCT), food requirement and food costs are increased by about 1 per cent. A slight draught over the pigs is equivalent to a reduction of 1°C, so that cold, draughty conditions can have a very depressing effect on performance.

## 10.  Boars Versus Castrates

Although castrates do not grow very much more slowly than boars, they are much less efficient because of their very slow growth of lean tissue and their poorer food conversion efficiency as illustrated in Table 2.11.

**TABLE 2.11   Comparison of castrates and entire males (20 to 90 kg liveweight)**

|  | Entire males | Castrates |
|---|---|---|
| FCR (kg food per kg liveweight gain) | 2.6 | 3.0 |
| Liveweight gain per day (g) | 800 | 720 |
| Lean tissue growth per day (g) | 280 | 230 |

## 11.  Management and Stockmanship

It is the role of management and stockmanship to control all important input components so as to provide the animals with the most comfortable and cost effective conditions. Thus, the manager and the stockman have a very crucial influence in planning the system of production and in applying to it the necessary high degree of attention to detail to ensure that the animals are well provided for at all times in terms of their overall requirements.

## CUMULATIVE EFFECTS OF ADVERSE INFLUENCES

A combination of all or even only some of the adverse influences on pig performance illustrated in Tables 2.3 to 2.11 will have a gigantic cumulative effect on the cost per unit weight of pigmeat produced relative to the perfect situation. The debilitating overall effect of adverse influences on the pig unit is illustrated in Figure 2.2.

The basic component of Figure 2.2 represents pigs of high genetic merit capable of producing a unit of lean meat at low cost (cost index = 100) if given perfect conditions. However, the various individual sources of inefficiency highlighted have a massive additive effect in terms of depressed pig performance and inefficient

Plate 2.1   To grow lean meat with maximum efficiency, the genotype, health, nutrition, housing, climate, penning, management and stockmanship must all be of a high standard.

use of basic resources. The cumulative effects result in a doubling of the costs of producing a kg of lean meat (cost index = 200).

Therefore, in the hypothetical situation represented in Figure 2.2, the cost index per kg of lean meat gain rises from 100 for the perfect situation to 200 as all the causes of depressed pig performances combine to create a very inefficient system, in which the cost per kg of lean meat produced is doubled relative to the perfect situation.

There is little doubt that such totally inefficient systems exist in practice, although, as the financial state of the business deteriorates, the owners of the business and/or their financiers would be forced to call a halt before matters deteriorated to their ultimate state of hopelessness. Although the worst situation depicted in Figure 2.2 is extreme, very large differences in efficiency of production of pigmeat exist between herds in practice. This can be demonstrated from the results of the largest independent pig herd recording and costing service in Britain, which is operated by the Meat and Livestock Commission and termed Pigplan. The results from rearing herds (from approximately 6 to 30 kg liveweight) and from feeding herds (from approximately 18 to 78 kg liveweight) are summarised in Table 2.12.

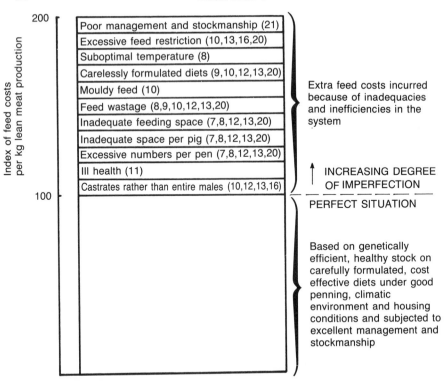

FIGURE 2.2   Feed costs per kg lean meat production for pigs between 5 and 100 kg liveweight. (Note: Numbers in brackets after each of the sources of inefficiency refer to later chapters in which these aspects which increase production costs of lean meat are fully discussed.)

Herds are divided into average, top third and top 10 per cent on the basis of feed cost per kg of liveweight gain. It can be seen that the top third and top 10 per cent herds tend to have lower mortality, better growth rate and feed conversion efficiency and cheaper diets (probably through a combination of wise purchase of raw ingredients and careful diet formulation and preparation). When the relatively small advantages which the top 10 per cent enjoy in each of the above aspects are brought together in their effects on the cost per kg of liveweight gain, this cost is over 22 and 20 per cent lower in rearing and feeding herds respectively relative to the average situation. The advantage in terms of cost per kg of gain which the top 10 per cent of herds have over the bottom 10 per cent could well approach the extreme situation depicted in Figure 2.2

It is clear that many factors can depress pig performance and collectively have a very substantial effect on the financial well-being of the pig enterprise. When pig production is very profitable the factors which contribute to depressions in performance cause reductions in profit margins. On the other hand, when the pigmeat value to feed price ratio is low, it may only be the unit with perfect genotype,

**TABLE 2.12    Overall Pigplan results to year ended September 1993**

**A.    Rearing Herd**

|  | Average | Top third* | Top 10%* |
|---|---|---|---|
| No. of herds | 214 | 71 | 21 |
| Average no. of pigs | 874 | 968 | 637 |
| *Pig performance* | | | |
| Weight of pigs at start (kg) | 6.5 | 6.5 | 6.5 |
| Weight of pigs produced (kg) | 34.7 | 35.2 | 33.2 |
| Mortality (%) | 2.8 | 2.5 | 1.9 |
| Feed conversion ratio | 1.79 | 1.67 | 1.52 |
| Daily gain (g) | 448 | 456 | 486 |
| *Feed usage & costs* | | | |
| Feed cost per tonne (£) | 220.27 | 208.73 | 203.10 |
| **Feed cost per kg gain(p)** | **39.44** | **34.96** | **30.84** |
| Feed cost per pig reared (£) | 11.12 | 10.03 | 8.23 |
| Feed per pig produced (kg) | 50.5 | 47.9 | 40.6 |
| *Sales* | | | |
| Sale price (£) | 38.47 | 37.48 | 35.77 |
| Sale weight (kg) | 36.1 | 34.9 | 32.6 |
| Liveweight price (p/kg) | 106.51 | 107.30 | 109.87 |

**B.    Feeding Herd**

|  | Average | Top third* | Top 10%* |
|---|---|---|---|
| No. of herds | 238 | 79 | 24 |
| Average no. of pigs | 1,144 | 1,253 | 1,239 |
| *Pig performance* | | | |
| Weight of pigs at start (kg) | 19.5 | 17.0 | 18.4 |
| Weight of pigs produced (kg) | 82.2 | 81.1 | 17.5 |
| Mortality (%) | 3.6 | 3.4 | 2.9 |
| Feed conversion ratio | 2.60 | 2.40 | 2.34 |
| Daily gain (g) | 586 | 599 | 615 |
| *Feed usage & costs* | | | |
| Feed cost per tonne (£) | 166.82 | 160.22 | 150.57 |
| **Feed cost per kg gain(p)** | **43.40** | **38.40** | **35.17** |
| Feed cost per pig reared (£) | 27.21 | 24.61 | 20.79 |
| Feed per pig produced (kg) | 163 | 154 | 138 |
| *Sales* | | | |
| Sale price (£) | 67.59 | 66.49 | 65.08 |
| Carcass weight (kg) | 63.4 | 63.4 | 63.5 |
| Deadweight price (p/kg) | 107.82 | 107.49 | 108.64 |

* Selected on food cost per Kg liveweight gain
(From: Meat and Livestock Commission *Yearbook*, 1994)

health, diet and conditions which is making a profit, while units with increasing degrees of problems which detract from performance make progressively greater losses.

The major factors which affect the efficiency with which pigmeat is produced will be discussed in turn in succeeding chapters. The next chapter deals with the biology of growth of the pig and this provides a basis for succeeding chapters which deal in turn with the pig carcass and breeding improvements.

## ADDITIONAL READING

*MLC Pig Yearbooks*, Meat and Livestock Commission, PO Box 44, Queensway House, Bletchley, Milton Keynes, England MK2 2EF.

*Chapter 3*

# The Biology of Growth in Pigs

Growth is central to the whole objective of pig production, because the meat which we eventually eat is produced by the co-ordinated increase in size of different tissues. The pig is kept exclusively for meat production and other benefits which we derive from the animal such as leather, bristles and hormones are trivial. This greatly simplifies the range of topics which are relevant in this complex field of biology. Even so, it is extremely important to those who wish to understand the changes in pig production and efficiency, both over recent years and expected changes in the future, to be aware of at least some of the basic principles. Many recent exciting scientific discoveries have greatly enhanced our understanding of the growth process, particularly the new information on how the animal controls growth by co-ordinated signalling using a variety of hormones (science of genetic engineering). However, we are still a long way away from understanding the fine control of growth. Indeed, such obvious phenomena as the symmetry between the left- and right-hand sides of the animal, or the precise shape and size of any organ or part, are well beyond our present ability to explain in terms of biological mechanisms.

GROWTH AND FORM

Growth can have the very simple meaning of an 'increase in size'. We see this aspect very readily by simply comparing our mental picture of the animal over successive periods of time. Many farmers become very skilled at this, and with practice can make reasonably accurate guesses of liveweight, growth rate and slaughter weight. Growth can be studied much more precisely by taking certain measurements, for example by using a rule to measure height, length or girth, or by weighing the animal on different occasions. If these observations are plotted on a graph with time on the horizontal axis (the X axis) and the measurement on the vertical axis (the Y axis), then very characteristic growth curves are produced (see Figure 3.1). If these extend across a wide range from conception to maturity, they resemble a rather badly shaped capital letter S which slopes forward and has a lower half rather smaller than the upper one. This has given rise to the term 'sigmoidal' growth curves, which simply means that they have the shape of an S. The shape of growth curves and how they may be altered will be discussed later under the heading 'Growth in Size'.

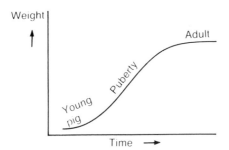

FIGURE 3.1  Typical growth curve of the pig.

To merely describe growth as the process by which animals get bigger is to lose sight of another important aspect which is that as animals grow, they also change in form. Some of the problems, and indeed many of the interesting features, of growth arise because the different organs and parts of the body grow at different rates (see Figure 3.2). Small pigs are not miniatures of large pigs but actually have different proportionate sizes of legs, head and body and also of organs, tissues and parts. It is usual, therefore, to consider growth as having two aspects, that is

- an increase in size
- a change in form.

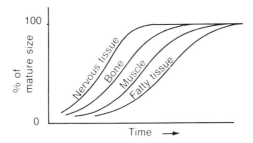

FIGURE 3.2  Order of maturity of various tissues.

The complexity of growth arises because these processes occur simultaneously within every part of the body right down to the different cell types and indeed the sub-cellular units. For our purpose, we must simplify and focus the process to relate it to the more practical issues in pig production. We shall consider the different components of the body and how their growth varies over time relative to one another. This is termed 'differential growth'.

## THE COMPONENTS OF GROWTH

An understanding of the main tissue types is important both for grasping the essential aspects of growth and for understanding the main features of carcass composition. For our purpose, the discussion will be limited only to five main categories or tissue groups. These are

Plate 3.1 The pig changes in shape as it grows. At birth the head, shoulder region, chest and limbs are well developed. These parts form a smaller proportion of the finished pig, in which the later maturing loin and hams are much better developed. (Finished pig courtesy of *Pig Farming*)

1. Nervous tissue, including the brain
2. Bone
3. Muscle
4. Fatty tissues
5. All the other parts, including the internal organs of digestion, circulation and respiration and the skin.

From the point of view of meat production, the main interest centres on the development of the muscle, which forms the red part of meat and which is usually referred to as the lean, and the fatty tissue, which is the white greasy part of the meat and which now is regarded as an undesirable component of joints, particularly if it is present in large prominent blocks.

The various tissues grow together in a coordinated way which, for pigs of similar breeding, produces typical patterns of growth and appearance. Much of modern thinking about growth in farm animals emanated from the very detailed dissections carried out by the late Sir John Hammond and his students at Cambridge University about 50 years ago and also from the group in the United States which was associ-

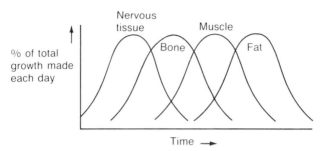

FIGURE 3.3   Hammond's picture of sequential maturity of different tissues.

ated with the very notable biologist Samuel Brody. The programme of growth of tissues was illustrated very simply by Hammond, who plotted the successive waves of growth of each tissue as it approached maturity in terms of the percentage of its total growth made each day (see Figure 3.3).

Each tissue has a specific function in the body and the relative importance of these functions changes as the animal grows. Each major tissue will now be discussed in turn.

### Nervous Tissue

The brain and nervous tissue of the body are absolutely critical for coordinating movement, generating the five senses and also orchestrating the whole activity of the animal and its behaviour. These tissues are relatively well developed in quite young animals, and they are the main reason why young animals appear to have a relatively large head. These tissues are described as 'early maturing' because they tend to make the majority of their growth early on and reach their mature size whilst other parts of the animal are still growing. It used to be thought that early under-nutrition could damage the development of the brain, but it is now clear that the animal is capable of protecting the growth of the brain and nervous tissue from severe nutritional deprivation. This feature is often described as the brain having a *relatively high priority for nutrients*, that is to say that if nutrition is poor, the animal will sacrifice other tissues such as fat and muscle before allowing damage to occur to the brain. Quite clearly, if any species is to survive in an environment of fluctuating food supply it must be able to protect the critical parts of its body whilst perhaps allowing other less important tissues to be depleted. Under conditions of severe undernutrition it is noticeable that the head appears to be disproportionately large in relation to the rest of the body and this can be explained by the tendency for nutrition to be diverted to this part because of its importance in the survival of the animal. Disporportionately large heads are particularly noticeable in young pigs at weaning when the piglet has had access to a poor teat and has only just managed to maintain itself.

The brain contains many rather special materials such as an unusually high proportion of phospholipids but this does not create any special nutrient demands, contrary to many popular beliefs about 'brain' foods. Damage to the nervous tissue is not usually associated with any specific nutrient deficiency, but is more likely to

arise due to the presence of toxic materials in the diet, such as those which are produced by poisoning with the heavy metals lead, cadmium and mercury, or from the
organic toxins of moulds or because of a specific infection such as streptococcal
meningitis. However, certain of the vitamins are connected with the nervous tissue
and we can give two examples. Choline is a precursor of a very important chemical
called acetylcholine which is important for the transmission of signals or impulses
along the nerves. There is also a role for vitamin A in a very special part of the
brain where the retina and optic nerves pick up light signals. The visual pigments
of the retina need vitamin A, and some forms of blindness can be attributed to a
deficiency of it.

## Bone and Skeleton

The bones give rigidity to the animal and form the basis of the system of levers
which allows the animal to move about. Strictly speaking, cartilaginous tissues
should be included in this category and also the strong tendons which attach the
bones to the muscles. The base material of bones is initially collagen, which is the
special type of protein found throughout the body. It is capable of forming extremely strong connecting units and thus is a large proportion of all connective tissue.
The feature of bone is that as the animal grows, it becomes mineralised by salts
of calcium and phosphorus. Almost all the calcium in the animal is located in the
skeleton, although there is a small proportion which plays a vital role in the
metabolism of cells and in the clotting of blood.

The skeleton is rather like the nervous tissue in that it is relatively early-maturing
and is quite well developed in many species at birth. The pig is actually rather immature at birth but its skeleton grows very rapidly whilst it is suckling. Growing
bones have special nutritional needs reflecting their composition. The diets of
young pigs should normally be supplemented with phosphorus and calcium to ensure that the bones are strong and to avoid the development of rickets, a condition
in which inadequate mineralisation of the bone causes bending of the long bones
in young animals and fractures in older animals. Vitamin D has a special role for
skeletal tissue in that it appears to affect the absorption of calcium from the gut and
is involved in allowing the animal to accommodate imbalances in the ratio of
calcium and phosphorus in the diet.

## Muscle

From the point of view of pig production, muscle is the most important tissue in
the body because it eventually becomes the lean meat of the carcass. Its main function is to provide the animal with movement. There are over 200 individual muscles
in the body of the pig and these allow it to perform the huge range of activities of
which it is capable. The main type of muscle of concern to us is the *skeletal muscle*,
but there are other types of muscle in the walls of the arteries and the gut, which
are classified as *smooth muscles*, and a unique type of muscle in the heart called
*cardiac muscle*. Muscles can contract up to about 15 per cent of their length and
this movement is transferred by tendons and bones into the actions of running,
jumping, rooting or chewing. In addition, by balancing the action of one muscle

against another, the animal maintains a particular posture. The structure of muscle is very complex and well beyond the scope of this book.

The main chemical components of muscle are proteins. In a dissected muscle, about 3 per cent of it is fat and the rest is water, protein and minerals, the proportions of which within a particular muscle are virtually constant at any given stage of maturity. There are minor differences between muscles in these respects but the greatest differences are with degree of maturity, as baby pigs have more water in their muscles than adult animals. On average, during the growing period, about 77 per cent of muscle is water, about 19 per cent protein and about 1 per cent ash. Almost every nutrient can have an effect on muscle growth. It is sensitive to the proportions of amino acids in the diet, particularly to any deviation of the essential amino acids from the ideal proportions (see Chapter 9). Similarly, a deficiency in almost any vitamin or mineral can in the end exert an effect on the rate of growth of muscle. For example, a severe deficiency of vitamin E can cause a type of muscular weakness variously called white-muscle disease or muscular dystrophy. There are also genetic or congenital defects in muscle development such as splay leg in baby pigs, and, in fact, some authorities regard the extreme muscling seen in Pietrain pigs and in some specialised sire lines as a muscle defect in a functional sense.

The main proteins which help muscles to contract are called actin and myosin and they obtain their energy via a complex series of biochemical reactions, either from glucose or from fatty acids. Energy is stored in the muscle either as a chain of glucose molecules called glycogen, sometimes referred to as animal starch, or in the form of lipid or fat, which must be converted to fatty acids before it can be of use to the animal. In newborn baby pigs which have little fat at birth, the glycogen in the muscle forms a very important energy reserve.

Muscles are made up of bundles of fibres which may be of different types. Some are called *fast glycolytic* because they can contract almost instantly in response to a nervous impulse and go on doing so until they run out of oxygen and become fatigued. Another type is called *slow oxidative* because, although they do not contract as rapidly as the ones just mentioned, they can utilise oxygen steadily for the oxidation of glucose or fatty acids and so provide long-term steady movements. The point here is that the muscle stores a limited amount of oxygen ready for use in a special pigment called *myoglobin* which gives muscle its reddish colour. In general, white meats are lacking in myoglobin. There are, however, some special reasons why on occasion the meat from pigs which are genetically sensitive to stress can appear pale and watery and this is dealt with later in relation to meat quality (see Chapters 5, 16 and 18).

## Fatty Tissues or Adipose Tissues

Fat is an essential storage tissue in the animal providing a buffer against variations in nutrient supply. It is the latest maturing of all the tissues in the sense that it may go on growing long after growth in all the other main tissues has ceased. In the pig, however, fat has a special role in that it also supplies insulation in an animal which is otherwise extremely vulnerable to environmental temperature. This is particularly true in the newborn pig, where there is a rapid increase in subcutaneous fat immediately after birth. In this respect, therefore, the pig is somewhat of an anomaly in relation to other species. Fatty tissue is not inert, nor is it totally made up of chemical lipid. The different fat depots vary in their exact composition and fatty tissue from these various depots contains between about 65 to 90 per cent of chemical lipid, between about 7 to 25 per cent of water and about 3 per cent of protein.

Despite its apparently homogeneous structure, fat is enclosed in little envelopes of connective tissue called locules which contain many thousands of fat cells or adipocytes. Each fat cell has a cell wall, a small amount of cytoplasm and a nucleus, but the volume is dominated by the relatively enormous globule of lipid. Although at first sight the main body of fat depots appears virtually devoid of blood supply, the peripheral areas are richly supplied with a capillary network of blood vessels. This provides nutrients to the adipose organ and also, very importantly during periods when the energy supply in the diet is below that required for maintenance, it allows for the resorption of lipid and transports it into the main bloodstream for use elsewhere in the body.

The chemical composition of fatty tissue can vary within certain limits in response to the diet. A diet which is rich in unsaturated fats which tend to be liquid at room temperature can produce fat in the carcass which is likewise also soft. This arises because the pig's metabolism allows the sub-units of the dietary fats, that is the particular unsaturated fatty acids, to be incorporated directly into the fat of its adipose depots. The fats present in whole-processed soya bean or rapeseed may cause the carcasses to have soft fat, particularly if the animals have low amounts of fat in the carcass.

The pattern of fatty tissue growth can be illustrated by reference to the classical data generated at Cambridge University nearly 50 years ago by C.P. McMeekan, who was a prominent member of the distinguished team of researchers in anatomical growth under the direction of the late Sir John Hammond. Although the exact numerical values are probably rather different from those of today's pigs, it can be reasonably assumed that the principles have remained unchanged and that the differences are of similar magnitude. Some selected organs and tissues are compared in Table 3.1 for piglets dissected at birth and at 16 and 28 weeks of age. Changes in the proportion of these organs and tissues are emphasised by considering the growth of each part as a proportion of the total muscle weight. It can be seen that the proportion of bone to muscle has halved at 16 weeks of age relative to that at birth and there is a much smaller drop between 16 and 28 weeks of age. However, for a given muscle weight, the proportion of bone remains relatively constant, independently of the amount of fat in the carcass. Fat is an extremely variable tissue and as the animal grows its proportion increases enormously. It rises from only 13 per cent of the muscle weight at birth to 109 per cent at 28 weeks of age. Like bone, the internal organs minus abdominal fat diminish in proportion to muscle as the animal grows.

The amount of fat in the body is of primary concern in determining the quality of the resulting carcass and is very variable depending on a wide range of factors. These include the protein content of the diet, the ration scale, the genotype and sex, the environmental temperature and the slaughter weight. All these aspects are considered in more detail in Chapters 4, 13, 14 and 16. In addition to the amount of

**TABLE 3.1  Weights and proportions of tissues at birth, 16 weeks and 28 weeks of age**

|  | Birth | Age 16 weeks Tissue weights (g) | 28 weeks |
|---|---|---|---|
| Empty body | 1,337 | 36,102 | 100,000 |
| Bone | 251 | 3,962 | 7,396 |
| Muscle | 388 | 12,669 | 31,649 |
| Fat | 51 | 7,127 | 34,513 |
| Internal organs | 241 | 6,208 | 13,702 |
| *Ratios of tissues (g : g)* |  |  |  |
| Bone/muscle | 0.646 | 0.313 | 0.233 |
| Fat/muscle | 0.131 | 0.563 | 1.090 |
| Internal organs/muscle | 0.621 | 0.490 | 0.397 |

(After McMeekan, 1940)

the fat, its composition, colour, texture, odour and flavour are also important. One role of vitamin E and also of selenium in the diet is to protect the fats of the body from oxidation. Failure to include adequate amounts of vitamin E in the diet can result in a browning of the body fat, particularly in diets containing a high proportion of unsaturated fats.

## Organs

The remaining category of tissue is rather imprecise because all the diverse, non-structural organs of the body are included in it. In this category are included the liver, spleen, the digestive tract, the heart, lungs, kidneys and the blood. It should be stressed, however, that although we consider the majority of these parts as offal, and in Western countries only regard a fraction of the total material as edible, these entities are vital to the animal. The proportion which they form of the total body varies largely in response to the nutrition of the animal. The digestive organs, for instance, can vary in size depending on the nature of the diet. Pigs fed on a bulky, fibrous diet may have an enormously enlarged hind gut which allows for the accumulation of large volumes of digesta so that fermentation can proceed on sufficient material to yield a reasonable amount of nutrient for the animal. Similarly, pigs offered diets which have a high water content, as is the case when skimmed milk or whey is used, may have kidneys which appear relatively enlarged.

These variations in size under special circumstances should not be allowed to obscure the general fact that the organs of the body tend to form a constant proportion of the lean body mass of the animal at any particular stage of growth.

The growth of the organs can be greatly affected by the quality of nutrition. Illustrations of this point are the reduced growth of the gut in response to toxins in the diet such as the lectins found in raw navy beans which severely damage the gut wall, and shortage of iron in the diet which causes anaemia because haemoglobin cannot be produced without it. Damage to organs in this way (blood can be regarded as an organ) has a knock-on effect on growth in general. The skin too can be damaged by an insufficiency of some of the B vitamins or of the trace mineral zinc. Although at first sight one would not suppose that growth would be affected overall by such effects on the skin, it is highly likely that such malnutrition has a secondary effect as the animal succumbs to infections which gain access through the damaged skin.

## GROWTH IN SIZE

The mature size of a species gives us quite an amount of biological information. Mice and elephants, which differ in mature size by a factor of about 80,000, are both mammals and have similar metabolisms. Yet we know that if we feed a mouse generously there is no possibility of it remotely approaching the size of an elephant. This rather crude and naive example does, however, illustrate an important aspect of growth in farm animals and indeed within a species. No matter how efficient a pig with a mature weight of 90 kg is when it is growing, it can never be a satisfactory animal if the market only accepts animals of more than 91 kg. Indeed it is likely that many of the so-called old-fashioned breeds of pig such as the Gloucester Old Spot, the Berkshire, the Small and Middle White and perhaps the Tamworth lost their place in the economy of pig production not particularly because they were intrinsically inefficient but because they had a small mature size. As the fashion drifted away from small pork pigs to heavier bacon pigs and heavy hogs, these breeds were therefore stranded.

## GROWTH CURVE

The S shape of normal growth curves was mentioned earlier. The shape is caused by the animal going through successive stages from conception to maturity during which the growth rate first accelerates, then remains constant and finally decelerates as the animal approaches maturity. Some growth curves for liveweight change are shown in Figures 3.4a and b.

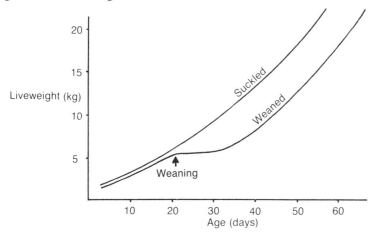

FIGURE 3.4a  Different growth curves of young pigs.

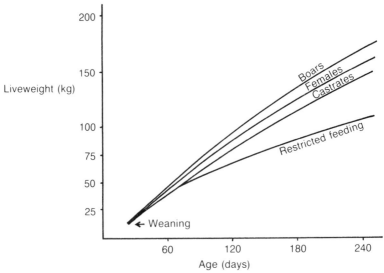

FIGURE 3.4b   Overall growth curves for typically healthy pigs.

It can be seen readily that, in general, growth from about 30 kg onwards is
almost a straight line, the exact slope depending on the sex of the animal. However,
many other factors play a part in determining the actual growth rate such as the
rate of feeding, and these aspects will be dealt with in much greater detail in
Chapters 10, 12 and 13. It is sufficient to state here that the natural curve is very
rarely expressed in the later stages of growth because the practice is to restrict the
intake of animals after they reach puberty and enter upon the reproductive phase
of their life.

## HORMONES AND GROWTH

The point at which the growth curve ceases to be straight is often associated with
the stage in growth when puberty occurs. This may be thought of as somewhat surprising since many will recognise that the sex hormones play a positive role in encouraging growth and for this reason are described as anabolic (muscle-building)
hormones. However, the major surge of production of the sex hormones which
coincides with puberty also appears to set in train the events which cause the bones
to stop elongating. A premature dose of high levels of sex hormones can cause
closure of the epiphyseal plates, which are the growing points of the bone usually
situated between the shaft and the head, and when these finally fuse no further
growth in length is possible (see Figure 3.5). This, however, is not the whole story
because castrated animals also stop growing eventually and it is likely that other
control factors take over.

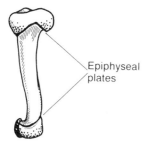
Epiphyseal
plates

FIGURE 3.5  Pig femur showing
epiphyseal plates, which are the
areas of active cell division.

The sex hormones are steroidal chemicals secreted almost entirely by the testis of the male and the ovary of the female. The male hormones or *androgens* are synthesised by the testicles which also produce quite substantial amounts of the female hormones. The ovaries, on the other hand, secrete the female hormones or *oestrogens*. The ovary also secretes other steroidal hormones but these have not been shown to have any major effect on the growth of the animal. The sex hormones can have a positive effect on growth, and this is apparent in the difference which exists in the growth characteristics of boars, castrates and gilts. Although the overall growth rate of each sex type may be quite similar, the growth rate of the bone and muscle tissue is quite different being about 15 per cent higher in the boar than in the castrate and 10 per cent higher in the boar than in the gilt.

Many of the hormones in the body have an influence on growth, the most obvious of these being the growth hormones, of which *somatotrophin* and the *somatomedins* are the most well understood. Extracts of the peptide hormone somatotrophin taken from the pituitary glands of pigs have been shown to increase the growth rate of pigs considerably, and it may be that the new science of genetic engineering will allow this hormone to be produced in greater quantity and with greater purity without the pig being involved at all, other than in providing the original genes. It may also be possible to promote a greater secretion of this hormone within the body by engineering extra copies of the gene complex which produces the hormone on to the genetic make-up of the pig so that this ability is fixed in its inheritance, thus constituting a genetic improvement.

Scientists have discovered a number of other substances which, when administered to the animal, affect its growth. *Cimeterol* and *Clenbuterol*, for instance, enhance the lean tissues of the growing animal. These discoveries are important in showing the scientist the mechanisms which may be involved in producing leaner pigs, but they raise a major area of the ethics of using growth-promoting agents in animal production. It should be pointed out that the risks to human health from possible residues resulting from the use of growth-promoting substances varies from nil for the protein type of hormones to something quite trivial for the steroidal types. However, recent legislation within the EEC which more or less bans the use of synthetic steroidal hormones in pig production is perhaps a pointer to the fact that it has been public attitudes which have condemned the use of such substances, rather than the available scientific evidence. In future, the scope for improving efficiency and obtaining faster growth may depend mainly on better genes, better feeding and better health rather than on the armoury of the biological chemist, although there are undoubtedly many exciting developments in our understanding of the physiology of the pig which could be beneficial.

## ADDITIONAL READING

Fowler V. R. (1968), *Growth and Development of Mammals*, Ed. G. A. Lodge and G. E. Lamming, Butterworths, London.

Fowler V. R. and Livingstone R. M. (1972), in *Pig Production*, Ed. D. J. A. Cole, 143−161, Butterworths, London.

Fowler, V. R. (1980), 'Growth in Mammals for Meat Production', *Growth in Animals*, Ed. T. L. J. Lawrence, 249−263, Butterworths, London.

*Chapter 4*

# The Pig Carcass as Meat

The function of the pig in terms of farming is to convert materials which are not directly attractive for human food into meat which is both attractive and nutritious. Unlike many other livestock, meat is virtually the only product of pig production which is valued. It is worth mentioning in passing, that there are minor exceptions to this which are usually regarded as by-products. These include leather from the hide, bristles for brushes, pharmaceutical products from the glands and the use of a certain amount of the fat in industrial processes such as soap manufacture.

It is usual for producers to remain relatively unaware of the problems of the slaughtering plant, or those of the meat processor, wholesaler or butcher. However, most producers have some experience from the point of view of a consumer of the end product. It is vital for the success of the industry that the producer maintains an interest and understanding of the intermediate phases of the production chain from farm to consumer.

PIGMEAT

The market for pigmeat is threefold: as fresh (or frozen) pork, as cured sides or cuts and for inclusion in processed meats. Butchering techniques differ enormously between countries and between regions within a country. The names applied to cuts of meat can be very confusing, particularly as the same name may be applied to different joints depending on the locality. The usual cuts are shown in Figure 4.1

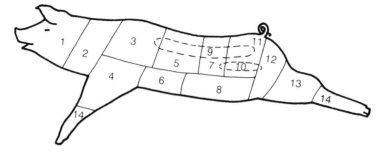

FIGURE 4.1   Parts of the pig carcass (see Table 4.1 for explanation of numbers).

39

**TABLE 4.1  Pork and bacon cuts**

| Cut | Anatomical region | COMMERCIAL CUTS Fresh pork | Cured |
|---|---|---|---|
| 1 | Head | Head | Cheeks |
| 2 | Neck | Neck chops Butt | Butt |
| 3 | Upper fore-limb | Shoulder Blade bone | Collar 'Picnic' ham Fore slipper Shoulder bacon |
| 4 | Lower fore-limb | Hand Hand and spring | Small hock |
| 5 | Dorsal thorax | Rib chops Loin chops (+ kidney) | Back and rib rashers |
| 6 | Ventral thorax | Belly | Streaky rashers |
| 7 | Lumbar | Loin Loin chops Chump chops | Short back rashers |
| 8 | Abdominal Wall | Flank | Thin streaky rashers |
| 9 | *Longissimus dorsi* | Eye muscle (large muscle in chops) | Special 'loin' bacon |
| 10 | *Ileo-Psoas* | Fillets | — |
| 11 | Pelvic | Chump Chump chops | Top back Gammon slipper Ham |
| 12 | Upper hind-limb | Gigot Leg | Corner-gammon Middle-gammon Ham |
| 13 | Lower hind-limb | Hock | Gammon hock Hock Ham |
| 14 | Feet | Trotters | |

and the names often applied to these cuts in Table 4.1. There is also a rather confusing nomenclature associated with the description of pigs slaughtered at different weights. These are shown in Table 4.2.

Details of carcass grading methods are given in Chapter 16. It is sufficient to note here that grading criteria differ profoundly between different countries. For example, within the United Kindgom there is often a very steep differential between the price paid for pigs which meet the criteria for the top grade and those which do not. In the United States, the grading standards are much less exacting and the price differentials between grades much less steep. A great deal of the difference found in grading techniques depends on whether the meat is sold with the skin on as in traditional pork with crackling, or as a trimmed joint with skin removed and some of the fat trimmed off.

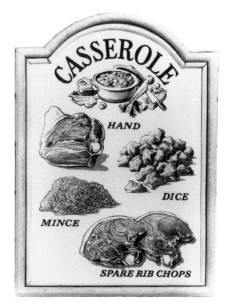
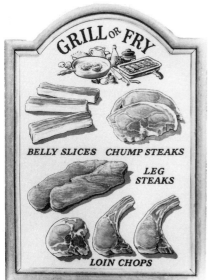

Plate 4.1   Some of the conventional and novel pork cuts of the pig carcass in the UK. In the curing process, the whole carcass, excluding the head, may be cured (as in the Wiltshire cure in the UK). Alternatively, only part of the carcass may be cured, for example the ham (e.g. for Parma ham in Italy) or the belly (e.g. for streaky bacon production in the United States). (Courtesy of Meat and Livestock Commission)

**TABLE 4.2  Live and dead weights of pigs for different markets**

| Liveweight range (kg) | Deadweight* range (kg) | Market |
|---|---|---|
| 10−20 | (eaten whole) | Sucking pig** |
| 58−68 | 40−50 | Light pork |
| 69−95 | 51−70 | Pork, cutters |
| 80−102 | 59−77 | Bacon |
| 95−106 | 70−80 | Heavy cutters |
| 106+ | 80+ | Heavy hogs |
| 120+ | 88+ | Cast sows |

* Weight of cold eviscerated carcass, includes head and abdominal fat; usually about 70−76% of liveweight after fasting overnight
**Very small but interesting connoisseur market
(Source: Fowler, 1982)

## Fresh Pork

In general, fresh pork reaches the consumer quite quickly after the animal has been marketed. Pork is not usually hung for a period after slaughter, as is often the case with beef. After slaughter, the carcass is usually graded and stamped, chilled overnight until it has become firm and then either transported as a fresh carcass or further processed to pre-packed joints which are then packaged according to type and marketed to the wholesaler or retailer. In this form the products may also be frozen, either for sale on the domestic market for home freezers or for export. In general, the export regulations to most-countries are very demanding, not only in terms of the standards applied by the abattoir and processor, but also in terms of the health regulations which apply to the live animal in respect of diseases which can be transmitted in raw meat such as foot and mouth and swine vesicular disease.

In many markets for fresh pork it is quite acceptable to utilise entire males (boars) provided that the final liveweight is not too high. The objection to boars, where it exists, is that the meat sometimes releases a strong, and to some people, unpleasant odour when it is cooked. The components of this odour are complex. One element is closely related to the sex-attractant chemical and has the abbreviated chemical name *androsterone*. Other factors which seem to be more associated with boar meat than with meat from castrates and gilts is the faint odour of *skatole* which, in much greater concentrations, is partly responsible for the odour of faeces. In many consumer trials and in many experiments with trained panels of assessors it has been shown that the problems associated with boar meat in the lighter weight ranges are trivial and easily offset by the greater leanness of the boar.

There is now little doubt that the eating qualities of pork can vary. The reasons for this are not entirely clear, but some retailers have argued strongly that it is affected by the amount of intramuscular fat in the muscles, that is the intrinsic and invisible fat (marbling fat) actually contained within the lean meat. It is said that the more of this fat there is, the greater the succulence and eating quality. If this assertion turns out to be true, then it is known that the trait differs between different breeds and crosses. It is claimed that some strains of the Duroc breed have more intramuscular fat than other breeds, and for certain highly discerning consumers, there may be a specialist market for meat produced with this concept in mind.

## Cured Products

Cured meat is usually produced from pigs which have a liveweight of at least 80 kg. The cure is effected by using a solution of different salts such as sodium and potassium chlorides and sodium nitrate and nitrite. Modern curing fluids may also contain polyphosphates which ensure that more of the curing fluid, which is said to increase the succulence, is retained in the product. The meat usually gains in weight during the curing process, and excessive use of these fluid-retaining elements can result in the meat shrinking alarmingly during cooking. This technique, known in the trade as 'pumping', has given some branded products a poor image and has, unfortunately, reflected badly on bacon as a whole. The producer can have little control over this kind of abuse, apart from ensuring that the problem is aired with the relevant processors at every opportunity.

In the traditional techniques used in the United Kingdom and in Denmark, bacon was produced by curing whole sides with the skin on, for example, the Wiltshire cure. This was done by careful trimming of the side, removal of the scapular (shoulder blade) and the ribs, injecting brine into the side and then immersing it in a tank containing brine for several days. The sides were then allowed to dry in a chill-room and, as an additional process, some sides were smoked in rooms filled with the smoke from smouldering oak sawdust. The whole sides were then sold for cutting up at the point of retail.

More recently, there have been developments in what is called 'in-bag' curing, whereby the carcasses are cut up into joints and trimmed of skin and excess fat. This is an important means of adding value close to the point of slaughter. Some manufacturers now go even further and package the sliced product on site. This allows great flexibility in the way in which different carcasses are used and opens up new possibilities for sophisticated grading systems whereby the particular attributes of a single carcass can be identified on the slaughter line and the carcass directed to that part of the plant which can most effectively add value to it.

There is considerable scope for some element of speciality in cured products. Dry curing is used in the production of York hams. This process is expensive because it involves repeatedly rubbing the hams in dry curing salt over a period of several weeks. The world famous Parma hams are similarly produced by a dry salting process. This market utilises very large pigs to produce hams of adequate size and requires very great attention to the health of the animals and to hygiene since the product is normally eaten without cooking.

## Processed Meat

The meat from pigs is extraordinarily versatile, and over the years a tremendous range of products has been derived from the carcass, the trimmings and the offal. The diversity of pork sausages available in Germany is justly famous, and many local reputations of companies and of family butchers have been founded on the production of delectable sausages. It is perhaps unfortunate that in these days of comparative plenty, some processors have been guilty of disguising low-quality offal parts behind the benign exterior of the sausage. Although this sleight of hand may not be detected by the unsuspecting consumer, it does little for the reputation of the good sausage or the industry as a whole when such practices come to light.

## PIG PRODUCTION, PIGMEAT AND SOCIETY

It is important that the producer keeps in touch with the perceptions of pig production as seen by the consumer. It is not an absolute right for the farmer to produce pigs and then demand that somebody somewhere must buy the pigs. It is not a basic requirement of human life to eat pigmeat or indeed any other kind of meat; it is a matter of free choice.

Meat eating is as much a cultural habit as anything else. In China, the pork at a meal is the high point of the cuisine, and enormous care is taken to ensure that it is presented as perfectly as possible. On a world-wide basis more than half the meat eaten is from the pig, despite the widespread but erroneous view that the pig competes with humans for food resources because it has a digestive tract which is similar to that of the human.

In certain societies, pork is regarded with either suspicion or indeed revulsion. Practising Jews and Muslims, in observing their faith, regard meat from pigs as unacceptable and unclean. Although this view is clearly founded on the origins of their religion, it is not difficult to see that there may at the outset have been some sound reasons for the precept.

The pig is an intermediate agent for the now rare pork tapeworm (*Taenia solium*). This parasite lives alternately in the human gut as a tapeworm and in the pig as an embryonic form, sometimes referred to as a bladder worm, which forms cysts in the meat. Each infects the other. The pig picks up the parasite when it is in the egg form by foraging amongst human excreta. The eggs hatch in the gut of the pig and the embyros migrate through the wall of the digestive tract into the various tissues of the body where they form cysts. If infected or 'measly' pork is not cooked properly, then these cysts develop in the gut of the human and form the classical tapeworm, the segments of which continuously shed eggs, and so the cycle is completed. A very serious condition results if the human is reinfected directly with the eggs because these can then cause cysts in any part of the body including the brain. The condition is known as cysticercosis. Fortunately, modern sanitation, meat inspection and efficient cooking methods have rendered the disease virtually extinct in developed societies.

## THE IMAGE OF PIGMEAT

With the removal of classical health hazards, it is easy to become complacent about the image of pigmeat. However, in some countries, new problems have come to the forefront. Three such areas are worthy of brief mention, namely the relationship between fat consumption and health, the possibility of drug residues in the meat and finally the public reaction against very intensive techniques of pig production which can be generically classed as the problem of perceived welfare.

## Pigmeat, Fat and Health

In recent years there has been considerable emphasis on the production of lean meat as the desirable objective of the production process. However, the traditional image of pigmeat is that it is associated with a large amount of visible fat, and there are still many examples in retail outlets which unfortunately reinforce this view. The public aversion to fat, although by no means universal, has been strengthened by the widely publicised opinion of several medical experts that excessive fat consumption is not only associated with an undesirable level of obesity, but also with a higher risk of coronary heart disease, high blood pressure and cerebral haemorrhage or a stroke.

It is therefore entirely understandable that strenuous efforts have been made to find techniques for making growing pigs as lean as possible. These have included breeding programmes for leaner pigs, restricting the feed, increasing the quality and amount of the dietary protein and the experimental use of certain anabolic materials. Each method has made a contribution, but it is often forgotten that modern methods of processing can also remove the fat to acceptable levels either by automatic trimming or by hand. In a production line which is subjected to proper quality control, there is really no excuse for packs of meat or bacon to be released which have unacceptable levels of fat. If the image of pigmeat is to improve in these terms, it is critical that all members of the production chain bear in mind the consumer view, because waiting in the wings are competing meats and meat substitutes which may appear preferable to a health-obsessed public.

It is fair to state, however, that impressive progress has been made in the leanness of pigmeat on offer to the public, and this progress must be maintained.

## Drug and Other Residues

In the same vein of ensuring the wholesomeness of meat, there have been a number of highly regrettable lapses in production technology which have focussed attention on the fact that farmers can abuse the use of drugs in relation to their livestock. Careless farmers who use dirty needles and faulty injection techniques may cause severe infection and poor performance and receive a notice from the factory about the high incidence of abscesses. The matter does not, however, end there. Sooner or later, these slovenly practices come to the attention of the public either through the staff or the media. Who can blame them for wishing to eat something else?

Some drugs have an entirely appropriate use on the farm and it is a tribute to the enormous skill of the pharmaceutical companies that they have solved very intractable health and welfare problems by producing effective antiparasitic and antibacterial drugs. The potency of these products puts a very special responsibility on the producer. Not only is he morally bound to ensure the safety of his own staff who administer these products, but it is of paramount importance to follow the instruction of the manufacturing company in ensuring adequate withdrawal times. Nothing could be more disastrous than the discovery that producers were flouting these regulations. The certain outcome will be that units will in time be subjected to cumbersome regulations and that more of the consuming public will have been alienated.

## Perceived Welfare and Meat Consumption

'I do not eat pigmeat because I do not like the way it is produced.' In many countries this statement would be almost incomprehensible, as public concern about the welfare of animals is not a major issue. Most farmers would consider the statement to be unfair and also an irrelevance. However, in many Western countries this is an issue which looms large and is likely to develop in scale. Many individuals do not belong to an active welfare movement but register their protest by purchasing some other food. There are at least three constructive responses. The first is to work towards systems which are generally agreed to cater for the reasonable welfare of the animal. The second is to vigorously reject the criticisms which are levelled on the basis of wrong information. The third approach is to see the problem as a market opportunity for producing pigs in a defined and verifiable way which appeals to this sector of the public. For example, one may foresee the production of pork labelled as 'non-intensive' and 'antibiotic free'. It is quite likely that if producers react in this manner, then new methods of production will be developed which will broaden the total appeal of pigmeat and which at the same time can also be profitable to the farmer.

## ADDITIONAL READING

Kempster A. J., Cuthbertson, A. and Harrington, G. (1982), *Carcass Evaluation in Livestock Breeding, Production and Marketing*, Granada, London.

*Pork Industry Handbook*, USA Co-operative Extension Service, University of Illinois at Urbana-Champaign, USA.

# Chapter 5

# The Principles of Genetic Improvement

## THE TWO BASIC APPROACHES IN PIG IMPROVEMENT

The efficiency of pigmeat production can be improved by two basic approaches:

1. Improving the genotype
2. Improving the environment (i.e. all non-genetic factors)

The genotype of a pig sets a ceiling on the extent to which it can be improved by such environmental factors as housing, nutrition and management so it is important always to strive to improve pigs genetically.

At first sight it may not seem appropriate to explain to pig producers and students the mechanisms of pig genetic improvement because there are many highly professional companies that make their first-class genotypes available throughout the world. These companies are backed up by geneticists and technical staff of the highest calibre. Also in many countries, pig producers have ready access to improved genes through cooperative or state-run artificial insemination stations. Why then should any pig production enterprise undertake genetic improvement on its own account?

The first point to make is that simple genetic improvement is not too difficult technically once the underlying principles are understood. Secondly, there are many circumstances where a farmer may be unable to obtain easy access to improved replacement stock because of isolation, trade embargoes or the unavailability of stock to suit his own special environment in terms of such factors as climate, dietary type and disease challenge from, for example, feral pigs. A producer may also be afraid of jeopardising a jealously guarded high health status. This is not to say that the purchase of high health stock is not possible but it is very difficult to ensure that the health status of the purchased stock is identical with that of the recipient herd. For example, immigrant pigs may have a higher health status than the receiving herd and suffer a setback when introduced. Conversely, an outbreak of disease at the multiplier level may be unwittingly transmitted to customers before the problem has been identified. Another factor is that breeding companies must charge for their expertise and services and this is not always recovered in improved performance. The final factor concerns the loss of possible options for production which may occur if one is totally reliant on the provision of improved genes from a breeding company. For example, a producer may wish to adopt a strategy which involves a major use of once-bred gilts and, to make a commercial success of such an enterprise, these would probably have to be bred on the farm to be cost effective.

One important area where large scale units may achieve savings is by achieving some genetic improvement on the female side through on-farm selection and crossbreeding strategies while attempting to stay in step with new genetic advances by purchasing semen from an AI organisation with outstanding boars at stud.

A factor which influences the choice of whether to purchase genetic improvement or practise it 'in-house' is the increase in size of many commercial units to very large businesses. These have a choice between concentrating entirely on production and marketing activities or taking on board also their own selection programme for genetic improvement. Many well-run production units already have in place much of the necessary equipment and facilities such as a computerised recording scheme, high class feed and pig weighing facilities and ultrasonic equipment for measuring backfat thickness, together with the appropriate organisational and management skills. The final choice depends on the interests and capabilities of the entrepreneurs themselves. It is interesting to note that many successful breeding companies started out as highly efficient producer units.

In concluding this introduction to the subject it should be pointed out that breeding companies have made a tremendous contribution to both genetic improvement and the dissemination of healthy replacement stock; in addition, a few outstanding companies have made their findings available for the benefit of all on a worldwide basis and have contributed enormously to the improvement in efficiency of pig production. These organisations will continue to lead the way in the genetic improvement of the pig and to cater admirably for the vast number of producers throughout the world who wish to concentrate on the highly demanding tasks of efficient production and marketing of high-quality pigmeat while purchasing the superior genes incorporated into high-health stock (which are basic to their objectives of efficient pigmeat production) from the successful breeding companies.

The purpose of this chapter is to review the underlying science of breeding improvement and the various techniques which are used.

## GENETIC IMPROVEMENT TECHNIQUES

A pig's genetic potential in terms of economically important traits is governed by many different genes and improving this potential involves manipulating these genes. Genetic improvement involves introducing new and useful genes into a breed or strain or family or increasing the frequency of existing favourable genes or gene combinations. This can be done by crossing with other breeds or strains or by selecting within existing breeds, strains or families. Thus, the basic methods of genetic improvement are crossbreeding and selection or a combination of these two approaches. Before discussing these approaches further we must decide on the aspects of the pig's genotype which we would like to change.

## TRAITS TO BE IMPROVED GENETICALLY

When we apply ourselves to think about all the aspects of performance and appearance that we would like to improve in our pigs we end up with a very long list. Usually in any walk of life, the greater the number of things we have to improve, the slower the improvement in each one if we spread our effort equally over all the factors. This approach may well be acceptable but if we use different approaches to achieve our overall objective, we can usually speed up the rate of improvement achieved. Thus, in tackling the many factors which we should improve in the pig, we will find that it is easier and more cost-effective to influence some through manipulation of environmental factors such as housing, nutrition or management, others can be improved most readily by crossbreeding, while selection within breeds or strains is the sensible approach to employ in the improvement of other traits.

Thus, from the list of factors in the pig that we would like to improve, we have got to decide on the most effective route for improvement. Of course, if we re-examine critically our original list of factors we might well decide that some are not really worth bothering about. Thus, we must rationalise our improvement objectives.

## RATIONALISING IMPROVEMENT OBJECTIVES BETWEEN ENVIRONMENTAL AND ALTERNATIVE GENETIC APPROACHES

In setting out to improve the efficiency of pigmeat production we must establish for each factor:

- its relative economic importance (economic weight)
- its heritability
- the degree to which it is correlated both genetically and phenotypically with other economically important traits
- the extent to which it can be influenced by heterosis through crossbreeding.

These considerations will now be dealt with briefly.

### 1. Relative Economic Importance

It is fairly easy to attribute an economic value to certain traits, e.g. an extra pig weaned per litter or a 5 per cent improvement in the food conversion efficiency of a particular diet. On the other hand, it is more difficult to place an accurate value on other economically important traits such as an extra 1 per cent of lean meat in the finished carcass or an improvement in the quality of lean meat, since, in most countries, payment for carcasses is not yet made directly on the basis of either lean meat or its quality. Nevertheless, if traits are of economic importance now or are likely to be in the future, an attempt must be made to place an economic value on them. Moreover, since improvement through selection, in particular, is a long term process, we must consider traits which may not be very important at present but may become much more so in the future. It is possible, for instance, that aspects related to the content, quality and composition of fat in pigmeat may become much more important in the future.

The relative economic values or weightings of several traits in pig production, based on 1988 values, are detailed in Table 5.1.

**TABLE 5.1  Relative economic weighting of pig production traits in the United Kingdom (based on 1988 values) (each calculated independently of the other)**

| Trait | Unit | Estimated value |
|---|---|---|
| Daily liveweight gain | +1 g per day | +£0.01 |
| Food conversion efficiency | | |
|    (kg food per kg liveweight gain) | −0.1 | +£1.00 |
| Percentage lean in carcass | +1% | +£0.60 |
| Pigs marketed per litter | +1 | +£1.50 |
| Area of eye muscle (*cm²*) | +1 | +£0.03 |
| Killing out percentage | +1 | +£0.55 |

(Source: Meat and Livestock Commission, 1988, and Webb, A.J., 1988)

If it was as easy to achieve a unit improvement in food conversion efficiency (0.1) as it was to increase eye muscle area by one unit (1 sq cm) then the priority for attention through changes in the genotype or environment (or by a combination of both approaches) should be in improving food conversion since it is worth more to the farmer.

## 2.  Heritability ($h^2$)

This is defined as the proportion of the superiority of the dam and sire in a particular trait (over their contemporaries) that, on average, is passed on to their progeny. Heritabilities of some important traits in pig production are outlined in Table 5.2.

The higher the heritability of a trait, the easier it is to improve it by selection through harnessing what are termed 'additive' genetic effects. Conversely, traits of low heritability are much more influenced by environmental factors and other genetic influences (non-additive) which cannot be exploited by selection. If we take litter size at birth, with a mean heritability of 10 per cent, this in effect means that

**TABLE 5.2  Heritability of important traits in pigs**

| | Level | Range (%) | Mean (%) |
|---|---|---|---|
| Litter size at birth | Low | 5−15 | 10 |
| Litter size | | | |
|    at weaning | Low | 5−15 | 10 |
| Daily liveweight gain | High | 45−55 | 50 |
| Food conversion | | | |
|    efficiency | Medium | 25−40 | 35 |
| Backfat thickness | High | 40−60 | 50 |
| Body lean content | High | 40−60 | 50 |
| Pig weight | | | |
|    at weaning | Low | 5−15 | 10 |

through genetic selection we have a 10 per cent influence over it. The remaining 90 per cent of the variation in litter size is due partly to non-additive genetic influences and partly to environmental factors, only some of which are understood and are controllable. Non-additive genetic influences can be exploited to some extent by well-planned crossbreeding schemes while one can also try to achieve more control over environmental factors which influence litter size such as service management, disease prevention, housing and nutrition. Given the choice between selection on the one hand and trying to control environmental influences combined with implementing sound crossbreeding schemes on the other in setting out to improve litter size, we should exploit the latter approaches to the fullest possible extent initially.

## 3. Heterosis and Crossbreeding

When individuals from two separate breeds or strains are mated and the performance of the resulting progeny in a particular trait is above the mean for the two parents, then heterosis or hybrid vigour is said to have occurred. The range of possible results from crossbreeding is illustrated in Figure 5.1.

The degree to which pig performance traits are influenced by crossbreeding and heterosis is indicated in Table 5.3.

It can be seen that traits associated with fertility, viability and lactation show

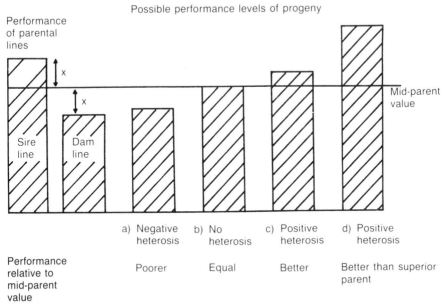

FIGURE 5.1 Possible consequences of crossing different breeds or strains in terms of a specific trait.

**TABLE 5.3 Heterosis estimates for pig production traits**

| Trait | Advantage of F1 progeny over mid-parent value (units) | (%) | Additional heterosis benefits from use of a crossbred dam (units) | (%) |
|---|---|---|---|---|
| Litter size at birth (pigs) | +0.30 | 3 | +0.75 | 8 |
| Litter size at weaning (pigs) | +0.45 | 6 | +0.85 | 11 |
| Individual piglet weight at weaning (kg)[a] | +0.5 | 5 | 0 | 0 |
| Litter weight at weaning (kg)[a] | +9 | 12 | +8 | 10 |
| Post-weaning growth rate (kg/day) | +0.04 | 6 | 0 | 0 |
| Age at slaughter (days) | −10 | 5 | 0 | 0 |
| Food conversion ratio (kg feed/kg liveweight gain) | −0.08 | 3 | 0 | 0 |
| Body composition and meat quality | 0 | 0 | 0 | 0 |

[a] Based on 6 week weaning
(From: Sellier, 1976)

higher heterosis following crossbreeding than feed efficiency and carcass traits, whereas the latter traits, being more highly heritable, are easier to improve by selection. This provides the animal breeder with an almost acceptable compromise since he can set out to improve the more heritable traits by selection while he can exploit crossbreeding and heterosis to improve many of the commercially important traits of low heritability.

Another very important genetic improvement technique involves selection between breeds or strains, and this can be followed by crossing boars from a breed or strain superior in a particular trait to another breed or strain lacking in this trait. An example of this approach is crossing a breed such as the Pietrain, which has excellent eye muscle area, with a breed such as the British Landrace, which is less well endowed in this respect. From such crossbreeding, one is not expecting heterosis to any extent but is merely looking for mid-parent value in the progeny in terms of eye muscle area.

From the foregoing discussions, therefore, three basic approaches to achieving genetic improvement emerge.

## THE THREE APPROACHES TO GENETIC IMPROVEMENT

### 1. Selection Between Lines or Breeds

Introducing into a country or to an individual farm a breed or strain which has already been improved in one or more economically important traits is nearly always the quickest and most efficient method of obtaining genetic improvement, provided that health aspects can be safeguarded. The new breed or strain can be used in purebreeding or it can be crossed with an existing breed or strain. A current example of this approach in the United Kingdom is the use of certain genotypes from Western Europe such as the Belgian Landrace and the Pietrain in crossing programmes with Large White and Landrace stock to achieve in the progeny significant improvements in carcass yield, eye muscle area, lean meat yield, increased proportion of ham and of lean to bone ratio.

## 2.  Crossbreeding

Crossbreeding is used for two basic purposes. It is employed where the lines to be crossed have different attributes and a good crossing system exploits the complementary nature of different lines by exploiting the strengths while hiding the weaknesses of each line. Crossbreeding can also exploit the phenomenon of heterosis which is most evident in traits associated with reproduction, fitness and viability. One of the best examples of crossbreeding is the use of two lines (e.g. A and B) which are strong on reproductive traits to form a *dam line* and the use on these A × B sows of boars from a *sire line* (C) which is strong on growth, food conversion efficiency and carcass traits. Thus, the system becomes:

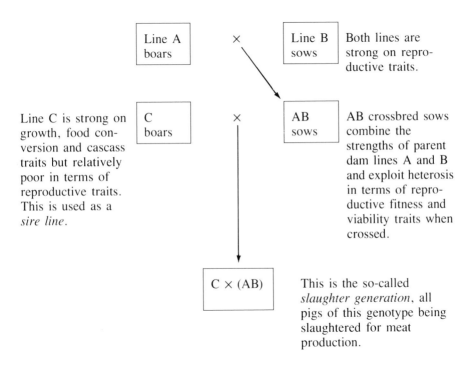

| Line A boars | × | Line B sows | Both lines are strong on reproductive traits. |

Line C is strong on growth, food conversion and cascass traits but relatively poor in terms of reproductive traits. This is used as a *sire line*.

| C boars | × | AB sows | AB crossbred sows combine the strengths of parent dam lines A and B and exploit heterosis in terms of reproductive fitness and viability traits when crossed. |

| C × (AB) | This is the so-called *slaughter generation*, all pigs of this genotype being slaughtered for meat production. |

In this system, while heterosis is exploited in terms of the traits which show the phenomenon, the strength of the crossbreds is very much dependent on the attributes of the original parental lines. Thus, improving parental lines will improve the quality of crossbred progeny resulting from the mating together of these lines. This brings us to the third approach to genetic improvement.

## 3.  Within Line Selection

Of the three basic methods of genetic improvement, this method is the most difficult and expensive since it attempts to influence the polygenic mode of inheritance (under the control of many genes) which controls most traits of economic impor-

*(text continued on page 58)*

A range of some of the world's most important pig genotypes

Plate 5.1 The British Large White (from which the American Yorkshire is descended). Up to now the incidence of halothane reactors in this breed has been negligible. (Courtesy of the Pig Improvement Company)

Plate 5.2 The British Landrace which when crossed with the Large White provides an excellent commercial sow. (Courtesy of Pig International)

Plate 5.3 The Danish Landrace was carefully developed in Denmark to constitute one of the import-ant components of the country's considerable reputation for high-quality pigmeat. It has a relatively low incidence of the 'halothane' gene. (Courtesy of *Pig Farming*)

Plate 5.4 The Pietrain is very well muscled but also has a high incidence of the 'halothane' gene.

Plate 5.5 The American Duroc is strong in the leg and has an excellent reputation for performing well in tough conditions. It also appears to have a higher proportion of marbling (intramuscular) fat than other genotypes. (Courtesy of Newsham Hybrid Pigs)

Plate 5.6 The American Hampshire is well muscled and has good carcass yield characteristics.

Plate 5.7 The British Saddleback has a reputation for good mothering ability. It is somewhat early maturing and is a popular component of commercial sows for outdoor ('Roadnight') production systems in the UK. (Courtesy of the Pig Improvement Company)

Plate 5.8 The Chester White, developed in the United States, is an alternative white strain to the American Yorkshire.

Plate 5.9   The Red Wattle from the United States is an example of selection for traits (e.g. the wattle) which bear no relationship to the efficiency of production of good quality pigmeat.

Plate 5.10   The Chinese Meishan has a reputation for very high prolificacy and early maturity. It is less strong on growth and carcass traits. (Courtesy of the Pig Improvement Company)

Plate 5.11a   A sire line hybrid boar developed by the Pig Improvement Company to produce the slaughter generation for the UK market. Its development has involved the integration of genes from various breeds to achieve efficient growth of lean tissue, combined with desirable carcass and meat quality characteristics.

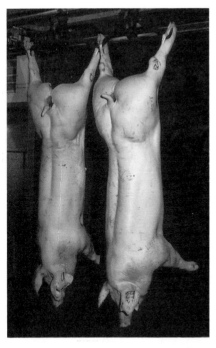

Plate 5.11b   The progeny of sire line boars showing the blocky carcasses and well-developed hams.

Plate 5.12   The Belgian Landrace, which is blocky and well muscled but has a fairly high incidence of the halothene gene. (Courtesy of the Pig Improvement Company)

Plate 5.13   The Welsh breed, which is similar in appearance to the British Landrace. (Courtesy of the Pig Improvement Company)

Plate 5.14 The Berkshire, which is an early maturing genotype and was an important breed in Britain in the past. (Courtesy of the Pig Improvement Company)

Plate 5.15 The Camborough Blue hybrid sow bred for modern outdoor pig production in Britain. (Courtesy of the Pig Improvement Company)

Plate 5.16 Sows of the European wild breed with their young.

tance. This approach should therefore be considered only when selection between lines or breeds and crossbreeding have been fully exploited. However, after these two methods are fully exploited, within line selection remains as the only way to make further genetic progress.

Genetic progress through selection in terms of the economic worth of the animal is maximised under the following conditions:

- Breeding animals are selected on the basis of the *most economically important traits*.
- These traits can be *measured accurately* before normal market weight in both sexes; there must be a large amount of *variation* in these traits within the line or breed and a high proportion of the variability must be *heritable*.

- Alternatively, a trait which is *closely correlated genetically* with the trait under selection can be measured accurately and relatively easily and can be used as the basis of selection (e.g. use of backfat thickness measured ultrasonically to predict total carcass fat content).
- As small a proportion as possible of the available animals are chosen as parents of the next generation, and the selected animals are the very best ones in terms of the traits we wish to improve. This is referred to as the *selection intensity* or the *selection differential*.
- New, genetically improved generations replace previous generations as quickly as possible. This is referred to as the *generation turnover*.

Thus, achieving maximum genetic progress in the economic worth of pigs through selection within lines or breeds is dependent on (1) deciding on the most economically important traits now and in the foreseeable future, (2) the ease and accuracy of measurement of these traits, (3) the variability in these traits in the population and their heritability, (4) the selection intensity which can be applied and (5) the speed of replacing older generations with new, genetically improved generations.

Some of these factors merit further illustration and discussion and this will be done after outlining the phenomenon of Mendelian inheritance by which genetic improvement can be made in some traits by a combination of crossbreeding and selection.

## MENDELIAN INHERITANCE

Some traits are not the result of many genes being expressed but of either a single gene or a small group of linked genes. This leads to a rather discrete pattern of inheritance first shown by Mendel in his classic work with green and yellow peas. The point is that a trait influenced by a single gene is expressed in one of three forms. These are the so-called homozygous dominant, the homozygous recessive and the heterozygous (or mixture of dominant and recessive). These terms are best illustrated using a simple example. In pigs, white colour is usually dominant to colours such as black, blue and red, these latter three colours being regarded as recessives.

Let us represent the genotypes as follows:

> White pig = WW (White colour in double dose
> i.e. a homozygous white)
> Black pig = ww (Black colour in double dose
> i.e. a homozygous black)

When these white and black pigs are mated together we get the following progeny:

| *Parents* | | | *Progeny* |
|---|---|---|---|
| WW ♂ | × | ww ♀ | → Ww |
| (White pig) | | (Black pig) | (Pig with colour genes from either parent, i.e. white colour from the male and black colour from the female parent) |
| (Homozygous) | | (Homozygous) | (Heterozygous) |
| (White) | | (Black) | |

The heterozygous (Ww) genotype should be white in colour since white (W) is dominant to black (w). However, 'dominant' and 'recessive' are not perfect descriptions in this situation since quite often the heterozygote (Ww) shows a mixture of parental types in that spotted or brindled pigs occur with moderate frequency. A much more exact version of Mendelian inheritance is shown in the case of pigs which are subject to porcine stress syndrome (PSS). This gene is very common in breeds such as the Pietrain and Belgian Landrace and in its pure recessive form is expressed as an extremely muscular animal which is also subject to stress and sudden death. Because such animals show an unusual response to the widely used anaesthetic halothane and after a few inhalations of this anaesthetic go rigid, it is widely known as the halothane gene. More details of the effects of this gene will be given later in this and also in the next chapter. It is important to know, however, that because it is a Mendelian gene we can breed for its presence or absence very accurately.

In simplest terms, the recessive gene (h) is expressed as follows when an animal with a double dose of this sensitive gene is mated with a normal animal without this gene:

| *Parents* | | | *Progeny* |
|---|---|---|---|
| hh | × | HH | → Hh |
| Boar with double dose of halothane gene (Positive to halothane test) | | Normal female Halothane gene not present (Negative to halothane test) | Heterozygote Halothane gene in single dose (Negative to halothane test) |

Thus, only the homozygous recessive animal (hh) is positive to the halothane test. However, when two heterozygotes are mated together the following occurs:

| *Heterozygous Parents* | *Possible progeny* |
|---|---|
| Hh ♂ × Hh ♀ | → HH (Normal) |
| | → Hh (Normal) |
| | → hh (Positive to halothane test) |

One can check for the presence of the halothane gene in what appears to be a normal boar, for example, by mating this boar with a known homozygous recessive sow (hh). If none of the progeny prove to be positive to the halothane test, then the boar is not carrying the halothane gene.

## WITHIN LINE SELECTION — FURTHER CONSIDERATION OF THE BASIS OF GENETIC IMPROVEMENT

### 1. Calculating Economic Value of Traits

As indicated earlier, under a particular set of economic conditions, it is a simple matter to attribute a financial value to a percentage increase in some factors, such as feed conversion efficiency on a particular diet. However, it is more difficult to attribute a financial value to a unit improvement in such an important factor as carcass lean content or in an aspect of lean quality since payment for carcasses is not yet based directly on these criteria in many situations. Nevertheless, an estimate of the economic worth of each trait must be made as a basis for decisions to direct selection policy.

### 2. Ease and Accuracy of Measurement of Traits

It is a simple and easy matter to measure some important traits such as liveweight gain. This is done by weighing the animal at intervals during its growth and carrying out a simple calculation of the liveweight gained per unit of time. This is often called *performance testing*, i.e. the assessment is carried out on the live animal. While liveweight gain is easy to measure, that of the gain in carcass weight or in lean meat is much more difficult. Moreover, measurement of such a vital trait as feed conversion efficiency is very laborious and expensive, involving as it does the measurement of feed intake on a family, group or individual basis. Recording feed intake of individual pigs involves penning pigs singly or individual feeding, both of which involve greater expense in housing. Accurate measurement of carcass attributes such as lean and fat content or lean-to-bone ratio involve slaughter and expensive carcass dissection into constituent tissues. Cheaper compromises which result in loss of accuracy involve dissection of a 'sample' joint to provide a measure of lean, fat and bone, while backfat thickness can be used to provide either an estimate of carcass fat content or an indirect estimate of carcass lean content.

Obviously, when potential breeding animals are being assessed for carcass attributes, estimates must be made on the live animal, such as with the use of ultrasonic machines to estimate backfat thickness. Alternatively, the close relatives of potential breeding animals can be slaughtered and their carcass measurements can be used to estimate breeding value. Thus, an animal's sibs (brothers or sisters) can be used in 'sib tests' or its progeny can be used in progeny testing to estimate the breeding value of their unslaughtered relative. This approach must be used to assess aspects of meat quality since, apart from testing for the presence of the halothene gene (see page 60), these characteristics cannot be assessed in the live animal.

Thus, many economically important traits are difficult and expensive to measure in providing a basis for selection.

### 3. Variability of a Trait in the Population Being Improved

The greater the variation in a heritable trait in a population of pigs, the greater the scope for selection and the easier it will be to achieve genetic improvement.

A population of pigs in terms of their performance in a particular trait, for example, liveweight gain, can be represented by Figure 5.2a. Most of the animals in Strain A have a liveweight gain which is fairly close to the mean. A small proportion will be very much worse than the mean, while a few pigs will have excellent growth rates very much higher than the mean. This shape of curve to describe a population of pigs in terms of a particular trait is called the 'normal distribution', which is symmetrical about the mean, i.e. the shape is the same on either side of the mean.

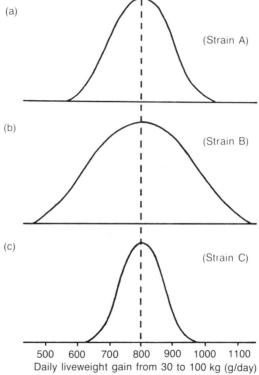

FIGURE 5.2   Three strains of pigs with identical mean growth rate under the same conditions of housing, nutrition, health control and management but with widely different degrees of variability in growth rate within the strain.

Each of the populations of pigs described by Figures 5.2b (Strain B) and 5.2c (Strain C) also has the same shape on either side of its respective mean. However, these two populations are very different. Strain C is much more uniform in growth rate than Strain B. While this greater uniformity in growth rate may be attractive from a commercial standpoint, from the point of view of the animal breeder trying to improve growth rate by selection in these groups of pigs, it will be much easier to make improvements in Strain B. While the very best pigs in Strain C have daily liveweight gains from 30 to 100 kg liveweight of 980 g, the best ones in Strain B have a daily liveweight gain of over 1100 g.

In selecting the best 1 per cent of boars for growth rate for siring the next generation within these strains, the best individual boars selected from Strain B will have very much higher growth rates than the best boars selected from Strain C. This degree of superiority of animals selected for breeding relative to the rest of the group is termed the *selection differential* or *selection intensity*.

The greater the selection intensity in a particular trait the greater the improvement which can be achieved by selection. Because a higher proportion of female breeding stock are required than males to produce the next generation, greater selection intensity can be achieved through the boars than through the gilts. Even greater selection intensity can be achieved through boars if AI rather than natural service is used because of the need for a very much smaller number of boars. With this reduced need, through AI, only the very best boars need be retained for breeding.

## 4. Heritability of Traits

Heritability is the proportion of the superiority of the selected boars and gilts over their contemporaries which, on average, can be passed on to their progeny. The higher the heritability of a trait the greater the improvement which can be made by sound selection. In two traits which have the same percentage variability, if we apply the same degree of selection intensity to one of moderate heritability (around 0.5), for example liveweight gain, as to one of low heritability (around 0.1), for example litter size, we achieve a much greater degree of improvement in the more highly heritable trait. However, if a trait has a low heritability but at the same time is highly variable, then it can be improved just as much as a trait which has a higher heritability but a very low level of variation in the population.

## 5. Generation Turnover

Generation turnover is the rate at which one generation of parents is replaced by the next and is defined as the average age of a parent at the birth of its offspring. If gilts and young boars are bred together and replaced by selected progeny after just one litter, then generation turnover will be approximately once per year. If gilts are kept for five litters and boars kept for an equivalent length of time before being culled and replaced by selected progeny, then generation turnover will be approximately two years. This assumes that progeny born in first to fifth litters are equally likely to be chosen as replacements. Hence the sow kept for 5 litters has them at 1, $1\frac{1}{2}$, 2, $2\frac{1}{2}$ and 3, but on average at 2 years of age.

In a situation of steady replacement of existing breeding stock with carefully selected superior progeny, then rapid generation turnover is desirable. On the other hand, rapid generation turnover involves a reduction in selection intensity since a higher proportion of each generation has to be selected as replacement stock. Thus, a compromise has to be reached between maximising generation turnover and selection intensity. Since breeding sows are most productive in their third to sixth parities, the temptation is to retain good sows for up to six parities before replacing them with improved, carefully selected gilts while boars may be turned over slightly more frequently. This slower turnover of breeding stock which is undesirable, in theory, from a genetic improvement point of view, is a possible compromise to adopt in some situations for it allows a greater selection intensity to be applied in deciding on replacement stock, while exploiting the superior reproductive performance of third to sixth parity sows. In practice, the pig breeder who is selling a lot of breeding stock often turns over his generations quickly so as to optimise his rate of genetic improvement and to enable him to sell genetically superior stock to customers. On the other hand, the producer who is purchasing replacements will probably find in most situations that it is more profitable to exploit the superior reproductive performance of middle-aged sows and will therefore turn over sows less frequently than the breeder.

## 6. Rate of Genetic Improvement

While the factors outlined above — variability, heritability, accuracy of measurement, selection intensity and generation turnover — all have an influence on the rate of genetic improvement which can be achieved in a particular aspect of pig performance, the most important influences the pig breeder can have is on the accuracy of measurement and the selection intensity applied. This is because in a given herd or population, the breeder cannot do anything to increase genetic variability in a particular trait other than by bringing in stock and genes from outside, nor can he influence the heritability of that trait. The point has already been made that factors associated with sow productivity are likely to discourage him from turning sows over too quickly.

### CALCULATING RESPONSE TO SELECTION

Estimated response to selection is calculated using the formula:

$$\frac{R}{\text{(Selection Response per year)}} = \frac{\text{Heritability } (h^2) \times \text{Selection Differential (S)}}{\text{Generation turnover in years (Y)}}$$

The following is a simple example of the application of this formula applied to reducing backfat thickness (measured ultrasonically on the live animals):

*Factor* *Backfat thickness* (mm) at the last rib at 90 kg liveweight (Point $P_2$)

| | | |
|---|---|---|
| 1. Mean for whole herd | = | 16 (A) |
| 2. Mean for selected boars | = | 12 (B) |
| 3. Mean for selected gilts | = | 14 (C) |

*Calculated Selection Differentials* (S)

| | | |
|---|---|---|
| 1. Boars (A−B) i.e. 16−12 | = | 4 |
| 2. Gilts (A−C) i.e. 16−14 | = | 2 |
| Total | = | 6 |
| mean for gilts and boars | = | 3 |
| *Heritability* ($h^2$) of backfat thickness | = | 0.5 |

*Generation turnover* (Y) = 2 years
(Sows replaced after 5 litters
i.e. at approximately 3 years of age
and boars replaced at same stage
but the average age of the parents
at the birth of the progeny is
2 years)

*Calculation of Selection Response*

Response (R)     = $h^2$ S

                 = 0.5 × 3.0

                 = 1.5 mm per generation

Response per year = $\dfrac{h^2 S}{Y}$

                 = $\dfrac{0.5 \times 3.0}{3}$

                 = 0.75 mm per year

It can be seen that by applying this degree of selection intensity and with the generation turnover of two years, the estimated response to selection in terms of reduced backfat thickness is reasonable at 0.75 mm per year.

## OTHER CONSIDERATIONS IN SELECTION

In addition to the factors discussed above, it is important in evolving a sound selection policy to be aware of traits which are correlated with each other genetically either in a desirable or an undesirable way. In addition, we must be conscious of the existence of genetic defects and decide whether these are important enough to worry about and, if they are, we must plan our tactics so as to deal with them.

### Correlated Traits

Many important traits are related genetically so that when we set out to improve one trait we also influence another which is connected with it in a genetic manner.

Geneticists often speak about *positive* or *negative correlations* between traits. An example of a positive correlation is that between food intake and both liveweight gain and backfat thickness. In increasing food intake we also increase the correlated traits of liveweight gain and backfat thickness. From a practical point of view, the importance of genetic correlations is easier to appreciate if we talk about *desirable* and *undesirable correlations* rather than about positive and negative ones. In the example given, food intake was positively correlated with (1) liveweight gain and (2) backfat thickness. While correlation (1) is a desirable one from a production viewpoint, correlation (2) is an undesirable one since fatter carcasses are discriminated against in most markets. Some examples of the two types of relationships are given below:

1. DESIRABLE GENETIC CORRELATIONS
   Food intake and liveweight gain
   Fat deposition and food conversion efficiency
   Lean tissue growth and feed conversion efficiency
   Lean tissue growth and carcass leanness

2. UNDESIRABLE GENETIC CORRELATIONS
   Food intake and fat deposition
   Per cent lean and quality of lean
   Growth rate and soundness of legs

It is important to be aware of these associations between traits but in practice there is only a limited amount which can be done to take them into account in genetic improvement programmes. To some extent, food intake is not an end in itself and it is only useful to the extent that it increases lean tissue growth rate (LTGR) and may improve lean tissue food conversion (LTFC). By choosing these 2 latter traits as selection objectives, only that component of food intake which is beneficial to LTGR and LTFC will be selected. The inverse correlation between per cent lean and quality of lean is much more difficult to accommodate. In general, the most important factor in this context is the incidence of the halothane gene since this is associated with higher lean percentage but poorer quality of lean.

Other criteria of lean quality such as intramuscular fat is at present very contentious in terms of its real importance to eating quality and therefore it cannot be given an appropriate economic weighting. The question of leg soundness is also controversial but can be accommodated in selection by a scoring system and an independent culling level, that is, a score which the breeder deems to be totally unacceptable.

The existence of desirable and undesirable genetic correlations are taken into account insofar as possible in the formulation of selection indices (see Chapter 6 page 80, Figure 6.10 and Table 6.6).

CONGENITAL DEFECTS

A series of defects which are found in pigs are sometimes termed 'congenital' defects. A Meat and Livestock Commission study in the United Kingdom examined the incidence of such defects in pigs sired by AI boars. The results of this study are presented in Table 5:4. It can be seen that the overall incidence of these defects was low, although a higher incidence was recorded in the Landrace than in the Large White breed, the apparent between-breed difference being mainly in the number of pigs affected by splay leg and Pityriasis rosea. The incidence of individual defects was very low. What is unclear about most of these defects is the relative parts played by genetics, by environmental factors and by a combination of the two. Of the defects listed, only Pityriasis rosea (which causes red ringworm like lesions on the pig and is relatively harmless) has been shown to be inherited in a simple manner.

In view of the uncertainty regarding the role of genetics, if any, in relation to many of these defects, apart from taking the sensible precaution not to use affected animals for breeding (nor their sibs where more than one piglet in a litter is af-

**TABLE 5.4  Observed incidence of congenital defects in pigs sired by AI boars**

|  | Large White | Landrace |
|---|---|---|
| Number of boars | 91 | 75 |
| Number of farms | 371 | 292 |
| Number of litters | 1,463 | 1,358 |
| Number of pigs | 15,206 | 13,830 |
| *Defect* | *Incidence (%)* | |
| Pityriasis rosea | 0.32 | 1.36 |
| Splay leg | 0.12 | 1.42 |
| Scrotal/inguinal hernia | 0.47 | 0.72 |
| No anus (Atresia ani) | 0.24 | 0.38 |
| Rig (cryptorchidism) | 0.22 | 0.20 |
| Umbilical hernia | 0.11 | 0.07 |
| Female genital defects | 0.07 | 0.17 |
| Hermaphrodite | 0.06 | 0.07 |
| Shakes (tremors) | 0.06 | 0.04 |
|  | 1.66 | 4.43 |

(Source: 'Developmental Abnormalities in British Pigs', unpublished manuscript by Reed, H.C.B. and Hill, W.G., 1976)

fected), there would appear to be no justification for manipulating breeding policy in any other way. However, if there appears to be an unacceptable incidence of any of these abnormalities, it would be prudent to examine very closely the possible existence of a genetic component from a particular family or strain.

Another defect known to be inherited in a simple manner is the previously mentioned porcine stress syndrome, which is caused by a double recessive gene (now called the halothene gene). While this gene is undesirable from the viewpoint of PSS, it is also associated with many desirable pig carcass attributes which are being exploited by appropriate selection and crossbreeding strategies. This will be discussed in more detail in the following chapter.

## ADDITIONAL READING

Dalton D. C. (1985), *An Introduction to Practical Animal Breeding*, Collins, London.

Fowler V. R., Bichard M. and Pease A. (1976), 'Objectives in Pig Breeding', *Anim. Prod.* **23**, 265.

Johannsen I. and Rendel J. (1968), *Genetics and Animal Breeding*, W H Freeman, London.

*Proceeding of the Third World Congress on Genetics Applied to Livestock Production* (1986), Volumes 9–12, University of Nebraska, Lincoln, Nebraska.

*Chapter 6*

# Achieving Genetic Improvement

## DECIDING ON OBJECTIVES IN PIG IMPROVEMENT

The criteria which should be used to decide which pig production traits should be improved by either between-line selection, crossbreeding or within-line selection were outlined in the previous chapter. They included economic importance, heritability and heterosis estimates, variability in the population and the ease and cost of measuring the trait.

Although this book does not concern itself with the breeding and lactating sow but rather deals with the pig from weaning to slaughter, nevertheless, in discussing the factors which should be improved by genetic means, aspects of sow productivity must be considered. Breeding improvement strategy must consider how best, in combination with environmental approaches, the overall efficiency of the pigmeat production process can be improved in the most cost-effective way. Thus, aspects of sow productivity must be incorporated, as desirable, into the breeding improvement plans.

To provide a basis for deciding on the traits which should be incorporated into breeding improvement strategies for pigmeat production and to decide on how best these strategies can be implemented in practice, the major groups of traits which merit consideration will be discussed.

### Groups of Important Traits in Pig Production

CARCASS TRAITS
The major components of the pig carcass are lean, fat and bone. Consumer demand in the future will almost certainly be for lean meat with just enough subcutaneous and inter- and intra-muscular fat (around 10 per cent of total fat) to give the essential properties of tenderness, succulence and flavour to the meat. Thus, high ratios of lean to bone and lean to fat will be required in the final carcass.

Improvements in the ratio of lean to fat, in particular, are likely to be achieved by the combined efforts of nutritionists and geneticists, with an important contribution also being made by a reduction in, and perhaps eventually a complete cessation of, the practice of castration of male pigs which are to be slaughtered well before the stage of sexual maturity is likely to be reached.

In achieving improvement in lean to fat ratio through selective breeding, it is important to have simple but accurate measures of lean content in the live animal, and further improvements in ultrasonic equipment are likely to make this possible in the near future. As well as providing a simpler and sounder basis for selection of such a trait, this will also facilitate accurate measurement of the growth of lean tissue.

Other traits in the finished pig and its carcass likely to increase in importance are killing out percentage, larger eye muscle area and a higher proportion of carcass weight in the more expensive areas such as the ham. This improvement, as well as some improvements in overall lean content and in lean to bone ratio, are likely to be achieved in a more cost-effective way by crossing the breeds which are strong in these respects with those which are less adequate. In Britain, such developments are likely to involve the use of sire lines based on suitable strains of such breeds as the German and Belgian Landrace and Pietrain with British breeds such as the Large White and the Landrace.

LEAN AND FAT QUALITY TRAITS

There is some evidence to indicate that, as breeds are improved in terms of leanness and the rate of lean meat growth, so meat quality has tended to decline.

Certain strains of Pietrain and European Landrace breeds which are extremely lean appear to have a high incidence of the porcine stress syndrome (PSS). When such animals are exposed to the stress associated with mixing, transport, violent exercise, mating or farrowing, an irreversible rise in temperature may occur followed by sudden death. In addition, these strains are associated with lower feed intake, lower liveweight gain, poorer food conversion efficiency and lower litter size, while carcasses from such animals have a higher incidence of PSE (pale, soft, exudative) meat. The muscles appear pale or two-toned, they suffer from high drip loss and curing difficulties are experienced. These problems appear to be associated with a recessive gene which, however, has beneficial effects on the quantity of lean meat in the carcass. The main problem arises in pigs which are homozygous for this recessive gene (see page 60). Pigs which are heterozygous for this gene have the superior lean meat qualities with only a low incidence of the meat quality problems associated with PSS. The presence of this recessive gene in homozygous animals can be identified with a high degree of accuracy at about 10 weeks of age through their reaction after inhaling the anaesthetic gas halothane. Stress-resistant pigs (i.e. those heterozygous for the gene or free from it) go to sleep in a completely relaxed state, while animals carrying the gene in double dose lie with their legs extended and rigid. Because of the test used to detect the presence of this gene in pigs, it has been termed the 'halothene gene'. The incidence of reaction to the halothene test by various breeds which have been tested by Dr Webb, formerly of the Animal Breeding Research Organisation in Edinburgh, is detailed in Table 6.1. It can be seen that the frequency of reactors varied from 0 to 100 per cent. While the British Large White had no reactors, all the Dutch Pietrains tested were positive reactors.

It would appear that the more obviously compact and muscular the breed, the higher is the average stress susceptibility. While pigs homozygous for the halothane gene are undesirable because of their stress susceptibility and other deficiencies, heterozygous animals, while having the advantages of good muscling, are not stress susceptible and have a very low incidence of muscle quality problems. It may be

**TABLE 6.1  Incidence of positive reaction to halothane anaesthesia in different breeds**

| Breed | Tested pigs reacting (%) |
| --- | --- |
| British Large White | 0 |
| Duroc | 0 |
| Hampshire (Europe) | 2 |
| Dutch Yorkshire | 3 |
| Swiss Large White | 6 |
| Landrace | |
| Norwegian | 5 |
| Danish | 7 |
| British | 11 |
| Swedish | 15 |
| Dutch | 22 |
| German | 70 |
| Belgian | 88 |
| Pietrain | |
| French | 34 |
| Dutch | 100 |

(Source: Dr A J Webb, Animal Breeding Research Organisation, Edinburgh)

possible to exploit the advantages of these heavily muscled breeds while avoiding their main disadvantages by using reactor boars as a sire line and mating these to female lines which are free from the gene but which are also lacking in the carcass attributes associated with this gene. Such a scheme suggested by the Pig Improvement Company (UK and USA) is outlined in Figure 6.1. Although there are stress susceptible pigs in the sire line, the Pig Improvement Company point out that this is likely to be more than compensated for by the positive benefits.

Compared with the British Large White and Landrace breeds, contemporary Pietrain and Belgian/German Landrace pigs have the following advantages:

1. Up to $5\frac{1}{2}$ per cent higher carcass dressing percentage
2. Up to 8 per cent more lean meat yield
3. Larger eye muscle area by up to 13 cm$^2$
4. Higher proportion of carcass weight in the ham
5. Higher lean to bone ratios (8—9:1 relative to 6:1 for the British breeds)

The slaughter generation progeny of such matings will demonstrate mid parent values for these traits, i.e. they will inherit half the sire's carcass advantages and at the same time remain entirely stress free.

PROBLEMS ASSOCIATED WITH VERY LEAN PIGS
A major objective in genetic improvement programmes for a considerable time has been increased carcass lean content and an increase in lean tissue growth. The effort to achieve increased carcass lean content has been very successful, and available data indicate a gradual and significant decline in carcass fatness over the years.

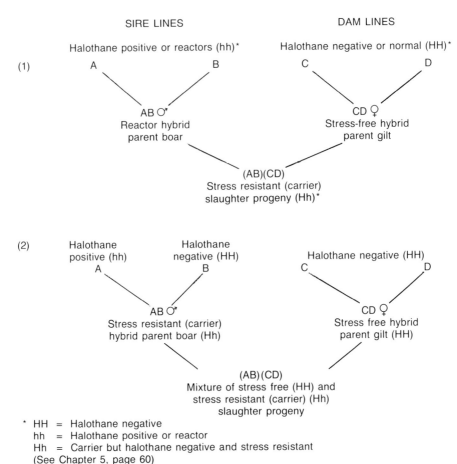

(1)

Halothane positive or reactors (hh)*        Halothane negative or normal (HH)*

A                    B            C                    D

AB ♂                          CD ♀
Reactor hybrid                Stress-free hybrid
parent boar                   parent gilt

(AB)(CD)
Stress resistant (carrier)
slaughter progeny (Hh)*

(2)      Halothane        Halothane
positive (hh)    negative (HH)              Halothane negative (HH)
A                B            C                    D

AB ♂                          CD ♀
Stress resistant (carrier)    Stress free hybrid
hybrid parent boar (Hh)       parent gilt (HH)

(AB)(CD)
Mixture of stress free (HH) and
stress resistant (carrier) (Hh)
slaughter progeny

* HH  =  Halothane negative
  hh  =  Halothane positive or reactor
  Hh  =  Carrier but halothane negative and stress resistant
  (See Chapter 5, page 60)

FIGURE 6.1  Two ways in which some of the high carcass merit of stress susceptible
lines can be utilised without incurring losses in commercial production (Source: Pig
Improvement Company (PIC).

There is speculation now regarding how far this effort to further reduce carcass
fatness and increase leanness should be allowed to proceed since there is increasing
concern among some processors and consumers of pigmeat regarding problems
associated with very lean pigs. Some of the reported associations with very lean
pigs include soft, floppy backfat; failure of carcasses to 'set' after chilling, which
makes cutting or slicing difficult; the occurrence of separation between backfat
layers, between backfat and muscle and between inter-muscular fat and muscle; un-
sightly fat distribution; lower yield of cured bacon and lack of succulence and
flavour in the cooked meat, which is dry and tasteless. These criticisms have focus-
ed attention on fat quality aspects, which have been closely examined by Dr Wood
and his associates at the Meat Research Institute in Bristol.

As pigs grow it appears that the content of connective tissue and water in 'fat' decreases while that of lipid increases. The lipid consists of fatty acids, some of which are synthesised mainly from carbohydrate, while others are obtained direct from absorption of dietary fatty acids. The main factor controlling the firmness of fat, which is the major aspect of fat quality subjected to criticism to date, is the balance between unsaturated and saturated fatty acids. The concentration of linoleic acid in fat appears to be particularly critical. This is usually less than 15 per cent and when this concentration is exceeded, firmness of fat is adversely affected. Increased linoleic acid content of fat is associated with underfeeding since it increases at the expense of the synthesised, mainly saturated fatty acids. In addition, when high fat diets, containing more linoleic acid, are fed at a low level, these combine to further soften the fat.

It would also appear that in genetically lean pigs and boars as opposed to castrates, the lipid component of fatty tissue is relatively unsaturated, but these differences seem to disappear when comparisons are made at the same fat thickness. In boars, it appears that the concentration of lipid in 'fatty tissue' is lower and that of water higher even at the same fat thickness. It is thought that this is due to extra connective tissue synthesis in the boar, particularly in the shoulder region. However, there are almost no differences in fat firmness between boars and castrates when comparisons are made at the same fat thickness. Similarly, problems with carcasses which are 'floppy' and do not 'set' appear to be closely correlated with fat thickness.

Thus, reported deterioration in fat quality appears to be very closely associated with lean pigs, whether such leanness is a function of breeding, diet or the amount fed. There would appear to be a limit, therefore, to the extent to which backfat thickness should be further reduced in breeding programmes, and this limit may have already been reached for some genotypes in the United Kingdom.

It is vitally important that the aspects of lean and fat quality which have attracted criticism from both meat processors and consumers be considered carefully by those involved in pig breeding improvement. Consumers are likely to become much more discriminating in the future on aspects of meat quality and, while it may be unrealistic to expect those concerned in genetic improvement to select positively for all of these quality aspects, it is important that they are fully aware of the trends in terms of selection and use of particular breeds in crossing programmes which have been mainly associated with reported deterioration in these aspects of fat, lean and meat quality. With such awareness, steps must be taken to halt and redress these undesirable trends.

GROWTH

Having outlined the requirements in the pig carcass in terms of its composition and quality, we are now in a position to define the objectives of the pig breeder in terms of the influence he should aim to have over the growth of tissues. Growth can be defined in a variety of ways.

While *liveweight gain* is one of the simplest parameters to measure, it can be an inaccurate measure of the obvious target end points for the animal breeder, whether this is the pig carcass, yield of edible meat or weight of lean tissue.

It would appear that the dressed carcass as a proportion of the liveweight or *killing-out percentage* does not vary a great deal within a breed or strain but, as indicated earlier in this chapter, marked differences in this aspect are evident between strains and breeds. In view of these considerations, and since killing-out percentage is difficult to estimate in the live animal, the most effective method of achieving improvement in this aspect is by exploiting superior lines in crossing programmes. In particular, the lines of pig which are strong in this aspect are an obvious basis for sire lines.

Because consumer demand in most countries of the world is for lean meat with minimum fat content, the *rates of growth of edible meat* (deboned meat with surplus fat trimmed off) *and of lean tissue* would seem to be obvious targets at which animal breeders and pig producers should aim. One reason why these parameters have not always been direct targets in the plans of pig breeders is that they are difficult and expensive factors to measure. A pig's breeding value in terms of growth of edible meat or in lean tissue growth rate (LTGR) can only be assessed accurately by either progeny or sib-testing and involves carcass dissection or sample joint dissection and careful and laborious weighing of dissected tissues. However, improved indices are now available for estimating lean meat content in the live animal within particular strains or breeds and these should facilitate direct selection in the future for LTGR.

Regarding improvement in growth rate of edible meat, this is likely to be achieved by exploiting lines or genotypes in appropriate crossbreeding programmes which are characterised by high edible meat yield (and therefore low bone and fat trim percentage) and which also have good growth rate properties.

With regard to the scope for improving the growth rate of edible meat by selection within lines or breeds, this could well be facilitated by current developments in alternative pig carcass processing methods. Such techniques are being developed by the Meat and Livestock Commission in the United Kingdom and involve deboning, fat trimming and subsequent rolling of the whole trimmed side of pig carcasses. The yield of such trimmed sides (or edible meat) from the carcass could well form a basis of payment for carcasses in the future. Such a development would provide an excellent index to the pig breeder as a basis for improving rate of edible meat growth by selection within his herd or population.

FOOD CONVERSION EFFICIENCY
Since food constitutes around 70 per cent of total pig production costs, food conversion efficiency is an obvious target for genetic improvement.

The measurement of the efficiency with which food is used in pig production can be based on liveweight gain, carcass weight, weight of edible meat or weight of lean tissue. Considerations regarding the usefulness of these parameters and of the relative ease and cost of their measurement have just been discussed.

The other component of the food conversion calculation is, of course, food intake. This can be measured on a group or individual basis (either by individual penning or by group penning and individual feeding), and such measurement is not inexpensive in terms of time and labour.

Because of the problems of knowing the composition of liveweight, there are strong arguments for basing the assessment of food conversion efficiency on carcass weight, weight of edible meat or weight of lean tissue. *Lean tissue food conver-*

*sion (LTFC)* was considered a very useful index of pig performance by Dr Vernon Fowler of the Rowett Research Institute in Aberdeen, since it incorporated in a single index the main target end product (lean tissue), the major item of input costs (food) and the efficiency of production element. If we were assessing pigs on the basis of LTFC on a specific diet, this would provide us with an index of cost effectiveness of lean meat production which is only lacking in one major element, this being the rate at which this lean meat is produced. This is important because some major costs in pigmeat production such as those on buildings and labour are time dependent.

The use of an index like LTFC in the same way as for lean tissue growth rate (LTGR) is dependent on obtaining an accurate estimate of lean tissue in the live animal or its slaughtered sibs or progeny.

FOOD INTAKE

The ability of a pig to consume food or nutrients at an adequate rate was not considered a limiting factor in pig production until comparatively recently.

The increase in interest in rate of food intake has been brought about by the realisation that the successful attempts by many organisations and private breeders to increase carcass lean and reduce fat content on ad lib. or 'to appetite' feeding systems has been associated with a reduction in food intake. In other words, part of the mechanism by which breeders have achieved a reduction in carcass fat content has been by subconsciously selecting pigs with lower appetites. It is considered that some genotypes with high lean and low carcass fat contents are unable to grow lean tissue at a sufficiently fast rate because of limited appetite.

With this realisation, breeders are now diverting their attention to the balanced objective of improving other desirable traits while maintaining or even increasing appetite at the same time.

REPRODUCTIVE TRAITS

Within-line or within-breed selection to improve reproductive traits was not given much consideration in the past because of the low heritability of these traits relative to that of traits related to growth, food conversion efficiency and carcass quality.

In addition, it was considered, with a lot of justification, that it was preferable to set out to improve reproductive traits by a combination of crossbreeding (to exploit heterosis in these traits) and manipulation of environmental factors and management. This left selection and management influences available to achieve improvement in growth and carcass traits.

However, now that heterosis and management influences have been exploited almost fully to maximise aspects of reproductive performance in many situations, interest is being rekindled in the possibility of improving reproductive traits by selective breeding. While earlier selection exercises on litter size in pigs failed to achieve any improvement, more recent studies involving highly prolific sows have been more rewarding. Sows which have achieved outstandingly high numbers of livebirths over a series of litters are used as the basis of 'prolific' boars and gilts. Using this approach, the Pig Improvement Company in the United Kingdom have produced a 'prolific' line which, on commercial farm trials, has given an advantage of over half a liveborn pig per litter relative to their conventional commercial hybrid.

Other breeding companies are also producing more prolific hybrids, and it is possible that there will be similar developments in the future to improve other aspects of reproductive performance through selective breeding. One possible target in this respect is earlier age at puberty.

Increased emphasis in selection on such reproductive traits will reduce selection pressure on growth, food conversion efficiency and carcass traits. However, in the light of earlier discussion in this chapter, the need to reduce selection pressure on decreased fat content in some lines and breeds may already be relevant.

The adoption by the pig industry of the concept of 'sire lines' and 'dam lines' is also likely to hasten developments to select for improved reproductive performance in the dam lines while concentrating on improving growth, food conversion and carcass traits in the sire lines.

## CRYSTALLISING SELECTION OBJECTIVES

The animal breeder who is setting out to maximise the rate of genetic improvement via selection has to establish clear priorities for attention. This is because the more traits he sets out to improve, the slower the progress he will make in each.

Andrew Coates of the Pig Improvement Company certainly crystallised the objectives of the animal breeder. He suggested that the breeder's clear objective should be 'to evolve stock which would produce the greatest number of market pigs with the genetic potential to produce the maximum amount of lean meat of acceptable quality, at least cost, in the shortest time'.

If we are to leave management, crossbreeding and between-line selection to carry their fair share of the responsibility for improving the overall efficiency of production of pigmeat of acceptable quality, the traits which we should concentrate on improving by within-line or within-breed selection are as follows:

1.  Lean tissue growth rate (LTGR) or growth of edible meat.
2.  Lean tissue food conversion efficiency (LTFC) or edible meat conversion efficiency.
3.  Appetite. It may not be necessary to select directly for this trait since, in achieving objectives 1 and 2 above, appetite might be improved simultaneously.

## USEFULNESS OF DIRECT OR INDIRECT SELECTION

In setting out to improve a particular trait, one can select directly for that trait or it may be simpler and less expensive to select indirectly for the target trait by selecting for a trait closely correlated to it.

Two selection studies will be cited to illustrate this principle:

1.  Drs Webb and King, formerly of the Animal Breeding Research Organisation

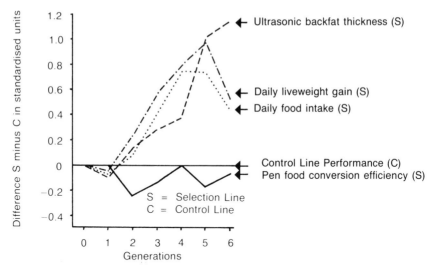

FIGURE 6.2 Cumulated selection responses in food conversion ratio, liveweight gain, food intake and backfat (Webb, A.J. and King, J.W.B., ABRO, Edinburgh, 1983).

in Edinburgh, set out to improve the food conversion efficiency of pigs on ad lib. group feeding. After six generations of selection (see Figure 6.2) no improvement was achieved in food conversion efficiency. However, daily food intake or appetite, daily liveweight gain and average backfat thickness (measured ultrasonically) all increased progressively over this period.

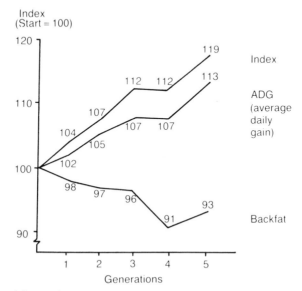

FIGURE 6.3 Selected line performance as a percentage of control line performance (Ahlschwede, W.T. and Johnson, R.K., University of Nebraska, USA, 1983).

2.   A University of Nebraska study set out to select pigs for fast rates of liveweight gain and low backfat. These two traits were combined into an appropriate index which formed the sole basis of selection. The response to selection is illustrated in Figure 6.3. It can be seen that the response to selection was very good in terms of the index and in both components of that index. Over the five generations of selection, backfat thickness was reduced by 0.2 of an inch (about 5 mm) and pigs grew 0.15 pounds (about 68 g) per day more rapidly. What was also very interesting from the results was that in food conversion efficiency (expressed as kg of feed required per kg of lean produced), the selected line showed an improvement of almost 20 per cent over the five generations.

Thus, it appeared from this and related studies that selection for lean growth (based on the index of backfat and liveweight gain) has been much more effective in reducing feed required per kg of gain than selecting directly for feed efficiency. This is a very pleasing result since lean growth (if based on the index of backfat and daily gain) is much easier and less expensive to measure than feed efficiency.

## Use of a Selection Index

Once selection priorities are decided, it is useful if these can be incorporated into a single index on which final selection is based.

If we wish to improve three or four major traits in our selection programme it is useful to formulate them into a single index on the following basis:

●   Their relative economic values
●   Their heritabilities
●   The existence of any correlations between them

The selection index will have to be reviewed and amended from time to time since the relative economic values may change.

## Assessment of Breeding Value

The basis of genetic improvement by selection within a herd or in any population of animals is the accurate assessment of breeding value. There are several methods for assessing breeding value.

*1.  Performance testing*
This involves measuring the animal's own performance or that of a family, e.g. a litter of pigs. Traits which can be assessed in this way include feed intake, liveweight gain and feed conversion efficiency while a measure of carcass quality can be obtained by using ultrasonic equipment to measure backfat thickness.

*2.  Sib testing*
This involves measuring the performance of a close relative (e.g. litter mates) of a pig that is being considered for breeding. Sib testing is useful for measuring traits

Pigs undergoing tests to estimate breeding value as a basis for genetic improvement by selection or crossbreeding.

(*Above left*) Plate 6.1   Young boars being evaluated in individual feeding facilities to assess feed intake, liveweight gain and feed conversion efficiency.

(*Above right*) Plate 6.2   Boar at 80 kg liveweight being assessed ultrasonically to estimate backfat thickness and depth of longissimus dorsi (eye muscle).

(*Left*) Plate 6.3   Young gilts being examined to assess number, spacing, conformation and normality of teats. (Plates 6.1–6.3 courtesy of Pig International)

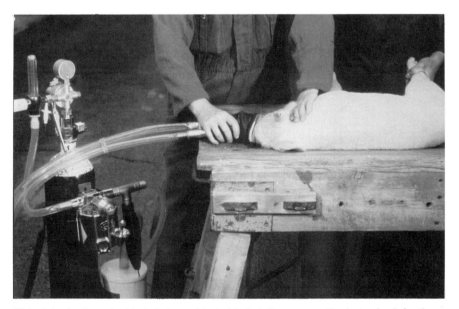

Plate 6.4   An 8 week old pig being subjected to halothane anaesthesia to check for the presence of the double dose of the recessive halothane gene. (Courtesy of the Institute of Animal Physiology and Genetics Research, Edinburgh)

which cannot be measured accurately on the animal being tested, such as carcass and meat quality. Obviously, these cannot be assessed with any degree of accuracy on the animal being considered for breeding but can be measured on the slaughtered sibs of the animal being evaluated. Thus, in the assessment of a potential boar for carcass quality traits, his gilt, boar and castrate litter mates can be slaughtered and their carcasses assessed.

### 3.  Progeny testing
This involves the examination of progeny to evaluate an animal, and it is obviously the ultimate test of an animal's breeding value. It is the only effective way to assess a boar's ability to transmit high merit in terms of reproductive traits to his female progeny. Along with sib testing, it can be used to provide extra growth and carcass information on a boar or sow.

### Comments on the alternative methods
Progeny testing is much more expensive than performance testing since the latter test only involves measurements on the animal itself whereas progeny testing can involve assessments on many animals. Also, another disadvantage of progeny testing is that it takes longer to obtain a measure of the breeding value of an animal than to do a performance test on the animal itself or on a sib.

Apart from the fact that progeny testing is the only effective way to assess the ability of a boar to transmit high merit in reproductive traits to female progeny, the progeny test tends to be more accurate in assessing breeding value than performance testing. On the other hand, performance testing for those traits which can be measured in this way gives a quicker result, it is cheaper and for traits of moderate to high heritability such as growth, food conversion and backfat thickness (measured ultrasonically) it is fairly accurate.

## NATIONAL GENETIC IMPROVEMENT SCHEMES

Many countries have organised national genetic improvement schemes for their nation's farm livestock species. A good example of such a scheme was the National Pig Improvement Scheme, which was organised by the Meat and Livestock Commission and its forerunner, the Pig Industry Development Authority, and which had been in operation in the United Kingdom for two decades until terminated in 1983.

The initial stages of the scheme involved comprehensive herd recording of reproductive performance, growth and carcass grading data. On this basis, herds were classified into the classical breeding pyramid (see Figure 6.4), with the very best herds being classified as nucleus herds, the next best stratum as reserve nucleus herds, followed progressively by the multiplier herds and the commercial producers.

Central test station facilities for assessing breeding value were made available only to nucleus and reserve nucleus breeders who submitted young boars and their sibs for testing (partly performance and partly sib-testing). Comprehensive information was collected and published on the test boars and their sibs (see Table 6.2).

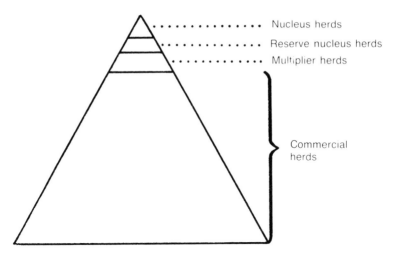

FIGURE 6.4   The classical pyramid of breeding herds.

On the completion of the test, boars were given an index rating based on two important traits:

1.  Economy of production (growth rate, feed conversion efficiency and killing-out percentage)
2.  Carcass quality (mainly backfat and lean percentage)

The average index score of any contemporary group of boars on test was set at 100 and those with less than 90 points, being considered inferior, were slaughtered.

Nucleus breeders were obliged to test a high proportion of their breeding boars, select on the basis of test results and achieve a good rate of genetic improvement in the traits under selection. Nucleus breeders who failed in this respect were demoted to the reserve nucleus category. On the other hand, Reserve Nucleus breeders who were achieving a good rate of genetic progress could gain promotion to Nucleus level. Thus, the system was a dynamic one with the top breeders under pressure to maintain a good rate of genetic progress while Reserve Nucleus breeders also had adequate incentive to improve.

Genetic improvement was not solely concentrated on boars. Part of the scheme involved an 'On Farm Testing Service' which was primarily designed for gilt selection but could also be used for boar selection. This test was based on assessing weight for age and backfat thickness (measured ultrasonically)at the equivalent liveweight for bacon production (approximately 90 kg) and the subsequent conversion of these two measures into a single index. The objective was to select from a contemporary group of tested animals those gilts which had the highest index rating and which were at the same time acceptable in terms of other essential characters such as the number, conformation and spacing of functional teats, soundness of feet and legs and normality in all other obvious respects.

The objective in the case of the multipliers was to purchase high index-rated

# MEAT AND LIVESTOCK COMMISSION

| FORM | TEST |
|---|---|
| CT 21 | 3456/ 1 |

**Report of Group Test** 3456/ 1 **Born** 30TH OCTOBER 1972 **Tested at** STIRLING **Report issued** 25TH APRIL 1973

**BREED:** LARGE WHITE

TESTED ON BEHALF OF:

A.G. NORRIE,
SLACKADALE,
TURRIFF,
ABERDEENSHIRE.

Tel: KING EDWARD 231
HERD PREFIX: SLACKADALE

EAR No. 426 5921
HERD BOOK No. 415847 162864

TEST REPORT 163 pts 158 pts

| | | HERD BOOK No. |
|---|---|---|
| Sire of Group | WESTPIT KING DAVID 380TH | |
| Dam of Group | SLACKADALE FANNY 162ND | |
| Sire's Sire | WESTPIT KING DAVID 330TH | 404679 |
| Sire's Dam | WESTPIT MELODY 97TH | 163372 |
| Dam's Sire | CAIRNHILL CHAMPION BOY 67TH | 400817 |
| Dam's Dam | SLACKADALE FANNY 128TH | 128800 |

## POINTS SCORE

| EAR No. OF BOAR | 8574 | 8576 | AVERAGE OF BOTH BOARS | CONTEMPORARY AVERAGE |
|---|---|---|---|---|
| ECONOMY OF PRODUCTION | 66 | 61 | 63 | 50 |
| CARCASE QUALITY | 69 | 66 | 68 | 50 |
| TOTAL | 135 | 127 | 131 | 100 |

## OTHER INFORMATION
### (DIFFERENCE FROM CONTEMPORARY AVERAGE)

| CHARACTER | | EAR No. OF BOAR | | CASTRATE AND GILT |
|---|---|---|---|---|
| | | 8574 | 8576 | |
| FOOD CONVERSION | | 0.11B | 0.04B | 0.09B |
| DAYS ON TEST (60-200 lb.) | | 2B | 2B | 4B |
| CONFORMATION SCORE | | AVE | AVE | AVE |
| C | (mm) | 1B | 2B | 1B |
| K | (mm) | 2B | 3B | 3B |
| LOIN 2 FAT | (mm) | 1B | 2B | 2W |
| SHOULDER FAT | (mm) | 2B | AVE | 3B |
| KILLING OUT % | | | | 4B |
| TRIMMING % | | | | 5B |
| LEAN % IN RUMP | | | | AVE |
| EYE MUSCLE AREA | (sq cm) | | | 3B |
| STREAK SCORE | | | | 1B |

| AVERAGE LENGTH (mm) | 834 |
|---|---|

B: Better
AVE: Average
W: Worse

TABLE 6.2 Typical performance test information on boars and their castrate and gilt sibs, as used by the Meat and Livestock Commission in their Pig Improvement Scheme

82

boars and some gilts from nucleus and reserve Nucleus breeders, to use the 'On Farm Testing Service' as a basis for selection of their home-bred gilts and to set out to win sales for their gilts, in particular, from the mass of commercial producers at the base of the pyramid.

The scheme, which was outstandingly successful, is now being modified. A summary of these modifications is presented later in this chapter. Meanwhile, the estimated genetic progress made under the scheme will be outlined.

## Estimated Genetic Progress

Details of the improvement in selected traits are presented in Table 6.3, which summarises improvements in food conversion efficiency and reductions in backfat thickness from 1958 to 1983 recorded in castrate and gilt pigs (sibs of test boars) tested at central testing stations.

**TABLE 6.3  Average performance of all castrates and gilts tested 1958–1983 in the United Kingdom Pig Improvement Scheme**

| Year | Feed conversion ratio (liveweight) | Shoulder fat (mm) | Loin fat (mm) | Eye muscle area (sq cm) |
|---|---|---|---|---|
| **Landrace** | | | | |
| 1958 | 3.40 | 42 | 25 | 27.36 |
| 1961 | 3.41 | 41 | 23 | 28.97 |
| 1964 | 3.03 | 41 | 22 | 30.36 |
| 1967 | 3.06 | 42 | 23 | 31.15 |
| 1970 | 2.81 | 40 | 20 | 32.10 |
| 1973 | 2.76 | 39 | 19 | 31.70 |
| 1977 | 2.59 | 33 | 18 | 32.15 |
| 1978 | 2.60 | 34 | 17 | 32.15 |
| 1981 | 2.61 | 33 | 15 | 32.50 |
| 1983 | 2.59 | 30 | 11 | 33.40 |
| **Large White** | | | | |
| 1958 | 3.31 | 46 | 26 | 26.71 |
| 1961 | 3.33 | 45 | 25 | 27.59 |
| 1964 | 2.92 | 45 | 24 | 29.14 |
| 1967 | 2.92 | 45 | 24 | 30.35 |
| 1970 | 2.71 | 42 | 21 | 31.80 |
| 1973 | 2.64 | 41 | 21 | 32.30 |
| 1977 | 2.50 | 34 | 16 | 33.25 |
| 1978 | 2.51 | 34 | 16 | 34.15 |
| 1981 | 2.53 | 33 | 15 | 34.15 |
| 1983 | 2.57 | 32 | 12 | 33.90 |

The extent to which backfat thickness has been decreased in British pigs from 1971 to 1986 is shown in Figure 6.5.

This information is based on carcass data recorded under the Pig Carcass Classification Scheme, which involves approximately 70 per cent of pigs

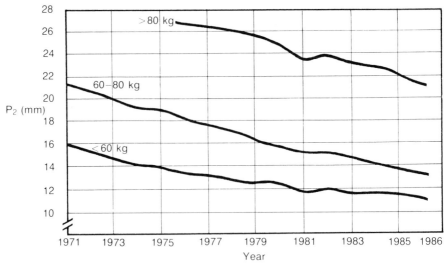

FIGURE 6.5   Trends in backfat depth of pig carcasses in Britain 1971–86 (MLC, 1987).

slaughtered in the United Kingdom. It can be seen that backfat thickness has been reduced in all types of market pig over the period studied, the average reduction in backfat for all market types being 0.45 mm per year. This has been achieved without any reduction in slaughter weight.

Of course, other things such as improved diet and control over feeding level will have contributed to this improvement, but the genetic contribution will almost certainly have been the major one.

**TABLE 6.4   Estimated annual genetic changes from 1971–1976 in British tested pigs***

|  | Improvement per year | | | |
|  | *Large White* | | *Landrace* | |
|  | *Economic value (pence)* | *Per cent* | *Economic value (pence)* | *Per cent* |
|---|---|---|---|---|
| 1. Daily gain | 0.3 | 0.04 | 5.9 | 0.75 |
| 2. Feed conversion ratio | 8.2 | 0.38 | 31.0 | 1.44 |
| 3. Killing out (%) | 6.9 | 0.14 | −1.0 | −0.02 |
| 4. Trimming (%) | 4.8 | 0.13 | 3.0 | 0.08 |
| 5. Estimated carcass lean (%) | 15.9 | 0.77 | 41.0 | 1.99 |
| 6. Daily feed intake | | −0.34 | | −0.68 |
| 7. Lean tissue growth rate | | 1.07 | | 2.84 |
| 8. Lean tissue feed conversion | | 1.41 | | 3.44 |

* Genetic change calculated by comparing pigs from control herds with all other tested pigs.
(Source: Jones, D W, 1977)

With environment as well as genotype changing, it is always difficult to estimate the respective contribution of these two factors to improvement in performance traits. One of the main methods used to assess the progress attributable to the Pig Improvement Scheme has been to compare the performance of pigs being improved through the scheme with pigs from two control herds (one Large White and one Landrace), which are kept at a constant genetic level over the years. On this basis, Jones (1977) calculated genetic progress in the scheme and his findings are summarised in Table 6.4. He calculated that food intake was being reduced by 0.51 per cent per year (by 0.34 per cent in Large White and 0.68 per cent in Landrace) but that lean tissue growth rate was being improved annually by 1.1 per cent for Large White and by 2.8 per cent for Landrace. Likewise, lean tissue food conversion efficiency was being improved by 1.4 per cent annually for Large White and by 3.4 per cent annually for Landrace.

## Cost-effectiveness of the Scheme

No genetic improvement scheme can be cost-effective unless the value of the improvements achieved more than covers the cost of the scheme. The scheme set out to test boars on 'their ability to produce more profitable progeny'. While it appears that the selection index used has been associated with a reduction in appetite in British pigs, significant improvements in food conversion efficiency and carcass leanness have been achieved with smaller improvements in growth rate.

## Criticisms of the Scheme

While the scheme resulted in significant improvements in feed efficiency and carcass quality in particular, it suffered from several disadvantages. The major problem was the disease risk in taking boars from many nucleus herds to a central test station with the consequent risk of spread of infection when some of these boars were returned to the farm of origin. The scheme is now being modified to reduce health risks and to improve it in other respects.

## Improvements to the Scheme

The changes being made in the scheme are as follows:

1.  Reduction of the size of the 'nucleus' to about 20 top 'super-nucleus' herds.
2.  These herds will be obliged to test a high number of boars annually and will have to subject their herd to rapid generation turn-over.
3.  The scheme will involve on-farm rather than central testing of boars and gilts so as to eliminate disease risks. The previous on-farm testing system has been rendered more accurate by incorporating measurements of individual feed conversion efficiency and the central testing of boar's litter-mates. 50 pigs (25 boars and 25 gilts) are submitted to the Central Test Station each year and at the end of the test period are slaughtered and carcasses evaluated to provide a measure of herd merit.

4.  Nucleus herds are under obligation to offer for sale to AI Stations the top 8 per cent of their boars on Performance Test (on farm). This is to ensure that the scheme will be of maximum benefit to those commercial producers who base their replacement policy on use of AI from top performing boars.

## PRIVATE BREEDING COMPANY IMPROVEMENT SCHEMES

### Background to Development of Breeding Companies

In many cases, the pedigree breeding herds of two to three decades ago were the embryos of the large private breeding companies in existence today. The main weaknesses of these herds were that they were small and were dependent on other herds for replacement boars and sometimes gilts.

Being dependent on bringing in replacements from outside, they were vulnerable from the health viewpoint, while their small size made it very difficult to make improvements through selection. Genetic variability in commercially important traits was likely to be limited in these herds and therefore scope for genetic improvement by selection was also limited. In addition, it is difficult for small herds to make an accurate assessment of the breeding value of even boars through progeny, performance or sib testing because of the considerable expense of these procedures.

### Breeding Company Development

Some breeding companies had their origins, therefore, in pedigree breeders that, either singly or in combination, decided that to improve their herds, they would have to improve their herd health status and the soundness and accuracy of their selection policy. They also saw the need to exploit the commercial advantages of heterosis through crossbreeding.

The beginnings saw a few breeders with healthier herds and superior genetic stock setting out to maintain and, if possible, further improve health status largely through a closed herds policy. It also saw them obtaining more accurate assessment of breeding value of boars by first using national progeny, performance and sib testing stations and then gradually establishing test premises of their own. They also realised that, apart from reaping the benefits of such improvements in health and performance in their own herds, they could only justify their investment in improved health control and in evolving superior genetic stock by selling this improved healthier stock to commercial producers.

The modest origins of these groups of breeders have lead to the present very large multinational breeding companies. Each company has a sophisticated and highly organised network of super-nucleus herds in which superior stock or genes are brought in from outside sources only through AI or hysterectomy. Strong selection pressure in these herds is based on comprehensive testing of stock for liveweight gain, feed conversion efficiency, carcass quality and, increasingly, for reproductive traits. Nucleus herds are populated by stock from super-nucleus herds increasingly by hysterectomy so as to minimise the risk of any disease organism inadvertently gaining entry at super-nucleus level finding its way to nucleus herds. Stock in nucleus herds are evaluated more often under group feeding conditions, selection being on an index based on liveweight gain and backfat thickness measured ultrasonically.

Selected purebred stock from nucleus herds are used to populate the multiplier herds where improved lines and breeds are crossed to produce first cross or hybrid gilts for sale to commercial producers. Purebred boars can be sold to commercial producers from either the nucleus or multiplier herds.

The basis of operation of one large international breeding company is illustrated in Figure 6.6.

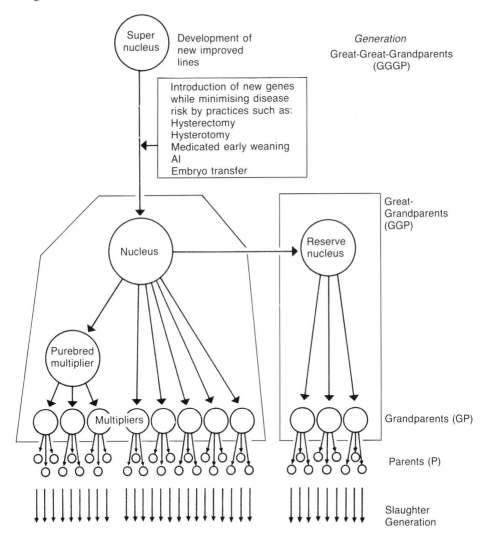

*Note:* Customers purchasing parent boars and gilts to produce the slaughter generation always have the opportunity of obtaining stock from the previous supplier (multiplier) within the same closed pyramid.

FIGURE 6.6  The breeding pyramid as practised by some large international pig breeding companies (adapted from Pig Improvement Company literature).

Pig breeding companies aim to pass on their genetic improvement to commercial producers by a process of rapid generation turn-over and a prompt transfer of this improvement to their customers through their multipliers.

The various stages in pig improvement can be summarised as follows:

*Generation (relative to slaughter generation)*

1. Super-nucleus herd          Great-Great Grandparents (GGGP)
2. Nucleus herds               Great Grandparents (GGP)
3. Multiplier herds            Grandparents (GP)
4. Commercial producers        Parents (P)
5. Slaughter Generation

While the interval between producing a generation at nucleus level to the stage their progeny are transferred to the multiplier herds may take between 1 to 5 years, the shorter the interval, the quicker is the transfer of genetic progress to the commercial producer. This is called the *genetic lag*. In a traditional purebred system where top purebred breeders sell boars to multiplier purebred breeders, who, in turn sell boars to commercial producers, the genetic lag is usually 7 to 8 years (see Figure 6.7a).

Genetic lag is reduced to less than 4 years in a modern system (see Figure 6.7b) where both boars and gilts are passed from a company nucleus herd to multipliers and where the commercial producer buys his replacement gilts in addition to his boars.

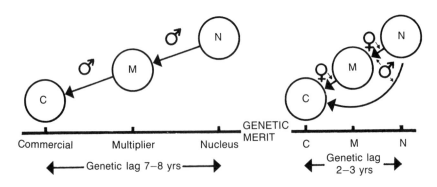

FIGURE 6.7  Genetic lag in 2 systems of boar and gilt replacement: (a) involving purchase of boars (1) by the multiplier from the nucleus and (2) by the commercial producer from the multiplier and (b) in a system whereby a commercial producer buys his replacement gilts and boars from a modern breeding company (adapted from Pig Improvement Company literature).

## Commercial Product Evaluation (CPE)

As well as being well organised in terms of genetic improvement and the maintenance of a high health status, breeding companies must invest in advertising and sales promotion to be successful. To provide an objective basis to their claims regarding the merits of their products and to guide prospective purchasers, it is important that the relative merits of the commercial products of breeding companies and private breeders are evaluated under standard conditions.

The Meat and Livestock Commission in the United Kingdom have operated such a Commercial Product Evaluation test, and the organisation of this test is summarised in Figure 6.8.

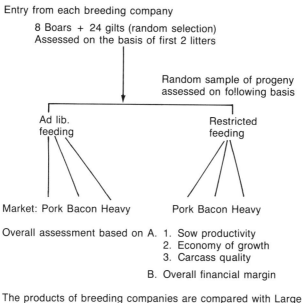

Entry from each breeding company

8 Boars + 24 gilts (random selection)
Assessed on the basis of first 2 litters

Random sample of progeny
assessed on following basis

Ad lib.
feeding

Restricted
feeding

Market: Pork Bacon Heavy          Pork Bacon Heavy

Overall assessment based on A. 1. Sow productivity
                                2. Economy of growth
                                3. Carcass quality

                             B. Overall financial margin

The products of breeding companies are compared with Large White purebreds and unimproved crossbreds.

FIGURE 6.8   The basis of Commercial Product Evaluation in the United Kingdom (organised by the Meat and Livestock Commission).

On the basis of the CPE test, it has been calculated that the genetic progress made by the participating breeding companies is equivalent to an annual benefit of between 55 and 75 pence per slaughter pig produced.

The CPE test was completed in 1980. It was replaced by a scheme which involved a comparison of stock based on conventional white hybrids (Large White, Landrace and Welsh) and on specialised meat type sires. These pigs were compared to a genetic control herd. Among performance parameters measured were growth, food conversion efficiency and carcass traits, and particular emphasis was placed on meat and eating quality aspects associated with very lean pigs. A summary of the results was presented earlier (Table 2.4, page 18).

## Usefulness of Artificial Insemination

Relative to natural service, artificial insemination (AI) helps to exploit the potential of a superior boar. Because high index rated boars from progeny, performance or sib tests can be used through AI to sire many more pigs, AI stations can, and should, purchase the best boars available.

Because superior stock can be obtained through purchasing semen, a handful of producers throughout the world use AI only, not only to produce their future breeding stock but also to produce their slaughter pigs.

More usually, however, AI is used on the best sows within a herd, as judged over a series of litters on breeding and rearing performance data but more particularly on the basis of the growth and carcass grading of their progeny. In this way, the very best boars can be used through AI to produce gilt replacements for the herd. AI could also be used in this way to produce replacement boars for a herd but, to make this feasible and sensible, the herd would have to be sufficiently large to avoid inbreeding.

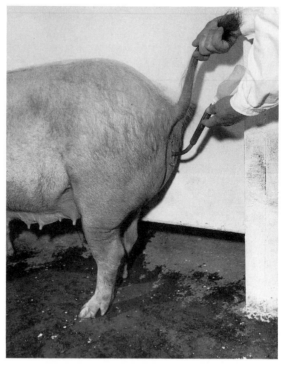

Plate 6.5   AI is a very effective means of introducing superior genes while minimising disease risk. The good AI stations will have a boar stud selected from the best available genotypes. (Courtesy of Tetra, Hungary)

## ON-FARM GENETIC IMPROVEMENT

### Calculating Number of Replacements Required

If a commercial herd is retaining sows for an average of 5 litters, this means that sows are being retained in the herd until they are 3 years of age. If they are sold after weaning their third or seventh litter, they will have been either 2 or 4 years old respectively at culling.

With a sow to boar ratio of 20 to 1, we can calculate the number of replacements required for a given average age at culling. We can assume that boars are being culled at the same age as sows (see Table 6.5). Thus, a very low proportion of the gilts and boars reared in the herd need to be retained for breeding to maintain herd size.

TABLE 6.5   Number and proportion of replacements required in a 100-sow herd

|  | *Average age of sows at culling* | | |
|  | *2 years* | *3 years* | *4 years* |
|---|---|---|---|
| Total piglets reared per year* | 2000 | 2000 | 2000 |
| Number of sows or gilts required to be replaced annually | 50 | 33 | 25 |
| Number of boars required per year | $2\frac{1}{2}$ | $1\frac{2}{3}$ | $1\frac{1}{4}$ |
|  | (say 3) | (say 2) | (say 2) |
| Proportion of total boars and gilts reared which must be retained for breeding: |  |  |  |
| Gilts $\dfrac{50}{1000} =$ | 5 | 3.3 | 2.5 |
| Boars $\dfrac{3}{1000} =$ | 0.3 | 0.2 | 0.2 |

* Based on rearing 20 pigs per sow per year

### A Simple On-farm Selection Programme

Let us work through a simple process for selecting improved breeding stock within a herd. In the herd, litters are recorded at birth and piglets receive an ear tattoo or ear notching system indicating their birth date. The only other pieces of equipment required are an ultrasonic machine and a weigher. Pigs are weighed when between 70 and 90 kg liveweight and at the same time their backfat thickness is measured ultrasonically at Point $P_2$ (see Figure 6.9).

Pigs are also checked to ensure that they are anatomically normal, that there are no obvious defects and that they are sound on feet and legs. They must also attain minimum standards for the number of functional teats and the spacing of teats.

Data on 20 such gilts are presented in Table 6.6.

### Calculating the Likely Response to Selection

If we require only 5 per cent of gilts for replacements, then we require only the best one out of this batch of 20 (or 10 out of a batch of 200).

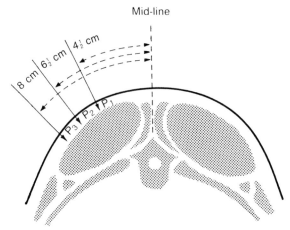

FIGURE 6.9  Cross-section of the carcass at the level of the last rib, indicating location of points $P_1$, $P_2$ and $P_3$ at which fat thickness above the eye muscle is measured.

While the mean index score (based on backfat thickness and weight for age) is 37, the highest index score of 50 is that for gilt 167.

If we sampled 200 such gilts and found that the mean index rating was the same as for a sample of 20 (37), while the mean for the best 5 per cent (10 gilts) on index rating was 50, then our:

Selection differential = 50 *minus* 37                    = 13
(Mean of selected individuals)     (Mean of population)

If we were selecting replacement boars from the same population we would only require the best 0.3 per cent or so (see Table 6.5). Our selection differential for boars would almost certainly be higher than that for gilts, but let us make the conservative assumption that it is the same as that for gilts. We can now calculate our estimated response to selection on this pig unit:

Response to selection  =  Heritability* × Mean selection differential
                                                of boars and gilts

$$= \ 0.5 \ \times \ \left( \frac{13 \ + \ 13}{2} \right)$$

$$= \ 0.5 \ \times \ 13$$

$$= \ 6.5$$

* Heritability of the index based on weight for age and backfat thickness is about 0.5.

Therefore, the estimated response to selection is 6.5 index points per generation.
The response to selection per year will depend on the rate at which one generation is replaced by the next. In Table 6.5 we considered replacing the whole herd within

*(text continued on page 95)*

**TABLE 6.6  On-farm evaluation of twenty potential replacement gilts**

| Ear number | 1 Liveweight (kg) | 2 Age (days) | 3 Backfat thickness at $P_2$ (mm) | 4 Index rating (based on 1, 2 and 3)† | 5* Feet/leg score | 6 Total teats | 7* Total functional teats | 8* Teat spacing score | Acceptable (A) or unacceptable (U) on the basis of criteria 5, 6, 7 and 8 |
|---|---|---|---|---|---|---|---|---|---|
| 141 | 70 | 125 | 11 | 41 | 3 | 14 | 14 | 4 | A |
| 144 | 76 | 150 | 13 | 31 | 3 | 16 | 16 | 4 | A |
| 145 | 80 | 161 | 10 | 37 | 3.5 | 14 | 14 | 3 | A |
| 146 | 81 | 158 | 13 | 34 | 3.5 | 14 | 14 | 2 | U |
| 149 | 78 | 148 | 13 | 35 | 3 | 14 | 14 | 3 | A |
| 150 | 79 | 149 | 13 | 35 | 1 | 16 | 16 | 1 | U |
| 152 | 82 | 151 | 14 | 35 | 4 | 16 | 16 | 4 | A |
| 153 | 71 | 124 | 15 | 36 | 3 | 14 | 14 | 3 | A |
| 154 | 71 | 125 | 8 | 48 | 4 | 15 | 14 | 3.5 | A |
| 156 | 75 | 156 | 15 | 26 | 3 | 14 | 14 | 3.5 | A |
| 157 | 71 | 148 | 11 | 34 | 4 | 15 | 15 | 3 | A |
| 158 | 85 | 161 | 12 | 37 | 4 | 16 | 15 | 4 | A |
| 161 | 72 | 130 | 12 | 39 | 4 | 14 | 14 | 4.5 | A |
| 162 | 81 | 166 | 18 | 24 | 4 | 13 | 12 | 3 | U |
| 163 | 70 | 140 | 11 | 36 | 4 | 16 | 16 | 4.5 | A |
| 164 | 77 | 135 | 12 | 41 | 4 | 14 | 14 | 3.5 | A |
| 166 | 70 | 150 | 12 | 30 | 2 | 16 | 15 | 4 | U |
| 167 | 83 | 146 | 6 | 50 | 4 | 14 | 14 | 4 | A |
| 168 | 75 | 121 | 11 | 48 | 4.5 | 14 | 14 | 4 | A |
| 169 | 70 | 115 | 12 | 45 | 4 | 14 | 14 | 3.5 | A |
| | | Totals | 242 | 742 | | | | | |
| | | Mean (÷20) | 12.1 | 37.1 | | | | | |
| | | Say | 12 | 37 | | | | | |

\* Traits 5 and 8 are scored on a continuous basis from 1 (very-substandard) to 5 (perfect). Scores below 3 make the animal unsuitable for breeding. Regarding Trait 7, the acceptable number of functional teats is 14.

† Derived from the use of the Nomogram illustrated in Figure 6.10.

Of the gilts evaluated, four are considered unacceptable for breeding for the following reasons: 146 Sub-standard on teat spacing; 150 Sub-standard on feet and leg score and on teat spacing; 162 Sub-standard on number of functional teats: 166 Sub-standard on feet and leg score.

FIGURE 6.10  Nomogram developed by the Meat and Livestock Commission in the United Kingdom to calculate an index rating on the basis of weight for age and backfat thickness.

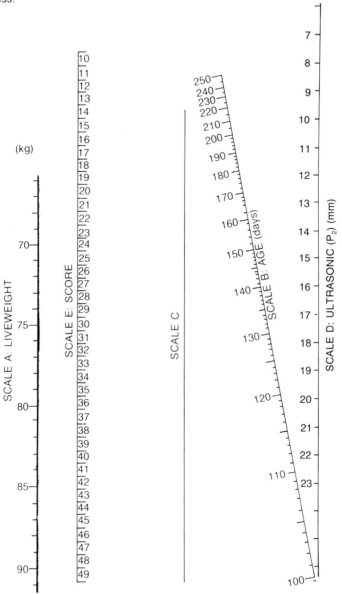

*Use of the Nomogram for constructing scores (index rating)*

(i) Place one end of the ruler at the appropriate point on the weight scale (scale A).
(ii) Place the other end of the ruler at the appropriate point on the age scale (scale B).

(iii) With a pencil held against the ruler where it crosses scale C, rotate the ruler until the end is at the appropriate point on the ultrasonic ($P_2$) scale (scale D).
(iv) Read off the score where the ruler crosses scale E.

*Formula for constructing scores* e.g. for Pig 141 in Table 6.6
$$(70 \text{ kg at 125 days and } P_2 = 11 \text{ mm})$$

$$I = \frac{(101.4 \times \text{Weight (kg)})}{\text{Age (days)}} - (1.784 \times P_2) + (0.02 \times \text{weight in kg}) + 2.6$$

$$= \left(101.4 \times \frac{70}{125}\right) - (1.784 \times 11) + (0.02 \times 70) + 2.6$$

$$= 56.78 - 19.62 + 1.4 + 2.6$$

$$= 41.16$$

(As indicated in Table 6.6 the index rating estimated from the Nomogram was 41 points)

---

2, 3 or 4 years (i.e after 3, 5 or 7 litters). The estimated response to selection per year for these situations is as follows:

| | | | |
|---|---|---|---|
| Average age at culling (years) | 2 | 3 | 4 |
| Average age at birth of progeny (generation turnover) (years) | 1.5 | 2.0 | 2.5 |
| Response to selection per year (Index points) | $\dfrac{6.5}{1.5} = 4.3$ | $\dfrac{6.5}{2} = 3.25$ | $\dfrac{6.5}{2.5} = 2.6$ |

Note: Generation turnover is defined as the average age of the parent at the birth of its progeny. A sow culled at 2 years of age will have litters at 1, 1.5 and 2 years of age, i.e. at an average of 1.5 years of age. Likewise, sows culled at 3 and 4 years of age will, on average, have their litters at an average age of 2 and 2.5 years respectively.

Thus, the longer the generation interval, the slower the response to selection per year. However, despite this slower response to selection per year with later culling, there are commercial advantages in terms of sow productivity for retaining sows over the most productive parities of from 3 to about 6.

The estimated response to selection per generation in this simple exercise of 6.5 index points is likely to lead to very useful improvements in terms of reduced backfat thickness and faster growth if continued over several generations.

Despite the useful genetic progress which, in theory, could be obtained by such a selection process in small herds, such procedures are rarely applied in these herds for a variety of reasons:

1. It would be impossible to apply this procedure to boar selection in small herds without running into inbreeding problems. Thus, the purchase of superior boars from other herds or breeding companies or semen from a top-ranking boar at an AI station is a more sensible policy.
2. Home-bred gilts could be selected as described above but this would be more straightforward if the herd was purebred. On the other hand, if this was done, it would mean that the herd was not cashing in on heterosis in reproductive and viability traits by having crossbred sows.

3.  It is not possible in a small herd to have the majority of the sows as first cross sows while having a small purebred nucleus as a basis for producing replacement first cross gilts out of another breed of boar.
4.  Despite the higher capital costs, many commercial producers prefer to purchase first cross gilts from private breeders and breeding companies. The major reasons for this practice are convenience and possibly the belief that, despite being more expensive than home-produced replacements, these purchased gilts are more cost-effective.

## CROSSBREEDING SYSTEMS

Crossbreeding systems are mainly designed to exploit heterosis in aspects of breeding and rearing performance. These aspects have shown relatively high levels of heterosis (up to 12 per cent above mid-parent value in the crossbred progeny), while growth and carcass traits have shown little heterosis (from 0 up to a maximum of 6 per cent above mid-parent value in the progeny of two different pure breeds).

The main relevance of crossbreeding systems to the growing pig and its resulting carcass is in relation to the sire line used in the final stage of the crossbreeding programme. Up to relatively recently, the traditional sire line breed used in the United Kingdom was the Large White and particularly boars of the breed that were of high proven merit in terms of growth, food conversion and carcass traits. One advantage of using such a sire line on Large White × Landrace sows was that the resulting 3/4 bred Large White gilts could be retained for breeding if necessary and, while heterosis is not as large as in the first cross, these 3/4 bred stock constituted a cost-effective commercial breeding sow in many situations.

Modern sire lines are, on the other hand, specialist meat lines and are specifically designed to sire the slaughter generation, sow productivity in these lines being less good that that of Large White × Landrace stock.

As noted earlier in this chapter, these sire lines are based on breeds and lines which are particularly strong in carcass traits. Many are based on combinations of German and Belgian Landrace and Pietrain lines with incorporation of useful traits from some Hampshire, Large White, Landrace and Welsh lines specially well endowed in carcass and lean meat quality traits.

One of the breeding companies that is now marketing such a sire line boar claims to have 'produced a good looking, well fleshed, stress resistant, continental type boar which transmits muscling, high quality lean and carcass yield to its progeny out of a conventional hybrid breeding sow. These benefits are achieved without sacrificing feed efficiency, liveweight gain, carcass length and liveability'. The company expects that all concerned − producer, meat trader and consumer − will benefit from the following advantages relative to the better types of Large White Landrace pig:

1.  Higher carcass yield − up to 2 kg more carcass from every 100 kg liveweight
2.  More lean − up to 2 per cent more dissectible lean
3.  Less backfat − up to 2 mm less

4. Higher quality lean, there being no problems with PSE
5. Lack of stress problems in boars and progeny when used on a conventional Large White × Landrace sow
6. Larger eye muscle area − up to 2 cm$^2$ more and hence better lean to fat ratios in loins and chops
7. Absence of strong colour marking
8. Active boars conferring hybrid vigour in the progeny when crossed with Large White × Landrace hybrid sows resulting in up to an extra 0.5 pigs weaned per litter.

These are typical of the claims made for the new sire line boars available in the United Kingdom. If only a reasonable proportion of these claims are borne out in practice, then the carefully evolved sire line boar will make an important contribution to the industry. These claims are based on sound evaluation work carried out by the breeding companies and will be validated or otherwise in due time through the medium of the commercial product evaluation tests operated by the Meat and Livestock Commission.

## EVALUATION OF PERFORMANCE AND SIB TESTING METHODS

Boars and sibs in the UK Pig Improvement Scheme have been evaluated at central testing stations on a twice daily to appetite feeding system. The major traits which have been evaluated directly in this test were food conversion efficiency, liveweight gain and backfat thickness. As indicated earlier in this chapter, all these traits have been improved steadily as a result of the scheme. Likewise, the correlated traits of lean tissue growth rate and lean tissue food conversion efficiency have been improved by between 1 and 3 per cent annually, and while these improvements have been taking place, food intake has been reduced by 0.51 per cent per year.

It appears that selection programmes which give greater emphasis to food conversion efficiency and lean content rather than the rate of lean tissue growth on ad lib. or 'to appetite' feeding systems appear to lead to a reduction in voluntary food intake. It appears that part of the improvement achieved in food conversion efficiency and lean content under such a selection procedure is achieved through a reduction in fat deposition consequent upon a reduction in appetite. Although the resulting achievement of improved food efficiency and of carcass lean content is very acceptable in the short term, the associated reductions in appetite may make further improvements in feed efficiency and lean tissue growth more difficult in the longer term.

The reasons why appetite tends to be reduced when selecting primarily for carcass lean content and food conversion efficiency is evident from Figure 6.11.

It can be seen that feed conversion efficiency is optimised as feed intake increases to a certain level but before appetite is attained. As the pig proceeds to satisfy its appetite on an ad lib. or 'to appetite' system, so its food conversion efficiency will start to deteriorate and its lean content to decline because of increasing fat deposition. Thus, selection for carcass lean content and food conversion efficiency on 'to appetite' feeding systems will tend to favour pigs with a lower appetite.

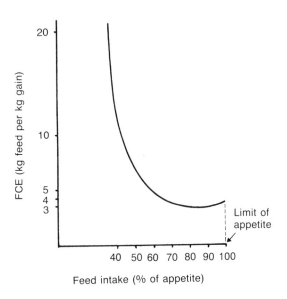

FIGURE 6.11   Trends in food conversion efficiency in relation to feed intake.

An alternative system of testing which might help to prevent this reduction of appetite associated with 'to appetite' systems of testing and selection is therefore desirable. The scheme proposed by Professor Kielanowski and Dr Kotarbinska of Poland appears to have gained most support in this respect. This scheme is based on a time scale feeding system using a feed scale close to ad lib. All pigs receive the same ration each day and all pigs are on test for the same length of time. The pigs which have gained most weight by the end of the test will be those which show the best combination of (1) ability to consume their ration (measure of a reasonable appetite), (2) lean tissue growth rate and (3) food conversion efficiency. A simple example of such a test if illustrated in Figure 6.12.

This system removes variation in food intake (apart from placing at a disadvantage those pigs which were unable to consume their full ration) and selection would favour animals which could deposit lean more efficiently at the same intake. Thus, this would be an effective system for selecting pigs on the basis of lean tissue growth rate and lean tissue food conversion efficiency.

This method of testing and selection is now being used by several pig breeding companies in the United Kingdom.

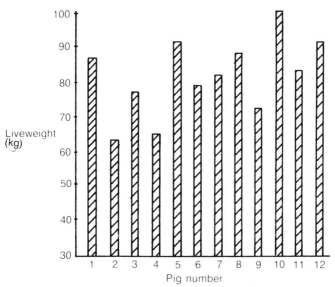

*Note:* Same total amount of feed (150 kg) available to each pig over the test period of 60 days from a starting weight of 30 kg. Numbers 2, 3, 4 and 9 failed to consume their 150 kg in the 60 days. Boar 10 had the best liveweight gain (65 kg) indicating that it had the best combination of appetite, growth potential, feed efficiency and carcass lean content.

FIGURE 6.12 Total liveweight gain of individual boars fed close to appetite over a fixed time period.

## SUMMING UP

Having an efficient, healthy genotype makes it possible to put expensive feed, buildings and labour to optimum use. The basis of any sound and successful system for growing pigs is a genotype which is capable of achieving a high level of biological efficiency during growth and which produces the type of carcass and meat most desired by the meat processor and the consumer.

## ADDITIONAL READING

Fowler, V. R., Bichard, M. and Pease, A. (1976), 'Objectives in Pig Breeding', *Anim. Prod.* **23**, 265.

Mitchell, G., Smith, C., Makower, M. and Bird, P. J. W. N. (1982), 'An Economic Appraisal of Pig Improvement in Great Britain. 1. Genetic and Production Aspects', *Anim. Prod.* **35**, 215–224.

*Pork Industry Handbook*, USA Co-operative Extension Service, University of Illinois at Urbana-Champaign, USA.

*Proceedings of the Third World Congress on Genetics Applied to Livestock Production* (1986), Volumes 9–12, University of Nebraska, Lincoln, Nebraska.

Smith, C., Gibson, A. and Mitchell, F. (1982). 'An Economic Appraisal of Pig Improvement in Great Britain. 2. Factors Affecting Estimated Benefits', *Anim. Prod.* **35**, 225–230.

*Chapter 7*

# Behaviour and Welfare

Pig welfare has been defined in a number of ways by different authorities. We feel that the following definition of Dr B. O. Hughes (1976) is particularly helpful: 'Welfare on a general level is a state of complete mental and physical health where the animal is in harmony with its environment'. An understanding of behaviour and appreciation of animal welfare is basic to good stockmanship which, in turn, is the most important component in ensuring the wellbeing of farm animals and their efficiency of production. Therefore, a good appreciation of pig behaviour is of vital importance in the planning and operation of efficient pig production systems. The purpose of this chapter is to give an outline of the ways in which animal behaviour can be described. There are critical periods when behaviour becomes exceptionally important as, for example, at weaning or when new groupings are formed following mixing. These latter aspects are dealt with in the later chapters on production systems.

## Systems of Behaviour

All systems of animal behaviour have been evolved to aid survival in the wild. The main systems of relevance can be classified as follows:

| | |
|---|---|
| *Ingestive behaviour* | Eating and drinking. |
| *Eliminitive behaviour* | Urination and defaecation. Pigs will keep their sleeping areas clean if given the proper conditions in colder climates. In hot weather they may deliberately create a wallow in their sleeping area so as to keep cool. |
| *Sexual behaviour* | Courtship and mating. |
| *Epimelectic or care giving behaviour* | The care of the sow for her piglets exhibited in the sow's protective attitude towards her young as in nesting and in the feeding call followed by nursing. |
| *Care soliciting behaviour* | This is mostly exercised by young pigs which, when separated from the dam, squeal in an attempt to attract the dam's attention and to regain contact with her. This can also be exhibited in older pigs when one has been separated from its group. |

| | |
|---|---|
| *Allelomimetic behaviour or behavioural mimicry* | This involves two pigs doing the same thing at the same time with some degree of mutual stimulation. Pigs readily follow each other, e.g. when one goes to the udder or to investigate a new object in the pen, the rest will follow. When one animal spots danger and issues a warning grunt, others in the group will quickly follow in issuing such a call. |
| *Shelter seeking behaviour* | In outdoor conditions, pigs will seek shelter from both hot and cold conditions. Pigs huddle together when cold, i.e. they obtain shelter or warmth from each other. |
| *Investigatory behaviour* | Pigs are very inquisitive and explore their environment or any new object which is introduced to their present situation. Such an object may be a plaything, e.g. a stone or a chain, it may be bedding material or it may be another pig. Introduction of fresh feed into a pen or trough also constitutes a new arrival in the pen and excites the natural curiosity of the pig. |
| *Agonistic behaviour* | Under this category are included reactions associated with conflict such as fighting and flight or retaliation following attack. Control of undesirable fighting is a very important objective in pig management and will be discussed in more detail later in this chapter. |

## GROUPING INFLUENCE OF VARIOUS SYSTEMS OF BEHAVIOUR

With the exception of agonistic behaviour, all other systems of behaviour tend to bring pigs together into a group. Pigs tend to feed and drink together, they have their preferred areas for urination and defaecation and they are attracted together for courtship and mating; care giving and soliciting behaviours have a particular influence in bringing together the sow and her piglets and also tend to keep any established group of pigs in social contact with each other; allelomimetic and investigatory behaviours usually involve many pigs in a group engaging in the same activity, while a group of pigs will also naturally seek shelter together, whether from hot sunny conditions outside or from cold, either in intensive or extensive conditions. Thus, pigs will naturally form groups even when not confined by pen walls.

The establishment of stability and order within such groups, whether formed naturally or created artificially in intensive pig systems, involves agonistic behaviour in the establishment of the 'peck' or social order or the social hierarchy.

## ESTABLISHMENT OF THE 'PECK ORDER' IN A GROUP OF PIGS

The 'peck order' involves a sort of chain of command within a group of pigs. When a group is first formed, a series of pig-to-pig combats develop from each of which one emerges as the conqueror and the other as the conquered. The greater the number of such contests won, the higher is the social rank of an individual and vice-versa.

Most pig hierarchies conform to the linear type (see Figure 7.1), although more complex triangular and square type arrangements have also been reported. In some situations, it is only the top and bottom pigs in the hierarchy which hold a stable position.

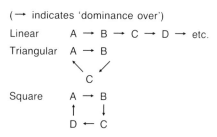

FIGURE 7.1 Types of social hierarchy.

## ATTAINMENT AND MAINTENANCE OF GROUP STABILITY

Immediately individual pigs from different pens are placed together in a new pen, a good deal of agonistic behaviour follows as animals strive for a high position in the pen group hierarchy. Once these paired combats are settled and the social order is established, each animal should know its place and appears to be kept in its place by social superiors by means of formal signals (visual or vocal), e.g. a harsh stare or adoption of a particular threatening posture, and it will maintain dominance over its inferiors by the same techniques.

Once this order of command is settled, the dominant individuals will have priority with regard to essential requirements such as feed, water and lying area. Whether or not pigs at the bottom of the order will suffer because of their low social rank depends on two main factors:

- *the adequacy of the facilities*, i.e. opportunity for feeding, watering, defaecating, urinating, exercising and resting
- *the number in the group*.

Therefore, if we want all pigs in a pen to perform well, we must ensure that low-ranking pigs have sufficient opportunity to obtain their necessary requirements. This places emphasis on good pen design and avoidance of excessive group size and stocking density.

Plate 7.1 Aggressive encounters between pairs of pigs are the basis on which pigs within a pen or group establish their 'peck' or social order.

Plate 7.2 Excessive stocking rate and inadequate feeding space and watering facilities combine to impose particular difficulties on pigs of lower social status. This is the most common cause of variation in feed intake and growth within a pen.

## GROUP SIZE

A 'group' for the purposes of the present discussion can be defined as a number of pigs sharing one set of essential facilities, i.e. feed and feeding space, watering points, lying and exercise space and opportunity for dunging and urinating so as to keep the lying area comfortable.

The maximum group size within which it is possible to achieve a stable social order would appear to be dependent on the number of its fellows an individual pig can recognise. While this number is not known exactly, it is thought to be about 30. When group size is above this number, one can expect instability and a higher than desirable level of agonistic behaviour and resulting restlessness.

When group size is below 30, the low ranking pigs will not be bullied provided they do not violate the space or territory of dominant individuals, i.e. they must keep their distance from their more dominant pen-mates. In other words, low ranking pigs must not challenge their superiors for feeding space and feed, for lying space and for dunging, urinating and exercise areas.

The basic requirement for the well-being and performance of low social status pigs within a group places great importance on pen design, on the facilities provided within the pen and on the stocking density of pigs in the pen. These should all be such as to prevent placing the lowest ranking animals at a disadvantage. The challenge in meeting this basic objective is taken up in the following chapters when the pig's specific requirements in these respects are outlined and housing, penning and management systems which conform to these requirements are outlined.

In addition, while, in theory, one can achieve stability within a group of pigs as large as 30, in practice, smaller group sizes may be preferable for several reasons. The old adage 'the smaller the group, the better they do' has much to support it in pig production, and the available information on optimum group size in various situations is discussed thoroughly in the following chapters.

As a general prelude to this discussion, however, it is important to outline some of the consequences of failure to meet the basic requirements for a stable social hierarchy within a group of pigs.

## FAILURE TO CATER FOR PIGS OF LOW SOCIAL RANK

When pigs of low social rank are not provided with adequate facilities and/or when group size is excessive, they are subjected to discomfort or *strain* as a result of the *stresses* imposed. If these stresses are not excessive, the pigs of low social rank may be able to adapt to them, e.g. if feeding space on ad lib. systems is limited, the low ranking pigs may circumvent this constraint with impunity by feeding at non-popular times. However, if the stresses imposed are severe enough or applied for a sufficient length of time, the pig is unable to adapt and will be subjected to strain, which is the ultimate effect of the stress or stresses imposed on it by the system of husbandry and housing. This strain may exhibit itself in a variety of production problems such as gastric ulceration, abnormal behaviour resulting in tail, flank or ear biting and depression in antibody production leading to greater liability to disease.

Plate 7.3   With a relatively low number of pigs per pen, liberal floor space, adequate
feeding space and opportunity for watering, little or no aggression is evident in a pen after
the 'peck' order is established, and even pigs of low social status can perform at or near
their potential.

Plate 7.4   Opportunity for watering may be less than adequate in many situations. In the
case of nipple drinkers, there should be at least 2 per pen, while in pens with large
numbers of pigs, one nipple drinker should be provided for every 10 pigs.

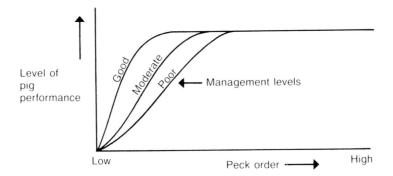

FIGURE 7.2   Level of pig performance according to position in the peck order and management conditions.

Glen McBride in Australia has provided a very simple but clear illustration of the failure to provide growing—finishing pigs with adequate facilities (see Figure 7.2).

McBride's example was based originally on data from poultry but has since also been validated for growing pigs. When pig performance was related to position in the peck order, the performance of lower ranking pigs varied according to the management conditions provided. At low levels of management, high ranking pigs performed well but pig performance progressively deteriorated from those in the middle of the order to the lowest ranking individuals. As management conditions were improved from poor to moderate to good management conditions, so progressively more pigs were able to perform to their full potential. It can be assumed from information on poultry that if management conditions were perfected (perhaps by individual penning and other approaches), performance of even the lowest rank-

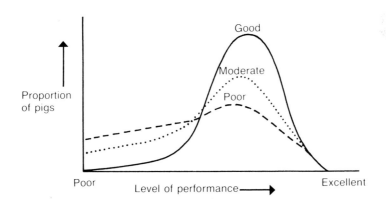

FIGURE 7.3   Frequency distribution of pigs according to performance level when subjected to good, moderate and poor management conditions.

Plate 7.5  Increasing variability in the size of pigs within a pen is often caused by inadequate floor or feeding space or by restricted opportunity for obtaining water. (Courtesy of Pig International)

ing pigs·would have been brought up to the level of that of the highest ranking individuals.

McBride further illustrated the performance of these three groups of pigs (i.e. under good, moderate or poor management) by depicting their frequency distribution in terms of performance levels (see Figure 7.3).

It can be seen that the frequency distribution of Group 1 (Good management) conformed closely to the normal distribution. The frequency distributions of Group 2 (moderate management) and Group 3 (poor management) were increasingly skewed to the left, indicating an increasing proportion of low performing animals among the lower ranking pigs. McBride accordingly suggested that the frequency distribution of performance in a pen of pigs could serve as a useful index of the adequacy of the facilities (housing, penning, feeding, watering, resting etc. and management) provided. While variation in growth of pigs within a pen is often attributed to differences in genotype or health, it is very likely that, in most situations, the greatest variation in performance is due to inadequate facilities and management.

Plate 7.6   In the case of restricted feeding systems, very liberal feeding space must be provided at the start of a growth period in a particular pen so as to ensure that space will still be adequate at the end of the period of occupation of the pen.

## SOME REASONS FOR INADEQUATE FACILITIES

Facilities and management may be inadequate for growing pigs in many situations because of a lack of knowledge or, more likely, a lack of understanding regarding their requirements. Another reason why facilities are often inadquate is that while pigs are, or should be, growing continuously, their provisions, in terms of pen and feeding space in particular, are often static for long periods.

## STATIC SPACE AND EXPANDING PIGS

Figure 7.4 provides a simple illustration of the growth of the pig from weaning at 3 weeks of age, when it weighs 5 kg, to the stage of slaughter at 90 kg liveweight. The pig's liveweight has been multiplied by eighteen-fold in this period. During stage 1 of growth the pig may increase from an average of 5 kg to 20 kg liveweight − a fourfold increase in weight. If it occupied the same pen, it is possible that lying and feeding space were very liberal at the start and still adequate by the end of this phase. However, facilities may well be adequate only up to 10 kg liveweight and become increasingly inadequate from then to the end of the growth phase at 20 kg.

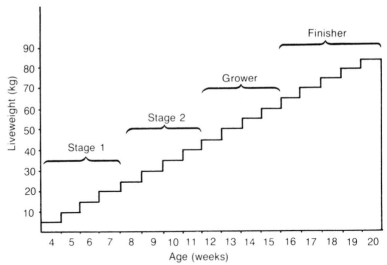

FIGURE 7.4   A simple illustration of the trend in pig liveweights at weekly intervals between weaning at 5 kg liveweight and 90 kg.

Such a possible situation in which feeding space has become limiting is depicted in Figure 7.5. This represents a pen of 20 pigs with the food intakes of each individual illustrated in relation to their maintenance requirement. It can be seen that the 12 more dominant of the 20 pigs are able to eat to appetite while the intakes of pigs 13 and 14 are slightly depressed. As we proceed down the peck order, pigs have increasing difficulty in achieving reasonable food intakes. Pigs 17 and 18 are able to consume only slightly more than maintenance requirements and will have very poor growth and food conversion efficiency. The lowest ranking pigs − 19

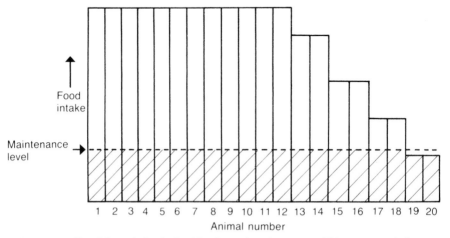

FIGURE 7.5   Possible variation in food intake and performance within a group of pigs associated with overstocking.

and 20 — are unable even to consume their maintenance requirements and will, as a result, be losing weight and will have negative food conversion efficiency. They are consuming food for absolutely no return.

This situation may prevail from the time a pen is first stocked if stocking is very excessive. However, we are more likely to find this state of affairs in the last few weeks of the occupancy of a pen when, with increasing growth, facilities which were adequate at the first stage of occupancy are now becoming increasingly inadequate. This adverse situation will persist until the eight or so heaviest pigs are taken out of the pen and either transferred to another pen or, if appropriate, sent for slaughter.

While in older pigs the situation depicted in Figure 7.5 might result only in a depression in liveweight gain and feed conversion efficiency, in pigs soon after weaning it would likely result not only in a depression in growth and feed conversion efficiency, but would also predispose to disease and mortality.

Further aspects of providing good feeding and other arrangements within a pen are dealt with in the later chapters on housing and on production systems.

## CORRECTING INEFFICIENCY AND IMPROVING WELFARE

It is likely that failure to provide adequate facilities for the pigs of low social status, at least during part of the overall period of growth, constitutes one of the most serious sources of inefficiency in the production of pigmeat. The solution to this problem lies in ensuring adequate facilities for the lowest ranking pigs within pens throughout their period of growth since, if their needs are satisfied, so will be those of their higher ranking pen mates.

This chapter has concentrated on the social behaviour of the pig and how knowledge on this subject must be more fully exploited if we are to achieve greater efficiency in the production of pigmeat.

If, through more careful housing and pen design, provision of adequate feeding and watering facilities and imposition of competent management and stockmanship, we can more adequately cater for the needs of all pigs, and of those of lower social rank in particular, we will at the same time be making a very important contribution to improving well-being and welfare of all pigs in the herd.

## ADDITIONAL READING

Wood-Gush D. G. M. (1983), *Elements of Ethology*, Chapman-Hall, London.

# Chapter 8

# Climatic Requirements; Housing Principles; Housing and Feeding Systems

All buildings are modifiers of the internal and immediately surrounding environment. They alter environmental space by changing the quality and the quantity of the space they enclose. Regardless of the designer's intentions, buildings will modify the climate in and around them, the resources used to build them and the behaviour and activities of the people and animals which occupy them.

Buildings modify environmental space by isolating a preselected portion of space within boundaries. Boundaries may take a variety of physical or perceptual forms. Whichever form the boundary takes, the aim is to prevent or reduce the passage of matter, energy or information, individually or collectively, between the enclosed space and the surrounding environment. Walls, for example, prevent the escape of animals (matter), reduce the flow of heat (energy) and distort the transmission of words or animal sounds (information). It is the job of the building designer to correctly assess the magnitude and acceptable rate of transmission of these three entities through the boundaries and to choose the most suitable resources to construct the boundaries. It is significant that, although it is the space within a building that is required, the resources go into constructing the boundaries and therefore the cost of the building is largely in the cost of the boundaries.

Boundaries enclose space, the quality of which differs from the surrounding environment by the degree to which the boundaries influence the rate of change of energy and information through them. The quality of an environment within a building is a function of the designer's intentions. These are an interpretation of the farmer or producer's expectations, the stockperson's operational requirements within the building and the efficiency with which it is managed. Several user requirements have already been expressed earlier in Chapter 1, e.g.

- Housing, penning and climatic control must be such that the pigs are comfortable at all times, with the most timid pig in the pen being well catered for.
- Prevention of disease is better than cure. One must set out to ensure healthy pigs in the first instance and maintain this desirable state by minimising risks of infection and by ensuring adequate nutrition, housing, management and stockmanship.
- A succession of optimum diets must be formulated to meet the pig's changing nutrient requirements as it grows and matures.

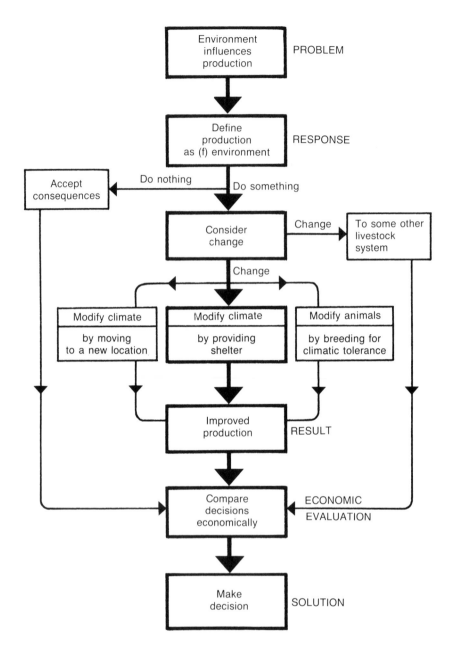

FIGURE 8.1   Decision-making process on the need to modify climate and on the most
cost effective approach. (Modified from Hahn, 1981)

● Stockmanship is the lynch pin in ensuring efficient production in that it is the controlling influence over all other vital components of production.

Housing must contribute to the attainment of these requirements. Buildings, however, cost money − to erect, operate and maintain. This investment must be justified by improved productivity. For example, considering the building as a climate modifier, the general decision-making process can be expressed in a series of step-by-step decisions as shown in Figure 8.1. It is clearly necessary to relate some or all of the parameters of productivity to the component to be modified − in this case climate. Such a relationship has been referred to earlier. The pig is comfortable and productive when it is kept in a thermal climate consistent with its zone of minimum metabolism (its thermoneutral zone). Such a climatic zone is generally described as that which lies between the pig's lower (LCT) and upper critical temperatures (UCT). When the external climate produces conditions above or below this zone for a significant proportion of time, then housing must be considered as a cost effective means of climatic modification when it succeeds in keeping the pig within its thermoneutral zone.

## THE MODIFICATION OF CLIMATE

The pig's response to the thermal components of its aerial and structural environment are reasonably well understood and documented. Pigs have a deep body temperature of 39°C and as the ambient temperature falls below or rises above this level, they will be increasingly subject to problems of sub-optimal (hypothermia) or excessive (hyperthermia) body temperature. Pigs will therefore go to great lengths to maintain their deep body temperature.

The pig's energy intake from food is largely fixed by its appetite. This energy will be used for the maintenance of its physiological state and for growth. The more energy that is needed for maintaining normal body temperature, the less there will be for growth. If the total energy intake is exceeded by the energy requirements for maintenance, then the animal will decline in body condition as it catabolises body fat and protein to meet its basic requirements for living. If this process is allowed to continue the animal eventually dies. How long the animal is able to survive by catabolising body reserves is dependent on the extent of these reserves at the start.

The process of feeding for maximum productivity will be most efficient when metabolic heat production is at a minimum. In a thermally neutral environment (between the LCT and the UCT), the minimum metabolic heat production is a function of pig size and energy intake and this has been established by experimentation. The lower boundary of thermo-neutrality is defined by the lower critical temperature and the upper level by either the wet or dry upper critical temperature (Bruce, 1981). In conditions below the lower critical temperature (LCT), heat loss by evaporation from the body surface or respiratory tract of the animal is at a minimum and all additional heat loss occurs by conduction, convection and radiation (non-evaporative). Above the LCT, evaporative losses increase and non-evaporative losses decrease with rising environmental temperature.

**TABLE 8.1  Upper critical temperatures (UCT) in dry and wet conditions for individual pigs at three feed levels housed on solid concrete floors**

| Liveweight (kg) | UCT (Dry)(°C) Feed level* | | | UCT (Wet)(°C) Feed level* | | |
|---|---|---|---|---|---|---|
| | $1 \times M$ | $2 \times M$ | $3 \times M$ | $1 \times M$ | $2 \times M$ | $3 \times M$ |
| 5 | 37 | 35 | 34 | 38 | 37 | 36 |
| 10 | 36 | 35 | 34 | 38 | 37 | 36 |
| 20 | 36 | 35 | 33 | 38 | 37 | 36 |
| 40 | 36 | 34 | 32 | 37 | 36 | 35 |
| 60 | 35 | 33 | 31 | 37 | 36 | 35 |
| 80 | 35 | 33 | 31 | 37 | 36 | 35 |
| 100 | 35 | 33 | 31 | 37 | 36 | 35 |
| 140 | 34 | 32 | 30 | 37 | 36 | 35 |
| 180 | 34 | 32 | 29 | 36 | 35 | 34 |

*Feed level: $1 \times M$ = Maintenance requirement; $2 \times M$ = Twice maintenance requirement; $3 \times M$ = Three times maintenance requirement
(Source: Bruce, 1981)

As the temperature rises to and begins to pass the upper end of the zone of thermo-neutrality, the pig must try to lose heat in order to maintain normal body temperature or thermal equilibrium. Unless provided with some means of cooling, the pig in this situation will resort to evaporative cooling by wallowing and, where no water or mud is available, faeces and urine in dunging areas provide an admirable substitute. Some idea of the UCTs in dry and wet conditions for pigs weighing from 5 to 180 kg on three feed levels and housed on solid concrete floors is given in Table 8.1. For similar-sized pigs on similar feed intakes but housed on perforated metal floors, UCTs are about 2°C lower.

In conditions below the lower critical temperature, the rate of heat production or heat loss from the pig is a function of the energy demand of the environment and the resistance to heat loss provided by the body tissues of the animal. Poorly insulated pigs will have a faster rate of heat loss than fatter or well-insulated animals.

The LCT for pigs at varying liveweights under various environmental conditions has been determined by experimentation, and several useful models have been developed to combine the influence of variables such as liveweight, energy intake, group size, floor type, air temperature and air velocity into a prediction of LCT. The model developed by Bruce and Clark (1979), for example, gives the following predictions of LCT for pigs weighing 20 to 100 kg in two group sizes, two floor types and three energy intake levels with air velocity constant at 0.15 m/s (virtually still air) (Table 8.2).

The following important relationships can be drawn from Table 8.2.

● For pigs of equal weight, on the same energy intakes and in the same size of group, the use of straw bedding can reduce the LCT by 3 to 6°C.
● For pigs of equal weight, on the same energy intake and on the same floor type, the benefits of grouping (huddling in a cold environment) can reduce the LCT by 3 to 8°C.

**TABLE 8.2 Lower critical temperatures for growing pigs based on the model by Bruce and Clark (1979)**

| Liveweight (kg) | Group size | Straw Feed level* $1 \times M$ | $2 \times M$ | $3 \times M$ | Concrete Feed level* $1 \times M$ | $2 \times M$ | $3 \times M$ |
|---|---|---|---|---|---|---|---|
| 20 | 1 | 26 | 22 | 17 | 29 | 26 | 22 |
|  | 15 | 23 | 17 | 11 | 26 | 21 | 16 |
| 40 | 1 | 24 | 19 | 14 | 27 | 23 | 19 |
|  | 15 | 20 | 13 | 7 | 24 | 18 | 13 |
| 60 | 1 | 23 | 18 | 12 | 26 | 22 | 18 |
|  | 15 | 18 | 12 | 5 | 22 | 16 | 11 |
| 80 | 1 | 22 | 17 | 11 | 25 | 21 | 17 |
|  | 15 | 17 | 10 | 4 | 21 | 15 | 10 |
| 100 | 1 | 21 | 16 | 11 | 25 | 21 | 17 |
|  | 15 | 16 | 10 | 4 | 20 | 14 | 9 |

Air velocity = 0.15 m/s
*M = maintenance requirement

- For pigs of equal weight, in similar group sizes and on the same floor type, changing the energy intake from a maintenance level to three times maintenance can reduce the LCT by 7 to 13°C.

Increasing the air movement across the body of the pig increases heat loss by raising the evaporative cooling from wet surfaces and by increasing the rate of convective heat transfer (the removal of heat by the passage of moving air). This is an advantage in hot conditions and a disadvantage in cold conditions.

Above the LCT but below the UCT, the pig's total metabolic heat production is at a minimum. When the environmental temperature increases above the LCT the pig must vary the means by which it continues to lose heat. With a rising environmental temperature, the difference between the deep body temperature and the temperature of the surroundings declines and so sensible heat production, e.g. heat loss by convection, conduction and radiation, also declines. The pig will vasodilate (expand the capillaries near the skin, so increasing blood flow), thus reducing the body's resistance to the outward flow of heat, and the insensible or evaporative component of heat loss will increase. The pig will then have to lose a greater proportion of its heat by sweating or panting, neither of which it does well.

Given suitable resources, however, the pig will turn to several other means of behavioural thermoregulation in hot climates. Pigs will seek cool, shaded areas in which to lie, exposing the maximum surface area to the coolest conditions. They will lie well apart from each other if space is available.

The pig will also wallow in water, mud or excrement, the latter to the consternation of many a stockperson without experience of these conditions but to the obvious delight of the pig. Finally, in hot conditions, pigs will reduce their food intake in order to save further energy embarrassment. Seldom, however, do natural climatic conditions match the ideal requirements for pig production all of the time, so some form of shelter becomes appropriate. Housing systems use three methods to modify climate:

1. Insulation
2, Ventilation
3. Heating or cooling.

To what extent some or all of these methods will be required depends on the magnitude of the difference between the natural climatic conditions and those required by the pig within the building. In very cold climates, for example, buildings will be well insulated, ventilation will be controlled and heating systems may be employed. Conversely, in hot climates, buildings will be insulated to reduce solar heating, they will have facilities to maximise the volume of air flow and they may need systems for cooling the pigs.

The three methods of modifying the climate will be dealt with in turn.

## Insulation

Buildings can gain or lose heat through the building fabric — walls, roof and floor. All materials provide some resistance to the passage of heat. Some, however, are good insulators and provide a high resistance to heat flow.

Thermal conductivity ($\lambda$ or lambda) is a specific property of a material defined in terms of a steady rate of heat flow through unit thickness of the material. A homogeneous slab of material conducts heat at a rate that varies with its conductivity and thickness. Materials with numerically large values of ($\lambda$) are poor insulators but, for the same material, greater thickness always means better insulation. The combination of these two values, conductivity and thickness, expressed as a ratio,

$$\frac{\text{thickness}}{\lambda},$$

gives the thermal resistance (R) of the slab of material.

When two or more materials are placed together to form a composite element, then the thermal resistance of the element is numerically equal to the sum of the thermal resistances of the individual materials plus the resistance of any air space also contained.

If an air space is provided between two materials, then its thermal resistance is influenced by the materials on both sides of the air space, the width of the air space, the direction of heat flow and whether the air space is ventilated or not. Unless the air space is lined with insulation having a reflective surface, such as aluminium foil, which will not become tarnished or coated with dust, a high emissivity (related to heat flow by radiation) should be assumed for all building materials.

In addition to the insulating properties of the various materials and any air spaces incorporated in their composite structure, thermal resistance is provided by the change in heat transfer at the external and internal surfaces.

For most agricultural buildings, normal exposure should be used, but where buildings are on the sea coast or on exposed hill sites, values for severe exposure would be more appropriate.

The total thermal resistance of a composite building element is then the sum of the thermal resistances of (1) the individual materials, (2) the air spaces and (3) the surfaces' resistances (heat exchange at the air/building surface inside and outside).

The value commonly referred to as the U value is a measure of the amount of heat transmitted through one square metre of complete structure for one degree (K) difference between inside and outside temperature. It is equal to the reciprocal of total thermal resistance, i.e.

$$U = \frac{1}{R},$$

and is called the thermal transmittance value.

## WALLS AND ROOFS

Unfortunately, most structures do not consist of homogeneous elements, and so a wall or a roof will have some parts where resistance to the transmission of heat is poorer than others. This situation occurs at what are termed thermal bridges, i.e. bridges for the passage of heat from one side of an element to the other (see Figure 8.2).

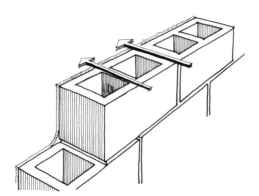

FIGURE 8.2   Thermal bridges in a hollow concrete block wall.

In many cases, thermal bridges do not make a significant contribution to heat loss, and, in view of the other assumptions and unknowns in the various calculations, too much accuracy in their calculation is hardly justified. Nevertheless, thermal bridges should be minimised in all structures especially if localised condensation is to be prevented. Thermal transmittance values for several wall and roof constructions are shown in Table 8.3.

## CONDENSATION IN WALLS AND ROOFS

Building materials and their composite fabrications used for wall and roof elements not only transfer heat from the hot to the cold side but they also transfer moisture in the form of vapour. The moisture passes from an area of high vapour pressure (usually the warm inside) to that of low vapour pressure (cold outside) and its rate

**TABLE 8.3   Thermal transmittance values (U) for external walls and roofs**

| Construction | U value $(W/m^2K)^*$ | |
| --- | --- | --- |
| | Normal exposure | Severe exposure |
| *Walls* | | |
| 1. Solid brick wall, unplastered 105 mm thick | 3.3 | 3.6 |
|                 220 mm thick | 2.3 | 2.4 |
| 2. Solid brick cavity wall (unventilated) with 105 mm outer and inner leaves with 13 mm dense plaster on inside face | 1.5 | 1.6 |
| 3. Weatherboarding on timber framing with 8 mm asbestos insulating board, 50 mm glass fibre insulation in the cavity and building paper behind the battens (assumed 10% of glass fibre bridged by timber) | 0.65 | 0.66 |
| 4. 5 mm thick corrugated asbestos sheeting on framing | 5.3 | 6.1 |
| 5. Double skin asbestos cement with 25 mm glass fibre insulation ( uncompressed) in between | 1.1 | 1.1 |
| *Roofs ($22\frac{1}{2}°$ pitched roof)* | | |
| 6. Corrugated asbestos cement sheeting on purlins | 5.43 | 6.41 |
| 7. Corrugated asbestos cement sheeting with cavity and 25 mm expanded polystyrene | 1.08 | 1.11 |
| 8. Corrugated double skin asbestos cement sheeting with 25 mm glass fibre insulation between (uncompressed) | 0.98 | 0.98 |

*Watts per $m^2$ per °C difference between inside and outside temperature

of passage is a function of the rate at which vapour passes through various materials. Even with impervious materials such as steel sheeting, moisture migrates through unsealed joints.

*Surface condensation*

Surface condensation is the most obvious and the most common type of condensation found in livestock buildings. Vapour barriers (materials which prevent the passage of vapour) do not prevent surface condensation. Surface condensation occurs where the surface temperature of a wall or roof cools the adjacent moisture-laden air to its dew point (temperature at which air is saturated with moisture vapour). To prevent condensation, the usual answer is to raise the surface temperature by adding further insulation to the wall or roof. In doing so, of course, it may also be necessary to add a further vapour barrier depending on where, in the construction, the additional insulation is added. Any change in the structure of a composite element will change the pattern of heat and moisture migration and therefore the position of the dew point within the construction.

*Interstitial condensation*

The vapour-carrying capacity of air is greater at higher temperature. Thus, when moisture diffuses through a building material, or passes through unsealed joints, it generally moves across a declining temperature gradient. At a unique point on this temperature gradient the vapour-carrying capacity of the air will reach dew point, and any further drop in temperature will result in the release of moisture as condensation. In constructions which allow the passage of vapour, this point is often reached within the structure, causing condensation where it cannot be detected. This may then result in the gradual deterioration of materials and a further reduction in the insulating value of materials like fibreglass. This type of condensation is known as interstitial condensation.

Some of the worst problems occur in low-pitched corrugated steel sheeted roofs, lined on the underside of the purlins with insulation boards but with badly sealed joints. Where the cavity between insulation and steel sheeting is badly ventilated, an accumulation of water vapour condenses on the cold, impervious inner surface of the steel roof sheeting. Cold, clear, frosty nights, with high radiant energy losses, exacerbate the problem by further reducing the surface temperature of the steel sheeting (see Figure 8.3a).

Problems such as this can be alleviated by preventing the migration of moisture into the roof cavity by installing a vapour barrier. As this is not always entirely satisfactory, ventilation of the roof cavity to remove as much residual moisture as possible may be needed (Kelly, 1973) (see Figure 8.3b).

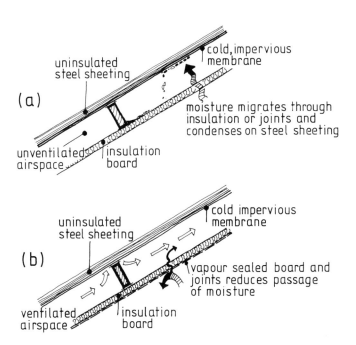

FIGURE 8.3(a)  Condensation on steel sheeting in a roof without a vapour barrier.
(b)  Eliminating condensation using a vapour barrier and ventilation.

Similar problems can occur within framed wall constructions and, although it is possible to design a wall structure that allows for the complete migration of moisture vapour from inside to outside, the occasionally unpredictable nature of materials and climate makes reliance on this migration risky. To minimise the risk, the installation of a vapour barrier on the warm side of the wall or material is a wise precaution.

### Insulation failure

Condensation is often a good indicator of the gradual deterioration or failure of insulation. Polyurethane foam, for example, may undergo an ageing process which results in a reduction of its thermal resistance. However, the overall thermal performance of this material is usually so good that such losses are insignificant except in exceptional circumstances.

In other cases, however, major reductions in thermal resistance can occur if insulants like fibreglass get wet. This can happen if the building leaks or if the moisture content of the insulant increases due to moisture migration. Where quilts of glasswool have been badly installed in vertical walls, sagging and thinning of the mat can occur. This may be further exacerbated by the additional weight of water in the mat as a result of moisture accumulation.

Finally, many insulants are prone to destruction by vermin. Although birds, mice and rats are unlikely to ingest glasswool or expanded plastics, they find it ideal for building nests or burrows. Polyurethane foam sandwiched between two layers of paper has provided a series of insulated burrows for mice when used as a ceiling liner in a piggery.

Insulants used in flat ceilings with a loft space above are particularly prone to damage by vermin and, as penetration of the insulation usually occurs from above, any protection in the form of metal sheeting or asbestos board should be on the top side. Where pipes or cables pass up through insulation boards these often provide runs for vermin to penetrate the ceiling from the underside and their occurrence should be minimised. Expanded polystyrene has also provided a useful substrate in which moths can pupate their offspring, particularly if the insulant is continually coated with organic dust on which the moths can feed. The lining of ventilation ducts is a favoured location were dust consisting of fine particles of food is deposited.

### FLOORS

Unlike walls and roofs, the insulation of floors must be considered from two different points of view. Like walls and roofs, heat is lost from a building by transfer through the floor to the outside air or to the subsoil beneath the piggery. There is also, however, the direct loss of heat from an animal lying on the floor. This condition is used in the assessment of the animal's lower critical temperature.

### Heat loss from within a building through the floor

Heat passing through the centre of a large area of floor passes into the subsoil but, near the edge of the floor, the heat flow moves laterally towards the external air. This edge effect becomes important within about 900 mm of the perimeter wall of the building. The larger and more nearly square a floor is, the smaller will be the average heat flow. For large floors, where the concern is solely with preventing heat loss from within the building, the use of a perimeter of edge insulation would seem to be an adequate and economical way of minimising this heat loss. Once the heat storage capacity of a floor has reached a stable condition, edge insulation has been found to be extremely effective in maintaining this condition. In very cold climates, where frost penetrates the ground to significant depths (in excess of 300 mm), vertical edge insulation can inhibit frost penetration beneath the building and reduce the likelihood of frost heave and failure of floors and foundations.

*The resting pig and thermal discomfort*
When the pig lies down on a floor it loses heat to the cooler floor mass. This can be beneficial in hot conditions but, when carried to excess in cool conditions, it can result in thermal discomfort. During the initial period of resting, the heat transfer from the pig to the floor varies gradually, getting less as the floor warms until a stable condition or steady state of heat transfer pertains. The duration of the transient period (i.e. until a stable condition is reached) is influenced by the construction of the floor. The amount of heat lost to the floor under steady state conditions is a good measure of the contribution of the floor to metabolic heat loss. For example, solid floors with no insulation, or those with the insulation embedded beneath a thick surface layer of concrete, create the worst thermal conditions whilst those floors liberally covered in dry straw bedding give the most satisfactory conditions. Perforated floors of metal mesh generally have a neutral value, having no more effect on the resting pig than the surrounding air has on the standing animal. Wet floors or floors covered with slurry will increase heat losses.

Plate 8.1 Various postures of pigs lying resting. Some are fully recumbent on their sides, some are lying on the sternum while others adopt an intermediate position as they lie in contact with pen mates.

When the pig is lying down, between 8 and 20 per cent of its body can be in contact with the floor, the amount of contact varying with the posture adopted by the pig (see Plate 8.1). In a cold environment, the pig will conserve energy by reducing heat loss to a minimum. Body contact with the floor will be reduced and the pig will assume a sternum lying posture with the body supported on all four legs.

In warmer conditions, the body/floor contact area will be increased as the pig adopts a more exposed, relaxed posture until finally, in a hot environment, the pig will lie fully recumbent with the maximum of body area in contact with the floor. It has been postulated that, under stable conditions, the major component of conductive heat loss from the pig is the lateral transfer of heat through the surface layer of the floor. Transfer of heat to the subsoil is not considered a significant factor (see Figure 8.4).

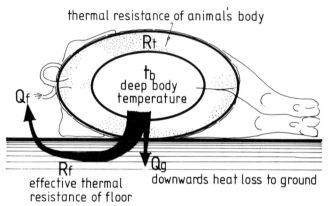

FIGURE 8.4   Loss of heat from a resting pig to the floor.

To use the commonly applied thermal transmittance value (U) to describe this condition is inadequate and a new, more appropriate value has been suggested, using a thermal simulator of the conductive heat transfer from the pig (see Plate 8.2). It has been proposed that floors should be ranked in accordance with their effective thermal resistance as measured by the simulated losses from a 45 kg pig. This is referred to as the $R_{f45}$ value. Using suitable adjustment techniques, this value can be modified to apply to animals of larger or smaller size. Table 8.4 gives a ranked classification of the $R_{f45}$ values for a range of floor types including those with applied insulation in the form of straw bedding.

When the simulator (see Plate 8.2) is raised above the floor to approximate a standing pig, the thermal resistance value to air is about 0.12°C m²/W. Floors with a $R_{f45}$ value equal to 0.12°C m²/W, such as metal mesh floors, are con-

**TABLE 8.4  Ranked classification of floors on the basis of thermal resistance measured using a simulated 45 kg pig**

| Floor type | Thermal resistance $R_{f45}$ (°Cm²/W)* | Approximate thermal advantage relative to a dry concrete floor (floor 16) |
|---|---|---|
| 1.  60 mm dry straw on concrete | 0.660 | +5°C |
| 2.  25 mm dry straw on asphalt | 0.520 | |
| 3.  25 mm dry sawdust on concrete | 0.230 | |
| 4.  Wooden slats 58 mm wide, 10 mm gap, 70 mm deep | 0.230 | |
| 5.  18 mm cement screed on 150 mm lightweight aggregate | 0.170 | |
| 6.  Metal mesh floors | 0.120 | +2°C |
| 7.  Slatted and T bar pvc slats | 0.110 | |
| 8.  Asphalt | 0.100 | |
| 9.  Concrete slatted panel | 0.086 | |
| 10.  18 mm cement screed on 150 mm no-fines concrete | 0.079 | |
| 11.  50 mm thick suspended concrete slabs | 0.077 | |
| 12.  110 mm tri-form concrete slats | 0.073 | |
| 13.  T-metal slats 24 mm wide, 12 mm gap | 0.067 | |
| 14.  Concrete slats 100 mm wide, 19 mm gap, 75 mm deep | 0.052 | |
| 15.  Muddy ground | 0.044 | |
| 16.  Concrete floor  − Dry | 0.042 | 0 |
|                  − Wet | 0.030 | −2°C |

*Values are measured in steady state conditions and are not appropriate to the immediate transitional state when a pig first lies on the floor.
(Source: Bruce, 1978)

sidered thermally neutral, and they will make little thermal difference to the animal, lying or standing. Floors with values higher than 0.12°C m²/W will feel warmer and will reduce heat loss, whilst those with lower values will feel colder because heat loss is increased.

Clearly, if solid floors are to be considered thermally effective for pigs, the insulation layer must be as near to the surface as possible. This is readily apparent from the high $R_{f45}$ value achieved with surface-applied insulants like straw bedding.

When screeds on insulation are compared with straw bedding approximately 60 mm thick on top of uninsulated concrete, the same thermal effect is achieved by using only a 5 mm cement topping on 50 mm of extruded polystyrene. For structural reasons, most existing cement screeds are 30 mm or more in thickness and therefore produce floors with poorer thermal properties than straw bedding. New materials and construction techniques can now produce floors with improved thermal characteristics.

Plate 8.2 Thermal simulator of a 45 kg pig resting on a floor of 'no fines' concrete finished on top with a cement screed. Instrumentation to measure heat transfer is located on top of the simulator. (Courtesy of Centre for Rural Building, Bucksburn, Aberdeen)

## THE RELATIVE IMPORTANCE OF BUILDING HEAT LOSS
## AND VENTILATION HEAT LOSS

Although some insulation of the building fabric is important in terms of reducing heat loss and condensation, just how much insulation one needs and the overall relevance of this to total heat loss must be considered. Ventilation is the other factor affecting transfer of heat from the building to the external air.

In buildings for growing—finishing pigs insulated with the equivalent of 100 mm of glasswool and ventilated at minimum levels in cold conditions, only about 10 to 15 per cent of the total heat lost from the building passes through the building fabric. In such a situation, it is wiser to concentrate on the heat lost through the ventilation system than to invest more money on extra insulation. Minimum ventilation rate is, however, not a standard quantity but one which varies with the system of production and its management. Over the years, a minimum ventilation rate of 0.375 m³/h per kg liveweight has proved satisfactory, but in very cold conditions, even lower values may be satisfactory for short periods of time.

Eventually, however, a minimum ventilation rate will be reached which then becomes independent of climate and, in regions like Canada and Scandinavia with particularly cold conditions in winter, further insulation of the building is the only other means of reducing heat loss. To establish the most cost effective way of maintaining animal performance, in this case, the cost of additional insulation must be compared with that of feeding the pig more or of adding heat to the internal environment.

### Ventilation

All pig buildings need to be ventilated and if management is to cope with the variation in climate, then all ventilation systems need to be controlled. The response, in terms of room temperature, etc., to a change in ventilation should be predictable.

Air moves into and out of a building as a result of changes in pressure distribution, since it moves from areas of high pressure to areas of low pressure. Changes in pressure may be brought about by the wind (see Figure 8.5), a heat source which changes the buoyancy of the air or pressure-modifying equipment like fans. Natural ventilation uses the pressure changes brought about by the first two effects and forced ventilation systems use fans to dominate all natural effects.

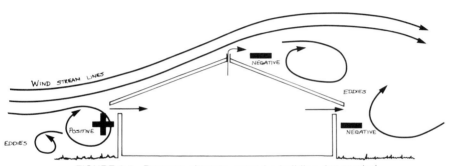

FIGURE 8.5   Pressure changes around a building due to wind.

Controlled ventilation is used to maintain aerial conditions within the piggery at specified levels. With some criteria like temperature and humidity, the conditions can be quantitatively described and automatically controlled by preset electronic devices. Other complex criteria like odours can only be described subjectively, and controls are either manually adjusted to cope with unusual circumstances or are preset on the basis of experience with some other measurable correlate like temperature or fan speed setting. Except under extreme conditions, controlling the ventilation system on the basis of temperature has proved adequate. Temperature thresholds (upper and lower acceptable levels) are set in relation to the zone of thermoneutrality of the pigs housed. The lower temperature level is usually about 2°C above the predicted LCT and the upper temperature level, if possible, is held at some 5°C or more below the UCT (dry). The effects of changes in temperature near the UCT are difficult to predict but, as the temperature in the piggery rises towards the UCT, food intake may decline and pigs may tend to lie in the wetter, cooler area of the pen. Maximum ventilation rates are generally chosen to maintain air temperatures within the building in the region of 2 to 3°C above external temperatures. Ventilation systems are best described by how well they can maintain ambient conditions within the temperature band described. Two important factors need to be considered in the design or choice of a ventilation system:

1.  How much air needs to be moved through the building?
2.  What pattern of air distribution will occur within the building and in particular near the pigs?

There is no unique solution to the question of how much air must be moved. Each case must be judged on the basis of other data pertinent to the problem such as:

● Weight and stocking density of pigs in the building
● Insulation quality of building and building heat loss per pig
● Temperature band (between lower and upper acceptable levels) selected for internal control and the probability and consequences of deviations from that setting
● Management's response to other aerial conditions such as high humidity, odours, dust or gases, assessed subjectively as individual or combined effects.

For many years, the practice in the United Kingdom was to choose a minimum ventilation rate based on 0.375 m³/hour/kg liveweight, and while this produced acceptable quality standards within the building it was an excessive rate in very cold conditions in relation to the growth, feed efficiency and health of the pig. More recently, with better insulated buildings and better control of ventilation, a minimum ventilation rate of 0.2 m³/hour/kg liveweight has proved acceptable in most conditions. In summer conditions in the United Kingdom, a ventilation rate 5 to 10 times greater than the minimum winter ventilation rate may be required, viz. about 1.875 m³/hour/kg liveweight. Controlling the ventilation rate over the full summer and winter range may be achieved in several ways. For fan ventilated systems, the following approaches have been used:

1.  Proportional speed control of all fans over the full range
2.  Proportional speed control of fans over half the range with a selection of fans being switched off completely
3.  Step control of fan speed with some preselected fans being switched on and off as necessary to obtain the full range of ventilation rates required.

With controlled natural ventilation systems, the following approaches have been used:

1.  Independent opening or closing of inlets and/or outlets
2.  Proportional controlling, i.e. small step control of inlet vents (ACNV) or automatically controlled natural ventilation
3.  Proportional controlling of inlet and outlet vents.

Where past experience cannot help a producer to arrive at a decision on the desired quantity of ventilation or its control, then advice should be obtained from specialists who can make the necessary calculations.

The configuration of a ventilation system, i.e. the position of air inlets and outlets and the direction of the air flow, together with the amount and velocity of the air

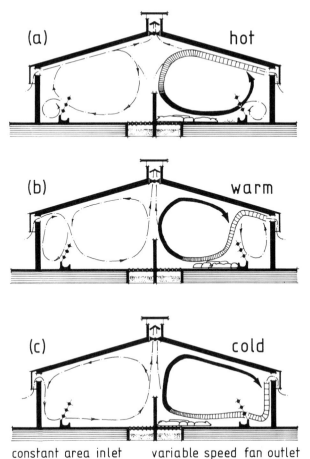

constant area inlet    variable speed fan outlet

FIGURE 8.6    Changes in air flow pattern with change in temperature and ventilation rate (note changes in pig lying position in an attempt to achieve greater comfort).

moved, will generate a particular air flow pattern in a building. In some systems, as the amount of air moving through the system changes in response to temperature conditions, the air flow pattern will also change (Figure 8.6). In other systems, the air flow patterns are unknown and unpredictable and in only a limited number of systems is the air flow pattern predictable and constant for both winter and summer ventilation. The significance of a changing air flow pattern lies in the conditions it creates at pig level. If the conditions at pig level remain within acceptable levels for the comfort of the pig, then a changing air flow pattern elsewhere will not be important. On the other hand, changing air movement at pig level can reduce pig performance by exposing them to greater cooling conditions in cold weather or it can alter their behaviour by encouraging them to lie where they usually defecate and vice versa.

The high-speed jet system developed at the National Institute of Agricultural

Engineering (NIAE) in Britain and the same principles incorporated in several proprietary systems aim to produce consistent and predictable air flow patterns at all ventilation rates. To do so, they usually incorporate the following principles:

1.  Fans operate at full speed only, and when switched off, they are protected by back-draught shutters (see Figure 8.7)
    OR
    Fans operate over a limited range of speeds, e.g. full to 60 per cent, and recirculate a mixture of internal and external air.
2.  Air velocity at inlets is maintained at approximately 5 m/s
3.  Inlets are evenly distributed along the length of a building, and air flow patterns are assumed to occur across the building only.

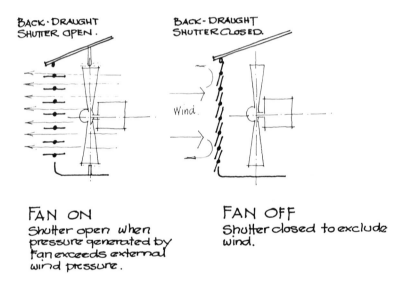

FIGURE 8.7   Operation of a back-draught shutter.

Natural ventilation systems have been operated in pig buildings for many decades and some systems have had simple manual control of air inlets and/or outlets. More recently, automatic control of vents in a system of natural ventilation has been developed (see Figure 8.8). The system, now referred to as ACNV (automatically controlled natural ventilation), usually consists of a controller, a differential thermostat, a drive unit and a system of movable covers at inlets and/or outlets.

The controller is regulated to measure house temperature at preset intervals. If the temperature deviates from preset limits, the drive units are actuated to run for a short prescribed time to open or close the ventilation covers at the openings. The cycle time and the run time of the drive units are chosen with regard to how quickly the system should respond to changing temperatures and how much variation in temperature is acceptable.

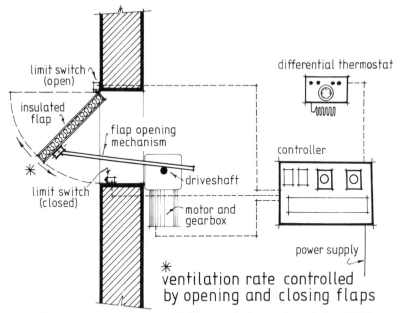

FIGURE 8.8 Schematic layout of automatically controlled natural ventilation (ACNV) system.

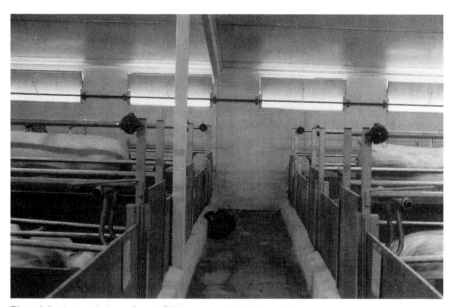

Plate 8.3 Internal view of an ACNV system of air inlets. The motor, gear box and associated driveshaft controlling the hinged flap are seen towards the top of the picture.

The drive system may be operated through geared motors and lay shafts or pulleys or through linear actuators. Covers at the ventilation openings may be top or bottom hinged to open out or in, or they may be pivoted around their centre line (see Plate 8.3). Covers may also be moved vertically on slides. Limit switches are used to disengage the drive units when the ventilation covers are either fully open or closed.

A balanced system operating movable covers at inlets and outlets has been operated in Denmark.

The system should be designed by a specialist and installed by a reputable manufacturer.

## Heating and Cooling

When a well-insulated building with a controlled ventilation system cannot maintain the prescribed thermal conditions in either hot or cold weather, then additional means of environmental modification need to be considered. The installation of a heating or cooling system, however, needs to be justified in economic terms and the following questions need to be considered:

1. Under what climatic conditions can the building not cope?
2. How often do these conditions occur?
3. What are the economic consequences of not being able to cope?
4. What are the costs of coping with all or only part of the conditions?

Any investment in further environmental control must be recovered within a reasonable period of time from the savings resulting from the investment, or alternatively the penalty for doing nothing must be less than the cost of doing something.

Before looking at further environmental control, it is worth reviewing the consequences of allowing the temperature in the building to deviate for significant periods from the prescribed thermal zone.

If the temperature falls below the LCT, then

- Pigs on controlled feed intakes will use energy to maintain heat production and so will grow more slowly, thereby occupying buildings for longer.
  OR
- Pigs fed ad lib. will consume more feed to produce the same growth.

If the temperature rises to and begins to exceed the UCT, then

- Pigs will consume less feed and grow more slowly, thereby occupying the building for longer.
- Pigs may attempt to lose more body heat by wallowing in faeces and urine in the dunging area. The resting area may also be used for dunging as discriminatory excretory behaviour gives way to behavioural change resulting from stress associated with excessive house temperature.

All four consequences will cost the producer money, either in reduced animal performance or in increased labour, but will these costs outweigh the costs of prevention through alteration of the climate? There are many factors which will influence the answer to this question, the most important of which will be the cost

Plate 8.4   A useful kit to check aspects of the climatic environment in a pig building.
(Courtesy of Centre for Rural Building, Bucksburn, Aberdeen)

of feed, the cost of fuel (for heating and ventilation) and the cost of investing in and maintaining additional equipment.

For example, in the United States in 1979, with feed costing $140 per ton and fuel (propane) at $0.55 per US gallon, but neglecting investment costs, it was concluded that it was less expensive to heat a building for young pigs than to allow the internal air temperature to decline to sub-optimal levels and to pay for increased feed costs. On the other hand, it was estimated in the United Kingdom that, when feed costs £175 per tonne and fuel £0.03 per kWh, then, heating a building for growing and finishing pigs cannot be justified since it would be more economical to provide extra feed to keep the pigs warm. These latter figures included £0.46 to £0.56 per pig per annum for investment costs. It is clear that as the relative prices of feed and fuel keep changing, the decision to invest in environmental modification needs to be reviewed continually.

HEATING

To make any decisions on the design and cost of a heating system, two essential factors must be estimated.

- Peak heating load
- Average annual heat production.

The estimate of peak heating load will be needed to prescribe the size and capital outlay on heating plant, and the average annual heat production will be used to calculate operational costs.

Several factors affect the calculation of supplementary heating requirements, some of which have already been discussed. The size of the pig, the stocking density and the feed (energy) intake will decide the production of metabolic heat; the quality of the building (insulation) and the ventilation rate will decide the heat lost from the building. The difference between the heat produced and that lost from the building will determine the temperature differential which can be maintained between inside and outside. The LCT of the pigs will define the lowest acceptable temperature within the building and this, minus the temperature differential which can be maintained between inside and outside, will give the lowest external temperature against which internal temperatures can be maintained. This external temperature is unique for any building and operational system and is referred to as t sup °C or, the temperature below which supplementary heating will be required to maintain prescribed internal conditions.

**TABLE 8.5  Desirable temperature; sensible heat production, heat loss and t sup for average weaner and finishing houses**

| Accommodation | Average liveweight (kg) | Desirable min. temp. °C | Sensible heat production (W/pig) | Total building heat loss W/°C/pig | t sup °C |
|---|---|---|---|---|---|
| Weaner | 23 | 25 | 55 | 3.69 | 10 |
| Finisher | 64 | 15 | 100 | 9.78 | 5 |

Data for both a weaner and a finishing house of average quality have been calculated and are shown in Table 8.5. In any particular location, the concept of degree days can be used to calculate the total average annual heat requirement. The base temperature for the calculation is taken as t sup °C. The degree day total below any base temperature is determined by adding the products of the temperature deficit below the base and the time over which it took place. A deficit of 10°C lasting 2 days is equivalent to a deficit of 4°C lasting 5 days. Both yield 20 degree days. At Aberdeen, Scotland, for example, in an average year there are about 1200 degree days at a base temperature of 10°C and 300 degree days at a base temperature of 5°C.

The average annual heat consumption (AAHC) in kWh per animal unit (weaner, dry sow, etc.) can be calculated from the following expression:

$$AAHC = \frac{24 \text{ (h/day)} \times \text{total building heat loss °C/pig} \times \text{degree days}}{1000 \text{ (W per kW)}}$$

The data for the two buildings shown in Table 8.5 are given in Table 8.6.

For a weaner or finishing house containing 500 pigs each, the AAHC would be respectively 53,000 kWh/pa and 36,000 kWh/pa, and at a cost of £0.03 per kWh, this would amount to £1590 and £1080 pa respectively.

In order to decide the size of heating plant to be operated, the peak load must be calculated. To do this some external design temperature for the particular location must be chosen. In the United Kingdom, for example, it has been suggested

**TABLE 8.6  Average annual heat consumption for average weaner and finishing house at Aberdeen, Scotland**

| Accommodation | Average liveweight (kg) | Desirable min. temp. °C | t sup °C | Degree days | Average annual heat consumption (kWh per animal unit) |
|---|---|---|---|---|---|
| Weaner | 23 | 25 | 10 | 1200 | 106 |
| Finisher | 64 | 15 | 5 | 300 | 72 |

that the external design temperature should be selected on a probability basis. Table 8.7 shows the design temperatures for several locations in the United Kingdom at different probabilities.

Where, for example, it is very important that a prescribed minimum internal temperature should be maintained (in a weaner house for example), then an external design temperature with a low probability of occurrence should be chosen to calculate the peak load capacity of the heating system. For the weaner and finisher houses considered in Tables 8.5 and 8.6 and using a design temperature at Aberdeen of $-3.3°C$ ($t_1$ only likely to occur for 1 per cent of the time) then the peak heating load of 40 kW and 25 kW respectively for 500 pig places would be expected to cope for 99 per cent of the time.

**TABLE 8.7  Design temperatures\* for several locations in the United Kingdom**

| Location | $t_1$ °C | $t_5$ °C | $t_{10}$ °C | $t_{90}$ °C | $t_{95}$ °C | $t_{99}$ °C[+] |
|---|---|---|---|---|---|---|
| Aberdeen | − 3.3 | 0.0 | 1.4 | 14.6 | 16.5 | 20.4 |
| Edinburgh | − 3.0 | 0.1 | 1.8 | 15.4 | 17.1 | 20.8 |
| Prestwick | − 3.0 | 0.2 | 2.1 | 15.2 | 16.8 | 20.8 |
| Carlisle | − 3.4 | 0.2 | 1.9 | 15.8 | 17.7 | 21.9 |
| Belfast | − 1.9 | 0.9 | 2.4 | 15.5 | 17.2 | 21.3 |
| Manchester | − 2.0 | 0.8 | 2.5 | 16.7 | 18.8 | 23.4 |
| Coltishall | − 1.8 | 0.8 | 2.4 | 17.0 | 19.1 | 23.0 |
| Plymouth | − 0.3 | 2.8 | 4.6 | 16.6 | 18.1 | 21.6 |

\*Temperatures are not adjusted for altitude
[+]Temperatures were below $t_n$ for n% of the time
(From: Bruce, 1983)

*Extra feed instead of heat*

Whether it is more economical to feed pigs more or to maintain house temperatures by heating is not only difficult to determine, but is always open to re-evaluation. On the assumption that a pig will consume about 0.4 g of extra feed/kg liveweight each day for every 1°C drop below its lower critical temperature, it has been calculated that, with feed costing £175 per tonne and fuel at £0.06 per kWh, then heating is not justified in the two cases previously used in Tables 8.5 and 8.6. Table 8.8 summarises this data.

**TABLE 8.8  Cost comparison of food or heat (per pig)**

| Accommodation | Weight (kg) | Extra feed cost per pig (£/annum) | Installation cost of heating (£/annum) | Fuel cost (£/annum) | Total heat cost (£/annum) |
|---|---|---|---|---|---|
| Weaner | 13.6 to 36 | 2.08 | 0.46 | 3.18 | 3.64 |
| Finisher | 36 to 91 | 1.33 | 0.56 | 2.16 | 2.72 |

The above assumptions, however, have been based on the notion that it is possible to give the correct amount of extra feed to each pig to compensate for cold stress. To achieve this, the amount of feed would need to be varied from time to time and also according to the weight of the pig. This is not normally possible in practical situations. Feeding pigs ad lib. might result in over-compensation when subjected to cold and this could lead to inefficient feed usage and poor carcass quality in heavier pigs. It would also be wrong to ignore the possible beneficial effects of maintaining house temperature on pig health and behaviour, although these factors are not easily measured.

*Heating systems*
In considering whether extra heating is justified in a pig building, several means of supplying energy may be considered. Typical heating systems may be fuelled by electricity, gas (natural or propane), oil or by solid fuels like coal, wood or straw. These systems vary little from their counterparts in industry and commerce. The energy generated at the boiler or primary source may be used directly as with electric or gas radiant heaters or indirectly through heated air in ducts or hot water in pipes in the floor or through radiators. Alternative energy sources such as solar, wind or hydro power can also be used to augment or replace the non-renewable sources of energy. Solar energy may be used directly but buildings must be specially designed as efficient passive collectors of solar energy.

In addition to heating systems, heat recovery devices may also be considered although the economics of such systems are still under consideration. Surface heat exchangers of various types have been used to collect heat from the outgoing ventilation systems of piggeries. Rockbed heat exchangers have been used in association with solar heating systems; other possible heat exchange devices which could prove useful on pig units but still await evaluation are heat recovery wheels, heat pipes and heat pumps.

COOLING
Cooling systems in piggeries may be classified by the means of heat exchange, i.e. radiation, convection, conduction or evaporation or whether they cool the pig directly or indirectly via the ambient air in the building.

Cooling the pig by conduction or radiation to a cold surface, either floor or wall panel units, is expensive, and the condensation which often occurs on the devices may prove disadvantageous to the maintenance of equipment although it may be useful as a further evaporative cooler to the pigs. Nevertheless, the pig loses a large part of its heat by radiation and such systems can prove useful in winter if they can be reversed to operate as heaters.

Cooling the pig by convection is possible if the ventilation system can be designed to direct cool air over the body of the pig. Some cooling can be achieved by air movement alone, and this has been incorporated into buildings using air mixing fans of large diameter revolving at slow speed.

*Evaporative cooling*
Evaporative cooling is perhaps the most common method now adopted in piggeries, and it has been used in three different ways for the cooling of pigs as follows:

- Evaporative air coolers
- Sprinklers
- Wallows.

Evaporative cooling operates by converting a liquid into a vapour by withdrawing the required heat for vaporisation from the surrounding medium (for example, the air or a pig). By injecting a fine spray of water into a warm stream of air, heat can be drawn from the air, or if the water is applied to the body of the pig, the heat may be drawn directly from the pig.

The simplest evaporative air coolers consist of large areas of wetted material through which the hot air is drawn (see Figure 8.9). In more refined equipment, the evaporative air cooler includes a heat exchanger through which the evaporative side cools a supply of unwetted air. This then enters the building as cool, dry air.

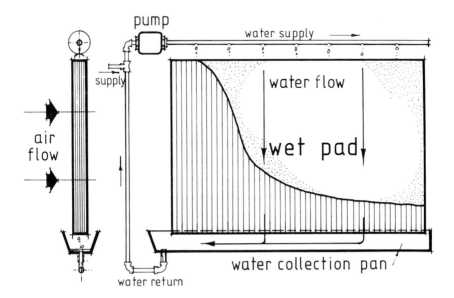

FIGURE 8.9   Simplified example of an evaporative cooler.

The quality and condition of the wet pads through which the air is drawn have a significant effect on the efficiency of the cooling process. Many materials are difficult to keep clean and free from dirt and dust, and all materials require regular maintenance. In hot, humid environments, the evaporative cooler is less effective than in hot, dry climates. In Canada, for example, the use of evaporative air coolers resulted in no beneficial effects on the growth and feed conversion efficiency of 60 kg pigs, but pigs sprinkled directly with water showed improved daily weight gain and feed conversion efficiency.

The benefits of direct sprinkling have been confirmed in the United States and Taiwan. Some of these studies have shown that at air temperatures greater than 21 to 25°C, growing–finishing pigs with access to sprinklers will maintain feed intakes and so gain weight faster than those pigs with no access to cooling. Feed conversion efficiency may also be improved. Although there have been some differences in the equipment used in the various experiments, all work confirms that only small volumes of water are required and that the intention is to subject the pigs to intermittent fine spraying at frequent intervals when the air temperature rises above pre-selected levels.

Sprinklers operating at a discharge rate of 150 to 200 ml/min for about 2 mintues every 45 to 60 minutes have proved satisfactory. One spray nozzle for 8 growing pigs (20 to 50 kg) or 5 finishing pigs (50 to 100 kg) appears to be sufficient with pre-selected operating temperatures of 25°C and 21°C for growing and finishing pigs respectively (see Figure 8.10).

The natural means of cooling adopted by the pig is to wallow in mud or any other suitable wet substrate. Where pigs are housed in yards and paddocks in hot climates, artificial wallows with and without the addition of shades have been tried. Unfortunately, although wallows have proved beneficial to the pigs, they require to be emptied and cleaned frequently to avoid heavy contamination. Water sprays under shades are more hygienic than wallows and appear to be preferred by the pigs.

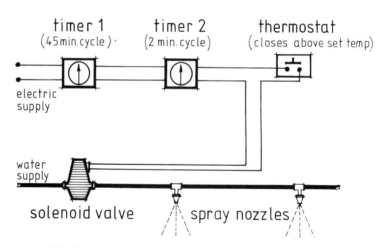

FIGURE 8.10   Schematic layout of a sprinkler cooling system.

## THE MODIFICATION OF BEHAVIOUR

Buildings and enclosures modify the behaviour of pigs by:

- modifying climate and therefore the pigs' response to climatic change
- constraining space and defining places within that space so attempting to confine specific behaviours like feeding and drinking to particular locations
- limiting or eliminating some behaviours like rooting, by the choice of materials used in construction, for example, the use of concrete instead of earth for floors.

The amount of space provided in a building is important. It has a significant effect on capital and operating costs, it can modify the behaviour of pigs in such a way as to affect the growth rate and feed conversion efficiency and it can influence the efficiency with which personnel carry out their tasks. In the United Kingdom, with houses for growing−finishing pigs costing from £140 to £200 per m$^2$ of floor area to build, producers are continually seeking ways of improving the efficiency of space usage. This can be achieved in several ways as follows:

- Increase stocking density or decrease space per pig
- Reduce working space or any other space not occupied by pigs
- Increase throughput of pigs.

To carry such intentions too far can result in several disadvantages, the costs of which will outweigh any savings which may have resulted from providing less space. Producers are continually seeking this illusive, optimum level, and so a closer look at the provision of space and its effects on behaviour, performance and welfare is needed.

### The Spatial Environment

Of the total three dimensional space in a piggery, we are primarily concerned with that volume of space occupied through time by the pigs and the people tending them. For people this is a layer of space approximately 2 metres deep at ground level and for growing−finishing pigs a layer say up to 1 metre deep. In most piggeries this space occupies between 35 and 65 per cent of the total volume. With tiered cages of pigs or double deck systems, the total usable volume of space may be as high as 80 per cent. If we regard space, however, as two-dimensional, looking at the plan of a building for example, then we can see that within the boundaries of the external walls, space may be used for the following purposes:

1. Pigs and their behaviours
2. People and their behaviours
3. Walls and fixed equipment
4. Movable equipment.

Whilst clearly the first two categories are the most important, the latter categories cannot be totally disregarded. For example, although 100 mm concrete block pen walls are robust and relatively cheap, they can occupy 8 times the space of preformed panel walls. In a typical piggery for 250 finishing pigs, the concrete block pen walls can occupy 11 m$^2$ of floor space (about 5 per cent of the total).

In addition, for the same stocking density, the larger the pen, the less space in the building will be taken up by pen walls. Fixed feeders also occupy varying amounts of space. Trough feeding for restricted-fed growing—finishing pigs, for example, requires about 0.075 m$^2$ per pig or about two or three times the amount of space occupied by ad lib. feed boxes. Floor feeding, with feed being delivered by pipeline and dropped from above the pen, requires no feeder space in theory.

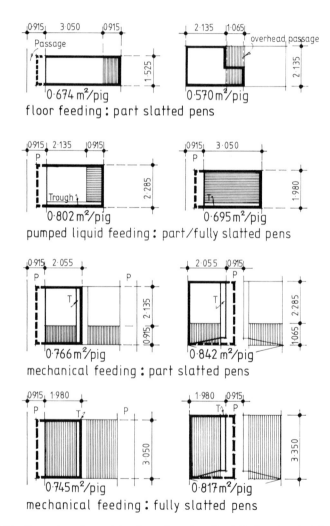

FIGURE 8.11  Examples of a variety of pen layouts with slatted and part slatted floors; also trough and floor feeding (areas shown are total building area per pig).

However, concentrating on the first two categories, we can say that nearly all piggeries consist of people-oriented and pig-oriented spaces. Although the use of these spaces is dominated by either people or pigs, neither space is exclusive. For example, feeding passages are clearly people-oriented spaces, but they may be used at times for moving pigs. Pens are pig-oriented spaces, but stockmen may have to enter them at times for various tasks. If the producer wishes to make the maximum use of his building without detracting from its operational efficiency, then, when fully occupied, pig-oriented space should form as high a percentage of total space as possible. For example, in the various layouts shown in Figure 8.11, pig-oriented space varies from less than 80 per cent to greater than 90 per cent of total space. Again, for the same stocking density, larger pens give, in many cases, better space utilisation figures.

This space, whether pig or people oriented, can be subdivided into several categories as follows:

1. Body space                  the space occupied by the volume of the occupant's body; whilst this does not vary with activity, in terms of area, a person or pig lying on the floor occupies more space than one standing.
2. Dynamic or ergonomic        the total space used by the body in performing
   space                       basic changes in posture without changes in position, for example, standing up or lying down.
3. Behavioural space           the total space used by the body to perform all behaviours including changes in position.
4. Social space                the space influenced or determined by the presence of other pigs or people.
5. System space                the space determined not by the pig or person, but by the system of management, e.g. pigs are given more space in straw-based pens than in slatted pens not because they need it but because straw would be used up too quickly if stocking density was too high.
6. Residual space              space which cannot be used effectively for a primary purpose, for example, space close to walls in passages cannot be used for walking.

For maximum efficiency, residual space should be reduced or designed in such a way that it can be used for secondary purposes. Where animals are housed individually, the need for social space can be perhaps eliminated in theory, but if adjacent animals can be seen, smelt or even touched, does the information so communicated still create a need for social space? This question remains unanswered at present.

Where animals have been housed individually in stalls, for example, space has been saved at the expense of behaviours, particularly those associated with changes of position. In some extreme situations, even dynamic space has been intruded upon with the consequent modification of behaviour and the possible development of physical trauma. Pigs provided with insufficient space to stand up or lie down in the appropriate manner often adapt their behaviours but may damage feet or legs in the process.

Body space, associated with particular postures, is clearly the minimum space which can be provided at that time, and it therefore forms the basis for determining minimum space requirements.

PIG-ORIENTED SPACE IN PENS FOR GROUPS OF PIGS

Recent work has shown that the space occupied by pigs can be estimated from their bodyweight and their posture at any moment. In this case there is no difference between the two-dimensional space (plan) occupied by a pig lying supported on all four legs (sternum) and a pig standing (see Figure 8.12). In either case this is the minimum superficial space possible and is that adopted by resting pigs in a very

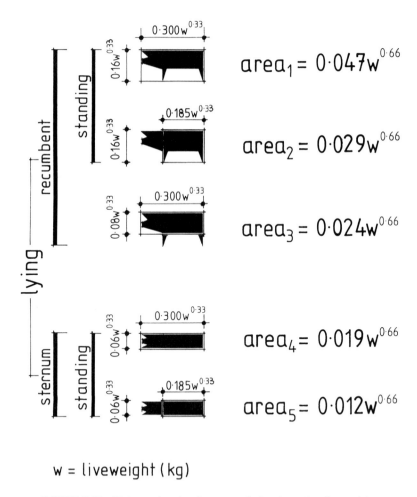

$$area_1 = 0.047w^{0.66}$$

$$area_2 = 0.029w^{0.66}$$

$$area_3 = 0.024w^{0.66}$$

$$area_4 = 0.019w^{0.66}$$

$$area_5 = 0.012w^{0.66}$$

w = liveweight (kg)

FIGURE 8.12   Pigtographs showing area of pig when standing or lying.

cold environment and by pigs standing at the feeder. When pigs are resting in a warmer environment, they lie on their sides in a recumbent posture but still in contact with each other. In a hot environment, pigs lie fully recumbent and away from each other to maximise environmental cooling and body heat loss. The superficial space occupied by a pig in all three postures is shown in columns (1), (2) and (3) of Table 8.9. The space occupied by groups of pigs in identical postures is obtained by multiplying the area required per pig by the number of pigs in the group.

**TABLE 8.9  Body space for Large White × Landrace pigs of 10 to 100 kg liveweight as determined from different body postures**

| Pig lw (kg) | (1) Area per pig for lying sternum or standing (m²) | (2) Area per pig for lying recumbent but closely packed (m²) | (3) Area per pig for lying recumbent but with no contact (m²) | (4) Area per pig: average of columns (1) & (2) (m²) | (5) Area per pig from Code of Recommendations for Welfare of Pigs, 1983 (m²) |
|---|---|---|---|---|---|
| 10 | 0.089 | 0.112 | 0.220 | 0.10 | |
| 20 | 0.141 | 0.179 | 0.350 | 0.16 | 0.15 |
| 30 | 0.186 | 0.234 | 0.460 | 0.21 | |
| 40 | 0.225 | 0.284 | 0.557 | 0.26 | 0.25 |
| 50 | 0.261 | 0.330 | 0.646 | 0.30 | |
| 60 | 0.295 | 0.373 | 0.730 | 0.33 | 0.35 |
| 70 | 0.327 | 0.414 | 0.810 | 0.37 | |
| 80 | 0.358 | 0.452 | 0.886 | 0.40 | 0.45 |
| 90 | 0.387 | 0.489 | 0.958 | 0.44 | |
| 100 | 0.416 | 0.525 | 1.028 | 0.47 | 0.50 |

In practice, all the pigs in a group rarely adopt the same posture. Some will lie in the recumbent position, some sternum and some in semi-recumbent positions often partly supported by the body of their adjacent companions. This would suggest that in an environmental temperature just above their LCT, pigs resting close together would occupy space somewhere between that estimated in column (1) and in column (2) of Table 8.9. This is shown in column (4) and can be compared with the guide figures for lying areas given in the UK Codes of Recommendations for the Welfare of Livestock − PIGS (1983). The estimates are in good agreement with some deviation at the heavier weights. It has been suggested that the heavier a pig becomes, the less likely it is to rest for long periods with its legs under its body. If this is so, then with more pigs of heavier weight lying in semi-recumbent or recumbent postures, the figures in column (4) should tend towards those in column (2) as bodyweight increases. This would bring them into closer agreement with welfare guidelines.

The figures given in columns (1), (2), (4) and (5), however, are only for resting postures and, in particular, those adopted in warm environments, i.e. just above the LCT of pigs in a group. For very hot environments, resting space areas should

increase towards those shown in column (3). But how much more space is needed
in a pen? In pens with part slatted floors or separate dunging areas, if pigs are not
to rest in the dunging area then total space requirement must exceed resting space.
As all pigs are unlikely to use the dunging area at the same time, then the dimen-
sions of the extra space required must be determined in some other way than on
an area per pig basis. The use of the part slatted area or dunging passage will be
determined by the shape of the area, the nature of the link with the resting area,
for example, whether it is via a pop-hole or with no barrier at all, and the location
of feeders and waterers. In practice, to allow for these variables, part slatted areas
usually have a minimum width of between 900 and 1200 mm.

Those pens screened on both sides with walls usually have the wider dunging
areas. The area of dunging space is then determined by pen shape and location of
dunging area (see Figure 8.11). In these layouts, the area per pig for dunging varies
between 0.11 m²/pig and 0.18 m²/pig. If an average value for dunging space in
part slatted pens of 0.14 m² per pig is added to the values in column (4) of Table
8.9, then the total area per pig for liveweights from 10 to 100 kg is shown in column (2) of Table 8.10.

**TABLE 8.10  Total area per pig in part and fully perforated floor pens**

| Liveweight (kg) | (1) Area per pig for lying (from col. (4), Table 8.9) (m²) | (2) Total area per pig in part slatted pens for 10 pigs/pen* (m²) | (3) Total area per pig in a fully slatted pen for 10 pigs/pen (m²) | (4) Total area per pig (suggested minimum level) (m²) |
|---|---|---|---|---|
| 10 | 0.10 | 0.24 | 0.16 | 0.14 |
| 20 | 0.16 | 0.30 | 0.25 | 0.22 |
| 30 | 0.21 | 0.35 | 0.33 | 0.29 |
| 40 | 0.26 | 0.40 | 0.40 | 0.35 |
| 50 | 0.30 | 0.44 | 0.47 | 0.41 |
| 60 | 0.33 | 0.47 | 0.53 | 0.46 |
| 70 | 0.37 | 0.51 | 0.59 | 0.51 |
| 80 | 0.40 | 0.54 | 0.64 | 0.56 |
| 90 | 0.44 | 0.58 | 0.69 | 0.61 |
| 100 | 0.47 | 0.61 | 0.74 | 0.65 |

*Includes allowance for dunging space of 0.14 m² per pig

These values for both part slatted and fully slatted pens are likely to prove excessive up to about 50 kg lw but perhaps hardly enough at liveweights of 80 kg or
more. This is clearly part of the problem which producers have experienced in
practice. In a part slatted system, if too much dunging space is provided, then the
house looks understocked; if too much resting space is provided, pigs will often
excrete on the solid lying area; if too little dunging area is provided, the same is
likely to happen. The problem is further compounded if temperatures in the pen
are outside the thermoneutral zone. If the temperatures are lower than the LCT,

Plate 8.5 Pens with movable fronts. The front is moved to avoid excessive lying space at the start of the growth period so as to minimise the risk of pigs fouling the lying area. As pigs grow, the lying area is extended gradually by moving the pen front towards the central pass. (Courtesy of A.M. Robertson)

pigs will tend to huddle into a smaller resting space, leaving part of the solid area on which they can excrete. If the temperatures are too high, then the pigs may end up resting in the dunging area. All this can happen, in addition to the pigs growing and changing body size over a period of weeks. Clearly the use of part slatted pens in particular needs good management and an understanding of pig behaviour, but even so there is no guarantee that pigs will not act in a contrary fashion to what is expected of them by stockmen. Two responses have been made to these difficulties. In the first case, the part slatted system is retained but the size of the resting area is adjusted by a movable pen front (see Plate 8.5). In the second, the part slatted system is rejected in favour of a fully perforated floor system if management is unconcerned where in the pen the pig excretes. It is often assumed, however, that because the system can cater for indiscriminate defecation, the pig will act in this way and that the total space in the pen can be reduced to resting space only. In practice, this does not appear to be true in all cases. In thermoneutral conditions, pigs, even on a fully perforated floor, will continue to defecate in discrete dunging areas. Where, however, space per pig is at a minimum, (i.e. equivalent to resting space only) defecation, because of the spatial constraints, may occur anywhere in the pen and this is only acceptable to management because the urine and excreta are pushed rapidly through the perforations and away from the immediate vicinity of the pigs. The pigs, therefore, remain reasonably clean.

Recent experimental work has suggested that even in fully perforated floor systems, the area per pig should not be less than the values shown in column (3) of Table 8.10. Comparing these values with those calculated for part slatted floors in column (2) suggests that with 10 pigs per pen, fully perforated floor systems require less area per pig up to 40 kg lw.

So far the calculation of pen space has been mainly theoretical but how do the areas suggested in Table 8.10 compare with those provided in experiments, and what are the likely effects on pig behaviour and performance of changing floor area per pig. The answers are inconclusive. There is no threshold value of floor area per pig below which, all of a sudden, the pig becomes behaviourally unstable and growth rate and feed conversion efficiency deteriorate rapidly. Indeed, where performance has deteriorated in experiments apparently comparing floor space allowances, there have usually been other factors which could just as easily or even more readily have adversely affected performance. Such confounding factors have included reduction of feeding space and opportunity for watering. Nevertheless, there is evidence to suggest that when area per pig is *severely* restricted, behaviour does change and feed intake, feed conversion and growth rate are adversely affected. From the somewhat conflicting evidence available the following suggestion is made to provide a rule-of-thumb on desirable floor space allowances. When the total area per pig in pens of up to 20 pigs with no bedding falls below the values shown in column (4) of Table 8.10, then management will have to be observant and skilful to avoid problems arising from abnormal behaviour. When the floor area per pig approaches the values shown in column (1) of Table 8.9, then feed intake and growth rate are likely to be depressed. Air temperatures near the pig's UCT and above will compound these adverse effects.

PRIORITIES FOR USAGE OF FLOOR SPACE
The total floor space within a pen is not behaviourally homogeneous but consists of several places where specific behaviours occur. Some of these are designed by and easily recognised by livestock personnel, for example, space primarily used for one of the following activities: resting, excreting, feeding and drinking. What is important, however, is how locations within a pen are perceived by the pig. There is rarely any doubt about feeding and drinking places as these are located in relation to the position of the feed and water supply. Resting and excreting places may be designed by management and recognisable by the placement of areas of solid flooring and of perforated floors, but they may not be used by the pig in the manner expected because the pig's perception of the spaces may be different. Finally, there may be some behaviours for which management has not planned and when pigs participate in these in a particular location, this upsets the original plans regarding the use of space. For example, if pigs have found a particular part of the pen ideal for grooming, and this coincides with part of the resting area, pigs may not rest here owing to the continual disturbance associated with some of their pen mates grooming. If planned resting space is reduced by this behaviour, then such a displacement may result in some pigs resting in an area planned for excretory behaviours.

Behavioural problems in pens may be the result of badly designed places for particular behaviours and activities rather than a shortage of total floor space. Very little is known about how the pig perceives locations within a 'barren' environment, and what little knowledge exists pertains to the pig's needs for the four activities of resting, excreting, feeding and drinking.

PLACES IN THE PEN

In modern housing there is a notable absence of locations for pigs to groom and play, and only such basic activities as resting, excreting, feeding and drinking are catered for. Some aspects of the requirements for these four activities will now be outlined.

### Resting place

As previously discussed, the pig is sensitive to changes in its thermal environment and this is likely to play a significant role in its choice of resting place. Both position and size of the resting place may be affected. Pigs will tend to avoid areas affected by cold air streams except in very hot conditions and, unless heat stressed, they will also avoid lying on wet, cold areas. They will generally avoid lying near a drinker where water spillage is inevitable and where there is often much activity. They will also avoid lying in the dunging area except under hot conditions. It has also been suggested that a further determinant of a resting place is security. Pigs will avoid lying in the centre of pens where activity may be greatest and will tend to gravitate to corners or alongside pen walls. Spaces near ad lib. feed hoppers may be avoided for the same reason. Where all pigs are fed at the same time, either once or twice per day, as distinct from 24 hour access to an ad lib. feeder, then there may be different influences on a resting place near the feeder. Lying beside the food trough when the feed arrives may be advantageous when securing access to the trough. So, where restricted feeding is practised, the food trough may be an attractant to resting. In addition, the food trough normally occupies as much as a quarter of the perimeter of the pen.

### Excretory place

Pigs tend to lie away from the excretory place for reasons of thermal comfort, but why do they excrete away from the resting area and where do they excrete in relation to other pen features? It has been suggested that the pig has a highly localised excretory habit and in general this is confirmed in practice. However, it seems that the larger the total area of space that pigs are given, the larger becomes the area they use for excretion. This suggests that they will excrete in any space that is not used for other purposes. However, within the total excretory area, individual pigs appear to have their own excretory place. Between pigs, these places differ only slightly in their position and degree of localisation and do not necessarily exclude use by other pigs. It has been suggested that the social rank of the individual pig affects the degree of localisation of its excretory habits, with the subordinate pig being more variable in its behaviour because it is not always able to gain access to its preferred excretory place. The choice of excretory site is thought to be determined by security. Though circumstantial, the idea that, in taking up a precarious stance, the pig should avoid others and place itself defensively next to a wall or corner seems plausible. As many as 80 per cent of all excretions have been noted as occurring when the pig stands with its back or side next to a wall, especially near a corner of the pen.

### Feeding and drinking places

The position and size of feeding and drinking places is determined by the location and size of the feeder and drinker. The feeding place, usually next to the passage-way, is often a fixed starting point for the design of the pen.

The size of the feeding place depends on whether limited (restricted) or ad lib. feeding is practised. In a limited feeding system, each pig must be given sufficient space at the feeder to allow all to eat at the same time. With ad lib. feed hoppers, the design of the feeding place is less straightforward. It is generally assumed that a number of pigs will share the same feeding position at different times during the 24 hour day. Problems arise, however, in trying to calculate the extent of time shar-ing in feeder use. For example, how long does a pig feed for each day and are there any limitations during the 24 hours when pigs will not choose to feed? More infor-mation on pig feeding behaviour is needed if these questions are to be satisfactorily answered. Practical experience suggests, however, that feeder space on ad lib. feeders with 24 hour access should be allocated on the basis of one place per four pigs.

How much space does a pig need at the feeder? Observations in practice indicate that pigs can feed successfully when packed shoulder to shoulder. The efficiency of feeding at such a space allowance has not yet been determined although with limit feeding there appear to be few problems. Table 8.11 gives the approximate shoulder width for British Large White × Landrace pigs from 10 to 100 kg liveweight and therefore an approximation for the calculation of feeder space per pig.

With restricted fed pigs in the United Kingdom, 10 to 12 inches (254 to 305 mm) of trough space per bacon pig of approximately 90 kg liveweight has been a com-mon recommendation and shows good agreement with the following data. Russian experiments suggest an optimum arrangement of 270 mm of trough space per 90 kg pig in pens containing 20 to 30 pigs at a floor space allocation of 0.75 m²/pig.

**TABLE 8.11  Shoulder width and feeder space for restricted and ad lib. feeders for pigs from 10 to 100 kg liveweight**

| Liveweight (kg) | Shoulder width of Large White × Landrace pigs (65 $W^{1/3}$)* (mm) | Feeder space/pig restricted feeding (mm)** | Feeder space/pig ad lib. at 1 space per 4 pigs (mm)** |
|---|---|---|---|
| 10 | 139 | 140 | 35 |
| 20 | 174 | 175 | 44 |
| 30 | 200 | 200 | 50 |
| 40 | 220 | 220 | 55 |
| 50 | 236 | 235 | 59 |
| 60 | 251 | 250 | 63 |
| 70 | 264 | 265 | 66 |
| 80 | 276 | 275 | 69 |
| 90 | 287 | 285 | 71 |
| 100 | 297 | 295 | 74 |

*   For a full explanation see Baxter (1984).
** Based on data in column 2.

Reducing the space at the feeder by 50 per cent reduced daily gain by about 12 per cent. Canadian recommendations for self-feeders (24 hour access) suggest 51 mm/pig up to 22 kg liveweight and 76 mm/pig up to 90 kg liveweight.

## FEEDING AND WATERING SYSTEMS

Before choosing any feeding equipment, the producer should first consider how this equipment will function within his overall management strategy on feeds and feeding. In formulating this strategy, decisions must be made on the following:

1. The dietary ingredients to be used and the basis of their selection.
2. How the ingredients selected will be stored, processed and mixed into the final diets.
3. The provisions which are required to ensure that feed is not spoiled during storage (by such agents as moisture, microbes, insects, vermin and wind borne material) nor subject to transport losses between storage and pigs.
4. How will the results of previous decisions under 1, 2 and 3 above be measured and can this lead to corrective action if required?
5. In arriving at a choice of feeding equipment can maximum flexibility be retained for the system as a whole?

A decision to feed pigs 1 kg of a particular diet means that all of this 1 kg of that diet, and no other, must be put into the pig's digestive system and not just into a bag or store or a feeder!

### Processing and Handling of Feed Ingredients

The physical characteristics of all feed ingredients before and after mixing or processing will influence the choice of distribution system and the means of presentation to the pig. From a materials handling point of view, some ingredients differ less before and after processing than others. For example, the conversion of cereal grains to meals is less of a change than processing whole potatoes or other root crops into flakes, powders or mash. In making decisions on handling and processing of feed ingredients, particular attention should be paid to the following characteristics:

- Particle size and shape
- Density
- Change of state or condition with time
- Change of state or condition when mixed with other ingredients, especially with liquids such as water, skim milk, or grass juice
- The tendency for particles to conglomerate.

The flexibility of a feed handling system is a measure of the system's capability of handling changes in ingredients and mixes, both qualitative and quantitative, without the handling system having to be modified. For example, systems using belt conveyors can readily cope with a change from cereals to potatoes (whether whole or mashed), but the same flexibility can hardly be claimed for smallbore chain and flight conveyor systems. Flexibility may, however, cost more than can be justified by the degree and nature of the changes which can be anticipated to occur in the system.

### Feeding Equipment and Feeding

In a large part of the world most pig producers feed cereal based feed mixtures in either dry or wet form in controlled or uncontrolled amounts to pigs, depending on their stage of growth. Water is usually available ad lib. from a separate system except in some wet feed systems where an adequate amount of water is mixed with the feed. Dry feed may be presented to the pig as a meal or as pellets, which are available in different sizes. The handling of feed from storage to feed dispenser is now carried out in large units by mechanical or pneumatic conveyor, but in smaller units it may still be handled manually by barrow or at best by a mechanically assisted trolley.

Finally, the feed may be presented to the pig in a trough or a feed hopper or distributed on the floor. In the 'river feeding' system, the liquid feed is presented in a trough which also acts as a gravity channel along which the feed flows as part of a liquid feeding circuit (see Figure 8.13). In some systems, the feed is delivered to the point of presentation as a dry meal, water being added before or during the time the pigs are fed.

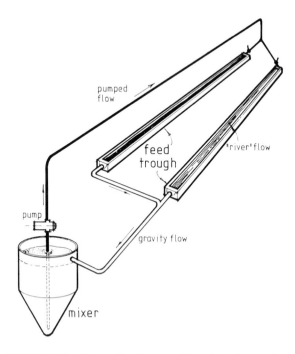

FIGURE 8.13   Schematic diagram of 'river' feeding system.

In limit feeding systems, a group of pigs may be fed automatically once or several times during the 24 hour day at preset times in preset amounts. In other systems, the presentation of the feed is carried out manually by the stockperson who also takes this opportunity to observe his pigs.

DRY AND WET FEED DISTRIBUTION SYSTEMS
Most feed distribution systems, wet or dry, consist of three parts:

1. Receiving hopper, container or mixer
2. Conveying system
3. Dispensing system

Most proprietary dry feeding systems can handle either meal or pellets up to 6 mm diameter. Pellets in excess of this size may limit the choice of suitable equipment.

Although some systems are designed to convey feed directly from the bulk storage container, many more use a smaller intermediate receiving hopper before conveying the feed to the dispensing points (see Figure 8.14). In dry feed systems,

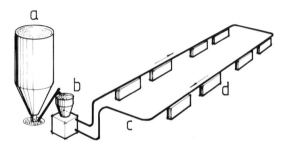

a ~ bulk storage      c ~ conveying system
b ~ receiving hopper  d ~ dispensers

FIGURE 8.14   Schematic diagram of dry feeding system.

these intermediate hoppers usually have a capacity of about 250 to 350 kg and they may be fitted with agitators to overcome problems of bridging. In liquid feed systems, the receiving hopper is also used as a mixer, operating as part of a batch or continuous process. Batch mixers are available in several sizes, the most common lying in the range of 1000 to 1500 litres capacity. In continuous flow systems, a smaller container occupying less space can be used but presoaking of the feed mix cannot be accomplished. Mixing of the contents of tanks can be achieved mechanically, hydraulically or pneumatically. Batch mixing takes from 5 to 15 minutes after meal and water in the correct quantities have been loaded automatically or manually into the mixer.

*Conveying systems*

With dry feed, meal or pellets, the conveying system may be mechanical or pneumatic. Most mechanical systems are of the chain and flight design, operating in galvanised steel box trunking or in plastic or steel tubular pipes. The chain may be of steel links or of stranded cable, and the flights, evenly distributed along the chain, are usually of steel or moulded plastic. Most conveyors operate at speeds of from 8 to 35 m per minute and the quantity of feed handled will depend on the type of feed, the size of the conveyor and the operating speed. At operating speeds of around 8 m per minute, a 40 mm diameter system will handle a typical dry cereal diet at a rate of about 150 to 200 kg per hour and a 75 mm diameter system will convey about 800 kg per hour. At an operating speed of 35 m per minute, 35 to 60 mm diameter ducting will handle between 400 and 2000 kg per hour. Although the larger systems have conveyor lengths up to 500 m long, the usual length of circuit is around 250 m. Most chain and flight conveyors have automatic tensioning devices to minimise chain drag and safety switches to prevent overflow of feed. An alternative to the chain and flight system is the auger tube. With a handling capacity of about 900 kg/h, this equipment consists of a 60 mm steel spring auger operating in a 70 mm heavy galvanised tube.

Pneumatic conveying systems usually operate at medium air pressure in plastic or galvanised spiral wound tubing in circuit lengths up to about 200 m. Using 38 mm diameter tubing, a 5.5 horsepower motor will convey light granular feed at rates of about 1.0 to 1.3 tonnes/hour. With more power and tubing of greater diameter, conveying rates of up to 3.5 tonnes/hour can be achieved.

In wet feeding systems, a mix of about 1:2.5 by weight of meal to water is usually pumped through 50 to 75 mm diameter steel or plastic pipes. Pump systems usually operate on a flow and return circuit with motors of 5 to 10 h.p. driving 50 mm or 75 mm self-priming centrifugal pumps. Compressed air systems usually operate a flow line only, with the pressure generated by a small motor operating an air compressor on a 50 mm diameter pipeline. In the simplest semi-automatic systems, each dispensing point has a manually operated valve controlled by the stockperson. Automatic control systems are also available where quantities are regulated by flow meters or electrically controlled, air-operated solenoid values. Systems can be programmed to feed pigs once or several times each day.

*Dispensers and feeders*

There are two main types of dispenser. The first deposits feed at a single point either into a feeder or directly to the pigs (see Figure 8.15) whilst the second deposits the feed in linear fashion (see Figure 8.16). Wet feed dispensers discharge at a point, and linear distribution occurs in the feed receptacle by gravity flow.

Dry feed dispensers indicate the quantity of feed they contain either on a volumetric or weight basis, the latter being more accurate if a wide range of dietary ingredients is used. Dispensers are available with capacities from 2 to 48 kg for a conventional dry cereal based diet: the smallest dispensers are used for individual feeding, and the most common capacities for group feeding of growing−finishing pigs are between 18 and 25 kg. The number of pigs per dispenser, their daily feed intake and the method of feed presentation will determine the size of the dispenser and the number of times it must discharge in 24 hours.

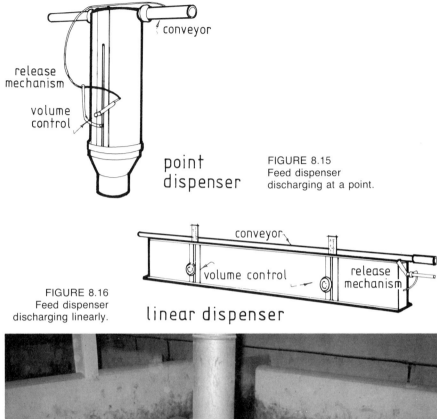

point
dispenser

FIGURE 8.15
Feed dispenser
discharging at a point.

FIGURE 8.16
Feed dispenser
discharging linearly.

linear dispenser

Plate 8.6   Floor feeding. The dry feed is transported via a pipeline and dispensed over a
cone in the middle of the feeding area. Pigs distribute themselves round the cone while
feeding. The cone helps to minimise trampling and scattering of the freshly delivered food
and achieves greater feeding space and more orderly feeding relative to delivery on to a
flat floor.

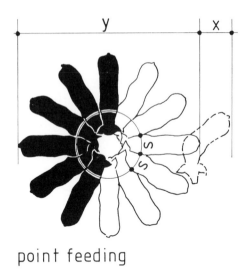

## point feeding

FIGURE 8.17   Theoretical distribution of pigs at point feeding depending on shoulder width (s), overall length of diametrically opposed pigs and the section of feeder in between (y) and additional space (x) for a pig leaving the feeder to take up a new position.

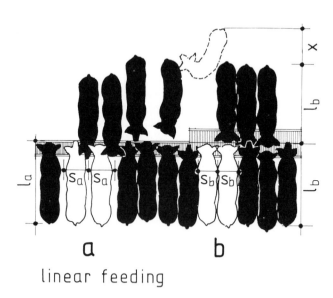

## linear feeding

FIGURE 8.18   Theoretical distribution of pigs at linear feeding dependent on shoulder width, on the feeding system (either Type A, single trough, or Type B, double trough), the length of the pig (l) and additional space (x) for a pig leaving the feeder to take up a new position.

Dispensers used in association with floor feeding where they drop feed from a height generate large quantities of dust unless the feed is dropped down an enclosed tube. To spread the feed sufficiently for all pigs to gain access, the feed is distributed by a cone at floor level placed directly beneath the tube (see Plate 8.6). Alternatively, the tube may be suspended and then moved by the pigs when feed is being dropped, so spreading the feed more widely.

The pattern of feed dispensed determines the distribution of the pigs at feeding and will often influence the shape of pen. Point feeding (Figure 8.17) requires a square shaped solid floor area on which to deposit feed, whilst linear feeding, i.e. in a trough, dictates that the pen be rectangular (Figure 8.18).

The amount of space required by pigs at the feeder has been discussed earlier, but what about the design of the various feed receptacles? Two types of feed receptacle are common, that used for limit feeding and that for continuous access ad lib. feeding. Apart from the size of the feeder, both types have a feed trough but in the latter case there is in addition a hopper to contain a supply of feed which discharges into the trough as the pigs consume the previous contents. The desirable capacity of the hopper is determined by the number of pigs supplied, their feed intake, the shelf-life of the feed before any deterioration occurs and the method of filling the hopper.

Ad lib. feeders may be made from wood, metal or concrete and they usually have an adjustable slide to control the discharge of feed into the trough. Edges of wood and concrete need to be protected from the pigs by metal to avoid erosion. Ordinary metal feeders deteriorate rapidly in pig units and have been replaced by feeders of stainless steel, heavily galvanised sheet steel or moulded plastic.

The traditional linear feed trough for restricted feeding is usually made of half-round glazed fireclay, and though it is robust and maintenance free, it is expensive and must be built on-site. Ordinary concrete troughs suffer the same on-site problems and do not last as well, especially when skim milk is fed because of the erosion caused by lactic acid. New prefabricated trough units made from polyester concrete are now available in several profiles and they appear to be more resistant to deterioration. Regardless of whether the trough stands on its own or is attached to a self-feeder, it must not only contain the amount of food deposited in it without spillage, but it must also contribute to efficient feeding and low wastage. Little work has been carried out on the most efficient design of trough shape but the following features would appear to be important:

1. The inside of the trough should be smooth and free from awkward angles into which feed can be deposited but not retrieved by the pig.
2. The trough should be large enough to contain all the feed deposited at one time. To reduce spillage, troughs should never be more than half full.
3. The front edge of the trough should have an internal lip to reduce spillage and the back of the trough should be high enough to prevent feed being thrown out.
4. Where self-feed hoppers discharge into the trough, the rate of discharge should be controllable and should not allow the trough to fill faster than the rate of consumption by the pigs.
5. The trough should have dividers to prevent pigs feeding along the length of the trough or lying in the trough.

Plate 8.7   A feed trough incorporating a hinged retaining board mounted above. After feeding, the retaining board is swung forward to prevent access to the trough by the pigs. The next feed can then be delivered to the trough immediately after the previous meal has been completed. This allows the new feed to be soaked if necessary and helps to minimise the time between feeding the different pens at the next meal, thus reducing excitement and stress for both the pigs and the stockman.

6.   The leading edge of the trough should be rounded to prevent injury to the pig and to facilitate access.

Where pigs are liquid fed from both sides of a communal trough, zigzag dividers may be used. Where traditional troughs have no dividers they are often provided with a swinging front which prevents entry of the pig except at feeding time (see Plate 8.7). Some self-feed hoppers have similar 'pig operated' lids over each feeding space to prevent contamination from excreta.

## Drinking Equipment

It is essential that all pigs should have access to an adequate and wholesome supply of fresh water. Growing pigs will consume between 2 and 6 kg water daily between 15 and 90 kg liveweight. At high environmental temperatures, voluntary water intake may increase by more than 100 per cent.

Care must be taken to ensure that drinking water is not contaminated at source, during storage, in its passage to the point of distribution or at the point of use.

Water storage tanks should be sited where there is no possibility of contamination from surface water or slurry and they should be covered to exclude airborne debris, birds' droppings, vermin or accidental contamination. They should be of sufficient capacity to meet the needs of short term disruption of supply and they should be inspected regularly. Contamination is most likely to occur at the point of use where pigs may pass infection to the dispenser or where excreta may foul the container.

Regular cleaning of water bowls and troughs is essential unless they are adequately protected with lids to prevent the ingress of excreta. Nipple drinkers, though less liable to contamination, should be checked regularly to ensure they are working. It is important to ensure that as little water as possible is wasted or discharged into the slurry system. Some drinkers are more prone to wastage than others. A comparison of nipple drinkers has shown that wastage rates can range from 50 to 200 per cent of the amount consumed. With types of nipple drinker which can only be operated by the pig when it is taken into its mouth, wastage is minimal. With inadequate maintenance, many nipple drinkers leak and the problem is compounded if the system is operated off a high pressure supply.

Some drinkers can only be operated from one position whilst others can be operated by the pig from several angles. This feature of the drinker will influence the position and amount of space needed around it (Figure 8.19). Pig drinkers fall into two categories, (1) bowls or troughs and (2) nipples or nozzles. In the former case, the pig drinks from a small container of water whilst in the latter the water is only available by operating the nozzle, etc. and no water is retained in the container.

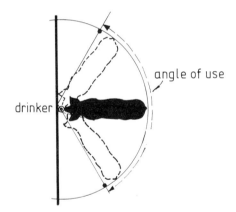

angle of use

drinker

FIGURE 8.19 Theoretical space use at the drinker showing possible limitation of drinking angle because of the type and position of the drinker.

TROUGHS AND BOWLS

Large exposed surfaces of water which can be readily fouled by the pigs or used as wallows in hot weather are rarely found in modern pig production units. The smaller receptacle in a bowl or cup shape is usually filled automatically by the operation of a pig operated plunger or by a water level control float. In all cases the water container must be so positioned as to avoid contamination or be provided with a lid to prevent it. In the former situation the level of the bowl must be above pig anus height or the bowl should be accessible only when the pig places its front feet on a raised platform at the drinker. Drinkers of this type placed outside must be well protected against frost using good insulation and/or small heaters.

Plate 8.8   A pig drinking from a bite drinker. As the name implies, the pig can obtain water only by biting the nipple. Relative to nipple drinkers which can be operated by the pig merely pushing the nipple, bite drinkers result in considerably lower wastage of water and a smaller volume of slurry.

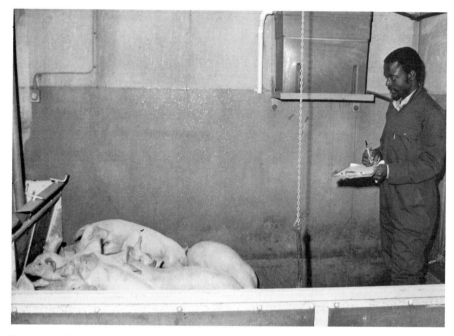

Plate 8.9   Where water pressure is high, provision of a header tank incorporating a float valve to supply nipple drinkers helps to reduce pressure at the nipple, prevents pigs being unduly wetted by spray when drinking and reduces water wastage.

NIPPLES AND NOZZLES

Nipples and nozzles are usually of two types. There are simple nipples whose operation requires only that a plunger should be pushed back or to the side, and then there are those which can only be operated when they are placed in the pig's mouth and the teeth are closed over the plunger to release the water (see Plate 8.8). The latter type are more expensive but usually result in less spillage.

With all nipple type drinkers, special attention should be paid to the water supply pressure, the fixing height and the location of the drinkers in the pen. Except where nipples are supplied for high pressure use, all nipple drinkers should be fed from a low pressure auxiliary water tank (see Plate 8.9).

Most nipple drinkers are fixed above the shoulder height of the pigs in order to prevent accidental operation and so as to direct the water into the upturned mouth of the pig. Where the same drinker is to be used by pigs of various sizes, then it should be mounted at the appropriate height for the largest pigs and raised platforms should be provided to cater for access of the smaller pigs.

Even the best nipple drinkers will leak when damaged or when the operating parts wear out. They should therefore be located where the spilled water can be readily observed and where it will do least damage. Siting the drinker in the dunging area may encourage pigs to urinate and defecate in this area.

When pigs only have access to one drinker of whatever type, it is important to rectify any malfunction as soon as it is discovered. When pigs are deprived of water for some time, salt poisoning occurs (see Chapter 11) and the signs of distress may not be seen in time, especially when routine inspection of the pigs is not carried out, e.g. over a weekend. No group of pigs should ever have less than two drinkers.

## Housing Systems and Layouts

There are many different housing systems for growing and finishing pigs and many reasons why this should be so. The simplest reason may be that each design will be an expression of the needs, perceived needs, ideas and perhaps idiosyncracies of the individual owner. The many differences in housing design are noticeable in the following features:

1. The methods of construction and materials used
2. The size, shape or structural form of the building
3. The feeding, watering, ventilation and waste handling systems
4. The internal layout, pen shapes and sizes
5. The management system

When one considers the number of variables in each of the above features and then the total number of systems which can be obtained from the combination of variables, then it comes as no surprise that so many different housing systems exist in practice.

Nevertheless, there are probably only a few major factors which have a significant influence on the development of specific combinations of features. Time, or geographical location and size of enterprise are important.

## Size of Enterprise

Producers with large numbers of pigs will usually have large buildings and these buildings will feature specific structural forms and shapes. Although large buildings can be very long and narrow (under 9 m in width), it is more common to find them with wider spans (up to 20 m). Such wide spans require ridged roofs, sometimes in multiple spans, whereas smaller buildings with spans less than 9 m often use monopitch roofs. Large, wide buildings will have multiple rows of pens and usually several passageways, and the layouts will need special consideration for animal handling, escape during fire, and ventilation. Large single span or multi-span roofs can provide special structural problems in areas of high wind or snow loads.

Where large businesses decide to build several buildings instead of one large structure, the location and climate may play a significant role in the orientation and spacing of the buildings.

## Geographical Location

Buildings in specific localities used to reflect the availability of local materials but now they are more likely to identify the existence of an individual manufacturer, supplier or even a keen adviser or consultant. However, buildings in different countries can still reflect the availability of materials and skills. Timber and framed structures are common in North America, bricks and blocks in the United Kingdom and Belgium and concrete in the Netherlands.

Where the climate in different localities is significantly different, buildings in these areas may differ not only in construction and insulation but also in the choice of ventilation or slurry handling systems. The building layout and its structural form will also be affected. In areas with long winters and large accumulations of snow, most activities are housed under one roof to minimise the inconvenience of regular passage between buildings in adverse conditions. Other climatic combinations also have their influence. Very cold climates result in well-insulated and control ventilated structures. However, if the low air temperatures are also combined with clear skies and good solar radiation, such buildings may also feature active or passive solar heating systems. In hot, humid regions on the other hand, buildings will provide overhead shelter against sun and heavy rain but will have the maximum amount of open wall area to allow cooling breezes to flow over the pigs. In such situations buildings will tend to be narrow span with their long axis facing the prevailing wind and will be well spaced from one another so as to maximise cooling.

Different geographical locations will also have different farming systems and this in turn may influence the choice of management system in the pig enterprise. The most common effect is that brought about by the utilisation of straw for bedding or the need to produce farmyard manure as a soil conditioner.

## Current Fashion

Buildings which were erected at approximately the same time, e.g. in the 1960s, will demonstrate the construction technology and production innovations of that time. In the United Kingdom, for example, pig buildings of the 1960s had brick or block walls and corrugated asbestos roofs and were insulated with about 50 mm of glasswool. In the 1970s the prefabricated framed building appeared and foamed plastic insulants became commonplace. Now, in the late 1980s, container type buildings with panel walls and roofs of bonded insulated panels are on the increase.

Systems, too, reflect changing ideas and responses to economic, managerial and even political changes. Part slatted floor and channels of stored manure are giving way to fully slatted floors, flush systems and storage lagoons. The current concern for animal welfare may influence further change in housing and penning systems. By promoting new management systems, new housing types to serve management will develop.

### Pen Shape and Size

Management clearly influences the layout of buildings and the shape and size of pens by making decisions on feed and waste handling systems, number of pigs in each pen and the duration of their stay in that pen.

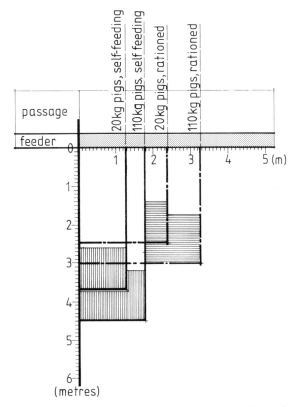

FIGURE 8.20   The effect of feeding system and pig size on the shape of part slatted pens (15 pigs/pen).

A decision to use straw bedding or to provide fully perforated floors will have a dramatic effect on the planning of materials handling facilities. Alternative systems such as restricted or ad lib. feeding and trough or floor feeding will influence decisions on pen size, shape and orientation with respect to passageways. For example, with a constant number of pigs in a pen (say 15), feeders located as close as possible to passageways for servicing, and part slatted floors, feeding method can influence pen shape to the extent shown in Figure 8.20. In both layouts for a specific weight of pig (either 20 or 110 kg), pigs have the same area of resting space. Each slatted excretory area has a minimum dimension of 1.20 m to ensure that a pig can position itself on the slats in any orientation, but yet the difference between the smallest and the largest area of slat for a given weight of pig is as much as $2\frac{1}{2}$ times. The area of slats provided is likely to have a significant effect on excretory behaviour or the cost of the slatted floor installation.

Several layouts for part or totally slatted floors have been presented in Figure 8.11. The varying layouts presented accommodate the same number and weight of pigs and yet the largest pen is 48 per cent greater than the smallest pen. This indicates that the shape or the design of the pen can have a considerable influence on space requirements per pig.

### Provision for the Stockman

The emphasis in this chapter has, with almost entire justification, been on providing for the needs of the pig. That is not to infer, of course, that the requirements of the stockman should be ignored. Wise planning to provide for the climatic, spatial, behavioural and nutritional needs of the pig provides a sound basis of a successful system. Adherence to the planning guidelines in the day to day management of the unit should help to contribute towards acceptable working conditions for the stockman in terms of temperature, regular air change, minimal risk of fouling of pig lying areas, maintenance of clean, healthy pigs and the minimal amount of onerous labour input in feeding and removing effluent. Additional provisions necessary for good working conditions are low dust and noise levels and ease of servicing and inspection of pigs to check wellbeing and to provide for special needs of individual animals. Thus, it is important that as well as providing for the needs of the pig, housing and all its components should allow for the development of good contact and relationship betwen the pigs and their attendant. Such a relationship is likely to enhance both the performance of the pig and the job satisfaction of the stockman.

### ADDITIONAL READING

Baxter S. (1984), *Intensive Pig Production: Environmental Management and Design*, Granada, London.

Brent G. (1986), *Housing the Pig*, Farming Press Books, Ipswich.

*Pork Industry Handbook*, USA Co-operative Extension Service, University of Illinois at Urbana-Champaign, USA.

Sybesma W. (Ed) (1981), *The Welfare of Pigs*, Martinus Nijhoff, The Hague.

*Chapter 9*

# Principles of Nutrition

## Feed in Relation to Total Costs

Up to 80 per cent of the costs of producing pigs for slaughter can be accounted for by the purchase of feed. The profitability of the whole enterprise may depend on whether the feed is good value for money and whether its formulation is suitable for the purpose. It is instantly apparent that nutrition is critical for the success of the enterprise, and yet it is often a subject upon which the producer is not well informed. It is, of course, perfectly feasible to be an excellent pig farmer and have absolutely no concept of the principles of nutrition. On the other hand, a farmer who has a feel for, and an understanding of, nutrition and its vocabulary is better placed to make judgements between different commercial options both in the choice of purchased diets and in the formulation of diets produced on the farm.

### Purchased Diets

A common and less demanding situation on a pig unit is the purchase of a series of proprietary feeds formulated by a professional nutritionist for a feed company. Usually the diets are satisfactory and the farmer is saved from much worry and anxiety about the quality of the constituents and the science of the nutrient balance. It is also useful for peace of mind to be able to purchase diets as and when the feed is needed, and have it arrive in either convenient loads for bulk storage or clearly identified bags. Many feedstuff companies have established excellent reputations for reliability and service. The larger companies often employ experts who will offer sound advice on production at either no charge or at minimal rates to the regular customer. For many producers, the extra costs associated with purchasing complete diets are completely offset by the security of being looked after by experienced professionals and by the implicit insurance that purchase of a branded feed offers, in terms of quality, reliability and backup service.

### On-farm Mixing

The other side of the economics of nutrition is that feed companies have high overheads and must extract from the farmer the price of keeping a large sales staff on the road, the considerable costs of advertising and the costs of transport of bulky materials to the mill and then after mixing out to the farm: none of these costs is incurred by the home mixer. This results in a diverse market place where farmers or small regional companies exploit local advantages either by mixing at least some of the diets on-farm or by the formation of small local cooperative mills. Economic judgements and comparisons between the options presented by this complex situation often require at least a basic understanding of the principles of nutrition and of its basic vocabulary.

The purpose of the rest of this chapter is to consider the underlying principles of nutrition. There are three components to this:

- Nutrients, what they are and what they do
- Nutrient requirements during growth
- Matching nutrients and requirements for growth in relation to genotype, sex and stage of development

## NUTRIENTS

Although it seems obvious to state that the tissues of the growing pig, such as bones, muscle, fat and skin, are all derived from the feed, it is one of the wonders of the natural world that materials as diverse as barley, soya bean and root crops such as mangolds and cassava can be transformed in this way. In fact, the diet, like the pig, is composed of basic building blocks and the processes of digestion and metabolism break down the complex structures of the plant to basic units and then reassemble some of them in the exact format of the pig's own tissues. This process, although extremely complex, is much simpler to understand if one thinks of the needs of the animal in terms of the basic building blocks. These are essentially the basic minerals such as calcium and phosphorous used in bone growth; the constituents of proteins, the so-called amino acids; a grouping of substances comprising fats and carbohydrates usually referred to as energy sources; and finally a group of rather complex molecules which the pig does not usually construct for itself called the vitamins. These simplified building blocks are usually referred to as nutrients, and establishing a reasonable balance between them and getting the quantities right is essentially the science of nutrition. The objective is to feed pigs so that they stay healthy and grow efficiently.

### Energy

The word 'energy' in the context of pig nutrition is loosely taken to refer to those parts of the diet represented by the cereals and added fat. Although this conveys an approximate idea of what is implied, it is a subject which is not well understood even by some professional nutritionists. There is much confusion over the units used and what all the different concepts mean. For this reason, some space is devoted to explaining the background to the nutritional concept of energy.

UNITS OF ENERGY
The history of nutrition has landed us with an awkward single word to describe a number of attributes of a feed. This word 'energy' is so ingrained in nutritional

language that we must go along with it, but the reader must be warned that in order to make it describe all the different aspects with which it is associated, it has to be qualified on almost every occasion in which it is used.

The most familiar concept of dietary energy is the 'calorie', which is usually cited without qualification in relation to human nutrition and found universally in media articles on dieting. Unfortunately, this familiar use is almost entirely misleading. Essentially, the units of energy used in nutrition refer to the heat released if a unit of food is completely burnt or combusted. The true calorie of science is the amount of heat required to raise the temperature of 1 gram of water from 14.5 to 15.5°C. This is a tiny amount of heat and historically a more useful unit was the kilocalorie, which was 1000 times greater than the true calorie. This value was usually designated either as a kcal or as a capital C. It is this latter use which has caused confusion since the calorie of the diet books is in almost every case the kcal. Even this is a relatively small unit and animal diets in the United States are often specified in terms of the Megacalorie (Mcal), which is 1000 times greater than the kcal.

To make matters worse, nutritional scientists in Europe have rendered the calorie almost obsolete by preferring the more fundamental unit of energy, the joule. One joule is defined as the amount of energy which is equivalent to one watt flowing for one second. Effectively there are 4.184 joules per calorie, 4.184 kilojoules per kilocalorie and 4.184 Megajoules per Megacalorie.

An example of how Megajoules or MJ relate to food is as follows. We shall consider one very simple and very pure nutrient although we could have taken many other examples such as starch or corn. One kilogram of soya bean oil contains a great amount of total energy amounting to about 39 MJ. This makes it a very energy dense material. If we were to burn it completely it would release 39 MJ of heat. Using the information given above on the definition of a joule, we can calculate that this is equivalent to the heat produced by a one kilowatt fire switched on for 10 hours and 50 minutes.

Now if the one kg of soya bean oil was fed to a pig over several days and was perfectly digested, then it could be used either to fuel the metabolism of the animal or to become part of the animal and be incorporated in some form into its tissues. If the whole amount was used for metabolism or, in other words, for maintaining the life processes of the animal, all the energy would eventually be lost from the animal as heat, equivalent in total to the heat produced by simply burning the oil. This process has been aptly called 'The Fire of Life' by Max Kleiber. In the end the animal itself burns the soya bean oil and yields 39 MJ of energy, again equivalent to the 10 hours and 50 minutes from the 1 kw fire, but of course spread over a longer time period. In fact, it would take a pig of about 60 kg liveweight about 4 days to dissipate this amount of energy. The heat would be lost in different ways, by convection (warming the air), conduction (warming the structures of the pen), radiation (invisible infra-red rays) or as the energy required to evaporate water, as occurs in breathing or in evaporating water off the skin.

However, if the animal was to use part of the soya bean oil to build its own tissues, then the energy would be effectively conserved. It will only be released as heat if the pig is fed a sub-maintenance amount of feed and starts to 'burn' its own tissues, or if the pig tissue is eaten and 'burnt' in the metabolism of another animal.

For example, if we ourselves eat meat then we become the furnace. If some part of the pig becomes meat meal then it may go round the animal cycle again. The energy stored in tissue can be released more directly by burning the tissue of the pig, either scientifically as in a calorimeter, which is a scientific instrument for measuring the heat released on combustion, or more dramatically as when a barbecued piece of meat catches alight.

A basic principle of physics is that energy cannot be created or destroyed and so, with any feedstuff given to an animal, all the energy which it contains at the start must emerge somewhere along the complex route of digestion and metabolism. The extent to which a feedstuff is useful to an animal depends to a large degree on how much energy it manages to extract from the food for its own purposes. Nutritionists attempt to describe the energy value of feeds by using rather specialised descriptive units all based on the fundamental one of the joule.

## UNITS OF ENERGY USED IN NUTRITION
### Gross energy (GE)

The gross energy of any feedstuff, as implied by the name, is the heat which would be released if unit weight of the feed was completely combusted. A typical value for a pig diet based on barley and soya bean would be about 15.5 MJ per kilogram of diet.

### Digestible energy (DE)

The gross energy of a feed is not usually all available to the animal for its use in metabolic processes. With the conventional constituents of pig diets, that is, cereals and the residues of oil seeds, the major loss is because about a fifth of the gross energy of the feed is contained in the associated faeces. Because this loss is easily determined in trials to measure the digestibility of feeds, and because it accounts for most of the variation in the utilisation of gross energy, digestible energy is widely used to describe the energy content of feeds and is usually abbreviated to DE. Thus,

digestible energy (DE) = gross energy (GE) minus faecal energy

The digestible energy of barley can be described either as 12.9 Megajoules of digestible energy or as 12.9 MJ DE.

A refinement of digestible energy is sometimes made to allow for the energy which is also lost in the urine and in the combustible gases, methane and hydrogen, which result from fermentation of some compounds of the feed. This is called metabolisable energy (ME) because virtually all this fraction of the energy can become involved in the metabolic or living processes of the animal. In practice, ME is difficult to measure precisely and few absolute determinations have been made. Much more commonly, just the urinary energy is accounted for. Even this is problematic because the urine is the route by which the animal excretes a break-down product of protein, urea, and this varies with the amount of protein in the diet and with the amount of growth being made by the animal. As an academic exercise, it is interesting to try to describe a feed in terms of its metabolisable energy adjusted for the use made of the protein by the animal, but in most cases it amounts to a frivolity and, if one must use metabolisable energy, then a useful approximation is that it is about 96 per cent of the digestible energy. Thus,

$$\text{metabolisable energy} = 0.96 \times \text{digestible energy}$$

*Other units of energy values*
In the United Kingdom, digestible energy is the most widely used way of describing the energy value of feeds, but some other countries prefer to use other units. Some of these are as follows:

*Total digestible nutrients (TDN)*
This unit was widely used in the United Kingdom and is still in use in the United States. It is calculated from the weights (g) of the apparently digested components in 100 g of diet as follows:

$$\text{TDN} = \text{CP}_d + \text{CF}_d + \text{NFE}_d + (\text{EE}_d \times 2.25)$$

where the elements of the right-hand side of the equation are apparently digestible grams of crude protein (CP), crude fibre (CF), nitrogen-free extract (NFE) and ether extract (EE) respectively per 100 g of feed.

*Net energy*
Systems based on net energy are used extensively in continental Europe. The basic idea is that feeds are ranked according to their relative ability to produce the equivalent of 1 kg of pure fat as body tissue. At first sight, this is rather a confusing idea because pig producers prefer to think that they are not in the business of producing fat. It is, however, an index of how much of the energy of the feed is finally useful to the animal whether it is used in driving the synthesis of tissues, or for maintenance, or incorporated in some form in the tissue itself. Starch equivalent or SE describes the potential of a feed to produce pure fat relative to a kilogram of pure starch. Scandinavian feed units, which relate feeds to the fat producing potential of a kilogram of barley, and oat units are similar except that the reference feed is oats.

Each system has its own particular merits, and to discuss them further is beyond the scope of this book. However, it is possible to interconvert the units for most practical purposes as shown below.

INTERCONVERSION OF UNITS OF FEED ENERGY

*Units of feed energy equivalent to 1 megajoule of digestible energy (1 MJ DE)*

1 MJ DE       = 0.96 MJ ME
                 = 55 g total digestible nutrients (TDN)
                 = 54 g starch equivalent (SE)
                 = 77 g Scandinavian feed unit
                 = 90 g oat unit

*Units of feed energy equivalent to 1000 g of total digestible nutrients (TDN)*

1000 g TDN = 18.49 MJ DE
     = 17.78 MJ ME
     = 990 g starch equivalent
     = 1.41 Scandinavian feed units
     = 1.65 oat units

Note that starch equivalents are often given as g/100 g of starch rather than per kg.


REQUIREMENTS FOR ENERGY

The energy-yielding nutrients in feed can be used for a variety of purposes. First, the materials can be transformed into the building blocks of the animal's body. For example, starch, sugars, fats and even proteins can become part of the fatty tissues or be made into glycogen, which is a fuel for the muscles. Food proteins, of course, can be broken down and reassembled as the proteins of skin, bristle, the internal organs or, most desirably of all, as muscle or lean meat. Apart from providing some of the structure, the energy-yielding substances can be 'burnt' or oxidised by the life processes of the animal and used as fuel. The energy used in this way eventually leaves the animal in the form of heat, either by evaporating the water in the lungs or in sweat, by radiation, convection or conduction and in the heat used in warming food and water and subsequently lost in the faeces and urine. Another loss of energy occurs if the animal does work, for example, rooting, walking, running or fighting.

*Maintenance*

If a pig is not fed and remains quiet in a comfortably warm environment, its metabolism maintains the basic processes of life. The energy which it uses is known as the *fasting metabolism*. This is, however, a very artificial circumstance and the animal, although staying alive, is not maintaining itself because it is having to supply energy from its body reserves to stay alive. If we feed the animal an exact amount of food which will exactly balance its losses of energy, this is called feeding the animal its *maintenance requirement*. Because eating, digesting and metabolising the food require energy, the heat lost from an animal kept at maintenance is about 25 per cent greater than the heat loss when it is fasted.

Although it would be rather foolish to give a growing pig only enough feed for maintenance, the cost of maintenance in terms of metabolisable or digestible energy is a useful value to know. Only that feed which is provided over and above maintenance can be used for growth. A well-established weaned pig can eat about four times as much feed as it requires to maintain itself. When the pig reaches 60 kg liveweight this has reduced to about three and a half times the maintenance requirement and at bacon weight (90 kg liveweight) to three times or less. This does not mean that the actual intake is getting less because the maintenance need increases as the animal grows.

A feature of the need for maintenance energy is that it does not increase as a fixed proportion of body weight but becomes proportionately less in relation to bodyweight as the animal grows. This can be seen from Table 9.1. The third col-

**TABLE 9.1  Maintenance requirement of growing pigs, expressed as Megajoules of digestible energy per day and in roughly the equivalent weight of barley**

| Liveweight (kg) | Maintenance MJ DE/day | MJ per day per kg of liveweight | Equivalent weight of barley feed (kg) |
|---|---|---|---|
| 5 | 2.06 | 0.413 | 0.160 |
| 10 | 3.20 | 0.320 | 0.248 |
| 20 | 4.94 | 0.247 | 0.383 |
| 50 | 8.81 | 0.176 | 0.683 |
| 100 | 13.63 | 0.136 | 1.057 |
| 150 | 17.60 | 0.117 | 1.364 |

(From ARC, 1981)

umn shows that the daily requirement for maintenance has reduced from 0.413 MJ/kg liveweight at 5 kg to 0.117 MJ/kg at 150 kg liveweight. The table also shows that a pig of 50 kg requires nearly 700 g of barley each day merely to stay alive and that a pig of 100 kg requires over 1 kg for the same purpose. These values are based on the assumption that the pigs are kept in a warm environment in what is called the thermo-neutral zone, that is, above the lower critical temperature (LCT) and below the upper one. (The effects of temperature on feed requirement were dealt with in Chapter 8.)

*Energy requirements for growth*
The feed that is supplied above the maintenance requirement is not converted totally into liveweight gain because the process of growth itself requires energy. A growing animal loses more heat to its environment than one which is only maintaining itself. There have been many elegant experiments to measure the energy cost of growth in pigs. Some of the most useful were conducted by two eminent Polish scientists, Professor Jan Kielanowski and Dr Maria Kotarbinska. They showed that it was possible to consider the energy costs in two parts, the cost of lipid or fat deposition and the cost of protein deposition. It turns out, not surprisingly, that fat is deposited with quite a high degree of energetic efficiency. For every MJ of energy deposited as fat (about 25 g), around 1.35 MJ of metabolisable energy or 1.4 MJ of digestible energy is required. This is an efficiency of 74 per cent. Retaining energy as protein is much more costly because the body has a considerable amount of work to do in servicing the elaborate machinery within the cells which is responsible for organising and connecting the amino acids in the precise sequence required for the immensely long chains which make up the proteins of the body. For each MJ of energy retained as protein in the body (about 42 g), 1.85 MJ of metabolisable energy or 1.93 MJ of digestible energy is required. This is an efficiency of only 54 per cent.

PREDICTING ENERGY REQUIREMENTS
The foregoing section is rather complex, but a knowledge of the efficiencies of fat and protein deposition allows predictions to be made of the energy requirements of animals growing at different rates and laying down different proportions of pro-

tein and fatty tissues. It is not our current purpose to show how this information relates to modelling techniques. However, it is worth pointing out that relating nutritional changes to growth responses can now be done by modelling with a precision which was inconceivable before this basic information was acquired.

SOURCES OF ENERGY

The four great classes of nutrients, that is, protein, carbohydrates, fats and fibre, can all supply the growing pig with energy, albeit in a different way. If protein is used for energy rather than as a direct constituent of tissue growth, then some of its total energy is lost to the animal because it is first deaminated* and the nitrogen lost as urea in the urine. The component left after deamination is a carbohydrate which is the equivalent of glucose.

Starch is a complex carbohydrate and to be utilised by the pig it must be broken down by hydrolysis† to its individual sugar constituents which are glucose units. In fact, starch and cellulose are both long chains of glucose units but with one vital difference, which is the nature of the chemical bond that links the units together. Alpha linkages occur exclusively in starch and beta linkages in cellulose. What this means in three dimensional organic chemistry need not concern us but it is all-important to the digestive enzymes. Pigs cannot digest cellulose but are very efficient at digesting starch. They do this with an enzyme called *amylase* which is secreted by the pancreas (Figure 9.1). Amylase is inactive against cellulose and indeed is ineffective against a whole family of carbohydrates collectively but inappropriately known as fibre.

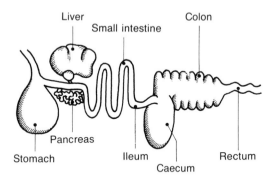

FIGURE 9.1   Diagram of the digestive system of the pig.

---

*Deamination* is the process whereby the amine grouping in protein is split off and converted to ammonia or urea.

†*Hydrolysis* of starch involves its separation into smaller units through the addition of hydrogen ions which break the original chemical bonds between the glucose units.

**TABLE 9.2   Approximate energy values of feeds (MJ per kg)**

| Feedstuff | Gross energy | Digestible energy |
|---|---|---|
| *Pure compounds* | | |
| Protein (lactalbumin) | 23.8 | — |
| Starch (corn) | 18.5 | — |
| Sucrose (cane) | 16.5 | — |
| Fat (anhydrous lard) | 39.5 | — |
| *Cereals* | | |
| Barley | 16.0 | 12.9 |
| Maize (whole) | 15.3 | 14.1 |
| Wheat | 15.8 | 13.9 |
| Oats (whole) | 17.0 | 10.9 |
| Oats (naked or groats) | 17.5 | 15.4 |
| Sorghum | 16.3 | 14.4 |
| Rice | 17.5 | 16.0 |
| *Cereal by-products* | | |
| Weatings | 16.8 | 12.8 |
| Wheat bran | 16.6 | 10.0 |
| Maize gluten (40%) | 16.9 | 13.5 |
| Distillers dark grains | — | 11.0 |
| Breakfast oat flakes | 17.5 | 15.0 |
| Rice bran | 14.8 | 9.6 |
| *Other energy sources* | | |
| Beet pulp (molassed) | 14.8 | 10.3 |
| Cassava (tapioca) | 14.6 | 14.0 |
| Corn oil | 39.0 | 35.0 |
| Molasses (75% DM) | 12.7 | 10.3 |
| Soya oil | 39.0 | 35.0 |
| Tallow | 39.0 | 34.5 |
| *Animal proteins* | | |
| Fishmeal (white) | 18.2 | 10.8 |
| Fishmeal (herring) | 20.5 | 11.5 |
| Meat and bone meal | | |
| 5% oil | 14.2 | 10.0 |
| 10% oil | 15.4 | 12.0 |
| Milk | | |
| Liquid skimmed | 1.8 | 1.7 |
| Dry skimmed | 17.0 | 15.8 |
| Whey liquid | 0.8 | 0.7 |
| Whey dried | 15.6 | 14.0 |
| *Vegetable proteins* | | |
| Beans (faba) | 15.6 | 12.6 |
| Beans (haricot) | — | do not feed |
| Lupins (yellow) | 15.1 | 13.0 |
| Peas (marrowfat) | 16.0 | 13.1 |
| Rapeseed (ext.* meal) | 17.7 | 12.1 |

*(continued on next page)*

**TABLE 9.2   Continued**

| Feedstuff | Gross energy | Digestible energy |
|---|---|---|
| Rapeseed (whole) | 24.5 | 16.1 |
| Soya beans (raw) | – | do not feed |
| Soya beans | | |
|    (cooked full-fat) | 21.5 | 16.9 |
|    (ext. meal 44) | 17.6 | 15.0 |
|    (ext. dehulled 50) | 17.8 | 16.0 |
| Sunflower (ext. dec†.) | 17.5 | 12.5 |

*Ext. = oil extracted
†Dec. = decorticated or dehulled

Fibre occurs in all plant material and the only way the pig can utilise it for energy is by waiting for the bacteria of its gut, mainly those in the caecum and colon, to ferment it. The bacteria do not produce glucose, but ferment the fibre to organic acids such as acetic (vinegar), propionic and lactic acid. These are then absorbed and metabolised by the pig but the whole process is very inefficient, only about 60 per cent of the fermented material providing energy which is utilised by the pig. In addition, the process of fermentation only affects a proportion of the fibre in the diet, and as far as the pig is concerned much of the fibre it gets is indigestible.

However, fibre is important in the biology of the digestive tract. It is a two-edged constituent of the diet: in small quantities it has a beneficial effect, but in large quantities a negative one. The beneficial effects stem from the fact that fermentation within limits creates a healthy gut environment partly because the end products like lactic acid inhibit pathogenic bacteria. The other positive factor is that the indigestible fraction binds with water and promotes a smooth passage of digesta and waste materials through the gut, often reducing the incidence of scouring and also preventing straining, constipation and prolapse of the rectum. The negative aspects of fibre include reductions in the digestibility of protein and energy in other constituents of the diet, the suppression of appetite and resulting reduction in growth.

For quick comparisons of the energy values of feeds, a list of the most common dietary constituents together with their respective values for gross energy and digestible energy is presented in Table 9.2.

## Protein and Amino Acids

The pig requires proteins in its diet to build very important structures in the body. The protein content of the body varies between 15 and 20 per cent of the total body weight, depending on the degree of fatness and on the age of the animal. Further details of the composition of the pig's body are given in Chapters 2 and 3. For the purpose of this section on nutrition, it is important to draw attention to the fact that the commercially desirable part of the carcass, that is the lean (or anatomically, the skeletal muscle), contains approximately 20 per cent protein, 75 per cent water, 3 per cent fat, 1 per cent ash and 1 per cent of other substances such as glycogen.

It should be noted that other less edible parts which are essential structures are also rich in protein; these include the internal organs, heart, lung, blood and liver and the external covering of the skin or hide, which, in fact, is the largest organ in the body. Proteins are giant molecules made up of relatively few basic units.

Amino acids are the sub-units of protein and there are about 20 different types. Proteins are made up of several hundred or even thousand animo acids linked together in enormously long folded chains. The most amazing fact is that each individual protein in the pig has a unique sequence of amino acids, which are as exact as the letters in a printed book. Just as a book can run to millions of copies, so also do the proteins, each one identical. The crucial point is that just as each book has a precise requirement for each letter of the alphabet, so the pig has a precise requirement for the amino acids of the proteins which it incorporates into its tissues.

IDEAL PROTEIN

Unfortunately, the pig can only synthesise some amino acids and the rest, the so-called essential amino acids, must be provided in the diet. There are some ten essential amino acids and from the above it is obvious that, ideally, they should be supplied in the diet approximately in the same ratio as they are required in the body. The proteins of plants contain rather different ratios of amino acids and, in particular, they are very deficient in the amino acid lysine relative to animal proteins. An ideal dietary protein for pigs would contain the amounts of the essential amino acids shown in Table 9.3. Shown also is the relative 'idealness' of the proportion of each amino acid in barley.

The first point to notice about barley is that, in addition to lysine, which is only 48.6 per cent of the ideal ratio, threonine is below the ideal (83.3%) as also to a lesser degree are methionine + cysteine (the sulphur-containing amino acids) (91.7%) and leucine (97.1%). This means that, purely in terms of the limiting amino acid, barley protein is only 48.6 per cent ideal as a balanced protein for

TABLE 9.3 **Amounts of essential amino acids ideally required in each kg of dietary protein for growing pigs compared with the proportions in the typical protein of barley**

|  | Ideal protein (g/kg) | Barley protein (g/kg) | % of ideal level in barley |
|---|---|---|---|
| Lysine | 70 | 34 | 48.6 |
| Methionine + cysteine | 35 | 33 | 91.7 |
| Threonine | 42 | 35 | 83.3 |
| Tryptophan | 10 | 12 | 120.0 |
| Isoleucine | 38 | 43 | 113.2 |
| Leucine | 70 | 68 | 97.1 |
| Histidine | 23 | 26 | 113.0 |
| Phenylalanine + tryosine | 67 | 82 | 122.3 |
| Valine | 49 | 54 | 110.0 |

(Source: ARC, 1981)

growing pigs. However, if the synthetic amino acid lysine is added, then the 'idealness' of the protein could be raised to 83.3 per cent (when threonine becomes limiting).

In general, except for specialist diets produced for young pigs, the amino acids are not normally added as separate entities, but as part of the protein of a protein-rich supplement such as extracted soya bean meal, meat-and-bone meal, fish meal or canola (rapeseed) meal.

PROTEIN DIGESTIBILITY

There are several additional factors to be considered in providing the pig with its needs for amino acids. First, the protein in a feedstuff is not totally available to the animal. As has already been shown for the energy fraction, digestibility is also important in determining the value of a protein source. This truth is made starkly apparent when one considers the well-known example of tanned leather (as in shoes) which is virtually 100 per cent ideal protein and about 100 per cent indigestible!

The declaration of protein content often found on feed bags as a statutory requirement does not take into account the extent to which the protein can be utilised by the pig or its digestibility. In fact, digestibility of protein in its simplest form can also be misleading. Digestibility is easily measured as the proportion of protein in the diet which apparently disappears on its way through the digestive tract. For example, if there are 300 g of protein in the feed consumed in 24 hours and 150 g of protein in the faeces produced in the corresponding period, then the apparent protein digestibility is 50 per cent (300 minus 150 divided by 300). If only 75 g of protein emerges in the faeces than the apparent digestibility is 75 per cent (300 minus 75 divided by 300). The protein which cannot be accounted for has certainly been digested, that is, broken down to its constituent amino acids and absorbed by the gut into the bloodstream. It may then be incorporated into body tissues (nitrogen retention) as part of the growth process. If the amino acids are not ideal or are surplus to the requirements of the body, then they are broken down (deaminated) and the nitrogen fraction removed from the body by the kidneys, which produce a solution of urea, this being the main nitrogen constituent of urine. The residue is used as a carbohydrate source for the energy metabolism of the animal.

Another possibility for absorbed amino acids is that they are re-excreted into the lumen of the gut in the form of enzymes (typically from the pancreas and the gut wall) or in the form of mucus. Because faeces also contain these protein secretions into the gut (the so-called 'endogenous' nitrogen), nutritionists usually describe the results of crude determinations of digestible protein as *apparent* protein digestibility. Some sources of protein, for example raw haricot beans which are toxic to pigs, cause an immense outflow of protein from the gut and can result in a negative digestibility (more protein excreted in the faeces than ingested in the feed).

ILEAL DIGESTIBILITY

It is a feature of the development of our nutritional knowledge that nothing remains quite constant or simple. It is easy to understand the basic principles of digestibility because we can almost see the protein in the food and the faeces. However, there are other important aspects which are less easily visualised. Essentially, the disruption of protein by the digestive tract of the pig is in two parts.

First we have the enzymic digestion in the stomach and small intestine, which is the result of the pig's own digestive juices working on the feed. Eventually the feed (or digesta) passes into the lower digestive tract, the large bowel, which anatomically comprises the caecum and the colon. This is where the nature of the digestive process changes and fermentation of the feed by micro-organisms takes over. Protein which fails to be digested in the small digestive tract down to its lowest part, that is, the terminal ileum, passes the ileo-caecal valve and can now no longer yield its amino acids to the pig. This is because in the large intestine the bacteria vigorously attack the protein with their own enzymes and either break it down to very simple nitrogenous substances such as ammonia or urea, or incorporate the amino acids directly or in modified form into their own structures. Experiments have shown that even infusing solutions of free amino acids directly into the upper colon is of no benefit to the animal because of the considerable activity of the natural micro-organisms, which either degrade these animo acids to ammonia and fatty acids or incorporate them into their own bodies.

For the reasons described above, in order to obtain an accurate description of the value of feedstuffs, it is important to incorporate an estimate of their potential ability to yield up their amino acids prior to the terminal ileum (before fermentation

**TABLE 9.4 Approximate ileal digestibilities of protein, lysine and threonine in different feedstuffs given as percentages and compiled from several sources**

| Feedstuff | Crude protein | Total lysine | Threonine |
|---|---|---|---|
| *Cereals* | | | |
| Barley | 75.0 | 74.0 | 69.0 |
| Maize (whole) | 80.0 | 78.0 | 72.0 |
| Wheat | 84.0 | 77.0 | 76.0 |
| Oats | 60.0 | 70.0 | 55.0 |
| Oats (naked or groats) | 84.0 | 82.0 | 78.0 |
| Sorghum | 75.0 | 81.0 | 72.0 |
| *Cereal by-products* | | | |
| Weatings | 70.0 | 74.0 | 55.0 |
| Wheat bran | 62.0 | 70.0 | 55.0 |
| Maize gluten feed | 52.0 | 40.0 | 45.0 |
| Maize gluten meal | 88.0 | 80.0 | 72.0 |
| Dist. dark grains | 70.0 | 68.0 | 67.0 |
| *Animal proteins* | | | |
| Fishmeal (white) | 80.0 | 88.0 | 82.0 |
| Meat and bone meal | 62.0 | 58.0 | 53.0 |
| Milk skimmed dried | 86.0 | 92.0 | 83.0 |
| *Vegetable proteins* | | | |
| Rapeseed (ext. meal) | 70.0 | 75.0 | 70.0 |
| Soyabeans (ext. meal 44) | 80.0 | 85.0 | 77.0 |
| Sunflower (ext. dec.) | 73.0 | 69.0 | 67.0 |

**TABLE 9.5  Approximate protein and amino acid values of feeds (grams per kg)**

| Feedstuff | Crude protein | Total lysine | Available lysine | Threonine | Ideal protein |
|---|---|---|---|---|---|
| *Pure compounds* | | | | | |
| Protein (lactalbumin) | 1000 | 97.5 | 97.5 | 52.5 | About 100 |
| Starch (corn) | 0 | 0 | 0 | 0 | 0 |
| Sucrose (cane) | 0 | 0 | 0 | 0 | 0 |
| Fat (anhydrous lard) | 0 | 0 | 0 | 0 | 0 |
| *Cereals* | | | | | |
| Barley | 100 | 3.7 | — | 3.1 | 53 |
| Maize (whole) | 90 | 2.3 | — | 3.3 | 33 |
| Wheat | 110 | 3.0 | — | 2.8 | 43 |
| Oats (whole) | 110 | 4.0 | — | 2.8 | 57 |
| Oats (naked or groats) | 155 | 4.5 | — | 4.5 | 64 |
| Sorghum | 110 | 2.7 | — | 2.7 | 39 |
| Rice | 74 | 2.5 | — | 2.7 | 36 |
| *Cereal by-products* | | | | | |
| Weatings | 160 | 5.5 | — | 4.5 | 78 |
| Wheat bran | 145 | 5.0 | — | 4.3 | 70 |
| Maize gluten feed | 210 | 5.3 | — | 7.0 | 76 |
| Distillers dark grains | 270 | 8.5 | — | 6.5 | 90 |
| Breakfast oat flakes | 145 | 5.5 | — | 5.0 | 79 |
| Rice bran (extracted) | 128 | 5.8 | — | 4.6 | 83 |
| *Other energy sources* | | | | | |
| Beet pulp (unmolassed) | 80 | 6.0 | — | 4.0 | 86 |
| Cassava (tapioca) | 24 | — | — | — | — |
| Corn oil | 0 | 0 | 0 | 0 | 0 |
| Molasses (cane) | 30 | 0 | 0 | 0 | 0 |
| Soya oil | 0 | 0 | 0 | 0 | 0 |
| Tallow | 0 | 0 | 0 | 0 | 0 |
| *Animal proteins* | | | | | |
| Fishmeal (white) | 660 | 45 | 36 | 26 | 500 |
| Fishmeal (herring) | 700 | 56 | 45 | 29 | 645 |
| Meat and bone meal | | | | | |
|   5% oil | 500 | 26 | 19 | 18 | 271 |
|   10% oil | 450 | 24 | 18 | 15 | 257 |
| Milk | | | | | |
|   Liquid skimmed | 35 | 2.6 | 2.6 | 1.8 | 31 |
|   Dry skimmed | 340 | 26.0 | 25.0 | 18.0 | 300 |
|   Whey liquid | 9 | 0.5 | 0.5 | 0.48 | 12 |
|   Whey dried | 125 | 7.2 | 6.8 | 6.7 | 95 |
| Pruteen (ICI) | 700 | 40 | — | 33 | 550 |
| *Vegetable proteins* | | | | | |
| Beans (faba) | 250 | 15 | — | 10 | 125* |
| Beans (haricot) | | | do not feed | | |
| Peas (marrowfat) | 210 | 15 | — | 9 | 150* |
| Rapeseed (ext. meal) | 360 | 22 | — | 15 | 300* |

**TABLE 9.5** Continued

| Feedstuff | Crude protein | Total lysine | Available lysine | Threonine | Ideal protein |
|---|---|---|---|---|---|
| Rapeseed (whole) | 215 | 13 | – | 9 | 180 |
| Soya beans (raw) | | | do not feed | | |
| Soya beans | | | | | |
| (cooked full-fat) | 370 | 24 | – | 15 | 240 |
| (ext. meal 44) | 440 | 29 | – | 18 | 286 |
| (ext. dehulled 50) | 485 | 32 | – | 19 | 315 |
| Sunflower (ext. dec.) | 420 | 17 | – | 21 | 220* |
| *Amino acids* | | | | | |
| Lysine hydrochloride | 780 | 780 | 780 | – | – |
| *Minerals* | | | | | |
| Dicalcium phosphate | 0 | 0 | 0 | 0 | 0 |
| Limestone flour | 0 | 0 | 0 | 0 | 0 |
| Salt (NcCl) | 0 | 0 | 0 | 0 | 0 |

predominates) and this is called *ileal digestibility*. Some examples of ileal digestibility are shown in Table 9.4 and of composition of major proteins in terms of key amino acids in Table 9.5.

PROTEIN/ENERGY RATIOS
The amount of protein per unit of digestible energy is more important nutritionally than the absolute concentration of protein because the animal requires these in an exact ratio to meet its requirements for maintenance and growth. Ideally, diets should not merely be described as being high or low protein or high or low in energy, but also in terms of the ratio of, for example, the most limiting amino acid, lysine, to the digestible energy of the diet. This means that the ratio of grams of lysine per MJ or Mcal of digestible energy is part of the formulation strategy. In this way, it is possible to link the diet composition with the real requirement of the animal. The body composition of the improved pig has a higher ratio of protein to energy (lean to fat) than the unimproved pig. Quite simply, this fact must be matched by increasing the protein to energy ratio of the diet.

As well as varying with genotype, the optimal ratio of protein to energy changes steadily throughout growth, being high in the young animal and low in the older animal.

This can be illustrated by the information presented in Table 9.6, which is calculated from data given in the review of the Agricultural Research Council (1981). The table gives the derivation of estimates of the amounts of lysine required daily, and also the ratio of lysine to energy for pigs of exceptionally good genetic potential (i.e. those with a very high rate of lean tissue growth).

It can be seen that the requirement for lysine and energy changes dramatically as the pig grows in that the g of lysine per MJ of DE falls continuously. If one were to meet the nutrient requirements exactly, then one would require a range of

**TABLE 9.6  Calculated lysine requirement per MJ of digestible energy in diets of growing pigs of exceptionally high genetic merit fed to appetite**

| Liveweight (kg) | Daily energy intake (MJ DE) | Daily liveweight gain (g) | Daily protein requirement for maintenance (g) | Protein* deposition per day (g) | Lean deposition per day (g) |
|---|---|---|---|---|---|
| 10 | 9.23 | 380 | 5.3 | 62.7 | 157 |
| 30 | 22.89 | 710 | 12.0 | 117.2 | 293 |
| 50 | 31.97 | 900 | 17.6 | 148.5 | 370 |
| 70 | 38.01 | 900 | 22.7 | 148.5 | 370 |
| 90 | 42.03 | 900 | 27.4 | 148.5 | 370 |

| | Requirement of | | | | Example dietary levels | |
|---|---|---|---|---|---|---|
| Liveweight (kg) | Total protein daily (g) | Ideal protein† daily (g) | Dietary lysine‡ daily (g) | Lysine per MJ DE (g/MJ) | Energy in diet (MJ DE) | Lysine (%) |
| 10 | 68.0 | 136 | 9.5 | 1.03 | 17 | 1.75 |
| 30 | 129.2 | 258 | 18.1 | 0.79 | 14 | 1.11 |
| 50 | 166.1 | 332 | 23.2 | 0.72 | 13 | 0.94 |
| 70 | 171.2 | 344 | 23.9 | 0.63 | 13 | 0.82 |
| 90 | 175.9 | 352 | 24.6 | 0.59 | 13 | 0.77 |

*Assuming 0.165 of daily gain to be protein (ARC, 1981)
†Assuming gross efficiency of utilization of ideal protein 0.5 (ARC, 1981)
‡Assuming lysine in ideal protein = 0.07
(Source: Fowler, 1985)

perhaps four or five diets during the growing period. In practice, many farmers feed but one compromise diet from 25 kg (e.g. 0.72 g lysine per MJ DE), causing lysine to be a limiting factor on growth in the early stages while wasting protein in the later stages since the excess lysine is merely deaminated and lost in the urine as urea.

## Vitamins

Vitamins are so called because earlier research workers, following their discovery of vitamin $B_1$ (thiamin), used the words 'vital amines' to describe the whole range of essential organic chemicals which are necessary in small amounts in the diet; 'vital amines' were later termed 'vitamins'. They fall into two broad categories, the fat-soluble and the water-soluble. This classification is self-explanatory. It has been fashionable to designate the vitamins by letter of the alphabet subscripted by numbers. For example, the so-called B vitamins range from $B_1$ to $B_{12}$. Unfortunately, this approach has become confusing as more vitamins have been discovered and it is now more usual to use a chemical name.

In terms of pig farming, it is not necessary for the producer to concern himself too much about the vitamins since most of them are now produced at a relatively low cost and a multi-vitamin supplement can usually be purchased at a modest price.

Before presenting the pig's requirement for vitamins (see Table 9.7), it is perhaps useful to emphasise which ones may actually be deficient in certain circumstances even when, superficially, the vitamin requirements have been met. The ones to watch are vitamin E (tocopherol) in diets which contain soft, unsaturated or even oxidised fats, particularly where antioxidants are absent; vitamin $B_{12}$ (cyanocobalamin) in diets which do not contain any animal protein, e.g. barley/soya diets; and possibly biotin in cases where sows or even boars show defects of the keratinous horns on the cleats of the feet.

A further factor to draw attention to is that there are two concepts in providing pigs with vitamins: the first is the requirement which is compatible with good health and which should meet its needs for maintenance and production; the second component is the daily allowance which is the requirement enhanced by an amount which will allow a margin of safety to account for variations in availability, storage losses, imperfect mixing, sub-normal health and stressful conditions. It is comparatively simple to quantify the requirement, but appropriate allowances are the subject of much debate between advisers, scientists and feed manufacturers. In general terms, it is probably sensible to increase the amount specified in the requirement by about 20 per cent, but this can, of course, add an appreciable cost to the diet, as in the case of biotin and vitamin E. There has been a tendency in recent years for manufacturers of feedstuffs to increase very substantially the amounts of inexpensive vitamins with the honourable objective of covering every conceivable contingency but, unfortunately, one suspects also with the less honourable objective of catching the eye of the purchaser with well-publicised rates of inclusion which are well above any concentration which could be biologically useful. Table 9.7 includes both the requirement and the recommended allowances for inclusion of vitamins in normal diets.

There are some circumstances whereby the pig can meet a tiny fraction of its requirements for some vitamins from the bacterial synthesis occurring in the gut. For example, biotin and some of the B-vitamins may be produced in this way and if pigs eat their own faeces or root about in strawed yards, where there is further fermentation, they may ingest appreciable quantities of these vitamins. However, it is safer not to expect the vitamins to be provided in this way and to ensure that adequate quantities are included in the diet. There is one notable exception in that it appears that the pig has little or no specific requirements for vitamin C, which it seems to be able to synthesise itself.

## Mineral Requirements

Mineral requirements are similar in principle to the requirements for any nutrient. Unlike some vitamins which the animal can synthesise itself, minerals are the basic inorganic molecules required for a specific purpose and in general cannot be substituted one for another. For example, the minerals in bone tissue are predominantly constructed from the elements calcium, phosphorous, hydrogen and oxygen. The hydrogen and oxygen are normal elements in any feedstuff but the

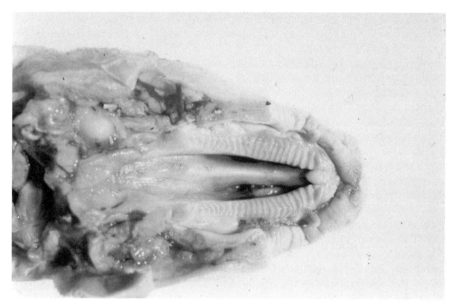

Plate 9.1   Diseases caused by mineral and vitamin deficiencies are now rare if pig producers purchase their vitamin/mineral supplements from reputable compounders. Among deficiency diseases sometimes encountered is cleft palate (see plate above), which is a defect sometimes produced by Vitamin A deficiency in the dam. The plate below shows a newborn piglet with oedema of the fore legs, which is sometimes associated with riboflavin deficiency.

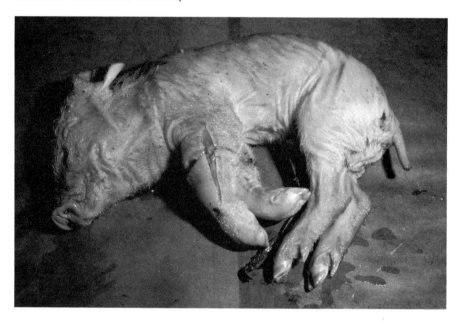

*calcium* and *phosphorus* may be totally inadequate. To ensure strong bones and healthy tissues it is necessary either to ensure that the diet includes at least some constituents which are rich in these elements such as fishmeal or meat and bone meal or to add a totally inorganic source like dicalcium phosphate which will supply a readily available source of both elements.

Another critical group of minerals is the one which maintains the stability of the cell fluids within the body, in particular *sodium, potassium, chlorine* and *sulphur*. These are normally found in their ionic form, that is, as soluble salts. Sodium and chlorine are frequently added as common salt or sodium chloride, whereas potassium and sulphur usually occur in adequate concentrations in normal dietary constituents. It is important to note that although it is not often harmful to add an excess of a vitamin, it can be extremely dangerous to do so with a mineral. *Selenium* is a mineral which is essential for the well-being of the animal and prevents its tissue fat from becoming oxidised. However, when given only slightly in excess it can be extremely toxic. Thus, it is important to know how much is in the basic constituents of the diet as well as the correct amount to add. Excesses of *common salt* can be dangerous, particularly if the water supply is in any way limited. In fact, deaths from *salt toxicity* can arise due to thirst even though there may appear to be adequate fluid in the diet. Pigs have died from salt toxicity even when fed on a diet containing a large amount of grass juice, which contains a very high proportion of potassium and sulphate. In particular, waste food products such as biscuit waste or reject potato crips can contain surprisingly high concentrations of salt and care must be taken to ensure that salt is not added to such diets.

Other critical elements are those which are required in relatively small amounts as key molecules in enzyme systems or in pigments. For example, *iron* is required for the formation of the red pigment haemoglobin in the red blood cells, also called erythrocytes, and without it in adequate quantities the pigs become anaemic, that is, short of properly functioning red blood cells. This makes the animals breathless during exertion because the blood is not transporting oxygen properly and may in extreme cases severely impair the growth.

Many of the elements listed in the mineral table are required in minute quantities but are absolutely essential to life. However, excesses are usually dangerous, and an apparently simple mistake such as confusing the units by a factor of 10 can be disastrous. One interesting exception is the pig's extraordinary tolerance of *copper*. Indeed, because the pig is so tolerant of it, it has been used in the past to suppress the proliferation of bacteria in the gut because the bacteria are less tolerant than the pig. This growth promotional effect was first observed by Dr Raphael Braude, who was largely responsible for the work which led to high levels of copper being adopted as a standard approach in diet formulation. However, sheep are much less tolerant of copper than are pigs, and because there have been a number of examples of contamination of sheep diets by residues from pig's diets and occasional reports of sheep dying after grazing pastures recently treated by the application of pig slurry, in many countries, including those in the EEC, the addition of copper has been restricted to levels which are above the strict nutritional requirement but which give a limited degree of growth promotion.

Another component of the diet can be regarded as a mineral and this is water.

**TABLE 9.7   Vitamins and minerals for growing pigs. Minimal requirements and, in brackets, the recommended degree of supplementation for normal diets (amounts per kg diet, 87% dry matter)**

| | Units | Liveweight 10 to 30 kg | | 30 to 90 kg | |
|---|---|---|---|---|---|
| *Vitamins* | | | | | |
| Thiamin (B$_1$) | mg | 2.5 | (0.0) | 1.5 | (0.0) |
| Riboflavin (B$_2$) | mg | 3.5 | (5.0) | 2.5 | (3.0) |
| Nicotinic acid (niacin) | mg | 20.0 | (20.0) | 15.0 | (10.0) |
| Pantothenic acid | mg | 15.0 | (20.0) | 10.0 | (7.5) |
| Pyridoxine (B$_6$) | mg | 3.5 | (5.0) | 2.5 | (2.0) |
| Cyanocobalamin (B$_{12}$) | μg | 20.0 | (40.0) | 10.0 | (20.0) |
| Biotin (Vit H) | μg | 200.0 | (100.0) | 100.0 | (0.0) |
| Folic acid (p-amino benzoic acid) | mg | ? | (1.0) | ? | (0.0) |
| Myo-inositol | – | ? | (0.0) | ? | (0.0) |
| Choline | – | ? | (0.0) | ? | (0.0) |
| Ascorbic acid (Vit C) | – | ? | (0.0) | ? | (0.0) |
| Vitamin A | IU* | 1980 | (5000) | 1320 | (4000) |
| (as Retinol)(IU) | μg | 600 | (1500) | 400 | (1200) |
| Vitamin D | IU | 200 | (1000) | 200 | (800) |
| or (as Cholecalciferol) | μg | 5.0 | (25.0) | 5.0 | (20.0) |
| Vitamin E (DL-α-tocopherol acetate) | mg | 15.0 | (20.0) | 10.0 | (10.0) |
| Vitamin K (Menaphthone) | μg | 300 | (1000) | 200.0 | (1000) |
| *Minerals* | | | | | |
| Calcium | g | 9.5 | (4.0) | 8.0 | (4.0) |
| Phosphorus | g | 7.5 | (2.0) | 6.0 | (1.5) |
| Chlorine | g | 1.5 | (1.75) | 1.5 | (1.75) |
| Sodium | g | 1.3 | (1.5) | 1.3 | (1.5) |
| Potassium | g | 2.5 | (0.0) | 2.5 | (0.0) |
| Magnesium | g | 0.4 | (0.0) | 0.4 | (0.0) |
| Iron | mg | 50 | (50.0) | 50 | (50.0) |
| Zinc | mg | 75 | (100.0) | 50 | (100.0) |
| Manganese | mg | 15 | (25.0) | 15 | (25.0) |
| Copper† | mg | 4 | (15.0)† | 4 | (15.0)† |
| Cobalt‡ | – | ? | (0.0) | ? | (0.0) |
| Iodine | mg | 0.5 | (2.0) | 0.2 | (2.0) |
| Selenium | mg | 0.2 | (0.15) | 0.2 | (0.15) |

*IU = International Units
†Copper may be increased in circumstances where it is a permitted growth promoter.
‡Cobalt has not been shown to be required other than as a component of the vitamin cyanocobalamin.

## Water

Water, as every school pupil knows, is made up of two critical elements, hydrogen and oxygen, and has a role in every function of the live animal. Up to 75 per cent of some tissues is water, and it is also required for the proper functioning of the kidneys and the excretion of waste materials such as the nitrogen excretory product urea resulting from the breakdown of surplus or inappropriate amino acids. Water is essential in adequate quantities to allow for the excretion of inbalances of certain minerals such as sodium, potassium, chloride, sulphate and phosphate, as well as a great range of other breakdown and waste materials. Water also has a function in the regulation of body temperature, in that evaporation from the lungs, from the sweat glands on the snout and from the surface of the skin, as occurs after wallowing, allows the animal to shed excess heat which would otherwise lead to a rise in body temperature and quite quickly to death. The provision of constantly available clean, fresh water is very important. Many pigs have died because water pipes froze or because drinkers were out of reach. One noteworthy example of the latter occurred after the deep straw litter was removed from a yard but the drinkers were not lowered to the new 'floor' level. Water can also be the means of transferring disease if it is contaminated, and it has been known to poison stock because it contained excesses of lead or other heavy metals when it was taken from an unchecked borehole or stored in unsuitable metal containers. The codes of welfare in force in the United Kingdom recommend that water should be available at all times to growing pigs. The one exception is for pigs on a wet feeding system where it is desirable to give about three times as much water as the weight of dry feed. In cases where salt levels could be higher than normal this should be increased.

RECOMMENDATIONS FOR VITAMINS AND MINERALS
Table 9.7 presents vitamin and mineral requirements for growing pigs, that is, the minimal amount compatible with good health and maximal performance, and also the recommended allowances for addition to a conventional diet to take account of possible losses in storage and errors of mixing.

## DIET IN RELATION TO GENOTYPE, SEX AND STAGE OF DEVELOPMENT

In order to obtain a clearer picture of the importance of matching the diet to the needs of the pig, the factors (in addition to nutrition) which influence the growth of tissues will now be outlined.

## GROWTH OF TISSUES

As outlined in Chapter 3, the major tissues of the carcass are lean, fat and bone. This section will concentrate on the development of lean meat in the carcass with the ancillary tissues of bone and fat being referred to only insofar as their development is influenced by the same factors which influence growth of lean. Lean tissue contains about 75 per cent of water whereas lipid or fatty tissue only contains some 10 to 15 per cent of water. Mainly as a result of the marked differences in water content, energy requirement for deposition of 1 kg of fatty tissue (50 MJ DE) is over three times greater than that required to produce 1 kg of lean (15 MJ DE).

Since (1) it is lean rather than fatty tissue which is in demand and therefore commands a considerably higher price and (2) lean tissue can be produced more economically than fat, the factors influencing efficient and economical production of lean tissue must be established as a basis for formulating diets and rationing.

## Factors Influencing Growth of Lean Tissue

The major factors influencing growth of lean tissue are as follows:

- Stage of development
- Sex
- Genotype
- Nutrition

The influence of these factors on the growth of lean tissue will now be outlined.

### Stage of Development

On an adequate diet and plane of feeding, the rate at which lean meat is laid down increases as the pig grows and reaches a maximum between about 30 and 100 kg liveweight (see Figure 9.2). After the fairly flat peak, the rate of gain in lean tissue declines to a zero level when the animal reaches maturity.

The actual daily rate of deposition of lean tissue and the exact stage when maximal growth is attained is mainly dependent on sex, genotype and nutrition.

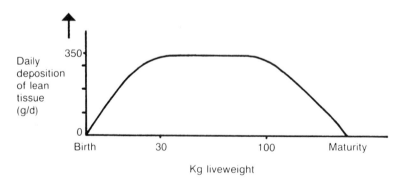

FIGURE 9.2   Trends in daily lean meat deposition with the stage of development.

## Sex

There are well-established differences in the development of lean tissue between the entire male, the castrate and the gilt. On the same level of nutrients, the entire male has the fastest and the castrate the slowest rate of lean tissue growth, with the gilt in an intermediate position.

In very young pigs between 2 and 7 kg liveweight, Williams (1976), working in Melbourne, Australia, did not find any differences in the rate of deposition of lean tissue between the sexes even when he gave them a full range of diets in terms of provision of energy, protein, essential amino acids and other essential nutrients.

At a further stage of growth between 20 and 50 kg liveweight, research workers, including Campbell and his associates in Victoria, Australia, found entire males and gilts to be similar in lean tissue growth rate when adequate diets were on offer at a high level of food intake (equivalent to about four times maintenance requirement for energy). However, when extremely high feed intakes were achieved ( up to 4.4 times maintenance requirement for energy), the entire male started to outgrow the gilt in terms of lean tissue.

Yen (1979), in a detailed experiment at the University of Nottingham, involving a wide range of dietary levels of protein and lysine at high levels of energy intake, found that over the 25 to 55 kg liveweight range, boars grew lean tissue at a 5 per cent faster rate than gilts and 7.5 per cent faster than castrates.

After the 50 kg liveweight stage, much larger differences emerge between the sexes in the growth rate of lean tissue. Campbell and his co-workers in Victoria examined pigs of a particular genotype over the liveweight range of 48 to 90 kg on well-balanced diets and high energy intakes and found the maximum rate of deposition of protein into lean tissue was 137 g per day in entire males and only 117 g per day in gilts. These levels are equivalent to daily growth rates of lean tissue in the entire male of 340 g and only 290 g in the gilt, an advantage for the boar of over 17 per cent. As energy intake was increased progressively from low levels to ad lib. intake, gilts (relative to entire males) used more of the energy for fat and less for lean tissue growth, grew more slowly and had fatter carcasses and much poorer food conversion efficiency. Yen found similarly large differences in the rate of lean tissue growth between the sexes. It can be calculated from the data of Yen that boars grew lean over 10 per cent faster than gilts and about 20 per cent faster than castrates.

## Genotype

As vast strides in genetic improvement have been made in some genotypes (particularly with regard to liveweight gain, feed conversion efficiency and carcass quality), with little or no improvement in other strains, there is no doubt that large genetic differences now exist between strains in the potential for growth of lean tissue. Campbell and his co-workers in Australia compared two contrasting genotypes over the growth period from 45 to 90 kg liveweight. The results are summarised in Figure 9.3.

Strain A had been subjected to intensive genetic improvement for commercial traits for some eight years, while little effort had been made to improve strain B

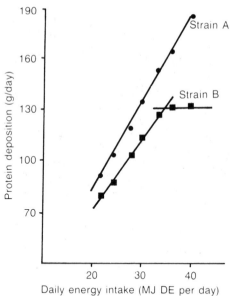

FIGURE 9.3   The relationship between energy intake and rate of protein deposition in two strains of entire male pig from 45 to 90 kg.

over the years. Campbell considered that the diets on offer were adequate in protein, essential amino acids and other nutrients. As energy intake was increased, Strain B appeared to reach its ceiling for deposition of protein in lean tissue at an intake of 33 MJ DE per day as there was no further improvement with further increases in energy intake. This ceiling for Strain B of 129 g of protein is equivalent to a rate of lean tissue deposition of 320 g per day. On the other hand, the improved Strain A showed no sign of reaching its maximum capability of laying down protein. At the highest level of energy intake (40 MJ DE per day) it was laying down protein at a rate of 187 g per day, which is equivalent to a lean tissue deposition rate of 464 g daily. If the Strain A pigs could have been persuaded to eat more, the indications are that they could have grown lean tissue at an even faster daily rate.

Thus, there are differences between sexes and genotypes in the rate at which lean tissue can be deposited. The important question now arises as to whether pigs with greater capabilities in terms of the rate at which they can deposit lean tissue require better diets and higher feed intakes to allow them to express fully their higher potential.

## Nutrition

### THE OBJECTIVES

One generally agreed objective of dietary and feeding strategy is that this should fully support a given pig's potential for muscle growth. As noted earlier, this potential changes with liveweight and is affected by sex and genotype and, indeed, varies between individuals of similar genotype and sex.

The role of the energy content of the diet and energy intake in helping to support the pig's potential for muscle growth will be outlined first.

THE ROLE OF ENERGY INTAKE

*Birth to 45 kg liveweight*

It would appear that up to around 45 kg liveweight one should strive to achieve maximum daily intake of digestible energy. When Campbell and his associates in Victoria progressively increased daily intake of digestible energy between 20 and 45 kg liveweight, daily deposition of protein tissue in entire males increased steadily up to a rate of 145 g daily (see Figure 9.4) with no sign of diminishing response up to ad lib. intake (34.2 MJ DE per day). Thus, maximum daily rate of protein

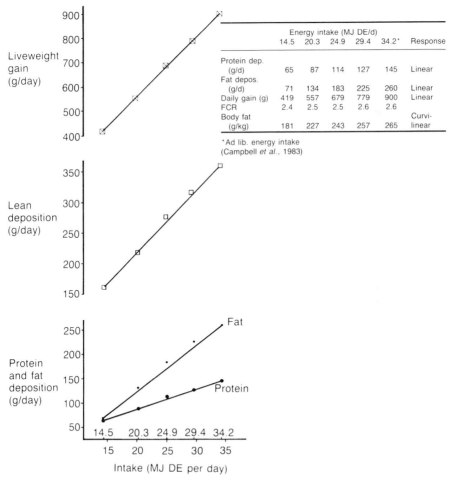

| | Energy intake (MJ DE/d) | | | | | |
| | 14.5 | 20.3 | 24.9 | 29.4 | 34.2* | Response |
|---|---|---|---|---|---|---|
| Protein dep. (g/d) | 65 | 87 | 114 | 127 | 145 | Linear |
| Fat depos. (g/d) | 71 | 134 | 183 | 225 | 260 | Linear |
| Daily gain (g) | 419 | 557 | 679 | 779 | 900 | Linear |
| FCR | 2.4 | 2.5 | 2.5 | 2.6 | 2.6 | |
| Body fat (g/kg) | 181 | 227 | 243 | 257 | 265 | Curvilinear |

*Ad lib. energy intake
(Campbell *et al.*, 1983)

FIGURE 9.4 The effect of daily intake of digestible energy by entire male pigs on daily rates of protein and lean meat deposition and on other parameters between 20 and 45 kg liveweight.

deposition was not established because of limitations of appetite. The general consensus is that up to 45 kg liveweight for boars of good genotype, the genetic ceiling for muscle growth lies beyond the limits of appetite or energy intake on ad lib. feeding (4 to 4.4 times maintenance requirement for energy).

Thus, over this wide range of energy intake, the rate of protein deposition shows a linear response as do estimated lean meat (protein deposition × 2.48) and fat deposition, as well as liveweight gain. Fortunately, estimated lean meat deposition shows a greater response to increasing energy intake than does fat deposition. If carcass grading standards based on backfat are strict and there are considerable financial incentives to produce carcasses with minimum fatness, the question arises as to whether it is desirable to reduce daily intake up to 45 kg liveweight in order to reduce fat deposition in the carcass. In the Australian work outlined in Figure 9.4, it was estimated that if daily energy intake is reduced by 27 per cent below ad lib. intake, other consequences would be as indicated in Table 9.8.

**TABLE 9.8   Consequence of reducing energy intake by 27 per cent below ad lib. intake for pigs between 20 and 45 kg liveweight**

|                                      | *Percentage reduction* |
| ------------------------------------ | :--------------------: |
| Body fat content                     |           8            |
| Daily liveweight gain                |           25           |
| Daily deposition of lean tissue      |           21           |
| Food to gain ratio                   |          nil           |

Thus, reduction in daily energy intake up to 45 kg liveweight would have resulted in an 8 per cent reduction in body fat content but this would be associated with considerable reductions in lean tissue deposition (21 per cent) and liveweight gain (25 per cent), with virtually no change in food conversion efficiency. Other workers have reached similar conclusions about restricting energy intake before 45 kg liveweight. Thus, while there would be some small advantage in reducing the energy intake of pigs up to around 45 kg liveweight in terms of reducing fatness, this would be greatly outweighed by the very substantial reductions in lean tissue and liveweight gains.

*45 kg liveweight upwards*
With relatively unimproved genotypes, there is evidence that as daily intake of digestible energy is increased up to about 2.5−3.0 times maintenance requirement for energy, the daily rate of deposition of protein, lean tissue and liveweight responds in a linear manner, while food to gain ratio also shows a progressive improvement (see Figure 9.5). However, as daily energy intake is further increased, there is no further increase in protein or lean tissue deposition. This critical level of daily energy intake (around 2.5 to 3.0 times maintenance) would therefore appear to be supporting the full potential for lean tissue growth of the unimproved genotype involved. As energy intake is increased further above these levels, lean tissue growth shows no further increase, the daily rate of fatty tissue deposition continues to increase and food conversion efficiency shows a progressive deteriora-

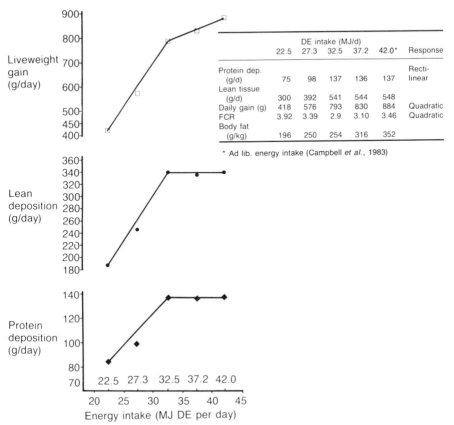

| | DE intake (MJ/d) | | | | | |
| | 22.5 | 27.3 | 32.5 | 37.2 | 42.0* | Response |
|---|---|---|---|---|---|---|
| Protein dep. | | | | | | Recti- |
| (g/d) | 75 | 98 | 137 | 136 | 137 | linear |
| Lean tissue | | | | | | |
| (g/d) | 300 | 392 | 541 | 544 | 548 | |
| Daily gain (g) | 418 | 576 | 793 | 830 | 884 | Quadratic |
| FCR | 3.92 | 3.39 | 2.9 | 3.10 | 3.46 | Quadratic |
| Body fat | | | | | | |
| (g/kg) | 196 | 250 | 254 | 316 | 352 | |

* Ad lib. energy intake (Campbell *et al.*, 1983)

FIGURE 9.5   The effect of daily intake of digestible energy by entire male pigs on daily rates of protein and lean meat deposition and on other parameters between 48 and 90 kg liveweight.

tion. These responses indicate that for such genotypes above about 45 kg liveweight, the pig's appetite exceeds its ability to grow lean tissue. Therefore, as energy intake goes above a certain critical level, the pig deposits progressively more fat relative to lean. Thus, in poor genotypes, energy intake must be restricted after a given stage of growth in order to avoid excessively fat carcasses. Such restriction would also seem to be desirable for poor genotypes in terms of optimising food conversion efficiency since over 45 kg liveweight, there would appear to be only a narrow range of energy intake over which food to gain ratio is minimal.

It has been suggested that the optimum level of energy intake for pigs over 45 kg liveweight should be that which just supports the pig's full potential for lean tissue growth. This is a sound concept although it suffers from the practical problem of determining this level of energy intake with increasing liveweight and for all genotypes and sexes. As indicated earlier, the optimum level of energy intake will vary between the sexes and between genotypes. Since entire males (relative to castrates and gilts) and improved genotypes (see Figure 9.3) have higher potential rates of lean tissue growth, they will justify higher levels of daily energy intake before feed restriction needs to be imposed.

It should be noted that for improved genotypes and especially for entire males, no food or energy restriction may be necessary because they are capable of responding by producing more lean tissue up to the limits of appetite. This is demonstrated by data from the Commercial Product Evaluation exercise of the Meat and Livestock Commission in the United Kingdom, where the three best genotypes, when fed at 80 per cent of ad lib. intake (an average of 21 MJ DE daily) between 25 and 118 kg liveweight, grew lean tissue at 239 g per day, whereas those fed ad lib. grew lean at a daily rate of 313 g.

THE INFLUENCE OF ENERGY CONCENTRATION OF THE DIET
*20 to 50 kg liveweight*
As indicated above, there are considerable incentives for setting out to maximise intake of digestible energy between 20 and 50 kg liveweight. The main advantage

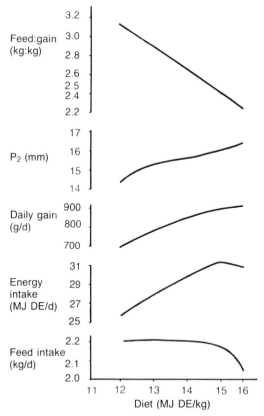

FIGURE 9.6   Responses to increasing energy concentration of the diet in entire male pigs between 22 and 50 kg liveweight. (Source: Campbell *et al.*, 1983)

is in terms of increased rate of gain in liveweight and lean tissue with only relatively minor increases in body fat content.

In order to maximise digestible energy intake, it is important that the concentration of energy in the diet is sufficiently high (see Table 9.9 and Figure 9.6). For these entire male pigs it can be seen that with increases of dietary energy concentration from 11.8 to 15.1 MJ DE per kg, maximum DE intake is not achieved until diets with 14.5 to 15.1 MJ DE per kg are offered.

**TABLE 9.9  Effect of dietary DE concentration on the voluntary feed intake and performance of entire male pigs growing from 22 to 50 kg**

|  | Dietary energy content (MJ/kg) | | | | |
|---|---|---|---|---|---|
|  | 11.8 | 12.7 | 13.6 | 14.5 | 15.1 |
| Voluntary feed intake (kg/day) | 2.19 | 2.21 | 2.19 | 2.17 | 2.05 |
| Voluntary energy intake (MJ DE/day) | 25.7 | 27.7 | 29.7 | 31.3 | 30.9 |
| Daily gain (g) | 695 | 776 | 847 | 898 | 913 |
| Feed:gain (kg:kg) | 3.16 | 2.89 | 2.61 | 2.39 | 2.25 |
| Carcass $P_2$ (mm) | 14.4 | 15.3 | 15.6 | 16.0 | 16.4 |

If we use a diet with 14.5 relative to one with 11.8 MJ DE/kg, the responses are summarised in Table 9.10. As energy concentration of the diet was increased from 11.8 to 14.5 MJ DE/kg, there was a 21.8 per cent increase in voluntary energy intake, 29.2 per cent higher liveweight gain and a 24.4 per cent reduction in food required per kg of liveweight gain. The only relatively small disadvantage associated with these considerable improvements was an 11.1 per cent increase in backfat thickness.

**TABLE 9.10  Responses from increasing dietary energy concentration from 11.8 to 14.5 MJ DE/kg for entire males between 22 and 50 kg liveweight**

|  |  | Per cent |
|---|---|---|
| Increase in: | energy intake (MJ DE) | 21.8 |
|  | liveweight gain (g/day) | 29.2 |
|  | backfat at $P_2$ (mm) | 11.1 |
| Reduction in: | food to gain ratio | |
|  | (kg food per kg gain) | 24.4 |

It would appear that over the liveweight range of 20 to 50 kg, a pig capable of growing at a rate of 900 g per day has a demand for energy which is 'a reflection of its potential for protein and fat growth' of between 30 and 32 MJ DE per day. However, since the maximum ingestive capacity of the pig over this weight range is between 2.0 and 2.2 kg per day of a normal diet, this means that this diet must have an energy concentration of between 14 and 15 MJ DE if energy intake is going to be sufficient to support maximum lean tissue growth potential.

As energy intake is increased over the same weight range for castrated males, there will be larger increases in backfat thickness. Responses in gilts will be midway between those of castrates and entire males. Despite responses to increased energy intake in castrates and gilts not being so attractive as those in entire males, there is no good practical reason for having different diets or feed levels for those up to 50 kg liveweight to those that operate for entire males since the theoretical difference in requirements between sexes is only about one percentage unit of protein in the diet.

Thus, between 20 and 50 kg liveweight, diets with energy concentration around 14.5 to 15.0 MJ DE offered on an ad lib. basis are recommended for gilts and castrates as well as for entire males.

### 50 to 90 kg liveweight
Over this liveweight range for average genotypes, the genetic potential for protein or lean tissue deposition lies within the limits of appetite. Thus, on protein adequate diets, with a wide range of DE levels, the pig's voluntary intake enables it to consume more than enough to support maximum rate of protein or lean tissue deposition. This being so, one must then decide on the optimum plane of feeding to achieve the best result in economic terms.

Reducing the feed intake in this period of growth does two things. First, in poor genotypes it prevents excess feed being wasted by not being converted into fatty tissue at all. Secondly, in the better genotypes it reduces the rate of fat deposition more than it reduces the rate of lean deposition, thereby making the carcass more lean. In this second case, although the carcass is more lean because of such feed restriction, it may not be associated with as good lean tissue food conversion efficiency as it would achieve on a higher level of feed intake. However, since a premium is often paid for lean meat when it is associated with an extremely thin backfat, restriction may be justified even with improved genotypes, and particularly with castrates.

### INFLUENCE OF PROTEIN AND LYSINE CONTENT OF THE DIET
The requirement of the growing pig for dietary lysine as well as its response to change in energy intake is determined largely by its capacity for muscle growth. Often the most profitable diet and feeding strategy for growing pigs is that which most closely matches the animal's potential for muscle growth. Thus, because potential for muscle growth varies with liveweight, sex and genotype, optimum dietary regime has to be considered in relation to these factors.

### Liveweight
It has been estimated that requirements for tissue protein vary with liveweight as indicated in Table 9.11. Thus at equivalent levels of energy intake the pig's requirement for protein declines with increase in liveweight. Since rate of muscle growth relative to voluntary energy intake declines continuously with increase in liveweight from birth to slaughter, the dietary concentrations of protein and essential amino acids can also be reduced. To meet the requirement of the pig more accurately there should be more frequent changes than at present in the amino acid

**TABLE 9.11   Estimate of requirements for tissue protein (growth + maintenance)**

| Liveweight range (kg) | Tissue requirement for protein* (g/MJ DE/day) |
|---|---|
| 1.8–6.5 | 10.3 |
| 7–20 | 7.2 |
| 20–45 | 5.4 |
| 45–90 | 4.8 |

*Requirement for a theoretical protein with a true digestibility and biological value of 1.0.
(From: Campbell, 1984)

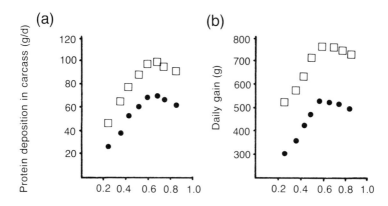

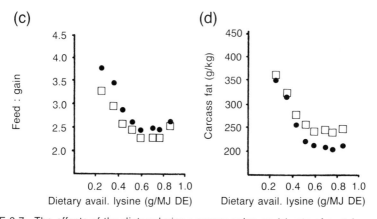

FIGURE 9.7   The effects of the dietary lysine : energy value on (a) rate of protein deposition, (b) growth rate, (c) feed to gain ratio and (d) carcass fat content of entire male pigs fed at 2.5 [ ● ] or 3.6 [ □ ] maintenance between 20 and 45 kg liveweight.

to energy ratio of the diet over the growth period. This has also been demonstrated very clearly by Fowler (1985) (see page 178).

The requirements for energy and protein are integrated in the formulation of a diet. Energy and protein do not act independently of each other, and one way of relating them sensibly is to consider the protein as a proportion of the energy supplied. This is sometimes called the nutritive ratio of the diet. The most useful means of expressing the relationship is as either protein in g of protein per MJ DE or as g of ideal protein per MJ DE or even as total or available lysine per MJ DE.

There is much confusion about what criteria should determine the optimum for the ratio of lysine to energy. This is illustrated in Figure 9.7. It can be seen that a higher ratio of available lysine to energy (7 g per MJ DE) is required to maximise the daily rate of protein or lean deposition in the carcass than is required to maximise the rate of liveweight gain (6 g per MJ DE).

*Protein requirement in relation to sex*
*Up to 50 kg liveweight.* From the data of Yen and others it has been clearly demonstrated that there are real differences between boars, gilts and castrates up to 55 kg liveweight, both in the growth rate of lean tissue and in the requirement for lysine expressed as g per MJ DE. However, in practical terms, one is considering a difference in requirement between boars and castrates of only about 0.1 per cent of lysine in the diet. Since the requirement is actually changing day by day over this whole growth period, it is not usually considered worthwhile to formulate separate diets for the different sexes.

*From 50 kg to 90 kg.* The differences in lean tissue growth rate between the sexes have already been shown to become much greater after 50 kg liveweight (see page 185). Because, for example, the boar is capable during this stage of growth of

Plate 9.2  Relative to castrates, entire male pigs grow lean more quickly, have less fat and convert nutrients more efficiently. To express their higher potential for lean meat deposition, they require higher levels of essential amino acids than castrates. (Courtesy of Pig International)

depositing 20% more lean tissue than the castrate, with the gilt intermediate, it is clear that matching the diets to these differences in lean growth potential is worthy of consideration. If we consider the work of Yen illustrated in Table 13.14 (page 365), the boar's requirement for lysine appears to be about 0.93% of the diet whereas requirements for the gilts (0.86%) and for the castrates (0.73%) are about 8% and 21% lower respectively. Since it is a widespread practice to separate the sexes so that they can be differentially restricted in feed allowance, these data also support strongly the case for providing diets which give extra lysine to gilts relative to castrates and to boars relative to gilts.

There is added support for this view from the work of Campbell in Australia involving the comparison of boars and gilts over the 50 to 90 kg weight range (see Table 9.12). The feed to gain ratio was optimised for the boars at a lysine ratio of 0.6 g of lysine per MJ DE, whereas that of gilts was optimised at a lysine to energy ratio of 0.5 g per MJ DE. These ratios correspond to lysine concentrations in a diet of 13 MJ DE per kg of 0.78 per cent and 0.65 per cent of the diet for boars and gilts respectively.

**TABLE 9.12     Effect of dietary lysine content on the feed:gain of boars (M) and gilts (F) growing from 20 to 50 and 50 to 90 kg liveweight**

|            |   | \multicolumn{8}{c}{Dietary lysine (g/MJ DE)} | | | | | | | |
|------------|---|------|------|------|------|------|------|------|------|
|            |   | 0.4  | 0.5  | 0.6  | 0.67 | 0.76 | 0.83 | 0.94 | 1.02 |
| 20–50 kg   | M | 3.3  | 2.9  | 2.6  | 2.4  | 2.2  | 2.2  | 2.3  | 2.3  |
|            | F | 3.3  | 2.9  | 2.6  | 2.4  | 2.25 | 2.3  | 2.4  | 2.4  |
| 50–90 kg   | M | 3.5  | 2.9  | 2.7  | 2.9  | 3.1  | 3.0  | 2.9  | 2.9  |
|            | F | 3.5  | 2.9  | 2.9  | 3.2  | 3.2  | 3.3  | 3.5  | 3.3  |

*Genotype*

With some strains of pig having been subjected to intensive genetic selection for lean tissue growth rate over the last decade in particular and with other strains being relatively unimproved, there is now wide variation between strains in lean tissue growth rate (see Figure 9.3). Strains A and B obviously differ markedly in lean tissue growth rate and it is expected that the levels of dietary lysine and of other essential amino acids required to support muscle growth would be higher for Strain A than for Strain B.

The work of Hardy, Bichard, Cooke and Curran (1979) similarly highlighted the potential of improved and unimproved genotypes (see Figure 9.8). Not only was there a marked difference in fatness at low daily intakes of protein between the improved (PIC Landrace) and the unimproved genotypes (Wye College Control Landrace), but also, as daily protein intake was increased, the unimproved genotype showed little or no response, whereas the improved genotype showed a marked reduction in backfat thickness. In other words, the improved pigs responded to more dietary protein by becoming even leaner. Indeed, the basic genetic advantage in terms of reduction in backfat at the lowest level of protein intake was doubled by increasing the daily protein intake.

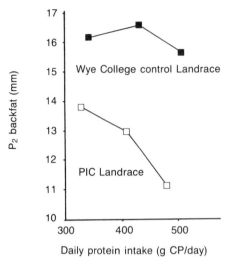

FIGURE 9.8 Comparison of backfats in a selected and control line in relation to daily intake of protein. (Source: Dalgety-Spillers Wye 6 Trial, 1979)

Thus, increasing attention must be paid to providing sufficient amino acids, energy and other essential nutrients in the diets of improved genotypes to allow them to express fully their superior genetic potential. Genetically improved pigs, therefore, even on the same diet and feed intake, can convert their feed to lean more efficiently than pigs which do not have the same amount of improved genes. In addition, improved pigs have the genetic capacity to respond economically to improved diets, whereas less developed strains show little response.

*Danger of providing excessive protein and amino acids*
As indicated in Figure 9.7, as the concentration of protein and essential amino acids was increased in the diet, there were marked responses in terms of higher protein deposition rate in the carcass, faster liveweight gain, reduced feed to gain ratio and reduced carcass fatness. However, after peak performance was attained in these traits, there were subsequent depressions in performance as protein and essential amino acid content of the diet were further increased.

The decline in performance when protein is in excess of the requirement is due to two factors. First, the excess protein must be removed from the body and this is done by a process known as deamination. This eventually leads to the kidneys excreting extra urea, which appears in the urine. This process uses energy which otherwise would be useful to the animal, and effectively the diet is less well utilised and performance impaired. The second factor is that some amino acids surplus to the tissue requirement circulate at high levels in the blood and exert the same effect as a toxin, making the animal feel unwell. This can be true of lysine, tryptophan and methionine.

Toxicity is much more likely to occur when the amino acid is supplied in the diet in a synthetic or crystalline form, as for example, lysine hydrochloride, than when it is a natural part of the dietary protein. The work of Batterham from Australia showed clearly that synthetic amino acids caused unnaturally high circulating levels of the amino acid in the blood shortly after feeding, with the further consequence that there was a rapid excretion of the amino acid via the urine. It is therefore very important to ensure that when additions of synthetic amino acids are made, the concentration is not allowed to exceed the recommended ratio to the other important amino acids in the diet which are represented in 'ideal protein' (see page 173).

The dilemma of the pig producer is to ensure that the diet supplies enough nutrients to allow the majority of his pigs to express their full lean tissue growth potential without at the same time wasting protein and possibly causing a reduction in performance in inferior pigs, e.g. castrates, which are receiving an excess of protein in relation to their needs. On balance, because the penalties for deficiency of protein tend to be greater than those for providing an excess, the economic optimum tends to be that which will meet or exceed the requirement of about 90 per cent of the pigs in the herd.

## Voluntary Feed Intake

The voluntary intake of feed by growing pigs has until recently been regarded as a problem for physiologists rather than one of concern to the pig producer. This was because the emphasis of the pig industry used to be directed towards the production of sides of bacon, and to produce the required degree of leanness it was necessary to restrict feed intake. A study of the feeding experiments on pigs conducted in the United Kingdom during the period from 1940 to the present time shows that a high proportion were concerned with finding optimal feeding scales for growing pigs. The classical experiments of McMeekan at Cambridge (1940 and 1941) were to a large extent responsible for giving authenticity to the strategy of feeding young pigs generously and older pigs very restrictedly.

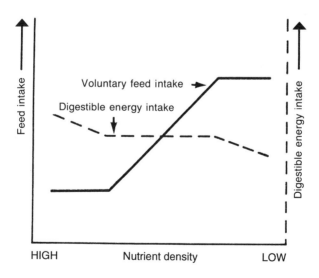

FIGURE 9.9   Relationship between the concentration of DE in the diet and the total daily feed intake. (From Cole, Hardy and Lewis, 1971)

## Reducing Voluntary Intake

Restricted feeding often entails additional work and expenditure compared with feeding to appetite because the feed must either be weighed or apportioned volumetrically to each pen. For this reason, bacon producers have been interested in alternative means of reducing intake. One approach is to incorporate in the diet certain ingredients which dilute the diet or which inhibit the intake of feed. Because the pig has only a very limited capacity to digest cellulose, plant materials which contain a high proportion of cell wall tend to be very indigestible. When the diet contains a high proportion of these materials, the pig may actually increase its intake in an attempt to compensate for a reduction in the digestible energy of the diet. However, if the digestible energy concentration is steadily reduced, then a point is reached when the pig can no longer compensate for the diluting effect and the total daily intake is thereby reduced (see Figure 9.9).

The subject has been extensively reviewed over the years, for example, by Cole, Hardy and Lewis (1972) and by Braude (1968 and 1972), and it is not our purpose to explore the quantitative aspects in depth. There are, however, some aspects of principle which merit some mention. The addition of materials to the diet which are low in energy may have an effect on other more positive components. For example, there may be a reduction in the utilisation of protein, because the fibre acts as a sponge, holding proteins and amino acids in its structure. It may also block the access of hydrolytic enzymes to the protein and physically prevent hydrolysed proteins being presented to the absorptive surfaces of the small intestine. The problem is not only related to protein but may affect other nutrients, for example, zinc can become unavailable because it is bound to the fibre.

In practice, it is extremely difficult for many commercial pig units to dispose of the effluent from intensive units even at its normal rate of production. The increase which would result from the use of indigestible materials would bring additional costs and exacerbate what is already a critical problem in many countries.

An alternative approach to reducing intake is to incorporate unpleasant but nontoxic substances in the diet. Blair and Fitzsimmons (1970) added a particularly bitter substance known commercially as Bitrex (benzyldiethyl 2:6-xylylcarbumoyl methyl ammonium benzoate) to the diet. This substance was claimed to be ten to twenty times more bitter than brucine or quassin. However, inclusion of this material had no long term effect on intake even when concentrations reached 50 ppm.

## Increasing Voluntary Intake

For the reasons discussed above, the problem of enhancing intakes has not until recently been considered a real one. However, several factors have come together in modern pig production which make it apparent that, in some circumstances, there could be an improvement in efficiency if the normal daily intakes of digestible nutrients could be increased. First, the new genetic strains of pig are substantially leaner than hitherto, and with them has come the suggestion from the processing industry that some pigs are too lean for the market. Secondly, the increasing use of boars instead of castrates leads to a shift towards leanness in the population and

**TABLE 9.13  Voluntary intake of feed by boars, castrates and gilts growing between 30 and 90 kg**

|                     | Boars | Castrates | Gilts |
|---------------------|-------|-----------|-------|
| MJ DE/day           | 33.4  | 37.8      | 37.1  |
| kg feed/day (13 MJ DE/kg) | 2.57  | 2.91      | 2.85  |

(Source: Fowler, 1985)

with it an actual reduction in voluntary food intake. The difference in the actual intake of boars, castrates and gilts is illustrated in data from the Rowett Research Institute given in Table 9.13.

It is evident that when pigs are sufficiently lean, it is no longer possible to increase efficiency by the substitution of energy-rich fatty tissue by lean tissue with a high water content. In this circumstance the only way forward is to improve the rate of production by increasing feed intake, thereby reducing the overhead costs of production associated with time. An obvious parallel is the broiler chicken and the turkey, where genetic improvement over recent years has been associated with a reduction in days to slaughter weight and an increase in daily feed intake.

## Carcass Weight and Meat Processing in Relation to Optimum Nutrient Intake

A third factor, but rather less obvious to those with a mainly biological outlook, is the change which has occurred in the technology of processing carcasses. For the bacon market, it was traditional in the 'Wiltshire' type cure for the side to be marketed whole with no further processing until it was cut on a slicing machine in front of the customer. This meant that the adjustment of the ratio of fat to lean was a primary responsibility of the farmer. However, modern methods of packaging, cutting and curing have introduced far greater flexibility within the factory for meeting the needs of the consumer. There are two interesting historical examples of the effect of this approach. In the 1960s there was a major initiative by an influential processing group in Britain to promote the so-called 'heavy hog' (Bellis, Friedlander and Trenchard 1960 and Friedlander 1961).

The purpose was to take pigs which had been fed to appetite to heavy weights (120 kg liveweight) and then during processing to direct the lean to one market and the fat to another. A detailed scientific investigation of this approach was conducted by Braude, Townsend and Harrington (1963).

These authors looked at the biological and economic efficiency of four systems of production, with pigs of bacon weight (about 91 kg liveweight) fed either to a scale or to appetite, and pigs fed ad lib. to a heavier liveweight (about 118 kg) with high or low protein in the diet. Their results showed that the pigs fed to 91 kg used quite a similar ratio of feed per kg of lean gain (11.4 and 11.9 kg respectively). The heavier pigs were notably less efficient at producing lean in terms of the amount of feed required per unit of lean tissue produced. Feed per kg of lean gain was 13.5 kg on the high protein diet and 14.7 kg on the low protein diet. This experiment was widely held to show that ad lib. feeding, particularly to heavy weight, was biologically and economically unsound.

This may well have been true at the time of the experiment, but since then many things have changed. First, the genotype of the animal has altered so that animals are now putting down more lean in each unit of liveweight gain even at these higher weights. This results in much greater efficiency of feed conversion in the later stages of growth than was possible only a decade ago. Secondly, in relative terms, the cost of feed is lower in relation to the value of the carcass. Although this is not a chapter based on economic criteria, it is easy to see that the optimal slaughter weight depends on the relative value of what is produced and what it costs to produce it. For example, if feed is almost infinitely expensive, then all other things being equal, one would wish to slaughter the animals as early as possible. However, if feed costs virtually nothing, then, provided that feeding the animals produces something of value, one would continue feeding pigs to as high a weight as possible. This simple example serves to give some idea of the underlying principle.

## LEAN TISSUE RESPONSES TO FEED INTAKE

In the results of many years' testing the commercial products of different breeding companies by the Meat and Livestock Commission in Britain (CPE tests), we have an accumulation of very important data on pigs of different genotypes killed at three liveweights, namely, 60, 90 and 113 kg, and fed at two levels, restricted and to appetite. Using these data, it is possible to show the effect of killing weight and feeding level on the efficiency of production of lean tissues.

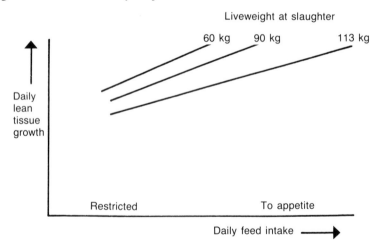

FIGURE 9.10   The lean tissue growth rate per day of pigs fed restrictedly and to appetite to three liveweights at slaughter (based on the mean of the CPE Results, Tests 6 to 8, MLC, 1980).

The results for CPE tests 3 to 6 were averaged over all companies and the lean tissue growth rate plotted against the daily feed intake for pigs up to the three finishing weights (see Figure 9.10). Although the slope of response of lean tissue growth is lower for the heavier pigs, it is still very positive showing that there is, even in these heavy pigs, an increase in the amount of lean deposited each day at the higher feed levels.

This is the biology of the response and it is important to appreciate it, since there is a widely held belief that increasing the feed intake of heavy pigs merely results in the production of fatty tissue. Whether it is economic or not to increase feed intake depends on the costs of feed and the value of the resulting carcass, and this aspect is developed further in Chapters 16 and 20.

## ADDITIONAL READING

Agricultural Research Council (1981), *The Nutrient Requirements of Pigs*, Commonwealth Agricultural Bureaux, Slough, England.

Campbell R. G. and King R. H. (1982), 'The Influence of Dietary Protein and Level of Feeding on the Growth Performance and Carcass Characteristics of Entire and Castrated Male Pigs', *Anim. Prod.* **35**, 177–184.

Campbell R. G., Taverner M. R. and Curic D. M. (1983), 'The Influence of Feeding Level from 20 to 45 kg Liveweight on the Performance and Body Composition of Female and Entire Male Pigs', *Anim. Prod.* **36**, 193–199.

Campbell, R. G., Taverner M. R. and Curic D. M. (1984), 'Effect of Feeding Level and Dietary Protein Content on the Growth, Body Composition and Rate of Protein Deposition in Pigs Growing from 45 to 90 kg', *Anim. Prod.* **38**, 233–240.

Cole D. J. A. and Haresign W. (Eds) (1985), *Recent Developments in Pig Nutrition*, Butterworths, London.

Fuller M. F. (1985), 'Sex differences in the Nutrition and Growth of Pigs', *Recent Developments in Pig Nutrition* Eds. D. J. A. Cole and W. Haresign, 177–189, Butterworths, London.

MacDonald P., Edwards R. A., and Greenhalgh J. F. D. (1988), *Animal Nutrition*, Longman, London.

*Pork Industry Handbook*, USA Co-operative Extension Service, University of Illinois at Urbana-Champaign, USA.

## Chapter 10

# Feeds and Feeding

Feeding pigs economically on appropriate diets is at the very heart of the business of growing pigs. Wrong judgements in this area can lead quickly to financial difficulty and a host of problems which may at first sight not appear to be related to the diet. The safeguards are either to buy expertise from a feed company or adviser or to familiarise oneself with the principles of nutrition, some of which are presented in the previous chapter; one must also become aware of the important characteristics of feed ingredients and the basis of diet construction and feeding methods.

### OBJECTIVES IN DIET FORMULATION

A great many decisions must be taken in arriving at a diet formulation although at first sight it may not appear so. The simplest situation is that which prevails in the United States, where it is economical to formulate diets by combining just three basic elements: an energy source (corn), a protein-rich source (extracted soya bean meal) and a mix of vitamins and minerals (some proprietary mixture).

At first sight these corn-soya diets are simplicity itself. However, even in this situation there are several problems for the farmer. They can be listed as follows:

1. What is the optimum ratio of corn to soya?
2. How many diets and different ratios of protein to energy (soya to corn) do I need to feed my stock adequately from 20 to 100 kg?
3. How good is my stock genetically?
4. What is the most cost-effective ratio of protein to energy in relation to the quality of pig which my market demands and which will help to maximise margin between carcass value and production costs?
5. Do I achieve the protein and protein quality I require in the final diet by the ratios of corn and soya that I use?
6. Should I feed the diet to appetite or should I restrict?
7. Is the mineral and vitamin supplement adequate?
8. Is the diet deteriorating during storage?
9. Is the soya bean adequately treated to remove trypsin inhibitor and other anti-nutritive factors?
10. Is the corn free of moulds and toxins such as vomitoxin, aflatoxin and zearalenone?

There are a host of other questions one might ask about the opportunities either for making the diet more cheaply by, for example, using by-products or for making it more effective by, for example, the use of synthetic lysine or the addition of a high fat supplement. Solving these problems or at least appreciating them well enough not to make grave mistakes makes the task of understanding nutrition worth while. In fact, a little understanding, though often rightly said to be dangerous, can protect the farmer from exploitation. The uncertainties, although real enough, make the farmer vulnerable to the unscrupulous salesmen who might manipulate the farmer's natural anxieties, and by a series of skilfully phrased remarks, persuade the farmer that he is on the brink of biological and economic disaster if he fails to buy some product.

## CHOOSING NUTRITIONAL TARGETS

The first step in formulating the basis of a feeding programme is to decide on the nutritional objectives. From the previous chapter on principles of nutrition it is clear that the diet should meet the nutritional needs of the animal after allowing a margin of safety for storage losses or inexact information about the raw materials used.

### Targets for Protein and Animo Acid Concentration and Protein to Energy Ratio

The danger of providing targets in a book is that they should somehow become a rule which holds regardless of circumstances. The secret of making pigs profitable is to choose the right balance between feed quality, feed price and the performance of the animals, including carcass quality and the price obtained for carcasses. However, there is always some value in providing guidelines for conventional circumstances even though one recognises that only rarely is a farmer's circumstance conventional.

### Energy Density

The concept of energy density relates to the amount of digestible energy which is contained in 1 kg of air dry feed. A conventional barley and soya bean diet would contain about 13 MJ DE per kg and a diet for early weaned pigs containing added fat might be as high as 18 MJ DE per kg. Many feedstuff companies make a great play on the phrase, 'high density diet', but such a description is useless unless the digestible energy content is specified. For some, a diet based on either wheat or maize rather than on barley is an adequate justification for calling it 'high energy' even though the MJ per kg may only change from 13 to 14 MJ of digestible energy (DE). The main determinants of energy density of a diet are the amounts it contains of relatively indigestible materials such as fibre and ash and of high energy components such as lipid or fat. Many equations exist to calculate the digestible energy of a diet from its chemical analysis. An example of such an equation is given in Table 10.1.

**TABLE 10.1  Prediction of DE in an air-dry diet (about 87 per cent dry matter)**

$$DE = 14.2 + 0.023\ CP + 0.22\ L - 0.28\ CF - 0.45\ A$$

where:

CP = % crude protein
 L = % lipid or oil or ether extract
CF = % crude fibre
 A = % ash.

For example, let us consider a diet containing:

Crude protein = 16%
Lipid         = 5.0%
Crude fibre   = 4.0%
Ash           = 3.5%.

Then DE = $14.2 + 0.023 \times 16 + 0.22 \times 5 - 0.28 \times 4 - 0.45 \times 3.5$,
giving          $14.2 + 0.416 + 1.1 - 1.12 - 1.575$,
which is        13.02 MJ.

Diets which have a high nutrient density are most suitable for young pigs and diets with a lower nutrient density can be used with pigs from 40 kg onwards. Baby pigs of 2 to 3 weeks of age do not digest rough fibrous material well and grow very slowly and can lose much of their body fat reserves if fed on a diet of a density of less than 14.5 MJ DE per kg. On the other hand, growing pigs can perform well on diets as low as 12 MJ DE. Diets of a lower DE than this may slow growth down because the daily intake of DE may be reduced. This latter feature is sometimes used in designing diets to improve the carcass grading of pigs fed under conditions of relatively free access to feed (so called ad lib. feeding). Suggested energy densities in diets for pigs of different liveweights are given in Table 10.2.

**TABLE 10.2  Useful targets\* for feed formulation**

| | | Nutrients per kg of fresh feed | |
| Liveweight range (kg) | MJ DE | Protein (g) | Total lysine (g) |
|---|---|---|---|
| 10–20 | 17 | 230 | 16.0 |
| 20–40 | 15 | 200 | 13.0 |
| 40–60 | 14 | 190 | 11.0 |
| 60–80 | 13 | 170 | 9.5 |
| 80–100 | 12.5 | 150 | 7.5 |

\* Note that the targets are set slightly above the theoretical requirements given in Table 9.5 to allow for variation in feed constituents and in availability of lysine.

### Protein and Amino Acid Concentrations in Diets

This is an area of great controversy because of the complexity of balancing the added cost of a diet containing more protein and amino acids with the added return of faster growth, better feed conversion and better carcass quality. There is no exact solution to suit a particular pig unit all of the time. This constitutes a great frustration to those whose manner of reasoning demands an unvarying rule to apply to their own situation.

There are several points to be borne in mind in trying to determine the most cost-effective level of protein and amino acids in the diet. The first is that every farmer is dealing with a population of pigs. At any one time, pigs within a herd on the same diet will be of different sex, genetic quality, weight, age, health status, appetite and social dominance. This means that the requirement of each individual pig is rarely met exactly by the diet.

This gives rise to a very important concept in nutrition, which is that it is the response of the group as a whole which is important, not that of the best individual. For example, a farmer who strives to increase the proportion of his carcasses in the top grade from 90 to 95 per cent by improving the quality of his diet is aiming to affect only 1 in 20 of his pigs. In other words, the added feed cost for 19 pigs produces no benefit from them and must be offset by the increase in value of the twentieth pig. The appropriate concentration of protein and amino acids in the diet is therefore decided by the point at which too few pigs in the population are showing a response, not when every pig has reached its full potential (see Figure 10.1).

If we could measure the response of a single pig or of a very similar group of pigs identical to each other in almost every material respect, then the response of lean tissue deposition to increasing concentrations of protein and amino acids in the diet is linear until the requirement is satisfied and then it settles on a plateau. (See Figure 10.1.) This has been shown by the very elegant work of Campbell and Taverner in Australia. However, when a normal population of pigs is considered, the series of plateaux for each individual pig combines to form a response curve. This is shown in Figure 10.1.

A guide as to what concentrations of energy and protein would produce maximum performance in about 85 per cent of a healthy population of high performance genotypes, kept in a thermoneutral environment and with high class accommodation, is given in Table 10.2.

## FORMULATING DIETS

The formulation of diets from a range of ingredients is more complicated than merely meeting the nutrient requirements. Ingredients differ in their suitability for providing nutrients. Some like rapeseed meal contain toxins. Others are not palatable, such as blood meal, and others are suitable for older pigs but cause allergic reactions in young pigs, as does, for example, extracted soya bean. There are also ingredients which may be damaged by moulding, for example, badly stored grain. Formulating diets then is combining those ingredients which not only meet the nutrient requirements at least cost, but also at least risk.

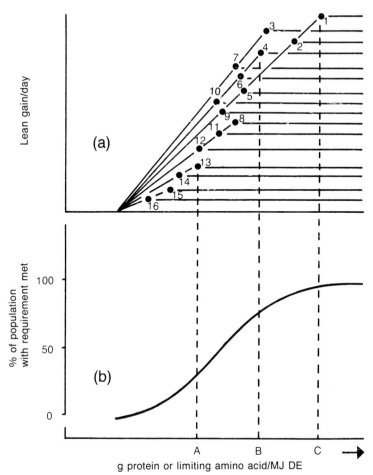

FIGURE 10.1   Diagram of the response curves of lean growth of 16 individual pigs to protein or the limiting amino acid (a) and the percentage of pigs which have their requirement met (b). It can be seen that each of the 16 individual pigs in this population or pen responds to increasing protein or limiting amino acid per MJ DE in a linear manner until their own specific requirement is satisfied, after which they show no further response, i.e. a plateau is reached. If the provision of protein or the first limiting amino acid is at point:

   A — the requirements of only pigs 12, 13, 14, 15 and 16 are met
   B — the requirements of all pigs except 1, 2 and 3 are met
   C — the requirements of all pigs are met

At level C the requirement of pig 1 is just met but we are wasting protein and essential amino acids on all the other 15 pigs.

At level A we are failing to meet the requirement of 11 out of the 16 pigs in the pen, i.e. of about 70%.

At level B we only fail to meet the requirement of 3 out of 16 pigs in the pen, i.e. less than 20%.

In many situations the most economical provision of protein and essential amino acids relative to energy in the diet will be around point B.

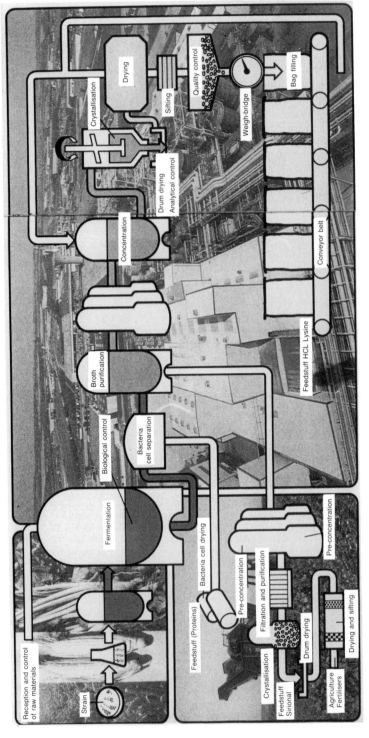

Plate 10.1 Synthetic lysine, methionine, cystine and threonine are now used widely in pig diets to meet nutrient requirements at lower cost. The picture shows an industrial plant producing synthetic lysine from purified carbohydrate and inorganic sources of nitrogen. (Courtesy of Eurolysine)

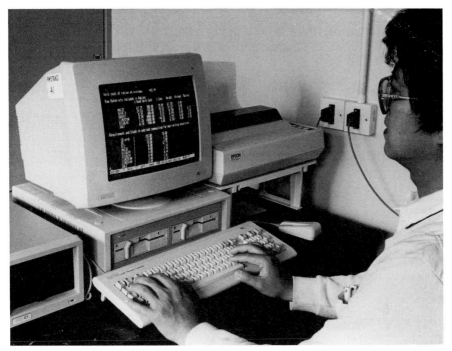

Plate 10.2   The computer is now a very essential piece of equipment in the hands of feedstuff manufacturers. It is used to guide the sounder purchase of raw materials and to formulate diets by linear programming which will meet the nutrient requirements of the pigs at lowest possible cost. It is also used to calculate the most cost-effective feeding programme for each class of pig.

## Least-cost Diet Programming

The tool that is most widely used in diet formulation by professionals is the computer-based least-cost ration programme. The essence of this technique is that one enters into the computer programme a set of rules and a data base on the composition of ingredients and their cost. The programme then solves a series of hundreds of equations, to arrive at a formulation which meets the specifications for the diet at a minimum cost. Generally, there is only one unique combination of ingredients which will do this, and this is the end product of the calculations carried out by the least-cost ration programme.

Because of the revolution in business computing it is possible that many readers may have some access to a least-cost ration programme and will at least wish to know some of the inputs which are necessary. To operate the programme, at least four types of information are required:

1.  The data base giving the nutrient composition of the available ingredients (see Tables 9.2 and 9.5 and Appendix 1 for example).
2.  The current prices of the ingredients.

*(text continued on page 212)*

**TABLE 10.3   Examples of constraints and solutions in formulating a least-cost early weaning (weaner 1) diet (6 to 12 kg liveweight)**

| | Constraints | | | |
| --- | --- | --- | --- | --- |
| | Min.* (%) | Max.† (%) | Price (£/tonne) | Solution (kg/tonne) |
| *Cereals* | | | | |
| Barley | 0.0 | 0.0 | 100.0 | 0.0 |
| Maize | 0.0 | 0.0 | 130.0 | 0.0 |
| Wheat | 0.0 | 0.0 | 100.0 | 0.0 |
| Breakfast oats | 0.0 | 9999.9§ | 251.0 | 326.0 |
| Flaked maize | 20.0 | 20.0 | 185.0 | 200.0 |
| *Protein sources* | | | | |
| Fishmeal | 15.0 | 15.0 | 300.0 | 150.0 |
| Soya bean | 0.0 | 0.0 | 200.0 | 0.0 |
| Soya bean (dehulled) | 0.0 | 0.0 | 220.0 | 0.0 |
| Soya bean (full fat) | 0.0 | 5.0 | 190.0 | 50.0 |
| Dried skim milk | 0.0 | 9999.9§ | 750.0 | 209.5 |
| Lysine hydrochloride | 0.12 | 0.12 | 2000.0 | 2.0 |
| *Others* | | | | |
| Weatings | 0.0 | 0.0 | 125.0 | 0.0 |
| Vegetable oil | 6.0 | 6.0 | 500.0 | 60.0 |
| *Minerals* | | | | |
| Salt | 0.0 | 9999.9§ | 300.0‡ | 0.0 |
| Dicalcium phosphate | 0.0 | 9999.9§ | 300.0‡ | 0.0 |
| Limestone flour | 0.0 | 9999.9§ | 300.0‡ | 0.0 |
| Copper sulphate | 0.10 | 0.10 | 400.0 | 1.0 |
| *Vitamins and Minerals* | 0.15 | 0.15 | 400.0 | 1.5 |
| *Additives* | 0.0 | 0.0 | 0.0 | 0.0 |
| *Analysis* | | | | |
| Digestible Energy (DE) MJ/kg | 17.0 | 9999.9§ | — | 17.0 |
| Crude protein          g/kg | 250.0 | 9999.9§ | — | 250.0 |
| Lysine                 g/kg | 16.0 | 9999.9§ | — | 16.0 |
| Calcium                g/kg | 10.0 | 9999.9§ | — | 13.7 |
| Phosphorus             g/kg | 8.0 | 9999.9§ | — | 9.7 |
| Sodium                 g/kg | 2.0 | 2.5 | — | 2.2 |
| Lysine (g per MJ of DE) | | | | 0.94 |
| *Cost per Tonne of Diet* | | | | £364.4 |

*Minimum percentage inclusion in the diet
†Maximum percentage inclusion in the diet
‡Artificially high price to prevent use as a filler.
§Excessive maximum to indicate no upper limit of inclusion.

**TABLE 10.4 Examples of constraints and solutions in formulating a least-cost grower diet (25 to 60 kg liveweight)**

| | Constraints | | | |
| | Min.* (%) | Max.† (%) | Price (£/tonne) | Solution (kg/tonne) |
|---|---|---|---|---|
| *Cereals* | | | | |
| Barley | 0.0 | 9999.9§ | 117.0 | 474.7 |
| Maize | 10.0 | 10.0 | 150.0 | 100.0 |
| Wheat | 10.0 | 10.0 | 125.0 | 100.0 |
| *Protein sources* | | | | |
| Fishmeal | 5.0 | 5.0 | 300.0 | 50.0 |
| Soya bean | 0.0 | 9999.9§ | 200.0 | 247.4 |
| Soya bean (dehulled) | 0.0 | 0.0 | 220.0 | 0.0 |
| Soya bean (full fat) | 0.0 | 5.0 | 250.0 | 0.0 |
| Dried skim milk | 0.0 | 9999.9§ | 750.0 | 0.0 |
| Lysine hydrochloride | 0.0 | 0.0 | 2000.0 | 0.0 |
| *Others* | | | | |
| Weatings | 0.0 | 9999.9§ | 150.0 | 0.0 |
| Vegetable oil | 0.0 | 9999.9§ | 500.0 | 0.0 |
| *Minerals* | | | | |
| Salt | 0.0 | 9999.9§ | 68.0 | 5.0 |
| Dicalcium phosphate | 0.0 | 9999.9§ | 200.0‡ | 19.0 |
| Limestone flour | 0.0 | 9999.9§ | 150.0‡ | 1.4 |
| Copper sulphate | 0.10 | 0.10 | 400.0 | 1.0 |
| *Vitamins and Minerals* | 0.15 | 0.15 | 400.0 | 1.5 |
| *Additives* | 0.0 | 0.0 | 0.0 | 0.0 |
| *Analysis* | | | | |
| Digestible Energy (DE) MJ/kg | 13.25 | 9999.9§ | – | 13.25 |
| Crude protein g/kg | 200.0 | 9999.9§ | – | 200.0 |
| Lysine g/kg | 10.5 | 9999.9§ | – | 10.5 |
| Calcium g/kg | 10.0 | 9999.9§ | – | 10.0 |
| Phosphorus g/kg | 8.0 | 9999.9§ | – | 9.0 |
| Sodium g/kg | 2.0 | 5.0 | – | 3.13 |
| Lysine (g per MJ of DE) | | | | 0.79 |
| *Cost per Tonne of Diet* | | | | £150.1 |

*Minimum percentage inclusion in the diet
†Maximum percentage inclusion in the diet
‡Artificially high price to prevent use as a filler.
§Excessive maximum to indicate no upper limit of inclusion.

3.  The nutrient constraints for the type of diet required, that is, maximum and minimum acceptable levels of such nutrients as protein, lysine, sodium and digestible energy.
4.  The ingredient constraints giving the maximum and minimum for each ingredient in terms of the permissible amounts in the diet, e.g. one may wish to include some whey powder and set the minimum for 5 per cent. However, because of the high ash content it would be advisable to set the maximum at 20 per cent.

In learning the technique, it is best to start with very simple diets containing three or four ingredients with few nutritional constraints, because it is very easy to pose problems which are not feasible, either because no combination of the ingredients available can meet the nutrient constraints or because the problem can be solved in more than one way.

Examples of constraints and solutions are given in Tables 10.3 and 10.4.

### Designing Diets

Although the least-cost ration programme has an important role in the construction of diet formulations, it cannot replace the insights of a skilled nutritionist. The solutions found by the programme are an exact solution of the problem, but the resulting diet may not make nutritional sense. The nutritionist in fact is not only trying to produce an inexpensive diet which meets the formal nutrient requirements, but is also trying to give due weight to the other aspects of the diet which are less easily defined. This includes factors such as the suitability of the final mix for the digestive tract of the pig, particularly in the case of early weaning diets, the risk involved in using certain ingredients of doubtful origin and also consideration of the palatability of ingredients. There are also the physical characteristics of the diet to be considered, such as whether it can be mixed easily or whether the final mix will be suitable for pelleting. Some of the important considerations are given below.

### Diets for Newly Weaned Pigs

Making up diets which are suitable for very young weaned pigs requires a certain understanding of the capabilities of the digestive tract of the baby pig. Because weaning pigs at three weeks of age or even less has been practised on a wide scale on a routine basis, it is easy to become convinced that the dietary requirements are fairly simple. In fact, the successful early weaning of pigs has depended very heavily on the skills of the feed manufacturer and the company nutritionist. A considerable amount of scientific attention has been given to the nutritional problems of the early weaned pig and it is only possible to give a very brief indication of this background. To understand the problems it is helpful to consider the developmental process from birth.

Sow's milk is a very special food. Most people are aware, of course, of the supreme importance of the milk secreted by the sow at farrowing and during the first 24 hours of the lactation. This milk, called colostrum, contains very important special proteins known as immunoglobulins. These help the piglet to combat disease and protect it against many of the specific potential diseases associated with any particular herd. There are several types of immunoglobulin, the main three being IgA, IgM and IgG, and the piglet needs a minimum amount of all of them. The really surprising aspect of this period of the piglet's life is that for the first 24 hours after birth, these proteins can cross the wall of the gut and enter the bloodstream. This is unique because in another day or two, the character of the gut changes and these proteins no longer can be absorbed intact. That is why it is so important for the piglet to gain access to them in the first 24 hours of life. Colostrum given later in life is digested in the normal way but is not of any special benefit apart from its nutritional value. In the bloodstream and tissues the colostral proteins have two effects. First they provide what is known as passive protection, that is, they protect the piglet directly from infections which gain access through the gut and lungs or even through damaged skin. Secondly, it now appears that the piglet can to some extent make its own copies of colostral proteins and so build up its own immune system and produce what is called active immunity. It can readily be appreciated that obtaining an adequate supply of colostrum is not only crucial to the immediate health of the piglet but also for its long-term health as well.

It is a surprise to some people that normal milk also contains immunoglobulins which are important to the piglet, the most important one being IgA, which as we have seen is also present in colostrum. IgA in milk exerts its important effect actually within the lumen of the gut, where it helps to prevent the growth of unfavourable bacteria, such as certain strains of *E. coli*, and also suppresses the effect of certain disease-causing viruses such as corona virus and rotavirus. When the piglet is weaned, the protection against infection conferred by the IgA is instantly lost, making the piglet very vulnerable to gastric and enteric infection.

The art of formulating diets for baby pigs is to recognise how vulnerable the immature gut is at this stage to digestive upset and formulate diets which simulate as far as is reasonable the composition of natural milk from the sow. It is not possible to provide immunoglobulins in the way the sow did but it is possible to go some way towards producing diets which mirror the nutrients provided in milk without using 100 per cent bovine milk but a proportion of cheaper ingredients. To do this, it is essential to understand the other important features of sow's milk.

The major nutrients in sow's milk and the basic chemical composition are shown in Table 10.5. This shows that if one considers the energy content, over half of this

**TABLE 10.5** **Composition and proportions of gross energy in each component of sow's milk**

| Component | g per kg fresh milk | kJ of gross energy per kg fresh milk | % of total gross energy |
|---|---|---|---|
| Lipid | 75 | 293 | 56 |
| Protein | 60 | 144 | 28 |
| Lactose | 50 | 85 | 16 |

is in the form of fat whilst the rest is divided between the highly digestible milk sugar, or lactose, and protein. The composition of milk indicates the capabilities of the digestive tract of the piglet at this age.

LIPID OR FAT

The lipid is presented by the mammary gland of the sow in an emulsified form. It is easily assimilated because the baby pig has an abundant supply from its pancreas of the very powerful fat-digesting enzyme called lipase, which partly breaks fats down so that they can be absorbed. It is not surprising, therefore, to find that some of the most successful diets for early weaned pigs contain in the formulation up to 15 per cent of high-quality lipid even though this makes the technology of diet mixing rather more difficult than it would be for lipid concentrations of 6 per cent or less. The most useful fats are those which have a low melting point such as the high-quality vegetable oils like soya, coconut or maize oil. It is crucial that these should be protected against oxidation by the addition of antioxidants such as ethoxyquin; otherwise during storage and in the heat of the pig housing they may oxidise and give rise to the fatal condition of mulberry heart.

PROTEINS

Sow's milk contains highly digestible proteins such as casein and albumins which are perfectly balanced in terms of their amino acid content. However, it is not enough just to provide alternative proteins in the diets which have a reasonable profile of amino acids. Proteins in plants, for example, are often difficult to digest because of their chemical structure. In some cases, specific proteins cause a violent reaction in the gut and are said to be allergenic because the reaction resembles that of an allergic response. When this happens, the gut wall becomes very inflamed and the surface cells become distorted. The finger-like projections from the lining of the gut called villi, which are important for absorption of nutrients into the bloodstream, collapse and the gut becomes very vulnerable to infection. Although in some animals almost any protein can cause this response, it is most frequently encountered when vegetable proteins are suddenly introduced into the diet. The immune system must become accustomed to the new protein, and this takes time. The reaction is quite common in very young pigs and much less likely to occur after they reach an age of about 40 to 50 days. In humans, some life-long allergies are now thought to be initiated by premature exposure of very young babies to non-milk foods. The condition known as gluten intolerance or coeliac disease, is an example of a condition which may be provoked in humans by giving babies food which contains wheat at too early an age.

In the pig, the major problems arise with proteins such as those in soya bean. Soya bean can cause severe allergenic responses in young pigs, whether it has been processed by heating or not. All categories of soya bean such as dehulled, full fat or just extracted and toasted can cause a violent reaction. Piglets so affected grow slowly, exhibit rapid loss of body fat and, in the absence of high concentrations of antibiotic, scour badly. The spine becomes prominent, the piglets become dejected and hairy and show a characteristic lack-lustre appearance.

Proteins which are much less likely to cause these symptoms are those derived from dairy products such as dried skimmed milk and whey. High-quality fishmeal, preferably made from fresh whole fish, is a good substitute for milk proteins. A small amount of very high-quality meat meal can also be used. Ideally proteins from soya bean, rapeseed or other oilseed residues should not be fed, particularly when the piglet is first weaned. However, as the piglet develops, a small amount of vegetable protein sources like soya bean meal may be incorporated but it must be introduced slowly into the feeding regime to allow the piglet to develop tolerance to it.

SUGARS

Milk sugar or lactose is a very special sugar uniquely found in nature in the milk of mammals. It provides energy for the piglet because enzymes in the gut split it into two absorbable units, glucose and galactose. However, it also encourages the development of a favourable bacterial flora, particularly associated with the presence of lactobacillus, which results in the conversion of lactose to lactic acid. This results in the contents of the gut having a tendency towards acidity, which is an environment in which many pathogenic bacteria do not flourish. In a sense, there is a natural antibiotic effect from the build-up of lactic acid in the gut. At weaning much of this beneficial effect can be lost just at the moment when it is most needed, especially if weaning around 3 weeks of age. It is therefore prudent to keep a proportion of the diet for early weaned pigs as milk powder and whey products.

CARBOHYDRATES

The natural carbohydrate in sows' milk is lactose. When weaned, piglets are often overwhelmed with a new carbohydrate, namely the starch in cereals. Piglets can handle starch only after they have developed a particular series of enzymes of which the most important is amylase. This takes a little time to develop properly and in sufficient amounts. Raw starch can be quite indigestible for the very young piglet because it is in the form of crystalline starch grains. Cooking, or heat treatment such as flaking, ruptures these grains and makes them much more digestible. Even adult humans are not in the habit of eating any quantity of raw grain and it is not really reasonable to expect the delicate digestive tract of a newly weaned piglet to cope with raw material the instant after being removed from a diet of milk.

Examples of starter (weaner 1) and second stage (weaner 2) diets for newly weaned pigs are included in Tables 10.6 and 10.7, and they reflect the principles outlined above. The high inclusion rate in the 'newly weaned' diet (6 to 12 kg liveweight) of cooked or flaked cereals (46 per cent), of milk by-products (25 per cent), of fishmeal (15 per cent), of high quality vegetable oil (8 per cent) and of glucose (5 per cent) takes the digestive capabilities of such immature pigs into account.

## DIETS FOR GROWING AND FINISHING PIGS

There is much more room for manoeuvre in the choice of ingredients for growing pigs than there is for pigs which have been recently weaned or which are relatively immature. The enzyme systems are much more effective and dietary factors which in a young animal might cause an allergic response, such as for example extracted soya bean meal, do not usually cause problems in older animals.

*(text continued on page 218)*

**TABLE 10.6　Specimen diets in Europe**

| | Weaner 1 | Weaner 2 | Early grower | Grower | Bacon | Heavy |
|---|---|---|---|---|---|---|
| Liveweight (kg) | 6–12 | 12–20 | 20–40 | 40–65 | 65–90 | 90–120 |
| | | | (kg per tonne) | | | |
| *Cereals* | | | | | | |
| Barley | – | 89.7 | 246.6 | 394.2 | 548.0 | 726.3 |
| Maize | – | – | – | – | – | – |
| Wheat | – | 100.0 | 200.0 | 350.0 | 200.0 | – |
| Breakfast oats | 262.4 | 125.0 | – | – | – | – |
| Flaked maize (ground) | 100.0 | 100.0 | 100.0 | – | – | – |
| Flaked wheat (ground) | 100.0 | 100.0 | 150.0 | – | – | – |
| *Protein sources* | | | | | | |
| Fishmeal | 150.0 | 150.0 | 125.0 | 50.0 | – | – |
| Soya bean | – | – | – | 81.8 | 125.9 | 50.7 |
| Soya bean (Dehulled) | – | – | 50.0 | 100.0 | – | – |
| Soya bean (full fat) | – | 92.8 | 75.0 | – | – | – |
| Dried skim milk | 200.0 | 100.0 | – | – | – | – |
| Rapeseed meal (Canola)‡ | – | – | – | – | 100.0 | 100.0 |
| Lysine hydrochloride | 2.0 | 1.7 | 2.0 | – | – | – |
| *Others* | | | | | | |
| Weatings | – | – | – | – | – | 100.0 |
| Vegetable oil | 80.0 | 85.5 | 46.0 | – | – | – |
| Whey powder | 50.0 | 50.0 | – | – | – | – |
| Glucose | 50.0 | – | – | – | – | – |
| *Minerals* | | | | | | |
| Salt | 2.6 | 2.3 | 2.4 | 3.7 | 4.6 | 5.3 |
| Dicalcium phosphate | – | – | 10.0 | 8.3 | 3.8 | – |
| Limestone flour | – | – | – | 9.0 | 14.7 | 15.2 |
| Copper sulphate (hydrated)* | 0.5 | 0.5 | 0.5 | 0.5 | 0.5 | – |
| *Vitamins and Trace Minerals* | 2.5 | 2.5 | 2.5 | 2.5 | 2.5 | 2.5 |
| *Additives* | † | † | – | – | – | – |
| *Analysis* | | | | | | |
| Digestible Energy (DE) MJ/kg | 17.25 | 17.0 | 15.0 | 13.3 | 12.9 | 12.5 |
| Crude protein　　　　g/kg | 230.0 | 230.0 | 210.0 | 190.0 | 16.5 | 145.0 |
| Lysine　　　　　　　g/kg | 16.5 | 16.0 | 13.3 | 10.2 | 7.4 | 6.0 |
| Calcium　　　　　　g/kg | 14.9 | 13.8 | 10.25 | 10.0 | 7.5 | 6.5 |
| Phosphorus　　　　g/kg | 9.7 | 9.3 | 7.7 | 7.0 | 5.0 | 4.6 |
| Sodium　　　　　　g/kg | 2.5 | 2.5 | 2.5 | 2.5 | 2.5 | 2.5 |
| Lysine (g per MJ of DE) | 0.96 | 0.94 | 0.88 | 0.76 | 0.57 | 0.48 |

*Or up to amount of copper allowed by legislation (175 ppm to 16 weeks of age and 100 ppm from 16 weeks to 6 months of age)
†Antibiotic additive if appropriate and with veterinary advice.
‡Low glucosinolate.

**TABLE 10.7  Specimen diets in North America**

| | Weaner 1 | Weaner 2 | Early grower | Grower | Bacon | Heavy |
|---|---|---|---|---|---|---|
| Liveweight (kg) | 6–12 | 12–20 | 20–40 | 40–65 | 65–90 | 90–120 |
| | | | (kg per tonne) | | | |
| *Cereals* | | | | | | |
| Barley | — | — | — | — | — | — |
| Maize | — | 200.0 | 420.0 | 536.6 | 603.7 | 721.4 |
| Wheat | — | — | — | 200.0 | 200.0 | — |
| Breakfast oats | 206.0 | 124.0 | — | — | — | — |
| Flaked maize (ground) | 100.0 | 100.0 | 100.0 | — | — | — |
| Flaked wheat (ground) | 100.0 | 100.0 | 150.0 | — | — | — |
| *Protein sources* | | | | | | |
| Fishmeal | 150.0 | 150.0 | 100.0 | 50.0 | — | — |
| Soya bean | — | — | — | 88.4 | 167.7 | 55.1 |
| Soya bean (Dehulled) | — | — | 85.5 | 100.0 | — | — |
| Soya bean (full fat) | — | 93.0 | 100.0 | — | — | — |
| Dried skim milk | 259.0 | 100.0 | — | — | — | — |
| Rapeseed meal (Canola)‡ | — | — | — | — | — | 100.0 |
| Lysine hydrochloride | — | 1.9 | 1.9 | — | — | — |
| *Others* | | | | | | |
| Weatings | — | — | — | — | — | 100.0 |
| Vegetable oil | 80.0 | 74.4 | 30.7 | — | — | — |
| Whey powder | 50.0 | 50.0 | — | — | — | — |
| Glucose | 50.0 | — | — | — | — | — |
| *Minerals* | | | | | | |
| Salt | 2.0 | 2.5 | 3.5 | 4.2 | 4.6 | 5.0 |
| Dicalcium phosphate | — | 1.2 | 4.1 | 10.3 | 8.8 | — |
| Limestone flour | — | — | 1.2 | 7.3 | 12.2 | 15.2 |
| Copper sulphate (hydrated)* | 0.5 | 0.5 | 0.5 | 0.5 | 0.5 | — |
| *Vitamins and Trace Minerals* | 2.5 | 2.5 | 2.5 | 2.5 | 2.5 | 2.5 |
| *Additives* | † | † | — | — | — | — |
| *Analysis* | | | | | | |
| Digestible Energy (DE) MJ/kg | 17.0 | 17.0 | 15.0 | 14.3 | 14.2 | 12.5 |
| Crude protein       g/kg | 230.0 | 230.0 | 210.0 | 190.0 | 150.0 | 145.0 |
| Lysine              g/kg | 16.0 | 16.0 | 13.25 | 10.0 | 6.3 | 5.4 |
| Calcium             g/kg | 14.5 | 14.2 | 10.0 | 10.0 | 7.5 | 6.5 |
| Phosphorus          g/kg | 9.7 | 9.5 | 7.5 | 7.0 | 5.0 | 4.2 |
| Sodium              g/kg | 2.3 | 2.5 | 2.5 | 2.5 | 2.5 | 2.5 |
| Lysine (g per MJ of DE) | 0.94 | 0.94 | 0.88 | 0.70 | 0.44 | 0.43 |

*Or up to amount of copper allowed by legislation.
†Antibiotic additive if appropriate and with veterinary advice.
‡Low glucosinolate.

## Mixing Diets

Farmers who mix diets for growing and finishing pigs on the farm usually grow or buy in cereals and balance this with bought-in protein concentrates and a bought-in package of supplementary vitamins and minerals appropriate for the class of stock. Milling of the cereal is usually carried out on the farm prior to mixing, often using a hammer mill.

Great care must be taken with mixing equipment to ensure that it is adequately guarded since accidents around the mill are unfortunately very common. There should be more than one instant cut-off button in a readily accessible place, and guards should always be replaced prior to switching on. No amount of saved time or increased profit can compensate for a lost life or severe injury. It is also important to cut down the hazards which arise from dust. Dust in enclosed spaces can be explosive, and several elevator disasters in the United States testify to this fact. In addition, dust is a health hazard causing chronic respiratory diseases such as farmer's lung. The provision of cyclones with a dust-capturing bag is one way to reduce the hazards and another is not to grind materials too finely. In general, grinding through a 3 mm screen is adequate.

There is a wide variety of mixing equipment and the different types fall into three categories:

1.  Vertical or horizontal dry mixers
2.  Wet mixers
3.  Proportioning mixers

1.   Vertical and horizontal mixers vary in the efficiency with which they mix the small additives within the diets, particularly if their capacity is greater than 0.5 tonnes. For this reason it is often sensible to have a small mixer of the type used in bakeries to form a premix of the vitamins and minerals required eventually for a larger mix. For example, the vitamins and minerals for a tonne mix can be added to 25 kg of the cereal fraction, mixed and then added to the main diet for further mixing.

The length of time the diet should be mixed is normally the subject of a manufacturer's recommendation but is usually about 15 minutes. Note that prolonged mixing in excess of the manufacturer's recommendations can cause separation of the ingredients again and layering of the mineral fraction.

2.   Wet mixers are usually fitted with a pump for driving the liquid round in the mixer and then down a delivery pipeline. Some are driven by an air pump which agitates the liquid in the mixing tank and then pressurises the tank prior to forcing the liquid under the accumulated pressure round a pipeline delivery system to the pig pens.

3.   Proportioning mixers work by taking the main ingredients and combining them in the right proportions (usually by volume and sometimes by weight) on a continuous or semi-continuous basis. One type combines the output of a series of small augers, each working at a different rate and taking its source material from either a cereal bin or a protein bin and, in some cases, from a mineral and a vitamin container. This is a very versatile system and can be used for materials which would not normally mix well in a horizontal or vertical mixer. For example, high-

moisture grain that is stored in a sealed or semi-sealed silo at 20 per cent moisture or more can be delivered at a very precisely determined rate into the mix.

A further application of this principle is the use of twin pipeline systems round the piggery, when feed is dropped into the pen from calibrated containers or augers supplied either by cereal from the one pipeline or concentrate from the other. The ingredients effectively mix as they drop into the pen, either into a hopper, onto the floor or over a fixed spreader cone placed in the centre of the pen. At first sight this may appear rather inaccurate but in practice it works quite well. It has the very considerable advantage that if it is linked to a computing system, then the changing nutrient requirements of each pen of pigs as they grow can be supplied very exactly.

It should be noted that for mixing small quantities of feed up to half a tonne, there is nothing unsophisticated about using a barn floor and a shovel. The rule is to make a neat conical pile of all the raw ingredients, with those required in small quantities such as vitamins and minerals spread carefully round the top of the heap when it is nearly complete. The heap is then turned by making a new heap about 2 metres from the first by shovelling from the bottom and throwing the meal to the new position. The second heap is then thrown back to the original position and, for perfect mixing, the whole operation is done again to give a total of four transfers, there and back, there and back.

## Formulating Diets, Including the Use of High-moisture Products

This is an enormous topic and to be comprehensive would require a book on its own. However, by applying the principles outlined in the previous chapter and getting a balance between the nutrient and economic objectives, the farmer can achieve a great deal. Examples of diets for growing pigs are included in Tables 10.6 and 10.7 (pages 216 and 217).

**TABLE 10.8  High-moisture waste products which may be of value to pigs**

Butter milk
Skimmed milk
Whey

Fish silage

Potato waste

Distillery wastes (e.g. pot ale and draff)
Wet brewers wastes
Wet distillers grains

Root crop waste (substandard vegetables, e.g. carrots, potatoes)

Wheat waste from starch manufacture

Wet sugar beet pulp

'Swill' products such as catering waste (must be heat processed to comply with regulations)

The farmer has several apparent advantages over the central compounder. The first and most obvious is that he can use home-grown crops for his stock. This means that wet stored grain can be used by the home mixer when it is not an option for the compounder. Similarly, many by-products of the food and feed industry are available at low cost if they are wet, but at high cost if they have to be dried. The farmer who is located close to a source of such material can take advantage of it providing the material is offered at no or little cost and transport costs are kept low. The room for error in pricing is small and transport over distances of more than 20 km can become prohibitive in many situations.

Examples of high-moisture waste products which may be of value for a farmer who has ready access to them are given in Table 10.8. Note that anything which may have meat or meat products in it must be heat processed according to the swill regulations to avoid the transmission of disease, particularly swine vesicular disease (SVD), foot and mouth disease and many forms of salmonellosis.

### Purchasing Diets or Home Mixing

Unless the farmer operates on a very large scale it is unlikely that he can justify the equipment for pelleting diets or for adding fat or molasses to diets. The latter products require special storage tanks and heaters and if diets require pelleting or the addition of fats or molasses it is often better to contract out this kind of work.

Obviously the margin between the cost of ingredients and the cost of the manufactured and delivered diet, which can amount to 20 per cent or more of the final cost, is an attractive potential area for additional profit for the farmer. However, the farmer should not be lured by this glittering prize into incautious investment in storage bins for raw ingredients and milling and mixing equipment. He should recognise his limitations and preferably proceed a step at a time. Many central compounders work against very fierce competition, and the real margins, after all the costs have been taken into account and due allowance has been made for the hidden factor of useful credit from the feed merchant, may in fact mean that the farmer has a lot of additional worry for only a small degree of financial gain.

## COMMON FEED INGREDIENTS

### Alfalfa (Lucerne) Meal Dry

The dried leaves and stems of the legume *Medicago sativa*. Though sometimes recommended as a source of fibre in sow diets, only under exceptional circumstances would alfalfa meal have a place in the diets of growing pigs. The material is high in indigestible fibre and low in useful energy and protein. Its green colour is sometimes regarded as giving a natural and healthy appearance to the feed, but this is a doubtful concept.

### Animal Fat

This rendered material can, with suitable equipment, be incorporated into pig diets. As with all fats, the quality can vary enormously and the purchaser must be satisfied

Plate 10.3 Although pig diets in highly industrialised countries are based mainly on cereals and protein concentrates, pigs are quite adept at processing a wide range of vegetables and by-products from the food and drink manufacturing industries. In the photograph below, Dr Vernon Fowler is being closely supervised as he prepares an array of vegetables for feeding to pigs in China.

that the material has been handled appropriately. For example, fat which has been used for frying in catering establishments is unsuitable because it can change its chemical structure by a process known as *polymerisation* which makes it indigestible. Fats that have been stored without antioxidant can become rancid, and this can make them unpalatable and cause vomiting or have more serious consequences.

For pigs, lard (from pigs) is more digestible than the tallows from ruminants, the latter often being very hard fats which are high in stearic acid. For feeding, the fat must be of a very high quality and preferably protected at the outside with antioxidants, the inclusion of which must be declared on the product. Any taint or suggestion of rancidity should be enough to reject the material. Oxidised fats are a certain way of inducing a fatal condition in pigs known as mulberry heart disease. This occurs because the natural antioxidants such as vitamin E are used up in the muscle and this interferes with the function of the muscle.

### Barley

This cereal grain (*Hordeum vulgare*) is an important one for pig feeding, although it is lower in digestible energy than either wheat or maize. It is usually obtained as the husked grain but can also be 'pearled', in which case the husk and the outer coating of the seed have been removed by milling.

### Beans

There are many botanical species of beans which are offered for pig feeding from time to time. The commonest are varieties of the field bean, *Vicia faba*. These are usually of two major types, spring sown and winter sown. However, it is more important to note that beans vary in the extent to which they contain various anti-nutritional factors such as tannins and proteins which are resistant to digestion or which interfere with the digestive process. In general, faba beans should not be included at concentrations above 15 per cent of the diet and then only from 30 kg onwards. White-flowered light-coloured beans contain smaller amounts of anti-nutritive factors than do pink and red-flowered varieties which produce small dark seeds. Field beans and tick beans are other names for faba beans. In general, bean hulls are worse than useless in pig diets because of the high concentration of anti-nutritive factors.

Haricot, kidney or navy beans (*Phaseolus spp*) are the beans used in the production of baked beans. In the raw state such beans are extremely toxic and contain very unpleasant substances called lectins which can seriously damage the intestine. On no account should beans of this kind be fed to pigs unless they have been thoroughly cooked. Even the toasting method or heat extrusion techniques used for soya beans may not process the beans sufficiently, so it is safer not to use them at all unless you have very expert advice.

For soya beans please see under that heading.

### Blood (Dried)

This is regarded as potentially a good source of animal protein, but it is subject to very great variations in quality due to differences in freshness at the time of drying, and also the temperature levels to which it is subjected during the drying process. Material which is insoluble and black is usually produced by an unsophisticated heat-drying process and is not at all suitable for incorporation in pig diets. Flash-dried material is often subjected to a preliminary water removal treatment before being finally dried at high speed. Under-processed material, however, has been known to cause outbreaks of salmonellosis, and over-heated material is highly un-palatable and of very moderate nutritional value. Unless the quality is very high and has some guarantee of suitability for pig feeding it is not wise to incorporate blood meal in diets. It is also prudent, even with high-class material, to restrict its inclusion to less than 5 per cent of the diet, particularly for young pigs. The amino acid profile is quite good, especially for lysine and threonine, but it is a poor source of isoleucine.

## Bread Waste

This is commonly available near large cities and from bakeries. It can be a very useful constituent of diets, but care must be taken to avoid any quantity of mouldy material and contamination with metal. If there is any likelihood of raw meat waste in any shape or form being part of this waste, then it must be treated as swill and cooked accordingly.

## Brewers Grains

A by-product of the brewing industry, these are the residue of the grain after it has been sprouted and the soluble materials such as the malt removed. Since they contain very little starch, the useful energy for pigs is very much less than it is for cattle. There is little role for them in the diets of growing pigs except as a source of fibre.

## Coconut or Copra Meal

This is the residue of the white flesh of the coconut after the oil has been extracted mechanically or with solvents. It can be usefully incorporated into pig diets provided it has been dried when fresh, and the very best quality has a feeding value close to that of barley.

## Corn and Corn By-products

In the United Kingdom the word corn may be used for any cereal grain, but the feedstuff industry in general takes the American usage and applies the word only to maize (*Zea mays*) or as an adjective to describe by-products from the maize or corn-processing industry, e.g. corn gluten meal.

## Corn (Ground)

This is used as the main energy source in the diets of growing pigs in the United States and quite extensively in the production of so-called high-energy diets in Europe.

## Corn (Flaked)

The flaking process gelatinises the corn starch and produces a highly digestible product which is particularly suitable for young pigs. The flakes should be reground to prevent selection for or against individual flakes in meal diets.

## Corn Gluten Feed and Meal

This is a by-product of the industrial extraction of starch from the grain but is very variable in composition. Its quality is determined by the concentration of protein, which should be declared, and this can vary between 25 and 50 per cent.

## Corn Hominy Feed

This is a by-product of the corn processing industry and has a variable composition but is of high feeding value. It consists of a mixture of the bran, germ and part of the starchy fraction of the grain.

## Cottonseed Meal

Cottonseed formerly had a poor reputation as a pig feed because of the toxic yellow and purple pigments known as gossypols. Low gossypol cottonseed meal (that is, less than 0.04 per cent of free gossypol) can be used in pig diets particularly in those countries where high protein ingredients are scarce. The protein content of about 35 to 40 per cent is not well digested nor is it high in lysine.

## Dicalcium Phosphate

A mineral supplement usually added to bring the phosphorus of the diet up to the requirement, this contains about 18 per cent phosphorus and about 32 per cent calcium. It is generally considered to be highly available and certainly more available than most organic sources of phosphorus.

## Distillers Dried Grains

This is the residue after the alcohol and liquid fractions of malted and fermented grains have been removed. The composition varies with the type of grain. Although it contains an appreciable proportion of the lipid in the grain, this is to a large extent offset by the high fibre content and the fact that virtually all the starch has been lost. In this case, the digestion of the non-lipid fraction can only be by means of fermentation in the gut, which is an inefficient process in the pig.

## Distillers Dried Grains with Solubles

This material is similar to the previous one except that, prior to drying, the thin liquor left after distillation is added to the more solid part. The soluble fraction tends to be non-hexose sugars and therefore is largely digested by fermentation in the gut, making it less valuable than starch or cane sugar.

### Dried Skimmed Milk

This normally expensive material can often be obtained for animal feeding after it has been degraded with substances which make it unpleasant for human consumption. The degrading agents can be fishmeal, rapeseed meal, which is high in glucosinolates, or grass meal. The intention of some techniques of degradation is to make the milk unsatisfactory for young animals so that it will be used as a substitute for conventional proteins in the diets of growing pigs (20 to 100 kg liveweight), without depressing the price of undegraded dried skim milk for use in expensive diets for early weaning. Cheap skimmed milk products must therefore be regarded with due caution, and it is best to avoid the most degraded products in specialist early weaning diets.

### Dried Whey

The liquid fraction remaining after the manufacture of cheese is described as whey. The dried product contains about 12 per cent of high-quality protein and 7 per cent of ash, a high proportion of which is derived from the salts of sodium and potassium. The rest of the material is mainly the milk sugar, lactose. Many versions of whey are available. Some are lower in lactose and higher in protein, and some have been to a certain extent demineralised. Whey can be used advantageously in the diets of early weaned pigs, provided the salt content is not allowed to rise too high.

### Feather Meal

Feather meal is only useful to pigs if it has been hydrolysed. It has a very low lysine content (about 1 per cent, which is about a fifth of that in fishmeal), although it is quite rich in threonine and the sulphur amino acids, cystine and methionine. It is not very palatable and it is not really suitable for the diets of young pigs; indeed, it should be used only sparingly, if at all, in any pig diet.

### Fishmeal

Next to milk and egg proteins, that from good fish is one of the most suitable of all proteins for growing pigs, but it is unfortunately a very variable product. The best quality is achieved when whole fresh fish are processed and dried at a relatively low drying temperature. Meals made from the remainder of the fish after filleting are less nutritious and tend to be higher in ash and have a lower protein digestibility and a poorer amino acid profile. The oil content of fishmeals can make a valuable contribution to the energy component of the diet, but there is a danger that if the oil is not properly protected against oxidation, there will be a loss of palatability and a real danger of the pigs developing mulberry heart disease due to the intake of oxidised fats. Meals made from fish which have been allowed to putrefy are particularly dangerous and may also contain toxic amines. The odour of fishmeal is some guide to its suitability for the pig, strong odours which suggest rancidity or putrefaction being indices of an unsatisfactory product. A dark product containing black particles is also an index of unsuitability because, in all probability, the sample has been overheated during processing and this will undoubtedly reduce the usefulness of the lysine, since some of it will be unavailable to the pig. It is also an advantage if the meal is relatively finely ground, silky to the touch and not gritty (grittiness is indicative of a high content of bone).

## Groundnut Meal

This material (also called peanut meal) is best avoided for pigs because of the danger of it containing aflotoxins from the development of the fungus *Aspergillus flavus*, which infects the grain even in the soil. Material which has been downgraded from the human market often finds its way into a potential material for pig diets but what is unsuitable for human consumption is also a risk for pigs. There are tests for aflotoxins and these must be satisfactory over a large number of samples if the material is to be used. Some countries, including the United Kingdom, have very strict regulations concerning groundnut, and may, in fact, prohibit it totally for livestock use.

## Hemicellulose

This is a major fibre in sugarbeet pulp and citrus pectin. It is more readily fermented than other fibrous materials and can therefore make a contribution to the energy nutrition of the pig provided the quantities are not too great.

## Hominy Meal (see Corn Hominy Feed)

## Linseed Meal

This is the residue after the extraction of oil from the seed of flax or linseed. It has a high fibre content and is also rich in protein. It can be used to a limited extent in the diets of growing pigs but not young pigs.

## Meat Meal

Meat meal is the dried product from meat separated from the bone. It may include all types of soft offal and is a very variable product. At its best, it is a high-quality product which can replace some fishmeal in the diet. The oil is usually reduced to about 8 per cent but even at this level it can provide useful additional energy in the diet.

## Meat and Bone Meal

This is a by-product of the meat processing industry and its value depends on its exact chemical analysis and the severity of the heat treatment. Some processing plants, in ensuring that there is no danger of transmitting salmonellosis or any other infection, overheat the material, thus reducing the nutritional value. It has properties which are similar to meat meal but because it contains ground bone it has a lower protein content (40 to 50 per cent) and a higher mineral content including useful amounts of calcium (about 10 per cent) and phosphorus (about 5 per cent).

## Molasses

Molasses is the uncrystallisable fraction from sugar refining. It can take the form of either cane molasses or beet molasses, and both have similar properties. The true protein content is negligible. Cane molasses is rich in calcium whilst beet molasses is rich in potassium.

## Oats

Oats (*Hordeum*) are not widely used in pig diets unless they have been dehulled or unless they are one of the so-called naked varieties such as Tibor or Rhiannon. Naked varieties can contain up to 15 per cent of protein and 8 per cent of oil.

## Oak Flakes

Flaked oats, which have been steam rolled, are alternatively known as porridge or breakfast oats. These have a special place as the cereal component of the diets of baby pigs because they are soft and readily absorb additional oil. In terms of cereals, oat flakes have a high concentration of protein (about 15 per cent) and the balance of the amino acids is quite good.

## Oils and Fats

These are very important in the formulation of pig diets because their inclusion provides the simplest way of raising the energy specification. There are many forms and the topic can only be given the briefest outline. Hard fats such as tallows are derived from ruminant carcasses and are rather indigestible for young pigs. Soft fats such as the lards are rather more digestible and vegetable oils such as corn or maize, soya and rapeseed which contain unsaturated fatty acids, are even more digestible. However, when using an unsaturated oil, it is absolutely imperative to ensure that it has been treated with an antioxidant such as ethoxyquin or BHT (butyl hydroxy toluene). Vegetable oils can be made hard by hydrogenation, which renders them more stable but also more difficult to digest.

## Oilseed Rape

The meal from oilseed rape is usually obtained after extraction of the 40 per cent or so of oil from the seed. It contains about 35 per cent of a well-balanced protein and would be ideal for growing pigs were it not for the toxic factors it contains. The main problem lies with the so-called glucosinolates which impart a strong, pungent, mustard-like flavour to the meal. Much progress has been made in developing low glucosinolate varieties and several spring sown varieties have relatively low concentrations of this material. The meals from some low glucosinolate varieties such as Tower and Candle are marketed by the Canadians as Canola meal. In the United Kingdom it has been more popular until recently to grow the high-yielding winter sown varieties such as Bien Venue and Rafal, both of which produce high glucosinolate meals. The winter sown variety Ariana is relatively low in glucosinolate as are the spring sown varieties Topas and Calypso.

Varieties are often given the description of being 'single' or 'double low'. This refers to the concentration of two negative factors, the above-mentioned glucosinolates and also to a specific fatty acid in the oil called erucic acid. Generally speaking, this toxic fatty acid has been virtually eliminated from all modern varieties grown for their oil for human consumption. However, the idea still lingers on in the 'single' or 'double low' description, 'single low' being low in erucic acid only, 'double low' being low in both erucic acid and glucosinolates, and also in the very new varieties called 'triple lows' in which the fibre content of the meal is also relatively low.

### Peanut Meal

See Groundnut Meal.

### Phosphorus and Phosphate (see also Dicalcium phosphate)

Phosphorus is an essential element for the building of the critical mineral of bones.

### Poultry Meal

This is produced from the offal of poultry processing plants. If meticulously processed, this can be a useful product in the formulation of diets for growing pigs. The raw product is illegal in most countries and unless processing is perfect there is a danger of transmitting salmonellosis.

### Rapeseed Meal

See Oilseed Rape.

### Rice

Rice is rarely used in pig diets but is roughly equivalent to corn.

### Rice Bran

This is usually available only after extraction of its high oil content and in this form is roughly equivalent to wheat bran.

### Soya Bean

Raw soya beans are totally unsuitable for growing pigs because they contain toxic factors which must be destroyed by heat treatment. Extracted soya bean meal is the residue left after removal of the majority of oil from the seed and it is very carefully heat treated to degrade the trypsin inhibitors and lectins which are the main toxic factors. This material is the main protein supplement used in pig diets, but one must be aware of the enormous differences which can occur between materials which have virtually similar descriptions. The problem arises because different samples contain different proportions of hulls. Soya bean meal from dehulled beans has about 49 per cent of protein and about 3.9 per cent of crude fibre. Material which is not dehulled usually has about 44 per cent of protein whereas material with additional hulls added back can be as low as 40 per cent of protein and, with this high fibre content, they have a low digestibility. It is a pity that a protein source which used to be so reliable as to be called the 'gold-standard' of protein supplements has been subjected to so much further processing that it may now be regarded as potentially a major pitfall for the unsuspecting buyer.

Whole soya is an attractive product made by roasting whole soya beans or by steam extrusion of the whole bean followed by drying. It has the problem of ensuring that the heat treatment is sufficiently adequate to denature the toxins but not so severe as to make some of the lysine unavailable. The whole-bean product contains about 18 per cent oil and about 37 per cent protein.

### Sunflower Meal

Extraction of oil from sunflower seeds leaves a meal which is quite rich in protein, containing about 42 per cent, but the lysine in that protein is relatively low, being only just over half the level in soya bean meal.

The hulls contain a great deal of fibre and it is only the meal from dehulled seeds which is really suitable for pig feeding. Even so, the crude fibre exceeds 12 per cent (cf. soya at 6.5 per cent) and the material is most suited to the heavier growing pig.

### Urea

There is no nutritional value in urea for pigs.

### Weatings

Wheat middlings or weatings are by-products of the milling process to produce white flour. Their composition can vary depending on the milling process. In general, they are less valuable than their chemical composition would suggest because the nutrients are locked up in a rather inaccessible fibrous matrix. The 16 per cent protein content makes the material a better source of protein than the basic wheat cereal, but the energy value is only about 80 per cent that of the whole wheat grain.

### Wheat

Wheat (*Triticum aestivum*) is a very valuable cereal in pig diets because it has a higher digestible energy per unit of weight than either barley or oats, the value being about 14 MJ. The protein content varies very much according to the type of wheat and ranges from about 11 per cent for a soft biscuit-making wheat to 15 per cent for a 'hard' breadmaking type.

It should not be ground too finely for pig diets because it can, when in contact with water or saliva, become very sticky and pasty. This makes it unpalatable and it also causes the area round the feeding trough to become very unhygienic. For grinding it is preferable not to use a screen size less than 2.5 to 3 mm.

Wheat is particularly good in the diets of young pigs, and it is even more useful if the deficiency in lysine is balanced by the addition of synthetic lysine hydrochloride. If 30 per cent of wheat is included in the diet, then about 1 kg of lysine hydrochloride should be added to one tonne of the total diet.

### Wheat Flakes

Flaked wheat, which is a very suitable cereal for young pigs, has a composition similar to that of the whole grain.

### Yeast

In the dried form, yeast has a protein content of about 44 per cent and a lysine content equivalent to that of extracted soya bean. It is, however, rather bitter and not greatly liked by pigs, particularly if it is instrumental in setting up a fermentation within the feed after it has been offered to the pigs. A ceiling of 5 per cent is suggested as an arbitrary maximum for inclusion.

## FEED ADDITIVES AND GROWTH PROMOTERS

Many substances are added to the diets of pigs which are not, strictly speaking, nutrients as such. The additions are made for a whole variety of reasons. At one end of the scale they have a very simple purpose such as adding colour or flavour to the diet and, at the other end, they can alter the efficiency and speed of growth of the animal. To examine this complex area in full would require a book in itself, but in this section we shall merely classify the types of substance available and consider the main purpose of each category.

At the outset, it should be stressed that perfectly satisfactory diets for growing pigs and sows can be produced without resorting to feed additives. They are widely used by feed manufacturers, often to allow them to include poorer ingredients in diets. In other cases, although the additives are effective at bringing about minor improvements, these improvements are often exaggerated by commercial organisations so as to obtain an apparent competitive edge for their product.

The producer should be extremely cautious about accepting the claims of commercial companies who produce glossy brochures describing obscure experiments which seem at first sight to support the use of a particular product. In many cases, only those trials which support the product are publicised, whilst those which show no advantage or which give negative results may well be suppressed.

A final preliminary warning about feed additives concerns the need to follow the manufacturers' instructions to the letter. Some products only receive a licence for incorporation in diets providing that certain conditions relating to their use are observed. For example, some products may be subject to a period of withdrawal prior to the slaughter of the animal or may have an absolute ceiling on the rate of inclusion in the diet. It is critical for the safety of the consuming public that the rules are followed. It only needs one producer that shows a disregard for the rules and is caught, to demonstrate that the level of trust expected is too great. If this action then results in the withdrawal from authorised use of a helpful material, those who run the risks must accept the blame not only for the removal from use of the additive, but also for the loss of a much more important commodity, namely, the goodwill of the consuming public for pig products.

Many products which were formerly used in animal production have been withdrawn. In virtually every case, this was done to appease a backlash of consumer anxiety based on the publicity which abuse had received. One exception to this was the very wise counsel of the Swann Committee Report on the use of antibiotics in animal production, published in the 1960s in the United Kingdom. This report pointed out the inadvisability of using antibiotics in animal production which were of importance in human medicine. They highlighted the dangers of resistance developing in the bacteria associated with animals and also the hitherto unappreciated danger of this resistance being transferred to bacteria associated with humans. Some materials now prohibited as a feed additive may, however, be prescribed by a veterinary surgeon to be used under his personal supervision, and then only on a limited scale and only in the particular circumstance of a clinical condition which would respond only to that antibiotic.

## Types of Feed Additive

There are many types of feed additive and several of these are shown in Table 10.9. Each will be considered briefly in turn. Note that any material mentioned in the description is not necessarily an approved product in all countries, nor does its mention imply an endorsement on the part of the authors. The legislation governing

**TABLE 10.9   Types of feed additives**

 1.  Preservatives
 2.  Flavouring and colouring agents
 3.  Texturing agents
 4.  Antimicrobial agents
 5.  Antibiotics
 6.  Antifungal and antiprotozoal agents
 7.  Enzymes
 8.  Probiotics (favourable organisms)
 9.  Substrates for micro-organisms
10.  Gut acidifying agents (citric acid, fumaric acid)
11.  Metabolic modifying agents
12.  Immune system stimulants
13.  Chelating agents for minerals
14.  Emulsifying agents for liquid diets

additives has been substantially modified in recent years and for the foreseeable future it will be under continuous review in almost every country.

## 1. PRESERVATIVES

Some feeedstuffs may be very subject to deterioration in storage, and are much more stable if protected in some way. An important group of preservatives includes the antioxidants such as ethoxyquin, which are very important for preventing the spoiling of fats, particularly oils and unsaturated fats. Some cereals which are stored in a moist condition are preserved with organic acids such as formic, acetic and propionic acid. It is also possible that some grain is stored by treating with ammonia. Some vitamins are packaged in special gelatin to protect them from deterioration when in contact with other materials in the diet such as copper sulphate.

## 2. FLAVOURING AND COLOURING AGENTS

These are quite common in the diets prepared for early weaned pigs. The flavours are often intended to give the flavour of milk but may also include vanillin or fruit flavours. Sweeteners are widely used and are included also in the water supply for young pigs. Colouring agents are sometimes used to impart a yellow cream colour to the diet, but this is probably more for the eye of the farmer than for the benefit of the pig. Sometimes colours are used to distinguish diets from one another, especially those which have been medicated.

## 3. TEXTURING AGENTS

The most common additives are those used to promote pelleting of the diet. For example, molasses and bentonite are used to help the passage of the pellets through the pelleting machine and ensure a firm pellet but not one which is heavily glazed and bullet-like. Fibrous materials such as sugarbeet pulp are sometimes used to improve the texture of pellets.

For liquid diets, gelling agents are sometimes added to hold semi-solid materials in suspension. Emulsifying agents are used to disperse fat globules in high-fat liquid milk substitutes.

## 4. ANTIMICROBIAL AGENTS

This term is used for a whole range of materials and, strictly speaking, includes the very large class of the antibiotics. However, as a group, these are so important that they are treated separately. In this classification, antimicrobial agents include all those materials which have antimicrobial activity but are not derived from fungi or micro-organisms as are the classical antibiotics.

Despite the widespread use of antimicrobial agents, there is still some dispute about their mode of action and the relative importance of each component. The possible modes of action include the following:

- They compensate for an immature immune system and keep potential pathogens under control.
- They prevent the degradation of nutrients by bacteria. This includes the all-important amino acids, and some experiments have shown them to be more effective when the diets are marginal for protein. They may also protect vitamins from bacterial degradation.

• They may have an energy-sparing effect, preventing sugars and starches from being subjected to inefficient fermentation when otherwise they would have been digested by the normal efficient enzyme systems of the pig.

Into this group of feed additives can be placed the following antibacterials:

Carbadox (Quinoxaline-1,4-dioxide) Not permitted in some countries
Furazolidone (Nitrofuran)
Nitrovin (Nitrofuran)
Olaquindox or Quindoxin (Quinoxaline-1,4-dioxide)

Copper is a very important feed additive because of its combined efficacy and cheapness as an antimicrobial agent. It is usually incorporated as copper sulphate (5 $H_2O$). Depending on price, it may also be incorporated as an oxide or as copper carbonate (7 $H_2O$) or copper chloride. The usual inclusion rate in Europe is 175 parts per million of added copper up to 60 kg liveweight and 125 parts per million after this weight. It is not permitted at this high level in the diets of breeding pigs.

5.  ANTIBIOTICS
The mode of action of the antibiotics is similar to that of the antimicrobials described above. There are many different types although they all interfere in some way either with the mechanism of protein synthesis in bacteria or with the formation of the cell wall. Some are more effective against certain types of bacteria than others but none are effective in controlling viral infections. Many of the antibiotics are produced by fermentation and the product used for addition to the feed is not the pure chemical but a dried product containing the mycelium of the fungus used in the fermentation. Table 10.10 provides a list of commonly used antibiotics.

**TABLE 10.10   Some commonly used antibiotics**

Avoparcin
Aureomycin (see also chlortetracycline)
Bacitracin (see also zinc bacitracin)
Bambermycin
Chlortetracycline (see also aureomycin)
Erythromycin
Eskalin (see also virginiamycin)
Lincomycin
Oleandomycin
Oxytetracycline (see also terramycin)
Penicillin
Spyramycin
Terramycin (see also oxytetracycline)
Tyamulin
Tylosin
Virginiamycin (see also Eskalin)
Zinc bacitracin

## 6. ANTIFUNGAL AND ANTIPROTOZOAL AGENTS

In this category are a range of antiprotozoals, anthelmintics and antifungal agents. These include:

Ronidazole (5-Nitro-imidazole)
Dichlorvos
Arsanilic acid (not now approved in most countries)
Gentian violet

## 7. ENZYMES

A relatively recent approach to improving diets is to add synthetically produced enzymes. These substances are capable of carrying out a measure of digestion of materials and can be complementary to the enzymes of the gut of the pig. They are particularly useful when the diet contains compounds for which the pig does not have a natural enzyme, but which are amenable to digestion when acted upon by the added enzyme.

The ones which are currently available are the $\beta$-glucanases which break down the $\beta$-glucans in cereals to glucose, various amylases which assist in the breakdown of starch to glucose and proteases which break down proteins to their constituent amino acids. These latter may be particularly useful in those cases where the proteins are in a form which causes them to be antigenic to the pig as, for example, occurs with lectins in extracted soya bean.

An exciting prospect for this type of additive is the possibility that it may be used to break down cellulose, which is otherwise very indigestible. Although some cellulases have been produced, the yield of glucose is not very high. However, if the technology is successful, then it may be possible to use some straw and hay in pig diets and obtain some nutritive value from them.

## 8. PROBIOTICS

This is a somewhat controversial name given to various materials which are the products of a special fermentation process. They usually consist of a mixed culture of bacteria of the lactobacillus types together with certain other species, many of which are regarded as trade secrets or special strains. The dried form is usually incorporated in the diet with the implied claim that the organisms multiply in the gut to form a favourable flora, thereby displacing unfavourable and potentially pathogenic bacteria. To some people they represent a more attractive means of modifying the gut flora than antimicrobials or antibiotics, but their efficiency over a range of practical conditions has yet to be proved.

## 9. SUBSTRATES FOR MICRO-ORGANISMS

Fibre is now thought to be more important in diets for pigs and indeed humans than was thought hitherto. This is not only for reasons of supplying bulk for the gut to work on but also because some fibrous materials ferment and cause a favourable change in the gut flora. Some additives are designed to promote this particular function.

10.  GUT ACIDIFYING AGENTS (CITRIC ACID, FUMARIC ACID)

When animals are stressed, as is the case at weaning, the normal functioning of the gut is impaired. One possible problem is that the cells of the stomach, which secrete acid into the gut to aid digestion and control the bacterial flora, fail to function properly. In an attempt to maintain the upper gut in an acidic state, certain feed additives have been developed based on the addition to the diet of organic acids. The organic substances citric and fumaric acids are among these and have the advantage of not interfering with the acid/base status of the animal which could occur if mineral acids were used. These materials also have the advantage of being well buffered so that they remain acidic in the presence of neutralising materials without being very strong acids themselves.

11.  METABOLIC MODIFYING AGENTS

Several substances can affect the metabolism of the animal and in some cases these alter the proportion of fat to lean in the liveweight gain. Some materials stimulate the hormonal system of the animal whilst others have a pharmacological effect. For example, the stimulant in coffee and tea, caffeine, has been used in pig diets and in some experiments was shown to improve leanness. More recently, orally active analogues of the sex hormones have been used subject to a period of withdrawal prior to slaughter. Public concern about the possible abuse of such products has led to their total withdrawal from sale in most countries. The hormonally active substances which were used included the analogue of the active female sex hormone, diethylstilbestrol, which is a member of the stilbene group of compounds and is now almost universally regarded as inappropriate for use in this way, because of the resistance of the molecule to breakdown and degradation. Other materials have included methyl testosterone, an orally active version of the male sex hormone, and zearalenone, an analogue of the female sex hormone found in some fungi.

A new approach is the use of a different series of compounds called $\beta$-agonists. These simulate the action of naturally occurring substances secreted by the adrenal glands and greatly enhance the proportion of the gain which is in the form of lean meat. They have a very rapid rate of degradation and excretion from the body. For this reason they incur no risk of leaving residues in the meat and seem to meet satisfactorily all the criteria for a safe and effective additive. At the time of writing, $\beta$-agonists have not received full approval for incorporation in pig diets and stringent tests are still being undertaken.

12.  IMMUNE SYSTEM STIMULANTS

Young and newly weaned pigs are much more susceptible to infection than older animals. This is due to the immune system being relatively immature and not always fully capable of producing enough immunoglobulin of an appropriate type to deal with the infection.

One novel approach has been to incorporate in the diet of young pigs a type of vaccine consisting of the killed cells of several different types of pathogenic bacteria. These dead cells have sufficient of the structures of the live bacteria to provide the immune system with the necessary information to form antibodies to the bacteria. If the piglet is then exposed to real infection from the relevant bacterial types, it has at least some protection from the antibodies it has already produced. One product already on the market which uses this principle is Intagen, produced by Unilever after pioneering work by Professor Philip Porter.

The effectiveness of this approach can be increased by exposing the sow to the killed bacteria prior to farrowing so that the colostrum she produces for the litter also contains antibodies against these specific pathogens.

13.  CHELATING AGENTS FOR MINERALS

In the view of some authorities, pigs may suffer from effective trace mineral deficiency even when apparently adequate quantities are provided in the diet. The reasons suggested for this are that the absorption of these minerals is impaired due to the presence either of fibre which binds the mineral or because other minerals in the diet are in excess and compete for the absorbing mechanisms. The claim is made that by binding the trace element in a molecule called a chelate it is protected from these interfering substances and released at the site of absorption. Some chelating agents are called proteinates, and the minerals most frequently offered in this form are manganese, zinc and iron. Although some experimental evidence is advanced to support their effectiveness, there is very little independent published work demonstrating that they are effective for pigs when the control diets contain adequate amounts of these minerals in a normal form and in balanced concentrations.

14.  EMULSIFYING AGENTS FOR LIQUID DIETS

Liquid diets are sometimes used for baby pigs, for example, when they are orphaned. If such diets are reconstituted from a dry powder and if they contain more than 3 or 4 per cent of lipid or fat, then it is often advisable to add an emulsifying agent to ensure that the fat is evenly dispersed throughout the liquid and also in a droplet size small enough to allow for easy digestion. There are a great variety of emulsifying agents including lecithin extracted from soya beans.

## Summary of the Effects of Feed Additives

Some additives are undoubtedly of value. Others are not. The effectiveness of antimicrobial agents and antibiotics is usually to improve growth rate and feed conversion by about 5 per cent in pigs growing from weaning to about 60 kg. After this weight they are much less likely to be effective. The response to antibiotics is likely to be greater in a herd which has problems than in one where the pigs are healthy and well cared for and where good diets are used. In general, the effects of antimicrobial agents are not additive and though one often sees cocktails of such products being used, this is a bad policy. If they are thought to be necessary, it is a far better policy to use one substance until its effectiveness wanes and then change to another. It cannot be stressed too strongly that the instructions provided by the manufacturer and/or the veterinary surgeon should be adhered to exactly, and any change in additive should be made in consultation with the veterinarian.

## Conclusions

Diet formulation and nutrition is central to the farmer's success. Whether he undertakes the task himself or pays someone else to do it is a very personal decision. The potential rewards are substantial for doing it one's self but the advantages may not be as great as suggested by a simple paper exercise.

Like everything else, mixing on the farm can (excuse the pun) be a mixed blessing. Time devoted to purchasing ingredients, coping with the volume of work involved in storage and mixing and worrying about pig performance, is time taken away from other crucial husbandry decisions. There are many farms with perfect feed mills but with the rest of the farm going to rack and ruin because the mill is taking more than its fair share of the managerial input. A neglected mill is an even greater hazard. Not only can it be dangerous, but poor stockkeeping, unduly long storage of ingredients, sloppy weighing and formulation, cheap 'buys' bought without proper analysis of the constituents, which turn out to be expensive, can all contribute to disaster.

For example, in our own experience, a farmer realising that raw soya bean on one occasion was the same price as cereal bought several hundred tonnes only to find that raw soya bean was toxic and that he had no facilities for heat extruding it. Rather than admit his error, he fiddled small amounts into his diets for a long period of time, a process which eventually removed the embarrassment but which probably did the pigs very little good and the profits no good at all. Another example was an enquiry from a farmer on the verge of buying raw haricot beans which were below standard for the baked bean industry. Fortunately, he had the good sense to make an enquiry about them and was just prevented from embarking on what would have been a total disaster, since haricot beans contain in the raw state a very toxic poison of the lectin type.

Simple diets such as those suggested in the examples in Tables 10.6 and 10.7 are usually quite cost effective. The main danger arises when cheaper ingredients or substitutes become available. These require proper chemical analysis and judgement to determine whether they can be incorporated advantageously into diets, and the farmer should not spurn the guidance of an expert independent adviser from either the national advisory services or an advisory agency.

## Additional Reading

Agricultural Research Council (1981), *The Nutrient Requirements of Pigs*, Commonwealth Agricultural Bureaux, Slough, England.

Campbell R. G. and King R. H. (1982), 'The Influence of Dietary Protein and Level of Feeding on the Growth Performance and Carcass Characteristics of Entire and Castrated Male Pigs', *Anim. Prod.* **35**, 177–184.

Campbell R. G., Taverner M. R. and Curic D. M. (1983), 'The Influence of Feeding Level from 20 to 45 kg Liveweight on the Performance and Body Composition of Female and Entire Male Pigs', *Anim. Prod.* **36**, 193–199.

Campbell R. G., Taverner M. R. and Curic D. M. (1984), 'Effect of Feeding Level and Dietary Protein Content on the Growth, Body Composition and Rate of Protein Deposition in Pigs Growing from 45 to 90 kg', *Anim. Prod.* **38**, 233–240.

Cole D. J. A. and Haresign W. (Eds) (1985), *Recent Developments in Pig Nutrition*, Butterworths, London.

Fuller M. F. (1985) 'Sex Differences in the Nutrition and Growth of Pigs', *Recent Developments in Pig Nutrition* Eds. D. J. A. Cole and W. Haresign, 177–189, Butterworths, London.

MacDonald P., Edwards R. A. and Greenhalgh J. F. D. (1988), *Animal Nutrition*, Longman, London.

*Pork Industry Handbook*, USA Co-operative Extension Service, University of Illinois at Urbana-Champaign, USA.

# Chapter 11

# Major Diseases and Principles of Maintaining Good Health

## INTRODUCTION

Many people believe that disease can only be caused by an infection and that the afflicted animal will develop certain clinical signs. Veterinarians specialising in pig problems have realised for some time that disease should be defined in a much wider sense. In fact, it is now generally accepted that herd performance data such as Food Conversion Efficiency (FCE) and Daily Live Weight Gain (DLG) are more sensitive and meaningful indicators of disease, especially sub-clinical diseases. The pig's performance may be affected by many factors besides infectious organisms. Detailed investigation of pig health problems over the last decade has led to the concept of multifactorial aetiology. In other words, the pig may only become diseased when it has been subjected to a number of factors or stimuli, some of which may need to act in sequence or even be synergistic in their effects, e.g. pneumonia may only become a problem in a herd after the stocking density has reached a certain level, the ventilation rate has dropped to a certain level, the dust level has risen to a certain level and the right combinations of organisms have colonised the respiratory tract. This complex combination of sequential events often makes it difficult for the veterinarian to establish the initial precipitating factor. Most of the problems causing economic loss come into this category.

## HEALTH STATUS

Health status may be categorised under a number of headings/titles which will mean different things to different people. Specific Pathogen Free Herds (SPF) are basically derived by hysterectomy/hysterotomy (surgical removal of foetuses) procedures and should be free of pathogens specifically named. Minimal Disease is another term used to describe herds derived by the same procedures although the term is more comparative than specific. Medicated Early Weaning (MEW), pioneered by Dr Tom Alexander and the Pig Improvement Company (PIC) is another procedure which has provided the basis for high health status herds. More recently another method of producing weaners relatively free of infectious disease, called Isowean 3 site production, has been pioneered in the USA by using a combination of early weaning, medication, and all in/all out procedures on three separate sites for breeding, weaner/rearing and finishing.

Pigs of high health status can be produced on a fairly regular basis from breeding herds with various diseases by this method. A modification of this process, segregated disease control or temporary partial depopulation, has successfully controlled disease on the same site.

No matter how high the health status is initially, any herd is likely to become gradually contaminated with infectious organisms, e.g. herds free of enzootic pneumonia can expect a breakdown rate of 5 to 10 per cent per annum unless situated in a remote area.

Once a high health status herd has been established, steps must be taken to prevent disease getting in to the unit. Obviously the site of the unit is important and where possible it should be at least 5 km away from other pig units or main roads. Pigs should only be bought from the same source as the original stock and a preventive medicine programme should be in operation. Briefly, this should include a regular veterinary clinical inspection and regular monitoring of pigs at the abattoir, particularly of snouts and lungs. The information gained from these inspections is linked with performance data to produce an assessment of herd health. (It is important to remember that a small change in FCE can produce a large change in financial returns.)

Signs should be erected indicating that visitors are not welcome, and those who can be tolerated, who should have been away from pigs for three days at least, should shower and change into unit protective clothing.

The compound perimeter fence should be vermin proof and strong enough to prevent the entry of wild pigs and other animals. Feed should be delivered from outwith the fence and pigs should only leave the premises via a loading bay at the perimeter on a freshly washed and disinfected lorry. Pig traffic at the loading bay should only be one way and at no time should transport personnel enter the pig compound via the loading ramp. (For more comprehensive health precautions, see *Diseases of Swine*, 1981.)

## PRINCIPLES OF DISEASE CONTROL

Many disorders can be controlled and prevented by taking certain precautions which will help to build up herd immunity, lessen the challenge by disease-causing organisms and lessen the effects of disease. The general principles are as follows:

### 1. Protection Against Exposure

REDUCTION OF WEIGHT OF INFECTION
The following steps should be taken with the above objective in view:

- Keep the herd closed if possible or buy from one source only.
- Ensure minimal contact between groups of pigs and avoid mixing pigs if possible and empty each house or unit completely at one time, i.e. try to establish an all in/all out policy.
- Maintain high standards of hygiene in houses and equipment.
- Reduce concentration of pathogens in the air by a combination of adequate ventilation and dust filters.

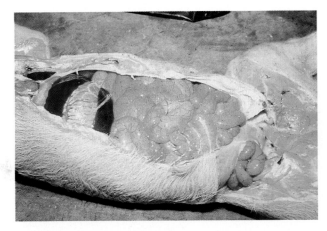

Colour plate 1  Post-weaning diarrhoea. Note small intestine grossly dilated with fluid.

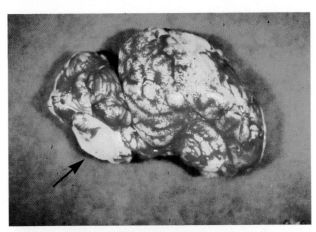

Colour plate 2 Streptococcal meningitis *(S. suis II)*. Brain from sudden-death case. Note intense congestion of membrane and blood vessels surrounding brain and pus at lower border of cerebellum (arrow).

Colour plate 3  Swine dysentery. Weaners suffering from chronic swine dysentery. Note severe loss of condition.

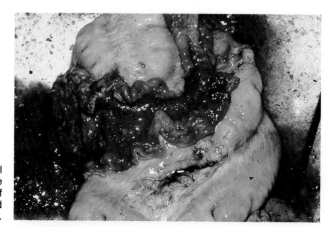

Colour plate 4 Large bowel from pig with swine dysentery. Note thickening of bowel and mucoid haemorrhagic contents.

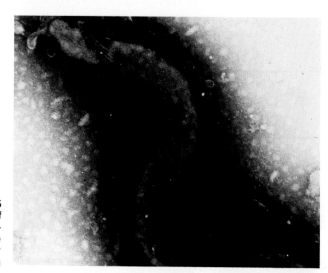

Colour plate 5 E.M. photograph of *Treponema hyodysenteriae* — the cause of swine dysentery. (Courtesy of Dr D.J. Taylor)

Colour plate 6 Snout of pig with atrophic rhinitis. Note shortening of snout, wrinkling of skin and tear staining.

Colour plate 7 Three snouts (cross-section) from pigs with atrophic rhinitis. Note severe destruction of turbinate bones (middle and left).

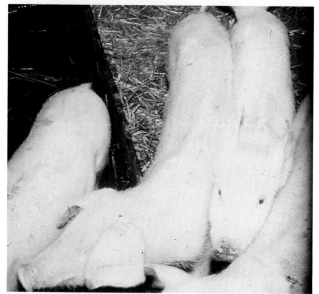

Colour plate 8 Porcine intestinal adenomatosis. Weaners suffering from necrotic enteritis. Note severe loss of condition.

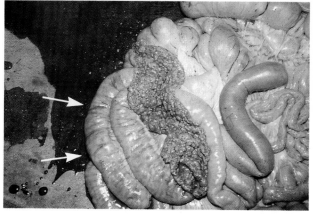

Colour plate 9 Terminal small intestine opened to show lesion of necrotic enteritis. Note thickening of affected bowel (arrow).

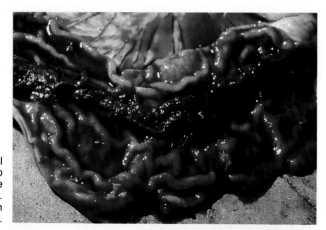

Colour plate 10 Terminal small intestine opened to show lesion of proliferative haemorrhagic enteropathy. Note haemorrhagic cast in lumen.

Colour plate 11 Young weaner with acute exudative epidermitis. Note reddening of skin and weeping of serum.

Colour plate 12 Weaner with exudative epidermitis showing multifocal chronic skin lesions.

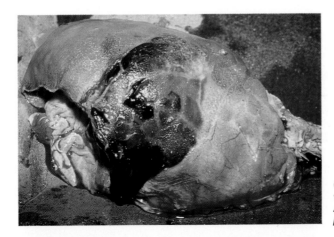

Colour plate 13   Pig lung with typical lesion due to *Actinobacillus pleuropneumoniae*.

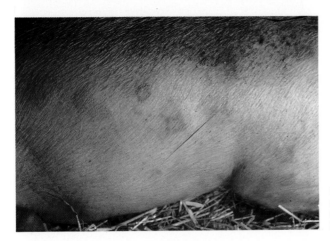

Colour plate 14   Pig with sub-acute erysipelas. Note characteristic raised skin lesions.

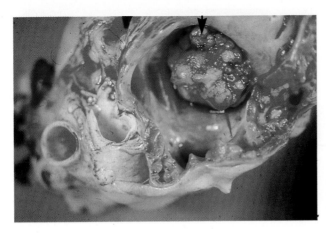

Colour plate 15   Pig heart opened to show lesion of chronic valvular endocarditis due to erysipelas infection (arrow).

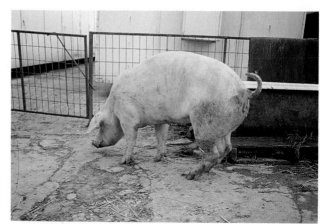

Colour plate 16   Gilt with arthritis due to *Mycoplasma hyosynoviae*. Note posture and arched back.

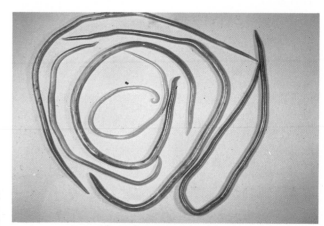

Colour plate 17A   Adult ascarids from a 90 kg pig. (Courtesy of Dr W. Beesley)

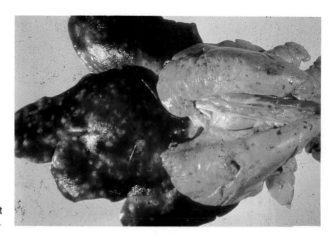

Colour plate 17B   Milk spot liver.

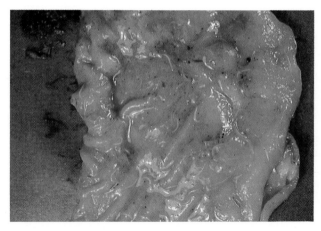

Colour plate 18  Caecum from 90 kg pig with heavy infestations of *Trichuris suis* (whipworms).

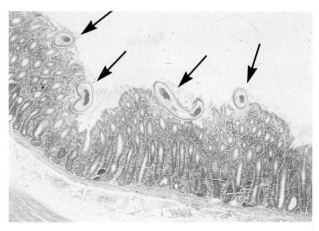

Colour plate 19  Section of caecum from 90 kg pig showing whipworms (arrows), embedded in epithelium.

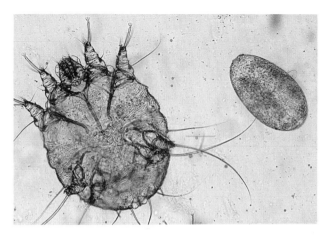

Colour plate 20  Adult sarcoptic mite and egg.

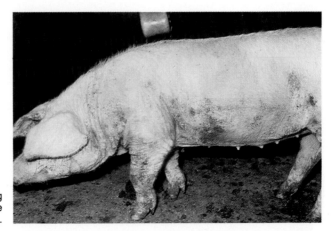

Colour plate 21   90 kg pig with typical skin lesions due to chronic sarcoptic mange.

Colour plate 22   Torsion of the mesentery: note the congestion and dilation of the whole bowel.

Colour plate 23   Torsion of the large intestine only. Note the relatively normal small intestine (arrow).

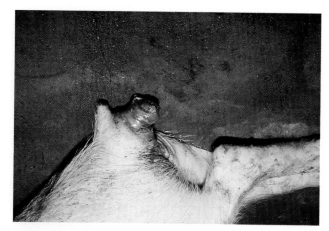

Colour plate 24   Weaner with prolapse of the rectum (5 hours' duration).

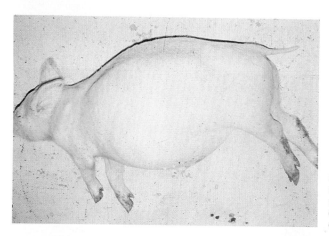

Colour plate 25   40 kg pig which died from complete rectal stricture. Note the loss of condition and severe distension of the abdomen.

Colour plate 26   Rectum from an 80 kg abattoir pig with partial stricture. Note narrowing of lumen near the anus due to scar tissue (arrow).

Colour plate 27    70 kg pig with severe damage
to tail due to tail biting.

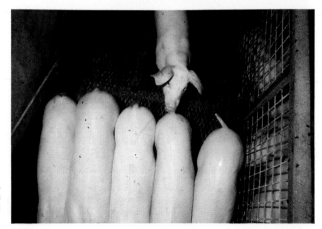

Colour plate 28    Weaner,
frustrated by lack of trough
space, actively biting the tail
of another.

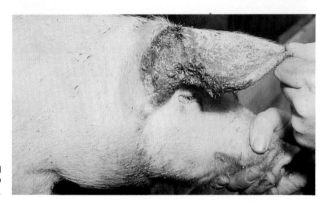

Colour plate 29    35 kg pig
with typical wounds due to
ear biting.

Colour plate 30   Pig with flank biting lesion actively rubbing the flank of a pen mate. Note apparent acceptance by pen mate.

Colour plate 31  These pigs fed on meal are relatively clean.

Colour plate 32   Pigs fed on the same diet as in plate 31 but this time as pellets. Note dirty appearance of pigs due to sloppy dung.

Colour plate 33 *(right and above)* Attractive presentations in retail outlets of a wide range of high-quality pigmeat products available at competitive prices assist greatly in improving the appeal of pigmeat to the consumer. (Courtesy of the Meat and Livestock Commission)

Colour plate 34 When it brings together the best in welfare, science, technology and marketing, pigmeat is unbeatable in terms of its potential and is likely to remain the most consumed meat in the world for a long time to come. (Courtesy of the Meat and Livestock Commission)

REDUCTION IN SUSCEPTIBILITY TO INFECTION

The important safeguards in this respect are as follows:

- Use vaccines if available.
- Avoid too many gilts in the breeding herd.
- Avoid stressful conditions.
- Avoid large numbers of pigs sharing the same air space.

## 2. Prevention of Infection

The following steps should be taken to prevent infection:

- Eliminate affected animals by test and slaughter.
- Repopulate with uninfected stock.
- Produce disease-free stock by hysterectomy, hysterotomy, medicated early weaning or Isowean 3 site production.

## 3. Mitigation of Effects of Disease

The effects of disease can be reduced in the following ways:

- Avoid exacerbating factors such as dust, extremes of temperature, under-ventilation, overcrowding, underfeeding, dietary deficiencies and stressful conditions.
- Reduce the severity and persistence of the disease process by medication of feed with antibiotics or chemotherapeutic agents.
- Minimise economic loss by slaughter and salvage.
- Avoid buying more affected pigs.
- Provide suitable 'sick pen' accommodation (note that removal of sick pigs to a hospital pen is a most important part of any treatment considered).

These principles will be discussed in more detail as they apply to the individual diseases outlined in the remainder of this chapter. Finally, it should be stressed that any treatment undertaken should be cost-effective. However, it is often impossible to determine this without a preventive medicine programme based on clinical inspections and accurate performance data.

## Bacterial Diseases

POST WEANING DIARRHOEA (PWD)

This disease reaches a peak 4 to 10 days after weaning – the younger the pigs are weaned, the shorter the duration between weaning and the occurrence of the disease. Toxins produced by certain serotypes of *E. coli* produce the gut damage and clinical signs.

*Signs*

Acutely affected pigs may be found dead without evidence of clinical signs. Others rapidly become listless, pass diarrhoeic faeces, which may vary from a dark loose consistency without mucus or blood to watery fluid, and lose condition rapidly. The eyes rapidly become sunken and the flanks hollow (see colour plate 1). Death is due to a combination of toxaemia and dehydration.

*Control and prevention*
The disease is a sequel to the normal changes which occur in the gut after weaning or after a change in diet. Briefly these are:

(1)  An increase in water content of the faeces
(2)  An increase in the output of amines (from protein)
(3)  An increase in the output of carbohydrate
(4)  An increase in the output of fat
(5)  Degeneration of epithelial cells lining the gut
(6)  In some animals, an increase in the numbers of *E. coli*, especially haemolytic, toxin-producing strains.

In addition, pigs weaned between 2 and 4 weeks of age have little or no circulating immunity. Efforts should be made to ensure that the piglets consume 'creep' feed before weaning to stimulate enzyme production and local immunity in the gut. The change of diet should be a gradual one. Water should always be available and all care should be taken to ensure that the piglets know where to get it.

The following procedures will help to control the disorder. Lactic acid (1 per cent), which will reduce the multiplication of *E. coli*, may be included in the water for 10 days after weaning. Zinc oxide added to the diet at 3,000 ppm for 14 days after weaning has proved to be particularly effective in preventing the disorder. Restriction of food intake has also proved helpful but this can only be done when adequate trough space is available to allow all pigs to feed at once. An antibiotic or chemotherapeutic agent may be added to the diet or water for 5 days before and 10 days after weaning. Finally, an *E. coli* vaccine may be used. This may be given orally or by injection, depending on the manufacturer's instructions. Parenteral vaccines have not proved very effective for controlling the problem. An oral *E. coli* vaccine has proved beneficial in some units in large-scale field trials.

BOWEL OEDEMA (OEDEMA DISEASE)
Although this disorder usually occurs 7–10 days after weaning, outbreaks have been noted in older pigs, frequently after a change in diet. The causal agents are again toxin producing strains of certain *E. coli* serotypes.

*Clinical signs*
One or even several of the fastest growing pigs may be found dead. Survivors show varying degrees of unsteadiness and appear blind and dazed. Pigs have a squeaky call and usually have puffy eyelids due to oedema. Constipation may be evident.

*Control and prevention*
In the experience of the author, the cause and development of the disease parallels that of post weaning diarrhoea. Prevention and control measures outlined for PWD are usually effective. However, this disorder can be a serious problem on occasions and may persist for as long as a year in spite of all known remedies being applied. The disease is due to toxins from rapidly multiplying strains of haemolytic *E. coli*.

STREPTOCOCCAL MENINGITIS (S. SUIS II)
This disease, which has recently become very prevalent in the United Kingdom,

may affect pigs of any age after weaning. Losses may vary from 1 to 20 per cent.

*Clinical signs*
Septicaemic cases are often found dead (see colour plate 2). Live affected pigs have a high temperature (40.6 to 41.7° C), nervous signs such as twitching, convulsions, paddling movements, opisthotonus and spasms. Pigs may show these signs for several days before death. In addition, affected pigs are often lame and show swelling of the joints. Some strains of the organism may be present in a herd without clinical cases arising.

*Treatment*
Penicillin by injection is the treatment of choice. It may be beneficial to use rapidly absorbed penicillin (crystalline) in conjunction with procaine penicillin. Some veterinarians have noted that corticosteroids given in addition to penicillin may be beneficial. Severely agitated pigs should be sedated and all should be given water. This is most easily administered by tube via the rectum. Affected pigs should be removed from their pen-mates and kept comfortable (for example on a straw bed) in isolation until they have fully recovered.

*Control and prevention*
The organism is usually carried on the tonsils of healthy animals and 75 to 100 per cent of weaners may be carriers in infected herds. Conditions such as over-stress, overcrowding, under-ventilation and wide variations in temperature tend to precipitate the disease. Outbreaks are often noted after the slurry level rises in flat decks and after mixing and moving.

Outbreaks can be minimised by avoiding the stressful situations mentioned or by the inclusion of penicillin in the diet. As procaine penicillin is largely destroyed in the gut, dose rates of up to 500 gm/tonne may have to be used for very young pigs whose feed intake is low. Phenoxymethyl penicillin is the drug of choice for feed inclusion provided it is not pelleted at temperatures above 55° C. So far, vaccination has not proved cost-effective. Herds free of the organism should avoid buying infected pigs. Before buying in new breeding stock a guarantee of freedom from the causal organism should be requested or, more realistically, freedom from the disease.

SWINE DYSENTERY
This disease occurs in pig rearing areas throughout the world and is caused by an organism called *Serpulina hyodysenteriae*.

*Clinical signs*
The first signs are those of inappetance and abdominal discomfort. These are followed by fever (40 to 41° C) and diarrhoea. Characteristically, the diarrhoeic faeces contain large amounts of mucus and fresh blood. Unless death occurs, the affected pigs rapidly become emaciated and dehydrated (see colour plates 3, 4 and 5). Mortality of infected animals varies from 5 to 40 per cent while morbidity can be as high as 90 per cent. Pigs usually become infected by ingestion of faeces either directly or indirectly through contamination from another carrier pig. Survivors may carry the organism for 90 days or more.

*Treatment*

Medication of the drinking water with drugs such as Lincomycin, Tiamulin, Dimetridazole and Ronidazole has proved effective and is the method of choice when pigs are clinically affected.

The disease may be controlled and prevented by inclusion of the same drugs in the feed. Monensin sodium and carbadox have also proved useful in preventive medication. Eradication may be achieved by depopulation, removal of all faeces and rodents, resting of the buildings and thorough disinfection followed by repopulation with disease-free stock. Eradication may also be achieved by a combination of medication and hygienic measures. The latter method can be time consuming and costly and should only be undertaken with veterinary supervision.

ATROPHIC RHINITIS (AR)

This disease, characterised by sneezing, nasal discharge (sometimes bloody) and nasal distortion, can cause severe depression of growth rate. However, the owner of a finishing unit can do little about controlling or treating the disease because this aspect must be tackled in the suckling stage as well as in the immediate post weaning stage. The treatment of pigs with snouts already distorted is a waste of time and money (see colour plates 6 and 7). However, feeding affected pigs on a liquid diet often helps to maintain expected growth rates.

Units can easily keep clear of the disease by avoiding the purchase of pigs from units with AR pigs. Problems are unlikely to develop if pigs are first infected after 15 weeks of age.

PORCINE INTESTINAL ADENOMATOSIS (PIA)

This disease, which is prevalent in pig rearing areas throughout the world, is responsible for considerable economic loss. It is often present in herds without the owner being aware of it. Morbidity is often high while mortality varies from 5 to 20 per cent.

*Clinical signs*

The disease may take several forms known as PIA, necrotic enteritis (NE), regional ileitis (RI) and proliferative haemorrhagic enteropathy (PHE) (see colour plates 8, 9 and 10). The first three forms usually appear in pigs of 8 to 16 weeks of age and clinically affected pigs become dehydrated, emaciated and 'runty' looking. They may pass loose, dark coloured faeces and have a depraved appetite. The disease is often sub-clinical at this stage and affected pigs may only show a drop in weight gain. PHE usually appears in older pigs (30 to 150 kg) and may present as sudden death but more usually as a haemorrhagic diarrhoea, severe depression and inappetance. The diarrhoea is of a dark tarry colour with a characteristic offensive smell and the pig itself rapidly becomes pale coloured because of blood loss. Outbreaks of PHE may be severe in MD herds or those of high health status.

*Control and treatment*

Pigs affected with PIA respond well to medication. Severely affected pigs should be removed from the group to an appropriate pen and given a glucose/electrolyte solution with soluble tetracycline for 2 days and no food during this time. This allows the gut to clear itself of any fibrous material consumed because of the depraved appetite. Then a wet mash should be gradually introduced with an antibiotic included for at least 7 days. Supportive therapy with vitamins and trace minerals will also help. Less severely affected pigs can simply be treated by the inclusion of tetracycline in the ration for 14 days.

PHE, however, is more serious and often fatal. Affected pigs may be treated with a variety of drugs including tetracycline, corticosteroid, vitamins, iron and fluids. Nursing must be of the highest standard. Unfortunately, animals which survive PHE may become runts (often developing NE).

### Control and prevention
The cause of the disease is an organism called *Lawsonia intracellularis* which is capable of multiplying in the absence of oxygen in the gut enterocytes. Vaccination has proved unsuccessful. Since the organisms are widely dispersed throughout the pig industry, the purchase of stock free from organisms is difficult, if not impossible, to achieve. Herds derived by hysterectomy acquire the organism fairly quickly in spite of all precautions. Where new MD herds have been set up, the gilts can be protected from PHE by strategic medication with tetracycline in the diet, one week in three, until they have farrowed.

#### EXUDATIVE EPIDERMITIS (GREASY PIG DISEASE)
Greasy pig disease is an inflammation of the superficial skin layers; it often affects suckling pigs but is also seen in pigs up to 12 weeks of age. Although outbreaks are sporadic, losses can be considerable when they do occur. The causal organism, *Staphylococcus hyicus*, can be found on the skin of many normal animals including sows. The disease appears to be precipitated by the organisms gaining entry through abrasions in the skin, which may be caused by fighting, sharp projections and self-inflicted wounds due to scratching from pruritus. Outbreaks are often prevalent during warm, muggy weather in the autumn.

### Clinical signs
Clinically affected pigs begin to show reddening or flushing of the skin, especially between the thighs, along the belly and behind the ears (see colour plate 11). Exudation of serum begins and this gradually gives the pig a greasy appearance. The exudate eventually forms a scab and the pigs rapidly become listless and inappetant. Death quickly occurs from toxaemia and dehydration. Both morbidity and mortality may be high but there is marked variation between outbreaks. The lesions may be generalised or multifocal in nature (see colour plate 12).

### Treatment and prevention
Treatment may be successful only in the early stages with the use of antibiotics including penicillin and lincomycin. Steroids will help to reduce the inflammatory response and lessen the shock.

Preventive measures will include avoiding the precipitating factors already mentioned and by medicating the feed with penicillin or lincomycin when the first cases arise. Dipping weaners in a mixture of mange wash and skin disinfectant has proved an effective preventive measure in some cases.

PNEUMONIA

Pneumonia or inflammation of the lungs can be caused by a number of infectious agents which may act singly or in various combinations. When one or more organisms are present, the phenomenon known as synergism or interaction is often noted, i.e. the effect is more severe than the effects of single agents acting independently of each other. There are several ways of describing the various forms of pneumonia but the most common method is by aetiology, i.e. the cause.

PLEUROPNEUMONIA

This type of pneumonia (due to *Actinobacillus pleuropneumoniae*) is present in most pig rearing countries and is highly infectious and often fatal (see colour plate 13). The severity of the disease may be increased in circumstances similar to those described for enzootic pneumonia (see page 248).

*Clinical signs*

High fever (39.5 to 41° C), respiratory distress and cyanosis of the extremities followed by death within 6 to 10 hours are in many cases the characteristic signs of the disease. The chronic form may present as pleurisy, which can be detected only at necropsy or slaughter. Although the organism may be sensitive to most of the antibiotics commonly used for treating enzootic pneumonia (see page 249), the response in many herds may be poor. The reasons for this are not yet known. Very sick animals should be treated by *injection* with antibiotic and supportive therapy, while animals in contact should receive medication via the water if possible.

*Control and prevention*

Exacerbating factors as described under enzootic pneumonia should be avoided or eliminated. Vaccination with commercial vaccines (if available) or autogenous vaccines has proved successful. The disease can only be eradicated by depopulation and purchase of stock from MD, SPF, MEW or Isowean 3 site production sources.

GLASSER'S DISEASE

This is an infectious, sometimes fatal polyserositis, caused by the organism *Haemophilus parasuis*. The organism is present in most herds but on entering a herd free of the organism (i.e. a non-immune herd) may cause a serious outbreak with high mortality in all age groups.

*Clinical signs*

Affected pigs quickly become ill with high fever (40–41° C), anorexia, shallow breathing and unwillingness to move. Some may be lame with obvious swelling of the joints. Occasionally some pigs will develop symptoms of meningitis. Cyanosis of the snout, ears and rump may be severe. Diagnosis can only be confirmed by special laboratory tests as other organisms may cause polyserositis.

*Treatment and prevention*
Outbreaks respond well to chlortetracycline in food or drinking water. Animals too ill to eat should be treated by injection of a suitable antibiotic. The disorder may be prevented by the strategic use of medicated feed after pigs are bought and mixed. There may be a suitable vaccine in some countries.

SWINE ERYSIPELAS (MEASLES)
This disease is found in all pig rearing countries of the world and is caused by the bacterial organism *Erysipelothrix rhusiopathiae*, which is found in soil, fishes, birds and carrier swine. Single animals may be affected or outbreaks may occur – especially in warm, humid weather.

*Clinical signs*
The disease may present as sudden death or more commonly as illness and fever (42° C) accompanied by characteristic skin lesions (see colour plate 14). These are usually raised, reddish areas often in the shape of a diamond. Infected individuals may eventually show signs of heart disease (see colour plate 15) or lameness due to arthritis.

*Treatment*
Pigs which are very ill should be injected with penicillin. Non-affected in-contact animals should receive an injection of antiserum or alternatively the feed may be medicated with penicillin for 14 days.

*Control and prevention*
Suggestions for control measures are difficult to make because of the sporadic nature of the disease. However, vaccines are available and are normally effective providing at least two doses are given.

SALMONELLOSIS
Salmonella organisms (of which there are many serotypes) are found throughout the world, and in the United Kingdom can be found in many pig herds if the search is diligent enough. On the whole, the organisms cause few problems; however, the disease may occasionally arise if the circumstances are right.

PARATYPHOID (SALMONELLA CHOLERAESUIS)
This form of salmonellosis may appear in finishing pigs and it causes high mortality in the septicaemic form.

*Clinical signs*
Affected pigs are listless, off food, fevered (42° C) and characteristically show a deep purple coloured cyanosis of the head, ears and rump. There is no diarrhoea.

*Treatment*
Mortality will be high in spite of treatment. The only effective drug may be chloramphenicol, which may not be available in some countries because of fears of transmissible drug resistance, as it is used for treating human cases of typhoid (*S. typhi*).

*Control and prevention*
Avoid continuous throughput in large overstocked groups if possible. Vaccination, if available, may be effective in preventing the disorder.

OTHER SALMONELLA INFECTIONS
These usually present as a gastro-enteritis and are often secondary to PRRS virus infection or to some stressful conditions, especially sub-standard management or husbandry. Antibiotics by injection and medication of the feed or water are the normal methods of treatment, while vaccines may be available for the control of some serotypes.

The presence of infection on a farm may be regarded as a public health threat in some countries and the authorities may take whatever control measures that are necessary for that particular unit.

ANTHRAX
Disease caused by this bacillus is rare; nevertheless, pigs may contract it following consumption of contaminated feedstuff. The septicaemic form, which is relatively uncommon, usually presents as sudden death. Occasionally the disease may take a pharyngeal form where oedema and swelling of the neck may be associated. Breathing is difficult and fever of 41.5° C may be noted. Vomiting, lack of appetite and severe depression will also be evident. In the intestinal form the infection causes acute inflammation of either the small or large intestine with loss of appetite and the passage of bloody, diarrhoeic faeces. Animals may recover spontaneously from the disease and transmission may then occur from pig to pig as carriers are established. The disease can only be diagnosed by a veterinary surgeon and clinical cases usually respond to parenteral treatment with one of the penicillins.

## Mycoplasmal Diseases

ENZOOTIC PNEUMONIA
This form of pneumonia is a problem in all pig rearing areas in the world and can be one of the major causes of poor productivity in finishing units. The cause is a mycoplasma organism, *Mycoplasma hyopneumoniae*. The disease is chronic in nature, except when introduced to high health status herds. Spread occurs by aerosol droplet from pig to pig. Its severity is markedly influenced by a number of factors:

- The presence of other organisms, e.g. *Haemophilus suis*, *Pasteurella multocida*, *Bordetella bronchiseptica*, *Mycoplasma hyorhinus* and viruses such as the swine influenza virus, the PRRS virus and the respiratory coronavirus
- The presence of other diseases, e.g. swine dysentery and PIA
- The purchase of pigs from many sources
- The purchase of diseased pigs
- When pigs are derived from a very young breeding herd
- Overcrowding
- Keeping large numbers of pigs in one air space
- Sub-optimal ventilation rates (it is important that coughed-up infective particles are carried to the exterior rather than being rebreathed by other pigs)

- High variation in temperature at pig level
- Low relative humidity (this dries up the mucous membranes of the respiratory tract and so increases the animal's susceptibility)
- Continuous throughput (this allows the build-up of infection and cross-infection of pigs as they enter the unit)
- Less than 3 cubic metres of air per pig

The incubation period, in the field, may vary from two weeks to three months. The disease can often be detected by regular lung inspections before it becomes clinically apparent or indeed may become clinically apparent long before lung lesions appear in slaughtered pigs.

### Clinical signs
In acute outbreaks, which occur when the organisms enter a herd for the first time, all ages of pigs may be affected. Respiratory distress, high temperatures (40.6° C to 42° C), depression and lack of appetite are often followed by death. However, on the other hand, occasional coughing may be the only evidence that a non-immune herd has become infected.

In the chronic form the only evidence of infection may be coughing and poor growth rate. This coughing is most noticeable when pigs are roused from rest or are moved. As secondary infection builds up, respiratory distress may become more apparent and the temperature usually rises. In ad lib. feeding situations affected pigs are not always easily detected but careful inspection will reveal a pig breathing heavily, disinclined to move, often mouth breathing and sometimes showing cyanosis (blue discolouration) of the extremities.

### Treatment
Clinical cases should be treated with antibiotics by injection and *removed* to an airy hospital pen. Supportive therapy with decongestants and corticosteroids is also useful. If clinical cases are arising frequently and many pigs are off food, then the treatment of choice is water medication. Treatment should continue for a minimum of 5 days.

Sub-clinical infection will respond to in-feed therapy with antibiotics. Treatment may be continuous at preventive levels or sporadic at therapeutic level. The intervals between the strategic treatments will depend upon a number of factors specific to each unit, but obviously the longer the interval between treatments, the less expensive treatment will be. However, before embarking on any mode of treatment, the person making the decision should ensure that it will be *cost effective*, and in a well-run herd with good records this can easily be determined. Regular routine lung inspections by unit veterinarians provide useful data which can be used in decision making. Drugs used to treat enzootic pneumonia successfully include the tetracyclines, tylosin, sulphadimidine, spectinomycin, potentiated sulphonamides, cetiofur and various drug combinations, e.g. tiamulin/oxytetracycline.

### Control and prevention
The severity of the disease can be lessened by pinpointing environmental and managemental deficiencies already mentioned and by rectifying weaknesses. Herds free of enzootic pneumonia should only purchase pigs from similar herds, i.e., pigs from herds of similar health status. Needless to say, all the other precautions such

as strict control of visitors, showering before entry into the unit and extermination of vermin should be taken. Even so, many units break down with enzootic pneumonia. The likely source of the organism in these cases is another infected unit less than 4 km away. It is possible that a passing lorry full of pigs may also be a source. Vaccines are now available in many countries and may prove cost effective.

### Eradication
The only certain method of eradication of this disease is to depopulate, rest and disinfect and repopulate with stock derived by hysterotomy, hysterectomy or MEW. The breakdown rate in densely populated pig areas is high (5–15 per cent per annum).

#### MYCOPLASMA HYOSYNOVIAE ARTHRITIS
This disorder is not uncommon and usually becomes clinically apparent when pigs grow heavier as they approach slaughter weight and puberty. The organism is commonly carried in the tonsils of normal pigs and when the right conditions occur, it migrates to the joints, especially the stifle, hip and elbow joints. Clinical signs are those of stiffness, stilted gait, swelling of the affected joints and occasionally a slight rise in temperature (see colour plate 16). Affected animals will continue to eat but will lose weight because of failure to compete for feed and unwillingness to walk to the feeding area. Outbreaks may be noted after selection and mixing of selected gilts in the 70–90 kg range. The disorder in this case may be prevented by the addition of tiamulin or lincocin to the diet.

### Treatment
Affected animals should be removed to a strawed hospital pen and given injections of corticosteroid and one of several antibiotics which may include tylosin, tiamulin and lincomycin.

#### MYCOPLASMA HYORHINIS
This organism is a common inhabitant of the upper respiratory tract in most herds. It is an opportunist pathogen in most cases and is usually secondary to some other invading organism. The organism may become established in the joints or other serosal surfaces, especially the pericardium and peritoneum. Pigs are most often affected within the first 4 to 6 weeks after weaning. Those with joint infection will show clinical signs of lameness, stiffness and unwillingness to rise, and the joints may be slightly enlarged. Other pigs with internal infection may show a reduction in appetite and a marked reduction in growth rate. There may be a rise in temperature (40.6° C) for 6 to 8 days. Pigs with chronic peritonitis or pericarditis may become runts. Chronic cases are difficult to cure because of the severe adhesions. Acute cases respond well to injections with suitable antibiotics. The percentage of pigs affected is rarely high enough to justify medication of the feed.

## Viral Diseases

#### SWINE INFLUENZA
This type of pneumonia is caused by the influenza virus. New strains of the virus frequently appear.

*Clinical signs*
Acute outbreaks usually affect 100 per cent of the pigs. Laboured, fast breathing is usually accompanied by high temperature (41.5 to 42° C), coughing and watery discharge from the eyes. When the pneumonia is complicated by other organisms, death may occur. Following treatment, affected animals make a quick recovery in 5 to 7 days.

*Control and prevention*
The virus is spread by carrier pigs and the pig lungworm. Antibiotic treatment will control secondary infection. A vaccine may be available in some countries.

SWINE FEVER
This is a highly infectious viral disease which is characterised by high morbidity and high mortality in all ages of susceptible swine. Although it has been eradicated from a few countries, it will probably always remain a constant threat.

*Clinical signs*
These may vary according to the pathogenicity of the particular strain of virus. In susceptible pigs, the peracute form will present as sudden death. The acute disease will present as dullness, lethargy, fever (42° C), conjunctivitis, ataxia and diarrhoea. Chronically affected pigs become emaciated over a long period and eventually die. The low-virulence form of the disease may cause only a mild inappetance and some vomiting in finishing pigs.

*Treatment, control and prevention*
There is no effective treatment. As the virus is mainly spread by carrier pigs or untreated swill (garbage), steps should be taken to avoid the former and eliminate the latter by proper treatment of swill.

In some countries, an eradication policy has been successful while in others, vaccination has kept the disease under control. Obviously, eradication is the control method of choice.

AFRICAN SWINE FEVER
This disease is caused by a virus which has no relationship to swine fever.

*Clinical signs*
Affected pigs have a high temperature for two days after incubation of the virus. However, pigs may remain bright during the pyrexic phase. As the temperature drops, the pigs huddle together and begin to show nervous signs. Coughing is sometimes followed by diarrhoea and occasional vomiting. The skin rapidly becomes blue and there may be a mucopurulent discharge from the eye and nose. Mortality is 95 to 100 per cent in *susceptible* herds.

*Treatment, control and prevention*
There is no effective treatment. The virus is spread by carrier pigs (including wild swine), untreated garbage, lice, ticks and wind. Appropriate steps should be taken to avoid these risks. The most effective method of control is slaughter of the whole

herd, disinfection of the premises and rest. A few pigs should be reintroduced and if they remain healthy for 4 weeks it can be presumed safe to introduce more stock. It should be noted that the virus is very resistant.

SWINE VESICULAR DISEASE

This viral disease is of little or no significance apart from the fact that the lesions may resemble those of foot and mouth disease and therefore can cause problems in the diagnosis.

*Clinical signs*

Pigs may become lame after developing vesicular lesions around the coronary band above the claw. In some cases, secondary infection causes under-running of the horn. The virus may be present in a herd without the owner knowing.

*Prevention, treatment and control*

The disease may be spread in various ways, e.g. via swill (garbage), carrier pigs, pork products, transport, direct or indirect faecal contamination and even invertebrate hosts such as earthworms. Steps taken to avoid these methods of transmission will effectively keep the disease out. Vaccines have not been very effective and there is no effective treatment.

FOOT AND MOUTH DISEASE

Foot and mouth is a very contagious viral disease characterised by an increase in temperature, lack of appetite, lameness due to vesicles and secondary infection on the coronary band and, much less frequently, lesions on the lips and tongue. Morbidity may be very high but mortality is usually low. Several serotypes of the virus exist and some are more pathogenic than others. There is no cross immunity between types and only partial immunity between sub-types. Pigs usually become infected from other carrier pigs or by ingestion of feedstuffs containing the virus, e.g. untreated swill (garbage). Wind-borne infection and infected transport can also play a role in the spread of the disease.

*Clinical signs*

Severe lameness is the most common finding. The infected pigs are obviously in some pain, and because of this they become reluctant to move and the gait may be stilted. Vesicles, which may be seen on the top of the tongue and alongside the snout, readily rupture to reveal small ulcers. After vesicles on the coronary band rupture, thimbling results in damaged horn which is shed. Secondary infection can cause lameness to become chronic and more severe. The disease can be confused with swine vesicular disease. Veterinary tests are usually required to confirm the diagnosis. Recovered pigs do not become carriers. Control procedures are usually based on either slaughter and repopulation or vaccination with a suitable vaccine or by a combination of the two, e.g. ring vaccination and slaughter.

RABIES

This is a rare but fatal disease of the pig in those countries of the world where rabies is endemic. Clinically the disease is characterised by nervous signs and death. Twitching of the nose may occur. Muscular spasms are often followed by prostration and death within 70 to 90 hours. The incubation period may be anything from 50 to 120 days. This disease can only be diagnosed post-mortem by a veterinary surgeon.

AUJESZKY'S DISEASE (PSEUDORABIES)

Aujeszky's disease, which is due to a herpes virus infection, is usually more serious in the breeding herd than in the finishing herd. The clinical signs vary according to the age of animal infected and are most severe in pigs up to 4 weeks of age, when a high mortality can be expected. After infection, pigs usually exhibit sneezing and coughing. As the temperature rises, lack of appetite and constipation follow. Some pigs vomit and gradually muscular spasms, convulsions, fits, loss of balance and prostration develop. In older swine or in herds with previous experience of the virus, the signs may be so mild that the disease may be difficult to recognise as such. Thus, in finishing pigs, mild inappetance, slight constipation and occasional vomiting should be considered as possible pseudorabies.

The main source of infection is other pigs. The virus may be windborne from nearby infected units; there is little evidence that rodents spread it. Although other domestic animals are very susceptible to the disease, they are not involved in its spread as the virus dies with them, i.e. they are dead-end hosts.

*Treatment and control*

There is no effective treatment apart from good nursing. Vaccination is a very effective form of control within the herd and live vaccines are particularly effective. However, vaccinated animals not only harbour the infection but also excrete the virus; thus they can still spread the disease.

PORCINE REPRODUCTIVE AND RESPIRATORY SYNDROME (PRRS) (BLUE EARED PIG DISEASE (BEPD), SWINE INFERTILITY AND RESPIRATORY SYNDROME (SIRS))

The causal agent, an arteri virus, is widespread throughout the world and the clinical signs in a finishing herd reflect the endemic infections of that herd. In high health status herds with no endemic pathogens, infection with the PRRS virus has produced few clinical signs. At the other end of the spectrum, in finishing herds infected with many pathogens or potential pathogens, mortality levels have trebled and many pigs have exhibited signs of respiratory disease. Food conversion efficiency and daily liveweight gain will be depressed in these herds.

The virus tends to persist in finishing herds, especially those which purchase pigs from several sources. The effects of the virus can be minimised by using in feed antibiotics to control secondary bacterial infection and by instituting an all in/all out policy in each section of the herd.

## Internal Parasites

In modern intensive systems, roundworms seldom cause clinical problems because of the widespread use of concrete or slatted floors, power washing and disinfection. However, if finishing herds are based on strawed yards or on dirt lots, helminths can cause serious economic loss, especially if weaner pigs have a high worm burden at purchase. Only the more important helminths will be discussed and then only briefly. For more specific details readers should consult *Diseases of Swine* (1981).

### HYOSTRONGYLUS RUBIDUS

This small red worm lives in the stomach mucosa. The adult females lay eggs which are passed out in the faeces and develop through stages into infective larvae. The whole cycle may be complete in 18 to 21 days. Heavy burdens may cause mild anaemia and growth rate depression.

### ASCARIS SUUM

This is the largest helminth of swine, females reaching up to 40 cm in length (see colour plate 17A). They spend their adult lives in the small intestine and can on some occasions make their way into the stomach. The pig may harbour many adults without clinical signs and interference with growth may often be surprisingly little.

Eggs from adult females are passed out in the dung and develop into infective eggs, which are extremely resistant and sticky and may survive in cold weather for up to 4 years. Upon ingestion, part of the development of the worm involves larval migration through the lungs and liver. Large numbers of migrating larvae will cause the pig to cough and show signs of pneumonia. The only result of liver migration is the so-called milk spot liver (see colour plate 17B), which is seen at slaughter providing the pig has been *killed within 35 to 40 days* of the liver migration.

Interestingly, ingestion of large numbers of infective eggs does not lead to large numbers of worms in the gut – in fact the very opposite. This is due to an immunosuppressive response. If weaners are wormed before being put into a *thoroughly clean* pen, 'milk spot' livers should not present a problem. Earthworms may occasionally harbour the infective larvated eggs.

### STRONGYLOIDES RANSOMI

Found exclusively in pigs, this threadworm has a remarkable method of ensuring the survival of the species which involves a free living stage outwith the pig. These free living adults may produce more eggs without ingestion by the pig. Larvae may enter the pig by mouth or through the skin. Newborn piglets may become infected through the colostrum and there is one report of prenatal infection (Store 1966). The life cycle may be complete in 4 to 6 days. Heavy infestation may lead to diarrhoea, anaemia, vomiting and unthriftiness.

Other helminths such as *Macracanthorhynus hirudinaceus*, *Trichinella spiralis* and *Globocephalus species* may be found in the small intestine of the pig.

### TRICHURIS SUIS

Also known as the whipworm, this nematode resides in the large intestine and rectum, where the whole development of the worm takes place (see colour plates 18 and 19). The eggs, which are present in the faeces, are extremely resistant. The life cycle is complete in 40 to 67 days. Large infestations produce a syndrome similar to swine dysentery. Blood-stained diarrhoea with spots of mucus is often noted. Clinical signs include anaemia, weakness, increased respiratory rate, loss of condition and occasionally death. The adult female worms are intermittent egg layers and a negative diagnosis should not be based on the absence of worm eggs, especially if pigs are diarrhoeic.

OESOPHAGOSTOMUM SPECIES

These worms are commonly found in pigs on a world-wide basis and are known as nodular worms because of the reaction in the large intestine. The eggs are passed in the faeces and hatch into infective larvae which are ingested by the pig. The life cycle is complete in 21 days. Heavy infestation results in diarrhoea and loss of weight.

LUNGWORMS

The adult worms of *Metastrongylus apri* live in the airways of the lung, where the females lay their eggs which are coughed up, swallowed and passed out in the faeces. The eggs must then be swallowed by an earthworm before further development can take place to the larval stage. After ingestion of the 'infective' earthworm, the larvae make their way to the airways of the pig's lungs and the life cycle is completed in about 4 weeks. Heavy infestations will cause signs typical of pneumonia but affected pigs are not likely to be fevered. Loss of weight may be severe and secondary bacterial infection may cause fatal pneumonia in some cases.

*Treatment and control of internal parasites*

Heavy burdens of internal parasites can be avoided by careful manipulation of grazing areas so that pigs are moved on to clean ground after dosing; otherwise they should be treated regularly with anthelmintics. Lungworms can easily be avoided by housing pigs on concrete or slatted floors. Contamination of pig muscle by the human tapeworm cyst (*Taenia solium*) can be controlled by preventing access of the pig to human excreta and/or sewage. Thorough treatment of garbage (swill) will prevent invasion of *Trichinella spiralis* larvae. There are many reliable, efficacious and safe drugs on the market for treating worms in the pig. Some are more useful than others against specific types of worms and veterinary advice should be sought if in doubt. There is only one drug on the market at the time of writing which will effectively treat all species of worms and external parasites and that is ivermectin.

## External Parasites

LICE

The pig louse, *Haematopinus suis*, is the only louse found on pigs. The adult (0.5 mm) is a light brown colour and can readily be seen on a white pig, especially behind the ears and over the shoulder. It is more difficult to detect on brown or black swine.

*Life cycle*

The adult female lays 80 to 100 eggs over a 20 to 30 day period. Each egg or nit (1 to 2 mm in diameter) is attached to a hair and hatches in about 10 to 20 days into a nymph. Unlike the adults, the eggs are easily seen on dark coloured pigs. After 3 moults the nymphs become adults, the whole cycle taking 23 to 30 days. The lice feed by sucking the blood in areas where the skin is soft. The lice can only live away from the pig for 2 to 3 days. Spread is from pig to pig.

*Clinical signs*
Affected pigs constantly rub and scratch. Very young pigs may be anaemic with heavy infestations. Growth rate may be reduced by up to 50 g/day.

*Treatment and control*
Lice will be effectively eliminated by control measures successful for mange (see below).

MANGE
Pigs may suffer from sarcoptic mange or demodectic mange – the latter being so rare that it will not be discussed further. Sarcoptic mange is caused by the mite *Sarcoptes scabiei* var. *suis*, and it is very common in all pig rearing areas of the world.

*Life cycle*
The adult female (a small, greyish white circular parasite, 0.5 mm in length and just visible to the naked eye) lays her eggs in tunnels in the skin (see colour plate 20). She may lay up to 50 eggs before dying at the age of one month. The eggs hatch in the tunnels into larvae, then moult to nymphs and adults. The whole cycle is complete in 10 to 15 days. Spread is from pig to pig by contact or by recently infected bedding. It has been demonstrated that mites may survive for up to 2 weeks away from pigs under laboratory conditions. However, under farm conditions, mite survival is likely to be much shorter. Chronic ear lesions are the main source of mites and it has been estimated that each gram of ear scraping material may harbour as many as 18,000 mites. It is often difficult to find mites in other parts of the body.

*Clinical signs*
The main clinical sign is scratching and rubbing – a sequel to pruritus and hypersensitivity. Research work by Cargill and Dobson (1979) has shown that there are two distinct forms of mange. The first is the chronic type, characterised by encrusted plaques inside the ears and thighs of some older breeding animals (see colour plate 21) – these lesions being the source of mites and therefore infection for the rest of the herd. The second type is due to the development of hypersensitivity of the skin, characterised by small focal reddish skin papules over the rump, flank and abdomen and may affect many pigs in the herd. Affected pigs may show intense irritation by scratching and rubbing themselves frequently. The skin gradually becomes more wrinkled and thickened with hair loss and skin abrasion occurring in some animals. Cargill and Dobson estimated that the deterioration in both growth rate and food conversion efficiency is approximately 10 per cent. In addition, there is the cost of treatment to consider.

*Treatment and control*

Mange can be effectively controlled and eradicated by thorough treatment of the breeding herd and effective isolation of treated animals from young infected stock or contaminated bedding. In practice, this is most easily achieved by the simultaneous treatment of all breeding stock twice with an interval of 10 days between treatments. Mange has been eradicated on a herd basis by the simultaneous treatment of all pigs in the herd with one injection of ivermectin (Hogg 1984). As this drug persists in the body of the pig for up to 3 weeks, a second injection is unnecessary. All other treatments should be preceded by thorough washing and scrubbing of chronic crusty lesions before washing, spraying or even the use of pour-on compounds. If spraying is the only method of treatment, it may have to be carried out at 4 day intervals for 3 months and even then may fail on a herd basis. It is important to note that boars must also be treated as part of the breeding herd.

## Miscellaneous Conditions

### TORSION OF THE MESENTERY

This disorder has been referred to as bloody gut and the intestinal haemorrhage syndrome or whey bloat (see colour plate 22). The problem usually presents as sudden death. On the few occasions when a pig is seen to be ill before death, it is obviously in great pain with abdominal discomfort and shock. Usually pigs of 35 to 70 kgs are affected, although smaller and larger pigs have been known to die. The carcass rapidly becomes bloated and very pale on the whole. Only rapidly growing healthy pigs succumb and the incidence is much higher with whey feeding. The incidence of such cases is rarely recorded but in one herd with a post-weaning mortality of 1.6 per cent, Smith (1976) noted that torsion of the mesentery was responsible for 50 per cent of the deaths, while in another herd with an 8 per cent post-weaning mortality, Jones (1976) noted that intestinal haemorrhage syndrome accounted for 15 per cent of the deaths.

The cause of the condition is not known but one theory is that the torsion of the whole gut around the root of mesentery is a sequel to fermentation followed by dilation of the large bowel. It is possible that a large dilated caecum could act like a lever pushing the gut round in a circle.

Because the cause is unknown, it is difficult to be precise about control and prevention, especially as the condition is so sporadic. However, reducing whey intake and feed intake in general seems to reduce the prevalence of the disorder. The addition of formalin to whey and antibiotics to the feed is said to have been beneficial in some instances. In one problem herd, the addition of monensin to the diet (100 ppm) prevented further cases arising. However, it should be borne in mind that any treatment considered should be cost effective. The condition can only be diagnosed by a veterinary surgeon. Torsion of the large intestine only (see colour plate 23) or a loop of the small intestine is not uncommon.

### RECTAL PROLAPSE

The majority of farmers in the United Kingdom will have experienced an outbreak of this condition.

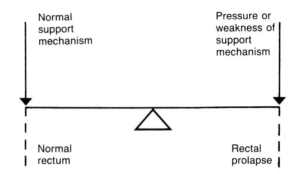

Pressure on the support mechanism will increase when:

Gut load increases
Straining occurs
Coughing is excessive
Constipation is present
Overcrowding occurs

Weakness of the support mechanism will occur when:

The structure becomes oedematous
Excessive deposition of fat occurs
Degenerative conditions arise
Genetic defects are present

FIGURE 11.1   Forces acting on the rectum.

Rectal prolapse is not an all or nothing phenomenon. Those cases which prolapse frequently represent the tip of the iceberg. The rectum itself is a very elastic piece of tissue which is held in place by a complex arrangement of muscles, ligaments and peritoneal fascia. In simple terms, this supportive apparatus may be referred to as the pelvic girdle. The girdle itself is elastic and every time the pig breathes, coughs or jumps up, the rectum will be displaced backwards. When the supportive mechanism fails, the rectal mucosa will evert and prolapse completely (see colour plate 24) – the amount of rectal mucosa extruded varying markedly from pig to pig.

In theory, the supportive mechanism will fail when (a) the pressure on it is too great or (b) there is an inherent weakness or instability. The degree of the problem is dependent on the balance between the strength of the support mechanism and the forces aligned against it (pressure, weakness) as illustrated in Figure 11.1.

Excessive straining in males will occur in cases of urethral obstruction. One outbreak in which calculi blocked the urethra is described by Wood (1979), but such cases are rare. Any diet which leads to constipation will increase the prevalence of rectal prolapse.

It has been suggested that the modern, genetically improved, rapidly growing pig tends to deposit excess fat in the pelvic area, so weakening the support tissues. In addition, many pigs are fed ad lib. to 90 kg liveweight and the relatively large intake of feed could increase pressure on the support mechanism. Overstocking and intense competition at feeders are other factors leading to an increase in the condition. Rectal prolapse may also be induced by some drugs. Oestrogens or compounds with an oestrogenic effect will induce prolapse. 'Mouldy corn' poisoning is one example (see page 265). The use of tylosin has occasionally been associated with the appearance of rectal prolapse, and lincomycin has also been linked with the problem (Kunesh 1981).

Some pig keepers in a few countries have noted a rise in incidence after a spell of cold weather. And finally, genetic susceptibility has been suggested by many pig keepers as the cause of rectal prolapse. In the few cases in Scotland where accurate data were available, there was no evidence that the cause was genetic. In one farm outbreak in Canada, however, it was shown that one particular boar was more likely to sire offspring with a tendency to rectal prolapse.

*Treatment and control*

Prolapsed cases should be removed to a hospital pen and treated by surgical means. Usually, replacement of prolapsed mucosa, followed by a purse string suture and antibiotic cover, will suffice to cure most cases. Surgical treatment can be made easier and more successful by inserting a piece of corrugated rubber hose into the prolapse and tying a ligature around the prolapsed portion. Occasionally a severely damaged rectal mucosa will have to be resected by a veterinary surgeon.

In the United Kingdom, many cases are treated by isolation and letting the prolapses resolve naturally. This takes anything from 10 to 20 days. In another outbreak described by Garden (1984), the number of cases dropped dramatically when pigs were given access to straw for 3 weeks between two periods in intensive housing systems.

Prevention is only likely to be effective when one can be specific about the cause. Steps taken are more often based on guesswork and intuition than on facts. In many cases the factor(s) responsible will have disappeared by the time the disorder becomes apparent. Pigs which recover naturally from rectal prolapse will successfully reach bacon weight in the majority of cases. However, Smith (1980) noted that 21 per cent of affected pigs developed complete rectal stricture. Partial rectal stricture is likely to be found in the majority of survivors which reach slaughter weight.

In a recent post-mortem survey of finishing pigs it was noted that 0.7 per cent of pigs with a history of sudden death had suffered fatal haemorrhage from a bitten-off rectal prolapse. Some cases may also resolve naturally in a very short time, so that they go unobserved by the pigman.

RECTAL STRICTURE

This disorder has always been thought of as an all or nothing phenomenon characterised by a gradual swelling of the abdomen, loss of condition and failure to pass faeces (see colour plate 25). However, as the condition becomes clinical only when the stricture is almost complete, clinical cases probably represent the tip of the iceberg. The prevalence of the condition always increases 5 to 6 weeks after an outbreak of rectal prolapse.

The cause of the condition is the natural healing of lesions in the rectum. Healing involves the formation of scar tissue which is fibrous and constrictive in nature. If the damage is severe, scar tissue will be more prevalent and complete stricture is more likely to follow. The cause of the lesion in the first place is nearly always traumatic damage to a prolapsed rectal mucosa. There is one report of the condition being due to salmonella infection in the rectum (Wilcock and Ollander, 1977) but this observation has not been confirmed by any other workers to date. In laboratory observations and in field investigations involving over 200 cases, the close relationship between rectal prolapse and rectal strictures (both complete and partial) has been confirmed (see colour plate 26).

### Treatment
Early cases can be kept alive by continually breaking down the scar tissue by rectal digital manipulation.

PORCINE STRESS SYNDROME (PSS)
This condition is closely linked with other syndromes known as malignant hyperthermia, sudden death in transport and pale, soft, exudative muscle (PSE). The condition is known in all areas of the world with some strains of genetically improved pigs. Deaths occur most frequently in pigs of 30 to 90 kg but have also been reported in breeeding gilts and young sows. There is a wide variation in the prevalence of the condition between genotypes.

### Clinical signs
These usually begin when some stressful situation arises, e.g. movement, mixing, fighting, transport and during anaesthesia. Initially, tremors of the tail and muscles may be noticed, followed by rapid, irregular breathing and changing patterns of skin discolouration associated with various levels of blood flow. This stage is followed by a bluish discolouration of the skin (cyanosis), especially of the extremities, a rapid increase in body temperature, marked muscle rigidity, collapse and death. Affected pigs are always in excellent condition. Another form of the condition appears as pale, soft, exudative muscle (PSE) after slaughter.

### Prevention
The gene can be eradicated from a herd by use of a blood test which identifies carriers. (For further reference to this condition see pages 60 and 67.)

Until such time as the gene can be reduced to tolerable levels, care should be taken with the mixing, movement and transport of pigs. They should be put on board lorries with care and patience and never forced. Loading on to the top deck is not advised, especially if the weather is hot. Indeed in warm weather it is worthwhile spraying the pigs with cold water at 10 minute intervals while they await transportation. Transport deaths can be reduced by ensuring adequate ventilation in the transporter, if possible avoiding transport when the temperature is excessive, avoiding undue physical exertion and excitement during loading and not feeding during the 12 hours prior to transportation. Periods in the lairage should be reduced to a minimum unless there is access to sugar solutions. Prevalence of PSE in the slaughter house is greater when carbon dioxide rather than electrical stunning is used.

GASTRO-OESOPHAGEAL ULCERATION
This condition has been recognised in all pig keeping countries and refers specifi-

cally to ulceration of the small area in the stomach around the entrance of the oesophagus. This area is lined with the same type of mucous membrane as the oesophagus itself.

*Clinical signs*

There appear to be few, if any, clinical signs until the ulcerated area starts to haemorrhage. If the haemorrhage is sudden and massive, the result is sudden death with the carcass appearing pale. Clinical signs of those which bleed chronically and intermittently include paleness, increased heavy breathing, loss of condition, occasional vomiting and the passage of dark-coloured faeces which are often hard and pelleted. These symptoms persist for 3 to 4 months before death. Once serious bleeding begins, the condition is invariably fatal. The condition may present as sporadic cases or as a severe and continuous outbreak.

There are many possible causes of gastric ulceration (see Table 11.1). Outbreaks in the United Kingdom, which have often been associated with nutrition, have been induced either by finely milled grain or by a deficiency of vitamin E of a primary or secondary nature. The cause of sporadic cases is unlikely to be found.

**TABLE 11.1   Factors which are claimed to predispose to gastro-oesophageal ulceration**

| Nutrition | Management | Infections | Other |
| --- | --- | --- | --- |
| High energy diets | Overcrowding | *Candida albicans* | Stress |
| Low fibre diets | Confinement | *Ascaris suum* | Pregnancy |
| Low protein diets | Cage-rearing | Erysipelas | Parturition |
| Heat-gelatinised grain | Restraint | Swine fever | Heredity |
| Pelleting | Handling and | | Reserpine |
| Winter pasture | transport | | Histamine |
| Small particle size | | | Ligation of |
| Whey and skim | | | bile duct |
| feeding | | | |
| Wet feeding | | | |
| High Fe, Cu, Ca, Zn | | | |
| Vitamin E and/or | | | |
| selenium deficiency | | | |
| Rancidity | | | |

(Source: RHC Penny)

*Treatment and control*

Clinical cases rarely respond to treatment and should be slaughtered. Sub-clinical cases with early stages of ulceration will respond quickly to removal of the offending ulcerogenic factor. Inspection of stomachs at the abattoir can provide useful early warning of an impending outbreak. Attempts should be made to avoid all situations likely to precipitate ulceration.

GROWER SCOUR

This disorder has become prevalent in the United Kingdom in more recent years and has probably been described under various names such as sticky dung syndrome and cow pat dung syndrome. These disorders may have different causes or indeed may be different manifestations of a common cause. The condition usually presents in pigs of 20 to 50 kg with nil mortality and variable but usually high morbidity. Pigs in a pen becoming dirty is usually the first indication of the disorder. The consistency of the stools may vary from sloppy, sticky dung to diarrhoea. The diarrhoea may often appear within 24 hours after the delivery of a new batch of feed – usually pelleted. Pigs may quickly cease to scour after removal of the suspect batch of feed. However, this same feed may be delivered to another unit where it is found to be wholly satisfactory. The condition becomes more obvious in pigs kept in pens with solid floors and scrape-through solid dunging passages.

Pigs fed meal instead of pellets have shown a remarkable improvement within hours even when the meal is made from exactly the same ingredients and to the same specifications as the pellets (see colour plates 31 and 32). Responses to treatment with antibiotics have been variable. Often a good initial response fades in a few days or weeks and the condition recurs. Improvement in pen hygiene has also given disappointing results. Some strains of spirochaetal organisms may infect the colon and cause a mild mucohaemorrhagic colitis in some pigs. In these cases, false positives to the Fluorescent Antibody Test for swine dysentery (SD) have been noted.

## Poisons and Toxins

SALT

Salt poisoning is also known as water deprivation, as both can produce the same clinico-pathological disorder.

### Clinical signs

Clinically the condition presents as blindness, staggering movements, fits and finally coma. The fits are aptly described by Done and Bradley (1984) as follows:

> The seizures of salt poisoning take a characteristic form, with the pig at first standing or sitting tensely and apprehensively, ears pricked, staring ahead and slightly upward as though seeing some object invisible to the human observer. Then the nose starts to twitch, the head nods, the eyes close and rhythmic chomping of the jaws produces a froth of saliva. As the clonic movements increase in strength and amplitude, the head is forced up and the pig moves backward. The body becomes increasingly rigid until the seizure reaches its climax and the animal falls down in apnea, often preceded by a hoarse cry. After an attack the pig lies quietly in a coma until normal respiration is restored; then it resumes the same behaviour as before the fit.

Affected pigs may attempt to climb the walls or press their heads into a corner. Mortality varies considerably but is not often more than 5 per cent before the source of the problem is rectified.

The disorder often arises when pigs are fed swill (garbage) with a high salt content or when water intake is reduced, e.g. through frozen pipes or lack of knowledge regarding the use of nipple drinkers by young pigs. The disorder can only be confirmed by a veterinary surgeon who will often require laboratory backup.

*Treatment and prevention*
Steps must be taken to ensure that all pipes are lagged so as to minimise risk of freezing and that young pigs are gradually introduced to nipple drinkers in the farrowing pen. The drinkers should be placed in an accessible place in the weaner house. Swill with a high salt content should be avoided. There is no effective treatment, although Shanks (1972) found that boiled water by intraperitoneal injection was of benefit.

MERCURY
All forms of mercury may cause poisoning in swine but the most likely source is cereal seed dressed with mercurial fungicide. Ingestion leads to diarrhoea due to gastro-enteritis followed by signs of central nervous system (CNS) involvement, e.g. blindness, ataxia, partial paralysis, coma and death. The disorder can only be diagnosed by a veterinary surgeon who may require laboratory backup.

*Treatment and prevention*
Care should be taken to avoid the use of cereal seed dressed with mercury. There is no suitable treatment.

COPPER
Copper toxicity usually arises when mistakes are made in mixing or inclusion rates. Pigs can tolerate high levels of copper (250 ppm or even higher), providing the levels of iron, zinc and calcium are also raised.

*Clinical signs*
Affected pigs become pale and listless. The stools may become dark coloured owing to altered blood. This stage is followed by collapse and death. The condition can only be diagnosed by a veterinary surgeon and confirmed by laboratory tests. It can be prevented by restricting feed levels of copper to 200 ppm.

COAL TAR (PHENOL)
Poisoning with coal tar derivatives such as phenol and cresol and ingestion of clay pigeons may present as an acute or chronic form depending on the amount ingested. In addition, piglets housed in recently disinfected pens may develop skin lesions characterised by small weals and papules. Acute poisoning very quickly results in death. In the more chronic form, pigs gradually lose condition, become pale or sometimes yellow coloured due to jaundice and sometimes show evidence of abdominal pain.

The condition can only be diagnosed by a veterinary surgeon. There is no effective treatment.

NITRATES AND NITRITES
Large quantities of both products may accumulate in water or plant sources and in

addition may come from substances such as fertiliser. Animal wastes, decaying vegetable matter, silage effluent and soils high in nitrogen-fixing material may hold high levels of nitrate and consequently may become the source of nitrate poison.

Nitrate is converted to nitrite in the body and the latter substance is very toxic. Haemoglobin is converted to methaemoglobin and death from hypoxia results. This results in increased respiratory rate, salivation, ataxia, the frequent passage of urine and finally convulsions. Diagnosis and treatment are best left to a veterinarian.

### WARFARIN
Pigs of any age between weaning and slaughter weight may contract warfarin poisoning if they have access to rodenticide containing the poison.

### *Clinical signs*
Affected pigs become pale due to internal haemorrhage. As they become more anaemic, the respiratory rate rises. Swellings over the joints are common and may also occur in any part of the body which has been traumatised. Bleeding from the mouth may be seen. Pigs with joint haemorrhage may become acutely lame.

### *Treatment*
Pigs will respond to vitamin K by both parenteral and oral routes.

### PIGWEED POISONING
Pigweed, more properly known as *Amaranthus retroflexus*, is a common weed in some swine rearing areas, and poisoning after ingestion tends to occur in the autumn.

Five to ten days after access to the plant, the affected pigs begin to lose coordination, tremble and become ataxic. They finally assume sternal recumbency (lying on belly or sternum) and posterior paralysis develops. Mortality of affected pigs may reach 90 per cent.

Post-mortem lesions are characteristic, the main one being perirenal oedema (another name for the disorder).

### *Treatment and prevention*
There is no effective treatment. Access to pigweed-contaminated areas should be prevented.

Other plants such as cockleburs, nightshade, hemlock and bracken may cause poisoning, but outbreaks are extremely rare and will not be discussed in this book.

## Mycotoxins

Many fungi are capable of producing toxins. Some of these fungi and their toxins have been identified; many have still to be identified. It should be noted that feedstuffs do not necessarily need to be obviously mouldy for toxins to be present.

### AFLATOXICOSIS
This disorder is produced by toxins from the fungus *Aspergillus flavus*. The fungus

may colonise the growing grain, and its presence will not be obvious in the finished feed.

Clinical signs include depressed appetite, wasting, palour, jaundice and collapse. These signs are mainly a sequel to chronic, irreversible liver damage.

### Treatment and prevention

Pig feed can easily be assayed for the presence of the toxin, and most large feed compounders carry out such assays on a routine basis. There is no effective treatment for affected pigs, which are best humanely destroyed.

### OCHRATOXIN

This toxin may be produced by several fungi often present in barley and oats.

Clinical signs are those due to kidney damage, i.e. frequent urination, increased thirst, dehydration and toxaemia. If offending feed is withdrawn in the early stages of the disease, most animals will recover. The disease has mainly been reported from Denmark.

### ERGOT

This toxin from the mould *Claviceps purpurea* is commonly found in cereal grains and grasses. In finishing pigs, the main clinical sign is gangrene of the extremities – mainly ear tips, feet and tail.

### Treatment and prevention

Badly affected pigs should be humanely destroyed. Others will recover if the contaminated feed is withdrawn. Feed can readily be assayed for the toxin.

### ZEARALENONE (F2 TOXIN)

This toxin is produced by the fungus *Fusarium graminearum* and has an oestrogenic effect on the body, i.e. it produces similar effects to the female hormone oestrogen. Clinical signs in finishing pigs include swelling and reddening of the vulva, enlargement of the teats and mammary glands and rectal prolapse. The condition is also known as mouldy corn poisoning.

### Treatment and prevention

Withdrawal of contaminated feedstuffs will cause the problem to resolve.

### FEED REFUSAL

This problem can be an embarrassment to both the veterinarian and the feed supplier. The circumstantial evidence that a new batch of feed is the cause can be quite overwhelming, yet, in some instances, the same feed can be taken to another farm where the pigs will readily consume it. Other cases of feed refusal have been linked with the presence of T-2 toxin, diacetoxyscirpenol and vomitoxin – all known as *Tricothecenes*. However, feed refusal may be linked to other ingredients in the ration such as feed additives, preservatives and others included by mistake. Feed refusal is often the only early symptom of an incubating disease. A diagnosis is rarely reached in the majority of cases. When it does happen, and it is clear that the pigs are not subclinically ill, the feed should be withdrawn. If tests fail to demonstrate the cause it may be fed to sows or to other pigs of the same age group, suitably diluted with other feed. Should a pigkeeper find that his own grain is contaminated with a fungal toxin, it will often be safe to feed it provided it is well *diluted* with uncontaminated grain.

## Drug Side Effects

All drugs may be toxic if the pig consumes more than the therapeutic dose for long enough. This is only likely to occur in cases of misuse or misformulation.

ANTIBIOTICS
Lincomycin may cause pigs to have loose stools for 2 to 8 days after administration, and some of these may develop prolapse of the rectum. Tylosin may cause oedema and irritation of the anus (see Rectal prolapse, page 257). Neomycin, when overdosed by injection, may cause kidney damage, while too much streptomycin may cause ear damage. Procaine penicillin may be toxic and even lethal to pigs because of the sudden release of toxic amounts of free procaine. Within hours of administration, affected pigs develop shivering, lassitude, inappetance, vomiting, cyanosis of the extremities and a high temperature (over 40° C). (Embrechts 1983 and Smith and Christie 1982.)

ORGANIC ARSENICALS
A number of these drugs are available as growth promoters or as therapeutic agents for treating swine dysentery and eperythrozoonosis. Sodium arsanilate may be added to the drinking water at 175 ppm for 6 days, arsanilic acid for feed therapy at 400 to 500 ppm for 5 to 6 days and 3-nitro 4-hydroxyphenylarsonic acid at 200 ppm for 5 to 6 days. These dosage rates are only guidelines and the appearance of toxicity will depend upon the intake and length of time for which ingested, e.g. signs of toxicity will appear with arsanilic acid if fed for 3 to 6 weeks at 250 ppm and differ from those of '3-nitro' in some ways.

*Arsanilic acid and sodium arsanilate*
Affected pigs may walk with a 'goose-stepping' gait as described in pantothenic acid deficiency. Most become blind and will circle round in an aimless manner. They are easily knocked over by healthy pen mates. Tremor of the head and more pronounced incoordination are followed by paralysis.

*3-nitro 4-hydroxyphenylarsonic acid ('3-nitro')*
Poisoning with this compound may produce not only similar symptoms to arsanilic acid poisoning but also signs which are markedly different. The description given by Gillet (1981) is similar to that seen by the writer (W.S.) and is given here verbatim.

> Veterinary advice was sought when the mortality rate in the five-to-eight-week-old age group of pigs weaned around 4 weeks of age rose markedly over a two to three week period. In one incident, when 40 pigs were moved from a flat deck house to the verandah house, 11 died within a few hours. When inspected under the increased illumination of fluorescent strip lighting, pigs in the flat deck pen became hyperexcited and squealed

excessively. Trembling, collapse and sometimes death followed. Restraint and parenteral administration of a vitamin E and selenium preparation (Dystosel:Intervet) to survivors resulted in further deaths within a few minutes of the procedure.

Detailed observation of the progress of the acute symptoms showed that after three to four minutes of introduction of the hyperexcitable state a small number of pigs from each of the groups stood still and trembled over the entire body. Simultaneously, irregular erythematous areas appeared on the skin of the back and hind quarters and showed a changing pattern of distribution. Skeletal musculature appeared prominent. The trembling became more severe until after two to three minutes the pigs became recumbent, usually lying on their sternum, after which the trembling ceased. Rectal temperatures varied between 39.5° C and 40.5° C and respiratory and heart rates were elevated. Within five to ten minutes of the onset of trembling, some pigs became comatose, heart and respiratory rates slowed and death occurred some 15 minutes from onset of trembling. There was no evidence of muscular rigidity preceding death.

The majority of trembling pigs recovered when left quiet and undisturbed but they remained susceptible to future intervention. Others, after one or more episodes of trembling and recumbency, survived to develop ataxia with paraparesis or paraplegia a few days later. Several cases showing the latter symptoms became evident among the pigs which survived the transfer from flat deck to verandah houses.

The histopathological changes are the same for each condition.

Most cases will survive if given access to non-medicated food and water. It is important to make sure that affected pigs get water, especially if they are semi-paralysed. This can easily be achieved by giving water per rectum.

As most cases arise from faulty inclusion rates, great care must be taken with mixing – especially the 3-nitro compound. In addition, the prescribed treatment time must not be exceeded.

## Vices

### TAIL BITING

Tail biting is a vice that was at one time confined almost exclusively to finishing pigs but is now becoming more common in early weaned pigs, particularly those reared in flat decks and cages. Most observers would express the view that it is a problem that has increased markedly with intensification, but the etiology is still obscure. It is rare in suckling piglets and breeding stock but occurs in all other ages of pigs (weaners, growers and finishers). Pigs of 12 to 16 weeks of age are perhaps at greatest risk, although well-documented evidence for this statement is scanty (see colour plate 27).

### *Incidence*

The literature indicates that the incidence of tail biting is highly variable, and many of the data have been collected on samples of pigs at the abattoir. However, it is clear that in most countries with intensifying swine industries there has been an increase in the condition.

In two large units in East Germany, tail biting was seen in 68.8 per cent of pigs housed on fully slatted concrete floors and in 34.8 per cent of pigs housed on solid concrete floors. Both groups were without bedding, and the sample sizes were 3874 and 784 respectively.

From the United Kingdom, reports on the frequency in abattoir samples have also varied. In a survey of cutter weight pigs (up to 75 kg liveweight), the frequency was 11.6 per cent. However, if the 34.6 per cent of tail-docked pigs had been included in the analysis, the overall frequency would have been 7.5 per cent. In another survey on heavy hogs (approximately 120 kg liveweight), the incidence of tail bitten pigs was 4.3 per cent. In both surveys the tails of males were about twice as frequently bitten as those of females (Penny and Hill 1974, Penny and Mullen 1976). This last observation has been confirmed on many commercial farms. According to the Ministry of Agriculture, Fisheries and Food figures, the condemnation rate for pyaemia in the United Kingdom during the 1960s rose from 0.012 per cent in 1964 to 0.135 per cent in 1968. Since that time the figure has fluctuated but, in general, has decreased quite markedly, and the change has been attributed to the now widespread practice of tail docking (Penny 1975).

### Economic effects
The economic effects are not well documented but arise through the paralysis and death of badly bitten animals following advanced infection and cannibalism, the decrease in feed efficiency and growth rate resulting from the bullying and restlessness precipitated, cost of treatment and control measures, loss of meat from total or partial condemnation at the abattoir, and additional meat inspection needed. Consideration must also be given to the economic and other pressures that may be exerted on the industry by the welfare lobbies over this unpleasant vice.

### Development of the disorder
Most observers agree that at least one pig, frequently below average size for the group, bites or chews the tail of another pig, often severely enough to produce a raw sore or to draw blood. The abnormal behaviour of one or more pigs may then develop into a vice, and a few or many in the pen will seek out the damaged tails and chew on them. In the early stages, those afflicted often seem unconcerned by gentle chewing; a case was observed in which 27 chewing movements were made on a pig's tail before it objected.

The initial cause of stimulus is often obscure, but overall opinion (both subjective and objective) suggests that tail biting is a form of maladaptive behaviour that turns into a vice and is aggravated or precipitated by a number of factors (stimuli), which, although individually not pathognomonic, are cumulative in their effect. The more important of these factors are discussed below.

### Physical environment
It has been demonstrated that tail biting becomes more common as the proportion of slatted floor in the pen is increased. This is independent of climatic factors (Madsen et al. 1970). In houses with partially slatted floors, the position of the slats seems important. Slats immediately behind the feeding trough lead to more tail biting than slats in the dunging area only (Hansen and Hagelso 1979). This finding may be related to the inability of pigs lower in social rank to compete successfully at the trough on slatted floors. It has also been observed that instability in the social order is more likely on totally slatted floors in a competitive feeding situation (Hansen 1977, Hansen and Hagelso 1979). Lower ranking pigs were noticeably

more aggressive, especially during feeding, and were observed to attack from behind in attempts to drive those higher in rank away from the trough (see colour plate 28). This they would have been unable to do in a normal head to shoulder confrontation on a solid floor. It is well accepted that tail biting is more common in pens not bedded with straw (Madsen and Nielsen 1970; Svengaard 1970; Von Hofsten 1970; Nielsen and Madsen 1971). The presence of straw may influence tail biting in a number of ways: it has occupational, comfort, hygienic and nutritional value.

The frequency of tail biting is known to be higher in units with large numbers of pigs per pen and high stocking densities. Such intensification can lead to instability in the social order. Nevertheless, it has proved extremely difficult to reproduce tail biting merely by reducing floor space per pig, and several cases of biting have also been noted in straw bedded pens in which the stocking rate was relatively low.

*Climatic environment*
At least one worker (Van Putten 1968) has demonstrated that lowering the temperature may increase the frequency of tail biting. Nevertheless, many outbreaks have been linked with unusually high environmental temperatures when pigs have no access to wallows or other means of keeping cool. Any extremes of temperature or large diurnal variation in temperature should be avoided.

Dry, dusty conditions may lead to more irritability and aggression, but pigs can tolerate a wide range of humidity without untoward reaction. In fact, there is no evidence that 'sweat box' conditions increase the severity of tail biting.

Ventilation rate, or the rate of air exchange, may exert an effect on liability to tail biting through relative humidity, temperature or the level of potentially toxic gases in the atmosphere. When the ventilation rate of climatically controlled or naturally ventilated buildings is reduced, the incidence of tail biting is likely to rise.

Although some workers have shown that there is a greater frequency of tail biting with increasing concentrations of gases such as ammonia ($NH_3$), carbon dioxide ($CO_2$) and hydrogen sulphide ($H_2S$), others have been unable to demonstrate any such correlation. It seems more likely that levels of gases will be linked to inadequate ventilation rates and changes in temperature, so the picture is a complicated one. Nevertheless, high levels of toxic gas should be avoided, not only from a human and pig health point of view, but also because of their possible involvement in tail biting.

In barren, uninteresting environments, bright light can act as a stressor and may precipitate tail biting. In pig houses the light intensity should be as low as possible but not so dark as to make inspection of the pigs difficult. Keeping pigs in the dark will reduce the overall activity of the group by some 20 per cent (Van Putten 1968).

*Nutrition*
Many nutritional factors have been blamed for precipitating outbreaks of tail biting. Deficiencies of vitamins, iron, copper, calcium, phosphorus, magnesium, salt and fibre and poor-quality protein have all been suspected. One worker suggested that tail biting could be induced by a vegetable diet high in energy and low in fibre. However, Ewbank (1973) failed to induce tail biting by feeding such a diet, and

other experiments have failed to substantiate this suggestion. When other contributory factors to tail biting are absent, there is no evidence that such biting will be a problem when diets up to National Research Council (NRC) or Agricultural and Food Research Council (AFRC) specifications are offered at normal levels. Common fallacies are that blood meal in the diet will lead to tail biting and that meat and fish meals will prevent it.

The quantity or availability of food probably plays a much more important role than the nutritional value of the food itself. Lack of trough space, over-restricted feeding, and lack of water are often implicated in outbreaks of tail biting. Some observers have noted severe aggression during competition at ad lib. feeders, probably because of the tendency to feed as a group from birth. The situation can be complicated by large group size and other factors such as a rough floor surface. Hansen and Hagelso (1979) demonstrated an increasing frequency of tail biting in pigs fed ad lib. with decreasing trough space. Malnutrition may therefore exert its effects through factors associated with the presentation of the food. Trough or hopper space and the number of watering points may interfere with availability of food.

*Concomitant disease*
Clinical or subclinical disease has often been suggested as a cause of tail biting, and internal and external parasites may play a role by causing increased irritability (Colyer 1970). It is unlikely that a disease state in itself will cause tail biting, but it may act as an additional predisposing factor.

*Treatment and control*
Consideration should immediately be given to the triggering factors mentioned, and glaring errors should be rectified. The incidence and severity of tail biting can be reduced by pinpointing and removing the culprits. Dimming the light may also help. Where pen design permits, the introduction of some straw may be useful. To prevent boredom, toys such as chains, wires, tyres, paper bags, tin cans, pieces of timber, etc. all have their advocates. Various preparations such as Stockholm tar can be applied to tails and rumps. Nutritional changes may be recommended and additional salt in the ration up to 2½ per cent has proved an effective control measure if water is readily available. Tranquillisers have been used, particularly where pigs have to be mixed or moved. Surgical amputation of the affected tail is recommended by Hagen and Skulberg (1960).

The docking of piglets' tails within the first few days of life is a commonly accepted preventive measure. The introduction of a cull sow to the pens may have a beneficial effect on group behaviour.

Management errors should be corrected one at a time, and an experimental approach may be needed, checking off the possible triggering factors discussed above.

EAR BITING
Ear biting is a more recently recognised vice than tail biting. The condition may be on the increase, particularly in units where early weaning is practised, and it tends to occur at an earlier stage than tail biting. In an abattoir sample, 12.2 per cent of

pigs showed evidence of the vice and in a farm sample, 27.7 per cent showed such evidence. There was no sex-related incidence, and in a farm sample the frequency declined after 10 to 12 weeks of age.

Ears may be bitten at two main sites: at the base where the lobe joins the cheek and at the ear tip (see colour plate 29). As would be expected, in most cases both ears are affected. Both sites may be bitten in some outbreaks, but in others a single site is the rule.

In mild outbreaks, damage is minimal and the lesions soon heal, but in some, the ear(s) may be lost, and occasionally attacks are fatal. In general, the economic effects are much less severe than with tail biting.

### Development of the disorder

The etiology is obscure and, like tail biting, is probably multifactorial, with many factors common between the two conditions. Large groups of early weaned pigs in intensive, barren and uninteresting environments are at particular risk; but the condition has been seen in pigs reared on straw and with both wet and dry feeding systems. An unsatisfied sucking reflex has been suggested as a precipitating factor. At first, the ear is sucked or nibbled very gently, and at this stage the attention may even appear to be appreciated. However, when a raw area is produced and blood is drawn, affected animals squeal and try to avoid their pursuers.

In some outbreaks, the pigs seem particularly restless and sarcoptic mange has been suspected as a precipitating factor, but treatment for these parasites does not always control the problem.

### Treatment and control

Treatment and control measures should be similar to those mentioned for tail biting.

#### FLANK BITING

This is another more recently observed vice that tends to occur mainly in groups of 20 or more pigs between 6 and 20 weeks of age. Outbreaks are usually sporadic, but some have been continuous in successive groups of pigs housed in the same pens within the same buildings. The condition is more common during the summer months. There is no sex-related incidence. Outbreaks are not confined to barren, apparently uninteresting environments. The condition is more common in docked pigs and can be found on straw based systems.

### Development

The site of the lesion or lesions varies from pig to pig but usually is the lower rib cage and flank (see colour plate 30), but lesions have been seen on the rump and also on the middle of the back. Lesions start as raised edematous plaques up to 2 inches in diameter, often with reddening of the skin. Eventually the skin becomes denuded, and subcutaneous edema with a central area of necrosis develops. Gradually the skin becomes ulcerated but haemorrhage is rarely a feature. Occasionally the ulcer may penetrate all muscle layers, and at this stage tissue decomposition is advanced and a putrid smell will be present. Infection may supervene, and an abscess may develop at the site.

The vice gradually progresses from snout rubbing to flank biting. Where outbreaks have been observed, snout rubbing by one or several animals in the pen is a common finding and the nose movement resembles that used by the piglet to induce milk 'letdown'. One animal was observed to receive 165 snout-rubbing movements at the same site by another pig without showing any signs of displeasure. The rubbing movements took place while the recipient animal was either lying on the floor or standing. Animals object only when rubbing reaches the stage of painful friction. Licking of the skin has also been observed during the snout-rubbing phase. Once the skin is broken and serum exudes, other pigs may bite the area and eventually an ulcer forms. Many secondary organisms including fungi have been isolated in these ulcers.

Once this vice becomes established, pigs may be seen moving from one affected animal to another and biting the lesions. In many outbreaks, ample bedding, trough space and drinking points are available. The snout rubbing does not occur around the feeding or drinking areas, and attempts to prevent further outbreaks by changing the diet have failed. When badly affected pigs are housed separately, rapid healing of lesions occurs. Lesions do not occur spontaneously as in outbreaks of spirochetal dermatitis, and spirochetes have not been present in flank-bitten lesions. Flank biting and ear biting have often appeared simultaneously, which suggests there are likely to be common precipitating factors.

*Treatment and control*
Attempts must be made to find the initial precipitating factors. Injured animals recover quickly after hospitalisation.

PEN FOULING
Contrary to uninformed opinion, the domestic pig is a remarkably clean animal. If provided with a suitable environment, the pig, either singly or as a group, will excrete in a small part of the pen away from the lying area. However, breakdown of this pattern of behaviour has become more common in intensive units, and the dirty conditions resulting have increased the disease hazard. It has also become apparent that there are many different causes of pen fouling and the problem is complex. However, irrespective of the cause(s), it can rightly be said that pen fouling is a fault of humans rather than pigs in that the social, physical or climatic environment must in some way be suboptimal. The two exceptions to the rule are the odd pig with an indiscriminate excretion pattern and the pig suffering from diarrhoea or dysentery.

*Etiology*
Many reasons have been offered to explain pen fouling, but the conclusions and observations of Baxter and Robertson (1979) given below are probably the most soundly based.

In colder conditions pigs lie away from their excretory area to prevent loss of body heat from dampness. An increase in ambient temperature may cause abnormal excretory patterns.

Individuals have personal excretory areas within the pen area. Indiscriminate excretion in a pen may be caused by actions of a single pig.

Pigs are unstable during excretion and so seek an area of minimal disturbance for that purpose. If such an area cannot be found, abnormal patterns may ensue.

Pigs excrete away from a drinker if at any time the demand for water exceeds its supply (i.e. a commotion area is created). If a drinker is placed in or near the excretory area, demand for water should not exceed supply.

A wall or corner away from disturbance may be used for excretion. If insufficient wall area is provided around a designated excretory area (e.g. on a partially slatted floor), pigs may excrete beside a nearby wall or corner.

In a cooler environment, pigs lie away from a drinker due to loss in body heat from spilled water and, with high stocking rates, this may force them to excrete beside the drinker to avoid the resting area. If the stocking rate is high and demand for water exceeds supply, the commotion in the drinking area may be greater than that in the resting area where excretion may then occur.

During the day pigs have two different lying areas. During feeding the commotion area around the feeder repels them. At all other times they lie near the feeder in anticipation of food. High stocking rates may not provide sufficient floor area for a mutually exclusive feeder and/or drinker/commotion area, lying area and excretory area.

Once established, an excretory area may be difficult to relocate because of the pig's excellent spatial orientation. If some individuals establish an excretory area in the 'wrong place', it would probably be better to put them in a new pen than attempt to relocate the excretory area in the same pen. However, complete deodorisation of the pen may possibly serve the same purpose.

The effects of faeces and olfactory stimuli on excretory behaviour are not fully understood. They are, however, believed to be responsible for location of personal excretory areas by individuals.

Idiosyncratic excretory behaviour is occasionally exhibited. Observations indicate that this does not occur frequently but may cause indiscriminate excretion in a pen.

Badly designed or worn slats with sharp edges and large gaps may prevent pigs from defecating in the expected area. Thus, abnormal eliminative behaviour may arise from one or a number of closely related causes. The stocking rate may be too low or too high, and either of these situations may be complicated by extremes of temperature. Needless to say, pen fouling is often a sequel to any form of gastro-enteritis/colitis, but in this case the cause is obvious.

*Control*

When pen fouling exists, the problem should be investigated by checking all aspects of the social, physical and climatic environment. The cause will often be simple and easily detected; however, sometimes the problem is more complex and difficult.

When pigs are moved into a new pen, simple procedures such as dampening the dunging area or placing faeces upon it and spreading food in the sleeping area are useful practices. It may also be good practice to move pigs late in the day so that they settle down more quickly.

## ADDITIONAL READING

Cargill C. F. and Dobson K. J. (1979), *Vet. Rec.* **104**:11.

*Diseases of Swine*, 5th edn. (1981), Iowa State University Press.

Hansen L. L. and Hagelso A. M. (1979), *Proc. Eur. Assoc. Anim. Prod.*, Harrogate, England.

Hogg A. (1984), *Proc. I.P.V. S.*

Kunsh J. P. (1981), *Diseases of Swine*, 5th edn., p 725, Iowa State Univ. Press.

Penny R. H. C. and Hill F. W. G. (1974), *Vet. Rec.* **94**:174–180.

*Pork Industry Handbook*, USA Co-operative Extension Service, University of Illinois at Urbana-Champaign, USA.

Smith W. J. (1980), *The Pig Vet. Soc. Proc.* **7**, 68–72.

*Chapter 12*

# Systems for Establishing the Newly Weaned Pig

The objective of this chapter is to outline suitable systems for the newly weaned pig up to the stage when we can consider it to be well established around 20 kg liveweight. The components of suitable systems in terms of such factors as diet and housing will vary with age at weaning. Age at weaning in practice has varied between the extremes of weaning soon after birth and as late as 12 weeks of age. However, with few exceptions on a global basis, weaning age varies between 2 and 8 weeks of age.

## THE PROCESS OF WEANING

The act of weaning implies the removal of the young from access to the milk provided by the mother. In nature, the wild pig normally becomes accustomed to foods other than milk by a process of exploratory behaviour which is associated with a decline in milk available from the mother and the increasing appetite of the developing pig. In commercial practice, the natural solid foods available to the wild pig have been replaced by creep feed or a balanced diet consisting of cereals, protein concentrates, vitamins and minerals. When pigs were weaned from their dam at 8 weeks of age, in the last week prior to weaning, with sow milk yield declining, they could be obtaining 70 to 80 per cent of their nutrient intake from creep feed. Thus, if the same creep feed was fed after weaning, the pigs would not be subjected to a major dietary change at weaning. When weaning at 6 weeks of age, in the last week prior to weaning, pigs would be likely to obtain 50 to 60 per cent of their nutrients from creep feed and so the act of weaning and being deprived of its mother's milk would be slightly more difficult for the pig. Progressively earlier weaning increases the extent of the nutritional change imposed on the pig at the point of weaning; the extreme situation in practice is reached when weaning at 2 weeks of age because, by this age, piglets will have consumed very little, if any, creep feed − no matter how high the quality is − and so the pig is subjected to a complete change in diet at weaning − from the sow's milk beforehand to the weaner diet following severance from the dam.

275

## THE MAJOR FACTORS INFLUENCING OPTIMUM AGE AT WEANING

The major factors to be considered in deciding on the most desirable age at weaning in a given situation have been outlined in detail in the book *The Sow: Improving her Efficiency* by English, Smith and MacLean and published by Farming Press Ltd. These factors, which will be referred to only briefly here, are as follows:

### Trends in Sow Milk Yield

Milk yield rises to a peak around 3 weeks of age. This peak is maintained for around 2 weeks and from 5 weeks onwards there is a gradual decline and milk yield is fairly low by 8 weeks following farrowing.

### Immunity Gap Around 2 to 3 Weeks of Age

The piglet receives its main immunity against prevailing infection from the immunoglobulins in colostrum, the three main ones being termed IgA (immunoglobulin A), IgG and IgM. These are absorbed through the gut as intact molecules by the pig in the first few hours of life and provide temporary protection against prevailing infection in the herd. Unfortunately these proteins are steadily degraded and diluted in the bloodstream and decline to low levels by 14 days of age. The immunity obtained from ingesting colostrum, being transient, is termed *passive immunity*. The young pig does not normally start to build up its own *active immunity* to prevailing infection until about 3 weeks of age and the level of immunity builds up rather slowly from this point. Thus, weaning at 14 to 21 days of age results in the piglet being weaned at a stage when its immunity is at the lowest level in its life (other than at birth). Another important consideration is that the act of weaning immediately deprives the piglet of its mother's milk which contains immunoglobulin A (IgA). IgA in milk serves the very important function of protecting the delicate lining of the small intestine against the toxins produced by pathogenic bacteria. When deprived of this source of IgA the weaned piglet is devoid of such protection and is thus subject to damage to the gut lining and consequent digestive upsets, unless perfect nutrition and conditions in general are provided following weaning.

### Weaning to Oestrus Interval and Conception Rate

Despite some popular opinion to the contrary, under good conditions of housing, nutrition and management, weaning to oestrus interval and conception rate to first service vary little between weaning at 14 days of age and at later stages.

### Subsequent Litter Size

There is a tendency for earlier weaning to be associated with smaller subsequent litter size. This is thought to be related to the fact that the uterus or womb takes some time to recover fully from the previous gestation, and the earlier that mating takes place following weaning, the less well prepared are the uterus and the endocrine support system to accept and nourish new embryos. The net result is higher embryonic mortality following very early weaning. In one study on a large commercial farm, litter size was reduced by about 0.4 pig for every 5 day reduction in age at weaning between 35 and 15 days of age.

## Housing Costs

The earlier that weaning takes place, the smaller the amount of farrowing space and the greater the amount of weaner accommodation required. Thus, fewer farrowing places are required for earlier weaning but such savings have to be offset against the cost of providing the more specialised weaner accommodation required. The very young weaner must be provided with a uniform high temperature for optimum performance, while ventilation and, to a lesser extent, humidity must be under control. The higher the cost of providing specialised piglet accommodation and of running costs, the less attractive earlier weaning becomes.

## Food Costs

By early weaning, the sow is removed from the responsibility of providing the piglet with nutrition from the time of weaning. Thus, savings can be achieved in sow food costs as a result of early weaning. On the other hand, the early weaned piglet must be provided with a substitute for its mother's milk. Suitable feeds for early weaned piglets tend to be very expensive, but they are utilised very efficiently by the piglet.

Whether the food cost of producing a weaner at the point of sale is increased or decreased by early weaning will depend on the balance between the value of the sow food saved and the cost of the extra 'milk substitute' required by the early weaned pig. Also affecting this calculation of the food cost per weaner is the number of weaners produced per sow per year.

If piglet food is very expensive relative to sow food and no great increase in sow output is likely to be achieved by weaning earlier, then there is less of an argument for early weaning. On the other hand, if the cost of weaner food is not too expensive relative to sow food and a marked increase in the number of weaners per sow per year is likely to be achieved following earlier weaning, then such earlier weaning is much more attractive.

## Attitude of Labour and Level of Husbandry Skill Available

Earlier weaning, to be successful, demands a higher degree of stockmanship and attention to detail for success than conventional weaning at 6 to 8 weeks of age. If the stockperson responsible is fairly resistant to change, then this is a very important factor to be considered. Thus, the attitude and skill of the available labour should be assessed carefully before taking decisions on the age at which weaning is to take place.

**Established or New Unit**

If a unit has a fair amount of life left in its buildings and it cannot be readily and cheaply adapted for earlier weaning, it would be much better to see the present position improved and consolidated before going for earlier weaning. We know that there is a great amount of slack to be taken up on existing 5 to 6 week weaning systems. This slack probably partly arises from a combination of a sub-optimal system and sub-optimal stockmanship. If the labour is not capable of making a job of 5 to 6 week weaning, then going for earlier weaning could be suicidal. It should be a case of improving the present system by ensuring adequate numbers born, reducing piglet losses and minimising the weaning to conception interval by paying all the necessary attention to detail.

When a unit approaches 100 per cent efficiency on an existing system, more consideration can be given to earlier weaning, but there are units which are producing 23 weaners per sow per year mainly in converted buildings on 5 to 6 week weaning. These are obviously operating very near 100 per cent efficiency for that age of weaning. They have almost reached the ceiling, and when the possibility of earlier weaning is mentioned the operators seem very unwilling to consider it, which is understandable: they have an easy-care system and in normal times they obtain a very worthwhile return.

For somebody who is setting up a new unit, the situation is different and early weaning becomes much more attractive. A producer considering a new unit should try to visit existing efficient units achieving around 25 weaners per sow per year. If they think they have the necessary dedication, skill and stockmanship to equal that performance and the resulting budgets show that the required return on capital will be forthcoming, then they should forge ahead.

## Is There an Optimum Age at Weaning?

This is a very difficult question to answer even if one is starting from scratch in planning a new unit and adequately skilled and motivated labour is available. The decision taken is likely to be very dependent on the relative costs of various inputs and the value of output, such as sow and piglet food, fuel and housing costs, labour costs and the value of weaners prevailing at the time. If these price relationships change, it might somewhat alter the validity of the first decision.

In Britain there are certain criteria which favour selecting a weaning age of between 3 and 4 weeks in setting out to plan a new unit. These criteria are based on several considerations.

## Weaning at 3 to 4 Weeks: Reasons for Preference in Britain

The immunity gap for weaned pigs exists around 2 to 3 weeks of age. The piglet's own immunity is beginning to increase by 3 to 4 weeks and so the piglet at this stage is likely to suffer less than at an earlier stage from the effects of the stress usually associated with weaning.

By delaying weaning until 3 to 4 weeks of age, there will have been a greater opportunity to encourage higher intake of solid food prior to weaning and so reduce the extent of diet change and associated check at weaning.

Following 3 to 4 week weaning, there should be no delay in appearance of heat in the sow and the depression in conception rate which is associated with very early weaning (before 14 days) should be avoided. In addition, numbers born are likely to be higher than following earlier weaning.

By 3 to 4 weeks of age, the piglet, as well as having better immunity and a more mature digestive system to minimise both the extent and the effect of post-weaning stress, is also not so demanding in terms of environmental temperature. It should be possible to arrange suitable housing/environment for such a piglet by harnessing its own heat production using a kennel-type arrangement either within pens or on a verandah principle so as to minimise dependence on expensive energy for providing heat. Energy costs are certainly increasing in most countries, and a 2 to 3 week weaning system is more vulnerable than 3 to 4 week weaning because of its greater dependence on expensive sources of energy to provide heat.

It is desirable to keep expensive accommodation filled to capacity, and since upsets are likely to occur in the regular flow of sows coming up to farrow, such upsets are likely to result in excess sows demanding farrowing space at certain times. This accommodation problem can be alleviated by weaning some litters earlier. If 2 to 3 week weaning was the standard practice, having to wean some litters at less than 2 weeks of age is likely to have adverse effects on both piglets and the rebreeding of the sow, whereas the change from a standard 3 to 4 week weaning system to weaning at around 3 weeks is likely to give rise to fewer problems.

The stronger 3 to 4 week old pig, possessing better immunity, a more mature digestive system and greater ability to withstand colder conditions, is likely to provide the stockman with fewer problems after weaning and therefore will make the job more acceptable and manageable.

Weaning at 3 to 4 weeks of age has been shown in several, although not all, studies to be the optimum age at weaning in relation to achieving the maximum number of weaners per sow per year. Although the number of litters produced is less than for 2 to 3 week weaning, this is often more than compensated for by the increased litter size and low mortality after weaning.

## OPTIMUM AGE AT WEANING — CONSIDERATIONS IN OTHER COUNTRIES

The same criteria for deciding optimum age at weaning in Britain apply to other countries, where some of the important variants of conditions prevailing are as follows:

### Sow Appetite in Lactation

In countries with hot summers, problems are experienced in encouraging sows to eat sufficient food in lactation to maintain bodyweight. Often sows will lose considerable weight as they catabolise body fat and protein from lean to help meet the requirements for milk production, and the longer lactation proceeds, the greater will be this weight loss. As a result, sows can be emaciated by weaning and there are often problems with rebreeding and depressed subsequent litter size as a result. Earlier weaning is one useful approach to minimise the extent of this loss in body condition during lactation.

### Availability and Price of Suitable Ingredients for Early Weaning Diets

In Britain and other EEC countries there has been a plentiful supply in recent years of dried skim milk which has been available at a reasonable price. This has made it possible to justify the inclusion of large proportions of this most excellent food in the diet of early weaned pigs. The availability at reasonable cost of cooked cereals such as breakfast oats and flaked wheat, maize and barley has made it possible to produce high-quality and cost-effective diets for pigs weaned around 3 weeks of age. Countries outside the EEC may not be quite so fortunate with regard to the availability and price of suitable ingredients for early weaning diets. This will obviously include Third World countries, such as China and some South American and African states, in which it is very sensible to allow the sow to use her intrinsic foraging ability, combined with the provision of crop by-products unsuitable for use by the human population, to produce milk over a longer lactation. Her nursing piglets will thus have a greater opportunity to wean themselves gradually from their mother's milk since, as milk yield declines, they will increase their intake of the same food material available to the sow. Thus, by the time they are finally weaned they will not be subjected to a major change in diet and their digestive systems will have matured sufficiently to no longer need the expensive and elaborate dietary ingredients necessary in the diet of the early weaned pig.

In countries in an intermediate position in relation to the supply and cost of suitable ingredients for early weaning diets, optimum age at weaning may be around 4 to 5 weeks of age. Since the relative availability and price of ingredients suitable for inclusion in the diets of early weaned pigs and of sows may change over time, an open mind must be maintained regarding optimum age at weaning.

## CATERING FOR THE WEANED PIG

In the remainder of this chapter, emphasis will be placed on the requirements for the pig weaned around 3 to 4 weeks of age (around 6 kg liveweight), for both the immediate post-weaning period and its subsequent development up to about 20 kg liveweight. In dealing with the requirements of such a pig over the 6 to 20 kg liveweight range, the requirements of pigs weaned at older ages and heavier weights within this range will also be covered. To cater for the fairly small proportion of pigs which are weaned before 3 weeks of age, either as part of routine practice or in response to emergency situations, some reference will also be made to very early weaning (weaning between 14 and 21 days of age).

## The Objectives of the Weaning Process and Subsequent Rearing

The objectives of the weaning process and subsequent rearing are best summarised by referring to the desirable growth curve of piglets from healthy, good-quality genetic stock as in Figure 12.1. Thus, the objective, with weaning taking place at any stage between 2 and 8 weeks of age, is to achieve steady, uninterrupted growth with no check following weaning and with liveweight gain accelerating steadily over the period. Mortality from birth should be minimal (around 5 per cent with only pigs having genetic and congenital defects falling by the wayside); pigs should remain healthy with no enteric or other problems; and a diet (first creep feed and then post-weaning diet) appropriate to the digestive capacity of the young pig (so as not to induce any digestive upsets) should be consumed in reasonable quantities and digested efficiently. By the end of this phase the young pig should have a strong, well-developed skeleton and a high proportion of good-quality lean meat and minimal fat in the carcass.

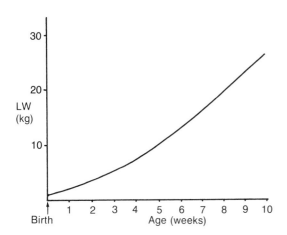

| Age (days) | Liveweight (kg) | Liveweight gain per day in previous week (g) |
|---|---|---|
| Birth | 1.5 | — |
| 7 | 3.0 | 214 |
| 14 | 4.5 | 214 |
| 21 | 6.0 | 214 |
| 28 | 7.5 | 214 |
| 35 | 9.5 | 286 |
| 42 | 12.0 | 357 |
| 49 | 15.0 | 429 |
| 56 | 19.0 | 571 |
| 63 | 23.0 | 571 |
| 70 | 27.5 | 643 |

FIGURE 12.1   Target weight for age and growth rates.

## The Basic Essentials in Suitable Systems for the Weaned Pig

In building up the basis of suitable systems for the newly weaned pig, it is important to summarise its needs in terms of the following:

1. Minimising stress at weaning
2. Climatic environment
3. Creep feeding
4. Post-weaning nutrition
5. Feeding system

6. Watering
7. Grouping at weaning
8. Penning
9. Floor space requirements
10. Feeding space requirements
11. Maintenance of health
12. Monitoring performance
13. Looking after the problem pigs at weaning
14. Variation in performance in a batch of weaners and development of management strategy

These important provisions will be discussed in turn.

## 1.  Minimising Stress at Weaning

The piglet suddenly removed from its dam at weaning is placed in a vulnerable state, and the earlier weaning takes place, the more serious its problem is. At weaning it is both socially and psychologically upset because it has lost the reassurance of its mother's presence and this can be accentuated by the disturbed behaviour of its litter mates. Secondly, it now finds itself in the alien environment of the weaner pen, often along with piglets from other litters, so that it no longer has the territorial rights which were established in the maternal environment of the farrowing/rearing pen. Finally, in this galaxy of disturbances it has lost its main source of nutrients (its mother's milk) and of external immunoglobulins (from the IgA of milk). The deprivation of its mother's milk and IgA is probably the greatest disaster of all, for the diet we now provide may bear little relationship, either chemically or immunologically, to the diet which it enjoyed from birth. Relative to artificial weaning in modern pig farming practice, if nature had been allowed to take its course, there would have been several more weeks for the piglet to remain on the sow, to gain experience of many different feed sources and nutrients and to adapt its digestive enzymes and immune system in preparation for being deprived finally of its mother's milk.

The challenge in artificial weaning, and especially at early ages, is therefore to simulate as far as possible the critical features of the weaning process. There are many vital components which must be fully appreciated to make the act of weaning less of an event and more of a process so that stress at weaning is minimised and the growth curve continues smoothly on its upward path with no undue deviations.

## 2.  Climatic Environment

As discussed in Chapter 8, the pig performs best when temperature is kept within its thermoneutral zone, that is, between its lower and upper critical temperature (LCT and UCT).

For a pig of a given liveweight and body composition, these temperatures vary mainly according to the energy intake of the pig and group size (see Table 12.1), the type of floor surface (see Table 12.2) and the draughtiness of the building.

These influences will now be dealt with in turn.

**TABLE 12.1    Critical temperatures for pigs on a solid concrete floor**

| Live-weight (kg) | Number in group | Lower critical temperature (°C) Feed level (multiple of maintenance) | | | | Upper critical temperature (dry) (°C) Feed level (multiple of maintenance) | | | |
|---|---|---|---|---|---|---|---|---|---|
| | | 1 | 2 | 3 | 4 | 1 | 2 | 3 | 4 |
| 5 | 1 | 30 | 28 | 26 | 23 | 37 | 35 | 34 | 33 |
| | 10 | 28 | 25 | 22 | 20 | 34 | 32 | 30 | 28 |
| 10 | 1 | 29 | 27 | 24 | 21 | 36 | 35 | 34 | 32 |
| | 10 | 27 | 24 | 21 | 17 | 34 | 32 | 29 | 27 |
| 20 | 1 | 29 | 26 | 22 | 18 | 36 | 35 | 33 | 31 |
| | 10 | 26 | 21 | 16 | 11 | 34 | 31 | 28 | 24 |

| Live-weight (kg) | Number in group | Upper critical temperature (wet) (°C) Feed level (multiple of maintenance) | | | |
|---|---|---|---|---|---|
| | | 1 | 2 | 3 | 4 |
| 5 | 1 | 38 | 37 | 36 | 36 |
| | 10 | 37 | 36 | 35 | 34 |
| 10 | 1 | 38 | 37 | 36 | 36 |
| | 10 | 37 | 36 | 35 | 34 |
| 20 | 1 | 38 | 37 | 36 | 35 |
| | 10 | 37 | 36 | 34 | 33 |

(From: J.M. Bruce, 1981)

GROUP SIZE, FEED INTAKE AND LIVEWEIGHT

The effects of these factors on LCT and UCT are outlined in Table 12.1. It can be seen that as the pig in a group of 10 progresses from 5 to 10 to 20 kg liveweight, on a feed intake equivalent to 3 times maintenance requirement, its LCT declines from 22 to 21 to 16°C. As a 10 kg pig in a group of 10 increases its feed intake from that equivalent to maintenance requirement to 4 times maintenance requirement, its LCT is reduced from 27 to 17°C. While a pig in a group of 10 has a lower LCT than one kept singly, as group size increases above 10 there is little or no further reduction in LCT. This is because a pig in a group of 10 can huddle with its litter mates (thus minimising the surface area from which heat can be lost) as effectively as it can in a group of 50.

Regarding the dangers of exceeding the upper critical temperature (UCT), there is little risk of this being a problem for the very young pig in most countries since the UCT is so high. Obviously, young pigs are less embarrassed by heat (a) if they have room to lie singly and avoid huddling with litter mates, (b) if they have low feed intake, (c) if they are lying in wet conditions, since evaporation of moisture from the surface of the skin will draw heat from the body and help to cool them down, (d) at lower liveweight and (e) with increasing fat content in the diet (digesting fat generates less heat than digesting other energy sources).

FLOOR SURFACE
In potentially cold conditions the advantages and disadvantages of alternative floor surfaces relative to a dry concrete floor are summarised in Table 12.2.

Relative to a *dry concrete floor*, it can be seen that the greatest advantage to the pig is conferred by having dry straw on top of a dry concrete floor (equivalent of +5°C). Lesser but not inconsiderable advantages are conferred by dry plywood (+3.5°C) and perforated metal (+2°C) floors. A wet concrete floor confers a net penalty on the pig equivalent to −2°C since body heat is drawn from the surface of the pig in contact with the wet floor.

DRAUGHTINESS OF THE BUILDING
Minimum air speed in pig units at floor level will usually not be less than 0.15

**TABLE 12.2   Thermal properties of a range of floor surfaces**

| *Floor type* | *Thermal resistance ($°C$ $m^2$ per watt) $(Rf_{45})^{(A)}$* | *Approximate thermal advantage relative to a dry concrete floor for 5 kg pigs$^{(B)}$ (Floor 9a)* |
|---|---|---|
| 1. Dry straw on top of a concrete floor | 0.66 | +5°C |
| 2. Glass reinforced concrete (GRC) screed (6 mm) over 50 mm polyurethane foam | 0.66 | |
| 3. Deep bedded straw on built-up litter | 0.42 | |
| 4. Plywood | 0.23 | +3.5°C |
| 5. 12 mm of dry sawdust on a concrete floor | 0.17 | |
| 6. 18 mm cement screed over 150 mm of lightweight aggregate | 0.17 | |
| 7. Perforated metal | 0.12 | +2°C |
| 8. Slatted floor a) plastic slats | 0.11 | |
|             b) concrete slats | 0.09 | |
| 9. Solid concrete (100 mm of concrete over 150 mm of hardcore aggregate) | | |
|             a) dry floor | 0.04 | 0 |
|             b) wet floor | 0.03 | −2°C |

[A] Calculations based on pigs of 45 kg liveweight in fully recumbent position and an air speed of 0.15 m per second
[B] Based on pigs on maintenance energy intakes and a group size of 20
(Source: A.M. Robertson, 1984)

metre per second (m/s), so this can be classed as virtually still air.

As air speed is increased at floor level from 0.15 to 0.5 m/s, this is equivalent to a drop in body temperature of 3°C, while a further increase in air speed from 0.5 to 1 m/s is equivalent to a further 3°C reduction in temperature.

## Conditions Which Help the Young Pig

TO KEEP WARM IN COLD CONDITIONS
From the above it is clear that the following conditions will help to keep young pigs warmer in cold conditions:

- a well-insulated floor
- being kept in a group with other pigs
- high feed or energy intake
- freedom from draughts
- higher liveweight

TO KEEP COOL UNDER VERY HOT CONDITIONS
The following factors are important in helping to achieve this objective:

- adequate floor space allowing pigs to spread out as individuals and avoid huddling
- increased air speed at floor level
- wet floors or wallows
- lower feed or energy intake
- substitution of fat for other energy sources in the diet
- avoidance of excessive protein content of the diet

## 3.  Creep Feeding

This refers to the provision of solid food to the piglet prior to weaning. The optimum strategy of creep feeding is very dependent on the age at weaning.

The practice of creep feeding was initiated when weaning took place at 6 to 8 weeks of age. Sound creep feeding practice was found to be essential to supplement the sow's declining milk yield after 3 to 4 weeks, so as to ensure reasonable growth to weaning and acceptable weaning weight. With the advent of very early weaning at around 3 weeks of age, it is perhaps more difficult to justify the practice of creep feeding. However, the justification on earlier weaning systems would be increased if the practice could be demonstrated to stimulate an earlier development of the mature digestive enzyme system.

The digestive system of the baby pig is equipped to deal only with lactose, casein and easily digested fats. The ability of the digestive system to deal with more complex carbohydrates, non-milk sugars, proteins other than casein and non-emulsified fats develops slowly, but there is evidence that earlier development of sucrase, maltase and amylase activity can be induced by encouraging earlier consumption of non-milk sugars, starch and protein.

The practice of creep feeding, using a diet that would be both acceptable and digestible to young pigs, might therefore be expected to stimulate an earlier development of the mature digestive enzyme system and result in a reduced growth

**TABLE 12.3   Formulation and composition of high digestibility diet for pigs weaned at an average of 19 days**

| Ingredient | % |
|---|---|
| Cooked oat flakes | 37.5 |
| Maize oil | 10.0 |
| Denatured skim milk IA | 20.0 |
| Milk substitute | 25.0 |
| Glucose | 5.0 |
| Salt | 1.0 |
| Tri calcium phosphate | 1.0 |
| Vitamin E ($\alpha$ tocopheral) | 0.1 |
| Vitamin/trace mineral supplement | 0.4 |
| | 100.0 |

check following early weaning. The work of Friend, Gorrill and MacIntyre (1970) and that of Okai, Aherne and Hardin (1976) did not produce strong evidence of such an effect, but that of English, Robb and Dias (1980) indicated that a sound creep feeding system using a highly digestible diet resulted in improved feed intake and performance following weaning. The reason for the failure of creep feeding to improve post-weaning performance in the work of Friend et al. (1970) and of Okai et al. (1976), in which weaning took place at either 3 or 5 weeks of age, might be associated with the relatively small creep feed intakes achieved in their work.

In the work of English and associates (1980), the highly digestible diet detailed in Table 12.3 was used as a creep feed in meal form. It was offered from 1 week of age to pigs which were to be weaned at 4 weeks of age. The creep feed was made readily available in shallow troughs and any uneaten feed was discarded and small quantities of fresh feed given twice daily. Over the suckling period, piglets consumed, on average, 610 g of the creep diet. At 28 days of age pigs were weaned into a flatdeck house with good environmental control and a rearing diet was introduced. Pigs remained in the flatdeck house until 47 days of age, at which stage they were transferred to a kennel or verandah house (naturally ventilated) until the com-

**TABLE 12.4   Effects of providing a highly digestible diet as a creep feed from 7 days to weaning at 28 days**

| Stage | | Advantage over control (%) |
|---|---|---|
| Suckling (to 28 days) | Piglet gain  Days 21–28 | +17 |
| | Litter gain  Days  7–28 | + 5 |
| Flatdeck house (29 to 47 days) | Feed intake | + 6 |
| | Piglet gain | +15 |
| | Food conversion efficiency | + 8 |
| Verandah house (48 to 69 days) | Feed intake | + 5 |
| | Piglet gain | + 5 |

pletion of the experiment at 69 days of age. A summary of the results of this trial is contained in Table 12.4.

It can be seen that creep feeding improved piglet liveweight gain during the rearing period, there being an improvement of 17 per cent in the last week of suckling. In both the flatdeck house and the verandah house, piglets receiving creep feed prior to weaning consumed more food and had higher liveweight gains.

Thus, the indications from this work were that sound creep feeding practice can help to acclimatise pigs to their post-weaning diet and help to improve food intake and performance following weaning. In terms of cost/benefit up to weaning, the practice of creep feeding could be considered marginal, but an important advantage of creep feeding is in its role in producing a weaned pig with a more mature digestive system which is likely to be less vulnerable to the rigours of weaning. Creep feeding may well confer on the piglet an improved intellectual appreciation of what solid food is at weaning. It may also help to familiarise piglets with the drinking device prior to weaning so that they may drink more water immediately after weaning.

The essential features of a sound creep feeding system would appear to be as follows:

- An acceptable and digestible diet
- A suitable form of diet, a flaky meal or small pellet being preferable to finely ground material
- Presentation in a suitable feeder which makes the creep feed readily visible and available
- Suitable placement of the creep feeder within the pen to minimise risk of fouling
- Feeding of creep on a 'little and often' basis with strict attention to cleanliness of the system, frequent and regular removal of any uneaten creep and replacement with fresh material
- Provision of a readily accessible supply of wholesome fresh water

As outlined in Chapter 9, Professor John Bourne and his colleagues at the University of Bristol have drawn attention to the possiblity of hypersensitivity reactions and subsequent intestinal disease after weaning in response to food antigens (e.g. as in soya and other vegetable proteins) offered in small quantities as creep feed before weaning. It would appear that the quantity of creep diet containing soya bean meal and other sources of food antigens consumed before weaning dictates the response to the effect of the same diet offered following weaning. The group at Bristol argue that if large quantities of the early weaning diet are consumed before weaning, the immune system will become tolerant to any food antigens and little hypersensitivity reaction should be seen. However, if only small amounts of this diet are consumed before weaning, then the immune system is primed and the response at weaning may be very damaging in some situations. Such damage can take the form of atrophy of the delicate finger-like villi lining the gut wall, resulting in malabsorption of nutrients and often subsequently complicated by enteric infections, either with *E. coli*, rotavirus or other infective agents. The outcome is a severe post-weaning diarrhoea which can only be controlled by restricting the food intake and incorporating antibiotics in the diet.

If such antigenic reaction is a problem, then the possible solutions are several:

- Ensure adequate creep feed intake before weaning
- Do not creep feed but introduce the solid diet for the first time at weaning
- Avoid using feed ingredients in creep feed with antigenic factors or use soya and other vegetable protein products which have been processed to reduce or remove the antigenic factors

Obviously the most desirable practice in the case of weaning at 4 weeks or later is to have a high quality creep feed, to manage its feeding efficiently and to ensure high intakes before weaning.

Plate 12.1  For creep feeding to be effective, the diet must be attractive, fresh and digestible. It should be offered on a 'little and often' basis in containers which make the feed very accessible and which allow communal feeding. The container should be placed in a position where the risk of fouling is minimised. A readily available supply of fresh water should also be provided.

SHOULD THE CREEP FEED AND THE POST-WEANING DIET BE THE SAME?

When weaning takes place at a young age (4 weeks or earlier), a strong case can be put forward for the creep feed being the same as the high-quality diet designed for the newly weaned pig, which such early weaning demands. Such a post-weaning diet should consist of high-quality ingredients like animal protein (dried skim milk and good-quality fishmeal), some vegetable oil and cereals (a proportion of them precooked). As well as being digestible to the young pig, these ingredients should also appeal in terms of palatability so that higher intake can be stimulated. As already indicated, as high an intake of creep feed as possible is desirable in the case of early weaning.

With later weaning (6 to 8 weeks of age), the important characteristics of a creep diet are that it should be complementary to milk and be consumed in reasonable quantities prior to weaning. Fowler and associates (1979) compared 4 creep feeds varying in protein content from 14 to 20 per cent for pigs weaned at 6 to 7 weeks of age and found that piglet gain to weaning did not vary greatly with protein content of the creep feeds. Therefore, a case could be made for cheaper creep feeds with lower protein levels for pigs weaned at 6 weeks of age and later. However, it is more convenient, and likely to be no less cost effective in most circumstances, to adopt the strategy of providing the diet to be used immediately after weaning as the creep feed prior to weaning. This makes for continuity and helps to minimise the dietary change at weaning.

IS CREEP FEEDING DESIRABLE IN THE CASE OF 2 TO 3 WEEK WEANING?

Pigs tend to consume very little solid food before 3 weeks of age and therefore the desirability of offering creep feed prior to weaning at this early age is questionable. This is especially so if the creep feed contains any vegetable protein sources which are likely to produce allergic responses in the newly weaned pig, as described earlier. As a general rule, because of the low intake likely to be achieved before weaning, creep feeding prior to such early weaning is unlikely to be justifiable.

However, if creep feed is to be offered prior to weaning at this early age, high-quality digestible ingredients must be used. There are some producers who use such high-quality diets and claim to achieve reasonable feed intakes prior to weaning at 3 weeks of age or earlier and also appear to escape any allergic reactions following weaning of the type highlighted by Professor Bourne and his fellow workers at Bristol University. Indeed, they feel that their creep feeding practice helps them to establish their pigs more effectively after weaning. On the basis of such an assessment, they are justified in continuing their practice of creep feeding.

## 4.  Post-weaning Nutrition

In formulating diets for early weaned pigs, the objectives of formulation should be to try to make nutritional weaning more of a *process* and less of an *event*. Ideally the piglet should receive a diet which is similar to the sow's milk. In practice, however, we have to balance biological ideals against economic realities; in other words, the composition of the diet should meet the needs of the young pigs as far as economic reality will permit. However, the consumption of feed in the first few days after weaning is only very small and it may take a week or more for piglets

**TABLE 12.5   Chemical analysis of early weaning diets**

|  | *Diet* | | |
|---|---|---|---|
|  | *Commercial 1* | *Commercial 2* | *High Digestibility (HD)* |
| 1. Determined values | | | |
|     dry matter (g/kg) | 930.3 | 909.5 | 928.7 |
|     Crude protein (g/kg) | 227.3 | 250.5 | 211.6 |
|     Crude fibre (g/kg) | 1.1 | 10.4 | 1.2 |
|     Crude fat (g/kg) | 115.9 | 106.4 | 159.4 |
| 2. Calculated value | | | |
|     Gross energy (MJ/kg) | 18.65 | 18.16 | 19.57 |

to consume 2 kg each. An investment in a high-class diet at this stage has a pay-off not only in healthier, more contented pigs, but also in faster throughput when housing is expensive, in reduced mortality and, not least, in a stockman's pride in his animals.

A diet which was formulated to match the requirements for high digestibility, low antigenicity and good palatability is shown in Table 12.3. It is characterised by its high content of milk products and high amount of vegetable fat. In addition, the chosen cereal has been hot-flaked and every attention given to the mineral and vitamin content. This diet has been widely used in the United Kingdom and is popular because, despite its rather high cost, it is not normally necessary to use any antibiotics.

The formulation which we shall term the High Digestibility or HD diet for the age of pig involved was first subjected to on-farm testing as the post-weaning 'starter' diet for pigs weaned between 17 and 21 days of age. It was compared with other commercial diets which were much cheaper because they contained considerably less of the suitable ingredients (such as milk by-products, partially cooked cereals and good-quality vegetable oil). The chemical analysis of the diets, which were evaluated on both an ad lib. and a restricted basis, are detailed in Table 12.5. It can be seen that diet HD tended to be lower in crude protein but had higher fat and energy levels than the commercial diets.

The results of this trial indicated interesting but expected differences between diets in the incidence of scouring as shown in Figure 12.2.

When commercial diets C1 and C2 were fed, which were assumed to contain less digestible ingredients than diet HD, a high incidence of scouring was experienced, and scouring was appreciably worse on ad lib. than on restricted feeding. In the case of diet HD, incidence of scouring was low and was no higher on ad lib. than on restricted feeding. This indicates that the need to restrict the feed intake of early weaned pigs mainly applies when a less suitable (less digestible) diet is being fed.

Although diet HD was much more expensive than alternative commercially available diets, the staff on the commercial unit on which this work was carried out were very attracted to diet HD because it could be fed ad lib. with minimum risk of scouring, it was associated with minimal mortality and it was converted very efficiently.

Accordingly, it was decided to evaluate the system based on diet HD fed ad lib.,

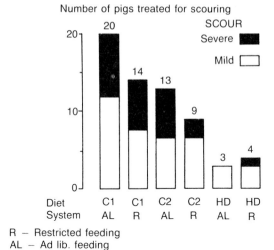

Number of pigs treated for scouring

FIGURE 12.2   Veterinary treatments for scouring. (Source: Deligeorgis, English and Davidson, 1978)

R – Restricted feeding
AL – Ad lib. feeding

and the results obtained from pigs weaned over a period of four weeks and managed on this system are detailed in Table 12.6. Pigs were weaned at an average liveweight of 4.37 kg and were transferred to a follow-on diet at 7.34 kg. The HD diet was converted at 0.95 kg food per kg gain so that less than 3 kg per pig of this diet was required to establish the pigs following weaning. Post-weaning scouring and mortality were both minimal.

Following the impressive results in terms of feed efficiency and survival obtained with the large number of pigs involved (over 700), the commercial unit on which the work was carried out adopted the system, and results in terms of monthly mortality before and after the change to this system from one based on restricted feeding of cheaper commercially available diets are detailed in Table 12.7. It can be seen that whereas post-weaning losses were averaging around 6 per cent before the changeover on to diet HD in month 5, losses after the change were around 1 per cent or less.

In practice it is found that although a very low incidence of scouring is experienced following weaning when using highly digestible diets fed ad lib., an outbreak

**TABLE 12.6  Commercial performance on a system based on ad lib. feeding of diet HD as the starter diet for pigs weaned at 17 to 21 days of age**

| Batch number | Number of pigs in batch | Liveweight (kg) at: start | finish | Liveweight gain (g/day) | Food: gain ratio (kg:kg) | Number of deaths | Per cent mortality |
|---|---|---|---|---|---|---|---|
| 1 | 158 | 4.26 | 9.27 | 239 | 0.890 | 1 | 0.63 |
| 2 | 186 | 4.29 | 6.31 | 156 | 0.983 | 0 | 0 |
| 3 | 184 | 4.25 | 6.92 | 178 | 0.988 | 0 | 0 |
| 4 | 175 | 4.68 | 7.21 | 194 | 0.991 | 0 | 0 |
| Overall | 703 | 4.37 | 7.34 | 189 | 0.952 | 1 | 0.14 |

(Source: English, Davidson, Fowler and Deligeorgis, 1980)

**TABLE 12.7  Trends in mortality of early weaned piglets on a 500-sow unit (age at weaning = 17 to 21 days)**

| Year | 1 | 2 | | | | | | | | | | | 3 | |
|---|---|---|---|---|---|---|---|---|---|---|---|---|---|---|
| Month | 12 | 1 | 2 | 3 | 4 | 5* | 6 | 7 | 8 | 9 | 10 | 11 | 12 | 1 | 2 |
| Number of pigs weaned | 856 | 655 | 730 | 793 | 699 | 749 | 842 | 970 | 844 | 721 | 827 | 851 | 1062 | 754 | 884 |
| Post-weaning deaths | 61 | 46 | 41 | 25 | 57 | 17 | 4 | 10 | 9 | 7 | 7 | 7 | 4 | 9 | 6 |
| Post-weaning deaths (%) | 6.7 | 7.3 | 5.6 | 3.1 | 7.9 | 2.5 | 0.4 | 1.2 | 1.1 | 0.8 | 1.1 | 0.8 | 0.4 | 1.1 | 0.7 |

* Change of diet and feeding system to diet HD fed ad lib.
(Source: English, Davidson, Fowler and Deligeorgis, 1980)

of scouring can be induced by a sudden drop in temperature caused by a breakdown of the environmental control system. Thus, a well controlled climatic environment, as well as a sound feeding policy, is essential in ensuring healthy, thriving pigs following early weaning.

Other advantageous points of the system of ad lib. feeding on highly digestible diets for very early weaning are the greater simplicity and ease of management of the system. In addition, ad lib. feeding tends to lead to a greater degree of contentment and a more peaceful situation for both pigs and stockpersons. An ad lib. system also makes possible more flexible house and pen design and it is easier in practice to ensure more equitable and adequate food intake for all pigs within a pen as the pigs grow than is the case with restriced feeding systems. With reference to the term ad lib., the point must be made that this does not involve putting several days' supply of food into a hopper but merely putting a 24-hour supply into a hopper to ensure that pigs obtain fresh feed daily.

PROGRESSION OF DIETS FOR EARLY WEANED PIGS

When very early weaning (under 21 days) is practised, pre-starter formulations along the lines of diet HD are desirable. Once such early weaned pigs become well established on a high-quality starter diet in the 10 days or so after weaning, one can phase the pigs gradually on to a diet using cheaper ingredients consistent with the age and stage of growth of the pigs. Such a follow-on diet, which might take the form of either diet A or B in Table 12.8, is designed for pigs weaned between 3 and 4 weeks of age weighing about 6 kg at weaning. It contains cooked cereals, between 25 and 30 per cent of milk by-products (dried skim milk and whey) as well as fishmeal, vegetable oil and glucose, and it would be fed up to about 12 kg liveweight, after which diets of type C and D in Table 12.8 would be introduced gradually. Diets C and D see the introduction of uncooked cereals and soya bean meal with considerably reduced quantities of milk by-products.

These pre-starter (for pigs weaned under 21 days of age), starter (for pigs weaned between 3 and 4 weeks of age and fed between 6 and 12 kg liveweight) and follow-on (for feeding between 12 and 20 kg liveweight) diets are suitable for feeding ad lib. or to appetite to healthy pigs in a good climatic environment.

Sometimes, and particularly in countries where milk by-products are both scarce and expensive, much less elaborate diets are fed to pigs weaned around 3 to 4 weeks of age. Simple corn and soya bean diets are sometimes used for such young pigs

**TABLE 12.8  Specimen 'starter and 'follow-on' diets for early weaned pigs**

| Liveweight range (kg) | Starter 6–12 | | Follow-on 12–20 | |
|---|---|---|---|---|
| Diet | A | B | C | D |
| | Europe | USA | Europe | USA |
| | | | (kg per tonne) | |
| Barley | – | – | 89.7 | – |
| Maize | – | – | – | 200 |
| Wheat | – | – | 100 | – |
| Breakfast oats | 262.4 | 206 | 125 | 124 |
| Flaked maize (ground) | 100 | 100 | 100 | 100 |
| Flaked wheat (ground) | 100 | 100 | 100 | 100 |
| Fishmeal | 150 | 150 | 150 | 150 |
| Soya bean (full fat) | – | – | 92.8 | 93 |
| Dried skim milk | 200 | 259 | 100 | 100 |
| Whey powder | 50 | 50 | 50 | 50 |
| Lysine hydrochloride | 2.0 | – | 1.7 | 1.9 |
| Vegetable oil | 80 | 80 | 85.5 | 74.4 |
| Glucose | 50 | 50 | – | – |
| Salt | 2.6 | 2.0 | 2.3 | 2.5 |
| Dicalcium phosphate | – | – | – | 1.2 |
| Copper sulphate (hydrated) | 0.5 | 0.5 | 0.5 | 0.5 |
| Vitamins and trace minerals | 2.5 | 2.5 | 2.5 | 2.5 |
| | 1000 | 1000 | 1000 | 1000 |
| *Analysis* | | | | |
| Digestible energy (MJ DE/kg) | 17.25 | 17.0 | 17.0 | 17.0 |
| Crude protein (g/kg) | 230 | 230 | 230 | 230 |
| Lysine (g/kg) | 16.5 | 16.0 | 16.0 | 16.0 |
| Lysine (g per MJ DE) | 0.96 | 0.94 | 0.94 | 0.94 |
| Calcium (g/kg) | 14.9 | 14.5 | 13.8 | 14.2 |
| Phosphorus (g/kg) | 9.7 | 9.7 | 9.3 | 9.5 |
| Sodium (g/kg) | 2.5 | 2.3 | 2.5 | 2.5 |

in the United States and Canada. In relation to the digestive capabilities of the young pig, such diets are inferior since the pig's ability to digest plant proteins and uncooked starch at this stage is limited. Such diets are therefore fed in very limited quantities in several feeds evenly spread throughout the day in the first week after weaning in an attempt to avoid overloading the pig's limited digestive capacity for such ingredients. Provided food intake is suitably restricted, this approach can be quite successful but it demands considerable managerial skill and is time consuming. Success in using such simple diets for early weaned pigs appears to be associated with the use of such diets as a creep feed when the efficiency of creep feeding management is very high and, as a result, high intakes of creep feed are achieved prior to weaning.

A third approach to early weaning diets is to virtually ignore the nutritional considerations and find a balance between cheap dietary constitutents and the inclusion of antibacterial agents. This is an unsound approach and should not be encouraged.

If suitable ingredients for early weaning diets are not available in a particular country or are exorbitantly expensive, then later weaning is the more sensible strategy. This allows piglets access to their dam's milk for a longer period, allowing their digestive systems to become more mature by weaning. One often gets the impression that early weaning is something of a status symbol in pig production. However, the point must be made strongly that there is nothing whatsoever inferior about later weaning and in many circumstances the latter is the more sensible and cost effective policy. An interesting experiment which demonstrated the importance of sound diet formulation for the young weaned pig was conducted by Okai, Aherne and Hardin in Edmonton, Canada. Among a variety of diets they offered to 3 week weaned pigs were two extreme types, one a simple diet based on wheat, barley and soya bean meal, the other a complex diet containing a proportion of cooked cereals and skim milk powder. The trends in growth of the pigs following weaning are illustrated in Figure 12.3.

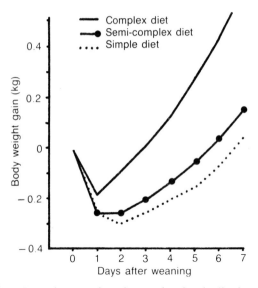

FIGURE 12.3   Post-weaning growth rate (first week) of pigs, weaned at 3 weeks of age, on 3 types of diet.

It can be seen that pigs on the simple diet lost weight following weaning and only regained their weaning weight a full 7 days following weaning. On the other hand, pigs on the complex diet settled down reasonably quickly following weaning, built up their food intake more quickly and were growing away from their contemporaries on the simple diet by the end of the first week following weaning. In addition, post-weaning mortality on the simple diet (5.6 per cent) was higher than that on the complex diet (1.4 per cent). It is obvious that pigs on the simple diet were losing body tissue (mainly body fat) in the week following weaning. The loss of such fatty tissue would reduce their insulation against cold and, in addition, their lower feed intake would make them even more vulnerable to cold conditions. In other words, pigs on the simple diet would require a much warmer environment.

MAKING THE CORRECT DECISION ABOUT CHOICE OF DIET FOR YOUNG PIGS

The choice in terms of the quality of diet that should be used with early weaned pigs rests with the producer, and the correct choice can be made only when objective physical data are available on which to base financial calculations.

Diets for pigs in the crucial period after weaning must be evaluated with all the following criteria in mind:

- Daily gain
- Feed efficiency
- Cost/kg gain
- Piglet losses
- Scouring
- Drug costs
- Consistency of results from week to week
- Simplicity of the system
- Ease of management
- Performance to slaughter

When post-weaning diets are evaluated on these criteria, the high-quality diets will almost invariably turn out to be the most cost effective. The particular ingredients and diets to be used will be dependent on the age at weaning and the relative availability and costs of alternative high-quality feed ingredients. However, milk nutrients should feature in these diets at a level depending on cost and age at weaning along with alternative good quality animal protein such as fish meal, low trypsin inhibitor soya flour and highly digestible energy sources.

Once piglets become well established on such a high-quality starter diet in the 2 weeks or so after weaning, one can phase them gradually on to a diet using cheaper ingredients consistent with their age and stage of growth. However, the cost of the diet is much less important than its cost effectiveness. Sound establishment of the weaner, minimal scouring, low drug costs and deaths and reduced cost per kg of liveweight gain are far more important considerations than lower cost per tonne of diet.

The advent of highly digestible, although expensive, diets for pigs weaned around 3 weeks of age and later has undoubtedly helped to minimise the incidence of post-weaning diarrhoea, reduced drug costs and post-weaning losses and may also have established a basis for more efficient performance in the later growing period by helping to maintain the integrity of the delicate villous lining of the gut, so increasing the efficiency of digestion and absorption of digested nutrients.

To conclude this section, the following quotation from John Ruskin on the subject of 'Values' applies very aptly to starter diets for weaned pigs:

> It's unwise to pay too much, but it's unwise to pay too little; when you pay too much you lose a little money, that is all. When you pay too little you sometimes lose everything, because the thing you bought was incapable of doing the thing you bought it to do. The common law of business balance prohibits paying a little and getting a lot. It can't be done. If you deal with the lowest bidder, it's well to add something for the risk you run. And if you do that, you will have enough to pay for something better.

## 5. Feeding Systems

The most common system for feeding newly weaned pigs is on dry diets, in either pellet or meal form, and on a restricted or ad lib. basis. More recently, feeding systems have been introduced in which feed and water are available in the same receptacle, and this provides the pig with the opportunity of wetting its feed before eating it.

AD LIB. FEEDING

Ad lib. feeding as applied to newly weaned pigs consists of placing in a feed hopper once daily just sufficient food to satisfy the appetite of the pigs in the next 24 hour period. In other words, feed in the hopper should be just finished or only a minute quantity should remain by the time the next day's supply is added. This is, in effect, feeding to appetite. The advantage of placing only sufficient food in the hopper to satisfy appetite in the next 24 hours is that this ensures that no stale feed accumulates in the hopper so that food is always fresh.

Plate 12.2　Ad lib. feeding of early weaned pigs tends to be a simpler system than restricted feeding since pigs are not competing so obviously for feed, provided feeding space is adequate. Ad lib. feeding for weaners should involve putting only one day's supply into the feeder so that it is just finished by the time it is due to be replenished. This approach ensures that food is always fresh and helps to minimise feed wastage. Aspects of feed hopper design also help to minimise feed wastage. These include adjusters on the feeder to control flow of feed from the storage section to the trough, an inturned lip on the trough, dividers at regular intervals along the length of the trough and sometimes hinged flaps above each feeding section.

Plate 12.3   Watching feeding behaviour provides the stockman with a good indication of wellbeing.

RESTRICTED FEEDING

With restricted feeding, feeding space must be sufficient to allow all piglets to feed at once so that equal intakes are achieved by all pigs sharing a feeder. Obviously, if all pigs are unable to obtain access to the feeder at the same time, some will obtain more and others less than their share.

The frequency of feeding and the quanitity offered at each feed vary. Restricted feeding of pigs in Britain usually involves feeding pigs 2 to 4 times daily. In the United States, on the other hand, sometimes in the first week to 10 days following weaning, pigs may be fed as frequently as 8 times daily with feeds being fairly evenly spread over the working day. Such frequent feeding is often practised with simple corn and soya bean meal diets for early weaned pigs. Only very small quantities are offered at each feed in an attempt to avoid overloading the limited digestive ability of the 3 to 4 week old pig. In addition, antibiotics are often added to such diets to help control scouring problems which may follow digestive upsets and further aggravate these.

RESTRICTED VERSUS AD LIB. FEEDING

As already indicated, on restricted feeding systems adequate trough space must be supplied to allow all pigs to feed at once, not only at the start but throughout the period over which such restriction is practised. Such feeding practice demands considerable managerial skill and tends to be time consuming. In addition, pigs can be more restless and noisy on this system, especially just before feeding. It has the advantage over ad lib. feeding that potential disease problems can be detected more quickly since individuals which do not come to the trough at feeding are immediately under suspicion of being off-colour. Thus, it may be possible to apply corrective therapy before a problem develops too far.

On ad lib. feeding, pigs can feed when they feel inclined and can satisfy their appetites. As a result they tend to be quieter and more contented and this is pleasing to the dedicated stockman. As already indicated, diets used on ad lib. systems should be highly digestible for the age and degree of maturity of the pig involved.

WET FEEDING SYSTEMS

Wet feeding systems for older pigs (discussed in the next chapter) usually involve meal and water being mixed in a slurry and delivered by pipeline to the pigs. In order to flow from mixer to the feed trough, the water to meal ratio should not be less than about 2.5 to 1. This consistency would be far too liquid for newly weaned pigs (unless milk rather than water was the liquid medium) and would limit dry matter intake. Thus, an alternative system is necessary for very young pigs.

Newly developed systems (see Plate 13.2) involve delivery of dry meal or pellets to the feed trough from a hopper mounted above, with nipple drinkers also mounted above the feed trough. Thus water spillage from the nipple drinkers ends up in the feed trough and wets the feed. The water to meal (or pellet) ratio will vary according to the speed of feed delivery to the trough, the rate of eating by the pigs and the amount of spillage from the nipple drinkers. The objectives of such systems are to encourage greater food intake and at the same time attempt to ensure adequate liquid intake. A further objective is to eliminate or at least minimise feed wastage on the premise that feed in dry form is more likely to be wasted than in wet form.

One very important requirement in wet feeding systems is that the trough be cleared of food at regular intervals for with weaner diets containing a proportion of milk products, wet feed left in the trough for any length of time could sour quickly in the high temperature prevailing in the weaner house. Thus, such systems involve delivery of dry feed and water for short periods at regular intervals during each day with the trough being cleared of feed before the next delivery. Keen stockmanship is also vital to ensure the proper working of the feed delivery equipment.

These wet feeding systems are in their infancy, and although the objectives are admirable, insufficient data are available to make judgements on their effectiveness relative to conventional ad lib. and restricted dry feed systems.

PELLETS OR MEAL?

Piglets may be more attracted to diets in meal than in pellet form at first. However, it is important in avoid both a dusty meal and a hard pellet. Materials such as breakfast oats and flaked maize will help to give the meal the open texture desirable to piglets.

Other very important considerations in making the choice between pellets and meal are the flow properties of each and the wastage factor. It must be remembered that diets for early weaned pigs usually contain 10 per cent or more of oil or fat and this renders them more sticky and less 'fluid' and makes them more liable to bridge in a feed hopper. Such bridging may from time to time severely limit the amount of food making its way to the trough part of the feeder. If the gap between the hopper and trough parts of the feeder is widened to increase the flow of feed, excessive quantities may be delivered and this can result in considerable wastage. It is very difficult to control the delivery of weaner diet in meal form so that enough but not excessive quantities end up in the trough. With pellets on the other hand, it is much easier to control flow to the trough so that only small quantities are always available at any one time. This always ensures fresh feed for piglets and helps to eliminate wastage. A high oil content (10 to 20 per cent) in the diet helps to reduce the dustiness of meal but makes the material difficult to pellet and often gives rise to a fairly soft pellet.

When one weighs up all the relative advantages and disadvantages of using pellets or meal for early weaned pigs, the balance of advantage comes out in favour of pellets of the right size and consistency mainly because of the ease of minimising wastage and so increasing the efficiency of feed usage.

## 6.   Watering

Piglets may not drink sufficient water to meet their requirements after weaning for a variety of reasons. Just prior to weaning their main liquid requirements have been satisfied by communal feeding on the sow on a warm, palatable liquid available every hour. They are subjected to a drastic change at weaning when they have to queue up at what is often a strange drinking point (nipple or bowl) from which a bland liquid such as water, perhaps of questionable purity, is available.

Just prior to weaning at around 3 to 4 weeks of age, piglets will have obtained daily quantities of liquid in the form of milk amounting to some 0.6 litre per head in addition to any water they may drink. After weaning their requirements could be even higher, especially if they are scouring, since such a problem is associated with dehydration of tissues.

Because of their high requirement for wholesome liquid following weaning and because of the drastic change in the type of liquid available and in the source from which it is available, considerable thought must be given to ensuring adequate liquid intake following weaning.

In some early weaning situations in commercial practice, a useful response has been obtained from making fresh clean water or dilute milk substitute readily available to piglets in the first few days after weaning in a container at which they can drink communally (see Plate 12.4). Strict hygiene and cleanliness should be exercised in such practice and it is usually desirable to make water or milk substitute available in this way for only about 1 hour each day with water being available from the standard drinkers in the pen (usually nipples) continuously.

When the communal drinking container is removed from the pen each day it should be thoroughly washed and disinfected so that a clean receptacle is always used. It is also important, of course, that the width of the trough of such a drinker allows adequate space to accommodate the piglet's head for drinking but is narrow enough to prevent the piglet from getting its front feet in the trough. The use of communal drinking in this way can also act as a carrier for antibiotic therapy where this is required.

As already indicated, the newly weaned piglet's need for liquid intake is increased if the piglet is subject to digestive upsets, later complicated by enteric infections
with *E. coli*, rotavirus, TGE (transmissible gastro-enteritis) or other infective
agents. The outcome is post-weaning diarrhoea. Such scouring can result in the
salts of sodium and potassium, which are secreted into the small intestine via the
bile, being flushed out in the scour rather than being reabsorbed in the large intestine. This lowers the blood content of electrolytes such as sodium and potassium
and tends to decrease thirst, thus discouraging water intake. Dehydration follows,
causing the wasting and 'sunken eyes' characteristic of many cases of post-weaning
diarrhoea. It is such dehydration which is the usual cause of death in scouring pigs.
This situation calls for the provision of electrolyte solution (often with glucose and
glycine, as well as antibiotics when appropriate and feed restriction) to restore
blood levels of sodium and potassium and so restore thirst and further liquid intake
so as to rehydrate the body. It is most important to have the correct concentration
of glycine, glucose, sodium and potassium in the electrolyte. The proportion of
these are very critical so it is best to purchase a standard product from a reputable
supplier.

If scouring piglets are too dehydrated and weak to drink, then the electrolyte
solution can be given by stomach tube or syringe. Rehydration of such weak pigs
is also possible via the rectum.

NIPPLES OR BOWLS FOR NEWLY WEANED PIGS
Water is more readily available from a small bowl situated at the correct height
above floor level for the young pig. However, because of their accessibility they
are also likely to be fouled by faeces. Nipple drinkers are certainly more hygienic
but they should be easy to operate and at the same time not be liable to excessive
waste of water. It is absolutely essential that daily checks are made to ensure that
nipples are functioning properly and bowls are clean.

It is a useful rule to have at least 2 nipple drinkers for even a small group (10
to 15 pigs). In larger groups, 1 nipple drinker should be provided for every 10
pigs. Brumm and Shelton (1986) at the University of Nebraska found in a comparison of 1 and 2 nipple drinkers in pens of 16 pigs weaned at 4 weeks of age that
those with 2 nipples were about 5 per cent heavier 5 weeks later and there was
greater uniformity in weight of pigs within pens.

It is therefore false economy to have only 1 nipple drinker per pen. A check
should be made to ensure that the drinker is at the correct height for the size (height)
of pigs occupying the pen. Newly weaned pigs can get off to a poor start at weaning
if the drinker design and/or the height cause the pig difficulty in drinking as much
water as it wishes. In order to ensure that water is readily available, some shrewd
managers adjust the nipple so that it drips continuously for the first few days after
weaning. The nipple drinker must be correctly positioned in relation to the feeder
so that piglets can readily alternate between feeding and drinking if they so desire.
If only limited amounts of top-quality water are available, then this should certainly
be diverted to the newly weaned pigs as a priority while taking urgent steps to improve the quality of water for other stock. Where intermediate storage (header)
tanks are located in the weaner house to help reduce water pressure at the nipples,
these tanks should be inspected and cleaned out regularly since putrefying rats or

Plate 12.4   In pens equipped with nipple drinkers, newly weaned pigs can benefit from having clean, fresh water readily available for a few days after weaning in a round drinker in the middle of the pen. This provides the opportunity for communal drinking to simulate the situation when nursing the sow. This approach can also be used to medicate via the water when necessary. In the interests of hygiene, the round drinker should remain in the pen only during working hours and, on removal, it should be thoroughly cleaned and disinfected in readiness for use on the following day.

mice in them will certainly not enhance the quality of the water available to vulnerable, newly weaned piglets!

## 7.  Grouping at Weaning

There is a general tendency in Britain to size pigs at weaning and place as uniform pigs as possible into a pen. Thus, pigs in a weaner pen may come from several different litters. In some parts of Canada, on the other hand, pigs tend to be housed as litter groups after weaning because of a belief that this will be less stressful than subjecting them to mixing at such a vulnerable stage. What evidence is available on the relative merits of these contrasting practices?

Wheatley (1987) went to the extreme in an attempt to answer this question. She studied the post-weaning performance of groups of 10 pigs made up as follows:

Treatment 1    10 pigs from the same litter
Treatment 2     5 pigs from each of 2 litters
Treatment 3     1 pig from each of 10 litters

Somewhat surprisingly, she found the best post-weaning performance in terms of growth and food efficiency in Treatment 2, the worst being in Treatment 3. She tried to explain this on the basis that a moderate degree of 'mixing stress' at weaning might help to stimulate appetite and growth, whereas if pigs originated from many litters, then individual pigs might be subjected to excessive strain and their performance could suffer as a result. It was interesting that in pens made up of groups of 5 from 2 different litters, the separate litters tended to segregate initially and lie separately within the pen. It could well be that individual pigs benefited from the security of being able to lie with their own littermates but were stimulated to compete for feeding space and feed with their 5 'rivals' in the pen which originated from another litter.

The best strategy to adopt in practice is likely to vary from one situation to another. If pens are constructed to take litter groups (around 10 pigs) and litters are very uniform in weaning weight, then they should be left intact. If litters are very variable in weaning weight, then groups of 10 uniform pigs should be made up from as few litters as possible, and this principle should also be applied in making up larger groups where bigger pens are used.

The advantage of putting pigs of uniform rather than very variable weight into a pen at weaning is that it will be easier to justify retaining them as an intact group throughout the growth period up to slaughter and, being more uniform, they can be disposed of within a short period of each other. This helps to make more efficient use of pen space. It also reduces the need for having to mix pigs at a later stage of growth, since mixing of older pigs can lead to serious fighting, poorer performance and death from injuries or stress on occasions.

Other arguments for regrouping pigs at weaning include (1) the need to get smaller and more vulnerable pigs together at this stage so that they can be given special treatment and (2) the desirability of separating the sexes if they are to be treated differently later in the growth period.

## 8.  Number of Pigs per Pen

What is the optimum number of pigs per pen for newly weaned pigs? Kornegay and Notter (1984) from Virginia State University in the United States closely examined many of the experiments carried out to try to answer the above question. The pigs in the various trials they studied averaged 14 kg liveweight and the weight range involved was from 7 to 21 kg. As the number of pigs per pen increased, the floor space allowance per pig remained constant. All the trials were carried out on either fully slatted or partially slatted floors. (See Figure 12.4.)

The overall picture indicated that from a baseline of 8 pigs per pen, with each additional pig in the group there was a 1.2 per cent decrease in feed intake, a 0.95 per cent decrease in daily gain and 0.27 per cent improvement in food conversion efficiency. On this basis, if we were to compare group sizes of, say, 8 and 16, the pigs in the larger group would be likely to eat 9.6 per cent less food, gain 7.6 per cent more slowly and convert their food 2.2 per cent more efficiently. Thus, apart from the small effect on feed efficiency these indications tend to support the old adage 'the smaller the group, the better they do'. The reason that the food conversion efficiency tended to improve with increasing group size while feed intake and

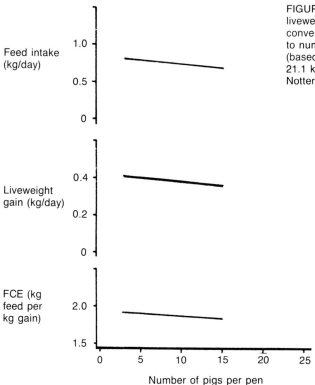

FIGURE 12.4 Feed intake, liveweight gain and feed conversion efficiency in relation to number of pigs per pen (based on growth from 7.6 to 21.1 kg liveweight). (Kornegay and Notter, 1984)

liveweight gain were reduced may indicate that in these various experiments individual piglets were able to keep warmer by huddling when in a larger group.

From Kornegay and Notter's findings, the main disadvantage of increasing group size was reduced liveweight gain which stemmed from depressed food intake. This calls into question the adequacy of feeding space and perhaps also the opportunity for obtaining water in these various experiments. It is possible that more liberal provision of these requirements would have considerably reduced the adverse effects of increasing group size.

In practice, newly weaned pigs are penned in groups from about 8 to 30. It is more expensive to provide smaller pens but, on the other hand, problems can be more readily and promptly spotted in a small group. This can often result in remedial treatment being applied more promptly and, therefore, with a more effective response. An argument for a larger group size (say 15 to 20 pigs) after weaning is that such a group could be kept intact right through to slaughter without the necessity of having to mix two smaller groups into one larger group at a later stage of growth when fighting following mixing would be more prolonged than at weaning and would be likely to have more serious consequences.

The argument for having larger groups (than say 8 to 10) in the growing and finishing stages (say 25 kg to slaughter) is that experiments have indicated little dif-

ference between group sizes ranging from 10 to 30 for growing—finishing pigs provided floor space per pig is kept constant and there is adequate feeding space and
opportunity for watering. These aspects of floor space and feeding space will now
be considered.

## 9.  Floor Space Requirements

Kornegay and Notter (1984) also looked closely at all the experiments conducted
on floor space allowances for weaned pigs over the weight range 7 to 21 kg (mean
14 kg). The studies were all on fully or partially slatted floors. Some studies were
conducted using different numbers of pigs in pens of the same size while others
looked at the same number of pigs in pens of different sizes.

It was found that as floor space per pig increased over the range 0.08 to 0.32 m²
per pig, there were steady increases in feed intake and, as a result, in daily gain
per pig. Taking a floor space allocation of 0.18 m² per pig as the baseline, for
each additional 0.1 m² of floor space provided, daily feed intake increased by 7
per cent, daily liveweight gain by 8.6 per cent while feed conversion efficiency
deteriorated by 1.2 per cent. The space allowance which made maximum daily
gains possible was equivalent to that which allowed all pigs to lie down comfortably
on their sides (fully recumbent) as calculated by Petherick and Baxter (1982).

Although daily feed intake and liveweight gain increased with more liberal floor
space allowance, less efficient use of floor space resulted as space per pig was increased. Again taking a baseline of 0.18 m² per pig, daily gain per m² of floor space
decreased by 32.6 per cent for each 0.1 m² increase in floor space allowance per
pig. This aspect is developed further in the next chapter (Figure 13.6, page 355).

The data calculated by Kornegay and Notter (1984) and the predictions of
Petherick and Baxter (1982) provide guidelines for floor space allocation for weaned pigs. However, many factors can influence optimum floor space allowance so
that this is likely to vary from situation to situation. Some of them are the following:

● When the temperature approaches and begins to exceed the UCT for the pigs,
greater floor space per pig will be beneficial as this allows pigs to spread out and
maximise the area from which heat can be lost.

● When temperature approaches and begins to fall below the LCT, reduced
floor space per pig could be beneficial, allowing a greater huddling effect and
reducing the surface area from which heat can be lost. If the building is kept full,
this increased stocking density will increase the overall number of pigs in the house
and so total heat production from the pigs will increase. This will help to warm
up the house if building insulation and control of ventilation are adequate.

● Floor space requirements per pig are less on slatted and partially slatted floors
than on solid floors.

● Where pigs are unhealthy and prone to respiratory problems, more floor
space per pig and therefore lower stocking density are desirable. If ventilation is
poor and there is insufficient air movement in the house, space requirements per
pig can increase further.

● Some workers have suggested that response to antibiotic therapy is greater
in crowded than in spacious conditions. The evidence on this possibility is,
however, contradictory and it is unsound practice to overcrowd pigs and expect that

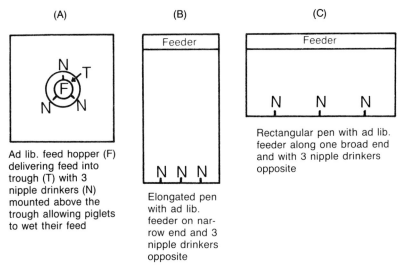

(A)                    (B)                    (C)

Ad lib. feed hopper (F)
delivering feed into
trough (T) with 3
nipple drinkers (N)
mounted above the
trough allowing piglets
to wet their feed

Elongated pen
with ad lib.
feeder on nar-
row end and 3
nipple drinkers
opposite

Rectangular pen with ad lib.
feeder along one broad end
and with 3 nipple drinkers
opposite

FIGURE 12.5    Three contrasting pen shapes with the same amount of floor space but varying in ease of access to feed and water supplies (all pens have fully slatted floors).

antibiotic therapy will counteract the adverse effects of such overcrowding. It is much more sensible to avoid overcrowding in the first place so that no growth depression occurs.

• Aggressive strains of pigs may require more floor space than less aggressive strains.

• The adequacy of provision of feed and the opportunity for watering are likely to have major influences on optimum floor space allowance per pig. Where feeding space is very liberal and watering points are numerous and well distributed, floor space requirements are likely to be reduced relative to a situation where these essential provisions are less adequate. Feeding space effects are discussed in the next section.

• The shape of the pen and the effect of this on the ease of access of each pig in the pen to feed and water are likely to have a major influence on optimum floor space allowance. Three contrasting pen shapes (see Figure 12.5) will illustrate this point. Regarding relative ease of access of any pig in the pen to feed and water supply, the most difficult situation prevails in Pen B, whereas ease of access to these resources is much improved in arrangements A and C.

In an experiment with arrangements as in Pen C, Hunt, English, Buckingham, Bampton, MacPherson and Ingram in Aberdeen found much lower floor space allowances to be acceptable than those suggested by Kornegay and Notter (1984) from their comprehensive review. Pigs were grown over the liveweight range 7 to 12.5 kg on one of three floor space allowances as shown in Table 12.9. Pig performance was good, there were no differences between treatments, while the incidence of abnormal and agonistic behaviour was very low and again there were no significant differences between treatments.

When compared to the floor space per pig estimated to provide the minimum requirements by Petherick and Baxter and relative to other recommendations, floor

**TABLE 12.9  Effect of floor space allowance on pig performance (Liveweight range 7.0 to 12.5 kg)**

|                              | Treatments | | |
|------------------------------|:----:|:----:|:----:|
|                              | A | B | C |
|                              | Floor space per pig ($m^2$) | | |
|                              | 0.21 | 0.14 | 0.10 |
| Pigs per pen                 | 10   | 15   | 20   |
| Feed intake (g/day)          | 412  | 421  | 445  |
| Liveweight gain (g/day)      | 271  | 270  | 266  |
| Feed to gain ratio (kg:kg)   | 1.58 | 1.53 | 1.54 |

space provided on treatment A would appear to be satisfactory while that on treatment C one would expect to be totally inadequate. Yet the results completely contradicted this expectation.

The most likely reasons that what appeared to be very dense stocking (treatment C) in this trial was associated with good pig performance were as follows:

1.  The pigs were very healthy.
2.  The climatic environment was excellent.
3.  Feeding space and watering points were liberal.
4.  The pen configuration was such as to make it easy for each pig in the pen to obtain its water and feed requirements without interfering unduly with its fellows.

Thus, like many other things in pig production, we can have no hard and fast rules about optimum floor space for a given size of pig. Many factors are likely to influence this requirement and the recommendations presented in Table 12.10 should be used as rough guidelines.

It is stating the obvious that floor space requirements increase steadily as pigs grow. However, this factor is not easy to cope with in practice. If we were going to make efficient use of floor space, we would be starting pigs off in very small pens at weaning and moving them to progressively larger pens almost weekly. This does not occur in practice and the tendency is to understock pens at weaning and

**TABLE 12.10  Recommended floor space allowances for weaned pigs ($m^2$ per pig) (on fully or part slatted floors)**

| Liveweight | 1 kg/.0084 $m^2$ or 25 lb/sq ft | MAFF | USDA | Minimum (Petherick and Baxter) | Adequate | Adequate (Hunt et al.) (see Table 12.9) |
|:----:|:----:|:----:|:----:|:----:|:----:|:----:|
| 5    | 0.042 | –    | –    | 0.100 | 0.141 | –    |
| 7.5  | 0.063 | –    | –    | 0.130 | 0.184 | 0.10 |
| 10   | 0.084 | 0.13 | 0.19 | 0.160 | 0.235 | 0.10 |
| 12.5 | 0.105 | –    | –    | 0.183 | 0.258 | 0.10 |
| 15   | 0.126 | –    | –    | 0.207 | 0.292 | –    |
| 20   | 0.168 | 0.19 | 0.32 | 0.253 | 0.357 | –    |
| 30   | 0.252 | –    | 0.46 | 0.332 | 0.469 | –    |

often these pens are overstocked before pigs are transferred to the next stage. This problem will be discussed and developed further in the next chapter.

## 10.   Feeding Space Requirements

Feeding space requirements are different for restricted and ad lib. feeding. For the latter, pigs have feed available all the time and, although there is a tendency for pigs to copy each other (allelomimetic behaviour) and therefore for others to follow when they see one pig feeding, the opportunity for sharing feeding space is much greater than on restricted feeding. When pigs are fed limited amounts once daily or more frequently, they must have sufficient space at the trough to allow them all to feed at once so that feed intakes are more or less equal. If feeding space is insufficient on restricted feeding systems, then some pigs will obviously obtain more than their intended share and others will receive less. Under some dietary regimes this may result in some pigs overeating and ending up with digestive upsets and scouring while others grow very slowly. This situation inevitably leads to wide variation in weight and even in body condition within the pen and consequent management problems including the need for regrouping to achieve pigs of uniform size within pens later on. This leads to fighting of mixed pigs as they strive to establish their peck order which at best results in a growth check and which can often result in injuries and even death.

Therefore provision of adequate feeding space helps to make more efficient use of lying space and reduces management problems.

FEEDING SPACE ON AD LIB. FEEDING

The most comprehensive studies on feed space allowance were carried out by workers at Virginia State University. In one of these they weaned pigs at 4 weeks of age and studied them over the next 5 weeks, during which time the pigs increased in weight from 7 to 18 kg. They were housed in groups of 10 in fully slatted pens with a floor space allocation of 0.15 m² per pig. A simple corn and soya bean diet was used. There was one nipple drinker in each pen and feeding space allocations of 3.0, 6.0 and 9.0 cm per pig were compared. The results of this comparison are summarised in Table 12.11.

It can be seen that feed intake, liveweight gain and feed conversion efficiency were virtually identical at the two highest levels of feeding space provision. However, when feeding space was further reduced to 3.0 cm per pig there were

**TABLE 12.11   Comparison of feeding space allowance on ad lib. feeding over the liveweight range of 7 to 18 kg**

|  | Feeding space per pig (cm) | | | Advantage of 6.0 over 3.0 cm (%) |
|  | 9.0 | 6.0 | 3.0 |  |
|---|---|---|---|---|
| Feed intake (g/day) | 590 | 586 | 572 | 2.4 |
| Liveweight gain (g/day) | 322 | 322 | 304 | 5.9 |
| Feed to gain ratio (kg feed per kg gain) | 1.84 | 1.83 | 1.89 | 3.2 |

(From Lindemann, Kornegay, Meldrum, Schurig and Gwazdauskas, 1984)

depressions in all traits measured, ranging from a 2.4 per cent depression in feed intake to a 5.9 per cent reduction in liveweight gain.

However, the mean figures over the 5 weeks' growth period do not tell the whole story. In the first 2 weeks, pig performance on the lowest feeding space allocation (3.0 cm per pig) was as good as or better than performance on the more liberal space provisions. It was obviously only from week 3 onwards that pigs on 3.0 cm per head began to run out of space.

The results of this experiment therefore provided an indication of the optimum feed space allowance on ad lib. feeding for weaned pigs from 7 to 18 kg liveweight. This optimum was somewhere between 3 cm per pig (which was too low) and 6.0 cm per pig (which was adequate). Further studies by the same workers came to the conclusion that a feed space allowance of 4.5 cm was adequate for pigs on ad lib. feeding over this liveweight range.

On this basis, width of the feeding face on ad lib. feeding for pigs in the first 4 or 5 weeks following weaning at around 7 kg liveweight would be as indicated in Table 12.12. These feeding space provisions should be looked upon as the minimum levels which should be considered.

TABLE 12.12   Minimum feeding space allowances on ad lib. feeding between 7 and 18 kg liveweight

| Number of pigs per pen | Width of ad lib. feeder (metres) |
| --- | --- |
| 10 | 0.45 |
| 15 | 0.68 |
| 20 | 0.90 |
| 25 | 1.13 |

(Based on studies of Lindemann and associates at Virginia State University)

Many pig producers will be extremely surprised by the very limited feeding space which proves quite adequate in some circumstances since feeding space provision is usually much more liberal in practice. That excessive feeding space can be detrimental to performance has been indicated by other studies. One consequence of excessive feeding space has been fouling of the feed with urine and faeces, especially at the ends of the feeder if it extends to the corner(s) of a pen. When this happens it takes time to clean out the feeder and feed has obviously got to be discarded. Even if the ends of the feeder are not fouled, pigs may neglect feed at the extremities of it and concentrate on feeding near its centre.

Producers are well advised to check feeders at very regular intervals and to take immediate steps to prevent fouling and of the build up of stale feed in any part of the food trough.

It would also be very worthwhile for producers to conduct an on-farm experiment comparing their present provision of feeding space with the more limited space allowances which the studies in Virginia (see Table 12.10) have suggested may well be adequate in many circumstances. At the same time they could examine the effect of increasing their feeding space above their present allowance.

FEEDING SPACE ON RESTRICTED FEEDING

Surprisingly, very little research work has been carried out to determine the feeding space requirements of newly weaned pigs on restricted feeding systems. The important requirement, of course, is that all pigs should be able to get into the feed trough at one time. The absolute minimum requirement for feeding space, therefore, can be calculated by multiplying the number of pigs in the pen by the shoulder width of the pig, this being the part of the body at which the pig is broadest. As pigs gain in liveweight, so they will increase in width and the requirement for feeding space will thus increase steadily.

Pigs of the same liveweight can vary markedly in shape, from the short stocky genotypes like the Pietrain to the long narrow types like the Norwegian Landrace. Feeding space requirements, therefore, vary according to liveweight and breed (or shape) and optimum feeding space allowance will change with circumstances.

Fortunately, it is easy in practice to make a judgement regarding the adequacy of feeding space on restricted systems. As feed in delivered to the trough and pigs come to feed, they should all be able to fit easily into the space provided. If this is not possible, one of two measures must be taken immediately: increased trough space must be provided or one or more pigs should be removed from the pen.

In practice, on restricted feeding systems, it is usual to provide more than adequate trough space at weaning so that by the time the pigs are about to be transferred to 'follow-on' pens, they can all just fit into the space provided at the trough.

Plate 12.5  For newly weaned pigs on restricted feeding, feeding space is critical. There may be sufficient space to allow all pigs to feed simultaneously at weaning but pigs grow so relatively quickly at this stage that feeding space can quickly become inadequate. This results in weaker and lower 'peck order' pigs being deprived of food while more vigorous pigs get more than their intended allowance.

To give some indication of approximate feeding space requirements on restricted feeding systems, the data of Baxter (1984) reproduced in Table 8.11 on page 148 should be studied. In this work the shoulder width of Large White × Landrace pigs was measured at regular liveweight intervals.

From this data, minimum feeding space allowances can be calculated for restricted feeding of the type of pig involved in the study. For genotypes which deviate in shape (mainly shoulder width) from those involved in the study summarised in Table 8.11, these allowances would need to be reduced or increased accordingly.

## 11.  Maintenance of Health

It will be clear from the foregoing that provision of adequate conditions for healthy pigs at weaning in terms of such factors as diet, climate, space and good stockmanship in general will make a major contribution to the maintenance of good health. Other important considerations in achieving this objective were outlined in Chapter 11.

## 12.  Monitoring the Weaner Pig System

Having set up a system for housing, feeding and managing newly weaned pigs, it is vital that it be monitored closely to ensure that all components of the system are fitting nicely together and, if not, to determine which components are proving faulty. The stockman and manager/farmer have several very useful tools at their disposal to help them detect faults in their system and to point the way to how best these can be remedied. It is something like the expert mechanic listening to and testing an engine as a basis for deciding how it can be more finely tuned to become more efficient and run more smoothly. The fine tuning of an early weaning system can be much more complex than that of a motor engine since not only are the principles of physics and chemistry involved but so also are the very complex laws of biology, involving as they do in this case the delicate interactions of the pig with a host of different micro-organisms and with the stockman. Thus, the complexity of the interactions between physics, chemistry and biology reach their zenith in an animal production system. While we can never expect to understand and harness these extremely complex interactions with 100 per cent efficiency, we can go some way to making most early weaning systems much more efficient than they are at present.

How then do we set about the fine tuning of our post weaning system? We have a few extremely useful and efficient tools at our disposal if we deploy them properly.

OBSERVATION OF PIG BEHAVIOUR
The ability to observe and interpret pig behaviour is one of our most effective mechanisms for first detecting and then pointing the way to the solution of problems. This is an excellent 'crypton' tester to guide the way to the fine tuning of the weaner pig system.

Pig behaviour and simple observations tell us a great deal about the adequacy of the system:

- Is it warm enough or is it too warm?
- Is there enough lying space?
- Is there too little or too much feeding space?
- Is the feeder correctly sited?
- Are watering facilities adequate?
- Are the pigs healthy and, if not, what is wrong with them?
- Are pigs losing too much body condition after weaning?
- Do pigs within a pen become much more variable in body condition in the week or so after weaning?
- Is the atmosphere stuffy and smelly? (stale air? ammonia? scour?)
- Are the pigs unduly noisy?

Some of these pointers to the adequacy of the system will now be developed further.

*Is it warm enough or is it too warm?*
Since many factors such as feed intake influence the comfort level or thermoneutral zone of the weaned pig, the best way to assess whether pigs are comfortable is to look at their behaviour. If they are huddling and some are tending to shiver, they are too cold. If they try to spread themselves out and are panting they are too warm. On the other hand, if they are lying on their sides and breathing very easily they are within their comfort zone.

The greatest likelihood of pigs being cold comes immediately after weaning when feed intake tends to be very low (see Figure 12.6). It can be seen that when 5 kg pigs in groups are only consuming enough food to provide for maintenance, then

Plate 12.6 Lying behaviour of pigs following weaning provides a very good indication of their comfort. If they are nicely spread out and breathing easily, this indicates that they are within their thermal comfort zone. Huddling and shivering indicate that they are too cold, while a tendency to lie very far apart and panting indicate that they are too warm.

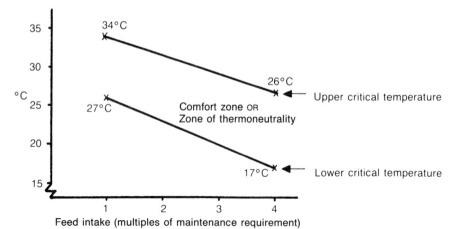

FIGURE 12.6   Upper and lower critical temperatures (UCT and LCT) of 5 kg pigs on different levels of feed or energy intake (pigs in groups of 10 and on mesh flooring). (From Bruce, 1982)

their LCT is as high as 27°C. The temperature can go up as high as 34°C before they become embarrassed by the heat. Thus, the range of acceptable temperature (range of comfort zone) is quite wide but the important point is that temperature should be at or above the LCT. If pigs have higher food intakes (2 to 4 times maintenance) then temperature requirements decrease steadily, so that stimulating higher feed intake is an obvious way to reduce temperature requirement for newly

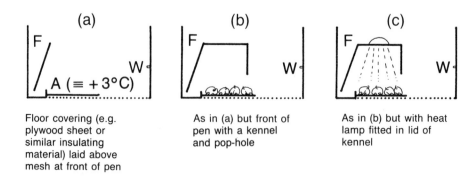

Floor covering (e.g. plywood sheet or similar insulating material) laid above mesh at front of pen

As in (a) but front of pen with a kennel and pop-hole

As in (b) but with heat lamp fitted in lid of kennel

A = Provision of plywood sheet is equivalent to raising temperature by 3°C relative to lying on a metal mesh floor
F = Feeder
——— = Floor covering
• • • = Mesh floor
W = Water

FIGURE 12.7   Approaches to providing the required temperature at pig level following weaning.

weaned pigs. On the other hand, some pigs after weaning will be consuming even less than their needs for maintenance and will be catabolising (losing) body tissue (mainly fat) to help provide their energy needs to keep vital body processes going. The LCT of these pigs will be even higher than the 27°C cited in Figure 12.6 for pigs on maintenance food intakes.

Thus, if young pigs are going to be warm enough immediately after weaning, temperature at pig level must be very high. Either the whole room can be heated to the temperature level required or else attempts can be made just to provide the necessary comfort at pig level. Some approaches to achieving the latter objective are illustrated in Figure 12.7.

If it is difficult or expensive to get the temperature at pig level in fully slatted pens high enough for newly weaned pigs, one should provide an insulated floor covering above the mesh (Figure 12.7a) even for the first few days after weaning until feed intake builds up. Observations of pig behaviour will tell the stockman whether this is the only modification necessary (without going to the length of increasing room temperature or else providing kennels and heat lamps).

If an insulated pad is provided above the floor at the front of the pen, the observer may see some pigs choosing to lie on the pad while others lie on the mesh floor. This indicates that the comfort zone for the individual pigs in the pen differ, perhaps mainly because of differences in feed intake, those with lower intakes choosing to lie on the warmer and those with higher intakes on the cooler areas. The modifications of the flat deck pen suggested in Figure 12.7 provide individual pigs with a choice of temperature within the pen which is a very useful provision to cater for variations in temperature requirement within a group of pigs.

If the behaviour indicates that pigs are too hot, then turning down any heaters, increased air flow over the pigs or provision of greater space, allowing pigs to spread out more, are obvious steps to take. If these are insufficient to keep temperature below the UCT then any of the approaches for cooling down buildings outlined on pages 136–138 should be implemented.

The penalties for allowing temperature to go outwith the comfort zone for newly weaned pigs can be severe. If temperature is excessive, feed intake will be reduced and both feed intake and feed conversion efficiency will be depressed.

If temperature is too low, pigs will use up energy from expensive food just to keep warm and feed efficiency will be depressed as a result. However, there can be even further drastic consequences in the form of increased liability to disease problems. It has been demonstrated that pigs which are exposed to cold or fluctuating air temperature have increased susceptibility to both bacterial and viral enteric diseases (Kelley, Blecha and Regnier, 1982 and Kelley, 1982). This increased susceptibility to infectious disease under cold exposure is probably brought about by changes in the endocrine system and subsequent stress-induced changes in the efficiency of the immune system in providing protection against disease challenge.

*Is there enough lying space?*
In trying to answer this question from observation of behaviour, one can check on the posture adopted by the pigs when lying and the general level of activity. In the evening when pigs are generally quiet and asleep for long periods, one can check their apparent comfort while resting. If they are able to stretch out into their

Plate 12.7   Flat decks are attractive from the health aspect in that they largely separate the pig from its own excrement. However, the provision of improved floor insulation above the mesh floor (e.g. a sheet of plywood) adjacent to the feeder in the first few days after early weaning helps to keep the pig more comfortable at a lower cost at a time when its temperature requirement is very high (see also Figure 12.7).

favourite fully recumbent positions (or semi-recumbent against their fellows) and they are quiet with only the occasional awakening of an individual to visit the feed trough or the watering point or to defaecate or urinate, one can be satisfied that floor space provision is adequate. On the other hand, if some pigs are lying on all fours (on the sternum) and almost all the floor space is occupied, if there are the regular short, sharp, high-pitched grunts or almost semi-squeals characteristic of annoyance and if there is more restlessness than normal during a period when almost perfect peace usually reigns, then one should be suspicious that floor space is inadequate. In periods during the day when there is normally a higher level of activity, one is on the lookout for the signs of more competitive and aggressive behaviour from the general activity and the physical and vocal interactions between the pigs. If these activities and interactions are indicative of a fairly peaceful co-existence, all may be well, but if they are indicative of strain and annoyance even in a proportion of the pigs, one must question the adequacy of floor space. Other factors which, of course, must also be under suspicion if such disruptive behaviour prevails include the adequacy of feeding space and of the diet, the opportunity for watering, excessive number of pigs in the pen and their general health.

Once inadequate lying space is suspected as being a problem, one can check the provision for space against the recommendations outlined in Table 12.10 as well as the other factors outlined earlier which influence the floor space requirement of young pigs.

*Is there too much or too little feeding space?*
Whether or not there is sufficient feeding space is easier to check on restricted feeding systems. When each feed is delivered to the trough it is very easy to check that all pigs can readily accommodate themselves at the trough simultaneously. This is something which has to be monitored constantly as pigs increase in weight and shoulder width. Excessive feeding space can cause more problems on ad lib. feeding systems where certain parts of the feeder may not be used. As a result, stale feed can build up in these sections resulting in waste. Worse still, pigs may dung and urinate in such sections, especially if these are in the corner of the pen. This fouls the feed in the immediate and adjacent areas and increases the labour input. If this occurs, either a smaller feed trough can be used away from pen corners or areas of the feeder being fouled can be blocked off, preventing dung and urine from entering the trough. If the fouling problem is confined to pen corners, placing a concrete block in front of the feeder in this area is a useful temporary remedial measure to adopt.

Stockmen must be constantly vigilant for the build-up of stale feed or fouling in particular areas of the feed trough. A daily check is essential.

*Are watering facilities adequate?*
If the observant stockman sees more activity than usual around the drinker, accompanied by slight squeals of apparent annoyance, improper functioning of the drinker must be suspected. Some types of nipple drinkers, in particular, are liable to block and the functioning of such drinkers must be checked daily. The rule of having at least two nipple drinkers per pen helps to cover for the possibility that one could be nonfunctional for part of a day until the problem is spotted.

If pigs are going to be short of water, this is most likely in the period immediately after weaning when they have to negotiate the major transition from getting a warm, nutritious (and apparently palatable) liquid from the teats of the mother every hour to obtaining sufficient for their requirements of a bland, often cold liquid (which is water) from a nipple drinker at which they may have to queue to obtain their needs.

Do they drink as much as is good for them in the first 24 hours or so following weaning? This is a difficult question to answer in the practical situation. Some attempt can be made by, say, 12 to 24 hours after weaning, introducing a round drinker containing clean water with the chill off at which all pigs in the pen can drink communally. If piglets investigate the container and the water and show little interest, they are probably obtaining enough water from the nipple drinkers. On the other hand, if one pig investigates it, starts drinking vigorously (and usually noisily), attracts its pen-mates and they in turn show an excited response and drink a reasonable quantity, this may indicate that the nipple drinkers do not constitute an adequate means of providing the pigs' liquid requirements in this very vulnerable period immediately following weaning. As part of routine practice, some pig producers make a wholesome supply of water available in drinkers from which pigs can drink communally in the first few days after weaning. This is sensible policy and gives piglets a chance to get fully adjusted to using the nipple drinkers or whatever drinker type is used in the pen.

*Are pigs healthy?*
The first sign of ill health is usually abnormal behaviour. The pig behaving differently from its pen-mates, its failure to come to feed with the rest when on a restricted feeding system, its different posture and activity level relative to the rest — all must be taken as possible signs of disease or the early stages of development of such. One should check one's suspicions by examining the pig for signs of scouring, although this is not at all easy either on fully slatted or straw-bedded floors. Early detection of disease problems is extremely important so that remedial treatment can be applied promptly before the problem develops too far.

*Detecting and responding to vices: tail, flank and ear biting; navel suckling*
Disturbed behaviour resulting in tail, flank and ear biting indicates that something is far wrong with the system. Further reference to these problems is made on pages 267–272, also see colour plates 27–30.

Suffice it to say here that all essential components of early weaning systems should be checked very carefully when such problems arise. They include the diet, feeding space, group size, stocking density, adequacy of ventilation (concentration of waste gases) and temperature (not too hot or too cold). Until the source of the problem is detected, bitten pigs should be removed from the pen, their injuries treated with antiseptic spray and they should be placed in isolation premises where they cannot be further molested by other pigs. The pens in which the problem develops should be watched carefully in an attempt to detect the main culprit(s).

Plate 12.8    Young pigs which have been subjected to flank biting by their pen mates. Vices such as flank, ear and tail biting must be taken as an indication that conditions for the pigs are inadequate. When this occurs there is a need to check whether it is too hot or too cold, along with such factors as the diet, feeding space, opportunity for watering, floor space allowance per pig and number of pigs per pen.

The rogue pig(s) may be caught in the act when it starts to bite a damaged ear or tail; if not, a pig with some blood stains around the nose and face must be under greatest suspicion. When suspicions are confirmed the defaulter must either be placed in solitary confinement or else be put in a pen with very much larger pigs which it cannot damage. Often, a smaller pig in the pen is the main source of the problem. Until the predisposing cause of the problem is isolated, short-term measures involve placing playthings such as stones or tyres in the pen with which the pigs can play. The suspension of chains or, better still, tough, thin strips of rubber gives the pigs something to play with and chew. Some claim that ear, flank and tail biting only occur in fully or partly slatted floor systems which they term barren environments. However, serious outbreaks also occur on well-managed straw-bedded systems.

Regarding the problem of navel suckling, this can be fairly common among pigs that are weaned very early. Generally, later weaning will reduce the occurrence of the problem. Such behaviour is probably analogous to thumb sucking in young children and is just as difficult to stop. The only treatment, as indicated later (page 323), is to foster the pigs back to a sow. This should be done as soon as possible after the problem is spotted for not only do these pigs fail to thrive themselves but they can greatly disturb their victims.

RECORDING ASPECTS OF THE CLIMATIC ENVIRONMENT

As well as monitoring pig behaviour, another set of tools which is useful in the fine tuning of a system for weaner pigs is the monitoring of climatic variables such as temperature, air flow patterns, air speed and, to a lesser extent, humidity.

Temperature should be recorded as near pig level as possible to determine the conditions to which the pigs themselves are subjected. Provided it is reset each day, a maximum/minimum thermometer is useful because it gives the overall range of temperature to which pigs are subjected over a 24 hour period.

The use of smoke bombs will help to check air flow patterns and, to some extent, air speed over the pigs to ensure that pigs are receiving an adequate supply of fresh air and that air speed over the pigs is not sufficiently high to constitute a draught.

The environmental specialist will use more sophisticated approaches in monitoring temperature and humidity trends continuously and in checking for the existence of draughts and foul air from the slurry pit passing over the pigs.

MONITORING PERFORMANCE

After behaviour and aspects of the climatic environment are checked, the actual performance of pigs on the system in terms of health and survival, food intake, liveweight gain and food conversion efficiency is the final arbiter in determining the efficiency of the system.

*Health and survival*

If pigs remain healthy and mortality during the establishment phase of the weaned pig (from weaning to about 20 kg liveweight) is kept to about the 1 per cent level, then this tells us much about the soundness of the system. When monitoring these aspects, it is vital that drug usage and drug costs are also fully recorded for it could be that a very impressive health and survival record is only made possible by the use of excessive drugs at an exorbitant cost.

*Feed and energy intake*

It is important to achieve high feed or energy intake consistent with good health after weaning for several reasons:

● to achieve faster liveweight gain and throughput of pigs
● to lower the cost of housing the pig per unit of time
● to keep the pig warmer
● to achieve improved feed conversion efficiency

The last point will be developed briefly. The pig must consume enough nutrients (including energy) to provide for its maintenance requirements (one way of describing maintenance is to define it as the food required just to keep all vital processes going with no surplus to allow body or liveweight gain). If it consumes food surplus to maintenance, it will gain weight and the higher the food intake, the greater will be the weight gain. The upper limit of food or energy intake is about four times the maintenance requirement. The higher the food intake up to the limits of its capacity, not only will the faster be the liveweight gain, but the young pig will be keeping itself warmer and will be converting its food more efficiently. The important relationship between food intake and food conversion efficiency is illustrated in Figure 12.8.

On food intake level 1, no food is available for liveweight gain since it is all re-

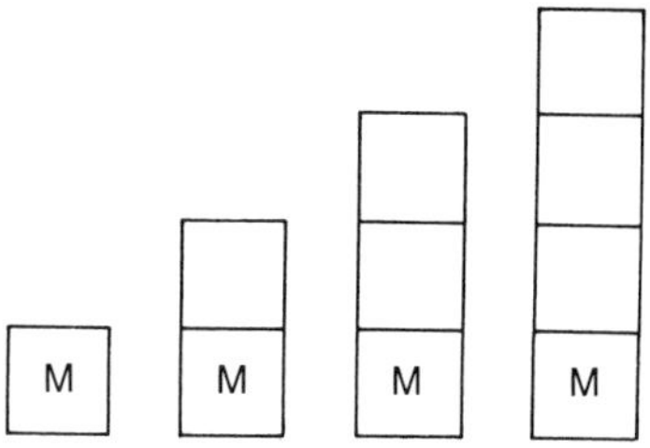

| Food intake level (multiples of maintenance needs) | 1 | 2 | 3 | 4 |
|---|---|---|---|---|
| Proportion of total intake required for maintenance (%) | 100 | 50 | 33 | 25 |
| Proportion of total intake available for body weight gain (%) | 0 | 50 | 67 | 75 |

FIGURE 12.8   Food intake (multiples of maintenance requirement) and the proportion of total food intake available for body weight gain. (M = Maintenance)

quired just to maintain the animal. The proportion of food available for liveweight gain increases steadily as one goes from feed level 1 to 4. On feed levels 2, 3 and 4, 50, 67 and 75 per cent respectively of the total intake is available for liveweight gain. Therefore, the efficiency with which food is converted into liveweight gain will also increase with increasing food intake. This is based on the assumption that the composition of liveweight gain (especially lean to fat ratio) will be very similar at different levels of intake for the young pig between weaning and 20 kg liveweight; this, in fact, is largely true. Therefore, there are many good reasons why we should try to achieve as high food (or energy) intake as possible in the young pig after weaning, provided this is consistent with keeping the pig healthy and free from enteric problems in particular.

Provided pigs remain healthy, high feed intake following weaning indicates that the post-weaning diet and such factors as group size, floor space and feeding space are adequate. These must be considered critically, however, if food intake is disappointing, along with the health of the pigs and the thermal comfort level (temperature and freedom from draughts).

*Liveweight gain*
Liveweight gain is not only one of the best indicators of the well-being of the system but it is one of the easiest to measure. Just as important as the average liveweight gain is the variation in gain for the different pigs within a pen. If pigs of uniform weight are put in a pen at weaning and they all grow well and evenly, then this tells us that our system is fairly sound. If growth within pens is very variable, on the other hand, this indicates some undue competition within pens and/or variability in health status. If there are no obvious disease problems, variation in liveweight gain could be due to inadequate floor or feeding space or opportunity for watering. These effects could be accentuated by a sub-optimal or variable temperature problem.

Thus, the detection of the problem of variable liveweight gain should set in motion the detective work to isolate the cause(s).

*Feed to gain ratio or feed conversion efficiency*
One component of this index of the adequacy of the system is liveweight gain. The other one is food intake for each pen which requires much more labour to measure, requiring the weighing of all food supplied to a pen and the weighing back of leftovers when final pig liveweights are recorded.

Nevertheless, it is a most important index for the pig farmer since food constitutes some 70 per cent of total costs, so it must be used efficiently. Poor food conversion efficiency could be due to one or more of many factors. Unhealthy pigs, poor-quality diets, low food intake, poor liveweight gain, inadequate floor and feeding space, poor watering facilities, sub-optimal temperature and draughts can all contribute. Thus, considerable and complex detective work is usually necessary to determine the main predisposing factors involved.

*Food cost per kg of liveweight gain*
This is the most important single index of how finely the pig weaner system is tuned. This is because the index incorporates many other variables already discussed. These include health and survival, food intake, liveweight gain and food conversion efficiency along with the cost of the diet.

While food conversion efficiency is a very useful index, it must be combined with the cost per tonne or per kg of diet as the data in Table 12.13 illustrates.

**TABLE 12.13  Cost per kg of liveweight gain at varying feed conversion efficiencies and food costs per tonne**

| Food to gain ratio (kg food per kg liveweight gain) | 1.0 | 1.5 | 2.0 | 3.0 | 4.5 |
|---|---|---|---|---|---|
| Cost of diet: *per tonne* | £450 | £300 | £225 | £150 | £100 |
| *per kg* | £0.45 | £0.30 | £0.225 | £0.15 | £0.10 |
| Food cost per kg liveweight gain | £0.45 | £0.45 | £0.45 | £0.45 | £0.45 |

Thus, we have food conversion efficiency varying very widely between the extremes of 1.0 and 4.5, but because the costs of the different diets also differ markedly, the different situations represented end up with exactly the same cost per kg of liveweight gain. Thus, food cost per unit of liveweight gain is a very good composite index of how well the system is operating. Additional, more comprehensive indices of the efficiency of the system include:

● Food and housing cost per unit of liveweight gain
● Food, veterinary, housing and labour cost per unit of liveweight gain

PROGRESS IN SYSTEMS FOR THE WEANED PIG OVER THE YEARS
The provisions made for early weaned pigs and their management have made considerable advances over the past decade or so. Performance in terms of liveweight

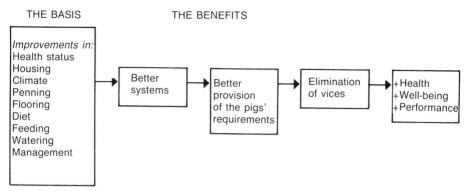

THE BASIS                              THE BENEFITS

*Improvements in:*
Health status
Housing
Climate          Better            Better              Elimination        +Health
Penning          systems           provision           of vices           +Well-being
Flooring                           of the pigs'                           +Performance
Diet                               requirements
Feeding
Watering
Management

FIGURE 12.9    The basis and benefits of improved systems for early weaned pigs. (From English, 1987)

gain, feed conversion efficiency and survival have been improved markedly. One of the biggest differences observed over the past decade in the apparent well-being of the weaned pig in Britain has been the virtual disappearance of vices such as tail, flank and ear biting on commercial farms. Whereas these problems were very common 5 to 10 years ago, they are found only very rarely in practice today. The reason for this considerable advance is obviously our improved understanding of the needs of the early weaned pig and the application of this improved knowledge in commercial practice by skilful farmers, managers and stockmen. In addition to improvements in health status, housing, climate, penning and providing for the social needs of the pig, there have been considerable advances in diets, in provision of feed and water and in general management. These improved provisions for the early weaned pig, when incorporated together into improved systems, have contributed very significantly to its enhanced health and well-being. The basis and benefits of these improved systems are summarised in Figure 12.9.

## 13.  Looking After the Problem Pigs at Weaning

Whatever the age at weaning, there are always some problem pigs which have not grown so well for a variety of reasons. They pose the problem of whether they should be weaned at all and, if the decision is made to wean them, then the question arises as to what special provisions must be made after weaning to meet their more complex requirements. There are other pigs which appear as mature and as prepared for weaning as their litter mates but which fail to thrive as well as their contemporaries after weaning and consequently create problems for the stockman. The objective of this section is to suggest the more useful approaches for looking after the interests of such 'misfits'.

EXTENDING NURSING FOR POORER PIGS

In most pig units, there is a strategy to wean pigs once weekly at a particular age which can vary in practice between 2 and 8 weeks of age. If the plan is to wean pigs at 4 weeks or 28 days of age once weekly, then litters between the ages of 24 and 32 (mean 28 days) will be weaned. If there are certain pigs in these litters which have not grown or thrived so well, and the stockman is concerned about weaning them, he may consider that they are better left suckling a sow. When this decision is made he can adopt one of two strategies:

1.  If he has a total of 8 such problem pigs from, say, 10 litters that are to be weaned, he can foster them on to a good milking sow that has just weaned 10 good pigs. It may be wise to leave unweaned one of the foster sow's own pigs (the smallest one) for a few hours or even a day, as the presence and nursing attempts of her own remaining pig will help her to become acclimatised gradually to the new litter and at the same time will help the new litter to settle down.

If one is careful enough in selecting a placid sow, there is usually no need to administer a sedative such as stresnil to facilitate the fostering process. A good milking sow that is due to be culled for some other reason is a good candidate to use as a foster sow. The new litter of poorer pigs should be left to suckle for 1 or 2 weeks until they are considered fit enough to wean. Producers sometimes grudge keeping a sow that is to remain in the herd back for, say, one week to do this important fostering job before finally weaning her. This attitude is difficult to understand for the following reason. If a sow rears 26 pigs in a year (52 weeks) she is producing, on average, half a pig per week. While doing this job of nursing 8 smaller pigs from various litters which have just been weaned from their own dams, she is helping to establish 8 pigs in a week or at least getting them to a condition at which they will be much fitter for weaning and much less vulnerable in the post-weaning period.

2.  If the stockman has only, say, 3 problem pigs at a weaning, he can look for a sow with strong 21 day old pigs which are due to be weaned the following week. If this sow has 9 pigs, the stockman can wean 4 or 5 of the strongest and foster the 3 problem pigs on to this sow. In doing this he is making a judgement (based on experience) that he will have less of a post-weaning problem by weaning 4 or 5 strong pigs from the younger litter than the 3 poorer pigs from the older litters.

PARTIAL WEANING

This refers to the practice, mainly used in the case of very early weaning (14 to 21 days), of weaning the stronger pigs some 5 to 7 days earlier than the poorer pigs. If, say, a farmer is weaning pigs at an average of 20 days he may wean the strongest half of the litter at 14 days and leave the poorer half on the sow for the next 6 days with less competition. The smaller pigs left on the sow will certainly benefit in terms of growth up to weaning as the data in Table 12.14 demonstrate.

**TABLE 12.14  Effects of partial weaning**

|  | *Timing of weaning (days)* | | | *% advantage of* | |
|  | *A* | *B* | *C* | *B over A* | *C over A* |
| --- | --- | --- | --- | --- | --- |
| Stronger pigs (5) | 17 | 14 | 11 | | |
| Poorer pigs    (5) | 17 | 17 | 17 | | |
| Daily liveweight gain of poorer pigs (g) | | | | | |
| 14−17 days | 170 | 232 | 246 | 36.5% | 44.7% |
| 11−17 days | 171 | 201 | 235 | 17.5% | 37.4% |

On treatment A, all pigs were weaned at the same time (17 days) so this acted as the control treatment. It can be seen in partially weaned treatments B (stronger pigs weaned 3 days earlier) and C (stronger pigs weaned 6 days earlier) that the liveweight gain of the poorer pigs in the last few days before weaning was between 17.5 and 44.7 per cent higher relative to the poorer pigs on treatment A, which had to compete with their stronger litter mates right up to weaning.

Resorting to partial weaning in this way must also be a matter of judgement by the stockman, who decides that he will have fewer problems after weaning by giving his poorer pigs a pre-weaning boost in growth even if he is weaning his stronger pigs somewhat earlier.

When partial weaning is practised at an early stage such as in the experiment summarised in Table 12.14, sometimes weaning to first oestrus interval in the sow is shortened and there can be a slight increase in litter size at the next farrowing. However, if partial weaning is practised too early or too many pigs are removed, the sow could well come into oestrus while still nursing the reduced litter in the farrowing pen and this causes obvious management problems especially in terms of heat detection. When half the litter is removed 4 or 6 days early, stockmen must be vigilant since some sows may be in oestrus on the day of final weaning or very soon afterwards.

FOSTERING BACK WEANED PIGLETS
Sometimes pigs are weaned with high expectations that few post-weaning problems will arise but things do not work out this way. One particular problem that arises is that of belly or navel suckling, as indicated earlier. Pigs which resort to this practice after weaning tend not to eat and they can greatly disturb their 'victims' so that the latter also suffer. Pigs that navel suckle, like thumb sucking in young children, take a long time to lose the bad habit and decisive and prompt action is essential. Whenever navel suckers are noticed they should be fostered back to a nursing sow and there they can turn their 'bad' habit into a good one by suckling a teat and obtaining excellent nutrition from it at the same time. If they remain on such a sow for a further 1 to 2 weeks they will be better grown and more mature and therefore better prepared for weaning, so that they are much less likely to revert to their previous bad post-weaning habit. The best way to accommodate such a pig when the decision is made to foster it back is to wean 2 or 3 strong pigs which are considered to be fit for weaning and to replace them with the navel sucker. In fostering on to an existing litter in this way, it is always desirable to wean more pigs off than you are fostering on, so as to give the fostered pigs a better chance of finding functional teats.

CATERING FOR PROBLEM PIGS AFTER WEANING
Apart from those pigs that resort to navel suckling following weaning, there are others which fail to adapt well to the post-weaning system, and they also impose problems for the stockman. The pigs which fail to thrive after weaning are, on average, the lighter ones but some of the heavier pigs also give problems as indicated in Table 12.15.

In this sample of weaners, when the 10 per cent of pigs which performed best were compared with the 10 per cent which had the poorest performance in the 4

Plate 12.9   The Chore-time Baby Pig feeder, developed in North Carolina, USA, is a useful piece of equipment for helping to establish the more vulnerable piglets at early weaning. Liquid milk substitute (of controllable dry matter content) is prepared automatically from milk substitute powder and water and delivered into a trough in predetermined quantities and at pre-set intervals. The equipment is relatively easy to clean and service.

**TABLE 12.15** Comparison of the best 10 per cent and the worst 10 per cent of pigs in a sample of 150 pigs weaned at 18 days of age

| | Liveweight at start (kg) | | Liveweight gain per day (g) | | | |
|---|---|---|---|---|---|---|
| | Mean | Range | Week 1 | Week 2 | Week 3 | Week 4 |
| Best 10% | 5.59 | 4.6–7.4 | 105 | 240 | 544 | 589 |
| Worst 10% | 4.54 | 3.6–6.6 | −38 | 85 | 164 | 61 |
| | | | Liveweight (kg) | | | |
| Best 10% | 5.59 | | 6.33 | 8.01 | 11.82 | 15.87 |
| Worst 10% | 4.54 | | 4.27 | 4.87 | 6.02 | 6.35 |
| Liveweight advantage of best 10% over worst 10% (%) | 23 | | 48 | 64 | 98 | 150 |

The pigs were on a high-digestibility starter diet at weaning which was offered ad lib. They were housed in groups of 10 to 12 in a comfortable environment. During week 3 they received equal quantities of the starter diet and a less expensive follow-on diet. During week 4 they received the follow-on diet only. (Source: English, Davidson, MacPherson, Birnie and Smith, 1984)

weeks after weaning, several interesting points emerged. At weaning, among the best 10 per cent were some light pigs while among the worst 10 per cent were some heavy pigs.

The best 10 per cent of pigs were only 23 per cent heavier than the worst 10 per cent at the start but were 150 per cent heavier after four weeks. The best 10 per cent of pigs increased their starting weight by a factor of 2.84 up to the 4 weeks stage, while the worst 10 per cent only increased their starting weight by a factor of 1.4 up of the four week stage.

While the worst 10 per cent of pigs were not very much lighter at the start, for one reason or another, they failed to adapt adequately to the post-weaning system. They lost weight in the first week after weaning and their rate of daily liveweight gain was lower in week 4 than it was in the previous week. Since week 4 was the first week that pigs were on the less digestible follow-on diet only (they received a 50:50 mix of the starter and follow-on diets in week 3), this would indicate that their digestive system was failing to cope with the follow-on diet. The worst 10 per cent of pigs gave every indication that they were the pigs with a lower level of digestive enzymes as described by Kidder (1981) (see Figure 12.10).

It would appear that the level of the digestive enzyme sucrase provides a good indication of the degree of development of the mature digestive enzyme system. It is clear from Figure 12.10 that the digestive system is increasing quite rapidly in maturity as age at weaning is increased from 3 to 5 to 8 weeks. Not only are the levels of the digestive enzymes which deal with non-milk nutrients low in the piglet around 3 to 4 weeks of age but they vary widely between piglets. It can be seen in Figure 12.10, at both 3 and 5 weeks of age, that the highest level of sucrase is over three times that of the lowest level. Thus, some pigs at these ages have only one-third of the level of mature digestive enzymes of other pigs so that the ability of pigs to adapt to post-weaning diets will vary very markedly.

Those piglets less well equipped in terms of digestive ability will be more likely

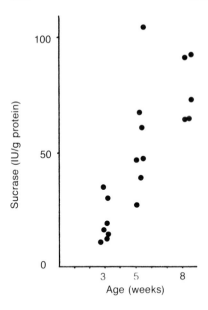

FIGURE 12.10   Mean sucrase levels in the small intestine mucosa of 19 suckled piglets of approximately 3, 5 and 8 weeks of age. Each dot refers to 1 piglet. (From Kidder, 1981)

to suffer from digestive upsets and scouring after weaning. Because of associated damage of the villi lining the small intestine, such developments will further reduce the production of digestive enzymes from the gut wall and so the initial problem of these pigs is further aggravated. Such pigs fall further and further behind their pen mates and die in greater numbers.

Most pig producers, to a greater or lesser degree, recognise the problem of a proportion of pigs failing to adapt after weaning. Whether or not poor digestive ability is the cause of this problem, these pigs must be given preferential treatment. If their failure to adapt after weaning is spotted early enough they could be fostered back to a sow. Otherwise they could receive any or all of the following advantages. They could be:

- kept in a warmer environment
- offered a higher quality diet
- left on the starter diet and the first stage of rearing accommodation for a longer period

As indicated earlier, monitoring the variation in performance of pigs after weaning is a useful basis for making a judgement about the adequacy of the system in general and for deciding on the best strategy to adopt.

### 14.   Variation in Performance in a Batch of Weaners and Development of Management Strategy

If we look at the post-weaning performance of all pigs in a unit and then plot the growth trends of the poorest and best performers relative to the average, the picture outlined in Figure 12.11 might emerge.

Let us assume in this case that pigs were weaned at 21 days of age and were on a high-quality starter diet in the first 2 weeks, got a 50:50 mix of the starter and

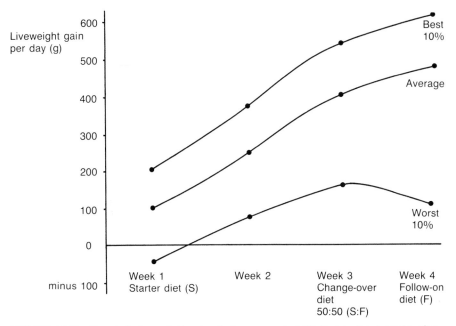

FIGURE 12.11   Trends in liveweight gain of pigs weaned at 18 days in the 4 weeks after weaning. (English, MacPherson, Birnie, Davidson and Smith, 1984)

follow-on diets in week 3 and received the follow-on diet only in week 4. It can be seen that the best 10 per cent of pigs grew reasonably in the first week after weaning (200 g per day), accelerated well thereafter, performing very well in week 3 and even better in week 4. The worst 10 per cent of pigs, on the other hand, lost weight in week 1 (40 g per day), began to pick up slowly in weeks 2 and 3 but got a check again in week 4 when they went on to the follow-on diet on its own.

This picture is a very typical one on many farms, some pigs in the post-weaning period performing well while others perform badly. The extent of the problem varies greatly between farms. In some you see virtually no passengers in the weaner pens, in others you see just a few problem pigs while in a few units there are far too many ill thriving pigs. Where there are no problem pigs after weaning, the system in terms of such components as diet, climatic environment, penning and management is very sound and obviously one should leave well alone. In the few units where there are many problem pigs, obviously the whole system needs to be examined critically and the weak points strengthened so as to make the whole system stronger. In units where there are some but not too many ill thriving piglets after weaning, two strategies are possible. One can make the whole system sound enough for the most vulnerable pigs by taking such steps as improving the climatic environment, the diet and perhaps by including antibiotics at low levels in the diet. These steps may well be over-extravagant since they are taken to cater for only a small minority of the pigs. The alternative approach is to leave the general system as it was before for the great majority of pigs but to strengthen part of it just for the small minority of problem pigs. Perhaps, as indicated in the previous section, this can be done by delaying the weaning of these problem pigs if they can be recognised at the time weaning is due. If this is not possible then it is vital that the stockperson detects these pigs as early as possible and improves their system before they deteriorate too far. Condition scoring or watching for signs of the backbone is as good a give-away as any that the system is not suiting some pigs. They should be picked out early and put in a special pen where they may be in a smaller group, have a better diet and a warmer environment; they remain on this special part of the system until the disappearance of the line of the backbone indicates they are established and ready to move on to the next stage.

Of course, it costs money and time to set up a special pen/pens for the small pro-portion of pigs which cannot adapt to the general system and to use this as a 'fluid' resource − transferring pigs from here to the general system as they become established and adding newly weaned pigs to this facility when they are showing the very earliest signs of failure to adapt to the general system. This special facility could be termed the 'hospital area' but a better term would be the 'special nursery', for the pigs are not really ill if their problem of failure to adapt is detected in the very early stages and such early detection of problems is the key part of such an approach.

So this special attention for problem pigs does cost a little time and money, but what is the alternative? A common approach when a few 'poor doing pigs' are noticed in most pens is to include appropriate antibiotics at low levels in the diet and, once started, this usually becomes a permanent feature of the system; the cost over a period of time can be very high. This general approach is adopted usually to simplify the system but it can also be done through overreaction to the problem because when most people with good stock sense see a pen of 20 pigs with 18 good ones and 2 poor ones, they focus much more on the 2 than on the 18. The 2 are in need of a better system but the 18 are not and it would be sounder husbandry and the most cost effective approach in many such cases to transfer the 2 to the 'special nursery' and leave the system as it was for the 18 than to incorporate an-tibiotics in the diet for the lot.

Since pens are understocked at the start of the period in a given stage, there is no harm in putting 10 per cent or so more pigs in at the start than you aim to have there at the end and be prepared to transfer those failing to adapt so well to the 'special nursery' as soon as they show the relevant signs.

Such an approach in recognising the poor doers in a group in the very early stages and making special provision for them was always a part of good husbandry as car-ried out by good stockpeople. There are always going to be the pigs at the bottom of the peck order which are in greater difficulties and, at the stage of weaning, some pigs are much less mature than others and will have greater difficulty in adapting.

The system is usually perfectly adequate for the great majority but not good enough for these special cases. Recognising these special cases early and trans-ferring them promptly to a more luxurious system must become a more common practice than it is currently on many farms.

## ADDITIONAL READING

Kornegay E. T. and Notter D. R. (1984), 'Effects of Floor Space and Number of Pigs per Pen on Performance', *Pig News and Information* **5**, 23–33.

*Pig News and Information* (Consulting Editor, R. Braude), Commonwealth Agricultural Bureaux, Slough, England.

*Pork Industry Handbook*, USA Co-operative Extension Service, University of Illinois at Urbana-Champaign, USA.

*Chapter 13*

# The Growing–Finishing Pig: the Basis of Efficient Systems

GROWTH FROM 20 KG LIVEWEIGHT – GENERAL CONSIDERATIONS

When the pig reaches about 20 kg liveweight it is usually very well established. On a well-designed and carefully operated rearing system in Britain it will reach this weight around 8 to 9 weeks of age. If it was weaned at 3 to 4 weeks of age, the post-weaning dietary regime and its own natural development will have ensured that its digestive system can deal effectively with a wide range of energy and pro-tein concentrates. If it was not weaned until 6 to 7 weeks of age, ingestion of creep feed prior to weaning and of the appropriate diet after weaning will likewise have ensured a competent animal producing all the digestive enzymes of the adult.

The main disability the pig has at 20 kg liveweight is a limited ability in the hind gut to process fibre since the potential to digest fibre increases as the animal matures. Thus, while the pig at 20 kg liveweight is reasonably competent in terms of its digestive capacity, it still requires concentrated and high-quality food if its remarkable potential for fast and efficient growth is to be achieved. For example, the animal may respond to the substitution of vegetable protein such as soya bean meal with a high-quality fishmeal (see Tables 10.6 and 10.7).

However, from the stage of 20 up to about 50 kg liveweight, on a sound system, if we provide balanced diets within an energy concentration range from about 14 to 16 MJ DE per kg and diets from about 12 to 15 MJ DE per kg from 50 kg on-wards, the pig on ad lib. feeding will maintain the same energy intake, by eating proportionally more of lower energy diets within these ranges. Only when energy level is below the above ranges and fibre content is high will the pig from 20 kg liveweight upwards fail to maintain the same energy intake (see Figure 9.9).

So if soundly formulated, well-balanced diets within the energy concentration range making possible maximum energy intake are on offer, the healthy pig based genetically on the white breeds such as the Large White and Landrace, from about 20 kg liveweight onwards on an ad lib. feeding system, will increase its feed intake with time in such a way that its growth will almost be a straight line up to about 120 kg liveweight as indicated in Figure 13.1.

As indicated in the figure, it is only as the pig reaches around the 120 kg liveweight mark that the growth pattern deviates from a straight line and starts to level off. The exact stage at which the growth curve starts to level off varies with

331

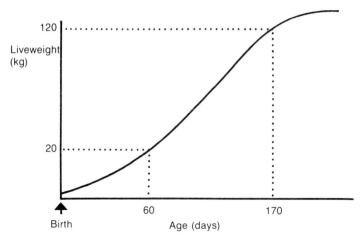

FIGURE 13.1   Typical growth curve of healthy, genetically improved Large White ×
Landrace type pigs fed ad lib. on good-quality diets.

both the genotype and the sex of the pig. Later maturing genotypes will level off
at a later stage than earlier maturing types. Entire males will level off in their
growth at a later stage than females. The deceleration of growth rate at this stage
is also influenced both by approaching puberty and, in some genotypes, by the
ever-increasing rate of fatty tissue deposition relative to lean. Up to the point where
growth starts to decelerate, the pig producer is often in a dilemma as to whether
or not he should set out to maximise the rate of liveweight gain in his pigs.

## The Case for Maximising the Rate of Liveweight Gain

There are strong arguments for setting out to maximise the rate of liveweight gain
between 20 kg liveweight and slaughter:

- The faster the growth and the shorter the time to reach slaughter weight, the
  more quickly the pig producer will obtain a return on his investment, i.e. it
  helps cash flow.
- The faster the growth, the more pigs the producer can put through his building
  in a year. Thus, building overhead cost per pig produced will be less, and other
  overhead costs may also be less. This will apply to labour costs if no more
  labour is employed as the throughput of pigs is increased.

## The Case for Controlling the Rate of Liveweight Gain

The main argument for controlling the rate of liveweight gain by limiting food intake is to reduce deposition of fatty tissue and therefore to improve carcass quality.
Some producers would claim that restricted feeding helps to achieve superior feed

conversion efficiency by eliminating feed wastage associated with some ad lib. feeding systems.

## THE DILEMMA OF THE PIG PRODUCER

The dilemma which the pig farmer finds himself in is summarised by the data presented in Table 13.1. It can be seen that as average daily feed intake over the liveweight range of 20 to 92 kg liveweight increased from 2.0 to 2.6 kg, so there was a progressive increase in daily liveweight gain, a proportional decline in days spent in the unit and consequent increase in the annual production from the unit. Unfortunately, these desirable trends were accompanied by the production of progressively fatter pigs (backfat at point $P_2$) as average daily feed intake was increased. In countries such as Britain which have carcass grading systems imposing severe financial penalties for surplus fat in carcasses, the dilemma of the pig producer is obvious. He would like the best of both worlds − quick throughput made possible by high feed intake on the one hand, and carcasses with minimum fatness consistent with excellent grading on the other. Unfortunately, the laws of biology are such as to prevent him achieving these two objectives simultaneously to the extent that he would like. So the producer's aim must be to find the optimum balance between the two desirable objectives of quick throughput and good carcass quality. The complex considerations necessary in finding this optimum balance are the subject of a later section (Chapter 20).

Fortunately, as indicated in Table 13.1, the pig producer can almost forget about food conversion efficiency in improved genotypes as he determines his optimum feed allowance to achieve the best balance between throughput and carcass grading. This is because there is unlikely to be much change in food conversion efficiency over a wide range of food intake between about 75 per cent of ad lib. intake and ad lib. Although slower growth induced by greater feed restriction would entail keeping the pig for a longer period, thus incurring higher feed requirements for maintenance, the pig at slaughter at a given liveweight (say, 90 kg) would have deposited less fat and more lean. Since lean meat requires considerably less feed than fat deposition, this improved ratio of lean to fat would effectively save feed and almost exactly balance out the extra food required for maintenance. It would

**TABLE 13.1  Output, daily gain and $P_2$ in a 600 pig place unit (liveweight range = 20 to 92 kg)**

|  | Average daily feed intake (kg) | | | |
|---|---|---|---|---|
|  | 2.0 | 2.2 | 2.4 | 2.6 |
| Daily gain (kg) | 0.64 | 0.71 | 0.78 | 0.85 |
| Days in unit | 112 | 101 | 92 | 85 |
| FCR | 3.12 | 3.12 | 3.12 | 3.12 |
| $P_2$ | 16 | 17 | 18 | 19 |
| Annual production | 1955 | 2168 | 2380 | 2576 |

(Fuller, 1984)

only be in cases of very severe feed restriction or with odd genotypes that food conversion efficiency would be affected by varying daily food intake over the range mentioned above.

The relative importance of throughput and grading will therefore have a major influence on the producer's selection of feed intake level for his stock between 20 kg liveweight and slaughter. However, even if carcass quality requirements were very demanding, it is most unlikely that a producer would impose feed restrictions from 20 kg liveweight. He would be much more likely to feed ad lib. up to at least 50 kg liveweight and to restrict feed intake as necessary thereafter. This approach allows him to exploit full liveweight gain potential in the early period of growth and impose food restriction in the later period when he can have a much greater influence in limiting the amount of fatty tissue deposited.

While carcass grading is a most important consideration since pig producers are in business to produce what the market demands, there are many other very important objectives. These will now be outlined before focusing on the most important components of an efficient system to comply with these objectives.

## IMPORTANT OBJECTIVES IN GROWING THE PIG FROM 20 KG LIVEWEIGHT TO SLAUGHTER

The important objectives are as follows:

Maintenance of good health
Minimal losses (less than 1 per cent)
Good carcass quality
Good meat quality
Fast liveweight gain and throughput consistent with good carcass quality
Good food conversion efficiency
Low food cost per unit of liveweight gain, carcass weight gain and
  lean meat gain
Low total (feed, labour, housing, veterinary, etc.) cost per unit of liveweight
  gain
Good return on invested capital

## COMPONENTS OF AN EFFICIENT SYSTEM FROM 20 KG LIVEWEIGHT TO SLAUGHTER

The important components of a system for growing pigs to slaughter from around 20 kg liveweight are as follows:

Genetic quality of the stock
Health of the stock
Diet
Feeding system and form of feed
Watering
Group size

Floor space and feeding space
Penning
Housing
Climate (temperature and air flow)
Management of different sexes
Controlling carcass quality
Monitoring behaviour and performance
Stockmanship

These components will now be discussed in turn so as to provide the basic ingredients of an efficient production system.

## Genetic Quality of the Stock

Assessment of the genetic merit of stock and genetic improvement techniques were fully discussed in Chapters 5 and 6.

In considering the pig over the liveweight range of 20 kg to slaughter, important traits which can be improved by genetic manipulation include carcass and meat quality, food conversion efficiency, liveweight gain and voluntary food intake. If a producer is operating a breeding herd as well as a growing–finishing pig enterprise, he must also be interested in the genetic merit of the stock as far as reproductive traits like prolificacy are concerned. The producer has the choice in many countries of achieving genetic improvement either by:

● selecting replacements from within his own stock. He may often select improved females in this way while purchasing high-quality sires evaluated on the basis of progeny, performance or sib testing (or a combination of any of these)

or

● purchasing improved genetic stock (boars and gilts) from a breeding company

A commercial producer might be involved in pure-breeding but he is more likely to be crossbreeding. The use of crossbred females confers advantages in terms of hybrid vigour or heterosis to improve such traits as litter size, breeding regularity and piglet viability. The producer may also be deploying crossbreeding in the form of a sire line boar which has been selected specifically for growth, carcass and meat quality characteristics. In this latter case, the progeny out of sire line boars constitute the 'slaughter generation' and must not be used for breeding because they are likely to be less well endowed with reproductive traits than alternative genotypes. It is vitally important that very serious thought is devoted to ensuring that efficient genetic stock are available for the growing–finishing pig enterprise so that all the expensive inputs such as those on feed, labour and housing will yield a good financial return.

The optimum genotype will vary with market demand. For example, in the United States the demand is for heavy pigs with little or no premium for reduced fat thickness. However, in West Germany shape and leanness are overriding criteria for bonus payments.

The importance of genotype is discussed further in Chapter 16 on 'Controlling Carcass and Meat Quality'.

## Health of the Stock

Although genes are important, probably more important still is the preservation of the status of a healthy herd. Obtaining healthy stock and keeping them healthy was the subject of Chapter 11. Healthy stock can exploit expensive inputs such as those on feed, housing and labour much more effectively than unhealthy stock. Therefore, very high priority must be given to high health status in any growing—finishing pig enterprise.

If stock are being purchased around 20 to 30 kg liveweight for a growing—finishing unit, every precaution possible must be taken to ensure that they come from a very healthy source. If the farm is a breeding—finishing enterprise, first locating a very healthy source of replacement stock and then sticking to this source for replacement gilts should be given very high priority. Alternatively, the enterprise might have a very healthy closed herd from which they breed their own replacements except for occasional boars. To eliminate any risk from buying in boars, the unit could become dependent on AI, purchasing semen from high-quality boars to be used on their best sows as a source of replacements for the herd.

## Diets

The principles of diet formulation for growing—finishing pigs have been outlined fully in Chapters 9 and 10. Specimen diets for early growers (20 to 40 kg liveweight), growers (40 to 65 kg), baconers (65 to 90 kg) and heavy pigs (90 to 120 kg) are detailed in Tables 10.6 and 10.7 (pages 216—217). These are specimen diets formulated to meet the nutrient and digestive requirements for these various growth stages specified in Chapter 9 and are not necessarily least cost solutions. As ingredient prices change relative to one another, different optimal diet formulations will apply but it is not worth changing formulations unless the financial advantage is significant.

Another important point with regard to these diets is that they meet the requirements for genetic stock of high quality in terms of lean tissue growth rate. It is clear that genetic improvement in lean tissue growth rate has resulted in a considerable divergence in this trait and in fat deposition between genotypes (see Figure 13.2). In this work, the relatively unimproved Wye College control Landrace was compared with the improved PIC Landrace.

It is clear that at a relatively low daily intake of protein and essential amino acids, the improved genotype (PIC Landrace) has a lower level of backfat thickness at $P_2$ than the relatively unimproved Wye College control line Landrace. It is also clear that as protein and essential amino acid intake per day is increased, the response in terms of reduction in backfat thickness is much greater for the genetically improved than for the control Landrace.

As genotypes have diverged in the United Kingdom in terms of lean tissue and fat growth, it has become obvious that one must treat each farm and its specific genotype on its merits with regard to the optimum dietary and feeding strategy for growing—finishing pigs. In many farms, carcass grading has been disappointing despite having apparently superior genetic stock. The initial response of the farmer to such a problem has been to impose further feed restriction.

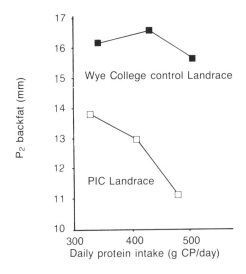

FIGURE 13.2 Comparison of backfats in a selected and control line. (Source: Dalgety-Spillers Wye 6 Trial, 1979)

However, the situation has often been transformed completely by effecting a considerable increase in the protein quality of the diet. Not only can there be a great improvement in carcass grading but a relaxation of feed restriction can be effected with consequent improvement of growth and throughput. In some such situations, the indications were that the previous diet and degree of feed restriction were resulting in an overstocking situation.

As carcass grading standards based on backfat have become more demanding in many countries in recent years, producers have tended to impose a greater degree of feed restriction in an attempt to maintain grading standards. Many have done this without reducing the number of pigs coming into the growing—finishing pig enterprise or increasing the floor or feeding space available. This has inevitably led to overstocking on many farms.

Thus, it has been an edifying and encouraging experience on many farms to increase the protein quality of the diet and often also the feed intake and then monitor the response. Those with superior genotypes in terms of lean tissue growth rate can find this a rewarding experience.

The work of Roger Campbell at Werribee in Australia has also demonstrated the great divergence in lean tissue growth rate between genotypes in Australia and he has determined the daily nutrient allowances required by these contrasting genotypes as a basis for evolving the most cost effective feeding system. This work will be referred to further later in this chapter.

HOW MANY DIETS OVER THE GROWTH PERIOD?

In Chapter 9 on the principles of nutrition it was pointed out that optimum lysine to digestible energy ratio was changing continuously. The ratio of lysine to MJ DE (g/MJ) specified in Table 9.6 for genetically improved genotypes was 0.79, 0.72, 0.63 and 0.59 for pigs averaging 30, 50, 70 and 90 kg liveweight respectively. Thus, if we were growing pigs for high lean tissue growth rate potential from say 20 to 100 kg liveweight, we could use a succession of four diets to conform with the above requirements. Pigs would proceed to the appropriate diet for their weight at 20 kg liveweight intervals.

Unless such frequent changes of diet could be demonstrated to be fairly cost effective, pig producers would not be enthusiastic, to say the least, about having to purchase or make up so many different diets. Apart from the extra work, one objection would be the scope for confusion which could be created and the mistakes which could be made.

One approach which might be more acceptable in practice is to have two diets only, one for the 20 to 40 kg liveweight stage and the other for the 80 to 100 kg stage and to cater for the stages in between by mixing the diets for the two extreme weight ranges in the appropriate proportions for the pigs of intermediate weight.

The existence of these diets for the different growth stages would also allow a producer to determine whether his pigs might respond favourably to a higher quality diet. For example, in some pens, the diet formulated for 40 to 60 kg pigs and for others that for 60 to 80 kg pigs could be continued to slaughter at 100 kg liveweight. The producer could determine from such a comparison whether his genotype was capable of giving an economic response to a higher quality diet in the finishing stages. If a large differential existed in prices for different carcass grades (based on backfat), some interesting findings could well emerge. Checking the cost effectiveness of the diets is discussed in more detail in Chapter 20.

## Feeding System and the Form of the Feed

Feeding systems include ad lib. and restricted dry feeding practices (pellets or meal) and wet feeding, using a slurry.

Some of these variations will now be described.

### AD LIB. FEEDING

Ad lib. feeding throughout the period of growth is a very convenient system and involves a low labour input. It has been a very common system for pigs up to the slaughter stage in the United States. In Britain, the system is normally used in producing pigs up to slaughter for the pork market around 60 kg liveweight. Pigs to supply the bacon market are normally slaughtered around 90 kg liveweight and the traditional system for such pigs has been ad lib. feeding up to about 60 kg liveweight followed by restricted feeding to slaughter in an attempt to control the fat content of the final bacon carcass.

It is important that ad lib. feeders are designed efficiently so as to eliminate feed wastage or, at least, reduce it to an absolute minimum. A badly designed feeder can result in the wastage of up to 15 per cent of the feed and this can convert a potentially handsome profit into a crippling loss.

Some features of design of ad lib. feeders which help to minimise wastage are illustrated in Plates 12.2, page 296, and 13.1, page 339. These design features include hinged lids above the trough, trough dividers, an inturned lip on the leading edge of the trough, the correct shape and depth of the trough and the control of flow of feed from the hopper to the trough. It is important that adequate feeding space is provided on ad lib. systems so as to ensure that all pigs in a pen have an equal opportunity to feed to appetite.

*Feeding space requirement*

The traditional rule of thumb used for feeding space on ad lib. feeders was one feeding space for every 4 pigs. Alternatively, as pigs approached 90 kg liveweight, an allowance of 4 pigs per foot or 0.3 m of trough space was recommended. This was the allowance (equivalent to 8 cm per pig) which Hanrahan (1985) working in Moorepark, Ireland, considered adequate for pigs on ad lib. feeding between about 35 and 85 kg liveweight.

Plate 13.1   It is very important to avoid both build-up of stale feed and other forms of wastage from ad lib. hoppers. Appropriate measures which can be taken to achieve this include (a) placing the feeder correctly so as to minimise risk of fouling by pig excrement; (b) checking the feeder daily and removing any feed fouled by excrement while redistributing any build-up of feed at extremities along the length of the feeder (the flow rate of feed from the storage section to the trough may also require adjustment); and (c) allowing the pigs to clear up all the feed in the hopper once weekly before refilling with fresh feed.

This, of course, is a very wide weight range and if a feeding space allowance of 8 cm per pig is adequate for an 85 kg pig, then somewhat less space should be sufficient for a pig around 35 kg liveweight. The studies of Lindemann and associates at Virginia State University on feeding space requirements on ad lib. feeding for pigs between 7 and 18 kg liveweight concluded that 4.5 cm was adequate. This being the case, a feeding space of around 6 cm per pig should be sufficient for pigs between 20 and 40 kg, with heavier pigs being allocated the 8 cm suggested by Hanrahan. Thus, available evidence and sensible extrapolation would suggest that the following should be considered as minimum feed space allowances per pig on ad lib. feeding:

| Liveweight (kg) | Minimum feed space allowance on ad lib. feeding (cm) |
|---|---|
| 7–20 | 4.5 |
| 20–40 | 6.0 |
| 40–85 | 8.0 |

### Managing ad lib. feeders

Some producers using ad lib. feeding operate the practice of allowing pigs to empty the feeder once per week before refilling. This is done to reduce the build-up of stale feed and to reduce feed wastage. Hanrahan in Ireland estimated that this practice improved feed conversion efficiency by 4 per cent. The problem of build-up of stale feed can often be associated with excessive feeding space.

### Restricting food intake from ad lib. hoppers

If a pig producer operating an ad lib. feeding system wishes to restrict feed intake in order to reduce fat deposition and so improve carcass grading, he can adopt one of two approaches without changing his feed hoppers:

1.  Restrict access to the hopper for a limited period of the day.

    Hanrahan restricted access to ad lib. feeders to 6 hours daily and compared the practice with 24 hour access to the feed hoppers for pigs between 35 and 83 kg liveweight. His results are summarised in Table 13.2, which shows that on 6

TABLE 13.2   Effects of 6 and 24 hour access to ad lib. feeders for 640 pigs

|  | 6 hour access | 24 hour access | Reduction on 6 hour access (%) |
|---|---|---|---|
| Total pigs | 640 | 640 | |
| Feed intake per day (kg/day) | 2.13 | 2.47 | 13.8 |
| Feed conversion efficiency (kg feed per kg gain) | 3.87 | 4.13 | 6.3 |
| Average backfat thickness (mm) | 25.5 | 26.5 | 3.8 |

hour access to feed, feed intake was decreased by 13.8 per cent, food conversion efficiency improved by 6.3 per cent and backfat reduced by 3.8 per cent. This approach would appear to be effective in reducing feed intake, and the duration of access to feed each day could be varied according to the reduction in daily feed intake required.

2.  Fill the hopper each day with the amount of feed which you wish the pigs to eat.

If in the finishing stages of growth a pig producer wishes to restrict food intake per pig to, say, 2 kg daily and there are 20 pigs in the pen, only 40 kg of food would be placed in the hopper each day. This amount could be weighed out and placed in the feeder each day or, if feed was being delivered by pipeline, the amount delivered to each feeder could be controlled volumetrically. The delivery of feed by pipeline could be simulated by pouring into the feeder, adjacent to the delivery pipe, 40 kg of feed out of a bag or container. The delivery pipe would be lowered to the point where the outlet is just touching the top of the cone of the 40 kg of feed just delivered manually (see Figure 13.3). The outlet of delivery pipes would be set at this height in all hoppers and feed would be delivered once daily supplying each hopper with a volume of feed equivalent to 40 kg by weight.

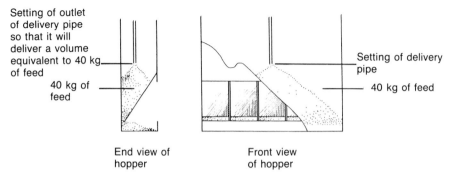

FIGURE 13.3   Calibration of ad lib. feeders and setting of delivery pipes to deliver a given volume of feed to each hopper daily.

The possible concern about either of the two approaches above for limiting daily food intake per pig on a system using ad lib. hoppers is that there might be unacceptable variation in food intake and therefore in growth and carcass quality within a pen. However, this problem does not seem to arise in practice. The probable reason for this is that on dry feed, a pig does not eat a big meal at one time. It has a relatively small meal and before it comes back to feed spends an interval drinking, urinating, defecating, wandering about and resting. This tendency to feed little and often on dry feed obviously results in reasonably equable intake of feed between pigs within a pen. Undue variation in food intake, growth and induced differences in carcass fatness are unlikely to be problems unless feed intake has to be very severely restricted.

*Inclusion of a fibrous filler in the feed*
Another approach to reducing intake of digestible nutrients on ad lib. feeding systems is to add a less digestible filler to the diet. In the past, such commodities as sand, sawdust and fibrous foods like oat husks or ground straw have been used for the purpose. The pig tries to respond to the incorporation of such ingredients in the feed by attempting to consume a higher total quantity so as to maintain the

same intake of digestible energy and other digestible nutrients as it could achieve without such fillers (see Figure 9.9). However, if sufficient filler is included, the pig's intake of digestible nutrients will be restricted with resultant reduction in liveweight gain and fat deposition. One problem with this approach, even when acceptable fillers are used, is that any filler costs money and fibrous fillers such as finely ground straw and oat husks can be very expensive. The other disadvantage of fillers is that they can reduce the digestibility of nutrients from the basic diet by binding up protein and also some of the minerals. Their use also increases substantially the amount of effluent, which in turn increases effluent storage and disposal costs.

Other approaches to reducing intake of digestible nutrients on ad lib. systems are the inclusion in the diet of natural foods with a reputed bitter taste, such as malt culms (dried roots and sprouts of barley germinated in the malting process).

DRY–WET AD LIB. FEEDING SYSTEMS

These are systems in which feed is delivered to the pig in dry form but which afford an opportunity to the pig to wet some or all of the feed before consuming it.

Types of feeders which come into this category are illustrated in Plates 13.2A and B. In A, dry feed is delivered on to a metal tray. Any which spills off this tray falls into a trough below. Nipple drinkers are mounted in the trough so that pigs cannot drink directly from the nipples but, in trying to operate them, cause water to be spilled into the trough. As pigs drink water from the trough, they automatically ingest any food which has spilled into the trough. The feeder in Plate 13.2B is simpler. Feed is contained in a funnel-shaped feeder which is fairly narrow at the point of delivery so that excessive food does not end up in the trough. Nipple drinkers are situated in the trough and pigs operate them in the same way as they do for the feeder in Plate 13.2A. Thus the feed is wetted and consumed in this form.

The objectives of these types of dry–wet feeders are several:

- reduction of dust in the house
- reduction of feed wastage
- faster eating and higher feed intake

TABLE 13.3  Comparison of ad lib. feeding systems (35 to 87 kg liveweight)

| | Dry feed | Dry–wet feed | Advantage (%) on: | |
| --- | --- | --- | --- | --- |
| | | | dry feed | dry–wet feed |
| Feed intake (kg DM/day) | 2.03 | 2.12 | | 4.2 |
| Liveweight gain (g/day) | 739 | 794 | | 7.0 |
| Feed conversion ratio (kg food per kg gain) | | | | |
| Liveweight basis | 2.77 | 2.70 | | 2.5 |
| Carcass weight basis | 3.58 | 3.48 | | 2.8 |
| Backfat at $P_2$ (mm) | 14.6 | 15.1 | 3.3 | |

(From: Patterson D C, 1987)

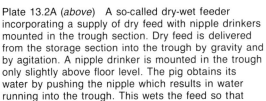

Plate 13.2A (*above*)  A so-called dry-wet feeder incorporating a supply of dry feed with nipple drinkers mounted in the trough section. Dry feed is delivered from the storage section into the trough by gravity and by agitation. A nipple drinker is mounted in the trough only slightly above floor level. The pig obtains its water by pushing the nipple which results in water running into the trough. This wets the feed so that while it is delivered into the trough dry, it is consumed as wetted feed. The claims for this approach are that, relative to dry feed, both dust and feed wastage are reduced.
B (*right*) An alternative design incorporating an upper tray on to which feed is delivered and from which pigs eat. Any food spilled from the tray falls into the lower trough section where it can be wetted by the pig operating the nipple drinker. (Courtesy of A.M. Warkup Ltd)

- faster eating and lower trough space requirement per pig, thus releasing extra floor space for lying and other activities

Patterson (1987) working in Northern Ireland studied a feeder similar to that depicted in Plate 13.2B and, relative to ad lib. feeding of a meal diet, found that most of the advantages that might be anticipated were borne out by his results as indicated in Table 13.3. Here we see that the advantages on the dry–wet system were better food conversion efficiency resulting from less wastage and higher liveweight gain resulting from higher food intake. The inevitable disadvantage associated with higher food intake and liveweight gain was fatter carcasses.

To obtain the main advantage of better food conversion efficiency from the dry–wet system without the main disadvantage of fatter carcasses, one would have to limit feed intake by restricting either feeding time or amount of food supplied each day by either of the approaches suggested earlier for modifying ad lib. dry feeding systems to reduce intake and improve carcass quality.

It is most important on these dry–wet systems that the risk of faulty watering

CHAPTER 13

systems which would lead to flooding of the trough and waste of meal as well as water is eliminated. The optimum feeding space allowance on these dry—wet systems has not yet been determined. It is already clear that space requirement is less than on ad lib. systems using dry feed.

RESTRICTED FEEDING

Where carcass grading is based on backfat thickness and particularly where there are substantial price penalties for producing overfat carcasses, a degree of restriction of food intake is usually desirable. Exceptions to this general rule would operate in the case of genotypes in which sustained genetic manipulation over several generations has greatly increased lean to fat ratio at particular stages of growth and which perhaps has reduced voluntary food intake at the same time. Very few pigs of such genotypes would have sufficient backfat at slaughter even on ad lib. feeding to cause downgrading.

The degree to which the intake of a well-balanced diet should be controlled during the growing—finishing period varies according to the genetic qualities of the stock, the price differentials prevailing for carcasses of different fat content and the liveweight at slaughter.

Different genotypes of pig vary in lean to fat ratio, the fatter genotypes requiring more control of feed intake during growth and finishing than leaner genotypes. Table 13.4 is based on data from MLC's Commercial Product Evaluation programme, which evaluated the hybrids produced by the pig breeding companies in the United Kingdom. The data indicate the effect of reducing feed intake on backfat thickness and other important traits.

TABLE 13.4  Effect of decreases of 0.1 kg in daily food intake from a mean daily intake of 2.5 kg of a balanced diet (13 MJ DE per kg) between 25 and 90 kg liveweight

| Factor | Effect of 0.1 kg per day reduction in food intake |
|---|---|
| Daily liveweight gain | minus 35 g |
| Food conversion ratio | 0 |
| Daily lean tissue gain | minus 11 g |
| $P_2$ backfat at 90 kg liveweight | minus 0.52 mm |

(From: ARC, 1981)

From this table it can be estimated that if a producer wished to reduce mean $P_2$ backfat at 90 kg liveweight by 1 mm he would have to reduce feed intake by an average of 0.2 kg daily between 25 and 90 kg. The penalties for achieving this reduction in $P_2$ backfat would be a reduction of about 22 g daily in lean tissue growth and a reduction in daily liveweight gain of about 70 g. When imposing this degree of restriction there could be no effects whatsoever on food conversion efficiency because, although the slower growth would entail keeping the pig for a longer period, thus incurring higher feed requirements for maintenance, the pig at 90 kg would have deposited less fat and more lean. Since lean meat requires considerably less feed than fat deposition, this improved ratio of lean to fat would effectively save feed and almost exactly balance out the extra food required for maintenance. It would only be in cases of very severe feed restriction or with odd genotypes that food conversion efficiency would be affected by varying daily food intake.

If, as is more common, a producer wished to feed ad lib. up to about 50 kg liveweight and restrict feed intake thereafter, he would have to reduce daily food intake by about 0.3 kg per day in order to reduce backfat at $P_2$ by 1 mm. Such a reduction in feed intake over this period would be likely to reduce daily liveweight gain by about 100 g and increase the period to reach 90 kg liveweight by about 7 days.

Thus, each producer in imposing greater food restriction must assess the balance between lower backfat, better grading and higher carcass value on the one hand and slower growth and lowered throughput on the other.

### Differences between boars, castrates and gilts
On the same daily intake of feed up to slaughter at, say, 90 kg liveweight, boars will have the least backfat and castrates the most. Thus, in order to produce carcasses of similar fatness from the 3 sexes, degree of feed restriction applied must be greater for gilts than boars and most severe for castrates. The alternative is to have the 3 sexes on the same feed allowance but to slaughter castrates at an earlier stage relative to gilts, with boars being grown to the heaviest weight. This aspect of managing the different sexes is developed further on page 368.

### Feeding space requirements
The criteria which dictate feeding space requirements on restricted feeding systems were outlined fully in an earlier section (page 309). Then main objective is to provide sufficient space so that all pigs can feed simultaneously. In turn, the main determinant of the space required will be the breadth of the pig across the shoulders. Baxter measured the shoulder width of Large White × Landrace pigs at different liveweights and these data are presented in Table 8.11 (page 148).

Other genotypes which are either longer and narrower or shorter and broader than the genotypes represented in Table 8.11 will have different shoulder width measurements. The shoulder width measurement should be looked upon as the absolute minimum space requirement on restricted feeding systems. More liberal provision of feeding space might be particularly important for socially inferior pigs if they are to obtain the same opportunity to feed and achieve as high feed intake as their social dominants.

### Restricted feeding using ad lib. hoppers
Methods for modifying feeding systems using ad lib. hoppers (providing either dry feed or dry–wet feed) to reduce feed intake and reduce fat deposition have been outlined earlier in this chapter (pages 340–342).

### Wet feeding systems
Wet feeding systems usually involve the delivery of feed ingredients to a central tank, thorough mixing of ingredients with water and subsequent delivery by pipeline or via a continuous trough (river feeding system) to the pens.

The optimum water to meal ratio varies with the means of propelling the liquid mix, in particular, whether it is actively pumped, driven by pressure or sucked. A higher proportion of water to meal is required if the system of delivery requires the mixture to distribute itself passively along the trough. This principle reaches its ultimate in the river feeding system whereby the mixture flows down a 10 cm diameter gutter from one end of the building to the other. In this case the mixture may be as dilute as 5 to 1. However, at such a high ratio, dry matter intake is likely to be restricted relative, not only to that on ad lib. dry feeding, but also to that on a wet feeding system with a water to meal ratio of less than 3 to 1.

Because of the low dry matter content of the final mix, wet feeding systems are confined to pigs in excess of about 40 kg liveweight. The wet feed tends to be too bulky for lighter pigs, resulting in lower dry matter intake and poorer liveweight gain.

Braude (1971) in a comprehensive review of feeding systems produced the summary of findings presented in Table 13.5. It can be seen that out of 44 trials in which dry and wet feeding were compared, liveweight gain and food conversion efficiency were improved on wet feeding in most of them. In the trials in which these traits were better on wet feeding, the advantage in liveweight gain relative to dry feeding ranged from 1 to 5 per cent, while the advantage in food conversion efficiency ranged from 5 to 13 per cent. Thus, the main advantage lay in better efficiency of feed utilisation, this being mainly due to reduced feed wastage.

**TABLE 13.5  Responses on change from dry meal to wet feeding in 44 trials**

| Response on wet feeding | Daily liveweight gain | Food conversion efficiency | Carcass quality |
|---|---|---|---|
|  |  | Number of trials |  |
| Improvement | 29 | 25 | 6 |
| Deterioration | 3 | 4 | 1 |
| No difference | 12 | 15 | 16 |
| No information | 0 | 0 | 21 |
| Total trials | 44 | 44 | 44 |

For pigs above 40 kg liveweight, no differences have been found between water to meal ratios ranging from 2:1 to 3:1 even when no additional water was available. The general recommendation is that the pig in a thermoneutral environment requires a water to meal ratio of 2.5 to 1*. This implies that if this is the consistency of the wet feed, no additional water need be provided. However, Gill (1987) found that at water to meal ratios in wet feed of 2:1, 2.5:1, 3:1 and 3.5:1, extra voluntary water intakes of growing pigs consuming 1.5 kg of meal daily were 1.26, 0.78, 0.44 and 0.24 litres per pig per day. This indicates that pigs will drink extra water even when water to meal ratio exceeds 2.5 to 1. It is interesting that recently Hanrahan (personal communication) found when using whey as part of the liquid medium that, between 40 and 90 kg liveweight, performance was better on a water ($H_2O$) to dry meal equivalent ratio of 2.7 to 1 than on a ratio of 2.2 to 1.

* Minimum acceptable ratio cited in 'UK Codes of Recommendations for the Welfare of Livestock: Pigs'. (MAFF, 1994)

Plate 13.3 A wet feeding system in which a predetermined quantity of feed is pumped to each pen 4 times daily. The troughs are made of non-corrosive PVC material. Note that the pigs are on fully slatted floors, which helps to ensure a dry floor and clean pigs. (Courtesy of G. Weeks, Bath, Avon)

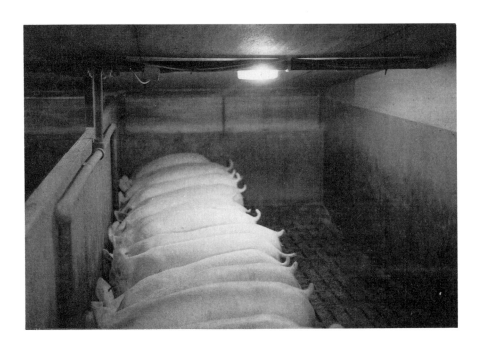

Braude (1985) listed the following advantages for controlled liquid feeding over dry meal feeding:

1.  Better performance − small, but significant
2.  Restricted water intake prevents wastage of water
3.  Reduced water excretion − amount of slurry can be drastically reduced
4.  Mechanisation made simpler and cheaper − transport of liquid more efficient than of dry material
5.  Automation of controlled feeding more accurate
6.  Water installation to individual pens unnecessary
7.  Pre-mixing of main dietary ingredients unnecessary
8.  Bulky ingredients easily incorporated into diets

Wet feeding using pipeline or the river system to deliver mixed feed to the pigs is attractive in a situation where cheap by-products such as skim milk, whey, distillery and brewery waste, yeast and fish waste are available. Wet feeding also helps reduce dust levels in piggeries and this contributes to a reduction in respiratory problems in both pigs and stockpeople.

Metal pipes used on such systems suffer from corrosion and subsequent replacement costs are high. For this reason plastic pipes are preferable.

### Floor feeding

As the name implies, this system involves delivery of feed either manually or automatically by pipeline and dispenser situated above each pen. The main advantage relative to trough feeding is the more economical utilisation of floor area. It is important that excessive amounts of food are not delivered at one time and it is recommended that pigs should be able to clear up the amount delivered within about 20 minutes if feed wastage is to be avoided. Even when this rule is applied, there tends to be 4 to 5 per cent poorer food conversion efficiency because of wastage than on trough feeding systems when meal is used, although there is no difference between trough and floor feeding systems for pellets.

### Frequency of feeding on restricted systems

The desirable frequency of feeding on restricted systems varies with the system as follows:

### Floor feeding

Meal frequency on the floor feeding system is dictated by the 20 minute rule that feed delivered at any one feed should be cleared up within 20 minutes of delivery so as to avoid wastage. Once-daily feeding is unsuitable when pigs are floor fed because they are unable to clear it up within 20 minutes and this results in fouling of the feed and subsequent wastage. Even twice-daily feeding may not be entirely satisfactory for the same reason although, if the feed is delivered by hand, this may be the most suitable compromise because of the extra work involved in more frequent feeding. When the feeders are controlled automatically, a more frequent feeding regime may be employed and 4 to 6 separate feeds have proved successful in practice.

*Wet feeding*
On wet feeding, because of the dilution of the diet, two or more daily feeds are usually necessary to allow pigs to consume their allowance.

*Restricted feeding of dry feed (meal or pellets) in troughs*
The major objective is to ensure even distribution of feed between individuals. This demands adequate trough space (see page 345) and may be helped by offering the feed only once daily. In this way, the most greedy pigs become satiated quickly and move away, thus ensuring that socially subordinate pigs obtain their ration. Some research work has indicated advantages in terms of elimination of feed wastage and better feed conversion efficiency from twice-daily (but not more frequently) as opposed to a once-daily regime.

One nutritional factor which influences the desirability of multiple feeds is the amount of synthetic lysine in the diet. The work of Batterham in Australia indicates that if excessive quantities of synthetic lysine arrive at the absorption sites in the gut at one time, lysine is used less efficiently than if quantities arrive on a 'little and often' basis. Thus, in such a situation, more frequent feeding is desirable on restricted systems. Of course, when fed ad lib. the 'little and often' principle will be followed since that is the natural habit of feed intake on such systems.

*Separate provision of cereal and protein-vitamin-mineral concentrate*
On restricted feeding systems, one can do away with the need for mixing the cereal with the other components of the diet by delivering the cereal component to the trough first and then spreading the protein-vitamin-mineral supplement on top. The work of Braude and Rowell (1968) in a coordinated series of experiments indicated that, for pigs between about 20 and 90 kg liveweight, there were no disadvantages from the separate provision of these components, thus economising on mixing costs. Furthermore, Lawrence and co-workers at the University of Liverpool showed that, even if the cereal was fed at one meal and the protein concentrate at the next, there was no adverse effect on performance.

PELLETS OR MEAL
Some 20 years ago, many trials were carried out comparing pellets and meal. Braude (1971) examined closely the results of these trials and produced the sum-

TABLE 13.6  **Response on pellets relative to meal in 57 trials**

| Response on pellets | Daily liveweight gain | Food conversion efficiency |
|---|---|---|
| | Number of trials | |
| Improvement | 39 | 48 |
| Deterioration | 2 | 1 |
| No difference | 16 | 7 |
| No information | 0 | 1 |
| Total trials | 57 | 57 |

mary presented in Table 13.6. It can be seen that out of 57 trials, liveweight gain and food conversion efficiency were superior on pellets in the great majority of cases. On the same feed intake of the same feed in meal and pelleted form, the average superiority of pellets in both liveweight gain and feed conversion was about 5 per cent. A major reason for better performance on pellets is lower feed wastage, particularly on floor feeding. It is also true that most ad lib. hoppers operate more reliably with pellets than with meal since the meal is liable to bridge. Another factor is that pellets have been subjected to heat treatment during manufacture and this may produce a partial cooking effect which may improve the digestibility of some constituents. In practice, one has to weigh up the generally better performance from pellets against their increased cost.

*Pellet size and quality*
More energy is required to produce pellets of smaller diameter and it is also more costly to produce durable pellets with a minimum amount of fine material. Hanrahan at Moorepark, Eire, in pigs between 30 and 85 kg liveweight compared pellets of 5 and 10 mm diameter and also pellets of different degrees of hardness as influenced by the amount of steam used in the pelleting process. No differences in pig performance were noted between either the 2 degrees of pellet hardness or between the 2 pellet sizes examined. However, pellets that are very soft and break up can cause problems in terms of bridging and flow in ad lib. hoppers. At the other extreme, pellets that are too hard may be unpalatable and result in reduced intake.

*Watering*
As discussed earlier in this chapter, some feeding systems (pipeline, river feeding and so-called dry−wet systems) also incorporate the provision of water.

While no difference in pig performance has been recorded in growing−finishing pigs on water to meal ratios between 2.0:1 and 3.0:1 when no additional water was available, it has been observed that pigs on wet feed with a water to meal ratio as high as 3.5:1 will still consume some extra water. Therefore, the general recommendation that no extra water need be made available with a water to meal ratio on wet feeding of 2.5:1 is probably not valid, particularly in hot environments. There seems to be no good reason to dispute the recommendations of the Welfare Codes of the United Kingdom which state that clean fresh water should be available at all times. Provision of 2 nipple or bite drinkers per pen is recommended for small groups of pigs (under 20) and for larger groups 1 nipple drinker for every 10 pigs.

Water usage is usually very much higher for nipple than for bite drinkers due to the considerable wastage which occurs even when these are situated at the correct height. Water wastage is expensive not only because of the supply costs but because of the additional costs of effluent storage and handling. Thus, while bite drinkers tend to be more expensive than nipple drinkers, they could well be more cost effective because of their effects in minimising water wastage. As well as minimising water wastage, of course, other very important requirements of drinkers are that they are hygienic and that they are fairly simple to operate, so enabling all pigs to drink readily and easily as much water as they require. It should not be assumed that because one is providing pigs with a liquid waste product that the water supply is, by definition, adequate. For example, silage effluent can be very high in potassium salts and, without extra water, it is quite possible to kill pigs with salt toxicity.

## Group Size

When Kornegay and Notter (1984) studied all the comparisons carried out on different group sizes of growing–finishing pigs, the consensus which emerged agreed with the old adage 'the smaller the group, the better they do'. Their findings are summarised in Table 13.7

**TABLE 13.7  Effects of increasing group size from a basal number of 16 per pen**

|  | Weight (kg) at | | Change (%) for each additional 10 pigs added to a basal group of 16 | | |
|---|---|---|---|---|---|
|  | Start | Finish | Feed intake | Daily liveweight gain | Food per kg of gain |
| Growing pigs | 27 | 54 | −1.6 | −3.0 | +1.5 |
| Finishing pigs | 44 | 92 | +1.3 | −1.6 | +1.8 |

(Source: Kornegay and Notter, 1984)

In the case of growing pigs, it can be seen that increases in group size from 16 to 26 show, on average, a 1.6 per cent reduction in feed intake, a 3 per cent reduction in liveweight gain and a 1.5 per cent deterioration in food conversion efficiency. Very similar responses applied to finishing pigs as group size was increased, the only exception being that feed intake in this heavier weight range increased slightly in larger group sizes. On the basis of this evidence the very small changes which are likely to occur in most circumstances as group size is increased from a group of 16 or so upwards should not discourage consideration of having growing–finishing pigs in fairly large groups. This is especially so since cost per pig place in terms of buildings and provision of essential feeding and watering facilities will tend to be less in large rather than in small pens.

However, group size should not be excessive and an upper limit of 30 should be considered. There is a belief that pigs can only recognise up to about 30 of their fellows and, therefore, when group size goes much above 30, a stable social order within a group is less likely to develop. This can result in more restlessness, aggressive activity and poorer performance. It is always useful, of course, to have sufficient smaller pens to accommodate the left-overs from a large pen after most of their faster growing pen mates have reached market weight and been consigned to the processing plant. Availability of such small pens helps to make more efficient use of expensive space within the building.

As group size is increased, it is vitally important that feeding space and watering and other essential facilities are increased proportionally so that each pig in the group has ample opportunity to obtain its feed and water requirements and to carry out all other essential activities.

**Floor Space Requirements**

As indicated in the previous chapter dealing with the weaned pig, many factors influence floor space requirements of growing–finishing pigs. However, Kornegay and Notter (1984) of Virginia State University provided some very useful guidelines on floor space requirements. They examined many of the experiments which have been carried out on this subject on fully and partially slatted floors and made a rough division between the growing and finishing stages as follows:

| Stage | Liveweight (kg) | | |
| --- | --- | --- | --- |
| | Start | Finish | Mean |
| Growing | 26.6 | 53.5 | 40.1 |
| Finishing | 44.1 | 92.3 | 68.2 |

A summary of the Virginia results is contained in Table 13.8, while the responses in terms of liveweight gain as floor space per pig was increased are illustrated in Figure 13.4.

**TABLE 13.8  Responses to increased provision of floor space for growing and finishing pigs**

| Stage | Liveweight range (kg) | Basic floor space allowance per pig (m²) | Improvement (%) per 0.1 m² increase in floor space per pig | | | Floor space allowance per pig at which maximum daily liveweight gain achieved (m²) |
| --- | --- | --- | --- | --- | --- | --- |
| | | | Daily gain | Feed intake | Food to gain ratio | |
| Growing | 27–53 | 0.3 | 5.2 | 3.2 | 1.6 | 0.92 |
| Finishing | 44–92 | 0.7 | 2.6 | 2.3 | 0.4 | 1.04 |

From Figure 13.4 it can be seen that, in the case of growing pigs, as floor space per pig was increased from a starting point of around 0.2 m² per pig, there was a steady increase in liveweight gain per pig as more floor space was provided. However, the rate of increase gradually fell off and it was estimated that maximum liveweight gain would be attained at a floor space allowance of 0.92 m² (see Table 13.8). Likewise for finishing pigs, there was a progressive increase in daily liveweight gain from a basal floor space allowance of about 0.4 m² per pig. The rate of increase in liveweight gain gradually falls off with more liberal space allowance per pig and it was estimated that maximum liveweight gain would be attained at a floor space allowance of 1.04 m² per pig.

Table 13.8 also shows the average improvements in food intake and food to gain ratio, in addition to that in liveweight gain, as floor space allowances are increased up to the level at which maximum performance level is attained. This floor space allowance is fairly close to the 'adequate' space requirements estimated by Petherick and Baxter (1982) for pigs at the upper ends of the weight ranges con-

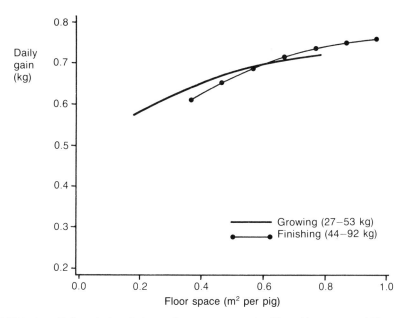

FIGURE 13.4   Daily gain in relation to floor space per pig. (From Kornegay and Notter, 1984)

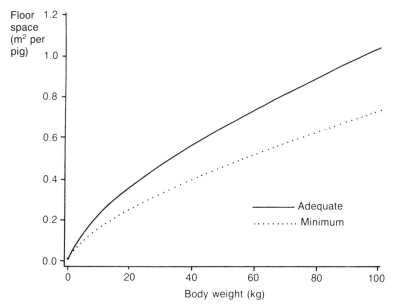

FIGURE 13.5   Estimated adequate and minimum floor space allowances per pig (housed in groups of 10–15). (From Petherick and Baxter, 1982)

sidered for growing (53 kg) and finishing (92 kg) by the Virginia workers. The basis of the requirements for floor space estimated by Petherick and Baxter were as follows:

*Adequate:* based on a pig in the fully recumbent resting position (lying fully stretched out on its side)
*Minimum:* based on a pig lying on all fours on its sternum

The estimated adequate and minimum floor space allowances which were calculated for Large White × Landrace pigs are summarised in Figure 13.5. Other recommended floor space allowances for pigs on fully or partially slatted floors (see Table 13.9) are very much less than that associated with maximum liveweight gain as estimated by Kornegay and Notter and the 'adequate' and even 'minimum' allowances suggested by Petherick and Baxter (1982).

**TABLE 13.9  Recommendations for floor space allowances for growing and finishing pigs on fully or partially slatted floors (m$^2$ per pig)**

| Liveweight (kg) | USA | MAFF (1983) | Petherick and Baxter Minimum | Petherick and Baxter Adequate | 1 kg/0.0084 m$^2$ or 25 lb/ft$^2$ |
|---|---|---|---|---|---|
| 20 | 0.33 | 0.15 | 0.253 | 0.357 | 0.168 |
| 30 | 0.38 | 0.20 | 0.332 | 0.469 | 0.252 |
| 40 | 0.44 | 0.25 | 0.403 | 0.568 | 0.336 |
| 50 | 0.48 | 0.30 | 0.468 | 0.660 | 0.42 |
| 60 | 0.52 | 0.35 | 0.528 | 0.746 | 0.504 |
| 70 | 0.57 | 0.40 | 0.586 | 0.827 | 0.588 |
| 80 | 0.63 | 0.45 | 0.641 | 0.904 | 0.672 |
| 90 | 0.69 | 0.48 | 0.693 | 0.979 | 0.756 |
| 100 | 0.74 | 0.50 | 0.744 | 1.050 | 0.84 |

There are many reasons for the large disparity in floor space recommendations for growing—finishing pigs. One of these is the compromise which is made in practice between maximising performance per pig in a pen and optimising the financial return from investment in a unit of floor space provided for pigs. This latter principle is illustrated in Figure 13.6 from Kornegay and Notter's work.

While individual pig performance (liveweight gain and food conversion efficiency) is improved steadily for both growing and finishing pigs as floor space per pig is increased over the floor space allowance represented in Figure 13.6, daily gain per m$^2$ of floor space shows a very marked decline with increased floor space allowance per pig. Thus, if pig producers are to obtain a worthwhile return on the considerable investment they have made in buildings, they must reach the right compromise between maximising individual animal performance and optimising financial return on their overall investment. Where this compromise position lies will vary with circumstances. For example, where buildings are cheap, one can be more liberal with floor space allowance per pig than if buildings are very expensive.

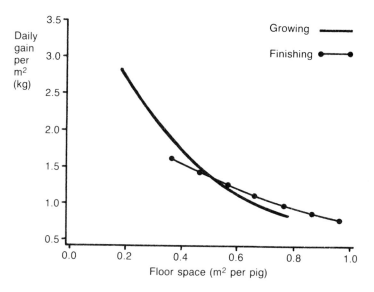

FIGURE 13.6   Relationship between floor space allowance per pig and daily liveweight gain per square meter of floor space provided.

Many factors influence floor space requirement per pig. When the combination of circumstances is optimal, the common recommendation of 10 kg per 0.084 m² of floor space (25 lb per square foot), can be quite satisfactory, whereas under more adverse conditions some of the recommendations in Table 13.9 for more liberal space allowance will be applicable.

The most important factors influencing floor space requirements of pigs from weaning to 20 kg liveweight were detailed in the previous chapter (pages 304–306). Since the same principles apply for growing–finishing pigs, the factors will be listed here with additional comments being made only on particular conditions which apply to growing–finishing pigs.

FACTORS WHICH INFLUENCE FLOOR SPACE REQUIREMENTS OF GROWING–
FINISHING PIGS
Floor space requirement per pig is:

- less on slatted and partially slatted floors than on solid floors
- greater where pigs are prone to respiratory problems, especially where ventilation and air movement in the house are inadequate
- less with more docile and less aggressive strains
- less where feeding space and opportunities for watering are very adequate in relation to the ability of each pig in a pen to obtain its full requirements
- less with more sensible pen shape which facilitates all pigs within the group obtaining their full requirements of feed and water and fulfilling all their other essential requirements with ease
- greater at high temperature

Where temperature tends to approach and fall below the LCT, having more pigs per pen and therefore less floor space per pig can be beneficial because of the greater huddling effects possible and greater total heat production per pen.

On the other hand, where temperature tends to approach and exceed the UCT, having fewer pigs in a pen and therefore greater floor space per pig can benefit the pigs by allowing them to spread out more and therefore increase the surface area from which heat can be lost.

This need to adjust floor space per pig according to temperature is often acted on in practice with pens being more heavily stocked in cold weather in winter and less heavily stocked in the heat of summer. Obviously, the greater the extremes of temperature between winter and summer, the greater will be the difference in the optimum number of pigs per pen in the two periods.

CHECKING THE ADEQUACY OF FLOOR SPACE PROVISION PER PIG

Because the optimum floor space provision per pig varies with the circumstances listed above and could also vary between summer and winter, individual pig producers, while using the recommendations in Table 13.9 as guidelines, are well advised to carry out some on-farm comparisons of stocking density. Hanrahan at Moorepark, Eire carried out such a comparison which serves as a good example. Over the growth period of 30 to 82 kg liveweight, the fully slatted pens examined were normally stocked with 16 pigs in a total floor space (excluding feeding space) of 10.25 m² (0.64 m² per pig). He decided to check the effect of increasing stocking density by having 18 pigs per pen (0.57 m² per pig). The temperature level prevailing throughout the experiment was within the thermoneutral zone of the pigs involved. The results are presented in Table 13.10.

Since the total feeding space per pen was the same in the 2 treatments, both lying and feeding space per pig differed between the treatments. There were small but consistent differences in terms of feed intake, liveweight gain and feed conversion ratio in favour of the smaller group size. Using current prices, the more heavily stocked pigs incurred an extra feed cost of 2.5 per cent or over 60 pence per pig which would have a considerable effect on the prevailing very small financial margins. Another basis for examining the effects of higher stocking rate in this ex-

**TABLE 13.10  Effect of stocking rate on pig performance over the liveweight range 30 to 82 kg**

| | | | |
|---|---|---|---|
| Floor area per pig (*m²*) | 0.64 | 0.57 | |
| Pigs per pen | 16 | 18 | 2 extra pigs* |
| Total pigs | 640 | 720 | |
| Feed intake (*kg/day*) | 2.15 | 2.09 | |
| Liveweight gain (*g/day*) | 686 | 649 | |
| FCR (*kg food per kg gain*) | 3.15 | 3.23 | 3.87 |
| Average backfat (*mm*) | 27.4 | 27.1 | |
| Feed cost per pig at £160/tonne | 26.21 | 26.88 | 32.16 |

*Attributes the poorer FCR on the 18 pigs per pen treatment entirely to the 2 extra pigs
(From: Hanrahan, 1980)

ample is to assume that the two extra pigs per pen in the second treatment are incurring all the extra feed used in their pen (relative to the control treatment). This would give the extra pigs a FCR of 3.87 and a feed cost per pig of £32.16 which is almost 23 per cent or £6 higher than the average on the control treatment. In most situations this degree of inefficiency associated with the extra pigs would result in the more heavily stocked pen having a lower margin per pen or per unit of building space than the more lightly stocked pen. Therefore, while output and financial margin per unit of floor space are important, depressions in individual animal performance as a result of inadequate lying and/or feeding space can seriously erode financial margins.

One very useful index of the adequacy of floor and feeding space in the practical situation is the degree of variation in growth within a pen. If a uniform lot of healthy pigs are placed in a pen in a healthy herd and these subsequently become very variable in size, the most likely cause of such variation is inadequate feeding and floor space. The low social order pigs suffer most in such a situation.

In times of very tight financial margins, no producers can afford slow growing passengers within a pen and a review of the adequacy of feeding space and floor space provision is called for on many pig units.

It is also important to ask the question: what can we do about the problem of overstocking at some stages of growth and understocking at others?

## THE PROBLEM OF UNDERSTOCKING AND OVERSTOCKING AT DIFFERENT PHASES OF GROWTH

Because feeding and lying space per pig is not increased gradually as pigs grow, these provisions are always a compromise. To ensure that feeding space and lying area are adequate at the end of the period of occupancy of a pen, these provisions must be over-liberal at the start of the period. Conversely, if feeding and lying space is just adequate at, or shortly after, the start of occupancy of a pen, it is likely to be very inadequate by the end of the period. Thus, fixing on provisions for feeding and lying space during a particular growth phase is always a compromise. This situation is depicted in Figure 13.7.

In this case, the compromise implemented in practice is to get the space allocation correct in the middle of each growth period. Thus, floor space allocation per pig during the growing and finishing periods corresponds with requirement at 40 (point X) and 80 kg liveweight (point Y) respectively. Below these mid points of each growth stage, pigs are understocked while above the mid points they are overstocked. This is a most unsatisfactory situation.

## APPROACHES TO MEETING FLOOR SPACE REQUIREMENTS MORE ACCURATELY AS PIGS GROW

Several approaches can be adopted in an attempt to avoid the alternate understocking and overstocking problem highlighted in Figure 13.7 and so make more efficient use of floor space:

1. Fill pens to capacity at the start of a period of growth and withdraw the smallest pigs regularly so as to maintain the exact match of pigs to floor space as pigs grow.

This certainly makes optimum use of the pen from which pigs are withdrawn but

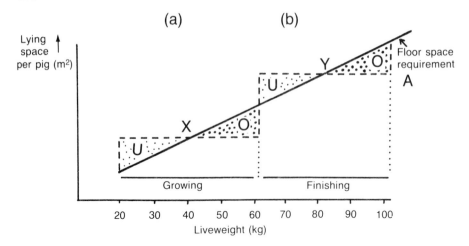

A = Floor space requirement based on 1 kg per 0.0084 m² or 25 lb/ft²
U = Period of understocking
O = Period of overstocking
X = Mid point of growing period
Y = Mid point of finishing period

FIGURE 13.7   Typical compromise in floor space allowance per pig during the periods of (a) growing (20–60 kg liveweight) and (b) finishing (60–100 kg liveweight).

another pen has to be found for the surplus pigs. In addition, when surplus pigs are transferred in this way they will amost invariably have to be mixed with equivalent pigs from other pens. Such mixing will lead to aggression as the newly transferred pigs fight in an attempt to establish the peck order. At best this will result in a growth check and there could also be injuries and even death on occasions as a result of such fighting.

2. There are several variants of the above approach:
   • Start off with an almost fully stocked pen and split the pen in two when stocking density becomes excessive. While this approach does not result in an exact match of requirement for floor space and provision of such space, it avoids the need to mix pigs.
   • In the finishing period, pens can be stocked almost to capacity at the start of the growth stage and, as pigs grow, the matching of floor space requirement and provision can be maintained by marketing the required number of pigs each week. The pigs marketed could be either the heaviest ones or the fattest ones, subcutaneous fatness being determined using an ultrasonic machine. This approach is discussed later in Chapter 16.

3. The provision of pens of different size in a house and transfer of pigs to progressively larger pens as they grow.
   Fritschen and Muehling (1978) in the United States suggested 2 alternative schemes which both involve pens of 2 sizes in a house. While this approach goes some way to making more efficient use of pen space, it does not provide as much flexibility as one needs in order to make optimum use of floor space.

Another approach was suggested by English and Fowler (1985) and this is illustrated in Figure 13.8. The features of this so-called 'xylophone house', its equipment and operation are as follows:

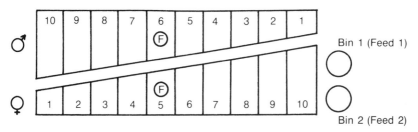

F = Round feeder

FIGURE 13.8   Suggested novel design for a growing-finishing house and facilities to accommodate pigs from 30 to 90 kg. (English and Fowler, 1985)

1. It is fully slatted.
2. Each pen has a round ad lib. hopper in the middle filled automatically by pipeline.
3. Water may be supplied from nipples on the back wall but preferably from nipples fitted round the circumference of the feeder. (These facilities for feeding, watering and the slatted floors are considered to be the best arrangements to keep pigs clean and comfortable and to ensure easy access to feed and water for all pigs within the pen.)
4. There are about 20 pigs per pen.
5. Pigs are introduced at the start (20 kg) into the small pens at one end and move along one pen per week as pigs from the far end are sent to market.
6. Castrates or boars on one side of the house and gilts on the other will allow differential nutrition if necessary.
7. Laggard pigs are withdrawn promptly and placed in the 'social rehabilitation section' of the unit or in the hospital premises as required.
8. Temperature is maintained at around 22°C, which is well within the comfort zone of all pigs (see Table 13.11). It is assumed that food intake of pigs is equivalent to 4 times maintenance up to 60 kg liveweight and 3 times maintenance thereafter.
9. The particular targets set for feed intake and liveweight gain depend on the genotype and carcass requirements.
10. The particular diet used for each weight group of pigs depends on sex, genotype, feeding level and carcass requirements.
11. One feed bin contains a starter and the other a finisher diet. The proportion of each diet delivered to each pen depends on the pigs' liveweight and sex.

This approach would certainly help to make more efficient use of floor space but has the disadvantage of weekly movement of pigs, albeit only to the next pen and

**TABLE 13.11  Lower and upper critical temperatures of pigs between 20 and 100 kg liveweight on perforated metal floors***

|              | *Liveweight (kg)* | | | | |
|--------------|----|----|----|----|-----|
|              | *20* | *40* | *60* | *80* | *100* |
| LCT (°C)     | 12 | 8  | 12 | 11 | 11  |
| UCT (dry)(°C) | 24 | 24 | 27 | 27 | 27  |

*Food intake of pigs up to 60 kg equivalent to 4 times
maintenance; above 60 kg equivalent to 3 times maintenance
(From Bruce, 1981)

with no change in climatic factors. Some producers feel that although the situation depicted in Figure 13.7 involves inefficient use of floor space, this approach has its compensations in terms of simplicity and ease of management. However, it is important to continue searching for a solution to the problem of inefficient floor space usage and to build into this solution the factors of simplicity, ease of management and other possible advantages. The principle of the xylophone house can be extended to include possibilities for improving the efficiency of pig production in other directions, including more efficient nutrition, and these are discussed in Chapter 22 (page 522).

## Important Differences Between the Sexes

For pigmeat production, gilts, boars and castrates are used. There are important differences between the sexes which must be appreciated if they are to be managed effectively. The most important are as follows:

1. MAINTENANCE REQUIREMENT.
Boars and gilts have higher heat production at maintenance levels of feed intake than castrates. It has been estimated that at around 60 kg liveweight, the maintenance requirement of boars is some 10 per cent higher than that of gilts and 15 per cent higher than that of castrates. The reason for the higher maintenance requirement of the boar is connected with its higher lean content and the fact that lean is more metabolically active tissue than fat.

2. APPETITE.
Castrates tend to have a higher voluntary food intake than boars and gilts (see Figure 13.9). The sex hormones − predominantly oestrogen in the gilt and androgens in the entire male − are mainly responsible for lower appetite relative to that of the castrate.

3. LIVEWEIGHT GAIN AND LEAN TISSUE GROWTH RATE (LTGR).
On the same daily intake of nutrients, liveweight gain tends to be considerably higher in the entire male than in the castrate and gilt (see Figure 13.10). It is obvious that differences between the sexes in liveweight gain up to about 45 kg

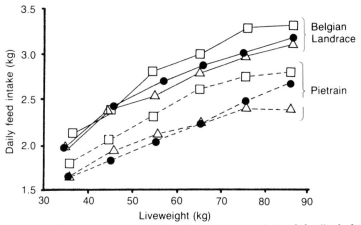

FIGURE 13.9   The differences in voluntary feed intake between boars [△], gilts [ ● ] and castrates [ □ ] of the Belgian Landrace and Pietrain breeds at various body weights. (From observations of Bekaert et al., 1974)

liveweight are almost negligible but the superiority of the entire male in terms of liveweight gain becomes very noticeable after this stage.

The superior liveweight gain of the entire male relative to the gilt over the growth period from 48 to 90 kg liveweight is also evident in Table 13.12 based on the work of Campbell in Australia. These data also demonstrate the higher deposition rate of protein tissue in the entire male relative to the gilt. It can be seen that at a daily energy intake of 31.7 MJ ME (on a diet with an excess of protein), the relative

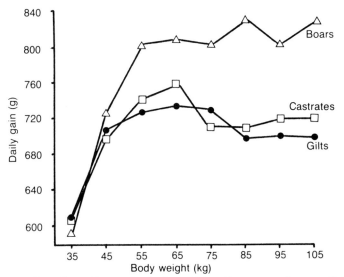

FIGURE 13.10   The effect of increasing body weight on the comparative growth rate of boars, gilts and castrates. (After Witt and Schröder, 1969)

rates of protein deposition were 129.5 g per day for entire males and 103 g for gilts, the deposition rate therefore being over 25 per cent greater in the entire male. These are equivalent to lean tissue growth rates of 321 and 225 g per day for entire males and gilts respectively. On the same feed intake, castrates would have lower rates of protein and lean meat deposition than gilts.

FATNESS

It can be seen from Table 13.12 that while entire males have higher liveweight gains and lean tissue growth rates relative to females from 48 to 90 kg liveweight, gilts deposit fatty tissue at a faster rate. On the same feed intake, castrates deposit fatty tissue at an even faster rate than gilts over this stage of growth.

**TABLE 13.12  Effects of energy intake between 48 and 90 kg liveweight on rate of protein deposition and the performance of entire male (M) and female (F) pigs**

|  |  | Energy intake (MJ ME/d) | | | | |
|  |  | 22.6 | 26.4 | 31.7 | 36.0 | Ad lib.[+] |
| --- | --- | --- | --- | --- | --- | --- |
| Protein deposition (g/d) | M | 69.4 | 94.8 | 129.5 | 130.0 | 132.0 |
|  | F | 63.4 | 84.5 | 103.0 | 102.0 | 99.0 |
| Daily gain (g) | M | 418 | 576 | 793 | 842 | 884 |
|  | F | 358 | 552 | 654 | 742 | 795 |
| Feed:gain | M | 3.9 | 3.4 | 2.9 | 3.1 | 3.5 |
|  | F | 4.6 | 3.6 | 3.4 | 3.5 | 3.6 |
| Body fat (g/kg) | M | 203 | 249 | 257 | 315 | 332 |
|  | F | 293 | 332 | 353 | 368 | 397 |

[+] 39.8 MJ ME/day for M and 37.9 MJ ME/day for F.
(Source: Campbell, 1985)

As one would expect from these differences in the relative growth rate of lean and fatty tissue between the sexes, percentage of lean in the carcass would be higher in entire males than in castrates, with gilts in an intermediate position. Conversely, castrates would have the highest fat content followed by gilts and then entire males. These trends in percentage content of fat and lean in the carcass are illustrated in Figure 13.11. It is obvious that the heavier the slaughter weight, the greater are the differences between the sexes.

These large differences in growth rate of lean and fatty tissue and in carcass fat and lean percentage are evident between the sexes when feed intake is equal. However, when castrates are allowed to express their greater appetite relative to entire males and gilts (see Figure 13.9), then differences in lean and fat percentage of carcasses of specific weights will be even more divergent between the sexes.

FEED TO GAIN RATIO

Since, relative to the gilt, the entire male lays down more lean tissue and less fat on the same feed intake, it tends to have a better feed to liveweight gain ratio (see Table 13.13). For the same reason, the feed to liveweight gain ratio of the castrate will tend to be poorer than that of the gilt. However, entire males have a smaller

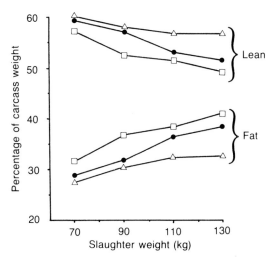

FIGURE 13.11   The difference in yields of lean meat and of fat by boars [△], gilts [●] and castrates [□] slaughtered at various bodyweights. (From data of Hansson, Lundstrom and Malmros, 1975)

advantage when food conversion efficiency is calculated on a carcass weight basis. Entire males have a lower carcass yield than gilts and castrates partly because of the weight of their testes and associated tissues and also, since they have less fat, they have a slightly higher proportion of head, feet and viscera. As indicated in Table 13.13, the superiority of entire males in feed conversion efficiency is reduced when this is expressed on a carcass rather than a liveweight basis.

RESPONSE TO INCREASING DIETARY PROTEIN
It has been noted above (see Table 13.12) that between 48 and 90 kg liveweight on the same daily feed intake, entire males have higher daily rates of deposition

**TABLE 13.13   Comparison of liveweight and carcass weight feed conversion ratios (FCR)**

|                       | Boars        | Gilts        | Castrates    |
|-----------------------|--------------|--------------|--------------|
| Restricted feeding    |              |              |              |
| Liveweight FCR        | 2.83 (100)*  | 2.94 (104)   | 3.04 (107)   |
| Carcass weight FCR    | 3.71 (100)   | 3.76 (101)   | 3.90 (105)   |
| Ad lib. feeding       |              |              |              |
| Liveweight FCR        | 3.18 (100)   | 3.29 (103)   | 3.39 (107)   |
| Carcass weight FCR    | 4.13 (100)   | 4.20 (102)   | 4.30 (104)   |

* Figures in brackets are indices of food to gain ratio. The figure for boars = 100.
(From: Walstra, Buiting and Mateman, 1977)

of protein and lean meat than gilts. Gilts in turn have higher lean growth rates than castrates. Therefore, entire males use dietary protein more efficiently than gilts and gilts in turn are more efficient in this respect than castrates. However, an important question is whether entire males and gilts require a higher quality diet in terms of protein and essential amino acids in order to express their higher potential for lean tissue growth. The results of relevant experiments are summarised in Figures 13.12 and 13.13, and indicate that sexes with higher lean tissue growth potential do, in fact, respond to diets with higher levels of protein and essential amino acids.

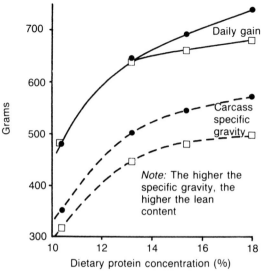

FIGURE 13.12   Responses of gilts [ ● ] and castrates [ □ ] to increasing dietary protein concentration. (From data of Fuller et al., 1976)

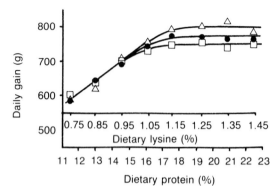

FIGURE 13.13   The growth rates of boars [Δ], gilts [ ● ] and castrates [ □ ] in response to increasing dietary concentration of balanced protein. (From Yen, 1979)

It is clear that in both experiments with diets containing relatively low levels of dietary protein and amino acids, no differences in liveweight gain are evident between the sexes. However, as the protein quality of the diet is raised, the gilt is able to express its higher growth potential relative to the castrate, while the boar demonstrates its superior growth relative to the gilt and the castrate.

The differential response to protein and essential amino acids between the sexes varies with liveweight, as indicated below.

*Up to 50 kg liveweight*
As indicated in Chapter 12, differences in lean tissue growth rate between the sexes are less noticeable up to about 50 kg liveweight, presumably because secondary sexual characteristics are not operating strongly at such an immature stage. The work of Campbell in Victoria, Australia found no differences in lean tissue growth rate between gilts and entire males on protein adequate diets at levels of intake up to 4 times maintenance requirement. It was only at very high levels of intake (4.4 times maintenance) that entire males grew lean tissue at a faster rate than gilts. Therefore requirements for lysine and other essential amino acids were very similar for boars and gilts at this stage of growth in the genotype examined by Campbell except at very high levels of food intake when entire males appeared to have a higher requirement for essential amino acids. The responses of the 3 sexes to different levels of protein (of constant amino acid composition) were examined in detail by Yen (1979) at the University of Nottingham, and over the liveweight range of 25 to 55 kg he estimated that the protein requirement of entire males was 7 per cent higher than that of castrates and just over 2 per cent higher than that of gilts (see Table 13.14).

**TABLE 13.14  Comparative requirements of protein (of constant amino acid composition, including 6.5 per cent lysine) by boars, gilts and castrates to attain their optimum in growth and carcass composition**

| | Boars | | Gilts | | Castrates | |
|---|---|---|---|---|---|---|
| | Optimum | Lysine (%) | Optimum | Lysine (%) | Optimum | Lysine (%) |
| *25–55 kg* | | | | | | |
| Daily gain (g) | 798 | 1.12 | 761 | 1.04 | 742 | 1.01 |
| FCR | 2.02 | 1.10 | 2.11 | 1.08 | 2.20 | 1.03 |
| Lean in ham (%) | 68.6 | 1.03 | 68.7 | 1.00 | 67.1 | 0.96 |
| Fat in ham (%) | 15.9 | 1.04 | 16.9 | 1.03 | 18.0 | 0.99 |
| Mean backfat (*mm*) | 13.7 | 1.04 | 14.8 | 0.99 | 15.6 | 0.97 |
| Longissimus dorsi area (*cm²*) | 22.3 | 1.04 | 22.2 | 1.07 | 21.0 | 0.95 |
| *50–90 kg* | | | | | | |
| Daily gain (g) | 958 | 0.92 | 870 | 0.83 | 816 | 0.75 |
| FCR | 2.57 | 0.90 | 2.92 | 0.84 | 3.15 | 0.72 |
| Lean in ham (%) | 67.8 | 0.93 | 66.3 | 0.87 | 63.5 | 0.70 |
| Fat in ham (%) | 19.3 | 0.92 | 22.0 | 0.87 | 24.5 | 0.73 |
| Backfat 'C' and 'K' (*mm*) | 34.0 | 1.00 | 37.0 | 0.88 | 45.6 | 0.77 |
| Longissimus dorsi area (*cm²*) | 33.5 | 0.90 | 33.5 | 0.84 | (28.9 | 0.70)* |

* Estimated by Fuller (1984).
(From Yen, 1979)

Thus, although there is some evidence of higher protein and essential amino acid requirements of the entire male and gilt relative to the castrate at this early stage, in practice growth tends to be limited by failure to achieve sufficiently high energy intake. Energy intake in practice may be limited by such factors as the inherent appetite of the pig, the energy density and general acceptability of the diet and feeding space. Thus, while in some circumstances a case can be made for formulating diets with slightly different concentrations of dietary protein and essential amino acids for entire males, gilts and castrates, the differences in nutrient requirement are likely to be so small in the reality of the practical situation that such refinement is not justified at this very early stage of growth. So there is no appreciable benefit of feeding different diets to the separate sexes before 50 kg liveweight.

*50 to 90 kg liveweight*
Figures 13.12 and 13.13 indicate that, at low dietary concentrations of protein and essential amino acids, there are no obvious differences in growth between entire males, gilts and castrates but, with increasing concentration of such nutrients, the gilt responds more than the castrate with the entire male showing the best response of all.

Therefore, there is a case for providing diets with different protein and essential amino acid concentrations for the 3 sexes. Fuller (1983) suggested that the economic optimum level of protein was that at which the cost of an additional increment of protein is exactly recovered by the value of the additional response. In most circumstances, the optimum level is likely to be at the point on the response curve at which the plateau is first reached (see Figure 13.13) and these optimum levels for different parameters in the work of Yen (1979) are indicated in Table 13.14. On this latter basis, the optimum dietary protein level for the entire male between 50 and 90 kg liveweight appears to be some 22 per cent higher than that of the castrate and 8 per cent higher than that of the gilt.

Campbell in Victoria, Australia made a similar attempt to estimate the optimum dietary lysine concentrations for the entire male and the gilt between 50 and 90 kg liveweight and his findings are summarised in Table 13.15. His criterion for deciding on the optimum dietary lysine level was that at which food to gain ratio was minimised. The optimum level for pigs between 20 and 50 kg liveweight was found to be 0.76 g lysine per MJ DE for both entire males and gilts. This is equivalent to 1.06 per cent lysine for a diet with 14 MJ DE per kg. However, for pigs between

**TABLE 13.15  Effect of dietary lysine content on the feed:gain of entire male (M) and female (F) pigs growing from 20 to 50 and 50 to 90 kg liveweight**

|  |  | *Dietary lysine (g/MJ DE)* | | | | | | | |
|---|---|---|---|---|---|---|---|---|---|
|  |  | *0.4* | *0.5* | *0.6* | *0.67* | *0.76* | *0.83* | *0.94* | *1.02* |
| *20–50 kg* | M | 3.3 | 2.9 | 2.6 | 2.4 | 2.2 | 2.2 | 2.3 | 2.3 |
|  | F | 3.3 | 2.9 | 2.6 | 2.4 | 2.25 | 2.3 | 2.4 | 2.4 |
| *50–90 kg* | M | 3.5 | 2.9 | 2.7 | 2.9 | 3.1 | 3.0 | 2.9 | 2.9 |
|  | F | 3.5 | 2.9 | 2.9 | 3.2 | 3.2 | 3.3 | 3.5 | 3.3 |

(Source: Campbell, 1985)

50 and 90 kg liveweight the optimum level of dietary lysine for gilts (0.5 g per MJ DE or 0.65 per cent lysine in a diet with 13 MJ DE per kg) was estimated to be some 15 per cent less than the optimum for entire males (0.6 g per MJ DE or 0.78 per cent in a diet with 13 MJ DE per kg). Therefore, provision of diets differing in protein and lysine content to entire males, gilts and castrates from 50 kg liveweight onwards would seem to be desirable if, on the one hand, we are going to allow the entire male to express its superior lean tissue growth potential, while on the other, we are going to avoid providing surplus protein and lysine to the gilt and the castrate.

RESPONSE TO INCREASING DIETARY ENERGY

Because the castrate, on the same feed intake, deposits more fatty tissue than the entire male (with the gilt in an intermediate position), energy requirements for liveweight or carcass weight gain are considerably higher in the castrate. It has been estimated that up to 90 kg liveweight, when pigs have the same daily food intake, food requirement per kg of liveweight gain is some 10 per cent higher for the castrate than the entire male. On a carcass weight basis, the advantage for the entire male is halved (5 per cent less food) because of its lower killing out percentage.

In order to produce carcasses of equal fat to lean ratio in the 3 sexes, daily food intake must be restricted more in the gilt than in the entire male, but the greatest food restriction must be imposed on the castrate. Fuller and Livingstone (1978) estimated that to produce gilts and castrates with equal subcutaneous fat, castrates would have to receive between 3 and 6 less MJ DE per day (between 0.25 and 0.5 kg less of a diet with about 12 MJ DE per kg) between 20 and 90 kg liveweight (see Table 13.16). Of course, a reduction of 0.5 kg per day in daily food intake for the castrate would reduce its daily growth rate by about 160 g daily relative to the gilt over the 20 to 90 kg liveweight range.

It is generally accepted that to produce carcasses at the same weight and of equivalent lean to fat ratio, it is necessary between 20 and 90 kg liveweight in most cases to reduce feed intake, relative to the boar, by 16 per cent in the castrate and by 8 per cent in the gilt.

**TABLE 13.16  Daily metabolisable energy needed to achieve equal carcass fatness in gilts and castrates**

| Measurement | Mean value (mm) | MJ ME required per day | |
|---|---|---|---|
| | | Castrates | Gilts |
| Shoulder fat | 46 | 22 | 25 |
| Midback fat | 22 | 20 | 26 |
| Minimum loin Intrascope | 24 | 21 | 26 |
| (P$_2$) | 19 | 21 | 26 |

(From: Fuller and Livingstone, 1978)

## Management of the Different Sexes

UP TO 50 KG LIVEWEIGHT

As indicated earlier, there is no strong case for managing the sexes differently before around 50 kg liveweight. The pig producer has almost every incentive to maximise intake of a balanced diet up to this stage for all sexes. By maximising intake, liveweight and lean tissue growth will be increased, food to gain ratio will be improved and the only disadvantage is a relatively small increase in body fat to weigh against all the considerable advantages.

FROM 50 KG LIVEWEIGHT UPWARDS

The basic factors which must be considered when deciding whether the different sexes should be managed in the same way or differently in the later phase of growth are the following:

1.  Lean tissue growth potential is highest in the boar, followed by the gilt and then the castrate. Differences between the sexes are considerable.
2.  Conversely, on the same daily food intake, the castrate deposits body fat at a much faster rate than the entire male, with the gilt being in an intermediate position.
3.  The castrate has a higher appetite than the gilt and entire male so that differences in carcass fatness between the sexes are accentuated when pigs are fed to appetite.
4.  Because of differences in lean tissue growth rate between the sexes, requirements for protein and essential amino acids differ. If lean tissue growth potential is to be fully expressed, then dietary provision of lysine and other essential amino acids should be some 10 per cent higher for entire males than for gilts and the requirement of the gilt in turn is some 10 per cent higher than that of the castrate.
5.  If protein and essential amino acids are provided in excess of requirement, this constitutes a comparative waste as these are then used as an energy source and, in addition, there is evidence of adverse effects on food to gain ratio if surplus protein and amino acids are provided. However, the penalties for not providing sufficient protein and essential amino acids are greater than those incurred by providing a small excess (see pages 196/197).

*Number of sexes to be considered*

The producer will normally have to consider only 2 sexes, either gilts and entire males or gilts and castrated males. There are few situations in which producers are justified in leaving some males entire while others are castrated. Obviously, it is somewhat simpler in the commercial situation to work out a sound strategy to deal with 2 sexes rather than 3.

*Separate penning*

If sexes are to be penned separately in the later stages of growth, they should be segregated at weaning since this avoids the need for mixing, with consequent fighting, at a later stage of growth. The only situation in which such segregation at weaning will not be necessary is where pigs are placed in large groups at weaning and are penned into smaller lots later on. In this latter situation, segregation of sexes can take place when the large group is being split up.

*Slaughter at different weights*
If boars, castrates and gilts are being offered the same diet at identical levels of intake, then in order to market carcasses with the same backfat thickness, gilts will have to be slaughtered at a lighter weight than boars and castrates at the lightest

Plate 13.4  Gilts and entire males are penned separately in this finishing house. This allows a higher-quality diet to be fed to entire males since they show greater responses in terms of lean tissue growth than gilts. Gilts are also restricted to a greater degree than entire males during finishing so as to produce leaner carcasses.

weight of all. At 90 kg liveweight on the same daily intakes of a well-balanced diet, a useful rule of thumb to use for average genotypes in the United Kingdom is that backfat at location $P_2$ (at the level of the last rib 6.5 cm lateral to the backbone and over the eye muscle: see page 92) will, relative to the entire male, be 2 mm higher in the castrate and 1 mm higher in the gilt. Since, on reasonable levels of daily food intake, the pig of average genetic merit approaching 90 kg liveweight will be increasing in backfat at $P_2$ by 1 mm for every 5 kg increase in liveweight gain (and every 4 kg increase in carcass gain), gilts would have to be slaughtered at a liveweight 5 kg less, and castrates at 10 kg less than entire males in order for carcasses from the different sexes to have the same average fatness at $P_2$. These differences are summarised in Table 13.17.

**TABLE 13.17   Differences in fatness between the sexes at 90 kg liveweight and approximate weights at slaughter to achieve the same average carcass fatness in pigs of average genetic merit in the United Kingdom (all pigs on the same diet at the same level of daily intake)**

|  | Difference at 90 kg liveweight in fatness at $P_2$ relative to the entire male (mm) | Approximate reduction in liveweight at slaughter to achieve same $P_2$ measurement (kg) | Equivalent liveweight at slaughter to achieve same $P_2$ measurement (kg) |
|---|---|---|---|
| Entire male | 0 | 0 | 90 |
| Gilt | +1 | 5 | 85 |
| Castrate | +2 | 10 | 80 |

These approximations will apply to pigs with an average $P_2$ at slaughter between 10 and 15 mm. If pigs are leaner than this, then proportionally smaller reductions in slaughter weight would be necessary in the gilt and castrate. On the other hand, where pigs are fatter, liveweight differences at slaughter would need to be larger in order to achieve the same fatness at $P_2$ from the carcasses of the 3 sexes.

*Feed intake*
The greater degree to which energy intake must be restricted in the castrate and gilt to achieve the same level of fatness at slaughter as in the entire male varies with the general level of fatness of the pigs and the growth period over which such restriction is to be imposed. In the great majority of situations it is usual and sensible to feed pigs to appetite up to around 50 kg liveweight, and if food restriction has to be imposed it is usually done after this stage.

Campbell in Victoria, Australia examined the influence of varying daily energy intake on body fat in entire males and gilts between 48 and 90 kg liveweight. His results were presented in Table 13.12. The genotype used (Large White × Landrace) was relatively unimproved in terms of lean tissue growth potential. It can be seen that body fat percentage was identical in entire males and gilts at respective energy intakes of 39.8 MJ ME (ad lib.) and 26.4 MJ ME, a difference in daily intake of 13.4 MJ ME. Similarly, body fat percentage was very similar in the 2 sexes at respective energy intakes of 36.0 and 22.6 MJ ME, a difference of 13.4 MJ ME in daily energy intake. Thus, for the genotype used by Campbell, gilts would have to receive approximately 13 MJ ME less daily than entire males over the growth period of 48 to 90 kg liveweight in order to produce carcasses with similar fat percentage. This reduction in energy intake is equivalent to about 1 kg of a balanced growing–finishing diet based on barley and soya bean meal. However, the reduction in daily energy intake to achieve similar backfat measurements in gilts and entire males is very much less than that required to achieve similar percentages of body fat and it is thickness of subcutaneous fat and not carcass fat percentage which is normally used as the basis of carcass grading.

The data of Fuller at the Rowett Research Institute in Aberdeen indicate that to reduce backfat at $P_2$ by 1 mm, it is necessary to reduce energy intake between 50 and 90 kg liveweight by about 4 MJ DE or about 0.3 kg of a balanced diet containing 13 MJ DE per kg. On the basis that in pigs of average genetic merit in the United Kingdom ($P_2$ fatness at 90 kg liveweight between 10 and 15 mm on to appetite feeding), gilts will have 1 mm more backfat at $P_2$ than entire males, with castrates having a $P_2$ a further 1 mm greater, this indicates that for such genotypes, gilts should receive 0.3 kg less and castrates 0.6 kg less than entire males between 50 and 90 kg liveweight if all 3 sexes are to produce carcasses with similar $P_2$ measurements. These proposed reductions in feed intake are equivalent to about 12 per cent for the gilt and 24 per cent for the castrate. The penalty for reducing energy intake by about 4 MJ DE between 50 and 90 kg liveweight will be a reduction of about 100 g per day in liveweight gain. The relative feed intakes of the 3 sexes to achieve the same backfat thickness at $P_2$ and the penalties for feed restriction are summarised in Table 13.18.

**TABLE 13.18** Degree of energy or feed restriction necessary between 50 and 90 kg liveweight for gilts and castrates to achieve the same backfat thickness at $P_2$ as entire males and the resultant penalties

|  | Reduction in daily energy intake (MJ DE) | Reduction in food intake (kg) (diet with 13 MJ DE/kg) | Reduction in daily liveweight gain* | Increase in days to slaughter | Estimated effect on food required per kg liveweight gain |
|---|---|---|---|---|---|
| Entire males | 0 | 0 | 0 | 0 | 0 |
| Gilts | 4 | 0.3 | 100 | 6 | NIL |
| Castrates | 8 | 0.6 | 200 | 14 | NIL |

* Based on the assumption that the daily liveweight gain of entire males = 875 g

A possible alternative to imposing greater food restriction on castrates and gilts is to offer them lower energy diets when on an ad lib. feeding system. However, in the later growth stages, pigs succeed in compensating for lower energy diets by eating more and the dietary energy level would need to be very low (below 11 MJ DE per kg) to have the desired effect. It must also be remembered, of course, that castrates have a bigger appetite than either gilts or entire males. Thus, providing castrates and gilts with lower energy diets on ad lib. systems would be successful in reducing backfat only if the energy density of the diet was very low.

*Protein and amino acid content of diet*
A useful global objective in pigmeat production is to provide during the growth period sufficient dietary protein and essential amino acids and a high enough feed intake to allow almost the full expression of lean tissue growth potential. If the potential for lean tissue growth is to be achieved in the later phase of growth by using dietary protein and essential amino acids as efficiently as possible, then the level of these nutrients should be varied for the entire male, the gilt and the castrate. Over the later period of growth (say from 50 kg upwards) the dietary level of protein and essential amino acids should be some 10 per cent higher for the entire male than for the gilt and, in turn, the dietary level of these nutrients for the gilt should be some 10 per cent higher than for the castrate.

While it is easy to state that the optimum dietary level of protein and essential amino acids should be that which allows almost full expression of lean tissue growth potential in a particular sex, it is by no means easy to determine this. To determine this optimum for a particular genotype would require extensive experimentation involving detailed carcass studies. Perhaps the most effective way in practice to determine optimum levels of dietary protein and essential amino acids would be to provide a range of dietary levels of these nutrients for each sex and to define the optimum level as that at which the food to gain ratio was optimised in both physical and financial terms. This principle can be demonstrated by referring to the data of Campbell (see Table 13.15 on page 366).

It was observed that between 20 and 50 kg liveweight, food to gain ratio was minimised with a dietary lysine concentration of 0.76 g per MJ DE in both entire males and gilts. However, over the 50 to 90 kg growth period, optimum lysine level was 0.6 g per MJ DE in entire males and only 0.5 in gilts. Although these levels may be the optimum in an important aspect of physical performance, one would need to check that they were also the optimum in economic terms. If such a trial was carried out only on entire males, one could use the rule of thumb that over the 50 to 90 kg liveweight growth stage, optimum lysine concentration would, relative to entire males, be about 10 per cent less for gilts and some 20 per cent less for castrates.

Since there would appear to be penalties for providing both too little and too much dietary lysine (and also other amino acids) for a particular sex, especially during the later stages of growth (see Table 13.15), it is desirable that greater attention is paid to catering more carefully for the different protein requirements in this period.

Determining optimum levels of protein and essential amino acids for pigs of different sexes and against varying economic backgrounds in terms of the relative cost of protein concentrates and price differentials between carcasses with varying lean percentage will be dealt with more fully in Chapters 16 and 20.

## ADDITIONAL READING

Kornegay E. T. and Notter D. R. (1984), 'Effects of Floor Space and Number of Pigs per Pen on Performance', *Pig News and Information* **5**, 23–33.

*Pigs News and Information* (Consulting Editor, R. Braude), Commonwealth Agricultural Bureaux, Slough, England.

*Pork Industry Handbook*, USA Co-operative Extension Service, University of Illinois at Urbana-Champaign, USA.

# Chapter 14

# Optimum Weight at Slaughter − Theoretical Considerations

## RANGE IN CARCASS WEIGHTS

Liveweight at slaughter and resultant carcass weights vary widely on a global basis from the very light carcass weights (5 to 20 kg) of the so-called 'suckling pig' to the very heavy ones (often over 100 kg) produced in Italy for the specialist Parma ham trade.

Average carcass weights in EEC countries are detailed in Table 14.1. It can be seen that carcass weights are heaviest in Italy and lightest in the United Kingdom, the Irish Republic and Greece. In the United Kingdom, pigs are slaughtered at very varied liveweights (see Figure 14.1) with some carcasses of less than 40 kg for the very light pork trade, a small proportion in excess of 100 kg for the 'heavy hog' trade and the great majority in the 60 to 70 kg range for the bacon and cutter markets. This is also the popular weight range in both Denmark and the Irish Republic since all 3 countries are heavily involved in producing Wiltshire bacon

**TABLE 14.1  Average carcass weights in EEC countries (1985)**

|  | *(kg)* |
|---|---|
| Belgium and Luxembourg | 85 |
| Denmark | 71 |
| France | 85 |
| Greece | 64 |
| Irish Republic | 64 |
| Italy | 106 |
| Netherlands | 84 |
| Portugal | 74 |
| Spain | 71 |
| United Kingdom | 64 |
| West Germany | 84 |

(Source: Meat and Livestock Commission, 1988)

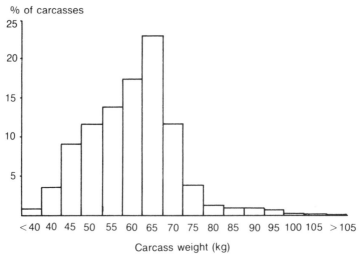

FIGURE 14.1   Distribution of carcass weights in a representative sample, year ended
September 1986, for the United Kingdom. (MLC Pig Yearbook, 1987)

Plate 14.1   Suckling pig is a
delicacy in many parts of the
world. (Courtesy of M.F.
Ngian)

which involves curing the carcass with the rind on. This requires that the pig has minimum backfat at slaughter since there is no opportunity to trim off surplus fat.

Another factor which dictates that carcasses should not be too heavy in some countries is the fact that male pigs are no longer castrated. This applies in Australia and the Irish Republic and limitations are imposed on carcass weight in an attempt to ensure that entire males are not too old at slaughter. Slaughtering entire males at a young age before they reach sexual maturity helps to minimise the risk of 'boar taint' in the meat.

## Is There an Optimum Weight at Slaughter?

The general answer to the above question must be 'no'. If, in relation to production costs, the price received for suckling pig to supply the high-class restaurant trade in Hong Kong is extremely attractive relative to that for pigs of heavier weight, then that may well be the optimum slaughter stage in that situation. On the other hand, if the price offered for very heavy pigs to supply the lucrative export trade in Parma hams in Italy makes this more attractive financially than slaughtering at lighter weights, then the 'Parma ham weight' is the optimum one.

However, the value of the carcass is only one side of the equation and we must look carefully at the factors which influence cost of production to reach various final weights. The most important of the factors influencing production costs of pigs slaughtered at a wide range of liveweights include feed intake, liveweight gain, food conversion efficiency, carcass lean to fat ratio, carcass yield and the original cost of the weaned pig per kg of carcass weight produced.

## Factors Which Influence Production Costs According to Liveweight at Slaughter

### Feed Intake

On a 'to appetite' feeding system, feed intake shows almost a linear trend with liveweight for many genotypes over a wide range of liveweights (see Figure 14.2).

In gilts there may be some interruptions in feed intake during oestrus periods at heavier weights if they reach puberty before slaughter. However, such oestrus periods will only impose short interruptions to normal feed intake.

### Daily Liveweight Gain

Daily rate of liveweight gain on 'to appetite' feeding tends to increase fairly rapidly from an early age and then reach a plateau, the level of which varies between the sexes (see Figure 14.3).

Over a wide range of slaughter weights, liveweight gain for a particular sex on 'to appetite' feeding will tend to be fairly constant. The fact that rate of liveweight gain remains fairly constant after this growth plateau is reached, although daily feed intake continues to rise, may seem surprising at first sight but this anomaly is explained by the fact that, as the pig matures, it is depositing progressively more fatty

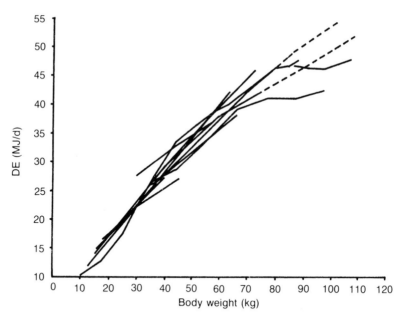

FIGURE 14.2  Relationship between daily intake of feed (MJ DE per day) and liveweight for data sets in which pigs had continuous access to feed. (ARC, 1981)

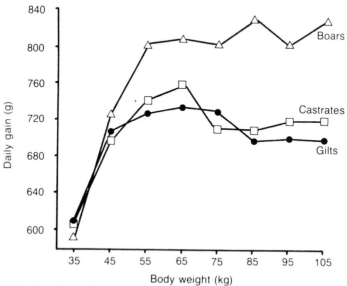

FIGURE 14.3  The effect of increasing body weight on the comparative growth rate of boars, gilts and castrates. (After Witt and Schröder, 1969)

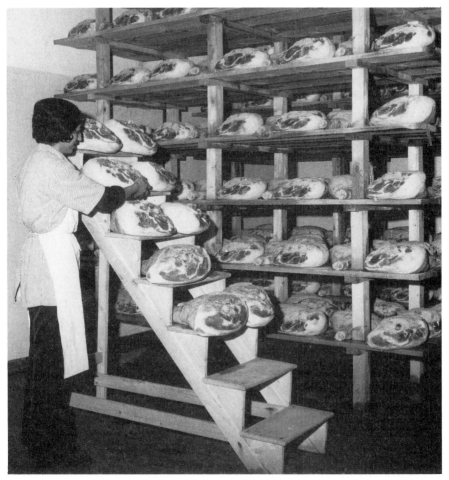

Plate 14.2   In Italy, pigs for Parma ham are grown to very heavy weights. The hams are highly prized both at home and by expatriates abroad. (Courtesy of Pigi Meat Factory, Italy)

tissue and proportionally less lean. Another factor which influences this trend is that energy intake as a proportion of the pig's maintenance requirements is falling all the time, starting off at about 4 times maintenance requirement after weaning and dropping to less than 3 times maintenance by 90 kg liveweight.

### Deposition of Fatty Relative to Lean Tissue and Food Conversion Efficiency

As the pig grows on a 'to appetite' feeding system, as noted above, it deposits progressively more fat relative to lean tissue. The contributes towards a deterioration in food conversion efficiency with increasing liveweight.

**Food Conversion Efficiency**

Useful information on food conversion efficiency trends in entire males comes from Pig Improvement Company data on boars on performance tests between 45 and 105 kg liveweight. These boars were housed in pairs and offered feed ad lib. Food to gain ratios were as follows during three particular liveweight stages:

| Stage | Liveweight range (kg) | Food required per kg of liveweight gain | Percentage increase in food per kg liveweight gain relative to stage 1 |
|-------|-----------------------|-----------------------------------------|------------------------------------------------------------------------|
| 1 | 45 to 50 | 2.40 | 0 |
| 2 | 68 to 73 | 2.76 | 11.5 |
| 3 | 95 to 100 | 3.45 | 43.8 |

Thus, in entire males, as with gilts and castrates, considerably more food is required per kg liveweight gain with increasing liveweight at slaughter.

**Carcass Yield**

Since the proportions of head, feet and offal tend to decrease relative to total liveweight with increase in weight, carcass yield or killing out percentage increases with increased weight at slaughter.

**The Cost of the Young Pig**

Young pigs are often purchased by operators of growing–finishing enterprises at around 30 kg liveweight in Britain. The overhead cost of this so-called weaner per kg of carcass produced varies with both the initial cost of the pig and the carcass weight as shown in Table 14.2. It is clear that the overhead cost of the weaner per kg of carcass produced is reduced if it can be purchased more cheaply and if carcass weight is increased.

## OVERALL EFFECTS OF INCREASING SLAUGHTER WEIGHT

The trends with increasing slaughter weight outlined above are demonstrated clearly in the data from a Canadian study (Sather, Martin, Jolly and Freedeen, 1980). Their Lacombe gilts and castrates were on ad lib. feeding and growth was almost linear from 21 kg liveweight with no indication of slowing down even to the heaviest liveweights examined (133.8 kg). Their findings are summarised in Table 14.3.

Backfat thickness increased progressively from 18 mm at 72.9 kg to 28 mm at 133.8 kg liveweight. As expected, food conversion efficiency deteriorated steadily with increasing liveweight at slaughter. Food required per kg of liveweight gain between 122.7 and 133.8 kg liveweight was 38 per cent greater than that required between 72.9 and 84.1 kg liveweight. Although the killing out percentage increased progressively with increased slaughter weight, food required per kg of carcass

**TABLE 14.2  Influence of cost of the weaner and final carcass weight on the weaner overhead cost per kg of carcass**

|  | Carcass weight (kg) | | | |
|---|---|---|---|---|
|  | 40 | 60 | 80 | 100 |
| Cost of 30 kg weaner | Weaner overhead cost per kg of carcass (pence) | | | |
| £25 | 63 | 42 | 31 | 25 |
| £30 | 75 | 50 | 38 | 30 |

**TABLE 14.3  Trends with increasing liveweight at slaughter**

| Weight class | Mean liveweight at slaughter (kg) | Feed efficiency to each slaughter weight (from 21 kg) | Incremental feed efficiency | Carcass weight (kg) | % yield | Approximate dead weight feed efficiencies (from 21 kg liveweight) | Average fat (loin and back) (mm) |
|---|---|---|---|---|---|---|---|
| 1 | 72.9 | 2.62 | )3.43 | 56.6 | 77.7 | 3.37 | 18 |
| 2 | 84.1 | 2.73 | )3.95 | 65.9 | 78.3 | 3.49 | – |
| 3 | 98.2 | 2.96 | )4.40 | 77.7 | 79.1 | 3.74 | – |
| 4 | 109.0 | 3.14 | )4.52 | 87.2 | 80.0 | 3.93 | – |
| 5 | 122.7 | 3.32 | )4.76 | 98.8 | 80.5 | 4.12 | – |
| 6 | 133.8 | 3.42 |  | 108.6 | 81.2 | 4.21 | 28 |
|  | 72.9 to 133.8 | 4.03 |  |  |  |  |  |

weight was 25 per cent greater when pigs were grown to 133.8 kg than to 72.9 kg liveweight. The main differences noted between the sexes over the period was (a) gilts tended to go off their feed in the fourth period (98.2 to 109.0 kg liveweight) (this probably coincided with puberty), and (b) the mean backfat thickness (loin and back) of castrates increased steadily by 2 mm for each 10 kg of liveweight increase from the lowest to the heaviest slaughter weight, while the gilts increased little in backfat thickness until after 109 kg liveweight.

Bichard of the Pig Improvement Company has provided a useful summary of some trends with increasing liveweight at slaughter on the basis of an examination of all the relevant information on the subject. He suggests the smallest and largest changes likely to occur with increasing liveweight at slaughter are as follows:

| Factor | Change per 5 kg increase in liveweight at slaughter between 50 and 150 kg | |
|---|---|---|
|  | Smallest change likely | Largest change likely |
| Food required (kg) per kg of liveweight gain | +0.03 | +0.10 |
| Backfat thickness (mm) | +0.5 | +1.0 |
| Carcass yield (%) | +0.25 | +0.5 |

These data are used in Table 14.4 to indicate the range of possible changes likely with increased liveweight at slaughter. The baseline is that from weaning to 50 kg liveweight:

Food to gain ratio                     =   2.5
Killing out percentage at 50 kg        =   73%
Backfat thickness at $P_2$ at 50 kg    =   8 mm

The degree to which the above factors are likely to change within the limits suggested by Bichard will vary with such factors as genotype, sex, feed level and quality of diet (particularly in terms of protein quality and ratio of essential amino acids to digestible energy level).

While the data in the table can be used to provide some estimate of likely changes with increase in slaughter weight, each individual producer considering an increase or decrease in slaughter weight is advised to carry out relevant studies on his own data to determine the precise changes likely to occur in factors such as food to gain ratio and backfat thickness in his own particular situation as he changes weight at slaughter.

**TABLE 14.4  Range of possible changes (relative to baseline) likely with increase in liveweight at slaughter**

| Liveweight at slaughter (kg) | Cumulative trends in food required (kg) per kg of liveweight gain | | Trends in backfat thickness at $P_2$ (mm) | | Trends in killing-out percentage | |
|---|---|---|---|---|---|---|
| | Smallest anticipated change | Largest anticipated change | Smallest anticipated change | Largest anticipated change | Smallest anticipated change | Largest anticipated change |
| 50 (*baseline*) | 2.50 | 2.5 | 8 | 8 | 73.0 | 73 |
| 60 | 2.56 | 2.7 | 9 | 10 | 73.5 | 74 |
| 70 | 2.62 | 2.9 | 10 | 12 | 74.0 | 75 |
| 80 | 2.68 | 3.1 | 11 | 14 | 74.5 | 76 |
| 90 | 2.74 | 3.3 | 12 | 16 | 75.0 | 77 |
| 100 | 2.80 | 3.5 | 13 | 18 | 75.5 | 78 |
| 110 | 2.86 | 3.7 | 14 | 20 | 76.0 | 79 |
| 120 | 2.92 | 3.9 | 15 | 22 | 76.5 | 80 |
| 130 | 2.98 | 4.1 | 16 | 24 | 77.0 | 81 |
| 140 | 3.04 | 4.3 | 17 | 26 | 77.5 | 82 |

## OTHER FACTORS WHICH VARY WITH SLAUGHTER WEIGHT

Other important factors which can vary with slaughter weight include:

- Carcass length
- Incidence of overlean carcasses
- Proportion of fat trim
- Incidence of boar taint in the meat from entire male pigs
- Value per kg of carcass
- Processing costs per kg of carcass
- Production costs per kg of carcass or lean meat produced

The relevance of these factors is outlined below.

## Carcass Length

Carcass length is taken into account in deciding grading on some systems. The longer carcasses in such grading systems are preferred mainly on the basis that long carcasses provide more (although smaller) rashers of back bacon. Over the carcass weight range of about 55 to 80 kg, length in Large White and Landrace pigs from the arterior end of the first rib to the anterior edge of the symphysis pubis increases by about 3 mm per 1 kg increase in carcass weight. Thus, if carcasses are being downgraded for being too short, a pig producer can estimate the increase in slaughter weight required to minimise this problem. Before a decision to increase slaughter weight is implemented, other associated changes, such as increased fatness, must be fully taken into account.

## Incidence of Overlean Carcasses

In Britain, backfat thickness of pig carcasses has been reduced markedly over the past 20 years in response to market demand. This has led to a situation at the present time in which there have been increasing complaints about reduced carcass and meat quality associated with very lean pigs. The meat processors' complaints about such pigs relate to floppy carcasses with soft fat which do not set and are difficult to butcher. In addition, in processing there tends to be separation of the layers of lean and subcutaneous fat which increases butchering problems and the difficulty of presenting attractive cuts in the retail outlet. Some consumers have complained about toughness and lack of succulence and flavour in the cooked meat. In addition, bacon curers have found that such very lean carcasses do not absorb the curing fluid as readily and so provide a lower yield of cured bacon.

If the demand from consumers and meat processors is to reduce the incidence of these problems, the producer can readily respond by producing carcasses with a higher percentage of fat. He can achieve this objective by manipulation of diet and feeding system or simply by growing his pigs to a heavier weight before slaughter.

## Proportion of Fat Trim

The extent to which carcass fat percentage increases with higher slaughter weight varies with such factors as genotype, sex, diet and feeding system (see Table 14.4). However, carcass fatness does increase markedly with increasing weight at slaughter and, as fatness increases above unacceptable levels, the surplus is wasted or at least can only command a relatively low price in the market relative to the cost of production. The amount of fat wasted relative to the backfat thickness ($P_2$) of the carcasses is highlighted in Figure 14.4.

The estimate of the amount of excess fat is based on the assumption that the average consumer eats one part of fat for every 5 parts of lean. The very marked increase in excess fat which either ends up as 'Retail trim' or as 'Preparation and plate waste' as backfat increases is obvious. The estimated amount of 'Retail trim'

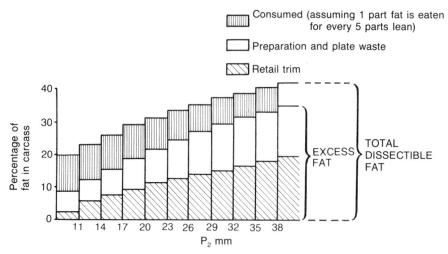

FIGURE 14.4  Estimates of excess fat in carcasses with different P₂ measurements. (From MLC, 1980)

from pig carcasses in Britain in 1980 was 67,000 tonnes with another 67,000 tonnes being lost in preparation and left on the plate. Increasing slaughter weight will, on average, be associated with thicker backfat and a higher proportion of waste fat.

### Incidence of Boar Taint in the Meat from Entire Male Pigs

The incidence of boar taint in meat from entire males increases as they approach and eventually reach puberty (see Plate 14.3, page 387). Since puberty is more a function of age than of liveweight, entire males must be grown quickly and slaughtered at a relatively young age if the incidence of boar taint is to be minimised. Thus, male pigs are not castrated in countries like Australia and the Irish Republic where weight (and age) at slaughter is relatively low. On the other hand, in countries such as Italy and the United states which produce pigs to heavy weights (and older ages) at slaughter, castration is standard practice. In Britain, on the other hand, male pigs for the light pork trade (40 to 50 kg carcasses) are normally left entire, whereas castration is more common when heavier carcasses (70 to 80 kg) are being produced for the bacon and 'heavy pig' markets.

### Value per Kg of Carcass

The value per kg of carcass of different weights will have a very large influence in helping the producer to decide on optimum weight at slaughter in his own particular situation. Average prices prevailing in Britain in November 1987 for pig carcasses in various weight ranges are summarised in Table 14.5, which shows that higher prices per kg prevail for lighter carcasses. The producer must examine these prices in relation to the cost of production per kg of carcass as a basis for deciding on optimum weight at slaughter in order to maximise financial returns.

**TABLE 14.5  Average price per kg for carcasses according to weight (based on prices prevailing in Britain in November 1987)**

| Carcass weight (kg) | Average price per kg carcass (pence) | Price index (Under 45 kg = 100) |
|---|---|---|
| Under 45 | 101.2 | 100 |
| 45—50 | 100.8 | 99.6 |
| 50—55 | 97.7 | 96.5 |
| 55—60 | 95.6 | 94.5 |
| 60—65 | 94.3 | 93.2 |
| 65—70 | 93.6 | 92.5 |
| >70 | 90.9 | 89.8 |

(From: MLC, 1988)

## Processing Costs per Kg of Carcass

The indications are that, at present, the labour costs involved in slaughtering and processing a light carcass are little different from those for a heavy one so that processing cost per kg of carcass or edible meat is less for heavy carcasses.

## Cost of Production in Relation to Slaughter Weight

Because food conversion efficiency in the growing—finishing pig deteriorates as the pig grows, the higher the slaughter weight, the greater the food cost per kg of pigmeat produced. However, the feeding herd cannot be kept in isolation from the breeding herd in trying to determine optimum slaughter weight. Hanrahan in Moorepark, in the Irish Republic, considered the breeding herd and the piglet up to 30 kg liveweight as well as the growing—finishing stage in determining optimum slaughter weight. On the basis of the data in Table 14.6, he claimed that in terms

**TABLE 14.6  Effect of slaughter weight on FCE — birth to slaughter including sow feed**

| Slaughter weight (kg liveweight) | FCE (kg food per kg liveweight gain) | |
|---|---|---|
| | 16W* | 18W* |
| 55 | 5.13 | 4.92 |
| 64 | 4.97 | 4.79 |
| 73 | 4.97 | 4.82 |
| 82 | 4.98 | 4.85 |
| 91 | 4.94 | 4.82 |
| 100 | 4.98 | 4.87 |
| 109 | 5.05 | 4.95 |
| 118 | 5.12 | 5.03 |

*W = weaners per sow per year
(From: Hanrahan, 1984)

of overall food conversion efficiency (for the breeding herd and from birth to slaughter) there was no real difference over a liveweight range at slaughter from 64 to 100 kg, whether this was based on a production of 16 or 18 weaned pigs per sow per year.

Within the growing–finishing period (30 kg to slaughter), incremental increases in slaughter weight of 9 kg were found to increase FCE by 0.15. However, if the sow's feed plus the feed consumed by the young pig up to 30 kg is taken into account, then it matters little whether pigs are slaughtered at 64 kg or 100 kg liveweight as shown in Table 14.6. This surprising result is due to the fact that the deterioration in food conversion efficiency as the pigs get heavier is exactly offset by spreading the overhead cost of the piglet over more kg of carcass.

Increasing sow output from 16 to 18 pigs is far more significant in that it improves FCE by about 3 per cent. If the boar advantage over the castrate is expressed in terms of total feed per kg carcass gain, the improvement is also about 3 per cent.

The Meat and Livestock Commission (1981) examined the total costs of producing pigmeat at different slaughter weights, basing their calculations on the records from their Pig Feed Recording Scheme. The results are summarised in Figure 14.5.

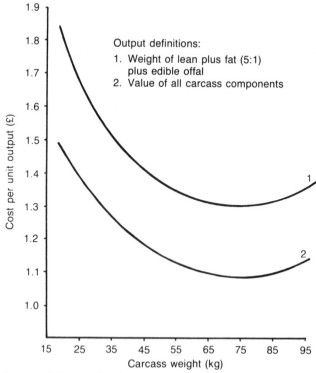

FIGURE 14.5   The relationship between cost per unit output and slaughter weight.

As indicated in the figure, calculations were based on the total costs of production per unit output of (a) lean meat plus fat (5 to 1 ratio) plus edible offal and (b) all carcass components including fat trim, bone and waste.

On both of these criteria it was found that optimum slaughter weight on the basis of lowest production cost per unit output applied to a carcass weight of about 75 kg with relatively little variation between 65 and 85 kg carcasses. Unit costs were considerably higher at light carcass weights (35 to 45 kg) and also at heavy carcass weights (95 kg and over). Thus, in order to justify slaughtering at light weights, the price obtained per kg of carcass must be considerably higher than that obtained for 65 to 85 kg carcasses. In the case of very heavy carcasses (95 kg and over) it is most unlikely that a higher price could be obtained per kg relative to that for 65 to 85 kg carcasses with the possible exception of Parma ham production in Italy. Therefore the only way production of such heavy carcasses can be justified in most circumstances is by reducing production costs such as those on feed, labour and buildings. As well as these foregoing considerations, optimum slaughter weight in any situation is likely to vary according to genotype and sex.

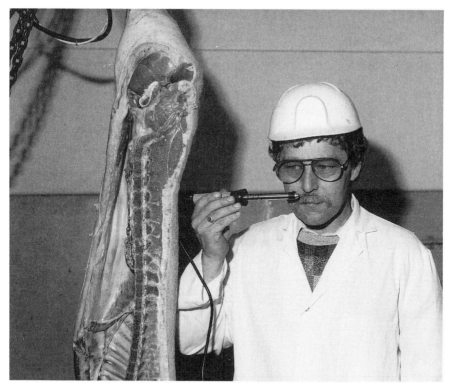

Plate 14.3  The hot wire test is used in some processing plants to test for the presence of boar taint in carcasses from entire male pigs. A heated wire is held against a small area of backfat. Sensitive testers can detect concentrations of androsterone as low as one part in several million. They may also look for other off-odours such as fish taint or the sewage-like odours skatole and indole.

## Optimum Carcass Weight — General Considerations

From the foregoing it will be appreciated that optimum carcass weight is likely to vary with circumstances, the main controlling variables being the price obtainable per unit weight of carcass and the production costs involved (including those of the breeding herd) in growing pigs to varying liveweights for slaughter.

## Additional Reading

Grimes, G., Carlisle, G. R., Ahcschwede, W. T., Philip, L. S. and Linden, O. 'Optimal Weight to Market Slaughter Hogs', *Pork Industry Handbook* **24**, Co-operative Extension Service, University of Illinois at Urbana-Champaign, USA.

*MLC Pig Yearbook* (1981), Meat and Livestock Commission, PO Box 44, Queensway House, Bletchley, Milton Keynes, England MK2 2EF.

*Chapter 15*

# Pigmeat Production Based on a Once-bred Gilt System

A major factor affecting the profitability of a growing−finishing pig enterprise is the cost of their incoming stock or weaners in relation to their quality. The lower the cost of a young pig of a specific quality, the more financially stable a growing−finishing enterprise becomes. While various approaches can be adopted to increase the efficiency of a conventional system of weaner pig production and so reduce the cost of production of the weaner, another method of producing weaners which is worthy of consideration is based on a once-bred gilt system. The possible basis and potential of such a system will now be considered.

It is logical to discuss such a system in a book on the growing pig because a once-bred gilt system could be considered as a means of extending an existing growing−finishing pig enterprise and of making it self-perpetuating without being dependent on a supply of weaners from a conventional sow-based system. However, there are several other arguments in favour of a system of meat production based on once-bred gilts.

## POTENTIAL ADVANTAGES OF A ONCE-BRED GILT SYSTEM

In theory, the efficiency of pig production can be increased by combining the two productive functions, growth and reproduction, simultaneously in the same animal. This is the underlying principle of the once-bred gilt whereby gilts are served at an early age and then, during their pregnancy, both nurture the growing foetuses and also grow their own tissues. These twin activities of growth and pregnancy are associated with only one element of maintenance food costs, thus spreading this considerable overhead over the two processes. The growth that is made is then exploited by slaughtering the gilts at the end of their first lactation and replacing them with another growing gilt for producing both piglets and meat. Following the process through, it can be seen readily that this is a biologically sustainable method of production since the replacement females for the system can be obtained from the litters born to gilts which were themselves bred at an earlier stage in the production cycle. An example of such a self-perpetuating system is outlined in Figure 15.1.

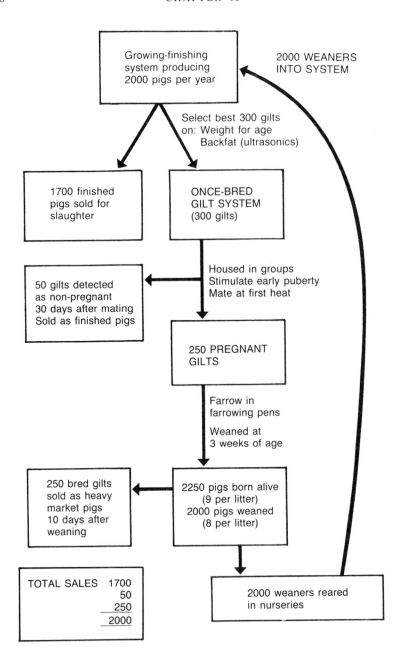

FIGURE 15.1  A self-perpetuating growing-finishing pig system involving once-bred gilts.

The production of once-bred gilts also serves to solve in a rather indirect way another problem emerging in Britain and other countries. This is associated with the difficulty of providing adequate welfare for the breeding sow over several parities. These problems arise because of the increasingly diverse size and body composition of members of the herd as they mature. Feeding in groups tends to increase this diversity and automatically results in fighting, particularly when sows are mixed after completing each lactation. Such problems of competition render individual feeding throughout pregnancy a virtual necessity, and to overcome these problems it is widespread practice to confine sows very closely in individual stalls during pregnancy and in farrowing pens during parturition and lactation over their working life. Problems associated with close confinement during pregnancy − a practice that has attracted considerable criticism on grounds of welfare − do not arise if the production system is based on the once-bred gilt.

Plate 15.1   A once-bred gilt system involves loose housing in fairly small groups during breeding and pregnancy.

## AN EXAMPLE OF A ONCE-BRED GILT SYSTEM

The example outlined in Figure 15.1 is that of a growing pig enterprise producing 2000 pigs for slaughter each year. The genotype used is a cross between Large White and Landrace strains. The unit is selling pigs for slaughter with a carcass weight varying from 70 to 130 kg. The system, which is basically a one-man operation, works as follows:

Plate 15.2 Once-bred gilts are biologically efficient. They can produce and nurse piglets and thereafter yield carcasses with an attractive lean content.

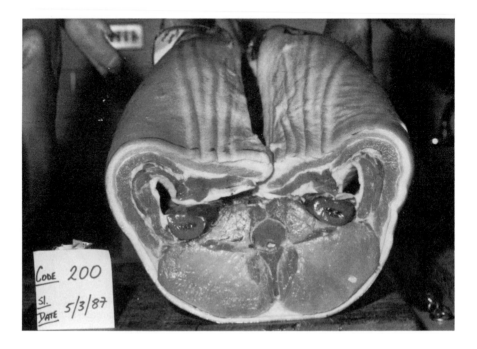

## Supply of Gilts

A total of 300 gilts are selected each year at about 140 days of age from the pig production unit. After ensuring that they possess the desirable attributes of sound breeding stock, based on visual examination, they are selected mainly on the basis of weight for age and ultrasonic backfat reading.

## Management to Service

Pigs are selected in uniform groups of 12 and placed in a conventional finishing pen of adequate size. They are trough-fed once daily on a level of 3.0 kg of a balanced diet (14 per cent crude protein and 13 MJ DE per kg). Two young fertile boars with a high performance rating are introduced to the pen from the time of selection and gilts are served at their first heat period. Service dates are recorded in so far as possible.

## Pregnancy

Gilts receive 3.0 kg of a balanced diet (13 MJ DE per kg and 14 per cent crude protein) daily given in one feed. Four weeks after service they are pregnancy tested and any found to be not in pig are culled and sold for meat.

## Farrowing

About 7 days before due to farrow date, or when udder development indicates imminent farrowing (if service date was not recorded), gilts are transferred to the farrowing quarters. Feeding level remains at 3.0 kg per day given in one feed.

At farrowing, piglet numbers and birthweight within litters are equalised by cross fostering so as to maximise piglet survival. Gilts suckle their piglets for about 21 days and during lactation are fed ad lib. on a diet with 16.5 per cent crude protein. Gilts are weaned in batches of 3 or 4 so as to secure uniform groups of piglets for the rearing pens.

At weaning, the gilt is penned along with others weaned at the same stage and fed ad lib. They remain in this group for a period of 10 days so as to dry off before slaughter.

Feeding and breeding policy over the whole period is designed so that at slaughter gilts will weigh 160 to 180 kg liveweight and thus yield 130 to 140 kg carcasses (assuming a killing out percentage of about 80).

## Rearing

On weaning at 21 days or about 5 to 6 kg liveweight, piglets are placed in conventional rearing accommodation and reared in a standard manner.

## ONCE-BRED GILT SYSTEMS IN PRACTICE

Once-bred gilt systems such as that outlined above have been suggested as a means of efficient production of pigmeat for a considerable time now, yet very few such systems are to be found in practice. There are several reasons for this.

A major criticism made on the basis of earlier research findings was that the quality of the carcass of the gilt after pregnancy and lactation was not good enough to merit a price above that paid for culled sows, this usually being 25 per cent or more below the price for carcasses of finished pigs. Most of the problems associated with the once-bred gilt carcass, however, could be attributed to the severely depleted body condition of the animals at slaughter as a result of attempts to keep the weight of the bred gilt carcass within the range of the traditional heavy pig (less than about 90 kg) and also because the length of the lactation was often 5 weeks or more.

New factors which now make the once-bred gilt a more attractive proposition are the following:

1. New methods of processing, for example, in-bag curing, now mean that the upper size of the carcass need not be the limiting factor it once was when whole carcasses were placed in curing tanks of limited size.
2. The increase in growth potential and mature size brought about by genetic selection now means that the gilt has more growth potential for lean tissue during the pregnancy period.
3. Better techniques of nutrition during lactation, for example, use of high density diets, make it possible to maintain body condition in lactation so that less fat is depleted and therefore the fat on the carcass does not become unacceptably soft and translucent.
4. New butchering methods have been developed along the lines used on the continent of Europe which allow heavier carcasses to be utilised efficiently in the production of a wide range of attractive retail joints.
5. There have been considerable advances in controlling the timing of oestrus so that gilts can be bred reliably at an early age.
6. If the gilts are allowed to eat at a rate well above maintenance, for example, at 4 kg of feed per day, then they will double their lean meat over pregnancy and the earlier criticism voiced by the meat trade relating to so-called emaciated carcasses and poor fat quality disappear.

## EFFICIENCY OF LEAN MEAT PRODUCTION FROM A ONCE-BRED GILT SYSTEM

Recent research work at the Rowett Institute and at the University of Newcastle now suggests that the cost of producing lean meat from the once-bred gilt is surprisingly efficient. Table 15.1 presents calculations of the relative efficiency of producing lean meat from conventional and once-bred gilt systems of pigmeat production.

Thus, the calculated lean tissue food conversion efficiencies are 8.6 from the conventional system and 3.99 from the once-bred gilt system. The relative efficiencies will change slightly if the assumptions on which the calculations are based change. The conventional system as laid out is already a very efficient one with a whole herd feed conversion efficiency (on a liveweight basis) of 3.1 (310 kg food, including share of sow and boar food per 100 kg carcass produced). Of course, food conversion efficiency based on both liveweight and lean tissue could be improved even further on this conventional system by increasing the output of weaners per sow per year and by improving food to gain ratio from 5 to 100 kg liveweight.

**TABLE 15.1   Relative lean tissue food conversion efficiency (LTFC) from conventional and once-bred gilt systems of pigmeat production**

**Conventional system**

Based on breeding sows in regular ages
Progeny slaughtered at 100 kg liveweight to produce a 75 kg carcass

*Feed requirements per pig produced to 100 kg liveweight*

a) Share of food allowance to sows and boars in herd
(to take pigs to 3 weeks of age and 5 kg liveweight)

| | | |
|---|---|---|
| Total food allowance per sow per year (including share of boar feed) | = | 1100 kg |
| Pigs sold per sow per year | = | 22 |
| Share of sow and boar feed per pig sold $= \dfrac{1.1 \text{ tonnes}}{22 \text{ pigs}}$ | = | 50 kg |

b) Food required per pig from 5 to 100 kg liveweight

| | | |
|---|---|---|
| 5 to 30 kg liveweight at food:gain ratio of 2:1 (2 × 25) | = | 50 kg |
| 30 to 100 kg liveweight at food:gain ratio of 3:1 (3 × 70) | = | 210 kg |
| Total food requirement per 100 kg pig (including share of sow and boar food) | = | 310 kg |

*Lean meat produced*

| | | |
|---|---|---|
| Liveweight at slaughter | = | 100 kg |
| Carcass weight (killing out percentage of 75) | = | 75 kg |
| Lean content of carcass (48%) | = | 36 kg |

*Lean tissue food conversion efficiency (LTFC)*

| | | |
|---|---|---|
| Total food requirement per 100 kg pig (including share of sow and boar feed) | = | 310 kg |
| Total lean produced by a 100 kg liveweight pig | = | 36 kg |
| LTFC $= \dfrac{310 \text{ kg feed}}{36 \text{ kg lean}}$ | = | 8.6 |

## Once-bred gilt system

a) *Food intake of a once-bred gilt*
   *from selection at 100 kg liveweight to slaughter*

|  |  |
|---|---|
| 120 days from premating through pregnancy at 3.0 kg per day | = 360 kg |
| 31 days from farrowing to slaughter at 5 kg per day (21 day lactation + 10 days for drying off) | = 155 kg |
| Total | = 515 kg (A) |

b) *Food allowance for piglets produced to 5 kg liveweight*

8 pigs weaned per litter
Allowance of 50 kg per pig produced
to equate with food requirement per
pig produced to 5 kg liveweight from
the conventional system

∴  8 pigs at 50 kg per pig                = 400 kg   (B)

c) *Net food requirement of extra lean produced*
   *from the once-bred gilt carcass*

(After allowance for production of
8 piglets at 5 kg)
i.e. Subtract (B) from (A)              = 115 kg

d) *Extra lean from once-bred gilt carcass*
   *relative to the carcass from the pig*
   *slaughtered at the conventional stage*
   *of 100 kg liveweight*

| Liveweight of once-bred gilt at slaughter | = 180 kg |
|---|---|
| Carcass weight of once-bred gilt (killing out percentage of 75) | = 135 kg |
| Lean content of carcass (48%) | = 64.8 kg (C) |
| Lean content of pig slaughtered at 100 kg liveweight on the conventional system | = 36 kg (D) |

∴  Additional lean from once-bred gilt carcass
   Subtract (D) from (C)                = 28.8 kg

e) *Feed conversion efficiency of additional*
   *lean produced from the once-bred gilt*

| Net food requirement of extra lean produced | = 115 kg |
|---|---|
| Additional lean from the once-bred gilt | = 28.8 kg |

LTFC                $= \dfrac{115}{28.8}$                = 3.99

Likewise, the efficiency of food conversion in the once-bred gilt system could be increased by rearing more pigs per litter and it could be reduced by such mismanagement as allowing the gilt to lose excessive weight in lactation by underfeeding or through the use of an inadequate diet in terms of protein quality.

However, if such mismanagement is avoided, the indications from the data presented in Table 15.1 are that lean tissue food conversion efficiency can be considerably better on a well-operated once-bred gilt system than from an equally well-run conventional system of pigmeat production.

A once-bred gilt system also has several additional interesting possibilities.

## ADDITIONAL ATTRACTIONS OF A ONCE-BRED GILT SYSTEM

### Genetic Improvement

It is obvious from the once-bred gilt system outlined in Figure 15.1 that a new generation of breeding gilts is produced from the base population each year. This very rapid generation turnover provides an opportunity to achieve fairly rapid genetic improvement, provided care is taken in the purchase of boars and in the within-herd selection of replacement gilts. If selection of replacement gilts is based on weight for age and absence of fat as detected by ultrasonics, this constitutes an effective way of increasing lean tissue growth rate. Improvement of lean tissue food conversion should be associated with this improvement in lean tissue growth rate. Replacement boars which are purchased should be selected on the same criteria. If boars have been partly evaluated on the growth and carcass attributes of sibs, then very useful information on lean and fat quality attributes should be available as a basis of selection. Attention to aspects of quality of lean and fatty tissue should ensure that these important characteristics do not deteriorate and might in fact improve in successive generations.

### A Complement to a Conventional Sow System

A possible variant of a once-bred gilt system which could improve its economic viability is its use as a complement to a conventional sow system. This would involve slaughter as once-bred gilts only of those animals with lower levels of output in terms of number and quality of piglets born and weaned. The most productive gilts would be kept as the foundation of the complementary conventional sow herd. This approach is likely to be more effective in a herd in which the repeatability of gilt litter size is reasonably high. The potential for using this approach in the appropriate circumstances can be demonstrated from the data in the following Tables.

In Table 15.2, it is clear that gilts which produce 12 or more pigs in the first litter averaged 11.4 in the second litter. Those producing between 9 and 11 piglets as a gilt had in excess of 10 born, on average, in the second litter. On the other hand, gilts having 8 or less in the first litter averaged less than 9 born in the second litter. Thus, if the less prolific sows in this sample were culled after weaning their first litter and the more productive ones kept to produce a second litter, performance of second litter sows would be enhanced relative to the situation which usually prevails in sow herds, that is, that gilts are not culled on the basis of first litter size

**TABLE 15.2  Number of pigs born in litter 2 relative to number born in litter 1**

| | Total pigs born in first litter | | | | | | | |
| --- | --- | --- | --- | --- | --- | --- | --- | --- |
| | <5 | 6 | 7 | 8 | 9 | 10 | 11 | >12 |
| Number of sows | 62 | 39 | 90 | 120 | 168 | 172 | 150 | 207 |
| Age at first farrowing (days) | 363 | 356 | 357 | 355 | 361 | 354 | 372 | 376 |
| Total pigs born second litter | 9.7$^{de}$ | 8.7$^{cd}$ | 8.2$^{c}$ | 8.6$^{cd}$ | 10.3$^{ef}$ | 10.4$^{ef}$ | 10.6$^{f}$ | 11.4$^{g}$ |
| Pigs born alive second litter | 8.7$^{d}$ | 8.1$^{cd}$ | 7.8$^{c}$ | 8.0$^{cd}$ | 9.4$^{de}$ | 9.6$^{e}$ | 9.8$^{e}$ | 10.4$^{f}$ |
| First farrowing interval (days)[a] | 160 | 162 | 164 | 162 | 164 | 164 | 165 | 165 |

[a] Farrowing interval calculated from one farrowing date to the next.
c,d,e,f,g Means on the same line with different superscripts differ significantly (P <.05)
(Source: Chapman, Thompson, Gaskins and Tribble, 1978, Texas Tech. University)

**TABLE 15.3  Average number born per litter in litters 2 to 6 relative to number born in litter 1**

| | Number Sows | Size of gilt litter | | | |
| --- | --- | --- | --- | --- | --- |
| | | Smallest 25% (Sector 1) | 2nd Smallest 25% (Sector 2) | 2nd Largest 25% (Sector 3) | Largest 25% (Sector 4) |
| Herd A | 200 | 10.5 | 10.7 | 10.7 | 11.5 |
| B | 267 | 9.4 | 9.7 | 10.1 | 10.5 |
| C | 155 | 11.1 | 10.8 | 10.9 | 11.7 |
| D | 117 | 11.2 | 10.8 | 11.3 | 11.7 |
| E | 129 | 10.2 | 10.7 | 11.2 | 10.9 |
| F | 132 | 9.1 | 10.4 | 10.0 | 11.1 |
| Weighted average | 1000 | 10.2 | 10.4 | 10.6 | 11.1 |

(Source: English, Bark, MacPherson and Birnie, 1984)

but are given at least a second chance to produce a litter with reasonable numbers.

The data in Table 15.3 relate first litter size to the average subsequent litter size in parities 2 to 6. It is clear in many herds that the more prolific gilts tend to be more productive in terms of numbers born in subsequent parities. Take, for example, Herd F. If a once-bred gilt system was in operation, the 75 per cent less prolific gilts (Sectors 1 to 3) could be slaughtered after weaning their litters. However, the most prolific 25 per cent of gilts (Sector 4) would not be slaughtered but would be retained as the replacements for a conventional breeding herd of sows. In this herd, the numbers born in parities 2 to 6 in the 25 per cent of sows which were the most prolific as gilts would result in an increase in average litter size of about 1.3 (11.1 for Sector 4 relative to 9.8 as the mean for Sectors 1, 2 and 3) relative to the situation where all sows were retained to produce more litters regardless of their level of prolificacy as gilts.

It is obvious, therefore, that while a system of meat production based on once-bred gilts can be justifiable in its own right in the appropriate situation, a once-bred gilt system can also be operated as a useful complement to a conventional sow herd in situations analogous to those outlined in Tables 15.2 and 15.3.

## Conclusions

A system of once-bred gilts adds a new dimension to the possibilities of meat production from pigs. There are clear biological advantages but these are to some extent offset by suspicion in the market place which results in the price offered by the processor being below the real value of the carcass. This suspicion arises because of a lack of trust between producer and processor whereby the processor feels that sows that have had several litters might be passed off as once-bred gilts. However, when the level of trust is sufficiently high, for example, where producer and processor are under the same overall management, then the technique has tremendous possibilities. For example, at present, Parma ham production requires a carcass of about 140 kg. This could be produced economically from once-bred gilts. There are also new opportunities for large joints not based on traditional butchering. For example, the large loin muscle can be removed easily as an entity and sold as a high-value fresh or cured product. The large muscles of the shoulder are also more easily removed in carcasses from these animals than from lighter carcasses and therefore can be manufactured more easily into added value products.

The system will not be popular with breeding companies which sell gilts, because the relatively high cost of an improved hybrid gilt cannot be justified if she only breeds once. However, the use of selected boars or AI and on-farm gilt selection can ensure that perfectly adequate genetic progress is achieved.

Finally, not only does the system produce cheaper lean meat but it provides greater flexibility in housing and feeding systems than can be used for the adult sow. In general, housing for pregnant gilts will be considerably cheaper than for a conventional sow herd.

*Chapter 16*

# Controlling Carcass and Meat Quality

Before describing the basic approaches for controlling carcass and meat quality, the main components of these parameters will be outlined.

## COMPONENTS OF MEAT QUALITY

Wood (1986) of the Meat Research Institute in Bristol defined meat quality as all those characteristics of the carcass other than its leanness or fatness which determine its value to the butcher and consumer. He divided these into (1) visual, (2) handling or butchery and (3) eating aspects. He pointed out that the importance attached to each of these varies with the requirement of the user.

Some of the characteristics will now be described in more detail.

### Visual Aspects

The most obvious aspect of quality as assessed visually is the ratio of lean to fat, but impressions of freshness and colour are also very important. In Britain, pale and dark meats are disliked and these characteristics can be associated with the respective problems of PSE (pale, soft, exudative) muscle and DFD (dark, firm, dry) meat. In cuts of meat which include the skin as in the 'crackling' of pork cuts, damage to the skin constitutes a serious problem.

### Handling or Butchery Aspects

Butchers like carcasses which are firm and well set because they are easier to cut and the joints maintain their shape as distinct from 'floppy' carcasses which do not 'set to the knife' and therefore increase problems in traditional methods of processing. Such carcasses which fail to set or firm up are often very lean and the fat soft. Separation often occurs between the different layers of subcutaneous fat and between fat and lean and thus makes it more difficult to present attractive cuts to discriminating customers in retail displays in shops and supermarkets. These separation factors and also soft fat are both features of very lean carcasses. Soft fat can also result from excessive restriction of feed intake during the finishing stages and from excessive amounts of unsaturated fats or oils in the diet.

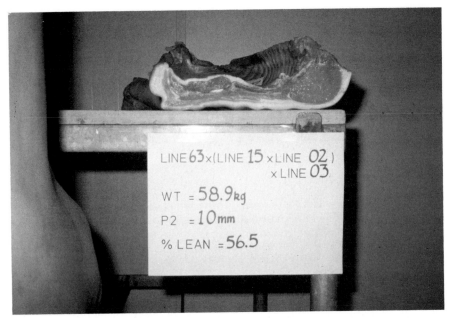

LINE 63 x (LINE 15 x LINE 02 )
                              x LINE 03

WT = 58.9 kg

P2 = 10 mm

% LEAN = 56.5

Plate 16.1   A carcass with good muscle depth and about 10 mm of backfat at $P_2$ which many experts consider the correct level of fatness to meet the requirements of most consumers in the UK. The general demand is for a low level of fatness but yet enough fat both to provide carcasses which set well after slaughter (which makes for easier butchering) and to produce cooked meat which has the desired qualities of tenderness, juiciness and flavour. (Courtesy of Meat and Livestock Commission)

## Eating Aspects

'Quality' from the consumer's viewpoint is difficult to define accurately, partly because tastes differ between consumers and partly due to the fact that the consumer distinguishes between 'good' and 'less good' meat on the basis of an overall assessment rather than on a careful analysis of what is good and less good about the many individual components of quality which are important.

The main features of quality to the consumer are tenderness, juiciness and flavour and these three tend to interact to form an overall impression during eating. All of these factors are influenced by the marbling and general fat content of the meat and by the method of cooking. The marbling fat is contained within the muscles and thus is termed the intramuscular fat. It cannot be trimmed off by the butcher as can subcutaneous and intermuscular (that between the muscles) fat. Marbling fat constitutes a small proportion (1 to 5 per cent) of the meat from which the subcutaneous and intermuscular fat have been trimmed by the butcher in the preparation of ultra lean meat.

Taint in the meat is also an important component of meat quality to the consumer. Such off-flavours include fishy taint, boar taint and that of skatole and indole. Fishy taint tends to be caused by inclusion of high levels of fish oils in the finishing diet, particularly when these have been oxidised or allowed to go rancid. The main com-

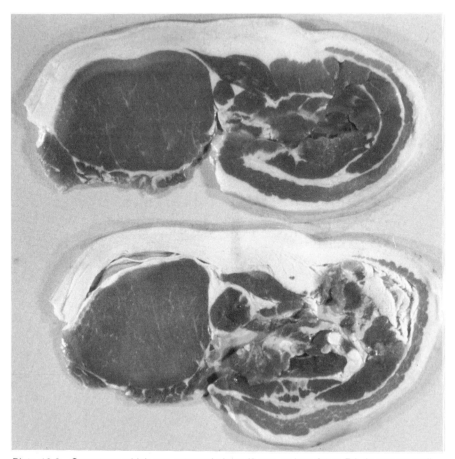

Plate 16.2 Carcasses which are extremely lean (6 mm or less fat at $P_2$) do not set well and are difficult to butcher. There is also a tendency for separation between fat and lean and between fat layers, which creates difficulties in terms of presenting attractive cuts in retail outlets. (Courtesy of Meat and Livestock Commission)

ponent of boar taint is a derivative of the male sex pheromone androstenone while skatole and indole are products of the bacterial breakdown of amino acids in the intestines. While boar taint tends to be associated exclusively with the meat from entire male pigs which approached sexual maturity at the time of slaughter, skatole and indole can be found in the meat of any of the sexes — gilts, castrates and entire males — although the concentration of these latter two tends to be higher in the meat of the entire male. As a guide to these odours, the smell of boar taint has been likened to that of stale perspiration or unclean urinals. Skatole and indole have the characteristic odour of sewage.

To an increasing degree, meat quality from the viewpoint of the consumer now includes nutritional or health aspects. Consumers are being made aware of the current medical opinion that the consumption of saturated fats is associated with coronary heart disease, high blood pressure and obesity.

Plate 16.3   Meat with PSE (pale, soft, exudative) muscle is characteristic of pigs which are halothane reactors (which have the recessive halothane gene in double dose). Following slaughter, the acidity of the meat of such pigs falls very sharply. This sudden fall in pH has an adverse effect on the water-holding capacity of the lean tissue, resulting in considerable 'drip' loss from the carcass and often an undesirable two-toned appearance in a cross-sectional cut of lean meat. (Courtesy of J.D. Wood, Food Research Institute, Bristol)

## CONTROLLING CARCASS AND MEAT QUALITY

The major component of carcass and meat quality is the lean to fat ratio and the control of this component will be outlined before dealing with the improvement of other aspects. Other important aspects include lean to bone ratio, the proportion of lean in the expensive parts and depth of muscle above the bone. Also of great importance is the image of pigmeat in the minds of consumers as influenced by such considerations as the method of production of the product (see Chapter 4).

### Consumer Requirements in Relation to Lean to Fat Ratio

Over the past 20 years in Britain, thickness of subcutaneous fat has been reduced at an average rate of 0.45 mm per year. Despite such an impressive reduction in fatness, average lean to fat ratio of slaughtered pigs at present (1988) is 3 parts of lean to 1 part of fat. Kempster (1987) of the Meat and Livestock Commission states that the typical consumer is almost certainly moving towards ratios greater than 5 parts lean to 1 part of fat, while the Super-Trim Campaign initiated by MLC and aimed at the highly lean conscious consumer is based on ratios of 10 to 1 or effectively the trimming of all 'trimmable' fat.

While there will continue to be wide variation in demand between consumers in Britain and in all other countries regarding the lean to fat ratio desired in pigmeat, there is undeniably a strong tendency for the average consumer to demand less and less fat in the meat.

The proportion of fat in pigmeat as presented in retail outlets can be controlled in two ways:

1. Controlled on the farm by manipulation of such factors as genotype, sex, diet, level of feeding and slaughter weight.
2. Controlled in the processing plant by trimming off surplus fat so that trimmed cuts have exactly the correct ratio of lean to fat demanded by the consumer.

The major factors involved in these two procedures to meet consumer demand and the main implications of each approach will now be outlined.

## 1. Producing the Correct Lean to Fat Ratio on the Farm

Certain pigmeat processing methods oblige the producer to 'tailor' the pig or control its growth on the farm so that the resulting carcass provides the consumer through the meat processor with the correct ratio of lean to fat. These methods in-

Plate 16.4 Carcasses undergoing the Wiltshire curing process in brine tanks. The Wiltshire cure, popular in both the UK and Denmark, involves the curing of the intact side with the skin on. Thus, carcasses with the correct lean to fat ratio for this market must be tailored on the farm by such practices as choice of genotype, correct diet formulation, controlled feeding and slaughter at the appropriate weight. (Courtesy of Pig International)

clude the production of pork in Britain with the skin or 'crackling' presented as an integral component of the pork joint. The Wiltshire type method of curing pigmeat also involves the curing of the whole side with the skin intact. To ensure that the resulting 'rind-on' rashers of bacon have the correct ratio of lean to fat required by the consumer, the deposition of fat on such pigs must obviously be controlled on the farm.

The traditional approach to achieve the correct lean to fat ratio in the carcass has been through the carcass grading system. This has been based on the thickness of subcutaneous fat which is closely related to the percentage of carcass fat. The lower the percentage of carcass fat, the higher is the percentage of lean.

## Methods of Reducing Fatness

The approaches to reducing fatness in pigs produced for such markets in order to improve grading are well established. They include genetic improvement, aspects of diet and control of feed intake, exploiting the differences between boars, castrates and gilts and controlling slaughter weight. These will be dealt with briefly in turn.

1.  GENETIC IMPROVEMENT

From about 1970 there has been a steady reduction of about 0.45 mm per year in the $P_2$ backfat measurement of pigs at slaughter in Britain. Advances such as improved diets, better control over feeding level and reduced incidence of castration will have contributed to this improvement, but the genetic contribution to this reduction in fatness will almost certainly have been the major one. This has been a magnificent achievement by the efforts of the Meat and Livestock Commission through their Pig Improvement Scheme, by private breeders and by the considerable strides made by the pig breeding companies. Thus, genetically, we have much leaner strains of pig in Britain now than we had 15 years or so ago. Similarly impressive progress in reducing fatness in pigs has been made in other countries where this has been a priority.

2.  RATIO OF PROTEIN AND ESSENTIAL AMINO ACIDS TO ENERGY LEVEL IN THE DIET

In any feeding programme, any restriction in the growth of lean meat should be minimised as far as possible, consistent with controlling fat deposition. The building bricks for lean tissue are the essential amino acids in the protein compo-

TABLE 16.1  Lysine requirement according to liveweight and energy intake (based on pigs of exceptionally good genetic quality)

|  | Liveweight (kg) | | | | |
| --- | --- | --- | --- | --- | --- |
|  | 10 | 30 | 50 | 70 | 90 |
| Lysine required per unit of energy (g lysine per MJ DE) | 1.03 | 0.79 | 0.72 | 0.63 | 0.59 |

(Source: Agricultural Research Council, 1981)

nent of the diet and the most limiting amino acid in the diet in the United Kingdom is usually lysine. The lysine requirement of the pig varies according to its stage of growth as indicated in Table 16.1. Thus, it is very important that the diet offered should have the correct ratio of lysine and other essential amino acids to its energy concentration in order to cater adequately for the lean tissue growth potential of the pigs involved.

The ability of a diet with the correct ratio of essential amino acids to energy to positively stimulate lean tissue growth and therefore result in a carcass with a higher ratio of lean to fat at a specific slaughter weight is illustrated in Figure 16.1.

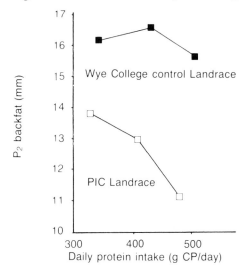

FIGURE 16.1 Comparison of backfats in a selected and control line. (Source: Dalgety-Spillers Wye 6 Trial, 1979)

It is obvious that increasing the daily provision of protein and essential amino acids by increasing their concentration in the diet achieved little or no response in terms of increased lean to fat ratio and therefore in reduced fatness in the relatively unimproved Wye College control Landrace. However, in the genetically advanced PIC Landrace, a marked improvement in lean to fat ratio and in reduced fatness in the pig at slaughter was achieved as a result of increasing daily provision of essential amino acids in relation to energy intake. As daily intake of protein was increased from about 400 to 480 g over the 30 to 90 kg liveweight range, backfat thickness at $P_2$ decreased by 2 mm (from 13 to about 11 mm).

The 'protein' referred to here is highly related to the concept of ideal protein described in Chapter 9. Whether or not a pig will respond to increased daily provision of protein and essential amino acids relative to energy is dependent on both its genetic potential for lean tissue growth and the adequacy of its present diet. This is exemplified in Figure 16.1. At the lowest level of daily protein intake, the Wye College control Landrace was already obtaining sufficient since increases above this basal level produced no further response. On the other hand, the lean tissue growth potential of the PIC Landrace was obviously not being fully expressed at this basal level of daily provision of protein and essential amino acids since the response in terms of lean to fat tissue growth and reduction in fatness by slaughter was quite dramatic with increased protein intake.

Thus, each pig producer must put his own specific genotype to the test in terms of optimum daily provision of protein. Providing progressive increases above present daily provision of protein and testing the response in terms of liveweight gain, food conversion efficiency, lean to fat ratio and thickness of subcutaneous fat in the carcass will provide the answer as to whether present daily provision of essential amino acids relative to energy is adequate or inadequate.

3. RESTRICTION OF FOOD OR ENERGY INTAKE

With any diet, the amount consumed daily by a growing pig has well-established effects on the lean to fat ratio of the carcass, and restriction of daily food intake during growth has been one of the most commonly used methods of controlling the thickness of subcutaneous fat and of fat percentage in bacon pigs produced for the demanding Wiltshire type cure market. As indicated above, different genotypes of pig vary in the relative rates of lean and fatty tissue growth and therefore in the lean to fat ratios of a specific weight of carcass (when the same diet has been fed at similar daily intakes). The fatter genotypes require more control of feed intake during growth than leaner genotypes in order to produce carcasses of similar lean to fat ratio. Food restriction succeeds in increasing lean to fat ratio in the final carcass because it reduces daily deposition of fatty tissue to a greater extent than that of lean tissue. Nevertheless, such restriction also results in serious reductions in the daily gain of liveweight and lean tissue (see Table 16.2). This data has been calculated from the results of the Commercial Product Evaluation Programme of the Meat and Livestock commission in the United Kingdom which evaluated the commercial products or 'hybrids' produced by United Kingdom breeding companies and private breeders.

**TABLE 16.2   Effect of decreases of 0.1 kg in daily food intake from a mean daily intake of 2.5 kg of a balanced diet (13 MJ DE per kg) between 25 and 90 kg liveweight**

| Factor | Effect of 0.1 kg per day reduction in food intake | Associated effects of reducing backfat at $P_2$ by 1 mm |
|---|---|---|
| Daily liveweight gain | minus 35 g | minus 70 g |
| Food conversion ratio | 0 | 0 |
| Daily lean tissue gain | minus 11 g | minus 22 g |
| $P_2$ backfat at 90 kg liveweight | minus 0.52 mm | minus 1.04 mm (say, 1 mm) |

(From: ARC, 1981)

From Table 16.2 it can be estimated that if a producer wished to reduce mean $P_2$ backfat at 90 kg liveweight by 1 mm he would have to reduce feed intake by an average of 0.2 kg daily between 25 and 90 kg. The penalties for achieving this reduction in $P_2$ backfat would be a reduction of about 22 g daily in lean tissue growth and a reduction in daily liveweight gain of about 70 g. When imposing this degree of restriction, there could be no effects whatsoever on food conversion efficiency because although the slower growth would entail keeping the pig for a longer period, thus incurring higher feed requirements for maintenance, the pig at 90 kg would have deposited less fat and more lean. Since lean meat requires considerably less feed than fat deposition, this improved ratio of lean to fat would effectively save feed and almost exactly balance out the extra food required for maintenance. It would only be in cases of very severe feed restriction (less than 70 per cent of appetite) or with odd genotypes that food conversion efficiency would be affected by varying daily food intake.

If, as is more common, a producer wished to feed ad lib. up to about 50 kg liveweight and restrict feed intake thereafter, he would have to reduce daily food intake by about 0.3 kg per day in order to reduce backfat at $P_2$ by 1 mm. Such a reduction in feed intake over this period would be likely to reduce daily liveweight gain by about 100 g and increase the period to reach 90 kg liveweight by about 7 days.

Thus, each producer in imposing greater food restriction must assess the balance between lower backfat, better grading and higher carcass value on the one hand and slower growth and lowered throughput on the other. Calculating where the optimum balance lies is discussed later in Chapter 20.

### 4. DIFFERENCES BETWEEN BOARS, CASTRATES AND GILTS

Relative to castrated males, on the same daily feed intake, boars will achieve considerably better feed conversion efficiency and at 90 kg liveweight will have at least 2 mm less backfat at $P_2$. Gilts will be in an intermediate position, with backfat thickness being about 1 mm less than that in castrates and 1 mm greater than that in boars. Thus, carcass grading based on backfat will be better in boars than in gilts and better in gilts than in castrates.

Before a producer can exploit these advantages of the entire male he must reach an agreement with his meat processor regarding (a) the acceptability of boars and (b) the level, if any, of any price penalty to be imposed on boars relative to castrates. It would appear that just over half the male pigs in the United Kingdom are now left entire but a higher proportion of entire males will be marketed at lighter weights for pork than at the heavier weights required for the bacon market. The proportion of entire males marketed relative to castrates is likely to increase further provided that they are grown quickly and slaughtered well before sexual maturity (so as to minimise the incidence of boar taint) and that they are not excessively lean. The quick growth required to ensure slaughter at a young age should help to ensure that boars also have adequate fat cover except at very low slaughter weights.

As indicated in Chapter 13, largely because of differences in lean tissue growth potential, the requirements of the entire male for essential amino acids from about 50 kg liveweight to slaughter are about 20 per cent higher than those of the castrate and some 10 per cent higher than those of the gilt. Thus, if lean tissue growth rate potential is to be expressed with minimal wastage of expensive protein, a sound case can be made for providing diets with different ratios of amino acids to energy for the three sexes, at least in the later growth stages.

If entire males, castrates and gilts are to be slaughtered at the same weight, then to achieve equivalent lean to fat ratio and thickness of subcutaneous fat, the feed intake of the gilt must be restricted relative to that of the boar while the most severe

**TABLE 16.3  Approximate degree of feed restriction to be applied to gilts and castrates to attain equivalent backfat ($P_2$) as entire males by 90 kg liveweight and the consequences of such restriction**

| | 25–90 kg | | | 50–90 kg | | |
| Reduction in: | Entire male | Gilt | Castrate | Entire male | Gilt | Castrate |
|---|---|---|---|---|---|---|
| Daily food intake (kg) | 0 | 0.2 | 0.4 | 0 | 0.3 | 0.6 |
| Daily liveweight gain (g) | 0 | 70 | 140 | 0 | 105 | 210 |
| Daily LTGR (g) | 0 | 22 | 44 | 0 | 33 | 66 |
| FCR | 0 | 0 | 0 | 0 | 0 | 0 |
| $P_2$ backfat (mm) | 0 | 1 | 2 | 0 | 1 | 2 |
| Increase in days to slaughter | 0 | 6 | 12 | 0 | 6 | 12 |

(Calculations based on an average daily feed intake of the entire male of 2.5 kg of a balanced diet (13 MJ DE per kg) between 25 and 90 kg liveweight and a daily rate of liveweight gain over this stage of 875 g)

restriction must be applied to the castrate. Since for pigs of improved genotype, $P_2$ backfat will be, on average, some 1 mm less in the gilt relative to the castrate and a further 1 mm less in the entire male, the relative degrees of food restriction which would have to be imposed on the gilt and castrate relative to the entire male can be calculated from the data presented on the effects of feed restriction on page 408.

Recommendations applicable to improved genotypes are summarised in Table 16.3. Here we see that while in terms of lean to fat ratio it is possible to produce as good carcasses from gilts and castrates as from entire males by feed restriction, this is not achieved without penalties. The penalties for the castrate are considerable reductions in the rate of gain of liveweight and lean tissue and almost 2 weeks longer to reach slaughter weight. The penalties imposed by feed restriction on the gilt are half those on the castrate. The provision of different diets (varying in the ratio of essential amino acids to energy), and/or the imposition of different degrees of food restriction to the different sexes, necessitates separate penning of the sexes or split-sex feeding. If pigs at weaning are put into large groups, the sexes can be separated into smaller pens at a later stage. Otherwise, penning the sexes separately from weaning is easier and has fewer potential post-mixing problems than repenning and mixing pigs at a later stage. The alternative approach for producing carcasses with the same lean to fat ratio in the three sexes is to slaughter the gilts and castrates at lighter weights. This approach to reduce backfat and improve lean to fat ratio will now be considered for pigs of varying genetic merit and for the different sexes.

5.  SLAUGHTER AT LIGHTER WEIGHTS

Since deposition of fatty tissue relative to lean accelerates as the pig matures, a useful approach to reduce carcass fatness and improve grading in some situations is to slaughter at a lower liveweight. For modern improved genotypes and for a given sex of pig within a farm, a useful approximation to use is that for each 5 kg reduction in liveweight at slaughter or each 4 kg reduction in carcass weight, backfat at $P_2$ will be reduced by about 1 mm.

Since following reasonable and equivalent levels of feed intake of good-quality diets during growth, boars from improved genotypes slaughtered around 90 kg liveweight will have about 2 mm less fat at $P_2$ than castrates and 1 mm less than gilts, this means that to produce carcasses of equivalent backfat at $P_2$, castrates should be slaughted at 80 kg and gilts at 85 kg liveweight.

### Producers' Reactions to Increased Demand for Less Fat Carcasses

Since meat processors in Britain have demanded lower and lower levels of backfat if pigs are to achieve top carcass grading and the highest prices per kg of carcass, pig producers have attempted to respond by slimming their pigs by some or all of the approaches cited above, including the reduction of slaughter weight. This has been an unfortunate trend since average carcass weight in some cases has been reduced below the most desirable range of 65 to 85 kg which, in most circumstances, is associated with maximum efficiency of production (see Chapter 14).

Thus, in responding to the need to produce leaner carcasses in Britain, some approaches can be applied without incurring penalties, whereas other approaches can incur considerable ones.

### Approaches to Increasing Lean to Fat Ratio in Carcasses which do not Incur Penalties in Other Directions

1. Genetic improvement for lean tissue growth rate
2. Cessation of castration (provided entire male pigs are grown quickly and slaughtered well before attaining sexual maturity so as to eliminate the risk of boar taint)
3. Provision of diets with the appropriate ratio of protein (and essential amino acids) to energy (although these may cost more per tonne of diet, they should be more cost effective)

### Approaches to Increasing Lean to Fat Ratio Which do Incur Penalties in Other Directions

1. Increased food restriction (because of reduction in liveweight and lean tissue gain and longer growth period)
2. Lower slaughter weight (because carcass weight may be reduced below the optimum range associated with maximum efficiency of production)

Because of the penalties imposed by some ways of reducing backfat thickness and increasing lean to fat ratio in slaughtered pigs, it is important to look at the strength of the incentives for reducing backfat and to consider alternative approaches to reduce carcass fatness which might help to minimise some of the adverse consequences of methods now employed.

## Basis of Carcass Grading Current in Britain

The carcass grading and pricing systems represented in Figure 16.2 represent the two basic approaches current in Britain in 1988. The system operated by Processor 1 is the traditional one. Carcasses with fat thickness at $P_2$ of less than 15 mm qualify for the top grade and the top price. Carcasses with a $P_2$ between 15 and 16 mm are demoted to Grade 2 and receive a 7 per cent price penalty per kg, while carcasses with a $P_2$ in excess of 16 mm go into Grade 3 and, relative to Grade 1, have a massive 21 per cent price penalty imposed.

Processor 2 is paying a bonus of 1 per cent relative to Processor 1 for top grade carcasses but excludes pigs which have a $P_2$ of less than 9 mm, these being subject to a 5 per cent price deduction because they are considered to be overlean. Processor 2 imposes a similar 5 per cent deduction on carcasses with a $P_2$ of between 15 and 18 mm and a 23 per cent penalty on carcasses with a $P_2$ in excess of 18 mm.

Because of the marginal economic situation of pig production which has prevailed in Britain in the last decade, Grade 3 pigs will be loss-making in almost all circumstances because not only are they commanding a very low price but, being fatter, their food costs will have been considerably higher because fat requires much more food for its production than does lean meat. In many circumstances, Grade 2 pigs will also be loss-making. Therefore, the producer has all possible financial incentives to reduce fatness and therefore to increase carcass lean percentage although, in supplying the needs of Processor 2, there is a limit to the extent to which fatness should be reduced because of the penalty imposed on overlean carcasses.

Thus, achievement of top carcass grades and the highest price per kg of carcass is becoming increasingly difficult for the British producer because not only are ever-increasing price penalties imposed for excessive fatness but an increasing number of processors are now imposing penalties on over-lean carcasses. This

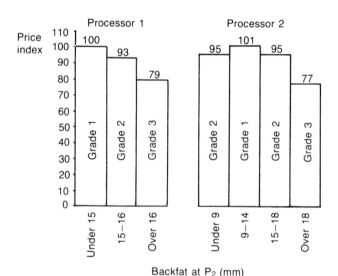

FIGURE 16.2  Typical bacon carcass grading systems in operation in Britain in 1988.

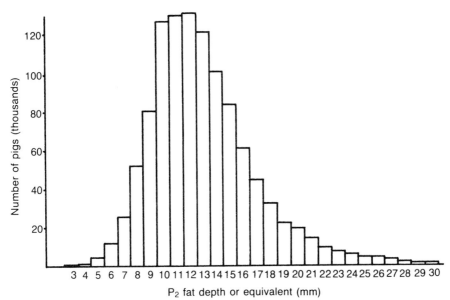

FIGURE 16.3   Distribution of $P_2$ fat depths in the classified sample, year ended September 1985. (From Meat and Livestock Commission Pig Yearbook, April 1986)

serious situation for the pig producer in Britain is well illustrated in Figure 16.3, which presents the Meat and Livestock Commission's data on classified carcasses.

It is clear that we still have a very wide range in fatness in our pig carcasses in Britain. In this sample, mean $P_2$ is about 12 mm but it varies from extremely lean carcasses with 3 mm to very fat carcasses with 30 mm. If this sample was subjected to the grading systems in Figure 16.2, there would be considerable downgrading for overfatness, while in the case of Processor 2, a significant proportion of carcasses would also be penalised for overleanness.

Against this background of failure to match backfat of pigs more closely with the requirements to achieve top grade and the highest price, a very relevant question may be asked: why are some pigs at slaughter still excessively fat and others excessively lean to meet current demand? The answer to this is that pig producers have tended to market pigs of the same sex on a liveweight basis rather than on the basis of fatness or degree of finish, the latter being the traditional basis used to decide optimum timing of marketing in sheep and cattle. One reason for this difference is that subcutaneous fat thickness or degree of finish has been much more difficult to assess in pigs. However, with the advent of ultrasonic equipment, it is now possible to measure backfat thickness with a reasonable degree of accuracy on the live pig.

## The Potential Usefulness of Ultrasonic Equipment to Improve Timing of Marketing of Pigs on a Demanding and Stepped Grading System Based on Backfat

The potential usefulness of ultrasonics can best be considered in Figure 16.4 in relation to two producers' carcasses averaging 12 mm at $P_2$ on Farm A and 14 mm on

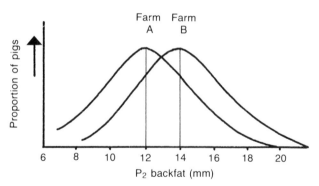

FIGURE 16.4   The frequency distribution of P₂ backfat thickness in pigs from two farms.

Farm B. The variation in $P_2$ at slaughter will have roughly the pattern shown which conforms to what is termed the 'normal distribution'. If both producers are selling pigs to Processor 1 (see Figure 16.2), they will be attempting to improve their grading and average carcass value by all the approaches cited previously.

An additional or alternative strategy they could adopt would be to identify the leaner and fatter pigs at an earlier stage using an ultrasonic machine. The fatter ones would then be restricted to a greater degree, or slaughtered at a lighter weight. As already stated, this is already done with castrates relative to gilts and gilts relative to entire males on many farms. However, some castrates are lean and some gilts fat so we might need a more sensitive approach than this.

Another possibility is to stock pigs in pens more densely at the start of the finishing phase (so that more efficient use is being made of pen space) but avoid overstocking later. This would be done by thinning out pigs at the right time by marketing the fatter pigs earlier before they run the risk of being downgraded.

It is interesting to look at the financial consequences of selling the fatter pigs at an earlier stage. It can be shown that in many situations it would be more profitable to sell lower grading pigs at 5 to 10 kg lower carcass weight if by so doing they could attain a higher grade and provided that these lighter carcasses were still acceptable to the processor (see Table 16.4).

With ultrasonic equipment it is possible to detect those pigs which are just in danger of slipping down a grade if kept for another week and to market them promptly. Of course, the same ultrasonic equipment could also be used to retain lean pigs to heavier weights (provided the maximum carcass weight is not exceeded) which would also reduce any problems associated with overleanness (as in the case of Processor 2 in Figure 16.2).

For those who decide on the timing of marketing by weighing pigs, measuring backfat thickness by ultrasonics during weighing would add about an extra minute per pig to the process. The cost benefit of this exercise would have to be evaluated carefully. However, in Britain, we might have little option but to adopt this approach if the penalties for overfatness and perhaps also for overleanness increase.

Historically, apart from the unavailability of ultrasonic equipment, there are several reasons why pig keepers have marketed on the basis of liveweight rather

**TABLE 16.4  Equivalent carcass weight of Grade A carcasses to Grades B and C carcasses to achieve the same total price**

| | *Grade* | | |
| | A | B | C |
| --- | --- | --- | --- |
| Value of a 68 kg carcass (£) | 77.52 | 71.40 | 63.24 |
| Value of a 62.63 kg carcass (£) | 71.40 | | |
| Value of a 55.47 kg carcass (£) | 63.24 | | |

Thus, if the pig yielding a 68 kg 'B' carcass could be sold much earlier to yield a 62.6 kg carcass at 'A' grade it would not realise less; and if the pig yielding a 68 kg 'C' carcass could be sold even earlier to yield a 55.5 kg carcass at A grade it would not realise less. When it is considered that such earlier marketing of these poor grading pigs would result in savings in feed costs (approximately £3 per week) and in housing costs in many situations (approximately 28 pence per week) it is clear that such earlier disposal is desirable.

than on apparent fatness or degree of finish. Pig processors in the past imposed rigid limits in terms of carcass length and maximum and minimum carcass weights and applied hefty financial penalties on carcasses which did not conform. Obviously, factors such as length and weight are closely related to liveweight, so the pig producer had to minimise the chances of incurring financial penalities by trying to ensure that he met these criteria and fatness thus became secondary.

Those marketing sheep and cattle in Britain never had so many restrictions imposed on them. They only had the degree of finish to consider. Thus, with only one target at which to aim, their job was made much easier.

It is gratifying to note that many pig processors in Britain have now dropped their carcass length standards altogether and have widened the range of acceptable carcass weights. However, if processors want carcasses within very narrow $P_2$ fat limits, they must be prepared to widen the acceptable carcass weight range, and many have already taken this step.

THE ACCURACY OF ULTRASONIC EQUIPMENT

Backfat thickness at $P_2$ or other points cannot be measured ultrasonically with perfect accuracy. A careful operator, experienced in using a good ultrasonic machine, will measure about 70 per cent of carcasses to within ± 1 mm and perhaps 90 per cent to within ± 2 mm of their correct fatness. Because such equipment and the operator cannot measure backfat with perfect accuracy, a 'margin of safety' must be applied on the farm. For instance, if pigs are downgraded from Grade 1 to Grade 2 when they exceed 14 mm at $P_2$, a farmer using ultrasonics might decide to market pigs at a maximum $P_2$ of 12 or 13 mm to minimise his chances of making mistakes which would result in some pigs going into Grade 2.

The application of ultrasonics is likely to be particularly useful in detecting very lean pigs and allowing them further growth. This would avoid any problems associated with overleanness and it would allow producers to take advantage of the opportunities which have been created by processors for accepting heavier car-

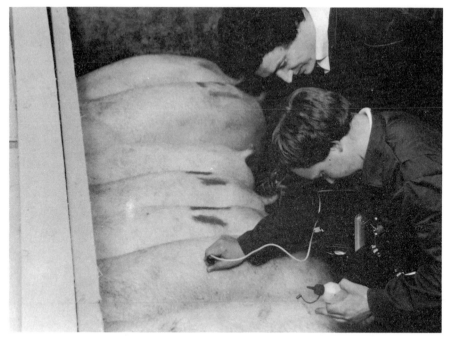

Plate 16.5   Pigs on a restricted feeding system having the backfat thickness at point $P_2$ assessed ultrasonically as they receive one of their 2 daily feeds. The readings are used to guide the timing of marketing so as to avoid overlean and overfat carcasses.

casses. Many such lean pigs could be grown on for several weeks without incurring risk of downgrading for overfatness or through being overweight. The necessary pen space to keep such pigs on to heavier weights could be created by putting fatter pigs off at lighter weights. The net result would be much more uniform pigs in terms of backfat, better grading and a higher average price per kg of pigmeat produced.

IMPROVING AVERAGE CARCASS VALUE AND MARGIN OVER OTHER COSTS
Some indication of the potential of the use of ultrasonics to improve timing of marketing, grading and average carcass value can be obtained by referring to Tables 16.5, 16.6 and 16.7. below.

In Table 16.5, the estimated proportion of carcasses falling into the different grades of Processors 1 and 2 (Figure 16.2) are presented according to the average fatness at $P_2$ within a herd. As expected, the greater the average herd $P_2$, the higher the proportion of carcasses downgraded for overfatness by both processors. However, in the case of Processor 2, reducing herd average $P_2$, while reducing downgrading for overfatness, now results in downgrading for overleanness (8 mm or less at $P_2$).

Average carcass value for herds with $P_2$ averages from 10 to 14 mm have been calculated (see Table 16.6) on the basis of the grading profiles in Table 16.5 and using prices for the different grades (pence per kg) equivalent to the price indices

**TABLE 16.5  Estimated proportion of pigs in different backfat and grade categories according to the average P$_2$ thickness in the herd**

| Mean herd P$_2$ (mm) | Processor 1 P$_2$ (mm) | | | Total |
|---|---|---|---|---|
| | 0-14 (Grade 1) | 15-16 (Grade 2) | >16 (Grade 3) | |
| | | Percentage of pigs | | |
| 10 | 93 | 6 | 1 | 100 |
| 11 | 87 | 10 | 3 | 100 |
| 12 | 79 | 14 | 7 | 100 |
| 13 | 69 | 18 | 13 | 100 |
| 14 | 57 | 22 | 21 | 100 |

| Mean herd P$_2$ (mm) | Processor 2 P$_2$ (mm) | | | | Total |
|---|---|---|---|---|---|
| | 0-8 (Grade 2) | 9-14 (Grade 1) | 15-18 (Grade 2) | >18 (Grade 3) | |
| | | Percentage of pigs | | | |
| 10 | 31 | 62 | 7 | 0 | 100 |
| 11 | 21 | 66 | 13 | 0 | 100 |
| 12 | 13 | 66 | 20 | 1 | 100 |
| 13 | 7 | 62 | 28 | 3 | 100 |
| 14 | 3 | 54 | 36 | 7 | 100 |

presented in Figure 16.2. Thus, a price index of 93 becomes 93 pence per kg. Average carcass value for the different grading profiles is compared to the optimum where 100 per cent of carcasses qualify for the top grade. In the case of Processor 1, a herd with an average herd P$_2$ of 10 suffers a fairly small shortfall of 43 pence per pig by failing to get all pigs into the top grade. Such a producer might consider that use of ultrasonics to detect fatter pigs at an earlier stage and the earlier marketing of these in an attempt to avoid downgrading would not be worthwhile in terms of cost benefit. However, as herd P$_2$ increases, grading deteriorates and the financial shortfall escalates relative to the optimum, an ever-increasing argument can be made for using ultrasonics to detect the potentially poor grading pigs earlier so as to market them more timeously and improve grading and price per kg. In the case of a herd with an average P$_2$ of 14 mm selling 10,000 pigs per year, the financial shortfall relative to the optimum is a staggering £4.02 per pig and £40,200 per year. While taking all available steps to reduce the average fatness of his pigs by all the methods outlined earlier, such a producer should also have one of his employees trained to operate ultrasonic equipment to detect at an earlier stage the 43 per cent of his pigs which at present are being downgraded (22 per cent to Grade 2 and 21 per cent to Grade 3), market them earlier and convert them from considerable loss-makers to profitable commodities.

It is interesting that in the case of pigs consigned to Processor 2, the financial shortfall relative to the optimum does not vary greatly (from £1.38 to £1.91 per pig) over the herd average P$_2$ range of 10 to 13 mm. This is for the obvious

**TABLE 16.6** Estimated average carcass value according to mean herd $P_2$ (prices for different grades are based on conversion of the price indices in Figure 16.2 into pence per kg)

| Mean herd $P_2$ (mm) | $P_2$ (mm) 0-14 | $P_2$ (mm) 15-16 | $P_2$ (mm) >16 | Processor 1 Average price per kg (p) | Value of 67.5 kg carcass (£) | Shortfall per pig (£) | Shortfall per 10,000 pigs |
|---|---|---|---|---|---|---|---|
| | | Percentage of pigs | | | | | |
| | 100 | | | 100.00 | £67.50 | | |
| 10 | 93 | 6 | 1 | 99.37 | £67.07 | £0.43 | £4,300 |
| 11 | 87 | 10 | 3 | 98.67 | £66.60 | £0.90 | £9,000 |
| 12 | 79 | 14 | 7 | 97.55 | £65.85 | £1.65 | £11,640 |
| 13 | 69 | 18 | 13 | 96.01 | £64.81 | £2.69 | £26,000 |
| 14 | 57 | 22 | 21 | 94.05 | £63.48 | £4.02 | £40,200 |

| Mean herd $P_2$ (mm) | $P_2$ (mm) 0-8 | $P_2$ (mm) 9-14 | $P_2$ (mm) 15-18 | $P_2$ (mm) >18 | Processor 2 Average price per kg (p) | Value of 67.5 kg carcass (£) | Shortfall per pig (£) | Shortfall per 10,000 pigs |
|---|---|---|---|---|---|---|---|---|
| | | Percentage of pigs | | | | | | |
| | | 100 | | | 101.00 | £68.18 | | |
| 10 | 31 | 62 | 7 | 0 | 98.72 | £66.64 | £1.54 | £15,400 |
| 11 | 21 | 66 | 13 | 0 | 98.96 | £66.80 | £1.38 | £13,800 |
| 12 | 13 | 66 | 20 | 1 | 98.78 | £66.68 | £1.50 | £15,000 |
| 13 | 7 | 62 | 28 | 3 | 98.18 | £66.27 | £1.91 | £19,100 |
| 14 | 3 | 54 | 36 | 7 | 96.98 | £65.46 | £2.72 | £27,200 |

reason that where herd average $P_2$ is greater, more pigs are being downgraded for overfatness, whereas where average $P_2$ is less, more pigs are being penalised for overleanness. The ultrasonic machine operator in this case has two jobs to do. He has to detect the fatter pigs to market them earlier and the very lean pigs to arrange for keeping them several more weeks to allow them to grow and deposit more fat. His ultimate target for the latter must be to avoid both overfatness and going above the highest acceptable carcass weight stipulated by the processor.

What about the economics of keeping these very lean pigs to heavier weights? Some guidelines are presented in Table 16.7. The assumptions on which these calculations are based is that after these overlean pigs are detected and the decision is made to retain them on the farm for a further period, they will continue to increase in liveweight and carcass weight by weekly amounts of 5 and 4 kg respectively and that timing of marketing will be such as to avoid downgrading for being either overfat or overweight. Taking an average price per kg of carcass of £1 and a feed cost of £150 per tonne (15 pence per kg), it is clear, whether food conversion efficiency over this further growth period is 3.0, 3,5 or 4.0, that there are very useful extra weekly positive margins of the extra carcass value over food costs. There would, of course, be slightly higher costs associated with housing (approximately 4 pence per day) and labour associated with retaining these overlean pigs

**TABLE 16.7  Possible extra margins from keeping overlean pigs to heavier weights before slaughter**

|  | FCR around 90 kg liveweight | | |
|---|---|---|---|
|  | *3.0* | *3.5* | *4.0* |
| Feed required/kg LWG | 3.0 | 3.5 | 4.0 |
| Feed required/5 kg LWG | 15.0 | 17.5 | 20.0 |
| Feed cost at 15p/kg | £2.25 | £2.63 | £3.00 |
| Value of 4 kg carcass (provided not downgraded) | £4.00 | £4.00 | £4.00 |
| Margin per week over food costs | £1.75 | £1.37 | £1.00 |

*Assumptions*
Liveweight gain  = 5 kg/week
Carcass gain    = 4 kg/week
$P_2$ gain        = 1 mm/week

for a further period, but in the great majority of circumstances, such a strategy would be very worthwhile.

## Controlling Lean to Fat ratio by Trimming Off Surplus Fat in the Processing Plant

The traditional method used in Britain, Denmark and other countries for tailoring pigs on the farm by the methods outlined earlier in this chapter have been subjected to critical evaluation by Fowler (1986) and others, who have argued that the on-farm methods used to produce the lean to fat ratio required by the consumer are not necessarily conducive to maximising the biological efficiency of production of lean meat or producing good-quality lean meat at least cost.

Lean meat is defined as skeletal muscle removed from the edible parts of the carcass by physical dissection. It is true, of course, that the value of lean meat can vary according to the part of the carcass from which it comes. However, it has been shown repeatedly that the actual proportions of the different muscles are virtually impossible to change by nutrition, and even quite determined attempts by genetic selection to alter the shape of pigs has resulted in only a small degree of change in the proportions of the lean part of the carcass.

### THE PROBLEMS OF RESTRICTING FOOD INTAKE TO REDUCE FAT DEPOSITION

As indicated earlier in this chapter, in order to meet stringent grading constraints for bacon pigs, many farmers find it necessary to apply some degree of food restriction during growth. This applies particularly to castrates. However, although restriction may improve grading it imposes a penalty because of the associated reduction in growth rate. On the one hand, there is an improvement in the average value of pigs sold and, on the other, a reduction in the number of pigs which can be sold from a given facility within a given time period (see Table 13.1 on page 333). The dilemma is reflected in the decisions which must be taken by breeders. They wish to supply pigs which grade well but they cannot supply pigs which genetically have low voluntary food intake and grow too slowly to be economic.

Plate 16.6 Trimming off surplus fat in the processing plant to produce super lean, deboned meat with virtually no visible external fat on the final joint. The joint has to command a high price to compensate for the low value of the trimmed bone and fat. (Courtesy of Meat and Livestock Commission)

The problems and also the solution to this dilemma can be illustrated by reference to data taken from the Meat and Livestock Commission reports on Commerical Product Evaluation. In these reports the commercially available products of the companies providing breeding stock in the United Kingdom were compared. One component of the test was to grow pigs of the slaughter generation under identical conditions. Half were fed ad lib. and half fed at about 80 per cent of the ad lib. intake. In tests 6 to 8, thirteen companies were represented together with the genetic control group (see Figures 16.5, 16.6 and 16.7). The control group was a good representative of the pig type available 20 years ago.

In Figure 16.5, it can clearly be seen that the percentage of lean decreased when pigs were fed ad lib. rather than restricted. However, restricted feeding was associated with a profound reduction in the growth rate of the lean tissue (Figure 16.6). This is the essence of the dilemma in that carcass lean percentage is higher on restricted feeding while daily growth of lean tissue is considerably higher on ad lib. feeding. One way of trying to resolve the dilemma is to determine the feed required for each kg of lean produced, i.e. the lean tissue food conversion efficiency (LTFC).

In Figures 16.5, 16.6, 16.7 and 16.9 each line represents a different breeding company. The solid circles on the left of each line refer to performance (lean percentage, lean growth per day, lean tissue food conversion efficiency or financial margin) on restricted feeding and those on the right to performance on ad lib. feeding. The open circles are the means of all companies.

Figure 16.7 illustrates the feed conversion to lean tissue. Rather surprisingly, it can be seen that there is very little difference between the feed levels although there are enormous differences between the participating companies. At one extreme,

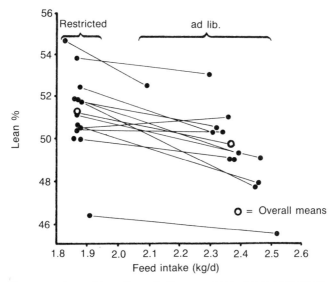

FIGURE 16.5   The percentage of lean tissue in the carcasses of pigs kept by 13 commercial companies at two levels of feeding, calculated from values from the Meat and Livestock Commission (1982).

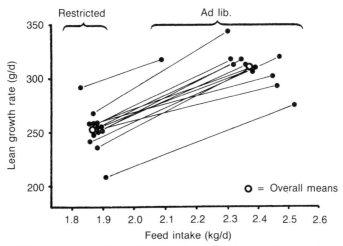

FIGURE 16.6   The growth rate of lean tissue in pigs at two levels of feeding by 13 commercial companies, calculated from values from the Meat and Livestock Commissiion (1982).

pigs from Company A have an LTFC of less than 7 while that from Company B is in excess of 9. However, feed utilisation, although important, is not the whole story. No allowance has been made for the time element. How does one balance the twin virtues of lean tissue growth rate and lean tissue feed conversion? An effec-

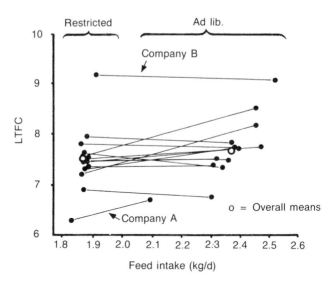

FIGURE 16.7   The feed required (kg) per kg of lean tissue gain (LTFC) in pigs kept by 13 commercial companies at two levels of feeding, calculated from values from the Meat and Livestock Commission (1982).

tive way of doing this is to calculate the margin between the value of lean meat produced daily and the food costs involved.

MARGIN PER DAY BETWEEN LEAN DEPOSITED AND FOOD COSTS

The balance between the value of lean produced per pig or per pig place daily and the cost of the feed required to produce it provides the margin out of which the fixed costs such as those for labour, buildings and so on must be paid, leaving the net profit. Since, by definition, the fixed costs cannot be manipulated by the strategy of feeding or the genetics, the only thing that need concern us is to provide the greatest possible margin between feed costs and the returns.

To calculate the daily margin between the value of lean deposited and food costs, one must assign values to the feed cost, which is easy, and to the lean meat, which is difficult. How can a value be given to the daily gain in lean meat when it depends on the grading profile? It becomes important to see the issues clearly. Grading systems in the United Kingdom, by intention, should reflect the value of the carcass to the consumer, and the consumer requires lean meat. The problem is that carcass grading in the United Kingdom makes a crude classification of carcasses into very few categories (see Figure 16.2 page 000) with sudden reductions in price per kg when a prescribed level of subcutaneous fat is exceeded. This stepped system of carcass grading and payment does not accurately reward or penalise carcasses according to content of lean. The only way round this problem is to state boldly that the true value of the gain is entirely described by the amount of lean which it contains. The assumption in this is that fat is a neutral commodity for which the farmer should neither be paid nor fined.

Fat actually has a positive value as a commodity in pig diets and in industries producing soaps, detergents, synthetic rubber, etc. The pig processing factory should easily recover the cost of removal of fat and more by selling it for human food, animal feed or industrial uses. This approach enormously clarifies the objectives.

The final step is to assign a value to lean meat and to feed. The ratio of feed consumed per kg of lean produced ranges between 10:1 and 6:1. If we take an intermediate value of 12:1 and assign a value of £2.20 per kg to lean and £0.16 per kg to feed, the average margin of lean produced per day relative to feed cost per day is shown in Figure 16.8 and the margins for each company are in Figure 16.9. Quite clearly, the highest margin between the value of lean and the feed cost applies to pigs fed ad lib. They provide a greater margin per day than those of the restricted-fed group. Of course, the margin between the value of lean deposited daily and feed cost is very dependent on both the value of the lean and the feed costs. If feed costs increase and the value of lean tissue is reduced, this will reduce the advantage for ad lib. feeding until it eventually disappears and becomes negative.

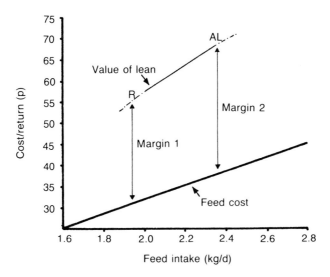

FIGURE 16.8  The relation between the daily cost of feed (16 p/kg) and the value of lean tissue produced daily (220 p/kg) for pigs at two levels of feeding: restricted (R) or ad lib. (AL), calculated from values from the Meat and Livestock Commission (1982).

BREEDING OBJECTIVES AND FEED INTAKE

The calculations given above have a profound effect on breeding objectives. The implications can be considered at two levels. First, the results at their face value show that although feed intake affected the margin between the value of lean deposited daily and food costs, it did not affect it as much as the source company. In fact, pigs from companies giving the highest margins were better on restricted feeding than others on ad lib. feeding.

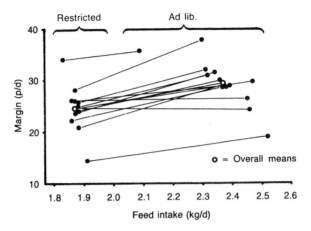

FIGURE 16.9   The margin (pence per day) between feed costs and the value of lean tissue produced for 13 commercial companies feeding pigs at two levels of intake, calculated from values from the Meat and Livestock Commission (1982).

The implications for the future are that when pigs have become lean enough by genetic improvement, there is only one route to improve efficiency. That is to make them grow faster and persuade them to eat more feed per day. To this end we must identify those pigs which not only grow more lean daily with less food but also those which grow a lot more lean daily with even higher food intakes. Eventually, we are looking for pigs which can grow at nearly 2 kg/day on 4 kg of ordinary feed, and grow lean at 0.75 kg/day between 30 and 90 kg liveweight. This may seem incredible, but a few pigs are already three-quarters of the way there.

The foregoing arguments may be labelled as academic in Britain but the approach suggested is no different from that employed in other countries. Ad lib. feeding to slaughter weights higher than those current in the United Kingdom have been the traditional method of producing pigmeat in the United States. Surplus fat is trimmed off carcasses to provide the precise ratio of lean to fat required by the consumer. In Europe, similar approaches to those prevailing in the States are employed in Holland and Italy, countries which, unlike Britain, have expanded their pig industries in the last decade.

## Grading Systems in Other Countries and Future Developments

Several countries now operate carcass grading and payment systems based directly on estimates of carcass lean content. The Canadians pioneered such a system. In Europe, Sweden and Denmark already operate carcass grading and payment schemes based on lean percentage, while such systems are about to be implemented in both Germany and the Netherlands (see Figure 16.10).

Britain adopted the EU Pig Grading Scheme in January 1989. This scheme involves an assessment of carcass lean content which is recorded either on the carcass or on the grading documents. Lean content is estimated from measurements of backfat (for example, $P_2$), eye muscle depth and carcass weight. Processors are

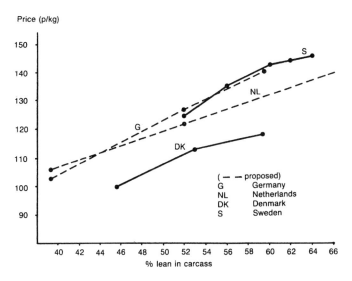

FIGURE 16.10   Carcass price schedules in three EU countries and Sweden. (Source: MLC Pig Yearbook 1987)

free to decide on the basis of payment for carcasses; some prefer to continue to base grading and payment largely on $P_2$ (or $P_1 + P_3$) backfat measurements while others have decided to change the basis of payment to carcass lean content.

The formula used in UK to calculate carcass lean percentage from $P_2$ and carcass weight is as follows:

% lean $= 65.5 - (1.15 \times P_2) + (0.076 \times \text{carcass weight})$

So that if $P_2$ was 10mm and carcass weight was 75g:

$$\% \text{ lean} = 65.5 - (1.15 \times 10) + (0.076 \times 75)$$
$$= 65.5 - 11.5 + 5.7$$
$$= 59.7 \text{ per cent}$$

Some processors in Britain are now making use of automatic grading devices such as the SKF Fat-o-Meater from Denmark and the Hennessy Grading Probe from New Zealand, which not only record backfat and muscle depth but can also detect problems such as pale, soft, exudative muscle (PSE) and DFD or dark, firm, dry meat. In addition to devices to measure muscle depth and colour, a Penetrometer probe has been developed to measure the texture or degree of softness of fat on the slaughter line. Thus, with the increasing ease of detection of both the merits and faults of carcasses and of lean and fatty tissues, the basis of grading and payment will be modified to take these factors into account. Those who produce carcasses with high lean content and lean and fat of excellent quality will, relative to the current grading system, get more of their pigs into the 'supergrade' category, while, conversely, greater price penalties will be imposed on inferior carcasses.

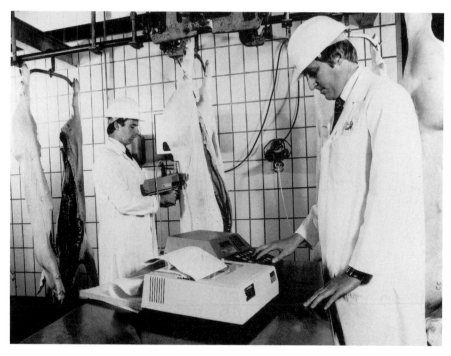

Various instruments used to assess carcass quality (courtesy of Meat and Livestock Commission): (*Above*) Plate 16.7   The Fat-O-Meater which is an automatic recording probe to measure both depth of fat and depth of muscle.

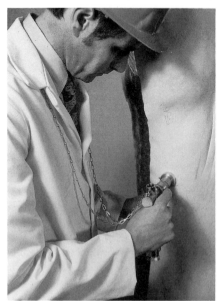

(*Left*) Plate 16.8   An optical probe usually used to measure the thickness of backfat above the eye muscle and also the depth of the eye muscle.

(*Below*) Plate 16.9   The Hennessy Grading Probe which is similar to the Fat-O-Meater.

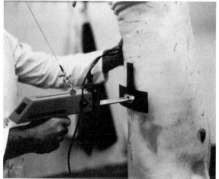

### Consumer Tastes Regarding Meat from Fat or Lean Carcasses

With the trend towards increased carcass leanness in Britain, there has been some debate regarding the relative acceptability of meat trimmed to similar levels of subcutaneous fat from lean and fat carcasses. Some argue that production of leaner and leaner meat is desirable, while those with more traditional tastes claim that high-quality meat is obtainable only from carcasses which have been well finished, that is, which have a reasonable amount of subcutaneous, intermuscular as well as intramuscular ('marbling') fat.

In an attempt to throw light on this issue, the Meat and Livestock Commission in Britain carried out comprehensive tests on meat from pigs finished to three levels of subcutaneous fat, representing the range from very lean to very fat pigs. These tests involved butchery assessment on meat processing aspects as well as consumer assessment of aspects of quality of the cooked product which had been trimmed prior to cooking to the same level of external (subcutaneous) fat. Results are presented in Table 16.8.

BUTCHERS' ASSESSMENT

From the butchers' viewpoint, joints from the very lean carcasses had a higher incidence of handling defects such as soft fat, lack of setting and excessive separation

**TABLE 16.8  Meat quality in 58 kg pork carcasses differing in fat thickness**

|  | $P_2$ (mm) | | | |
|---|---|---|---|---|
|  | 8 | 12 | 16 | Differences |
| Joints not set[a] | 60 | 28 | 17 | *** |
| Excessive tissue separation[a] | 46 | 18 | 11 | *** |
| Firmness of shoulder fat (g) | 432 | 637 | 913 | *** |
| Marbling fat (% of muscle) | 0.5 | 0.7 | 1.0 | *** |
| *Consumer panel*[b] |  |  |  |  |
| Tough | 18 |  | 12 | ** |
| Dry | 39 |  | 28 | ** |
| Poor Flavour | 9 |  | 9 | NS |
| Low acceptability | 10 |  | 10 | NS |
| *Taste panel*[c] |  |  |  |  |
| Tenderness | 1.0 |  | 1.1 | NS |
| Juiciness | 1.1 |  | 1.3 | ** |
| Flavour | 1.5 |  | 1.7 | NS |
| Overall acceptability | 0.7 |  | 1.0 | NS |

[a] Butchers' assessments − % of loin joints not set or with excessive tissue separation.
[b] MLC consumer panel of 500 families − % of loin chops with low scores for tenderness, juiciness, flavour and overall acceptability.
[c] FRI(B) = Food Research Institute Taste Panel − mean scores for loin chops on scale −7 (low) to +7 (high), except juiciness which was scored 0 (dry) to 4 (very juicy).
*** Differences significant at 99.9 per cent level of probability.
** Differences significant at 99 per cent level of probability.
NS Difference not significant.

between fat layers and between the fat and lean. Marbling fat in the eye muscle of a loin chop from the last rib region was slightly greater with an increase in fat thickness. On the basis of their assessment of the handling qualities and appearance of the meat, butchers predicted that, relative to the fattest carcasses, a higher proportion of the leaner ones would have poorer eating qualities.

ASSESSMENT OF EATING QUALITY

The consumer panel, who cooked and ate chops in their own homes, found a higher proportion of the leaner carcasses 'tough' and 'dry' relative to the fattest carcasses. However, they detected no difference in either flavour or general acceptability of the meat.

The taste panellists, who sampled chops cooked under controlled conditions, found those from the leanest carcasses to be slightly less juicy and tender but, despite this, found no difference in overall acceptability between the samples from carcasses varying widely in fatness. The absence of a difference in overall acceptability between the samples was thought to be brought about by consumers trading off the slightly increased eating quality in terms of juiciness and tenderness of meat from the fatter carcasses against the leanness of the meat from carcasses with least fat. The results did not resolve the debate about the importance of marbling fat, which is increased slightly in fatter carcasses. Some discriminating consumers appear to appreciate the attributes of marbling in terms of improving flavour, juiciness and tenderness of meat; others put less store on these aspects and place more emphasis on the meat being lean and almost devoid of fat.

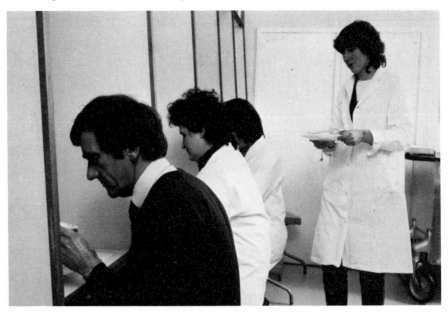

Plate 16.10   A taste panel in operation scoring meat cooked under standardised conditions for such traits as tenderness, juiciness, flavour and general acceptability. (Courtesty of J.D. Wood, Food Research Institute, Bristol)

## Influence of Cold Shortening and Cooking on Meat Quality

The care taken with pigs during loading, transportation and in lairage has very important influences on meat quality, and these are outlined in Chapter 18. Sometimes the texture of pork is unusually tough and, in many cases, this is due to the process known as cold shortening, which occurs when pork is frozen too quickly and before adequate 'conditioning' (associated with the interruption of the normal biochemical changes in the meat following slaughter) or maturation of the meat takes place.

It is not the purpose of this chapter to be a manual for the cooking of pork and bacon products but it is important to recognise that meat can be enhanced enormously by skilful preparation and cooking and, conversely, ruined by inept culinary procedures.

## Summing Up

The producers of pigs and the processors of their product are very dependent on each other. The producer, for his part, must be fully aware of the problems of the meat processor and, as far as possible within the limits of biological variation, must supply pigs of uniform quality of the type required to allow the processor to operate an efficient system and, in turn, supply the consumer with a wide range of attractive products at a competitive price. The processors, for their part, must be fully aware of the problems of the pig producer and of the production methods which are conducive to the most efficient and economical production of good-quality lean meat on the farm. Such increased understanding of their respective problems will lead to much more effective communication between the pig producer and the pigmeat processor. Both parties will benefit from such increased cooperation and, in turn, the consumer will be satisfied by being supplied with an attractive range of pigmeat and pigmeat products at a competitive price.

## ADDITIONAL READING

Kempster A. J., Cuthbertson A. and Harrington G. (1982), *Carcass Evaluation in Livestock Breeding, Production and Marketing*, Granada Publishing Ltd, London.

*MLC Pig Yearbook* (1988), Meat and Livestock Commission, PO Box 44, Queensway House, Bletchley, Milton Keynes, England MK2 2EF.

*Pork Industry Handbook*, USA Co-operative Extension Service, University of Illinois at Urbana-Champaign, USA.

Wood J. D. (1984), 'Fat Deposition and the Quality of Fat Tissue in Meat Animals', *Fats in Animal Nutrition*, Ed. J. Wiseman, 407−435, Butterworths, London.

Wood J. D. (1985), 'Consequences of Changes in Carcass Composition on Meat Quality', *Recent Advances in Animal Nutrition*, Eds. W. Haresign & D. J. A. Cole, 157−166, Butterworths, London.

*Chapter 17*

# Effluent Storage, Treatment and Disposal

Pig effluent consists of variable proportions of solid and liquid depending on the housing and feeding system and the method of storage and treatment. The solid material consists of organic and mineral matter. Traditionally, the material has been used as a fertiliser and soil conditioner in crop and vegetable production. However, in more recent years, the range of uses of pig effluent has widened. In liquid form, pig effluent can be used for biogas production and as a medium for the growth of algae (which can be harvested and used in animal feeds after drying), while 'ponds' of pig effluent support enterprises for growing ducks and special types of fish in some parts of the world. The solid matter in pig effluent is used as a compost in horticulture and, following appropriate processing, is used as a component of the diet of ruminants and sometimes pigs.

## Offensive Nature of Pig Effluent

Raw pig effluent is offensive in terms of its odour and also as a potential pollutant in water courses. The oxidation of its organic matter content in water courses uses up oxygen in the water and, as a consequence, places at risk fish and other aquatic life. Because of its potential to pollute air and water, therefore, disposal of pig waste is subject to regulations in many countries of the world. In the United States, for example, pig odours and waste disposal are subject to both public and private legislation. Public pollution regulations specify minimal tolerance levels for measurable components of air and water pollution from pig enterprises. Under private regulations, all landowners have a right to be free from unreasonable interference with the enjoyment of their property. Such unreasonable interference is termed a 'nuisance' and might involve such factors as foul smells, dust, flies, manure spillover and water contamination. The onus is thus on pig-keepers to avoid causing 'nuisance' to their neighbours or others who may be downstream or downwind.

Appropriate attention must be given, therefore, to the effective and acceptable management and disposal of pig effluent.

## MANAGEMENT OF PIG EFFLUENT

In addition to the need to control pollution, increased pig unit size and the scarcity and expense of labour have stimulated much thinking and development work in terms of the management of pig effluent. Pig manure can be handled as a solid (over 20 per cent dry matter (DM)), as a semi solid (10–20 per cent DM), which can be pumped using a piston pump, or as a slurry with up to 10 per cent DM. The latter material can be handled by centrifugal pump; however, if DM is as high as 10 per cent the slurry must be well mixed before pumping begins and even this is too high a concentration of solids for many practical situations. Centrifugal pumps can deal more easily with material with less than 8 per cent DM. On slatted floor systems (no bedding), few pig farms can produce slurry with over 4 per cent DM unless specially designed to do so. Slurry on such systems more usually contains less than 2 per cent DM. This is typical of the dry matter content of slurry on lagoon systems after the solid material has settled or of the run-off material from open or semi-open yard systems.

How best to handle pig effluent depends on the objectives of each producer. Possible objectives might be to:

- make the most efficient use of the material as a fertiliser
- minimise land area involved, the capital required or the labour requirement
- control undesirable odours
- minimise risks to the health of both stockman and pigs
- achieve any combination of two or more of these objectives

Because resources and circumstances vary greatly in different situations, there will be no 'best' pig effluent management system which will suit every pig farmer.


## PIG EFFLUENT MANAGEMENT ALTERNATIVES

A range of some of the more common pig effluent management systems is sum-marised in Figure 17.1.


### Pasture Based Systems

Pigs attend to their own effluent disposal in such systems with no harmful effects on the land or the environment provided that (1) stocking rate is not excessive in relation to the conditions of climate, soil and pasture, (2) pigs are rotated at ap-propriate intervals from one area to another and (3) effluent does not pollute field drains and water courses.


### Semi-intensive Systems

These systems can be defined as those with housing systems with outside runs. Pig effluent may be handled in either solid or liquid form and will be diluted by rain water collected in the outside runs. If handled in liquid form, appropriate storage facilities must be available.

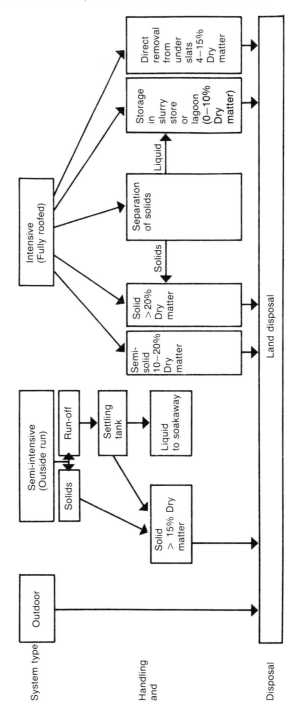

FIGURE 17.1 A range of some of the more common pig effluent management systems. (Adapted from Melvin, S.W., Humenk, F.J., White, R.K., Day, D. and Orr, D., 1979)

If effluent is handled mainly as a solid, facilities for storing liquid run-off must also be available as this will contain high levels of solids and polluting materials which must be prevented from getting into water courses.

## Intensive, Wholly Confined Systems

Pig effluent from such systems will consist of faeces, any residues of bedding used, urine, wash water and any spillage from drinkers. It may be handled primarily as a solid, with appropriate storage for surplus liquid, or as a liquid in the form of slurry.

Liquid storage may take the form of underfloor storage pits or shallow collection pits which are either mechanically scraped or hydraulically flushed to liquid stores outside the building. Such liquid effluent can be pumped or transported by tanker to fields and spread as a fertiliser or it can be treated in a variety of ways:

- stored anaerobically for later application to land for cropping. Before spreading, the material will have to be agitated to achieve adequate mixing of liquid and solids (which will have settled in the intervening period)
- stored in shallow lagoons where most solids are allowed to settle, after which the remaining largely liquid component (less than 4 per cent solids) can be pumped or transported for spreading on cropping land.
- stored following mechanical separation of the bulk of the solid material from the original effluent.
- subjected to aerobic digestion by incorporation of air into the mass. This results in oxidation of some of the organic matter and removes undesirable odours from the mass.
- subjected to anaerobic digestion. Under the appropriate conditions, this results in the production of biogas (approximately 70 per cent methane and 30 per cent carbon dioxide) from the organic matter of the effluent.

The resulting liquid from aerobic and anaerobic digestion can be used directly as a fertiliser and has been put to a variety of other uses such as:

- recirculation to pigs as drinking water or for wallowing in hot climates or for washing or flushing purposes
- recirculation to pigs of liquid treated aerobically as a source of nutrients such as bacterial protein, calcium, phosphorous and B vitamins
- a liquid medium for growing algae or bacteria or for ponds to support particular types of fish with a low oxygen demand

## VALUE AS A FERTILISER

About 80 per cent of the nitrogen (N) and phosphorous (P) and 90 per cent of the potassium (K) in a diet based on cereals and protein concentrates is excreted by pigs and therefore provides a very useful source of nutrients for plant growth. In addition to these major plant nutrients, pig effluent supplies other minor elements and organic matter which contribute to soil fertility and soil structure. These improve the nutrient and moisture holding capacity of the soil.

Pig manure applied to the surface of the soil helps in preventing soil crusting (the formation of soil granules into an impervious layer on the surface of the soil). If it is mixed with the soil, it will decompose more rapidly and the resulting products will improve soil structure and general physical condition. Thus, whether applied to the surface or mixed with the soil, the organic and inorganic components of pig effluent will help to conserve water and soil by reducing liquid run-off and soil erosion caused by either water or wind.

Pig manure provides a source of nutrients for soil micro-organisms while the organic component provides these organisms with a source of energy. This energy is fully exploited by these organisms as they transform components of soil and manure to release nutrients for plant growth and contribute to improving the physical structure of the soil. These processes enhance production of crops, some of which will be consumed by pigs, and so the plant $\rightarrow$ pig $\rightarrow$ soil $\rightarrow$ plant cycle is perpetuated.

## Content of Major Plant Nutrients

The output and average dry matter content of effluent from various categories of pigs are presented in Table 17.1.

**TABLE 17.1   Amount and dry matter content of effluent from pigs**

| Stage | Liveweight (kg) | Faeces & Urine per day (kg) | Dry matter (kg)* |
|---|---|---|---|
| Weaner | 15 | 1.0 | 0.09 |
| Grower | 30 | 1.8 | 0.16 |
| Finisher | 70 | 4.3 | 0.39 |
|  | 90 | 5.7 | 0.51 |
| Sow in gestation | 130 | 4.2 | 0.38 |
| Sow and litter | 170 | 15.1 | 1.36 |
| Boar | 160 | 5.3 | 0.48 |

* Based on dry matter content of 9 per cent
(Source: Adapted from Melvin, S.W., Humenik, F.J., White, R.K., Day, D. and Orr, D., 1979, *Pork Industry Handbook Leaflet PIH-67*, University of Illinois)

The average N, P and K content of undiluted pig effluent is detailed in Table 17.2. The original composition of pig effluent is dependent on the type of diet and will be altered if mixed with bedding or if diluted with water. It will also be altered if any waste feed finds its way into the final manure.

The composition of the manure ultimately available for plant growth is influenced by the method of collection and storage, the time and method of application, the climate and the characteristics of the soil to which it is applied.

The nitrogen content of pig effluent is influenced markedly by the type of housing and waste handling system in operation (see Table 17.3). There can be considerable loss of nitrogen from urine (up to 30 per cent) in the form of ammonia before it ever gets into the slurry or alternative storage system. Subsequently, much loss of

**TABLE 17.2  Average composition of undiluted pig effluent\* (70 kg pigs on a barley-based diet)**

|            | N    | $P_2O_5$ | $K_2O$ |
|------------|------|----------|--------|
| %          | 0.80 | 0.47     | 0.33   |
| kg/tonne   | 8.0  | 4.7      | 3.3    |
| kg/pig/year| 12.0 | 7.0      | 5.0    |

\* Moisture content = 90 per cent
(Source: Svoboda, 1988)

nitrogen occurs when manure is dried by sun and air movement or is leached by rain, all of which can occur in 'Open lot' or outdoor systems. In contrast, comparatively little nitrogen is lost from manure in an intensive system involving a 'manure pack' (built-up litter) or when a liquid pit (i.e. anaerobic pit) storage system is used. Nitrogen loss is greatest in long-term treatment or storage systems such as oxidation ditches or shallow lagoons. The main problem is that nitrogen in fresh manure becomes volatile when temperature is high enough. Alternatively, it can be converted to ammonia which also escapes into the air. Nitrites and nitrates are lost after conversion into nitrogen.

Phosphorus and potassium losses are minimal (5 to 15 per cent) in all except outdoor systems and those involving lagoons. In outdoor systems, between 40 and 50 per cent of the P can be lost through liquid run-off and leaching. In the case of lagoons, between 50 and 80 per cent of the phosphorus can settle out in the sludge layer and thus will be unavailable if only the liquid is applied to the land.

**TABLE 17.3  Approximate nitrogen losses from swine manure as affected by handling and storing methods**

| Handling, storing methods | Nitrogen loss (%)\* |
|---------------------------|---------------------|
| *Solid systems*           |                     |
| Manure pack               | 35                  |
| Open lot                  | 55                  |
| *Liquid systems*          |                     |
| Anaerobic pit             | 25                  |
| Oxidation ditch           | 60                  |
| Lagoon (shallow)          | 80                  |

\* Based on composition of manure applied to the land relative to composition of freshly excreted manure.
(Source: Sutton, A.L., Vanderholm, D.H., Melvin, S.W., Miner, J.R., and Kornegay, E.T., *Pork Industry Handbook Leaflet PIH-25*, University of Illinois)

## Effect of Method of Application

Nitrogen losses are minimised when pig effluent is incorporated into the soil immediately after application (see Table 17.4). Such immediate incorporation of manure into the soil minimises both run-off and nitrogen loss to the air and also allows soil micro-organisms to start decomposing the organic matter content, thus making nutrients available to the plant sooner. Such immediate incorporation into the soil also minimises loss of phosphorus and potash through run-off, and another increasingly important consideration is that it minimises the adverse odour problems associated with the spreading of pig effluent.

**TABLE 17.4 Approximate nitrogen losses from swine manure to the air as affected by application method**

| Application method | Type of manure | Nitrogen loss (%)* |
|---|---|---|
| Broadcast *without* cultivation | Solid | 20 |
|  | Liquid | 25 |
| Broadcast *with* cultivation† | Solid | 5 |
|  | Liquid | 5 |
| Knifing | Liquid | 5 |
| Irrigation | Liquid | 30 |

\* % of total nitrogen in manure applied which was lost within 4 days after application
† Cultivation immediately after application
(Source: Sutton, A.L., Vanderholm, D.H., Melvin, S.W., Miner, J.R. and Kornegay, E.T., *Pork Industry Handbook, Leaflet PIH-25*, University of Illinois)

## Timing of Application

Nitrogen in pig effluent is either in the ammonium or organic forms. All the ammonium nitrogen, except that lost to the air, can be utilised by plants in the year of application. However, nitrogen in the organic form must first be released under the influence of micro-organisms and must be in a water-soluble form before it can be taken up by plants. Between 20 and 50 per cent of this organic nitrogen may become available in the year of application with some being carried over and becoming available in the next cropping season. On the other hand, almost all the phosphorus and potassium in pig manure are ready for plant use in the year of application.

To exploit the readily available nutrients for plant growth it is preferable to apply pig manure to land near the start of the growing season, this being especially important in high rainfall areas with light soils. However, applications in autumn or winter, although resulting in a nitrogen loss of between 5 and 10 per cent, allow soil micro-organisms time to decompose the material and release nutrients for use in the following growing season. This is especially important where the manure has a high content of organic matter.

## Application Rate

As a guide to application rates of pig effluent, Table 17.5 provides details of average nutrient content according to the handling system in use, while Table 17.6 indicates the nutrient content available for plant growth (fertiliser value) according to the storage and disposal system used. While the figures in these tables are useful guides to average composition, it is always preferable to obtain an analysis of the pig effluent available on a particular farm just before land application is due so that application rate is appropriate to the crop and the expected yield response.

On land receiving heavy applications of pig manure, it is desirable to monitor not only the nitrogen, phosphate and potassium content of the manure and soil but also the concentration of other heavy metals and salts. Thus, the levels of copper, arsenic and inorganic salts of sodium, calcium, magnesium and chloride should be monitored so as to avoid toxic effects and maintain the optimum balance of nutrients in the soil. For example, several cases have been recorded of sheep suffering from copper toxicity after grazing pasture which has had recent and heavy application of pig slurry. Even harvested forage following such treatment can still be toxic.

## Monetary Value of Pig Manure

In some situations, it may be necessary to place a monetary value on pig effluent. Probably the simplest basis for this is to transpose the cost of a unit of plant nutrients in artificial fertiliser and apply it to the estimated fertiliser value of the

**TABLE 17.5   Approximate average (and range) dry matter and fertiliser nutrient composition of swine manures at time applied to the land**

| Manure handling system | Dry matter | Available N† | $P_2O_5$‡ | $K_2O$§ | Total N# |
|---|---|---|---|---|---|
| *Solid* | | | *kg/tonne manure* | | |
| Without bedding | 18(15-20) | 3.2(2.5-4.0) | 4.1(3.2-5.9) | 3.6(2.7-4.5) | 4.5(4.0-5.0) |
| With bedding | 18(17-20) | 2.7(2.2-4.5) | 3.2(2.3-4.6) | 3.2(2.7-4.1) | 3.6(3.2-4.6) |
| *Liquid* | % | | *kg/1000 litres manure* | | |
| Anaerobic pit | 4(2-7) | 3.1(2.6-3.6) | 3.3(1.5-3.5) | 2.7(1.4-3.5) | 4.3(3.4-6.6) |
| Oxidation ditch | 2.5(1-4) | 2.0(1.5-2.7) | 3.3(1.2-3.5) | 2.7(1.2-3.0) | 2.9(2.2-4.1) |
| Lagoon | 1(0.3-2) | 0.5(0.2-0.6) | 0.2(0.1-0.4) | 0.4(0.2-0.7) | 0.4(0.3-0.6) |

† Primarily ammonium-N and 35% organic nitrogen which is available to the plant during the growing season
‡ To convert to elemental P, multiply by 0.44
§ To convert to elemental K, multiply by 0.83
# Ammonium-N plus organic N which is slow releasing
(Source: Sutton, A.L., Vanderholm, D.H., Melvin, S.W., Miner, J.R. and Kornegay, E.T., *Pork Industry Handbook, Leaflet PIH-25*, University of Illinois)

**TABLE 17.6  Approximate nutrient value of swine manure per animal unit (1000 kg average liveweight) per year***

| Handling and disposal method | Total N | $P_2O_5$ | $K_2O$ |
|---|---|---|---|
| | | kg/animal unit | |
| Manure pack | | | |
| Broadcast | 84 | 107 | 124 |
| Broadcast & cultivation | 102 | 107 | 124 |
| Open lot | | | |
| Broadcast | 58 | 61 | 80 |
| Broadcast & cultivation | 70 | 61 | 80 |
| Manure pit | | | |
| Broadcast | 95 | 111 | 119 |
| Knifing | 124 | 111 | 119 |
| Irrigation | 92 | 111 | 119 |
| Lagoon | | | |
| Irrigation | 24 | 25 | 89 |

\* Based on initial nutrient content and subsequent losses due to method of handling and disposal
(Source: as Table 17.5)

pig effluent available on a particular farm. As an example, let us take from Table 17.6 the values for pig effluent stored in a 'manure pit' and applied to land by the broadcast method. The value of the annual production of effluent from an animal unit (1000 kg average liveweight) is calculated in Table 17.7. Therefore, the estimated total value of the major plant nutrients in the output of one animal unit was £83.77. This type of calculation might be useful for such purposes as examination of the cost/benefit of applying pig manure to land.

## TREATMENT OF PIG EFFLUENT

Pig effluent can be in solid or liquid form. Solid floored housing systems usually involve scraping of effluent and the resulting material can be carried in solid form or flushed to storage facilities. On slatted floored systems, where a deep storage

**TABLE 17.7  Estimated value of fertiliser from one animal unit (1000 kg average liveweight) per year. Handling system: manure pit; disposal system: broadcast**

| | Total N | $P_2O_5$ | $K_2O$ |
|---|---|---|---|
| Output per animal unit (*kg*) | 95 | 111 | 119 |
| Value per kg (£)* | £0.33 | £0.29 | £0.17 |
| Estimated value of output per animal unit (*) | £31.35 | £32.19 | £20.33 |

\* Based on prices for artificial fertiliser in the United Kingdom in May 1988

pit exists under the slats, slurry can be sucked out at intervals by vacuum pump. Where storage below slats is minimal, slurry can be flushed out several times daily to outside storage facilities.

When slurry is not transported and spread on fields directly, decomposition processes take place until the mass is stable. Organic matter is decomposed by bacteria while the undesirable odours associated with such digestion are given off. Slurry can be processed in different ways as follows:

### Separation

This involves the separation of some of the solid material from the slurry (see Figure 17.2). The solid material can be stored or spread directly. The liquid residue, deprived of much organic matter, will not be subject to the same degree of bacterial action and will emit less offensive odours during digestion. The liquid can be stored or used immediately for irrigation or processed further and recycled for flushing.

Separation can be carried out by the use of processes such as settling tanks, screens, mechanical sifters and presses.

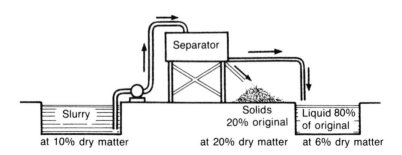

FIGURE 17.2   The process of separating some of the solid material from the rest of the slurry. (Source: MAFF, 1980)

### Treatment of Liquid

Pig effluent is usually cheaper to process than municipal sewage because of its higher solids and organic matter content. However, it is extremely difficult to reduce pig waste to an inoffensive end product. Pig wastes have a high BOD (biochemical oxygen demand), which is the amount of oxygen required for bacterial decomposition of organic matter. It is expressed usually as the grams of oxygen required for the complete oxidation of biodegradable organic matter in 1 litre of liquid. Pig slurry can be processed in various ways:

Plate 17.1   An aerobic digester in operation. The digester incorporates agitators to achieve adequate aeration of the liquid and in turn the oxidation of fermentable material. Such processing reduces the undesirable odour appreciably. In some tropical/sub-tropical countries, following digestion, the liquid is recirculated to provide wallows while the solid material is sifted out and is used as a component of the diet for cattle in feed lots or as a high-grade compost for the horticultural industry. (Courtesy of Centre for Rural Building, Bucksburn, Aberdeen)

AEROBIC LAGOONS

These oxidation ponds are designed and operated to maintain dissolved oxygen in the water all the time. They are relatively odour free but require extensive surface areas. Aerobic bacteria degrade the organic components cellulose and lignin very slowly. Other less complex organic compounds are degraded more quickly with the production of new bacterial cells, water, carbon dioxide and the conversion of protein nitrogen to nitrites and nitrates or free nitrogen.

Aerobic systems can be naturally or mechanically aerated. Natural systems are aided by turbulence and growth of algae which utilise waste and the sun's energy to produce oxygen by photosynthesis through a complex process which involves splitting water into its components of hydrogen and oxygen. To make possible adequate aerobic action such lagoons should be between 0.9 and 1.5 m in depth. In mechanically aerated aerobic lagoons, oxygen is incorporated into the liquid by means of floating surface aerators or air diffusers which are capable of aerating ponds up to 6 m in depth. An alternative to the mechanically aerated lagoon is the oxidation ditch which involves mechanical aeration of a continuous channel under slatted floors within a building.

Under all aerobic systems, non-biodegradable solids form a sludge which must be removed periodically as required. These systems reduce the amount of effluent to be handled due to the evaporation of liquids. However, their main attribute is that they are essentially odourless.

ANAEROBIC LAGOONS

These lagoons should be deep (6 m or more) and should have as small a surface area as possible. Anaerobic digestion is performed by a group of bacteria falling

Plate 17.2  Slurry store and adjacent anaerobic digester and storage tank for the methane gas produced. In the UK, a considerable proportion of the methane produced in winter is used to heat the liquid in the digester to achieve more efficient fermentation. The surplus methane is used to provide energy for heating in the piggery. (Courtesy of Hamworthy Engineering Ltd)

into two categories, viz. acid-forming and methane-forming bacteria. The acid-forming bacteria metabolise the organic matter to carbon dioxide, water, methane, hydrogen sulphide and organic acids. The methane-forming bacteria produce carbon dioxide and a small quantity of mercaptans in addition to methane from organic acids. The methane-forming bacteria are inactivated by oxygen and this can lead to foul odours because of excessive production of sulphur compounds.

In properly designed and operating anaerobic lagoons, however, carbon dioxide and methane are the primary gases produced and such lagoons have a musty odour. An adequate temperature is necessary for anaerobic digestion since low temperature inhibits bacterial action.

METHANE PRODUCTION FROM ANAEROBIC DIGESTION

Systems involving the collection of methane require an airtight digestion tank with internal mixing devices and heat controllers to maintain a temperature of between 30 and 40°C*. Methane is collected in a gas receptor tank (see Plate 17.2). At this temperature, complete digestion of the biodegradable component of organic matter takes about 1 month. The gas produced contains 60 to 70 per cent of methane with the bulk of the remainder being carbon dioxide. The amount of gas produced is dependent on the organic matter content of the slurry, the size of the bacterial population and the temperature of the digester. Under good conditions, 1 kg of slurry dry matter should produce about 300 litres of gas. the digested waste is odourless and the dry matter contains, on average, about 6 per cent of nitrogen, 5 per cent of $P_2O_5$ and 1 per cent of $K_2O$. The high nitrogen content is due to the fact that there is no gaseous escape from the airtight digester and the nitrogen is present in an organic form.

## Uses of Liquid Following Digestion

Following either aerobic or anaerobic digestion, the resulting liquid is put to a variety of uses:

- directly as a fertiliser
- recirculated into buildings for flushing purposes
- a medium for growing fish with a low oxygen demand, e.g. tilapia
- a medium for growing algae, bacteria, yeasts and fungi which are later harvested, dried and processed before incorporation into animal feedstuffs
- recirculated into buildings to provide a wallow in warm climates
- recirculated to provide part of the drinking water requirements and also as a source of nutrients

In addition, the solid component following digestion has been used as:

- a source of nutrients for ruminants and pigs
- a medium for growing fly pupae and earthworms, which are subsequently used as a source of protein following appropriate processing

*Fermentation is slower at 30°C than at 40°C and so less gas is produced per unit of time. Although gas production is faster as temperature is increased from 30° to 40°C, one has to balance this against the added cost of heating the liquid up to 40°C in colder conditions.

Some of these uses of the liquid and solid components of pig slurry following digestion merit brief comments.

SOURCE OF NUTRIENTS FOR RUMINANTS AND PIGS

Conventional pig diets are between 85 and 88 per cent digestible. The indigestible component (12 to 15 per cent of the original diet) subjected to bacterial degradation in aerobic systems results in a considerable conversion of the nitrogenous component to bacterial protein. In most studies, the major nutrients in recycled liquid from aerobic digestion systems have been found to be amino acids (in the form of bacterial protein), minerals and B vitamins, with very low levels of carbohydrate. The dry matter content of such recycled material is often only 2 to 4 per cent and, while research studies have not conclusively demonstrated that this material is a useful source of nutrients for pigs, such liquid material produced following appropriate aerobic digestion has not been associated with any obvious harmful effects. Thus, the material at least constitutes a promising source of the water requirements of pigs. Not only is this useful in relation to reducing requirements for fresh water but it could have a substantial influence in reducing the amount of liquid effluent to be disposed of.

Regarding the liquid material resulting from the anaerobic digestion of pig slurry, this has a fairly high content of fatty acids, especially acetic acid. The material tends to have a somewhat 'tarry' smell, mainly because of its content of ammonia and hydrogen sulphide. However, the preliminary indications from research studies are that pigs will drink as much of this material daily as they will of fresh water.

In relation to possible problems from infectious organisms, it would appear that, because of the extreme anaerobic conditions, digestion constitutes a very cleansing process. Salmonella organisms are destroyed and work has demonstrated that the concentration of other pathogenic bacteria are reduced considerably following digestion. It is possible, however, that the more resistant viruses such as rotavirus may survive the digestion process. While any problems associated with potential pathogens in digester liquid may be less in a closed herd situation, the effects of recycled digester liquid on pig health must nevertheless be carefully monitored.

Another potential problem likely to be associated with the recycling of digester liquid through pigs is the probable increase in concentration of the electrolytes sodium and potassium. While it would appear that pigs are able to tolerate dietary levels of sodium and potassium which are very much above the published requirement levels before toxic effects are measurable, an increased concentration of these elements in the diet increases the water requirement, which, in turn, would increase the amount of effluent produced and thus somewhat defeat the initial objective. Of course, it would be possible to prevent such an increase in intake of sodium and potassium by controlling, as far as possible, the content of these elements in the diet. Other problems may arise because of the concentration of potential toxic materials such as copper and certain organic compounds such as indole and skatole. These offensive smelling compounds may be dissolved in the body fat of the pig and contribute to off-odours in the meat.

PRODUCTION OF BIOGAS

Undiluted pig effluent contains about 10 per cent of dry matter of which 70 per cent is biodegradable. Bacterial degradation of this organic material under anaerobic conditions first results in production of organic acids followed by a mixture of gases (biogas) which usually consists of 50 to 60 per cent methane, 40 to 50 per cent carbon dioxide and about 1 per cent by volume of hydrogen sulphide, ammonia and other trace gases. If necessary, carbon dioxide, trace gases and water can be removed by chemical means. The methane-producing bacteria are most sensitive to improper operating conditions and when they are inhibited, organic acids accumulate.

The main requirements for efficient anaerobic digestion are:

● Maintenance of temperature of slurry in the digester at between 30° and 40°C (digestion is faster at the higher temperature)
● Slurry of high dry matter content

The temperature is especially important in colder climates since slurry must be heated to 30° to 40°C to achieve a satisfactory rate of digestion. Under the correct conditions, 1 kg of organic dry matter produces 300 litres of biogas. If slurry contains 6 rather than 3 per cent of dry matter, it will produce twice the amount of biogas per 1000 litres of slurry. During an average winter in the United Kingdom, slurry with about 3 per cent of dry matter is required to produce enough biogas to raise slurry temperature to the required level of 30° to 40°C. Only when slurry contains over 3 per cent of dry matter is a surplus of biogas generated to produce heat and/or electricity. Thus, in temperate climates in winter, the dry matter content of slurry is particularly critical.

The problem of low dry matter slurry, however, is not so critical in tropical countries in which slurry may be within the desirable temperature range of 30° to 40°C without providing additional heating. In one example in the Philippines, it was reported that 1000 finishing pigs produced about 655 tonnes of manure dry matter annually. Since 0.07 m³ of biogas is produced per kg manure dry matter, these pigs will produce 45,850 m³ of biogas annually. Since slurry temperature will usually be maintained between 30° and 40°C without extra heating, this biogas is available for family use for cooking or other purposes. In view of the fact that in the Philippines the average family of 6 uses about 0.7 m³ of biogas each day and 256 m³ each year, the biogas output from the effluent of 1000 finishing pigs will be enough to meet the needs of

$$\frac{45,850}{256} = 179 \text{ families.*}$$

* In this example, the biogas production from 1 kg of manure dry matter of 0.07 m³ or 70 litres is lower than the 300 litres of gas per kg of dry organic matter cited earlier. The low production of 70 litres might be associated with factors such as short fermentation period, a high content of fibrous bedding material in the slurry or sub-optimal slurry temperature at night or during some periods of the year.

Thus, biogas production from pig effluent can constitute a most useful source of energy for domestic or farm use in tropical countries. However, in temperate regions, particularly in winter, slurry of adequate dry matter content is essential to make biogas production from anaerobic digestion an economically viable proposition.

## Dangers Associated With Pig Effluent

It is salutary for all pig producers to remember that toxic gases are produced from stored pig manure. When such manure is stored below the slatted floors of a pig unit, gas concentrations can be such as to cause illness or even death to both pigs and humans. Where gas concentrations are not sufficiently high to cause obvious illness in pigs and stock people, it is possible that they could still predispose to respiratory problems. The gases generated from pig effluent which can lead to these problems are ammonia, carbon dioxide and hydrogen sulphide, while carbon monoxide can also accumulate in pig houses where defective or oxygen-starved gas or diesel space heaters are used.

### AMMONIA

Although levels of ammonia of up to 50 parts per million (ppm) in pig house air probably do not affect the growth of healthy animals, corrective action is needed once the concentration exceeds 20 ppm because of possible effects on the stockman. Ammonia is colourless but can be readily detected by its characteristically pungent smell. However, stockmen vary in their ability to detect this gas at potentially harmful levels although it is a powerful irritant, particularly of the eyes.

### CARBON DIOXIDE

This gas is both colourless and odourless, and normal concentration of it in the atmosphere is 0.03 per cent. While concentrations of 0.5 to 1 per cent have no apparent effect on the pig, upper limits in the piggery of 0.3 to 0.5 per cent have been proposed. Higher than desirable levels have been blamed for outbreaks of tail biting in growing and finishing pigs, perhaps because this indicates a low rate of air change which makes the animals uncomfortable.

### CARBON MONOXIDE

This gas is also lacking in both colour and odour but is extremely poisonous. A concentration in air of as low as 1 per cent can cause death if breathed for any length of time. This gas is usually only a danger in farrowing houses where the ventilation rate is reduced to maintain temperature level and where gas or diesel-fired heaters are badly maintained. It is possible that concentrations as low as 150 to 200 ppm could be harmful in the farrowing house, and a concentration of 100 ppm (0.01 per cent) might constitute the upper limit of acceptability.

In the case of ammonia, carbon dioxide and carbon monoxide, it should be possible to keep the concentration of these within acceptable limits if the experienced and competent stockman uses his judgement to adjust the ventilation so as to remove staleness in the atmosphere and achieve instead an obvious freshness.

HYDROGEN SULPHIDE

The concentration of hydrogen sulphide in the atmosphere can increase rapidly when manure channels and pits are stirred or emptied. This happens because the gas remains dissolved in slurry until it is agitated. At a concentration of 500 to 1000 ppm this gas can cause dizziness, nausea, respiratory paralysis and unconsciousness. Higher levels than 1000 ppm result in immediate loss of consciousness and then death.

Concentrations as low as 20 ppm can bring about a loss of appetite; irritation of the eyes and respiratory tract can occur at a concentration of 50 to 100 ppm, while 150 ppm could prove fatal if exposure is prolonged. An upper tolerance level of 5 ppm is normally suggested and even that would be found unacceptable by most workers. The greatest caution is required when the slurry system is investigated, particularly when the operator descends into a slurry channel or pit and his head is below the general level of the piggery floor. In all cases, one person should be in attendance outside the pit or channel when a colleague is making the investigation. Ideally, respirators should be used.

Many people mistakenly assume that the characteristic 'rotten eggs' odour of this gas makes it readily detectable. It is true that this rule of thumb can be used to detect low concentrations (around 1 to 5 ppm). However, above this level the sense of smell tends to be paralysed by the gas and, at still higher levels, breathing control is paralysed, leading to a loss of consciousness.

Because it is so difficult to detect rising levels of hydrogen sulphide when slurry pits inside are being emptied or agitated, one should assume a build-up of the gas in such situations and exercise the utmost caution. If the animals cannot be removed from the building when slurry is being removed, then ventilating fans should be turned up to their maximum speed and doors, windows and ventilation inlets and outlets left wide open.

Hydrogen sulphide is heavier than air and therefore remains in highest concentration in the atmosphere immediately above the slurry. Therefore slurry pits under animals should not be allowed to become overfull.

METHANE

Methane is only produced in small quantities during normal storage of slurry. It is odourless, colourless and highly inflammable, a 5 per cent mixture of it in the air being explosive. There is a need to maintain good ventilation at animal level and to avoid slurry levels rising within 300 mm of the slats in stores under the pig building. One should never smoke or expose naked lights near slurry stores. Another problem which has arisen in practice involves fermentation in slurry tankers. Unless these have a proper safety valve and venting system, gas pressure from fermentation can build up and cause an explosion with sometimes fatal consequences.

FLIES

As well as making working conditions very unpleasant, flies can be vectors of disease organisms. Sound hygiene, regular cleaning of pig pens and avoiding the drying out of slurry and dung below slats can all help to minimise the incidence of flies. If these preventative measures fail, an appropriate insecticide can be used.

## Pig Effluent and Pollution

Of all farm animal manures, that from pigs has the most pungent odour in the opinion of most people. In addition, water courses can be polluted by effluent from pig enterprises because of failure to contain effluent adequately on the farm or through run-off after effluent is applied to fields. Air and water pollution are always greater in areas of dense pig population while associated problems are exacerbated when pig units are close to centres of human population.

In such situations, therefore, special measures must be taken to minimise environmental pollution and the 'nuisance' element to the human population. Probably no single area of the world has been affected more by these problems than the city state of Singapore and no region has taken more positive steps to deal with the problem. A brief outline of the relevant problems associated with pig production in that locality would therefore seem appropriate in that the special arrangements which Singapore was obliged to make within the last decade may have to be repeated by other countries with large concentrations of intensive pig enterprises in the future.

Singapore has a population of 2.5 million people and a population density of 3800 people per square kilometre. It has only 9000 hectares of agricultural land which is rapidly diminishing with the expanding population demanding more housing, development of public projects, factories and leisure and recreation areas.

Over 80 per cent of the population eat more pork than any other meat and consumers prefer 'warm' pork from pigs killed only a day or two previously. They dislike frozen meat which militates against meeting pigmeat requirements through imports from other countries. A total of 1.2 million pigs are produced for slaughter annually.

Previously, pig production was concentrated in the main water catchment area of the state. The resulting risk of serious water pollution and the need to control environmental pollution in general for the benefit of the population and to safeguard the considerable tourist industry demanded drastic official action. The possibility of becoming almost completely dependent on imports to meet their requirements for pigmeat was dismissed on the basis of the general dislike of frozen pork and because of the attendant financial risks of placing themselves at the mercy of outside suppliers, despite being almost entirely dependent on the import of feed ingredients for pig diets.

The action taken by the appropriate government agency was to ban pig production in the main water catchment area and resettle pig farmers, with payment of appropriate compensation and grants, in a relatively uninhabited area of the country. It became obligatory for producers to set up units above a minimum size and a minimum stocking rate per hectare of land occupied (about 2500 pigs per hectare occupied).

The objective of the government was to contain pollution from pig production and preserve the quality of the tropical environment at minimal cost. Accordingly, the Government provided grants for pig producers to build waste treatment facilities and producers who failed to build such a plant by 1984 were obliged to cease production. Grants were available only for units above 5000 pigs as this was considered to be the minimum unit capacity to make a waste plant an economically feasible proposition. Thus, smaller units had to amalgamate if they were to become eligible for such grants and stay in business. In addition to being under obligation to control pollution, pig producers were also subject to production targets.

Associated with the waste treatment operations were ancillary developments such as the growing of algae on treated pig effluent for protein production. The algae grown was processed using energy from biogas produced from solid components of pig effluent. Among the advantages of this approach was that algae add oxygen to the waste water while removing dissolved nutrients. This resulted in the removal of odours while the processed algae could make an important contribution to protein feed supplies and save on expensive imported soyabean meal. Also, following the culture of algae, the treated water could be recirculated as wash water and was also used for fish culture. Further developments involved fermentation of both liquid and solid pig wastes to produce high grade plant proteins suitable for animal feed.

Despite the very comprehensive arrangements which the Singapore authorities made to control pollution from pig farming activities in their very densely populated country, it would seem at the time of writing (1988) that they have had eventually to admit defeat; the decision appears now to have been taken to abandon pig production in the country and to rely on imports instead.

### Control of Undesirable Odours

Undesirable odours emanating from pig buildings stem mainly from the decomposition of pig effluent. Compounds causing these odours rarely, if ever, exceed safe air standards and are not injurious to human health. They can be regarded as nuisance pollutants and the pig producer has a moral and social responsibility to adopt an understanding and cooperative attitude to any complaints from the general public. Pig producers who adopt such an attitude and who operate well-designed and well-maintained facilities seldom experience any difficulty with the general public.

The main compounds which are produced from the decomposition of manure and which have objectionable odours to some people include ammonia, hydrogen sulphide, skatole, indole, the amines and mercaptans. Odour control measures include the reduction of the moisture content of the manure (anaerobic biological decomposition is largely halted when moisture content of manure is less than 40 per cent), covering of manure storage tanks and aerobic digestion. While properly designed and managed anaerobic lagoons are not free of undesirable odours, they seldom cause an odour problem. Other approaches to reducing the nuisance of undesirable odours include careful selection of the sites of new piggery units, selection of a field downwind from centres of human population when spreading manure, spreading in the morning rather than later in the day (since people tend to be most sensitive to undesirable odours in the early evening) and direct injection of effluent into the soil or immediate covering of the material after it is applied to land.

## Additional Reading

*Pork Industry Handbook*, USA Co-operative Extension Service, University of Illinois at Urbana-Champaign, USA.

Robertson A. M. (1977), *Farm Wastes Handbook*, Centre for Rural Buildings, Aberdeen, Scotland.

*Chapter 18*

# Transport, Lairage and Slaughter

There may be a tendency for pig producers to lose interest in their pigs when they are taken from their finishing pens in readiness to be transported to the slaughter house, apart from the obvious interest in subsequent carcass weight, grading and price. However, producers should maintain a keen interest in their pigs as they are being marshalled to the loading area, as they are being loaded for transport to the slaughter house, during such transit and off-loading at the slaughter house, in the period of lairage at the slaughter house and right up to the completion of the slaughter process. Organisation, procedures and facilities during this period must be such so as to cause minimal distress to the animal. This is in the interests both of the welfare of the animal and the ultimate quality of the meat. Serious problems can occur in this period in the form of deaths in transit and in lairage, injuries, carcass shrinkage and in carcass and meat quality if special care is not exercised.

### DEATH IN TRANSIT

The most obvious effect of lack of sufficient care in this period is the death of the pig. In the United Kingdom, it is estimated that about 9000 pigs die in transit each year. In one survey carried out by the Meat and Livestock Commission involving a total of 723,510 pigs being transported, a total of 530 or 0.07 per cent died in transit (see Table 18.1). It can be seen that the incidence of losses did not vary

**TABLE 18.1  Number of pigs carried, injuries and deaths**

| Class of pig | Number | Number injured | Number dead on arrival | Percentage deaths |
|---|---|---|---|---|
| Pork | 141,324 | 1 | 71 | 0.05 |
| Cutter⎱<br>Bacon⎰ | 548,040 | 10 | 442 | 0.08 |
| Heavy | 34,146 | 0 | 17 | 0.05 |
| Total | 723,510 | 11 | 530 | 0.07 |

(Source: Sains, A., Meat and Livestock Commission, 1980)

451

greatly between pork pigs, cutters, baconers and heavy pigs. The indications of predisposing factors to death in this survey were as follows:

### Location in Transporter

More deaths occurred immediately behind the driving cab, while losses were greater on the lower deck (see Figure 18.1). A possible reason for this might be the greater restriction of air flow in these positions. If this is the case, designers should pay attention to providing more positive ventilation in this area. Simpler reasons might be that these compartments are used more frequently and that pigs in these locations (especially just behind the driver's cab) are loaded first and are often in the transporter for longer periods.

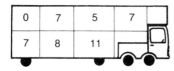

FIGURE 18.1   Number of deaths in relation to location on two types of transporter. (Source: Sains, A., Meat and Livestock Commission, 1980)

### Other Factors Associated with Death in Transit

FIGHTING
There were indications that two-thirds of the pigs which died had been involved in fights.

TEMPERATURE
Losses tended to be higher in hotter conditions, particularly where the container was made of alloy rather than wood.

FEEDING ON THE DAY OF TRANSPORT
Pigs which were fed on the day of transport tended to suffer higher losses and this tended to occur regardless of the distance travelled.

FEEDING SYSTEM
Feeding systems involved included ad lib. dry feeding systems, wet feeding by pipeline and once and twice daily restricted feeding. There were no indications of differences in losses in transit between these systems.

A similar survey in Saskatchewan, Canada, undertaken by the Saskatchewan Hog Marketing Commission, indicated that losses amounted to 0.4 per cent and were therefore considerably higher than in the British survey. Seventy per cent of the losses occurred in transit and the remaining 30 per cent at lairage in the abattoir between arrival and slaughter.

Losses were highest in both very hot and very cold weather conditions. The post-mortem examinations carried out by Dr Clark of the Saskatchewan College of Veterinary Medicine indicated that in about 16 per cent of these pigs there was evidence of pre-existing disease, while about 10 per cent were apparently injured during transit or in the lairage. Most of the remaining deaths applied to pigs which had apparently been thriving on the farm and were in excellent body condition. The indications in most of these was that they had died from acute heart failure.

Incidence of deaths during transit and lairage are reported to be higher in other countries than those detailed above for Britain and Saskatchewan. Losses between 0.5 and over 1 per cent have been reported from countries such as Belgium, West Germany and Holland. It is most unlikely that less adequate transport and lairage facilities are to blame, and the most likely cause is the greater proportion of pigs suffering from the porcine stress syndrome (PSS) in these countries because of the high incidence of PSS in particular extreme meat-type strains, such as types of Pietrain, Belgian and German Landrace.

Some of the causes of death in transit in these studies in Britain and Canada have been substantiated in various studies, while other predisposing factors have also been highlighted as follows:

*1. Timing of last feed*
When pigs are on controlled feed intakes, involving either once or twice daily feeding of fairly large quantities of food at a time, feeding such a meal soon before loading appears to predispose to a higher incidence of deaths in transit (see Table 18.2). It would, therefore, appear that on controlled feeding systems, the withholding of feed within 6 to 12 hours of loading is advisable so as to avoid loading and transporting pigs with a full stomach.

**TABLE 18.2  Number of bacon pigs dead on arrival, classified by time interval between last feed and loading**

| Time interval last feed to loading | No of pigs despatched | No of deaths | Deaths per thousand |
|---|---|---|---|
| >12 hours | 9394 | 16 | 1.7 |
| 6−12 hours | 3007 | 4 | 1.3 |
| 2−6 hours | 8569 | 57 | 6.7 |

(Source: Robertson, 1987)

*2. Load density*
Load density is defined as the number of pigs being transported in relation to the recommended stocking in the available space. The data collected by Robertson

(1987) in the north of Scotland indicated the dangers of stocking the transporter up to or over recommended capacity (see Table 18.3). The adverse effects of overstocking can be accentuated by both the distance travelled and high temperature.

**TABLE 18.3  Deaths in transit of bacon pigs in relation to load density**

| Vehicle load density | No of pigs despatched | No of deaths | Deaths per thousand |
|---|---|---|---|
| 80–89% | 9,243 | 16 | 1.7 |
| 90–99% | 10,702 | 36 | 3.4 |
| ≥ 100% | 9,679 | 52 | 5.4 |

(Source: Robertson, 1987)

*3.  Distance travelled*

The data of Robertson in the north of Scotland also indicated that deaths in transit were considerably higher when transit distance exceeded 200 miles (322 km) (see Table 18.4).

To minimise the adverse effects of long transit distance it is important to be particularly careful during the loading process, to avoid overstocking in the transporter and to ensure good environmental conditions (adequate air flow and a suitable temperature) during the journey.

**TABLE 18.4  Deaths in transit of bacon pigs in relation to farm-to-processor distance**

| Distance (miles) farm to processor | No of pigs despatched | No of deaths | Deaths per thousand |
|---|---|---|---|
| ≤ 99 | 1,933 | 4 | 2.1 |
| 100–199 | 24,599 | 55 | 2.2 |
| 200–299 | 10,256 | 63 | 6.1 |
| ≥ 300 | 3,075 | 20 | 6.5 |

(Source: Robertson, 1987)

*4.  Temperature during transit*

The data in Figure 18.2 indicate increasing mortality during transportation as air temperature rises above 20°C. It is therefore important to ensure good control of air flow and temperature within the transporter and/or to travel during the cooler periods of the day in hot periods of the year. Wet sand on the floor of the transporter in hot weather also helps to keep pigs cooler. The adverse effects of

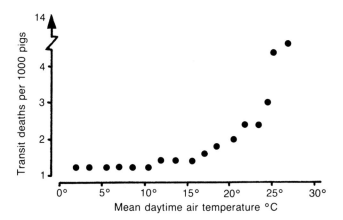

FIGURE 18.2   The relationship between mean daytime air temperature and transit deaths per thousand pigs, January to June. (From Smith, J.P. and Allen, W.M., 1976)

excessively cold conditions during transportation in the Canadian study cited earlier are indicated in Figure 18.3. The problems in the hot months of June and July are obvious but deaths also tended to be higher in the colder months of December and January. More adequate protection from air flow and cold during transportation in severe winters such as those experienced in Western Canada is therefore most desirable.

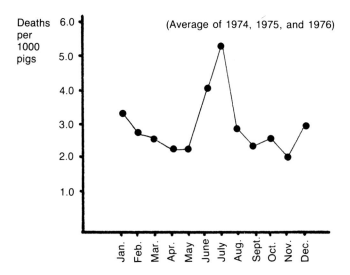

FIGURE 18.3   Monthly variation in transport deaths in Saskatchewan market weight hogs. (Source: McClung, 1980)

## SHRINKAGE IN LIVEWEIGHT AND CARCASS WEIGHT

During transit from farm to abattoir, pigs can lose between 2 and 10 per cent of their original liveweight. Much of this weight loss is due to defaecation and urination but there is also loss of carcass weight. The amount by which the deadweight is reduced due to transport is known as shrinkage.

The effects of different degrees of deprivation of feed and water on shrinkage in liveweight and carcass weight and on other carcass traits are summarised in Table 18.5. It can be seen that 24 hour deprivation of food effects a shrinkage in carcass weight of 0.9 kg while longer food deprivation and deprivation of water in addition accentuate the effect.

**TABLE 18.5  Effect of withholding feed, water or both before slaughter on liveweight and carcass shrink**

|  | | *Treatment* | | | *Difference owing* |
|---|---|---|---|---|---|
| *Feed removed hrs before slaughter* | *0* | *24* | *24* | *48* | *to withholding* |
| *Water removed hrs before slaughter* | *0* | *0* | *24* | *0* | *feed and/or water* |
| Final weight (*kg*) | 93.2 | 90.8 | 92.1 | 91.6 | — |
| Weight after feed and water withheld (*kg*) | — | 86.3 | 86.9 | 84.3 | yes |
| Liveweight shrink (%) | — | 5.0 | 5.7 | 7.9 | yes |
| Apparent carcass shrink (*kg*) | — | 0.9 | 1.5 | 2.8 | yes |
| Carcass length (*cm*) | 77.2 | 76.2 | 77.2 | 77.2 | no |
| Back fat (*cm*) | 3.7 | 3.7 | 3.7 | 3.3 | no except at 48 hours |
| Area of loin eye (*sq cm*) | 25.9 | 25.0 | 24.3 | 25.9 | no |

(Source: Bowland and Standish, 1966)

Environmental temperature during transit and duration and length of journey also affect shrinkage (see Tables 18.6 and 18.7). This work was carried out in Indiana, USA and indicates that temperature extremes below $-7°C$ and above $27°C$ increase shrinkage while a combination of low temperature and long duration of

**TABLE 18.6  Effect of variation above or below 10°C (50°F) over time on in-transit shrinkage of slaughter weight market pigs: 232 observations**

| | *Percentage weight loss by temperature range* | | |
|---|---|---|---|
| *Hours in transit* | *minus 17—minus 7°C (1—20°F)* | *20—27°C (69—80°F)* | *over 27°C (over 80°F)* |
| Up to 1 | 0.96 | 0.54 | 0.87 |
| 1—2 | 1.17 | 0.84 | 1.00 |
| 2—4 | 1.24 | 1.26 | 1.54 |
| More than 4 | 3.27 | 1.75 | 1.51 |

(Source: Stout and Cox, 1959)

**TABLE 18.7   Per cent in-transit shrinkage of pigs shipped from Indiana concentration points**

| Distance shipped (miles) | % in-transit shrinkage |
|---|---|
| 100 | 1.7 |
| 200 | 2.0 |
| 600 | 3.8 |

(Source: Stout and Armstrong, 1960)

travel has a particularly adverse effect. In very hot weather, provision of wet sand on the floor of the transporter is useful in reducing shrinkage. As might be expected, the greater the distance travelled, the greater the shrinkage.

## ADVERSE EFFECTS ON MEAT QUALITY

In Chapters 5 and 6, the problem of porcine stress syndrome (PSS) in pigs was discussed in the context of genetic improvement. It was noted that although strains of pig with PSS have desirable carcass characteristics in terms of high lean to fat ratio, good eye muscle area, high killing out percentage and higher proportion of high-priced cuts, they suffer from problems of poorer reproductive performance and meat quality while being liable to sudden death when subjected to stress. The problems of PSS in relation to meat quality and liability to sudden death will be further developed in this chapter. A comparison of some breeds with high and low incidence of PSS is presented in Table 18.8.

It can be seen that the Pietrain and Belgian Landrace, which have a higher proportion of lean cuts than the Large White and Norwegian Landrace, also have a considerably higher incidence of death loss in transit. Those pigs with PSS produce a higher level of lactic acid (lactate) when subjected to exercise or stress and this tends to accumulate in the muscle, causing a form of cramp. This can be fatal when it affects the heart muscle and hence the liability of these genotypes to heart attack. This higher accumulation of lactic acid in the muscle also increases the acidity of the muscle (i.e. lowers the pH). While it is normal for the pH of meat to fall below

**TABLE 18.8   A comparison of some breeds with high and low incidence of PSS**

| Breed | Number of pigs | Lean cuts (%) | Lactate (μmol/g) | Death loss during marketing (%) |
|---|---|---|---|---|
| Large White | 96 | 54.72 | 7.91 | 1.05 |
| Norway Landrace | 80 | 54.39 | 11.21 | 0 |
| Dutch Landrace | 112 | 54.58 | 11.43 | 2.68 |
| Pietrain | 96 | 59.37 | 18.45 | 5.21 |
| Belgian Landrace | 80 | 57.85 | 14.35 | 10.37 |

(Source: Sybesma, 1972)

5.8 within a few hours of slaughter (it is also beneficial because it improves the keeping quality of meat), a sudden drop in muscle pH to 5.8 or less within 45 minutes of slaughter reduces the ability of the lean meat to hold water and this results in fluid loss or 'drip' loss from the meat. The pre-slaughter stress, through the action of adrenalin, also restricts blood flow in the muscle which will result in a pale-coloured muscle following slaughter. Thus, the meat of such a pig following slaughter is said to be pale, soft and exudative (PSE).

While pigs with PSS are particularly prone to stress and therefore to problems of PSE in their meat, preslaughter stress can also lead to PSE problems in pigs which do not have PSS. As indicated above, this comes about through the effects of pre-slaughter stress in stimulating production of adrenalin which causes the blood vessels to contract, thus restricting blood flow to the muscles. This results in muscle paleness and a build-up in lactic acid in the muscle brought about by incomplete oxidation of muscle glycogen due to a shortage of oxygen reaching the cells. Pigs subjected to considerable physical exercise prior to slaughter (e.g. following fighting) can also end up with meat quality problems. This is because they may have used up most of their muscle glycogen so that, within a few hours after slaughter, muscle pH may still be at 6 or above because there is insufficient glycogen left in the muscle for production of lactic acid. This problem is associated with the incidence of what is termed DFD (dark, firm, dry) meat and can have adverse effects on the keeping quality of the meat. Thus, in normal pigs, pre-slaughter stress can have adverse effects on meat quality, and it is therefore vitally important that the degree to which pigs are stressed prior to slaughter should be reduced to an absolute minimum. Careful handling and good conditions are essential at all stages from the time they leave their home pens, during loading, transporting, off-loading and in lairage right up to the time of slaughter.

## BEHAVIOUR OF PIGS WHILE PREPARING FOR LOADING, DURING LOADING AND TRANSPORTATION AND IN LAIRAGE

Before deciding on optimum provision during these phases, it is important to establish some details on pig behaviour at this time.

Harassment of pigs in transferring them from their pens to the loading facilities is stressful, this being indicated by a rise in corticosteroids in the blood. With good arrangements and patient, competent stockpeople using stock boards to provide a solid barrier behind pigs being moved in fairly small groups, devices such as electric goads should certainly not be necessary.

When pigs from different pens are mixed, they fight prior to loading. Therefore, they should be taken from their pens immediately before loading or else pigs from different pens should be penned separately in the loading area. Once the journey begins, pigs originating from different pens will stop fighting and, if space permits, pigs will tend to group together at first in the centre of the area and avoid standing against the side of the container. Non-slip floors in the transporter will help to maintain this position. As the journey gets under way, pigs with adequate space will tend to lie down for most of the time while the vehicle is in motion.

When the transporter stops, pigs will start to fight again, so that the fewer stops there are, the less fighting occurs and the fewer the biting injuries sustained. Fighting among strange pigs will tend to restart while in lairage and is more intense between entire male pigs. This can result in serious skin damage as well as meat quality problems. As indicated earlier, during transportation in very hot conditions, pigs can suffer from heat stress. Specially ventilated transporters are necessary to prevent this occurring. Alternatively, in such weather, pigs can be transported at night when it is cooler.

## LOADING FACILITIES FOR PIGS

Fighting among pigs will be minimised if pigs are loaded directly from their pens, transported direct to the abattoir without any stops and slaughtered almost immediately after arrival at the abattoir.

Plate 18.1  Pigs being collected from various pens into a well-bedded area adjacent to the loading ramp in preparation for transport. (Courtesy of Pig Improvement Company)

However, if pigs are left in their pens until the transporter arrives, the stockman is likely to be under pressure to get the pigs out so as not to delay the driver of the transporter unduly. As a result, pigs could well be subjected to undue disturbance and rough handling to get them into the transporter quickly. It is more satisfactory if a special loading facility exists, and there is evidence that mortality during transport is lower if pigs are collected into special holding pens a few hours before loading. Features of this area to facilitate pig movement should be good lighting, solid walls to the race and pens to avoid distraction, good floors while avoiding excessive gradients.

An example of such special holding pens is illustrated in Figure 18.4. It consists of a sequence of holding pens leading to the loading area, each pen preferably holding the pigs from a single pen in the piggery. Thus, mixing of strange pigs and resulting fighting while awaiting loading is avoided. Where mixing of pigs from different pens prior to loading is unavoidable, time in the loading area should be minimal and, during this period, distracting materials such as bunches of straw thrown among the pigs as soon as they are mixed will help to take up their attention and distract them from each other. It is important to avoid an excessive slope in the loading area since the greater the angle of the slope, the more reluctant pigs will be to walk up it. The gradient should be between 1 in 9 and 1 in 5 (see Table 18.9). It is clear from this data that the steeper the slope at loading, the greater the increase in heart rate.

While these holding facilities may appear to be very elaborate, it is in the interests of both pig welfare and ultimate meat quality that adequate attention is paid to holding and loading facilities and to careful handling when pigs are drawn in readiness for transport to the abattoir. In a 1977 study, the Meat and Livestock Commission in Britain estimated that the annual cost of carcass condemnations caused by careless handling was £420,000. There would, of course, be considerable additional penalties in the form of deaths in transit and inferior meat quality.

TABLE 18.9  Heart rate of pigs directly after climbing a loading bridge up to a height of 122 cm (the angles of the loading bridges are different). Each animal was accompanied by three other pigs

| Angle of loading bridge (°) | Number of animals | Heart rate (% of basic value) | Difference (progressive) |
|---|---|---|---|
| 15 | 20 | $139 \pm 19$ | |
| 20 | 19 | $160 \pm 17$ | 21** |
| 25 | 20 | $177 \pm 16$ | 17* |
| 30 | 21 | $202 \pm 23$ | 25** |

** Difference significant at the 99 per cent level of probability.
*  Difference significant at the 95 per cent level of probability.
(From: Van Putten and Elshof, 1978)

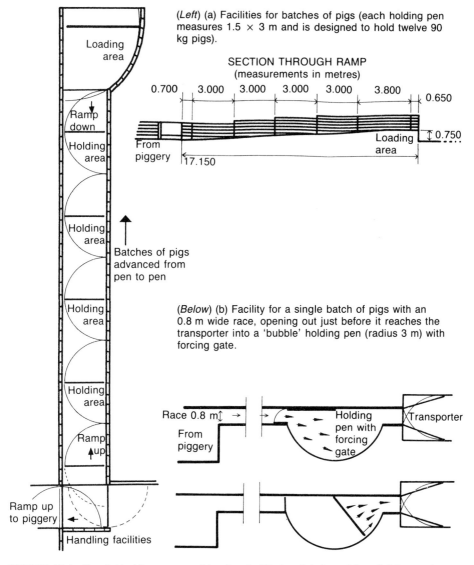

(*Left*) (a) Facilities for batches of pigs (each holding pen measures 1.5 × 3 m and is designed to hold twelve 90 kg pigs).

**SECTION THROUGH RAMP**
(measurements in metres)

(*Below*) (b) Facility for a single batch of pigs with an 0.8 m wide race, opening out just before it reaches the transporter into a 'bubble' holding pen (radius 3 m) with forcing gate.

FIGURE 18.4   Special holding pens and loading facility to minimise mixing, fighting and stress. (Courtesy of MAFF, 1983)

## LIVESTOCK TRANSPORTERS

In many countries vehicles used for the transport of livestock are the subject of legislation, and details are specified to safeguard the welfare of animals during loading, unloading and carriage. Although specific deck heights are not usually

Plate 18.2 Pigs en route to the processing plant should be handled very carefully during loading, offloading and at lairage if stress-related meat quality problems are to be avoided. (Courtesy of Pig International)

given in the United Kingdom, in transporters carrying animals on more than one level, the decks must be constructed in such a manner as to enable any animal being transported to stand in its natural position with sufficient space above to allow for the proper circulation of air. Deck heights of containers will therefore vary and will be dependent on the type of animal to be carried.

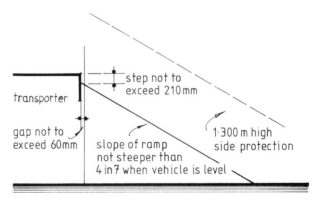

FIGURE 18.5 Livestock vehicle ramp constraints.

Legislation in the United Kingdom allows for animals to be loaded or unloaded from a container by a variety of means. This includes a ramp, which may or may not be carried on the vehicle, a loading bank, mechanical lifting gear or manual lifting. However, irrespective of the method employed, vehicles are obliged to carry a ramp of suitable design for unloading livestock in an emergency. The normal solution is to provide a full height tailgate which in effect becomes a ramp when in the lowered position. The legal constraints in the United Kingdom imposed on such a ramp are shown in Figure 18.5. Although the maximum permissible gradient is given as 4 in 7 when a vehicle is standing on level ground, commonsense would suggest that the gradient should be as near to the horizontal as possible to facilitate the loading and unloading operations. The data in Table 18.9 indicate the adverse effect of excessive gradient on heart rate.

Adequate precautions must be taken to ensure that animals are afforded a proper foothold on any ramp. Figure 18.6 illustrates a vehicle in position against a loading ramp. The variation in the height of vehicle platforms should present no difficulty provided the height of the loading ramp does not exceed the lowest vehicle platform height. It is desirable to have the vehicle stance as level as possible with only sufficient slope to drain surface water.

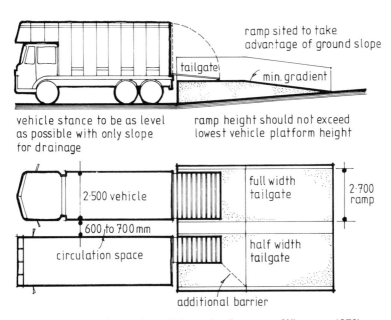

FIGURE 18.6  Space for vehicles at loading ramp. (Wiseman, 1978)

Where space for static ramps and loading bays is not available, hydraulically operated lifting platforms may be used, with lifting heights capable of 'off and on' loading livestock from and to most multi-decked transporters. A typical hydraulic platform is shown in Figure 18.7. Such lifting platforms may also be attached to the vehicle. They can greatly facilitate the loading and off-loading operations resulting in a time saving, a reduced degree of stress on the pigs and improved meat quality.

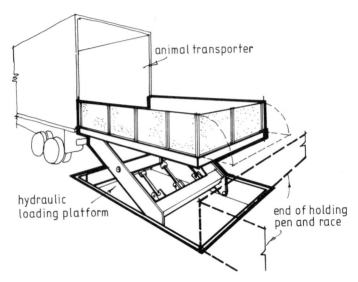

FIGURE 18.7   Hydraulic loading platform.

Since there will be increasing emphasis on aspects of meat quality in the future by both the processor and consumer, improved handling, loading and transport facilities, including the use of hydraulic platforms for loading and unloading, are bound to be increasingly emphasised.

Overstocking in transporters has been mentioned earlier. This problem is not helped by lack of sufficient ventilation in some vehicles, and it has been recommended that the space per pig be increased by up to 15 per cent in hot weather conditions. The materials used in vehicle construction are also important. British work has shown that above 17°C there is an increase in mortality in vehicles of single-skin alloy construction compared with vehicles constructed of wood or composite materials.

## HANDLING AT LAIRAGE

### Desirable Timing of Slaughter After Arrival

As pigs have been subjected to stressful conditions of varying degrees during loading, transport and off-loading and possibly a degree of dehydration on long journeys, it is usually considered desirable to give them a short period of rest in lairage before slaughter. If conditions are suitable in lairage this should help the pig to recover its physiological balance and, as a result, problems with meat quality following slaughter should be reduced.

In Polish work, pigs transported up to 100 km from a farm and slaughtered immediately on arrival at the abattoir had a 1 per cent higher killing-out percentage and better muscle colour than those in which slaughter was delayed for 24 hours. However, the latter group were superior in terms of both pH and moisture content of meat. It was inferred in this work that if conditions at lairage were better for the pigs, such as improved penning and provision of water, then the merits of delaying slaughter for up to 24 hours after arrival might have been greater.

It was also found that delaying slaughter for 24 hours after arrival had greater adverse effects on pigs from large industrial farms than on those from small family farms. It was inferred that the latter pigs were more amenable to handling and less affected by the change in environmental conditions between farm and abattoir.

## Special Treatment in Lairage

As indicated earlier, it has been recognised for a considerable time that prolonged stress prior to slaughter can adversely affect the quality of pigmeat. Such conditions result in the depletion of muscle glycogen reserves and a consequent lower than optimum production of lactic acid in the carcass after slaughter. The resulting low ultimate level of acidity in the meat (pH above 6.0) makes the meat and bacon from it more susceptible to the problem of DFD and to bacterial spoilage than normal pigmeat, the ultimate pH of which should be between 5.4 and 5.8. Attempts have been made to correct this problem by feeding a readily assimilated carbohydrate prior to slaughter in an attempt to enhance muscle glycogen reserves for subsequent breakdown to lactic acid after slaughter.

At the University of Newcastle upon Tyne, Fernandez, Smith, Ellis, Clark and Armstrong found that, relative to slaughter immediately after arrival at the abattoir and to a 'water only' treatment for 14 hours before slaughter, the provision of a solution of sucrose (about 902 g per pig) or of glucose syrup (about 704 g per pig) for 4 hours, followed by a 10 hour period of access to water only, resulted in a reduction in muscle pH and an increase in liver weight. A longer period of access to glucose or sucrose solution (12 hours), followed by a 2 hour period of access to water only before slaughter, resulted in a reduction in carcass yield, probably because of an initial transfer of water from the body into the intestinal lumen brought about by the hypertonic nature of these sugar solutions. Access to a glucose syrup solution for the first 4 hours in lairage followed by 10 hours access to water only before slaughter can increase carcass yield compared to access to water only prior to slaughter, provided that the intakes of sugar and subsequently water are high.

Similar treatment has also been shown to increase bacon yield relative to immediate slaughter on arrival at the abattoir and overnight lairage with access to water only before slaughter. This increase appears to be due entirely to the influence of this treatment in increasing carcass yield since these carcasses actually gained less weight during the curing process.

There is general agreement that the feeding of sugars before slaughter results in

Plate 18.3  Pigs at lairage drinking sucrose solution made available for a limited period to
restore muscle glycogen reserves prior to slaughter in pigs subjected to stressful
conditions during loading and in transportation. This provision of a readily assimilated
carbohydrate source helps to improve keeping quality of meat following slaughter.
(Courtesy of Pig International)

increased liver weights due to the great capacity of the liver to store glycogen and
associated water. Consumer studies indicate that the heavier liver produced in this
way, despite being higher in glycogen and lower in protein, is generally as acceptable to the consumer as is normal liver. Thus, where pigs are in lairage overnight,
provision of a glucose syrup solution followed by water may reduce slightly the
weight gain of the carcass during the curing process, but this is more than offset
by a favourable response in carcass yield, the net result being a higher yield of
bacon. Glucose feeding in this way results in an increase in liver weight and reduction in the ultimate pH of lean meat. It is difficult to generalise on the cost effectiveness of this practice, which will be dependent on the conditions provided in
overnight lairage and on the degree of exhaustion of pigs on arrival at the abattoir.

    Some experts would argue that if handling and conditions were improved be-
tween the farm and the processing unit and at lairage, resulting in a considerably
lower degree of stress in the pigs, there would be less need for such special
'remedial' treatment in the lairage. In some situations, much-improved facilities

and better cooperation between the farmer, haulier and processor, followed by slaughter within a few hours of delivery at the processing plant, have resulted in a lower degree of shrinkage, fewer deaths and superior meat quality, thus benefitting the producer, the processor and the consumer.

## Slaughtering Procedures

For reasons of humanity and animal welfare it is forbidden in most countries to bleed slaughter pigs without stunning. There are three main forms of stunning.

MECHANICAL STUNNING
This is carried out with a type of pistol which crushes the skull rendering the animal unconscious immediately on impact.

CARBON DIOXIDE STUNNING
Animals are led into a tunnel with an atmosphere of 70 to 80 per cent carbon dioxide. On inhaling this gas, pigs become unconscious within 2 seconds.

ELECTRICAL STUNNING
This involves the use of a pair of tongs to apply an electrical charge to the pig's head. Effective stunning using this method results in unconsciousness within 1 second of application and unconsciousness persists for 66 seconds, on average. A current of 1.25 amps is necessary and equipment must be of at least 180 to 220 V and preferably 300 to 600 V; 600 V equipment can now be made perfectly safe.

Effective stunning makes possible prompt and more complete bleeding which are important in relation to minimising blood splashes (the rupture of capillaries resulting in staining of fatty tissues). It also minimises intensive muscle contractions and resulting PSE problems.

### MOVEMENT OF ANIMALS FROM LAIRAGE TOWARDS LOCATION OF STUNNING

This must be carried out very carefully so as to minimise problems of PSE and DFD meat. In Denmark, automatic moving fences push the animals slowly in the right direction in single file. The pig moves between 2 moving belts and this 'restrainer' presses the animal on both sides, lifting it from the floor and bringing it smoothly to the stunning operator. In the Netherlands, an automatic stunning device based on the 'restrainer' is being developed. No human manipulation of the apparatus is necessary so that it can be used with very high voltages resulting in immediate stunning. Such procedures are in the interests of both humane slaughter and of good meat quality.

### WELFARE

The processes of loading, transport and slaughter have with good reason caused some worries among those of us concerned with welfare. Unfortunately, an uncaring attitude in some people has given leverage for adverse media coverage. It is important from the point of view of presenting pigmeat as an acceptable food that every possible care be taken to make transport and slaughter as humane as possible.

## ADDITIONAL READING

Bacon and Meat Manufacturers Association (1986), *Code of Practice for the Hygienic Manufacture of Meat Products*, BMMA, London.

Gregory N. G. (1985), 'Stunning and Slaughter of Pigs', *Pig News and Information* **6**, 407–413.

Moss R, (Ed.) (1981), *Transport of Animals Intended for Breeding, Production and Slaughter*, Martinus Nijhoff, The Hague.

*Pork Industry Handbook*, USA Co-operative Extension Service, University of Illinois at Urbana-Champaign, USA.

# Chapter 19

# Marketing

## INVOLVEMENT OF PRODUCERS IN MARKETING

Up to comparatively recently, the main interest of farmers in their finished pigs ended when they left the farm gate on their road to market. They certainly looked forward to receiving market returns in terms of carcass weight, grade and price but they did not involve themselves in marketing. They left that task to the abattoir, the meat processor, the meat wholesaler and the retailer. Such an attitude is understandable in situations in which pig production is very profitable or where there is a guaranteed price for the product or in an expanding market in terms of demand where pigmeat of almost any quality can be sold successfully at a reasonable price. However, pig producers have been accused for a long time of not taking sufficient interest in marketing and in the preferences of the final consumer.

There are many reasons why the producer should become more involved in marketing, and he can help to stimulate some of the functions of an efficient marketing system. Among such functions are the following:

1. Consumer requirements must be signalled through the entire marketing system to the producer.
2. Pigs must be transported from the farm at minimum cost and handled carefully in lairage consistent with maximum safety and no adverse effects on carcass and meat quality.
3. Pigmeat must be processed, packaged and presented in retail outlets under very hygienic conditions so that the wholesomeness of the meat and the health of the consumer are fully safeguarded.
4. Pigs must be converted into an attractive variety of pork and processed products at low cost, consistent with good hygiene and high quality in the final product and maximum appeal to the modern consumer.
5. Adequate information must be available to forecast demand, supply and price to aid planning of production and marketing.
6. The marketing system should undertake an appropriate level of promotion of pigmeat and pigmeat products to foster demand.

The links in the chain between producer and consumer must not be considered as independent but as interdependent entities.

469

## The Producer to Consumer Marketing Chain

The possible links in this chain are shown in Figure 19.1. The producer to consumer chain can be direct, as in the case of the producer who is licensed and has the facilities to slaughter his own pigs, or it can involve many intermediate stages.

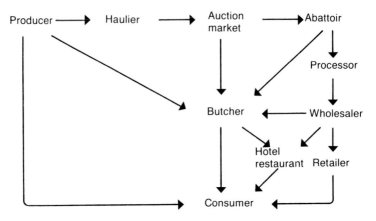

FIGURE 19.1    Possible links in the chain from producer to consumer.

Each component of the chain has an important influence on the quality, range and acceptability of products reaching the consumer and all must therefore be considered as interdependent organisations which control the products finally offered to the consumer. They must also be seen as interdependent entities so that consumer requirements can be relayed efficiently up through the chain in order that each component of that chain can organise its operation to ensure that demands are met as nearly as possible for the price the consumer is willing to pay. Since demands may vary greatly between different sectors of the consuming public (perhaps according to age grouping or social stratum) and because demands may change seasonally and over time, this communication from consumer through the interdependent links in the chain to the producer must be rapid and efficient.

The more all components of the production, processing and marketing chain can cater for consumer requirements, the greater will be the demand for pigmeat. Increased demand has a favourable effect on the price paid for pigmeat and creates opportunities for expansion of the industry. Some of the factors affecting demand for pigmeat will now be outlined.

## Factors Affecting Demand for Pigmeat

### 1.  Price

One way of increasing consumption of pigmeat is for producers to reduce the price relative to other meats and competitive products. The extent to which demand can be increased for a unit reduction in price is called the *price elasticity of demand*. For the United Kingdom, estimates of the price elasticity of demand for pork and other pigmeat products have been estimated by the National Food Survey. A recent estimate (1987) gave a value of minus 0.6. This means that for each 10 per cent reduction in price, the consumption will rise by 6 per cent.

## 2. Competitive Meats and Meat Substitutes

The main alternative meats to pigmeat are mutton and lamb, beef and chicken. In the developed countries which are fairly self-sufficient in cereals and, to some extent, in protein concentrates, lamb and beef tend to be more expensive to produce and therefore have to be sold at a higher price than chicken and pigmeat. Meat 'substitutes' containing cereals, soya bean protein, cheese or very small proportions of real meat are providing an increasing challenge to real meat in the market place.

The *cross-price elasticity of demand* is the term given to the change in demand for a product per unit increase or decrease in the price of a competitive product. For example, if the cross-price elasticity of demand for pigmeat in a specific country at a given time was 0.4, then if the price of poultry meat rose by 10 per cent, the demand for pigmeat would increase by 4 per cent.

## 3. Income

The quantity of pigmeat consumed will increase much faster as incomes rise in a developing country like Mexico relative to countries which are already affluent, such as many in the EEC. This change in demand for a product for a unit change in income is called *income elasticity*. For a relatively low income country like Mexico, demand for pigmeat might increase by about 15 per cent for a 10 per cent rise in income. For a relatively prosperous country such as Britain, income elasticity of demand for pigmeat has been around 0.4 in recent years, that is, for each 10 per cent rise in income, demand for pigmeat has increased by about 4 per cent. However, the amount spent on pigmeat might increase by more than 4 per cent – perhaps by about 6 per cent. The amount spent on the product tends to rise more than the quantity consumed since, as consumers become more affluent, they tend to change from buying cheaper pork products, such as belly of pork and lard, to more expensive components like chops and fat-trimmed loins.

## 4. Consumer Taste

Apart from intolerance to pigmeat on the grounds of religion, a variety of other objections have also been levelled. Some are based on superstition, for example, the belief that pork should not be consumed during the months of May, June, July and August when the letter 'r' does not appear in the name of the month as it does in the other months of the year. Some associate pork with a high fat content, with being high in calories and with problems of coronary heart disease. Others consider that pork is difficult to cook and that it is a meat only for special occasions.

An increasing proportion of consumers, mainly of younger generations, object to eating meat on moral grounds in relation to animal production in general and to aspects of animal welfare in particular.

## 5. Quality

Aspects of carcass and meat quality and the major factors influencing these were dealt with thoroughly in Chapters 4 and 16. Important aspects of quality which influence demand for pigmeat include high lean to fat and lean to bone ratio, the depth of lean meat above the bone, the quality of lean and the quality of fat. With regard to aspects of fat quality, the subcutaneous fat layers should not separate, in the interests of both ease of cutting and presentation, the fat should not be soft and 'floppy', while the connective tissue content in fat should be minimal. The lean meat should be neither pale, soft and exudative (PSE) nor dark, firm and dry (DFD). The meat should be well endowed with the qualities of tenderness, juiciness and flavour.

In many countries, including the United Kingdom, there is likely to be a fairly static market for meat in the future, and, given adequate total supplies of meat, consumers are likely to become increasingly quality conscious. Thus, the meats and meat products which best come up to the quality expectations of the consumer at a price he or she can afford will gain an increased market share. All components of the pigmeat production chain, including the original breeders of the stock, must become more conscious of producing meat and meat products of higher quality at an increasingly competitive price.

## 6. Processing, product range and packaging

In developed countries, where the market is adequately supplied with meat, consumers become more discriminating in their choice. This choice is influenced by such factors as price, quality, the range of products available, packaging and appearance, ease and quickness of cooking and absence of waste. These characteristics have become even more important with the gradual change in retailing from butchers' shops to self-service supermarkets. This change in retailing has made such factors as shelf-life, size and attractiveness of the pack (see colour plate 33) and consistency and repeatability of product even more important. Dr Geoffrey Harrington, Marketing Director of the Meat and Livestock Commission in the United Kingdom, claims that, against the background depicted above, increased market share will be gained by the meat industry sector which is most attractive to consumers in terms of having 'the best range of competitively priced, consistent, well-presented products that meet their needs most closely'.

These requirements present a formidable challenge to all components in the chain of production of pigmeat from breeder to retailer. Only by rising to this challenge will product retail prices be stimulated and an increased market share won.

## 7. Sales Promotion

In a situation where demand for a product is outstripping supply, little or no effort in terms of sales promotion is necessary. On the other hand, in the present situation where demand for meat in many developed countries is no longer rising but static, and where export markets are difficult to obtain, meat promotion activities which appeal to both the home consumer and potential customer overseas are essential if demand is to be increased to stimulate price and justify further expansion of the industry.

Many countries are now becoming active in meat promotion. This takes the form of generic promotion of all meats or of a specific meat, for example 'British Bacon' or 'Danish Bacon'. It also involves promotion of particular brands of pigmeat from different processors, e.g. of bacon, pork or processed pigmeat products such as sausages, pies, salami and pâté.

Promotion of pigmeat in its various forms and of particular companies' branded products is carried out using all media sources. This involves advertising through television, radio, newspapers, magazines, point of sale displays in the butcher's shop or the supermarket and special promotions at the retail end. Other promotional techniques include cookery demonstrations and the issue of free information booklets on the product and recipe leaflets. These promotions are aimed at consumers in general, but some appeal particularly to young housewives and school children since the younger generation in many countries tend to be more antagonistic to meat-eating.

Some promotions have the objective of educating doctors, dieticians and home economists and emphasise characteristics such as the nutritional strengths, variety, versatility, ease of cooking properties and 'value for money' of good-quality pigmeat products. Promotions for the catering and food service establishments likewise focus on the versatility and appetite appeal of pigmeat products and their profitability to the caterer.

Pigmeat promotion exercises are often financed by statutory levies on producers and the meat trade. Such promotion can often be more successful when carried out by cooperatives or joint organisations, sometimes vertically integrated, involving producers and all sectors of the slaughtering, processing and retail trades.

Vital to the success of promotion of pigmeat products are consistency of product and a constant availability of supply at all retail outlets where consumers have been stimulated to seek such a product.

In most countries, the amount of money spent on pigmeat promotion has been relatively small (a fraction of 1 per cent) in relation to the value of the final product. It is likely that the pig industries in most countries can justify spending more on pigmeat promotion in the future if pigmeat products are to win a bigger share of the total meat and meat substitute market and if expansion possibilities for the indigenous pigmeat production industry are to be created.

Evaluating the success of a promotional campaign is always difficult because of simultaneous changes in the availability and price of competitive meats. However, most soundly designed and well-conducted pigmeat promotional exercises have been shown to be cost effective. In one pork promotion exercise in Britain in 1979 during a period when a surplus of pork in relation to market demand was in danger of developing, purchases of pork increased by 16 per cent while prices were 5.5 per cent higher relative to the equivalent period in the previous year. Thus, pigmeat promotions are likely to be useful in influencing short-term demand during a period when surplus supplies are available so as to prevent an oversupply situation since only a very small surplus can have a devastating effect on price.

Pigmeat promotion techniques used to increase demand within a particular country can also be applied to increase pigmeat export opportunities to other countries.

## The Producer's Role in the Marketing of Pigmeat

The main steps the producer can take to aid the marketing of pigmeat have been outlined by Dr Geoffrey Harrington as follows:

1. Continuously strive to reduce production costs
2. Produce carcasses within a desirable weight range which provide the appropriate lean to fat ratio required by the market and which are of good quality in all other respects
3. Organise production in such a way as to ensure a steady supply of the required type of pig to the market
4. Support, with adequate finance, soundly designed and well-executed pigmeat promotion activities, of both a generic and brand-related nature

Pig producers must contribute to the marketing effort for their product in these and other ways for, in doing so, they will be stimulating their industry and helping themselves. Further specific aspects of marketing strategy from the point of view of the individual producer are discussed in Chapter 20.

## Summary

It is vital that information on the requirements of the consumer in terms of the quality, type and presentation of pigmeat products is conveyed quickly to all components of the production chain from breeder, producer, abattoir, processor, and wholesaler to the retailer and that all the sectors fully coordinate their efforts in such a way that the products required by the consumer are available at the right place, at the right time and at the right price.

## Additional Reading

Harrington G. (1987), 'Meat and Meat Products: Changes in Demand and Supply', *Diets in Transition*, Proceedings of Nutrition Society/British Society of Animal Production Meeting, University of Reading Nutrition Society, Cambridge University Press, Cambridge.

Kempster A. J., Cuthbertson, A. and Harrington G. (1982) *Carcass Evaluation in Livestock Breeding, Production and Marketing*, Granada, London.

*Pork Industry Handbook*, USA Co-operative Extension Service, University of Illinois at Urbana-Champaign, USA.

*Chapter 20*

# Monitoring the Pig Enterprise

Aspects of monitoring the pig enterprise were referred to in Chapters 12 and 13 which dealt with the weaned and growing-finishing pig respectively. If one is going to run a successful pig business, one must pay considerable attention to the inputs and the output in both physical and financial terms.

INPUTS

A good indication of the relative importance of the resources for a pig enterprise can be obtained from comprehensive pig enterprise recording schemes. One example of this in Britain is the Pig Management Scheme operated by the University of Cambridge under the direction of Mr Bob Ridgeon. The 1986 results of this were based on a total of 144 recorded pig herds and the proportional costs of the major inputs in all herds are summarised in Table 20.1. Since no charge has been added for interest on capital in the analysis, the real cost of some inputs will be

**TABLE 20.1   Inputs for pig enterprises and their proportional costs**

| Input | Proportion of total costs* |
|---|---|
| Feed | 73.1 |
| Labour | 13.0 |
| Building depreciation | 4.7 |
| Power and water | 2.3 |
| Veterinary expenses (including medicines) | 1.5 |
| Maintenance | 1.2 |
| Transport | 1.1 |
| Equipment and fittings | 0.8 |
| Bedding | 0.8 |
| Miscellaneous items | 1.5 |
| | 100.0 |

\* No charges have been included for interest on capital or for replacement stock.
(From: R.F. Ridgeon, Pig Management Scheme)

underestimated and this will apply particularly to buildings which normally involve a considerable investment and therefore a substantial interest charge. The data in Table 20.1 apply to both breeding and finishing herds, the latter growing pigs to the slaughter stage. If one examined the cost profile of finishing herds only (taking pigs from around 25 kg to slaughter), then the proportional contribution of inputs to total costs would be slightly different. The main anomalies relative to Table 20.1 would be that the proportion of veterinary and labour costs would be slightly lower and that of feed costs higher.

FEED
While one must deploy all inputs very carefully in a successful business, it is obvious from Table 20.1 that very particular attention must be paid to the diet and feed costs.

LABOUR
Labour must also be given careful thought. This constitutes a fairly high proportion of total costs, and cost effective labour saving approaches in operating the enterprise must always be sought. However, it is as important, if not even more so, to ensure that high-quality staff are attracted to the enterprise, that they are afforded proper incentive and encouragement to improve their efficiency even further and that their skills are deployed effectively in the running of the enterprise. Thus, rather than the emphasis being on the reduction of labour costs, the priorities should be providing skilled labour with the opportunities to improve the very considerable influence they can have in increasing the quantity and quality of output and the efficiency with which such expensive inputs as feed and buildings are utilised.

BUILDINGS
The annual cost of buildings, incorporating the depreciation and interest charges, are considerable on most pig enterprises. This places emphasis not only on the need to pay much attention to careful initial planning and regular maintenance of the fabric but to ensuring that the buildings are fully utilised. The latter objective will be achieved if they are kept fully stocked, since the pigs being produced from a building that is only half full have to carry a much larger housing overhead charge and so are likely to be less profitable. Similarly pigs that grow more slowly than the planned rate occupy the building for a longer period and also have to carry a higher housing overhead charge. Thus, fast growth, while being desirable for many other reasons, also results in a lower housing charge per pig.

## Outputs

The output from the growing-finishing pig enterprise consists not only of live pigs on their way to market but also of heat, waste gases, moisture, effluent and dead pigs. The relevance of other outputs such as effluent, has been dealt with in previous chapters; here we are only concerned with minimising the number of deaths and with optimising the number, quality and value of pigs sold. Therefore, monitoring of the pig enterprise must pay much attention to the incidence, timing and cause of deaths. It must pay very considerable attention to the growth of pigs, since fast growth can help to reduce housing, labour and other overhead charges per pig produced and can contribute very usefully to improving feed conversion efficiency.

The efficiency with which food is converted into liveweight gain, into carcasses and into lean meat must be given paramount importance in monitoring the enterprise. This is because the parameter of food conversion efficiency embraces the major item of costs, which is feed, and the only useful output from the pig enterprise, which is liveweight or carcass or lean. However, important as FCE is, its relevance must be qualified by the need to attach financial values to it. On the one hand, the cost of the feed and the food cost per unit of liveweight, carcass and lean meat produced must be under constant surveillance; on the other, the value of live pig, the carcass or lean meat produced must be set against the input costs. Thus, measures such as food cost per unit of gain and margin of carcass value over food and weaner costs begin to tell the producer more about the success of his business in financial terms.

The main deficiency in the last two financial parameters from the pig producer's point of view is that they do not give him any indication of the financial margin he is making per day on a per pig and/or on a per pig place basis since these would take the growth of his pigs into account. This objective could be achieved by regular calculation of such parameters as:

• total margin of carcass value over feed and weaner costs divided by the number of days in the growth period
  or
• total margin of value of carcasses produced each year over total feed and weaner costs divided by the number of pig places on the unit.

Thus, in summary, the main output parameters which should be monitored are the following:

Deaths
Liveweight gain
Food conversion efficiency
Food costs
Carcass grading and carcass value
Food cost per kg of liveweight, carcass and lean meat gain
Margin of carcass value over feed and weaner costs
Daily margin per pig of carcass value over feed and weaner costs
Daily margin per pig place of carcass value over feed and weaner costs

## MONITORING THE ENTERPRISE

The most successful producers are those who are most critical of themselves. The signals that the farmer gets of success or of indifferent performance come in many forms. Each is important in its own way. However, there is a continuing danger that unless the farmer consistently questions what he is doing, he can become com-placent and lapse into a loss-making situation without being aware of it.

There are three essential forms of monitoring in the pig enterprise. These are as follows:

1. Qualitative
2. Quantitative
3. Financial

These three forms of monitoring will be dealt with briefly in turn.


## 1. Qualitative Monitoring

ROUTINE OBSERVATIONS

A great variety of qualitative monitoring takes place on a pig unit. Stockmen use the following criteria in this type of assessment of the animals under their care and the housing of these:

Behaviour
Posture
Respiration
Appearance (e.g. shininess or hairiness of coat)
Body condition
Consistency and colour of faeces
Noise level and type of sound
Smell (e.g. of scour or ammonia)
Warmth
Humidity
Condensation on the walls or roof
Draughtiness
Adequacy of lighting for stock inspection


Stockmen use these criteria to make the following assessments (many of these have been outlined in some detail in the section on 'Monitoring the weaner pig system' in Chapter 12):

Is it warm enough?
Is it too warm?
Is it draughty?
Is the air fresh?
Is the atmosphere smelly?
If the pigs have a separate lying and dunging area, are they keeping the lying area clean?
Has something gone wrong with the ventilation system?
Are the pigs noisy or restless?
Are they healthy?
If unhealthy, what is wrong with them?
Do any pigs require veterinary treatment?

Is there any sign of vices such as tail or ear biting?
Are the pigs overstocked?
Are the pigs within a pen getting more uneven in size?
Have they enough feeding space?
Are they getting sufficient water?
Should some ill-doing pigs be removed from the pen and given better
    conditions?
Are the pigs losing too much body condition after weaning?

The answers to these and other questions posed by the qualitative assessment will indicate what action, if any, needs to be taken.

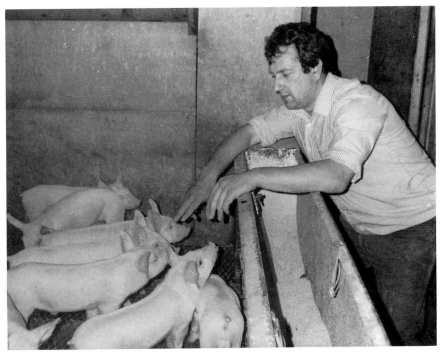

Plate 20.1   Keen scrutiny of pig behaviour by a dedicated and observant stockman can often detect problems in their very early stages and lead to corrective action being taken before any serious consequences ensue.

THE IMPORTANCE OF SECOND OPINIONS
The questions listed above often have rather subjective answers, and familiarity can lead to a form of blindness or complacency. This can be remarkably altered by inviting comments from an informed and respected colleague, friend or adviser. The extra pair of fresh eyes and different approach can often raise new issues and possibilities for improvement that would not otherwise have been considered. Fear of criticism is natural but can be a great hindrance to improving performance. In-

deed, the farmer who is progressive enough to pay for critical advice will often take far more notice of it and benefit far more than the one who believes (wrongly) that all that can be thought about the issues has already crossed his mind.

ROUTINE CHECKS ON EQUIPMENT
Among other parts of the qualitative monitoring should be the following:

### Ad lib. feeders
These should be checked to ensure that the feed is flowing at the correct rate from the hopper to the trough. If the food is bridging in the hopper and so not flowing to the trough, or if the flow to the trough is too copious with the result that the trough is too full and wastage is occurring, then the flow rate needs to be altered by adjusting the delivery gap between the hopper and the trough.

To avoid build-up of stale feed in the trough, particularly in the corners, pigs should be obliged to empty the hopper and trough once weekly. This practice also reduces wastage and improves food conversion efficiency according to the work of Hanrahan in Eire. It also results in small holes developed through normal wear and tear being detected promptly in wooden and metal feeders so that a repair can be made before damage gets worse and considerable feed wastage occurs.

Checking feeders daily also results in any fouling of the feed with faeces and urine being detected promptly and prompt corrective action being taken.

### Drinkers
It is important to check that nipple drinkers are working effectively and that bowl drinkers are not fouled and are functioning properly.

### Ventilation system
Ventilation fans or air ducts with automatically controlled opening and closing mechanisms must be checked regularly and bearings greased or oiled to keep them in efficient working order.

## 2. Quantitative Monitoring

This involves keeping a check on supplies of feed, stock purchases, numbers of stock of different liveweights on the farm, performance of the pigs including feed usage and number and weight of pigs sold. Also coming into this category would be the monitoring of energy use (electricity, gas or fuel), this being especially important in nurseries for newly weaned pigs where energy costs can be considerable. Brief comments on the major items monitored under this heading are as follows:

PIG STOCK
Detailed records must be kept of purchases of pigs in terms of their origin, date purchased, their liveweight and cost. Similar details must be kept on any deaths and sales. An inventory of numbers and weight of stock on hand will be essential as a basis for estimating the value of pigs on hand at the beginning and end of an accounting period. Such financial accounts are often only prepared on an annual basis; however, larger pig businesses intent on keeping a very close check on their

financial performance will calculate detailed costs, returns and financial margins on a three monthly or even a monthly basis. Detailed records of stock on hand including liveweights will also help the enterprise in planning to ensure a regular sale pattern, as their contract with the meat processor will almost certainly involve the sale of a prescribed number of pigs of a given weight each week.

FEED SUPPLIES

The amount and type of each feed (both raw ingredients and mixed diets) on hand must be recorded at regular intervals for several reasons. Such records of opening and closing stocks will be essential in the preparation of financial accounts covering a specific time interval (monthly, quarterly, half yearly or yearly). They will also be used as a basis for deciding on the need for further purchases, whether of raw ingredients or complete diets. Skilful and timely purchase of ingredients when they are available at an attractive price is one of the hallmarks of the successful pig producer who is home-mixing his diets. Details of opening and closing feed stocks over a given time period, along with records of purchases within such a period, provide a record of the total feed used within such a period. If pigs on the farm are weighed at the start and end of this period and account is taken of the weight of pigs purchased and of those sold, the total liveweight gain of pigs within this period can be calculated. With these details of total liveweight gain and total feed used within the period, the whole herd food conversion efficiency can be calculated. This is a very useful measure which can be compared with equivalent figures from similar farms covering the same period. The figure can also be compared with previous figures from the same farm to assess whether feed efficiency is static, deteriorating or improving.

Regular assessment of feed stocks is also useful in several other respects. Checks can be made that storage conditions are adequate and that no spoilage of feed supplies is taking place. A close check can also be made to ensure that the valuable food purchased and stored for the pigs is not being consumed by birds or rodents.

LIVEWEIGHT GAIN

When pigs grown to supply pigmeat processors have been born on the farm, are identified at birth and their birth date recorded, a useful measure of their liveweight gain is their age and weight at slaughter. However, this does not tell us anything about the pattern of their growth between the start and finish. They may have grown extremely well while suckling their dam and only moderately thereafter or vice versa.

It is essential in determining the adequacy of the growth of the pig on a farm to draw up a target level of performance and then compare the actual growth achieved with the targets. An example of target growth is illustrated in Figure 20.1. This merely sets out targets in terms of weight for age. Therefore the only two pieces of information required are liveweight and corresponding age. If age is unknown, then a record of the date at each weighing is all that is required.

While it may seem very straightforward to collect this information, weighing does involve considerable time and effort and imposition of a degree of strain on the pigs, depending on the adequacy of the handling and weighing facilities and the accessibility of the pigs. Checks on growth can be carried out in one of three ways:

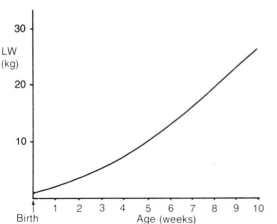

| Age (days) | Liveweight (kg) | Liveweight gain per day in previous week (g) |
|---|---|---|
| Birth | 1.5 | – |
| 7 | 3.0 | 214 |
| 14 | 4.5 | 214 |
| 21 | 6.0 | 214 |
| 28 | 7.5 | 214 |
| 35 | 9.5 | 286 |
| 42 | 12.0 | 357 |
| 49 | 15.0 | 429 |
| 56 | 19.0 | 571 |
| 63 | 23.0 | 571 |
| 70 | 27.5 | 643 |
| 77 | 32.5 | 714 |

FIGURE 20.1   Target weight for age and growth rates.

1. Weigh all pigs at the start of the period of occupancy of a house and again at the end. If this is a finishing house, this approach will only involve one extra weighing at the start of the period, for pigs will be weighed at the end of the period as they are being consigned to the meat processing plant. This approach, however, suffers from the disadvantage that there is no knowledge of the growth pattern between the starting and finishing points.

2. Weigh a sample of pens at the start and finish of the period of occupancy of a house and, if at all possible, at several stages in between.

3. Weigh a random sample of pigs in each pen (e.g. 2 males and 2 females chosen randomly out of a pen of 20) at the start and finish and at several intermediate stages. This system necessitates that the four randomly selected pigs be clearly identified from the start (e.g. by an ear tag). In methods 2 and 3, if sexes (e.g. boars and gilts) are penned separately, it is important to ensure that an equal number of pens of each sex are monitored.

When actual growth is compared with the target there are several possible outcomes:

*Possibility 1. Actual growth is equal to or better than target*
No action is necessary except that subsequent targets might be raised.

*Possibility 2. Actual growth is poorer than the target set in most pigs*
If the target set is realistic and based on what the genotype in use is capable of achieving on the prescribed diet and the predicted feed intake, then detailed detective work must be carried out. This will involve the following analyses and questions:

a) Having the diet analysed to ensure that it contains the level of nutrients specified.

b) Checking the quality of the raw ingredients of the diet. Has any deterioration (e.g. from mould) taken place in any of the raw ingredients or in the mixed diet in storage?

c) Has the diet been too finely ground?

d) Is the quality of the climatic environment adequate for the weight of pig involved and its energy intake? Particular factors to be checked in this regard are temperature at pig level, freedom from draughts and adequate ventilation and air change. Monitoring of these aspects is dealt with in more detail later in this chapter.

e) An assessment of health status including the possibility of some subtle sub-clinical problem.

f) Checking on the quality of stockmanship with regard to such factors as the functioning of the watering devices and the adequacy of the water supply, signs of build-up of stale feed, or fouling of the feed troughs.

*Possibility 3. Actual growth is poorer in some pigs and adequate in others relative to the targets set*

The same factors can be checked as under outcome 2 above, especially the possibility that although some pigs are perfectly healthy, others have sub-clinical (e.g. respiratory or enteric) problems. The particular aspects which should be checked when growth of pigs is quite variable are the following:

a) The adequacy of feeding space. This may be sufficient for all pigs at the start of the growth period but as pigs grow, they run out of space and, while those at the top of the peck order are able to obtain their full allowance, those lower in the social hierarchy are unable to obtain their fair share, with the inevitable consequence of variation in growth.

b) The adequacy of floor space and the opportunity for obtaining water. This problem is similar to (a) above. Floor space may be adequate at the start of the growth period but conditions become progressively overcrowded. In this situation, the pigs of higher social rank can obtain their full requirements but their social inferiors may not only find it difficult to find a comfortable lying area at all times but also experience increasing difficulty in getting to the feed trough and watering points.

The consequences of pigs failing to grow as quickly as reasonable target levels are several:

*Consequences of failing to achieve target growth rate*

1. Pigs will have to be kept for a longer period than anticipated and this can result in an overstocking situation if the original stocking of the buildings was based on target growth rates.

2. Reduction in sales in a given period of time.

3. Deterioration in food conversion efficiency, particularly in the period from weaning up to about 50 kg liveweight.

Thus, careful monitoring of growth rate is extremely important to check its adequacy in relation to the targets set and to ensure that there is not undue variation between pigs of the same sex and starting weight. When careful monitoring indicates that there is a problem, this sets the necessary wheels in motion to investigate and isolate the source and to rectify the contributory factors with the minimum possible delay.

FOOD CONVERSION EFFICIENCY

Earlier in this chapter (page 481), a basis for estimating whole herd food conversion efficiency in a given time period was outlined. It was indicated that this can be a useful figure for comparing with earlier periods on the same farm or over the same time period with similar pig enterprises. However, of more value for management purposes are more detailed measures of feed efficiency. For example, it is important to know the conversion efficiency of the succession of diets used over the growth period, the relative efficiency with which gilts and entire males convert the same or different diets, the conversion efficiency in two houses occupied by pigs of a similar weight range or that in two different seasons (e.g. winter and summer) in the same house. When the pig farmer is contemplating a change in his system, for example, a change in diet, he will want to evaluate the wisdom of such a change by comparing pigs on the proposed new diet with equivalent pigs on the original one. This comparison must be based on food conversion efficiency as well as on feed intake and growth, with carcass grading being an additional parameter when a finishing diet is being assessed.

To obtain accurate assessments of food conversion efficiency for any of the purposes outlined above, the pig producer has no option other than to monitor a number of pens of pigs. Pigs will have to be weighed at the start and end of the evaluation period so that the total liveweight gain can be determined. All food supplied to the pigs must be weighed, and any food remaining in feed hoppers at the end of the period must be weighed and subtracted from the total supplied to calculate the total amount consumed. This procedure necessitates accurate weighing of both pigs and feed and meticulous recording. Careful calculation of total feed intake and liveweight gain and then the ratio of total intake to total gain will give the feed to gain ratio or feed conversion efficiency.

If the pig producer monitors a sample of pens at different stages of the growth process in this way on a regular basis, by appropriate comparison with past results, he can readily determine if efficiency is static, improving or deteriorating. If he spots deterioration in feed efficiency then he must undertake detective work in the same way as he did in trying to determine why growth of his pigs was lower than target levels. Thus he will want to check the following:

Have there been changes in the diet relative to specifications?
Has the climate changed within the house because of faulty ventilation or deteriorating insulation?
Are the pigs growing more slowly and, as a result, is a degree of overstocking or inadequacy in terms of feed space creeping in?
Is his stockman becoming somewhat more careless and paying less attention to detail?
Is the health status of his pigs deteriorating and, if there are no obvious problems, are sub-clinical levels of respiratory disease or enteric problems to blame for the deterioration in food conversion efficiency?

His painstaking monitoring of feed conversion efficiency has at least detected a problem and he, along with his feed supplier, specialist pig adviser and veterinary practitioner, must systematically examine all the most likely reasons until the major predisposing factor is detected and corrective action taken.

CARCASS GRADING

In countries like Britain, there is increasingly severe discrimination against excessive fat in carcasses, this being applied through substantial price penalties as indicated in Chapter 16.

Because grading in Britain is not based on a gradually sliding scale on the basis of backfat but on a stepped pattern, with considerable reductions in price whenever a specific range of backfat level is exceeded, there can be quite marked week to week variations in grading without average backfat for the batch of pigs changing greatly over time. This can happen particularly on small pig farms which consign only a few pigs weekly to the abattoir. This week to week variation in grading can occur because, in one week, a high proportion of pigs have a backfat which just gets them into the top grade, whereas in the following week, a high proportion have a very slightly thicker backfat which just relegates them to grade 2. Because of this almost fortuitous week to week variation in grading, it is more useful to monitor the backfat measurement (e.g. $P_2$ as recorded on the grading sheet) rather than the grade. Thus, the average backfats should be calculated for each week, each month, each 3 months and each year. This will provide a very useful indication of short- and long-term changes in backfat. The small producer, in particular, should place more emphasis on long-term than on short-term changes in backfat. If backfat is tending to increase, he should check the influence of factors outlined in Chapter 16 which might explain this trend. For example, is carcass weight increasing, is he selling a higher proportion of castrates relative to gilts and entire males, has he reduced the protein quality of the diet or increased the feeding plane in the finishing stages?

On the other hand, if backfat is showing a useful reduction over time he should be very satisfied, provided his meat processor does not impose price penalties for over-lean pigs. Of course, the reduction in backfat would be expected if in the interim he had done away with castration and was now selling entire males instead. If the reduction in backfat, on the other hand, was brought about by imposing a greater restriction on feed intake in the finishing stages of growth or by reducing liveweight and therefore carcass weight at slaughter, then he will have to assess very carefully the wisdom of such tactics. For example, by imposing a greater degree of feed restriction during finishing, he will be slowing up the growth of his pigs, his throughput and annual sales will be reduced and he may well be creating an undesirable overstocking situation which is having adverse effects in terms of greater variation in growth within pens, an increase in the incidence of sub-clinical disease and a deterioration in food conversion efficiency. Thus, the impact of the change he has made must not only be assessed in terms of carcass grading but the associated detrimental consequences of the change must be set against the favourable response in terms of improved grading. Calculation of the net influence of the change requires detailed aspects of physical performance and intricate financial evaluation which will be described later in this chapter.

THE CLIMATIC ENVIRONMENT

Details of the climatic requirements of pigs were outlined fully in Chapter 8. Tables 8.1 and 8.2 outlined the thermoneutral or comfort zone of pigs, this being bounded by the lower (LCT) and upper (UCT) critical temperatures. In Britain, apart from the occasional very hot summer or buildings with unnecessarily high heat input from non-pig sources or in which the ventilation system has broken down, we are mainly concerned with keeping temperature above the LCT. The LCT varies with the weight of the pig, its energy intake and insulation value of its lying area. A slight draught such as an increase in air velocity from 0.2 to 0.4 metres per second (m/s) (air velocity up to 0.2 m/s is considered to constitute 'still' air) is equivalent to a reduction in effective temperature of 1°C and therefore has the effect of increasing the LCT by 1°C; that is, the temperature at pig level must be kept higher to compensate for draughty conditions. The penalties for failing to achieve the LCT at pig level have been calculated by Holmes and Close (1977) and their estimates are presented in Table 20.2.

**TABLE 20.2   Calculated equivalent weight of feed\* required or decrease in liveweight gain caused by a decrease of 1°C below the lower critical temperature**

| *Liveweight* *(kg)* | *Extra feed required* *(g/day/°C)* | *Decrease in liveweight gain* *(g/day/°C)* | |
|---|---|---|---|
| | | (a) | (b) |
| *Groups of pigs* | | | |
| 20 | 13 | 4 | 28 |
| 60 | 25 | 8 | 16 |
| 100 | 35 | 11 | 18 |
| *Individual pigs* | | | |
| Sows 140 thin | 59 | — | — |
| fat | 34 | — | — |

\* Energy of feed = 12 MJ ME per kg
(a) Assuming only fat deposition affected
(b) Assuming all tissue deposition affected
(From: Holmes & Close, 1977)

It can be seen that a drop of 1°C below the LCT for 20 kg pigs necessitates an extra daily intake of 13 g of a diet with 12 MJ ME. This extra feed will be used just to keep the pig warm and so will not contribute to growth and will result in a deterioration in food conversion efficiency. Of course, if the temperature is 5°C below the LCT, the 20 kg pig will have to consume an extra 65 g (5 × 13 g) daily just to keep warm.

If the pig does not have the opportunity to eat more food to compensate for the cold conditions, then it will have to divert some of its present food intake to keep warm and less will be available for growth. In this situation, if it is subjected to a deficit of 1°C below its LCT, a 20 kg pig will deposit 4 g less fatty tissue per

Plate 20.2 Pieces of equipment which can be of assistance to the manager and stockman in monitoring aspects of the pig enterprise:

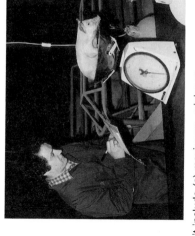

(Right) Weighing machines to monitor liveweight and to weigh feed inputs of a sample of pigs to assess liveweight gain, appetite and food conversion efficiency.

(Below, left to right) Computer to obtain a regular update on costs, returns and margins and to assess the most cost-effective means of protecting the pig from adverse climate; vane anemometer (to measure ventilation rate); smoke tubes with puffer (to check detailed air flow patterns); smoke pellets (to check overall air flow pattern); stopwatch (used along with vane anemometer and with sling psychrometer); distilled water for use with the sling psychrometer; sling psychrometer (to measure wet and dry bulb temperature and then relative humidity); clinical and digital thermometers; ultrasonic equipment for backfat measurement. (Courtesy of Centre for Rural Building, Bucksburn, Aberdeen)

Other useful pieces of equipment for the pig unit include (a) maximum–minimum thermometers to check overall range in temperature in a given period (e.g. to check the extremes between day and night temperature at pig level) and (b) a thermograph to obtain a continuous record of temperature near pig level.

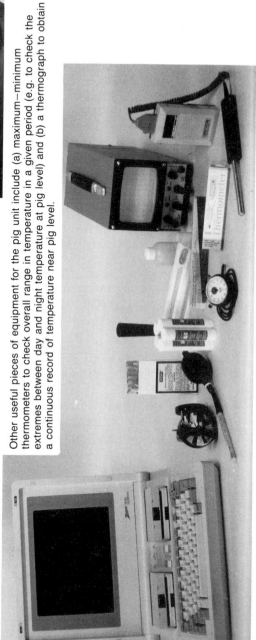

487

day or 28 g less in overall liveweight gain. If the pig is kept 5°C below its LCT, then fatty tissue deposition will be depressed by 20 g (5 × 4 g) daily and liveweight gain will be depressed by 140 g (5 × 28 g) daily. Thus, the penalties for a sub-optimal temperature (below the LCT), in terms either of food conversion efficiency or of liveweight gain can be considerable.

Among the simple approaches for monitoring aspects of the climatic environment and housing and possible responses to such recording are the following.

*Temperature*
As indicated in Chapter 12, a useful assessment of the adequacy of temperature at pig level can be made on the basis of pig behaviour. However, one is normally assessing such aspects of pig behaviour during the day, and night-time temperature could be lower if temperature control mechanisms are not as effective as they should be. A maximum-minimum thermometer reset each day will provide a measure of the overall range in temperature in the previous 24 hour period. A ther-mograph is even more useful. When properly calibrated, this clockwork mechanism records temperature continuously over a 7 day period on a graph (see Figure 20.2). From this, the average temperature over a week can be estimated as can also the proportion of time, if any, that temperature dipped below the LCT. Of course, it is important to try to record temperature as near pig level as possible without putting the equipment at risk. It is also important to record temperature in pens in different parts of the house to check on trends in different locations. If temperature within the house tends to be very variable and to drop below the LCT on occasion, then the thermal performance of the building is called into question and remedial measures must be considered.

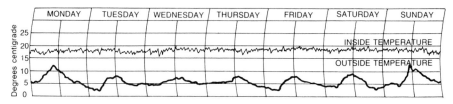

FIGURE 20.2   Continuous thermograph readings over a 7 day period of temperature inside and outside a finishing house.

'Temperature lift' is the term given to the average increase in temperature within the house relative to the outside temperature. This can be determined by recording maximum, minimum and average temperatures inside and outside the building over a period. The temperature lift within the building is influenced by:

● the number, liveweight and energy intake of the pigs within since this will deter-mine total heat production from the pigs
● the thermal insulation of the building and
● the ventilation

The influence of these factors on temperature lift is indicated in Figure 20.3,

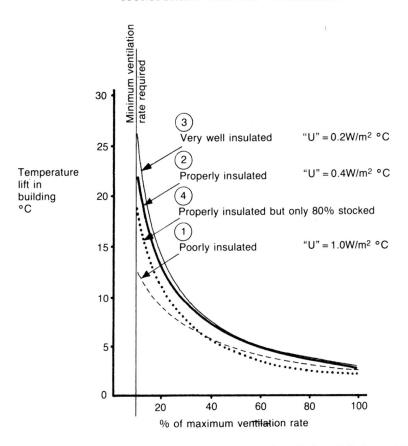

FIGURE 20.3  Temperature lift in a finishing house for 360 pigs. (J.E. Owen, 1978)

which shows the calculated temperature lift that can be achieved in a finishing house for 360 pigs under different insulation, ventilation and stocking conditions. Curve 1 shows the temperature lift that can be achieved if the house is poorly insulated (overall U value of 1.0 W/m²/°C) and fully stocked, the maximum lift possible being 13°C at the minimum ventilation rate required, i.e. 10 per cent of maximum ventilation rate.

Curve 2 shows that by improving the insulation to an overall U value of 0.4 W/m²/°C, a much higher temperature lift can be achieved, i.e. 23.5°C at the minimum ventilation rate. This is considered by Dr Jeff Owen of the University of Reading to be the proper insulation level since for a required house temperature of about 18°C, the pig heat alone is sufficient to maintain the desired house temperature at outside temperatures down to −5°C (the normal minimum design temperature for United Kingdom conditions).

Curve 3 shows that the effect of insulating the house very well, to an overall U value of $0.2 \text{ W/m}^2/°\text{C}$, is to achieve a maximum temperature lift of $26.5°\text{C}$ at the minimum ventilation rate. However, in this case Dr Owen considers that the house is over-insulated, the temperature lift being greater than required for this house in normal United Kingdom conditions and the insulation cost required to gain an extra $3°\text{C}$ temperature lift above the situation represented in Curve 2 being twice as much as for the properly insulated house.

Curve 4 shows the effect of understocking the house; these figures show that if the properly insulated house is only stocked to 80 per cent of its full capacity, then the maximum temperature lift that can be achieved drops to $19°\text{C}$ at the minimum ventilation rate. Dr Owen has found that in buildings where special management considerations demand low stocking policies, e.g. early weaning rooms, heating may have to be used to maintain the required house temperature, since even with perfect insulation there is insufficient pig heat to raise the internal temperature to the desired level. In these buildings the same considerations will apply as for the 360 pig finishing house since one will be seeking to minimise running costs of the heating.

Finally, the major effect of ventilation rate on the temperature lift that can be achieved under any insulation conditions should be noted. It can be seen that if the minimum ventilation rate that can be achieved in the building is 30 per cent (often the minimum achievable with many commercial ventilation control systems is 30 to 40 per cent), then the maximum achievable temperature lift in the poorly insulated building will only be $7°\text{C}$ and even in the very well-insulated building only $9.5°\text{C}$. In other words, the insulation is virtually a waste of time at such ventilation rates. The respective temperature lifts at 20 per cent ventilation rate for the poorly and very well-insulated buildings will be $9°\text{C}$ and $14°\text{C}$ respectively as opposed to $13°\text{C}$ and $26.5°\text{C}$ at the correct minimum ventilation rate of 10 per cent.

Dr Owen points out that the means of improving the thermal performance of a building are specific to the particular building, but in general the approach that should be adopted is as follows:

1. Insulate the building adequately; as a guide an overall U value of $0.4 \text{ W/m}^2/°\text{C}$ should be aimed for in most pig houses.
2. Ensure that the minimum ventilation rate required can be achieved by the ventilation system and its associated controls and windproof the building to prevent extraneous ventilation.
3. Utilise to the full the free heat available from the pigs by ensuring that the building is fully stocked, particularly during the winter period.

If temperature lifts in buildings fail to come up to expectations, one possibility is that the original insulation has deteriorated either through damage by rodents or because the insulation is wet due to moisture penetration through poorly sealed walls and/or roof spaces.

*Ventilation*
The lower limit of ventilation is designed to prevent the carbon dioxide ($CO_2$) concentration of the atmosphere in the pig house exceeding 0.3 per cent (10 times higher than in ordinary air). In practice, the stockman normally objects to condi-

tions in the piggery before they affect the pigs themselves. This is not cussedness on the part of the pigman but a perfectly natural desire to work in a reasonably pleasant environment.

Instruments are available to measure the $CO_2$ concentration of the air in the pig house and, if it exceeds the limit, it indicates inadequate air change which might be associated with higher than desirable levels of the dangerous gas hydrogen sulphide ($H_2S$) in the atmosphere. Ammonia ($NH_3$) may also be at a noticeable level detectable by smell, while the general staleness of such air may also predispose to respiratory problems.

It is most unlikely that the pig farmer will have equipment to measure $CO_2$ or $H_2S$ concentrations. However, he should be capable of detecting undesirably high levels of ammonia and of making a judgment on the general staleness or freshness of the air in the building. If he considers that the air is reasonably fresh, temperature is above the estimated LCT for the pigs in the house and their lying behaviour indicates that they are within their comfort zone, then all is well. If, on the other hand, the atmosphere is somewhat stale and smelly and ventilation can be increased slightly without resulting in temperature falling below the LCT for the smallest pigs in the house, then such a ventilation adjustment should be made.

When dealing with newly weaned pigs, as ventilation is increased, to the necessary level to maintain an adequate air change and freshness in the atmosphere, several modifications can be made fairly quickly to maintain temperature at pig level above the LCT. One simple approach is to increase heat output from the electrical, gas or central heating mechanisms. Another is to cover part of the slatted floor with an insulated board and to place an insulated cover above the lying area to create a kennel. Such a simple approach can increase the temperature in the kennel about 5° C above the house temperature (see pages 312 and 313).

When house temperature tends to become excessively hot and approach the UCT for the pigs in the house, then increasing the ventilation rate helps to reduce temperature lift within the house (see Figure 20.3) and manipulation of an efficient ventilation system, with only rare exceptions, should be capable of preventing excessively hot conditions in pig houses in Britain.

*Air movement and draughts*
Pig producers are unlikely to possess the specialist equipment necessary to obtain an accurate measure of air speed at various locations within the pig house. A useful tool in the hands of the producer is a smoke making device such as a smoke bomb or even the exhalation of tobacco smoke. Smoke tests in various locations of the building will provide useful indications of both the adequacy of the supply of fresh air and the speed with which this is supplied. Slow wafting of fresh air from air inlets, falling gently on the pigs to replace the warm air rising from them, will provide a fair indication that the air is reaching the pigs at no more than 0.2 metres per second, which is considered equivalent to still air and therefore does not constitute a draught.

These, then, are some of the comparatively simple measurements the pig producer can take to assess the adequacy of the climatic environment for his pigs. If he comes across an obvious climatic problem which he finds impossible to solve, then an environmental specialist must be called in. Such specialists now have the support of very useful computer programmes which can quickly take into account all the very complex interacting effects of the nutrition and stocking rate of the pigs, their heat output, the thermal characteristics of the building, the ventilation system and the influence of the external climate to arrive at the most cost effective solution to the problem.

## Financial Monitoring

THE PIG ENTERPRISE

In most countries, farm businesses must be fully evaluated in financial terms once per year to determine profit margin and liability for taxation. A pig enterprise might, of course, be only part of the farm business and it would therefore not be obligatory to assess the net profit margin of the pig enterprise on its own. However, although not obligatory, such an assessment is absolutely essential to assess the performance of the pig enterprise in financial terms. As stated earlier in this chapter, some large pig producers will carry out a full financial appraisal of their pig enterprise at 6 monthly, 3 monthly and sometimes even at monthly intervals. Such frequent monitoring can provide the producer with very early warning that all is not well, and, if the causes are not obvious things such as a sudden decrease in pig prices or an increase in feed prices, these alarm bells will stimulate a thorough search for the contributory factors. The sooner such a search gets under way, the more quickly the causes of the problem will be identified and corrective measures applied.

The causal agents might be some of those discussed earlier in this chapter. Possibilities include depressions in growth and therefore in throughput and sales, deterioration in food conversion efficiency or in carcass grading. As indicated earlier, these depressions in pig performance or in carcass grading can be brought about by a variety of changing circumstances, and skilful diagnostic and analytical work is necessary to isolate the basic predisposing factors and to suggest solutions.

THE FEEDING SYSTEM

While regular financial appraisal of the whole farm enterprise is extremely important for the reasons just outlined, financial appraisal of the feeding system is just as important for very obvious reasons. Feed is the predominant cost item in pig production and it has an overwhelming influence on all major aspects of pig performance such as growth, food conversion efficiency and grading. One important question which must be asked is: Can I feed more cost effective diets or have a more cost effective feeding system? One way to try to answer this question is to carry out some experiments on the farm.

CONDUCTING ON-FARM EXPERIMENTS TO DETERMINE THE ADEQUACY OF YOUR PRESENT FEEDING SYSTEM

Although detailed information has been presented earlier on nutrient requirements for pigs according to such variables as stage of growth, sex and genotype, the best diets to use are likely to vary from farm to farm. This is because no two farms have identical genotypes, housing, disease status or management. Recommendations on diets may therefore be correct on average, but rarely ideal for the individual farm.

It is necessary to lay down a few principles and guidelines so you can, by paying attention to a few simple rules about the conduct of on-farm experiments, tune your feeding system and diets to suit your own particular requirements.

Many farmers conduct their own experiments to try and find the feeding system most suited to their conditions. There are many pitfalls in this approach, and we shall start by examining the snags associated with the commonest type of on-farm experiment.

It quite often happens that the farmer gets a hunch that a different feeding system or a different diet would be an improvement. To try out his idea he decrees that on a certain date the whole unit will switch from the existing system to a new one. In due course the performance of the pigs on the new system is assessed and a comparison made with the old system. The farmer may conclude that any improvement has resulted from the change in the feeding system. In actual fact, so many changes may have occurred which were not related to the change of system that the comparison may well be worthless, or worse still lead to entirely the wrong conclusion. For example, the comparison may be invalidated by changes in the following: feed quality, the source of barley, the influence of a particular sire, the grading system, the season of the year − or even a new pigman!

The only method which stands a real chance of helping you tune your system with any degree of accuracy is to do very simple comparisons on a contemporary basis, i.e. to compare the new and the old systems under similar conditions at the same time. This may sound rather formidable at first, but the rules are extremely simple even if putting them into effect requires a little care. In essence, the technique involves making sure that the only difference between the systems is the one in which you are interested. The experiment should have the simplest possible design and should be of the A-versus-B kind.

The first thing to decide is which two diets or systems are to be compared. One of these will, of course, be your existing system, which we will call the standard treatment. The other treatment or test treatment will depend on the change in your system which you feel would either cheapen your diet, speed up growth rate or improve the carcass grading.

The trick at this stage is to make the test treatment more extreme than that which you anticipate you may adopt in practice. In other words, you should test a difference which you are reasonably confident will produce an effect. If, contrary to your expectation, there is no effect following the change, then you can be reasonably sure that changes of lower magnitude would have produced no effect either. If there is a difference, then you can reasonably assume that intermediate changes would have given intermediate results on a *pro rata* basis. For example, if you are using a 14 per cent crude protein (CP) diet at present and you wish to test the effect of using a higher protein diet, then you should test one with 18 per cent rather than one with 15 per cent of CP. In the same way, if you wish to assess the effect of using a more restricted ration scale for your pigs during finishing, choose one which will cause a delay to bacon weight of not less than two weeks or one which will reduce growth rate by 100 g per day.

The important thing to keep in mind when setting up the experiment is that the only difference you want between the pigs on the standard and those on the test treatment is the one item in which you are interested. The best way to test the dif-

ference between the two treatments is to select pairs of pens and then toss a coin
to allot the pens to either treatment. It is desirable to make the two pens of pigs
which form a pair as similar to each other as possible. For example, the difference
in the average liveweights should be no more than 2 kg and there should not be
a marked difference in the numbers of males and females in each pen.

In Table 20.3 are set out examples based on 10 pigs per pen indicating where
the pairing is satisfactory and where it is less than satisfactory. To obtain a satisfactory comparison between two treatments, it is necessary to have at least six pairs
of pens.

**TABLE 20.3  Examples of pen pairs**

| Pair number | 1 | | 2 | | 3 | | 4 | | 5 | |
|---|---|---|---|---|---|---|---|---|---|---|
| Treatment | A | B | A | B | A | B | A | B | A | B |
| Average liveweight (kg) | 25 | 25 | 22 | 22 | 24 | 26 | 22 | 23 | 23 | 26 |
| Males | 4 | 4 | 7 | 7 | 5 | 4 | 6 | 3 | 6 | 6 |
| Females | 6 | 6 | 3 | 3 | 5 | 6 | 4 | 7 | 4 | 4 |
| Comment | Ideal | | Ideal | | Satisfactory | | Unsatisfactory sex ratio | | Unsatisfactory liveweight | |

One important point to consider is that the results can be biased by any factor
which affects only one of the pens in a pair. For example, the pens of ten receiving
one treatment must be distributed evenly throughout the piggery. A further hazard
which can unbalance the experiment is if an outbreak of scouring occurs or if the
growth rate of one particular pen of pigs is very much lower than the remainder
in the experiment. If you consider that this reduction in performance could not be
attributed to the treatment, then this pair of pens should be eliminated from the trial.
Very poor performance by a single wayward pig is not usually an effect of the treatment. The results from such an animal are best ignored, but when calculating the
intake of others in the pen, do not forget to allow for the food it has consumed.

The more accurate the measurements, the more confidence you will be able to
place in the results. Among the important measurements are the starting and
finishing weights of the pigs. Measurements of the feed intake can be extremely
tedious and very upsetting routine-wise − at weekends. One way of overcoming
this is to weigh accurately one week's supply for a pen and then sub-allocate this
each day by rough weighing or by volumetric measure. A very accurate record of
feed intake can be made by counting the number of pre-weighed bags of feed consumed and weighing back any remaining at the end of the trial.

RUNNING THE EXPERIMENT

The details of the day-to-day running of an experiment depend very much upon the
type of comparison being made. So let us consider two different situations.

1. Comparing diets for ad lib. fed pigs. This is one of the easiest types of on-farm
experiment. The main problem arises from feed wastage around the feeder. This
source of error can be greatly reduced by allowing the feeders to run-out for a 12
hour period each week to encourage the pigs to eat up the spilled material.

2. Comparing diets for restricted fed pigs. This can best be done by using a feeding scale based on time rather than liveweight. This time-based scale has an enormous advantage in that pigs need not be weighed other than at the start and end of the experimental period. As the pigs on the two diets eat the same amount of feed over the same period of time, any difference in liveweight gain during the experimental period is a direct measure of the difference between the two diets.

WORKING OUT THE RESULTS

One of the most useful figures to calculate is the relative cost per kg of liveweight gain. Improvements in growth rate potentially allow a greater throughput of pigs per year. This is only true if you can buy in additional pigs to fill the vacated space. If you manage to achieve this with perfect efficiency, then a 10 per cent improvement in growth rate should yield a 10 per cent improvement in profit (when pigs are in fact profitable) and provided all other things remain equal.

The simplest way of measuring the effect of the treatments on grading is to calculate the average financial return per pig for each of the treatments. Another additional useful measure is average backfat thickness.

The final step in assessing the relative merits of the two treatments is to calculate what the effect of changing from system A to B would have on your annual profits. Quite large differences in performance may disappear when you compare the treatments on this basis. A difference of 2 per cent or more in annual profits would provide a good reason for changing systems; do not place too much store on the results if the financial difference is less than this.

By a succession of exploratory steps away from your present system or diets, you can readily see in which direction improvements in profitability lie. You may find that movement away from your system in any direction produces no benefit. In this case you are lucky − you are at the optimum! The chances are, however, that you will find, quite unexpectedly, that your present system is well wide of the optimum for profitability.

PREDICTING THE EFFECT OF CHANGING THE DIET AND FEEDING SYSTEM ON THE BASIS OF THE BEST AVAILABLE DATA

For those producers who either do not have the time or are not prepared to go to the considerable trouble and effort of conducting a well-planned and carefully executed on-farm trial, they can use the best available data to predict the consequences of a change in diet or in the feeding system.

*Predicting the effects of a change in diet*

For improved genotypes in Britain, the estimated effects of changing the protein quality of the diet for pigs over the growth period from 55 to 90 kg liveweight are outlined in Table 20.4. It can be seen that the data predict that, as one changes from diet 1 (20 per cent CP and 1.3 per cent lysine) to diet 2 (18 per cent CP), there will be no change in any of the parameters; however, as one reduces protein quality further, there will be progressive deterioration in daily gain, food conversion efficiency and backfat thickness (i.e. more fat). Likewise, if one is feeding a diet with 12 per cent crude protein and 0.78 per cent lysine to improved pigs, by increasing the protein and lysine concentrations to 18 per cent and 1.17 per cent respectively,

**TABLE 20.4  Effect of reductions in protein and lysine between 55 and 90 kg liveweight on performance and carcass backfat thickness (relative to Diet 2)**

| Diet | Crude protein (%) | Lysine* | Daily gain | FCR | Average carcass backfat at $P_2$ |
|------|-------------------|---------|------------|-----|----------------------------------|
|      |                   |         | *Percentage deterioration in* | | |
| 1    | 20                | 1.30    |            |     |      |
| 2    | 18                | 1.17    | 0          | 0   | 0    |
| 3    | 16                | 1.04    | 2.5        | 2.5 | 8    |
| 4    | 14                | 0.91    | 5.0        | 5.0 | 16   |
| 5    | 12                | 0.78    | 10.0       | 10.0| 20   |

* Lysine as % of protein in each diet = 6.5%

one can predict useful improvements in growth, food efficiency and leanness. It is possible to put financial values on the improvements in growth and food conversion efficiency, but to put a value on the reduction in backfat it is necessary to relate average backfat at $P_2$ to a grading profile. This procedure will now be described.

A common grading system for bacon pigs in operation in Britain at present and the prices for different grades are outlined in Table 20.5, in which we see that considerable financial penalties are incurred when carcasses have more than 16 mm backfat (to be relegated to Grade 3) or between 15 and 16 mm (when they end up in Grade 2).

**TABLE 20.5  An example of a carcass grading and pricing system in Britain**

|                              | Grade 1   | Grade 2 | Grade 3 |
|------------------------------|-----------|---------|---------|
| Backfat at $P_2$ (mm)        | Up to 14  | 15–16   | Over 16 |
| Price per kg of carcass (p)  | 100       | 93      | 79      |

If a herd has a mean backfat ($P_2$) at slaughter of 12 mm, this does not mean that all pigs will have a $P_2$ of 12. Many carcasses will be slightly fatter and many slightly leaner, while a few will be very fat and a few extremely lean. To calcaulate the likely spread of backfats around the mean for a given herd, simple statistical principles can be applied. The estimated proportion of carcasses ending up in different grades for herds with different average $P_2$ levels is summarised in Table 20.6.

On the basis of the grading system outlined in Table 20.5, it can be predicted that herds with a mean $P_2$ of 9 mm will have almost all their pigs (97 per cent) in the top grade. On the other hand, the estimate for a herd with a $P_2$ of 16 is that only 31 per cent of pigs will be in the top grade, while 43 per cent will be relegated to grade 3. Having estimated the proportion of pigs in the different grades accor-

**TABLE 20.6** **Estimated proportion of carcasses in different grades for herds with different mean backfat thickness ($P_2$)**

| Mean herd $P_2$ (mm) | Grade 1 0–14 mm | Grade 2 15–16 mm Percentage of pigs | Grade 3 >16 mm | Average price per kg (p) | Value of 67.5 kg carcass (£) |
|---|---|---|---|---|---|
| 9 | 97 | 3 | 0 | 99.79 | 67.36 |
| 10 | 93 | 6 | 1 | 99.37 | 67.07 |
| 11 | 87 | 10 | 3 | 98.67 | 66.60 |
| 12 | 79 | 14 | 7 | 97.55 | 65.85 |
| 13 | 69 | 18 | 13 | 96.01 | 64.81 |
| 14 | 57 | 22 | 21 | 94.05 | 63.48 |
| 15 | 43 | 26 | 31 | 91.67 | 61.88 |
| 16 | 31 | 26 | 43 | 89.15 | 60.18 |

ding to mean herd $P_2$, and taking the prices for the different grades outlined in Table 20.5, it is then a straightforward calculation to obtain the average price per kg and the value of a 67.5 kg carcass, and these values are also presented in Table 20.6. A 67.5 kg carcass is chosen in this example since a pig of 90 kg liveweight with a killing out percentage of 75 would provide such a carcass.

We are now almost in a position to calculate the cost effectiveness of changing the protein quality of the diet on the basis of figures presented in Table 20.4. However, we still need to calculate the cost of the diets providing different levels of protein and lysine and this is done in Table 20.7. We shall ignore diet 1 since it is estimated that there will be no advantage in terms of pig performance in providing this relative to diet 2, which will be cheaper. We can now estimate the net effect of making a dietary change over the finishing stages from 55 to 90 kg liveweight

**TABLE 20.7** **Simple diets designed to provide protein and lysine levels specified for diets 2 to 5 in table 20.4 and their costs**

| | Diet 2 | Diet 3 | Diet 4 | Diet 5 |
|---|---|---|---|---|
| *Inclusion in diet (%)* | | | | |
| Barley | 74.00 | 80.00 | 86.00 | 92.00 |
| Soya | 24.00 | 18.00 | 12.00 | 6.00 |
| Lysine hydrochloride | 0.25 | 0.25 | 0.25 | 0.25 |
| Crude protein | 18.20 | 16.10 | 14.00 | 11.90 |
| Lysine | 1.17 | 1.04 | 0.91 | 0.77 |
| Cost per tonne (£) | 154.60 | 150.80 | 146.80 | 143.00 |
| | | | | |
| Ingredient prices used – | | | | |
| Barley | = | £110/tonne | | |
| Soya | = | £180/tonne | | |
| Vitamin/mineral supplement + milling/mixing charge | = | £24/tonne | | |

on a particular pig farm. Let us suppose that the diet being used at present on this farm is diet 4 (14 per cent CP and 0.91 per cent lysine) and we wish to estimate the cost benefit of providing either diet 2 or 3. At present the average backfat thickness ($P_2$) in the 67.5 kg carcasses produced is 14 mm, while the current food conversion efficiency and liveweight gain over this phase of growth are 3.15 and 760 grams per day respectively. The impact of changing the diet is summarised in Table 20.8.

The calculated margin of carcass value over food and housing costs has to cover the cost of the 55 kg pig at the start, labour and all the other costs. Relative to diet 4, the estimated extra margin from changing to diet 3 is £1.32 while a change to diet 2 is worth an extra £2.40 relative to diet 4. Therefore, the indications are very strong that under the present circumstances on this farm, a change to a higher protein/lysine diet would be very cost effective. The increase in the financial margin as calculated in this example would be likely to have a major proportional

**TABLE 20.8   Estimated effects of changing from diet 4 to diet 2 or 3 over the liveweight range 55 to 90 kg**

| Diet | CP/lysine[A] (%) | FCR[B] | Food[C] required (kg) | Food[D] cost per pig | Liveweight[E] gain (g/day) | Days to[F] grow from 55 to 90 kg liveweight |
|---|---|---|---|---|---|---|
| 4 | 14.0/0.91 | 3.15 | 110.25 | £16.18 | 760 | 46 |
| 3 | 16.1/1.04 | 3.075 | 107.63 | £16.23 | 780 | 45 |
| 2 | 18.2/1.17 | 3.0 | 105 | £16.23 | 800 | 44 |

| Diet | Total[G] housing cost per pig from 55 to 90 kg | Feed[H] + housing costs | $P_2$[I] backfat (mm) | Grade[J] 1, 2, 3 (%) | Average[K] carcass value | Margin of[L] carcass value over food and housing costs |
|---|---|---|---|---|---|---|
| 4 | £1.94 | £18.12 | 14 | 57 '22 21 | £63.48 | £45.36 |
| 3 | £1.90 | £18.13 | 13 | 69 18 13 | £64.81 | £46.68 |
| 2 | £1.86 | £18.09 | 12 | 79 14  7 | £65.85 | £47.76 |

(A)   From Tables 20.4 and 20.7
(B)   Based on Table 20.4 and the fact that food conversion efficiency on the present diet (diet 4) is 3.15
(C)   Based on food conversion efficiency and the gain of 35 kg from 55 to 90 kg liveweight
(D)   Based on estimated costs of the different diets in Table 20.7
(E)   Based on Table 20.4 and the fact that liveweight gain on the present diet (diet 4) is 760 g/day
(F)   Divide total liveweight gain (35 kg) by liveweight gain per day
(G)   Based on a cost per pig place of 4p per day
(H)   (D) + (G)
(I)   Based on Table 20.4 and the fact that the average carcass $P_2$ in the herd at present on diet 4 is 14 mm
(J)   Derived from Table 20.6
(K)   Derived from Table 20.6
(L)   (K) minus (H)

effect on net margin per pig, the latter being equivalent to the profit margin after all cost items including interest and depreciation charges have been levied.

Using the basic relationships between the protein quality of the diet and growth, food conversion efficiency and carcass backfat as outlined in Table 20.4., it is possible to carry out similar calculations for any specified circumstances. The answers obtained will be dependent on:

1. The grading system and the level of price penalties imposed on surplus carcass fat. If price deductions for surplus fat are less severe than in the above example, then the advantages of improving the protein quality of the diet will be less.
2. The present average level of carcass backfat in the herd. If carcasses are already very lean and therefore carcass grading is very good, the impact of improving protein quality will also be less.
3. Feed costs and particularly the cost of protein sources including lysine. Where protein concentrates are cheap relative to cereals, there will be greater financial incentive to improve the protein quality of the diet than if protein concentrates are very expensive.

*Predicting the effects of a change in daily feed intake during the finishing stages*

The estimated influences of different feed or energy intakes during the finishing stages of growth of improved genotypes in Britain are summarised in Table 20.9, which shows that as food intake is restricted to a greater degree during finishing, carcass quality improves (backfat reduced) while liveweight gain and throughput decrease. Food conversion efficiency is about 2 per cent better at 80 and 90 per cent of ad lib. intake relative to ad lib., but at 70 per cent of ad lib. intake, food conversion efficiency is about 3 per cent worse than on ad lib.

One can examine the impact of changing from an ad lib. system and imposing a varying degree of feed restriction over the 55 to 90 kg finishing period. Let us

**TABLE 20.9   The effect of reductions in feed or energy intake between 55 and 90 kg liveweight on daily gain, feed conversion ratio (FCR) and carcass backfat thickness at $P_2$**

| Percentage reductions from ad lib. intake | Percentage changes in | | |
|---|---|---|---|
| | Daily gain | FCR | Average carcass backfat $(P_2)$ |
| Ad lib.* | 0 | 0 | 0 |
| 90 | − 8 | +2 | + 6.7 |
| 80 | −17 | +2 | +13.3 |
| 70 | −26 | −3 | +20 |

* Average daily intake of a diet with 13.0 MJ DE/kg from 55 to 90 kg liveweight is 2.4 kg
+ = Improvement
− = Deterioration (both relative to ad lib.)

**TABLE 20.10  Calculated effects of imposing increasing degrees of feed restriction between 55 and 90 kg liveweight**

| Percentage reductions from ad lib. intake | FCR[(A)] | Food[(B)] required (kg) | Food[(C)] cost per pig (Diet 2 Table 20.7) | Liveweight[(D)] gain (g/day) | Days to[(E)] grow from 55 to 90 kg liveweight |
|---|---|---|---|---|---|
| Ad lib. | 3.0 | 105 | £16.23 | 800 | 44 |
| 90 | 2.94 | 103 | £15.92 | 736 | 47.5 |
| 80 | 2.94 | 103 | £15.92 | 664 | 53 |
| 70 | 3.09 | 108 | £16.70 | 592 | 59 |

| Percentage reductions from ad lib. intake | Total[(F)] housing cost per pig from 55 to 90 kg | Feed[(G)] + housing costs | $P_2$[(H)] backfat (mm) | Grade[(I)] 1, 2, 3 (%) | Average[(K)] carcass value | Margin of[(L)] carcass value over food and housing costs |
|---|---|---|---|---|---|---|
| Ad lib. | £1.76 | £17.99 | 15 | 43 26 31 | £61.88 | £43.89 |
| 90 | £1.90 | £17.82 | 14 | 57 22 21 | £63.48 | £45.66 |
| 80 | £2.12 | £18.04 | 13 | 69 18 13 | £64.81 | £46.77 |
| 70 | £2.36 | £19.06 | 12 | 79 14  7 | £65.85 | £46.79 |

(A)  Based on Table 20.9 and the fact that current FCR on the ad lib. system is 3.0
(B)  Based on FCR over the 55 to 90 kg liveweight range
(C)  Based on diet 2 in Table 20.7
(D)  Based on Table 20.9 and the fact that current daily gain on the ad lib. system is 800 g
(E)  Divide total liveweight gain from 55 to 90 kg (= 35 kg) by the daily liveweight gain
(F)  Based on cost per pig place of 4p per day
(G)  (C) + (F)
(H)  Based on Table 20.9 and the fact that the average carcass $P_2$ on the present ad lib. system is 15 mm
(I)  Derived from Table 20.6
(K)  Derived from Table 20.6
(L)  (K) minus (G)

take a herd producing 67.5 kg carcasses with an average backfat thickness at $P_2$ of 15 mm and a food conversion efficiency of 3.0. The pigs have a liveweight gain averaging 800 g daily over this growth stage. The data in Table 20.10 outline the impact of imposing increasing degrees of feed restriction.

The calculated margin over food and housing costs has to cover the cost of the 55 kg pig at the start and all other costs. The smallest margin is achieved on the present ad lib. system and the estimates indicate that the financial margin would be increased by £1.77 and £2.88 by reducing daily feed intake by 10 and 20 per cent respectively. Such feed restriction would reduce growth rate and increase the time taken to grow from 55 to 90 kg liveweight. If buildings are already fully stocked, any imposition of feed restriction will result either in overstocking or necessitate sale at a lower liveweight. Such overstocking would be counter-productive, and lowering liveweight at slaughter is probably also likely to be an unwise option. However, the financial impact of selling lighter carcasses will have to be evaluated as will also the cost effectiveness of providing extra accommodation. The only other option is to consider reducing herd size.

The results summarised in Table 20.10 apply to one specific set of circumstances but the procedures used can be applied to check on current feeding strategy in terms of degree of feed restriction on any unit. There will be less argument for imposing greater food restriction either when carcass grading is already very good or when price differentials between carcass grades are smaller than those applied to the situation summarised in Table 20.10. Of course, where genetically improved pigs are not subjected to grading but are paid on a flat rate basis, regardless of level of fatness, then it is very desirable that they be fed to appetite and grow as quickly as possible. This helps to avoid overstocking and to improve throughput.

EVALUATING A CHANGE IN BACKFAT THICKNESS AND GRADING PROFILE

In addition to being able to change carcass backfat by manipulating the protein quality of the diet and feed or energy intake during the finishing stages of growth, one can bring about such changes by a variety of other approaches. These include genetic manipulation, ceasing to castrate and leaving male pigs entire and reducing the slaughter weight. As with manipulation of feed intake and diet quality, one can make a reasonable prediction of the effect of any such change on backfat thickness, and it is useful then to be able to calculate the impact of such a change on grading profile and hence on average carcass value.

Let us consider the two somewhat contrasting grading and pricing systems outlined in Table 20.11. It can be seen that system 1 is identical to that shown in Table 20.6. System 2 imposes a penalty not only on overfat pigs but also on overlean ones (carcasses with a $P_2$ backfat of 8 mm or less).

**TABLE 20.11  Contrasting carcass grading and pricing systems**

|          |                            | Grade 1   | Grade 2              | Grade 3  |
|----------|----------------------------|-----------|----------------------|----------|
| System 1 | Backfat at $P_2$ (mm)      | Up to 14  | 15–16                | Over 16  |
|          | Price per kg carcass (p)   | 100       | 93                   | 79       |
| System 2 | Backfat at $P_2$ (mm)      | 9–14      | Under 9 and 15–18    | Over 18  |
|          | Price per kg carcass (p)   | 101       | 95                   | 77       |

Relative to system 1, system 2 is paying 1 per cent (or 1p) more for grade 1 carcasses but grade 1 only applies to pigs in the $P_2$ backfat range of 9 to 14 mm. Pigs with less than 9 and between 15 and 18 mm backfat at $P_2$ are relegated to grade 2. Grading systems operated by other processors may have yet different standards, so it is thus important that a pig producer can decide fairly quickly and easily where he should consign his pigs to command the best price. One such ready-reckoner approach which will help him do this is outlined in Figure 20.4.

*Component 1* This consists of a simple calibrated *backfat grid* ranging over a wide $P_2$ backfat range.

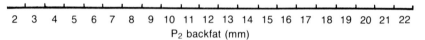

2   3   4   5   6   7   8   9   10  11  12  13  14  15  16  17  18  19  20  21  22
$P_2$ backfat (mm)

*Component 2* This consists of a *transparent sheet* of a standard frequency distribution of a normal population of pigs with the highest proportion concentrated around the mean value and with ever-reducing proportions towards the tails of the distribution.

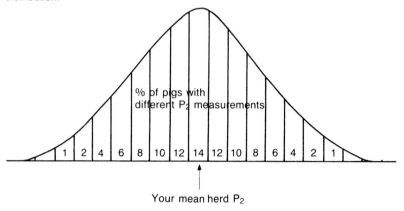

% of pigs with different $P_2$ measurements

1 | 2 | 4 | 6 | 8 | 10 | 12 | 14 | 12 | 10 | 8 | 6 | 4 | 2 | 1

Your mean herd $P_2$

FIGURE 20.4   Simple Ready Reckoner to help a pig producer predict his carcass backfat profile and grading on the basis of mean herd backfat ($P_2$) thickness.

PROCEDURE TO CALCULATE PROPORTION OF CARCASSES WITH DIFFERENT
BACKFAT THICKNESS AT $P_2$

1. Calculate your present mean herd $P_2$.
2. Superimpose component 2 (transparent sheet) over component 1 (backfat grid), making sure that your mean $P_2$ (highest column in bell-shaped distribution) coincides with this specific $P_2$ backfat thickness on the backfat grid.
3. Holding the transparent sheet in position over the backfat grid, the figures on the transparent sheet (bell-shaped distribution) provide a good estimate of the proportion of your pigs with different levels of backfat.

**TABLE 20.12   Proportion of carcasses with different backfat thickness at $P_2$ and predicted grading profile on grading system 1 in Table 20.11**

|  | \multicolumn{10}{c}{$P_2$ Backfat (mm)} |  |  |  |  |  |  |
|---|---|---|---|---|---|---|---|---|---|---|---|---|---|---|---|---|
|  | 5 | 6 | 7 | 8 | 9 | 10 | 11 | 12 | 13 | 14 | 15 | 16 | 17 | 18 | 19 | Total |
| Proportion of carcasses | 1 | 2 | 4 | 6 | 8 | 10 | 12 | 14 | 12 | 10 | 8 | 6 | 4 | 2 | 1 | 100 |
| Proportion in different grades |  |  |  |  | 79% Grade 1 |  |  |  |  |  | 14% Grade 2 |  | 7% Grade 3 |  |  |  |

If mean herd backfat at $P_2$ is 12 mm, then your pigs are likely to show an overall range in backfat at $P_2$ from 5 to 19 mm. The proportions of pigs likely to fall into the different backfat levels can be read off the transparent sheet and they are summarised in Table 20.12. It is calculated that on grading system 1, when herd mean $P_2$ equals 12 mm, 79, 14 and 7 per cent of carcasses will end up in grades 1, 2 and 3 respectively. If, on the other hand, the producer decides to consign his pigs to the processor operating grading system 2 (Table 20.11), he will end up with $1 + 2 + 4 + 6 = 13$ per cent of his pigs relegated to grade 2 because they are overlean. A further $8 + 6 + 4 + 2 = 20$ per cent of pigs will end up in grade 2 because they have a backfat between 15 and 18 mm, while 1 per cent of pigs (above 18 mm) will be relegated to grade 3, so that his grading profile will be:

|  | *Per cent* |  |
|---|---|---|
| Grade 1 (9 to 14 mm) | 66 | |
| Grade 2 (<9 and 15 to 18 mm) | 33 | $\left( \begin{array}{l} 20 \text{ from 15 to 18 mm} \\ +13 \text{ under 9 mm} \end{array} \right)$ |
| Grade 3 (>18 mm) | 1 | |
| Total | 100 | |

Similar estimates can be carried out for any mean herd $P_2$, based either on the present average level or expected $P_2$ following a change, for example, in the protein quality of the diet, which is being contemplated. The reader who wishes to test out the above ready-reckoner system will obtain the answers outlined in Table 20.13 if the carcass grading and pricing systems outlined in Table 20.11 are put to the test.

**TABLE 20.13  Grading profiles estimated from the Ready Reckoner and average carcass prices based on the data in Table 20.11**

| Processor 1 (Grading system 1) | | | | *Average* | *Value of* |
|---|---|---|---|---|---|
| *Mean herd* | *Grade 1* | *Grade 2* | *Grade 3* | *price* | *67.5 kg* |
| *$P_2$ mm* | *0–14 mm* | *15–16 mm* | *>16 mm* | *per kg (p)* | *carcass (£)* |
| | | *Percentage of pigs* | | | |
| 10 | 93 | 6 | 1 | 99.37 | 67.07 |
| 11 | 87 | 10 | 3 | 98.67 | 66.60 |
| 12 | 79 | 14 | 7 | 97.55 | 65.85 |
| 13 | 69 | 18 | 13 | 96.01 | 64.81 |
| 14 | 57 | 22 | 21 | 94.05 | 63.48 |

| Processor 2 (Grading System 2) | | | | | |
|---|---|---|---|---|---|
| | *Grade 2* | *Grade 1* | *Grade 2* | *Grade 3* | |
| | *0–8 mm* | *9–14 mm* | *15–18 mm* | *>18 mm* | |
| | | *Percentage of pigs* | | | |
| 10 | 31 | 62 | 7 | 0 | 98.72 | 66.64 |
| 11 | 21 | 66 | 13 | 0 | 98.96 | 66.80 |
| 12 | 13 | 66 | 20 | 1 | 98.78 | 66.68 |
| 13 | 7 | 62 | 28 | 3 | 98.18 | 66.27 |
| 14 | 3 | 54 | 36 | 7 | 96.98 | 65.46 |

The Ready Reckoner in Figure 20.4 will estimate grading profile fairly accurately from knowledge of mean $P_2$ backfat in most circumstances. It will be slightly less accurate in situations in which a producer is very adept at detecting lean pigs and retaining them to heavier weights before slaughter and in selling fatter pigs at a lower liveweight. It is not easy to make such judgements about leanness and fatness by eye and, as stated in Chapter 16, good ultrasonic equipment has to be used by a skilful operator before more accurate assessment of backfat can be made. Ultrasonic measurement of backfat is certainly called for in the case of processor 2 using grading system 2 in Table 20.13. On this grading system, it can be seen that there are no great incentives for reducing average herd backfat since average carcass value increases very little (from £66.27 to £66.80) as backfat is reduced from 13 to 11 mm. As backfat is decreased further to 10 mm, average carcass value is less than it was at a mean $P_2$ of 11 mm. The obvious reason for this is that as backfat thickness is reduced, downgrading for overfatness decreases but downgrading for overleanness increases. In this situation, ultrasonic measurement of backfat would be used to ensure that lean pigs were kept to heavier weights until they laid down more backfat, while fat pigs would be sold at lower liveweights before backfat increased to a level to cause downgrading. The objective of using ultrasonics in this specific situation is therefore to change the normal, fairly wide distribution of backfat in carcasses from a particular herd as illustrated by the wide bell shape in Figure 20.4 to the very narrow, somewhat skewed bell shape illustrated in Figure 20.5. This latter backfat distribution in carcasses avoids carcasses being downgraded because they are overlean and, at the same time, minimises the proportion downgraded for overfatness (in excess of 14 mm).

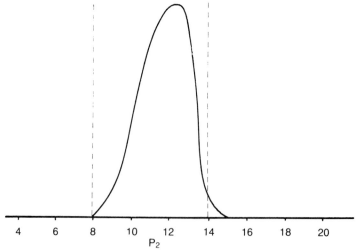

FIGURE 20.5   Desirable distribution of backfats both to cater for the needs of Processor 2 (see Table 20.11) and to improve grading and average carcass value.

Thus, in attempting to evaluate a change in the system likely to influence average backfat thickness, or in assessing which processor has the best deal on offer for pigs from a particular herd, it is important to be able to relate average backfat thickness to grading profile and average carcass value. Such assessments may also indicate the desirability of adopting new technology, such as the use of ultrasonics, to help improve the timing of marketing of individual pigs on the basis of their estimated backfat thickness.

PREDICTING FINANCIAL CONSEQUENCES OF OTHER CHANGES

In addition to carrying out partial budgeting to assess the consequences in physical and financial terms of changing backfat thickness by a variety of approaches, or of amending the protein quality of the diet or of altering the feeding level during the finishing stages, it is important to carry out a partial budget to estimate the effects of other changes under consideration on the pig unit. For example, if the trough section of ad lib. feed hoppers is wearing thin and likely to spring a leak very soon, whereas the remainder is in very sound condition, it is probably going to be much more cost effective to repair the worn parts using heavy duty non-corrosive metal than to purchase expensive replacement feeders which are no more efficient and which are unlikely to last any longer than the reconditioned originals. Shiny new ones may improve the appearance for a while and act as useful status symbols but are unlikely to be any more effective in ensuring efficient use of feed and will be less effective in controlling bank borrowings and interest changes. On the other hand, for the overworked, dedicated stockman, investment in automated manure handling could pay a handsome dividend in that the time so saved could be used by the stockman to give much more attention to critical detail in the care of the pigs, which in turn could provide a handsome return on the investment. In the same way, if several hours each day are devoted merely in transporting feed to the pigs within the piggery, then an investment in a more time-saving and less energy-sapping feed delivery system could be extremely cost effective.

CASH FLOW CALCULATIONS

Most pig producers who are indebted to the bank are under obligation to produce forward budgets and cash flows so that some prediction can be made on the amount of bank credit required in the months ahead. However, even if not required by the bank, such forward budgets are an essential basis for the forward planning and organisation of any farm business. It is unwise to base these forward budgets on the most optimistic possibilities just to impress the bank manager or to delude oneself at the time, since the disappointment of everybody concerned will be all the greater when the moment of truth arrives at the end of the year and actual performance is compared with what was predicted. One effect such anomalies can have is that the bank manager may have less faith in future in the client and, as a result, adequate bank credit for the proper running of the business may be harder to obtain.

Therefore, it is wise in such forward budgeting to make estimates on the basis of the most pessimistic, the most likely and the most optimistic scenarios and discuss all these possibilities with the bank manager. Together, banker and client can then decide on the most probable situation on the basis of all the most likely eventualities they can think of. Many producers, as well as keeping a monthly check on how closely their actual income and expenditure tally with their cash flow predictions, represent the predicted and actual performance graphically in the farm office so that the pig unit manager and staff are kept fully up to date with the picture (see Figure 20.6). This approach is useful educationally since results which are better than predictions are encouraging and motivating for dedicated staff. If results are worse than predictions, then provided the main source of the problem can be identified, such trends, while being disappointing, will not demotivate staff with the right attitude, but should spur them to further efforts to get results back on course as soon as possible, if it is within their control to do so. Such occurrences as unexpected increases in feed prices or decreases in price per kg of pigmeat on offer can cause serious distortions to predicted cash flows about which the stockman can take little, if any, corrective action.

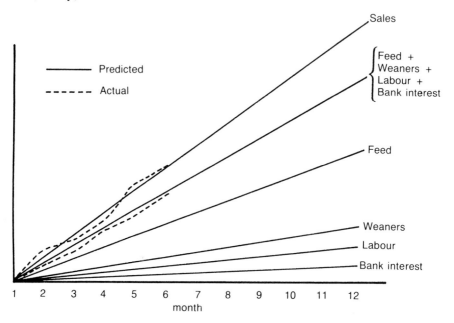

FIGURE 20.6   Cash flow predictions and actual performance.

It can be seen in Figure 20.6 that actual sales, although showing slight variations from month to month are conforming closely to predictions. Expenditure on the major cost items in this particular unit (feed, weaner pigs, labour and interest changes) is tending to keep below predictions. The latter trend is encouraging and may be explained by a change to a more cost effective range of diets which is resulting in a lower cost per kg of liveweight gain, or it may have been brought about by staff paying more attention to the fine tuning of the climatic environment in the housing to reduce undue diurnal and seasonal variations in temperature at pig level.

THE COMPUTER AS AN AID TO MONITORING

If properly programmed and if data is entered meticulously, the computer is a great time-saver in helping to keep farm records and results right up to date. It is used in the computation of predicted cash flow, and if details of sales and expenditure (itemised according to category) are entered promptly, the monthly cash flow chart (Figure 20.6) can be kept right up to date so that the state of the business is known.

Computer programmes such as those available at the centre for Rural Buildings in Aberdeen can aid in checking the adequacy of the climatic environment for pigs at different stages of the production process and to calculate the relative cost effectiveness of alternative ways of modifying the climate if it is found to be faulty and resulting in depressed pig performance.

The computer is also an essential tool in diet formulation and in the detailed fine tuning required to produce a range of diets to suit pigs of different genotype and sex at different stages of the growth period. It is also useful in assisting with the determination of the most cost effective dietary regime for a particular situation as in the case studies presented in Tables 20.8 and 20.10 on the optimum dietary protein/lysine and feed levels respectively. Identifying the meat processor who has the most attractive grading and pricing system to suit your pigs (see Figure 20.4 and Table 20.13) is also a job the computer can carry out promptly and accurately. However, like the pig unit, the computer must be properly operated and, with a competent programmer and operator, it is now an essential tool in assisting with the wise planning, careful operation and monitoring of many major pig production enterprises.

## ADDITIONAL READING

*MLC Pig Yearbooks*, Meat and Livestock Commission, PO Box 44, Queensway House, Bletchley, Milton Keynes, England MK2 2EF.

*Pork Industry Handbook*, USA Co-operative Extension Service, University of Illinois at Urbana-Champaign, USA.

Ridgeon R. F. (1987), *Pig Management Scheme Results*, Agricultural Economics Unit, Department of Land Economy, Cambridge University, 19 Silver Street, Cambridge.

# Chapter 21

# Management, Labour Motivation and Deployment, and Stockmanship

## INTRODUCTION

A production unit involving a number of people immediately becomes a social unit with a character and even a personality of its own. Most people do not want to be miserable, but wish to be associated with success and attainable goals. The management of a pig unit involving a manager/stockperson interface is a peculiarly difficult relationship to get right, and 75 per cent of the responsibility rests with the management system and attitude. A slack manager cannot demand 110 per cent performance from his staff.

The most important area is for management to establish two kinds of objective. The first is that of numerical objectives, for example mortality rate, growth rate, feed conversion and grading percentage. The second is more difficult but of critical importance. These are the subjective targets which include appearance and health of the pigs, tidiness of the unit and, above all, clarity of the messages flowing between management and staff.

The pig unit involves a very high capital outlay. To be efficient, the communication systems must be clear and effective. The purpose of this chapter is to draw attention to the importance of effective dialogue between staff, and to stress how that mysterious but essential ingredient of good stockmanship can be identified and promoted.

## MANAGEMENT

It is the role of management to make available to stockmen genetically efficient and healthy stock, good facilities, a sound system and to provide the stockmen with the necessary motivation and time so that they are given every incentive and opportunity to exercise their skills.

The stockman should know exactly to whom he is answerable. Too often he gets conflicting messages and in pleasing the one master he annoys the other. For example, the manager should not bypass the head stockman and berate an individual or undermine the head stockman's authority. It is the duty of management

509

Plate 21.1   Regular meetings of management and staff to discuss problems, successes and results in physical and financial terms can be very helpful to all concerned if they are conducted in an open, constructive manner. Such meetings, say, at monthly intervals, can help to foster good team spirit. The picture shows Mr Arthur Simmers of J.A. Simmers & Sons, Aberdeenshire, who has been a pioneer of such interactive sessions in the management of his very large pig enterprises in the north of Scotland.

to ensure that the head stockman is given responsibility and then held accountable. If he is not able to cope with this responsibility, then it is wise to train someone else for the post. The margins in pig production are too small to allow passengers in responsible positions.

## LABOUR MOTIVATION AND DEPLOYMENT

It is much easier to motivate and deploy labour effectively if the objectives of the job are well defined. In setting out to achieve a high level of efficiency in pigmeat production from the weaner stage, the objectives are very clear cut.

What is basically required is the sound establishment of young weaner pigs and their development to the market stage so that one maintains good health, minimises mortality, achieves maximum feed intake and growth consistent with keeping food cost per kg of liveweight or lean meat gain as low as possible and produces a finished pig which is wholly acceptable in terms of carcass and meat quality. However, in setting out to achieve these straightforward objectives there is no single magical formula for success. Success in achieving each of these objectives depends on applying a multiplicity of small factors.

Thus, in order to achieve a high level of performance, there must be full appreciation by the stockmen of the factors involved, a system incorporating these factors must be developed carefully, preferably through the joint efforts of management and staff, and there must be implicit belief in this system on the part of the stockman who must then apply it rigorously in practice.

In order to apply the system properly, the stockman should be allocated sufficient time to pay the necessary attention to detail. The philosophy of getting one person to look after more and more pigs has proved to be false economy on many units because, in this situation, there is increasingly less time to pay the necessary attention to detail. Individual pigs which are not performing optimally because of such factors as ill health, excessive stocking density or group size or inadequate feeding space are not spotted timeously, if at all, and less efficient production and increased mortality are the outcome.

Personnel with traditional, preconceived ideas which may be less than half-truths are often difficult to motivate in an alternative but well-proven direction. Conversely, intelligent and energetic personnel entering the modern pig industry without any preconceived ideas often perform excellently, given the proper guidance and training.

From the manager's point of view, it is very important that he gives the stockpersons a formal and regular opportunity to be praised and encouraged. At the minimum, monthly meetings should be held and some form of written record of decisions be kept. Management should be aware that requests for, say, a supply of light bulbs or switches to be mended are critical to the men involved and they should allow themselves to be held to account if they have not responded to a reasonable request. Similarly, criticisms of the diets should be listened to with sympathy. The good stockperson is very aware of subtle changes in the behaviour of pigs and his unease about the diet may precede serious trouble if not acted upon.

Figures quoted at such meetings should be realistic and preferably derived without argument from an objective recording system. Computer programmes provide a measure of anonymity and objectivity which can often allay suspicion. Performance targets set for stockmen should be realistic and attainable, and care should be taken not to over-react to temporary problems when the longer-term figures are good. Numbers have a natural variation and blistering abuse can look very stupid when all returns to normal retrospectively or when a substantial mistake is found in the summary of performance for that month.

Careful recording and monitoring of the pig herd in both physical and financial terms and the involvement of all pig unit personnel in regular discussion on the trends in performance and on possible reasons for failure to achieve target performance levels can be an extremely useful exercise in terms of providing adequate motivation.

Subjective targets like tidiness, quality of and timeliness of maintenance and appearance of the animals are important but difficult to discuss sensibly in the central office. Time devoted by management walking round the unit is well spent. Again, notes should be kept of any decisions made and the manager must be prepared to fulfil his part of any duty which he agrees to undertake. This generates a sense of partnership and of common commitment and purpose.

Another point is worth making on the subject of motivation. To the urban com-

Plate 21.2  Premises which are kept clean, tidy and hygienic are attractive to both management and staff and help to bring the best out of them in tending the stock. (Courtesy of National Pig Development Company)

munity, a person who works with pigs, however expertly, can often be assigned a poor social standing. Employers and managers can help here by widening the responsibility of stockmen to include a degree of added status such as feed purchasing and ordering, organising production records to give greater clarity, e.g. producing graphs. In addition, the term 'stockman' has a more pleasant ring than that of 'pigman' and 'livestock manager' has a bit more style than 'head pigman'.

## STOCKMANSHIP

Of all the vital components for achieving a high level of efficiency in pigmeat production, stockmanship is undoubtedly the most important. The leading scientists who have grappled with the requirements of the pig in terms of its nutrition, housing and maintenance of its health are the servants; the good stockman is the master. The buck has to stop somewhere and it is the good stockman who, at the point of practical application, has the responsibility for moulding existing knowledge on disease prevention, feeding, housing and provision of an adequate environment into a system of operation in the actual commercial production of finished pigs. The behaviour and performance of the stock act jointly as his main barometer of well-being and he adapts and amends the basic system according to the needs of individual animals within the herd.

Stockmanship is one of those terms which are extremely difficult to define and, despite the universal recognition of its great importance in animal production, it has been the subject of only limited investigation.

Working in Holland, Paul Hemsworth subjected 11 to 22 week old pigs penned in groups of eight to 'pleasant' and 'unpleasant' treatments three times per week over a period of 2 months. The 'pleasant' treatment consisted of entering the pen and stroking a pig when it approached while the unpleasant treatment consisted of entering the pen and slapping or giving a shock to the pig as it approached. At 25 weeks of age, the pigs in the unpleasant handling treatment were less willing to approach the experimenter when he entered the pen for 3 minute test periods. In addition, the pigs subjected to the 'unpleasant' treatment had a lower growth rate and had higher corticosteroid concentration in the blood both at rest and in response to the presence of the experimenter (see Table 21.1). It was concluded that the unpleasant handling by humans resulted in both chronic and acute stress responses. Other experiments with young pigs (Table 21.1) have since confirmed the earlier findings of Hemsworth.

**TABLE 21.1  Effects of handling treatments on the level of fear of humans and performance of pigs in four experiments**

| Experiment | Handling treatment | | |
| --- | --- | --- | --- |
| | *Pleasant* | *Minimal\** | *Unpleasant* |
| *1. Hemsworth et al. (1981)* | | | |
| Time to interact with experimenter (sec)† | 119 | - | 157 |
| Growth rate from 11−22 weeks (g/day) | 709 | - | 669 |
| Free corticosteroid concentrations (ng/ml)‡ | 2.1 | - | 3.1 |
| *2. Gonyou et al. (1986)* | | | |
| Time to interact with experimenter (sec)† | 73 | 81 | 147 |
| Growth rate from 8−18 weeks (g/day) | 897 | 888 | 837 |
| *3. Hemsworth et al. (1987)* | | | |
| Time to interact with experimenter (sec)† | 10 | 92 | 147 |
| Growth rate from 7−13 weeks (g/day) | 455 | 458 | 404 |
| Free corticosteroid concentrations (ng/ml)‡ | 1.6 | 1.7 | 2.5 |
| *4. Hemsworth et al. (1986)* | | | |
| Time to interact with experimenter (sec)† | 48 | 96 | 120 |
| Pregnancy rate of gilts (%) | 88 | 57 | 33 |
| Age of a fully co-ordinated mating response by boars (days) | 161 | 176 | 193 |
| Free corticosteroid concentrations (ng/ml) ‡ | 1.7 | 1.8 | 2.4 |

\*  A treatment involving minimal human contact
†  Standard test to assess level of fear of humans by pigs
‡  Blood samples remotely collected at hourly intervals from 0800 to 1700 h

(From: Hemsworth, 1988)

Similar 'pleasant' and 'unpleasant' treatments were imposed at a similar age by Hemsworth and his associates on potential breeding stock, and a further 'control' treatment was examined in which stock had little contact with humans apart from that associated with routine husbandry practices. Relative to the 'pleasant' handling treatment, the control and 'unpleasant' treatments were associated with greater reluctance to approach humans, higher blood corticosteroid level following contact with humans, later sexual development and poorer conception rate to service at second oestrus (Table 21.1). The results of Hemsworth and his colleagues therefore suggest that the behaviour of the pigman, the degree and nature of contact he has with his animals and the relationship he establishes with them, have an important influence on the welfare and productivity of the animals in his care.

While the characteristics of good stockmen have not been clearly established in the case of pigs, Dr Martin Seabrook has made suggestions on the basis of studies with dairy cows regarding the characteristics of high achievement cowmen (see Table 21.2). Seabrook's studies were based on single stockman dairy herds which were almost identical in terms of genotypes of cow, nutrition, facilities and management.

**TABLE 21.2   Average characteristics of high-achievement cowmen (x)**

| | | | | | | |
|---|---|---|---|---|---|---|
| Not easy-going | x | | | | | Easy-going |
| Adaptable | | | x | | | Unadaptable |
| Inconsiderate | | | | x | | Considerate |
| Meek | | | | x | | Not meek |
| Patient | x | | | | | Impatient |
| Unsociable | x | | | | | Sociable |
| Not modest | x | | | | | Modest |
| Independent minded | x | | | | | Not independent minded |
| Persevering | x | | | | | Giving up easily |
| A worrier | | | | x | | Not a worrier |
| Cheerful | | | | x | | Grumpy |
| Talkative | | | | | x | Not talkative |
| One who speaks one's mind | | x | | | | One who keeps quiet |
| Difficult to get on with | | x | | | | Easy to get on with |
| Lacking confidence | | | | | x | Confident |
| Co-operative | | | | x | | Uncooperative |
| Liking change | | | | | x | Suspicious of change |
| Forceful | | x | | | | Giving in easily |

(From: Seabrook, 1984)

The indications from Table 21.2 were that cowmen who achieved the best results in terms of milk yield from their herds tended to be somewhat introverted, with a high degree of confidence in their own ability. It is highly likely, of course, that different characteristics are desirable in a stockman who is the sole employee on a one-man unit than for one who is a member of a team of workers on a large farm. The relationship the stockman is able to develop with his animals is one very important component of stockmanship. Good stockmanship also involves a well-moulded combination of

- a sound basic knowledge of the subject
- a basic attachment for and patience with the stock
- an ability to recognise all individual animals and to remember their particular eccentricities
- a keen sensitivity for recognising the slightest departure from normal behaviour of individual animals
- an ability to organise his working time well
- a keen appreciation of priorities combined with an almost constant willingness to be side-tracked from routine duties as pressing needs arise to attend to individual animals in most need of attention

The basic desire is to make each animal as comfortable and contented as possible and to strive constantly for higher levels of performance and efficiency.


## TRAINING OF STOCKMEN

Stockmanship, being such a vital component in achieving high efficiency in pigmeat production, creates a pressing need for ensuring a good flow of suitable personnel into the industry and the appropriate training of such is brought into focus. Stockman training should involve a combination, preferably in tandem, of a sound apprenticeship on the pig unit and of well-organised courses, aimed at increasing understanding of the animal in terms of its structure, physiology and behaviour and of its requirements in terms of nutrition, climatic environment, housing and maintenance of good health. It is important that the apprenticeship is spent working with stock under the guidance of a patient, knowledgeable and experienced stockman with the ability to train others in his skills and to impart to them the secrets for his success.

The value of skilled stockmanship has always been recognised by those who knew how to get the best out of their stock. In this age of automation, stockmanship has become not less important, but even more so, if we are to get the most out of expensive stock, buildings and feed. Good stock and a sound basic system can very readily end up in disaster in the hands of inadequate management and labour. Good stockmanship, on the other hand, can be looked upon as a vital cog in a wheel which gets the very best out of mediocre stock and a mediocre system and makes sure that a potentially good system fulfils its full promise in terms of efficient pigmeat production. The need for effective recruitment and training of stockmen thus becomes paramount.

Plate 21.3  To attract and retain young, good-quality personnel, the apprenticeship served
in working alongside senior colleagues in the pig unit must be supplemented with a
continuing education programme which involves a regular afternoon or evening session
held, say, once monthly, designed to increase the understanding of the stockpeople about
the physiological processes of the pig and its basic requirements for high health and fast,
efficient growth of lean tissue.

## NEED FOR A CLEARER DEFINITION OF 'STOCKMANSHIP' IN RELATION TO IMPROVING TRAINING AND RECRUITMENT

While the importance of good stockmanship is universally recognised, much further work is necessary in order to define the characteristics of the efficient pig
stockman more clearly. Such clearer definition of the essential characteristics of
such a stockman is necessary to guide the training of young recruits for the
industry.

Further clarification of the essential traits of a good stockman is also important
to provide a basis for drawing up efficient interview and selection procedures when
a new stockman is being recruited to a pig farm. Present selection procedures tend
to be very subjective and therefore many expensive mistakes result from making
what is proved by hindsight to have been the wrong choice. Interview and selection
procedures should, at least, be effective in differentiating between those individuals
who interview well but are really looking for any kind of job and those who may
not interview so well but are really very enthusiastic about embarking on a career
in the pig industry.

## Conclusions

To date, most research and development effort and finance have been devoted to nutrition and feeding and this has been justified on the grounds that feed constitutes about 70 per cent of total production costs. However, it is not an overstatement to claim that the stockman has at least a 70 per cent influence on how efficiently such feed is converted on the pig unit into pigmeat. This being so, studies aimed at defining the characteristics of the excellent pigman should be encouraged and improved training schemes must be implemented on the basis of the findings so as to ensure for the future a steady supply of good recruits for the pig industry who will be capable of achieving in the animals under their care the inseparable objectives of a high standard of pig welfare and efficient production.

## Additional Reading

English P. R., Burgess G., Segundo R. and Dunne J. H. (1992), *Stockmanship: improving the care of the pig and other livestock*, Farming Press, Ipswich, UK.

English P. R. (1995), Stockmanship and its importance to profitable pigmeat production. Proceedings Iowa State University Conference on 'Swine Breeding Herd Management', Module 3: Stockmanship. Des Moines, Iowa, USA. Sept. 1995, 9 pages.

English P. R. (1995), Stockmanship: The 'Achilles Heel' of the pig industry and the role of training, education and motivational procedures in enhancing pig care and performance. Proceedings Iowa State University Conference on 'Swine Breeding Herd Management', Module 3: Stockmanship. Des Moines, Iowa, USA. Sept. 1995, 13 pages.

English P. R. (1995), Stockmanship: Its importance in improving health, welfare and production efficiency and the role of training in enhancing the quality of farm animal carers. Proceedings British Pig Association Conference, ICI Conference Centre, Peterborough, Nov. 1995, 23 pages.

English P. R. (1996), How can we improve stockmanship care? Proceedings of the Joint Meeting of the Ordre des medecins veterinaires du Quebec and the Association des medecins veterinaires practiciens du Quebec, University of Montreal, Sept. 20–22, 1996, 16 pages.

Gonyou H. W., Hemsworth P. H. and Barnett J. L. (1986), 'Effects of Frequent Interactions with Humans on Growing Pigs', *Appl. Anim. Behav. Sci.* **16**, 269–278.

Hemsworth, P. H., Barnett J. L. and Hansen C. (1981), 'The Influence of Handling by Humans on the Behaviour, Growth and Corticosteroids in the Juvenile Female Pig', *Horm. Behav.* **15**, 396–403.

Hemsworth P. H., Barnett J. L. and Hansen C. (1986), 'The Influence of Handling by Humans on the Behaviour, Reproduction and Corticosteroids of Male and Female Pigs', *Appl. Anim. Behav. Sci.* **15**, 303–331.

Hemsworth P. H., Barnett J. L. and Hansen C. (1987), 'The Influence of Inconsistent Handling by Humans on the Behaviour, Growth and Corticosteroids of Young Pigs', *Appl. Anim. Behav. Sci.* **17**, 245–252.

Hemsworth P. H., Brand A. and Williams P. J. (1981), 'The Behavioural Response of Sows to the Presence of Human Beings and Productivity', *Livestock Prod. Sci.* **8**, 67–74.

*Pork Industry Handbook*, USA Co-operative Extension Service, University of Illinois at Urbana-Champaign, USA.

Seabrook M. F. (Ed.) (1987), *The Role of the Stockman in Livestock Production and Management*, Report No. EUR 10982, CEC Luxembourg.

*Stockmanship in Pig Production* (1988), Proceedings of RASE/ADAS Conference, Royal Agricultural Society of England, Stoneleigh, Warwickshire, England.

# Chapter 22

# Future Perspectives

Where are we going in pig production? Will the consuming public still wish to eat meat? Has production technology reached a plateau? These are questions which many forward-thinking people are asking, and the purpose of this chapter is to address some of them.

Some trends are already clear. For example, those countries which have developed a high level of technology have become models for other countries with a lower level of technical back-up. A whole range of technologies including complete feed-mixing plants, complex buildings for accommodation, total breeding programmes and carbon-copy pigmeat processing plants have been installed in countries where people barely have adequate housing and nutrition themselves. This represents an enormous moral dilemma because, in some cases, technical elaboration has become mixed up with status and political symbols. There is a danger that this book could contribute to the view that only pig production at the very frontier of technology can be justified. The truth is that though it is very important to understand the basic principles and underlying science, the final assembly of the concepts in this book into a functioning system depends on the specific country and includes such diverse features as tradition, politics, finance, technical ability and market possibilities.

The various scenarios described below are obviously not applicable to all groups but should be taken to represent the possibilities for change even in the most sophisticated pig industries. Particular attention is given to the possibilities for further technical innovation and changes in the ethical perceptions of meat production in many of the most industrialised countries.

## FUTURE DEMAND FOR PIGMEAT

Cultures which traditionally consume pigmeat and which are not greatly urbanised, although probably consuming the greatest amount of pigmeat of any sector, have very limited impact on the world market for pig products because the animals are produced by indigenous rural producers for home consumption. For them the pig is still what Gervase Markham described in his book *Cheap and Good Husbandry* published in 1614, as '... Troublesome, noisome, unruly and great ravenours ... the husbandman's best scavenger, and the huswife's most wholesome sinke'. There is every reason to suppose that in countries such as China, this aspect of the rural economy will continue and as feed becomes more available and less competitive with human need, this area is likely to expand. Indeed it is quite possible in such countries that the peasant economy will be substantially boosted by better organisation of small-scale production so that, to some extent, the urban market will also be supplied.

### Change in Ethical Views

In Europe and North America, pigmeat is in fierce competition with poultry and beef and retains its competitive edge because the meat is interesting and capable of being produced at low cost. The pursuit of low cost has, however, damaged the image of intensive production in the eyes of the public. Some systems of production are so intensive that they are perceived as being unduly repressive and beyond the bounds of reasonable human behaviour towards animals. Although welfare issues are taken extremely seriously in some countries, in others they are not. Even within those countries where welfare of livestock is an important issue, a minority of producers have been reluctant to move towards those systems which are widely regarded as offering improved welfare, sometimes on the grounds of cost, but sadly in some instances because they are insensitive to the arguments and do not see the future consequences of their failure to react. There is a view that if farmers do not respond to gentle persuasion, such as that contained in the welfare codes of some countries, then the politicians may consider it necessary to introduce legislation which greatly limits what a farmer is allowed to do on a livestock unit. To ensure that farmers conform, some form of inspection and licensing will then be required. Of course, good farmers with an insight into the needs of stock have little to fear from such changes other than the inconvenience it will incur and the costs which will be involved, because these will almost certainly be levied on the industry. Unresponsive farmers, however, may find themselves unable to continue in stock farming and, much as they might regard such measures as undue interference in their chosen way of life, they will find very little sympathy from the general public.

### Changes in the Perception of Meat as a Healthy Food

Human nutritionists have not produced consistent nutritional objectives for the consuming public. Sometimes this has worked for the benefit of meat producers, but more recently it has tended to incline away from their interests. In the United Kingdom, there have recently been a number of government reports on diet and human health. Virtually without exception, they have recommended a reduction in the intake of fat, with the emphasis upon fat in animal products. The hazard which those reporting thought they saw was an association between fat intake and the incidence of a number of potentially killer diseases such as coronary heart disease, certain vascular disorders including an increased risk of impaired blood supply to the brain which could culminate in a stroke, enhanced risk of cancer of the large intestine and a greater tendency towards obesity and its associated disorders.

Although some members of the medical profession considered that the recommendations were based on debatable evidence and failed to take sufficient account of other correlated factors in a sophisticated life-style, these reports and similar ones in other countries have had a profound effect on the attitude of the public to the quantity and quality of the meat which they consume. Some consumers even regard good-quality lean meat with suspicion from the health aspect, notwithstanding the universal consensus that such lean meat constitutes a nutritious and safe food.

## Fat Consumption

The switch from accepting that fat contributes substantially to the flavour and eating quality of meat and to the satisfaction derived from the meal as a whole to the view that almost any visible fat is verging on the immoral has been nothing short of a revolution. Its effects on production and processing methods have been profound, and it will continue to dominate the argument about the role of meat in human health. It is of little import whether the arguments are right or wrong or exaggerated, if the balance of demand in some countries has swung to pork and bacon products which have virtually no fat. There is no sign that this trend, once begun, is going to be significantly reversed, although there are some counter-arguments. For example, it has been claimed that meat from very lean pigs lacks succulence because it lacks intramuscular fat, that is, fat actually within the muscle. In the United States, streaky bacon has a special role in the 'great American breakfast', but such is the weight of reaction against animal fat, that even this traditional market may also diminish unless the product is changed. It is clear that the demand from most consumers is for lean meat and for joints which have been very carefully trimmed of fat so that it is either hardly visible or appears as an even, very thin layer over the outside of the joint or rasher.

## Growth of Vegetarianism

Whilst in many countries the populace is striving to increase its proportion of meat in the average diet, in others, vegetarianism is being held up as a desirable nutritional objective. It must be conceded that with modern nutritional understanding, and the use, if necessary, of vitamin and mineral supplements, a perfectly satisfactory diet can involve the consumption of little or no meat. This, of course, disposes of a favourite view which used to be widely held, that meat was essential for a healthy diet and was essential for a sense of well-being.

Unfortunately, the proponents of vegetarianism often elevate their opinion to that of a pseudo-religious cause and harness any possible argument to bring the consumption of meat into disrepute. The basic scientific position is that meat eaten in moderation and without too much attendant fat can make a valuable contribution to a nutritious and interesting diet. There are a number of so-called moral issues advanced but basically the structure of our society allows individuals to choose what they wish to eat. However, opponents of meat eating often gain leverage for their position by publicising any dubious aspect of the production chain or by playing on public hysteria generated by such evocative words as hormones, drugs, antibiotics and genetic engineering. Developments in the science and technology of production must take these attitudes into account. Public relations have become very important in deciding the acceptability in practice of a technical advance.

It is also true that opponents of eating meat are often helped in their stance by the casual attitudes of some producers, who perpetuate the view that, somehow, everyone involved in the food production chain should be a protected species, free to operate as they see fit with no constraints. Such people fail to realise that, in the eye of the public, they are in a position of trust. The indiscriminate use of drugs, careless pollution of the environment and lack of sufficient concern about farm animal welfare are all problems which cause people to reconsider their automatic acceptance of the meat-eating habit. A recent informal survey of students in the agricultural faculty of a university revealed that one-third did not normally eat meat, many taking this position on what they perceived to be moral grounds. If this is a reflection of the view of a wider section of thinking young people, then it must be taken extremely seriously. It possibly indicates that the presentation of meat and the associated advertising is not directed at the appropriate targets and that more market research is required to establish how young people arrive at their attitudes.

## THE FUTURE POSSIBILITIES FOR TECHNICAL ADVANCE

### Nutrition

The application of many ideas advanced in earlier chapters would in many circumstances greatly improve the performance of growing pigs. New technology based on computers can now bring what were formerly rather idealised nutritional concepts to the ordinary farm. For example, twin feed conveying systems, delivering to different pens varying proportions of one high and one low protein diet, give scope for very fine tuning of the actual diet received by pigs based on their weight, age, sex or genotype. The same principle could be used to deliver different proportions of raw materials (such as barley, soya bean meal and vitamin-mineral premixes) to each pig pen, thus eliminating the need to mix before delivering to the pigs.

Genetic engineering of crops is at an early stage of development. New strains of familiar crops could be produced which are much more closely aligned to the needs of the pig. For example, the protein content and protein quality of wheat could be changed to be much more similar to that required in a complete diet. Completely new crops may become available and existing crops may not only be modified in terms of their composition but also in relation to the areas in which they may be grown. For example, it is quite possible to think of soya bean strains which can grow at much higher latitudes than the varieties currently available.

Genetic engineering may also affect the ease with which certain nutrients such as the amino acids threonine and lysine can be produced by fermentation of cheap substrates, thus making them very much cheaper and therefore more realistic options for least-cost diet formulation.

There are also possibilities for cheaper options in low-cost production systems. For example, harvesting cultured worms from organic wastes or the production of algal protein could produce less expensive sources of valuable nutrients.

## Technology and Growth

The way in which the body controls the types of tissue it produces is now much better understood than it was. It has been shown that the regulation of speed of growth and the proportion of fat to lean are largely associated with the protein-like growth regulator somatotrophin. Pigs have a special version of this substance, and one of the remarkable achievements of modern technology is to persuade bacteria to produce the precise molecule for us. Trials have already shown that this material can dramatically raise the potential for lean tissue growth. The big technical problem is how to provide growing pigs with this substance without having to resort to daily injections. It cannot be added to the diet because it is a protein-like substance which will be made ineffective by the digestive processes. Although it is a scientific fact that growth hormones stimulate the production of lean meat without risk to the humans who eat it, there is a major problem regarding the image of the product. For example, there is an ethical issue as to whether the public should be informed that this material was being used in the production process.

Other substances shown to have a profoundly beneficial effect on the rate of muscle growth and so on the leanness of the meat include the so-called B-agonists. These have been produced by many pharmaceutical companies and have the potential advantage that they are destroyed very rapidly indeed in the tissues and leave no residue in the meat. Again the ethical question of acceptability must be considered. It is important to see these developments in perspective. All animals control their own growth in one way or another and these factors are present in all meat. For example, the testicles and ovaries of the animal produce quite natural but very potent growth substances which mankind has been consuming over the millennia without ill effect. The argument is really more about the acceptability of physiological technology in animal production than about whether there is any risk to the consumer.

## Building Developments

The environment which we provide for growing pigs is critical and ultimately dependent on the type of protection we provide in the form of buildings. There have been, and will continue to be, enormous developments in innovative design and in the techniques of prefabricated or 'system' building. Many of the best innovations derive from an understanding of the animal's physical and physiological needs. For example, it is well known that the space requirements of the growing pig change as they grow. This means that during the period of occupancy of a pen, pigs have the correct space allowance for only a short period of time during their growth and most of the time their pens are either understocked or overstocked. One way round this problem is to opt for a flexible though stable layout and this is what is achieved in the xylophone house, so called because it has the appearance in plan view of two xylophones placed in counter matching positions (see Figure 13.8).

Many novel designs combine the provision of cheap space with the construction in one part of the pen of a well-insulated nest, so allowing the animal to choose its environment. An example of this is the so-called family pen for sows and growing pigs developed at the University of Edinburgh by Professor Wood-Gush and Dr Stolba.

A further factor which is increasingly being taken into account is the need of the operator to work in a healthy, dust-free environment. Cynics may regard this as an unnecessary elaboration since protection could be given by the wearing of masks. This, however, is symptomatic of an uncaring attitude since few would opt to pursue the whole of their working life encumbered by a mask unless it was absolutely necessary. Nor should it be presumed that the environment which humans find distressing is suitable for pigs. It is probably not, and is almost certainly responsible for sub-optimal production and the exacerbation of respiratory disease. Two environments, one suitable for humans, can easily be designed into buildings. For example, warm kennels can provide for the basic thermal needs of young pigs while the stockperson can perform almost all his activities in a well-lit, well-ventilated covered service passage. If high-quality staff are to be recruited and retained, it is essential that their working environment is made satisfactory and free from health hazard.

## Breeding

There are many exciting possible developments in breeding. First there are the combinations of specially bred lines to give good reproductive performance on the female side, but with good meat characteristics in the slaughter generation. The best sire lines combine good distribution of meat with good meat quality.

The possibilities for genetic engineering or highly selective breeding are illustrated by the potential of certain of the Chinese breeds of pigs. If, for example, their greater prolificacy and sexual precocity could be transferred to the advanced white breeds, without too great a cost in terms of growth and efficiency, then there would be an enormous increase in potential.

Genetic engineering might also be used in other ways. For example, it could be used to enhance the effects of natural growth substances such as somatotrophin or perhaps improve the immune system of pigs to make it even more effective and thus reduce losses due to poor performance associated with disease. The possibilities are endless, but all are subject to the procedures and the products being acceptable to the consumer.

## Meat Processing and the Image of Pigmeat

Probably the most critical area for the future of pigmeat as a marketable commodity is the role played by the processing industry. Every fat carcass can be converted into lean joints by the processor if he applies the appropriate technology. Although fat may be an embarrassment to the processor, he could turn it into an asset. Fat has a value in its own right even if it does not continue in the human food chain. At the worst, it can be recycled through the animal feed chain where it has a considerable value as a high-energy constituent of pig and poultry diets, particularly for younger growing animals and also for lactating sows. Many retailing chains have demonstrated their requirements by rejecting the meat products of some processors, and concentrating on obtaining the product they want from any country in

Plate 22.1 To meet the requirements of an ever more demanding consuming public, it is essential that the pig is accorded maximum care and attention on the farm, in transit to the slaughter plant and at lairage. (Courtesy of Cranswick Mill Group)

the world which can meet their standards. The new situation is that markets which have been based on home-produced supplies have become complacent but now must face up to increasing international trading in high quality produce. In the world of supermarket and hypermarket chains, the new royalty of the production chain are the buyers. They have virtually absolute discretion over what is bought and sold, and their views must be fully respected not only by the processors but also by the producers. The buyers are motivated largely by economic pressures and not by loyalty to the domestic producers.

It may seem extraordinary to those who understand the science that meat labelled as 'naturally produced' has any kind of consumer preference. One could argue that the only natural meat is that obtained from a wild animal shot in the forest and riddled with all the natural diseases. However, the term 'natural' is, romantically, whatever the buyer chooses to define as natural, and there are undoubtedly considerable market opportunities for those who are prepared to go along with their view. Again, one must concede the right of choice to the buyer, even when such a choice involves an element of gimmick and charade. If by following this type of lead, pigmeat can be reinstated in the purchase preferences of those who have otherwise lost confidence in the product, then this is all to the good. Again one must stress that the producer who has contracted to raise pigs naturally (according to the rules) must not break faith, for in so doing he may, when found out, alienate many of the consuming public to the detriment of his fellow producers.

## CONCLUSIONS

The future of pig production depends on all components of the production chain acting harmoniously together with a common objective, namely producing attractive, wholesome, cheap meat for the consuming public. To achieve this, it is necessary for all sectors to accept some discipline and to do their utmost to improve communication between all the components of the chain. The starting point in all this is to be absolutely sure what consumers want and what influences their choice. If consumers have to eat the pig or starve, they will eat the pig. If there is a surfeit of choice in meats, then pigmeat has to be something exceptional in this range. Pigmeat is undoubtedly the most versatile of all meats, capable of gracing the most noble dishes in the land (see colour plate 34). It is also very economical to produce. Bringing together the best of science, technology and marketing, it is unbeatable in terms of its potential and is likely to remain the most-consumed meat in the world for a very long time to come.

## ADDITIONAL READING

*Pig News and Information* (Consulting Editor, R. Braude), Commonwealth Agricultural Bureaux, Slough, England.

# Appendices

## APPENDIX 1

## Composition of ingredients for pig diets (adapted from Feedstuffs, 1986)

| Ingredients | Dry Matter % | Crude Protein % | Crude Fat % | Crude Fibre % | MJ DE/kg | Calcium % | Total Phos. % | Ash % |
|---|---|---|---|---|---|---|---|---|
| Alfalfa Meal, Dehy | 93.1 | 20.0 | 3.5 | 20.0 | 8.94 | 1.5 | 0.27 | 10.5 |
| Alfalfa Meal, Dehy | 93.0 | 17.0 | 3.0 | 24.0 | 5.82 | 1.3 | 0.23 | 9.6 |
| Alfalfa Meal, Dehy | 93.1 | 15.0 | 2.3 | 26.0 | 5.86 | 1.2 | 0.22 | 8.5 |
| Alfalfa Meal, Suncured | 90.7 | 15.0 | 1.7 | 29.0 | 5.62 | 1.4 | 0.2 | 9.0 |
| Bakery Product, Dried | 91.0 | 10.0 | 13.0 | 0.7 | 15.66 | 0.1 | 0.35 | 4.0 |
| Barley, Grain | 89.0 | 11.5 | 1.9 | 5.0 | 12.64 | 0.08 | 0.42 | 2.5 |
| Barley, Grain, Pacific Coast | 88.0 | 10.0 | 2.2 | 6.0 | 12.95 | 0.06 | 0.4 | 2.5 |
| Barley, Malt, Dehy | 91.0 | 13.7 | 1.9 | 3.3 | 14.44 | 0.06 | 0.46 | 2.2 |
| Bean, Broad (Vicia faba) | 89.0 | 25.7 | 1.4 | 8.2 | NA | 0.14 | 0.54 | 6.0 |
| Beet, Pulp, Dried | 90.8 | 8.0 | 0.5 | 21.0 | 10.33 | 0.6 | 0.1 | 3.8 |
| Blood Meal, Animal | 89.3 | 80.0 | 1.0 | 1.0 | 8.49 | 0.28 | 0.22 | 4.4 |
| Brewers Dried Grains | 93.0 | 27.9 | 7.4 | 11.7 | 9.87 | 0.30 | 0.66 | 4.8 |
| Brewers Dried Yeast | 93.0 | 45.0 | 0.4 | 1.5 | 11.67 | 0.1 | 1.4 | 6.5 |
| Buckwheat, Grain | 88.0 | 11.0 | 2.5 | 11.0 | 12.46 | 0.1 | 0.3 | 2.1 |
| Buttermilk, Dried | 89.0 | 32.0 | 5.0 | 0.3 | 13.26 | 1.3 | 0.9 | 10.0 |
| Casein Dried | 90.0 | 80.0 | 0.5 | 0.2 | 12.07 | 0.6 | 1.0 | 3.5 |
| Cassava, Tubers, Meal | 87.3 | 2.4 | 0.3 | 7.6 | 14.61 | 0.15 | 0.08 | 3.0 |
| Cattle Manure, Dried | 90.0 | 16.6 | − | − | NA | 1.6 | 0.75 | 7.6 |
| Citrus Pulp, Dried | 91.4 | 6.0 | 3.7 | 12.2 | 8.26 | 1.4 | 0.1 | 4.6 |
| Coconut Meal (Mech) | 93.0 | 22.0 | 6.0 | 12.0 | 11.01 | 0.17 | 0.6 | 7.0 |
| Corn, Yellow, Grain | 88.0 | 8.9 | 3.5 | 2.9 | 13.95 | 0.01 | 0.25 | 1.5 |
| Corn Dent Yellow, Ears Ground | 87.7 | 7.5 | 3.0 | 10.0 | 11.01 | 0.04 | 0.2 | 1.5 |
| Corn Cobs, Meal | 89.3 | 2.3 | 0.4 | 35.0 | 1.34 | 0.11 | 0.04 | 1.5 |
| Corn, Fermented Extracts, Cond. | 53.0 | 23.0 | 0.0 | 0.0 | NA | 0.14 | 1.8 | 10.0 |
| Corn Germ Meal (Wet Milled) | 90.0 | 20.0 | 1.0 | 12.0 | NA | 0.3 | 0.5 | 3.8 |
| Corn Germ Meal (Dry Milled) | 90.8 | 17.7 | 0.9 | 10.9 | 11.51 | 0.03 | 0.5 | 3.5 |
| Corn Gluten Feed | 88.0 | 21.0 | 2.0 | 10.0 | 10.57 | 0.2 | 0.9 | 7.8 |
| Corn Gluten Meal − 41% | 90.0 | 42.0 | 2.0 | 4.0 | 13.52 | 0.16 | 0.4 | 3.0 |
| Corn Gluten Meal − 60% | 90.0 | 60.0 | 2.0 | 2.5 | NA | 0.02 | 0.7 | 1.8 |
| Corn, Distillers Dried Grains | 93.8 | 27.0 | 9.0 | 13.0 | 16.17 | 0.09 | 0.41 | 2.2 |
| Corn, Distillers Dried Grains with Solubles | 92.5 | 27.0 | 8.0 | 8.5 | 14.93 | 0.35 | 0.95 | 4.5 |
| Corn, Distillers Dried Solubles | 91.5 | 27.0 | 9.0 | 4.0 | 12.78 | 0.35 | 1.30 | 8.2 |

NA − Data not available.

| | | | | | AMINO ACIDS | | | | | | |
|---|---|---|---|---|---|---|---|---|---|---|---|
| Methionine % | Cystine % | Lysine % | Tryptophane % | Threonine % | Isoleucine % | Histidine % | Valine % | Leucine % | Arginine % | Phenylalanine % | Glycine % |
| 0.33 | 0.23 | 0.87 | 0.46 | 0.88 | 0.98 | 0.42 | 1.19 | 1.5 | 0.98 | 1.04 | 1.0 |
| 0.28 | 0.18 | 0.73 | 0.45 | 0.75 | 0.84 | 0.35 | 1.04 | 1.3 | 0.75 | 0.91 | 0.88 |
| 0.23 | 0.17 | 0.6 | 0.38 | 0.6 | 0.68 | 0.3 | 0.84 | 1.1 | 0.58 | 0.66 | 0.72 |
| 0.2 | 0.17 | 0.6 | 0.38 | 0.6 | 0.60 | 0.22 | 0.60 | 1.1 | 0.58 | 0.58 | 0.7 |
| 0.16 | 0.16 | 0.3 | 0.09 | 0.28 | 0.36 | 0.2 | 0.4 | 0.8 | 0.4 | 0.4 | 0.9 |
| 0.18 | 0.25 | 0.53 | 0.17 | 0.36 | 0.42 | 0.23 | 0.62 | 0.8 | 0.5 | 0.62 | 0.36 |
| 0.18 | 0.22 | 0.39 | 0.15 | 0.29 | 0.40 | 0.20 | 0.46 | 0.6 | 0.45 | 0.47 | 0.3 |
| 0.2 | NA | 0.5 | 0.2 | 0.4 | 0.6 | 0.3 | 0.7 | 0.7 | 0.4 | 0.6 | NA |
| 0.25 | 0.14 | 1.52 | 0.24 | 0.98 | 1.0 | 0.6 | 1.22 | 1.6 | 2.2 | 0.98 | 1.0 |
| 0.01 | 0.01 | 0.6 | 0.1 | 0.4 | 0.3 | 0.2 | 0.4 | 0.6 | 0.3 | 0.3 | NA |
| 1.0 | 1.4 | 5.3 | 1.0 | 3.8 | 0.8 | 3.05 | 5.2 | 10.3 | 2.35 | 5.1 | 4.4 |
| 0.6 | 0.4 | 0.9 | 0.4 | 1.0 | 2.0 | 0.47 | 1.69 | 3.2 | 1.3 | 1.82 | 1.20 |
| 1.0 | 0.5 | 3.4 | 0.8 | 2.5 | 2.2 | 1.3 | 2.37 | 3.2 | 2.2 | 1.86 | 1.7 |
| 0.18 | 0.2 | 0.6 | 0.18 | 0.44 | 0.35 | 0.26 | 0.53 | 0.53 | 0.8 | 0.44 | NA |
| 0.7 | 0.38 | 2.4 | 0.5 | 1.6 | 2.7 | 0.9 | 2.8 | 3.4 | 1.1 | 1.5 | 0.6 |
| 2.7 | 0.3 | 7.0 | 1.0 | 3.8 | 5.7 | 2.5 | 6.8 | 8.7 | 3.4 | 4.6 | 1.5 |
| – | – | – | – | – | – | – | – | NA | – | – | – |
| 0.06 | – | 0.33 | NA | 0.21 | 0.21 | 0.09 | 0.29 | NA | 0.14 | 0.06 | 0.37 |
| 0.08 | 0.11 | 0.2 | 0.06 | NA | NA | NA | NA | NA | 0.28 | NA | NA |
| 0.33 | 0.2 | 0.54 | 0.2 | 0.6 | 1.0 | 0.3 | 1.0 | 1.49 | 2.3 | 0.8 | 1.1 |
| 0.17 | 0.13 | 0.22 | 0.09 | 0.34 | 0.37 | 0.19 | 0.42 | 1.0 | 0.52 | 0.44 | 0.33 |
| 0.14 | 0.13 | 0.16 | 0.05 | NA | NA | NA | NA | 1.0 | 0.3 | NA | 0.28 |
| – | – | – | – | – | – | – | – | – | – | – | – |
| 0.5 | 0.8 | 0.87 | 0.05 | 0.96 | 0.76 | 0.72 | 1.26 | 2.0 | 1.12 | 0.88 | 1.07 |
| 0.6 | 0.4 | 0.9 | 0.2 | 1.1 | 0.7 | 0.7 | 1.2 | 1.7 | 1.3 | 0.9 | 1.1 |
| 0.43 | 0.4 | 1.1 | 0.25 | NA | NA | NA | NA | NA | 1.4 | NA | 1.1 |
| 0.5 | 0.5 | 0.6 | 0.1 | 0.9 | 0.6 | 0.7 | 1.04 | 1.9 | 1.0 | 0.8 | 1.0 |
| 1.0 | 0.6 | 0.8 | 0.2 | 1.4 | 2.3 | 0.9 | 2.2 | 6.6 | 1.4 | 2.9 | 1.5 |
| 1.9 | 1.1 | 1.0 | 0.3 | 2.0 | 2.3 | 1.2 | 2.7 | 9.4 | 1.9 | 3.8 | 1.6 |
| 0.45 | 0.32 | 0.9 | 0.21 | 0.3 | 0.93 | 0.6 | 1.2 | 2.6 | 1.0 | 0.6 | 0.49 |
| 0.6 | 0.4 | 0.6 | 0.2 | 0.95 | 1.0 | 0.6 | 1.33 | 2.7 | 1.0 | 1.2 | 1.0 |
| 0.6 | 0.6 | 0.9 | 0.20 | 1.0 | 1.20 | 0.6 | 1.60 | 2.1 | 1.0 | 1.5 | 1.1 |

| Ingredients | Dry Matter % | Crude Protein % | Crude Fat % | Crude Fibre % | MJ DE/kg | Calcium % | Total Phos. % | Ash % |
|---|---|---|---|---|---|---|---|---|
| Cottonseed Meal − 41% (PrePress Solvent) | 89.9 | 41.0 | 0.81 | 12.7 | 10.28 | 0.17 | 1.0 | 6.4 |
| Cottonseed Meal − 41% (Mech Extd) | 91.4 | 41.0 | 3.9 | 12.6 | 10.80 | 0.17 | 0.97 | 6.2 |
| Cottonseed Meal − 41% (Direct Solvent) | 90.4 | 41.0 | 2.1 | 11.3 | NA | 0.16 | 1.0 | 6.4 |
| Cottonseed Hull | 90.4 | 4.0 | 4.4 | 43.0 | NA | 0.14 | 0.09 | 2.5 |
| Crab Meal | 95.0 | 30.0 | 2.2 | 10.5 | NA | 18.0 | 1.5 | 31.0 |
| Distillers D.grains w/Solubles | 91.2 | 29.0 | 8.4 | 7.8 | 15.72 | 0.27 | 0.78 | 4.3 |
| Fat, Animal | 99.5 | 0.0 | 99.4 | − | 34.79 | − | − | − |
| Fat, Vegetable | 99.5 | 0.0 | 99.4 | − | NA | − | − | − |
| Feather Meal, Poultry | 93.2 | 85.0 | 2.5 | 1.5 | 10.0 | 0.2 | 0.7 | 3.9 |
| Fish Meal (AAFCO) | 88.4 | 59.0 | 5.6 | 1.0 | 10.17 | 5.5 | 3.3 | 20.2 |
| Fish Meal, Herring (Atlantic) | 93.0 | 72.0 | 10.0 | 1.0 | 11.01 | 2.0 | 1.0 | 10.4 |
| Fish Meal, Menhaden | 92.0 | 62.0 | 10.2 | 1.0 | 9.82 | 5.0 | 3.0 | 20.0 |
| Fish Meal, Anchovie (Peruvian) | 91.0 | 65.0 | 10.0 | 1.0 | 10.79 | 4.0 | 2.85 | 15.0 |
| Fish Meal, Red Fish | 92.0 | 57.0 | 8.0 | 1.0 | 11.23 | 7.7 | 3.8 | 26.0 |
| Fish Meal, Sardine | 92.0 | 65.0 | 5.5 | 1.0 | 11.01 | 4.5 | 2.7 | 16.0 |
| Fish Meal, Tuna | 93.0 | 60.0 | 7.0 | 1.0 | 11.01 | 8.9 | 4.7 | 23.0 |
| Fish Meal, White | 91.0 | 61.0 | 4.0 | 1.0 | 10.83 | 7.0 | 3.5 | 24.0 |
| Fish Meal, Freshwater, Alewife | 90.0 | 65.7 | 12.8 | 1.0 | 14.71 | 5.2 | 2.9 | 14.6 |
| Fish Meal, Freshwater, Sheepshead | 90.0 | 62.4 | 8.4 | 1.0 | 10.57 | 7.5 | 3.6 | 20.5 |
| Fish Meal, Freshwater, Maria | 91.0 | 66.2 | 6.6 | 1.0 | 13.21 | 6.0 | 3.1 | 16.3 |
| Fish Meal, Freshwater, Tullibee | 89.0 | 68.2 | 7.8 | 1.0 | 14.75 | 5.0 | 2.7 | 13.8 |
| Fish Solubles, Condensed | 51.0 | 31.0 | 4.0 | 0.5 | 6.17 | 0.1 | 0.5 | 10.0 |
| Fish Solubles, Dehy | 93.0 | 40.0 | 6.0 | 5.5 | 14.05 | 0.4 | 1.2 | 12.5 |
| Hominy Feed, Corn Expeller | 89.0 | 11.5 | 6.5 | 5.0 | 14.82 | 0.05 | 0.5 | 3.0 |
| Kafir Grain Sorghum | 89.5 | 11.8 | 2.9 | 2.0 | 12.74 | 0.04 | 0.33 | 1.5 |
| Kelp Meal, Dehy | 91.3 | 6.5 | 0.5 | 7.0 | NA | 2.5 | 0.21 | 35.2 |
| Linseed Meal Flax (Expeller) | 90.0 | 32.0 | 3.5 | 9.5 | 10.57 | 0.4 | 0.8 | 6.0 |
| Linseed Meal Flax (Solvent) | 88.3 | 33.0 | 0.5 | 9.5 | 8.81 | 0.35 | 0.75 | 6.0 |
| Malt Sprouts, Barley Dried | 92.3 | 25.0 | 1.2 | 15.0 | 6.19 | 0.2 | 0.7 | 7.0 |
| Meat and Bone Meal (45%) | 92.4 | 45.0 | 8.5 | 2.5 | 10.79 | 11.0 | 5.9 | 37.0 |
| Meat and Bone Meal (50%) | 92.6 | 50.0 | 8.5 | 2.8 | 10.72 | 9.2 | 4.7 | 33.0 |
| Meat Meal (55%) | 92.8 | 55.0 | 7.2 | 2.5 | 11.19 | 7.6 | 4.0 | 25.0 |
| Milk, Whole, Dried, Feed Grade | 96.2 | 25.5 | 26.7 | 0.1 | NA | 0.9 | 0.72 | 5.6 |
| Millet Grain | 90.0 | 11.5 | 3.6 | 6.5 | 12.69 | 0.05 | 0.3 | 3.2 |
| Molasses, Beet | 78.5 | 7.6 | 0 | 0 | NA | 0.1 | 0.02 | 10.5 |
| Molasses, Cane | 73.5 | 2.9 | 0 | 0 | 10.32 | 0.82 | 0.08 | 8.1 |
| Molasses, Cane, Dried | 91.0 | 7.0 | 0.5 | 9.0 | 11.28 | 1.18 | 0.9 | 8.0 |

| | | | | | AMINO ACIDS | | | | | | |
|---|---|---|---|---|---|---|---|---|---|---|---|
| Methi-onine % | Cystine % | Lysine % | Trypto-phane % | Threo-nine % | Iso-leucine % | Histi-dine % | Valine % | Leucine % | Arginine % | Phenyl-alanine % | Glycine % |
| 0.52 | 0.64 | 1.71 | 0.47 | 1.32 | 1.33 | 1.10 | 1.88 | 2.4 | 4.59 | 2.22 | 1.70 |
| 0.55 | 0.59 | 1.59 | 0.5 | 1.30 | 1.31 | 1.07 | 1.84 | 2.5 | 4.33 | 2.20 | 1.69 |
| 0.51 | 0.62 | 1.76 | 0.52 | 1.34 | 1.33 | 1.10 | 1.82 | 2.4 | 4.66 | 2.23 | 1.69 |
| – | – | – | – | – | – | – | – | – | – | – | – |
| 0.5 | 0.2 | 1.4 | 0.3 | 1.2 | 1.2 | 0.5 | 1.5 | 1.6 | 1.7 | 1.2 | 1.8 |
| 0.46 | 0.52 | 0.81 | 0.2 | 1.12 | 1.93 | 0.81 | 1.83 | 2.34 | 1.12 | 1.93 | NA |
| – | – | – | – | – | – | – | – | – | – | – | – |
| – | – | – | – | – | – | – | – | – | – | – | – |
| 0.55 | 3.0 | 1.05 | 0.4 | 2.8 | 2.66 | 0.28 | 4.55 | 7.8 | 3.92 | 2.66 | 4.76 |
| 1.72 | 0.57 | 5.17 | 0.67 | 2.49 | 3.64 | 1.53 | 3.26 | 4.69 | 3.73 | 2.68 | 3.93 |
| 2.2 | 0.72 | 5.7 | 0.8 | 2.88 | 3.00 | 1.91 | 5.7 | 5.1 | 5.64 | 2.56 | 4.6 |
| 1.8 | 0.6 | 4.7 | 0.72 | 2.34 | 2.83 | 1.44 | 3.43 | 5.0 | 3.23 | 2.28 | 3.88 |
| 1.9 | 0.6 | 4.9 | 0.75 | 2.7 | 3.0 | 1.5 | 3.4 | 5.0 | 3.38 | 2.39 | 4.07 |
| 1.8 | 0.4 | 6.6 | 0.6 | 2.6 | 3.5 | 1.3 | 3.3 | 4.9 | 4.1 | 2.5 | 4.0 |
| 2.0 | 0.8 | 5.9 | 0.5 | 2.6 | 3.3 | 1.8 | 3.4 | 3.8 | 2.7 | 2.0 | 4.5 |
| 1.5 | 0.4 | 3.9 | 0.71 | 2.5 | 2.4 | 1.8 | 2.8 | 3.8 | 3.2 | 2.5 | 4.3 |
| 1.65 | 0.75 | 4.3 | 0.70 | 2.6 | 3.1 | 1.93 | 3.25 | 4.5 | 4.2 | 2.8 | 2.7 |
| 1.93 | 0.47 | 5.49 | 0.63 | 3.29 | 3.4 | 1.93 | 3.58 | 4.8 | 4.69 | 2.91 | 3.7 |
| 1.64 | 0.36 | 5.24 | 0.51 | 2.79 | 2.87 | 1.71 | 3.09 | 4.6 | 4.95 | 2.5 | 4.45 |
| 1.89 | 0.49 | 5.96 | 0.59 | 3.18 | 3.11 | 1.98 | 3.41 | 4.9 | 4.71 | 2.83 | 5.04 |
| 1.95 | 0.45 | 6.22 | 0.65 | 3.27 | 3.3 | 2.19 | 3.5 | 4.9 | 4.47 | 3.02 | 4.71 |
| 0.45 | 0.19 | 1.46 | 0.11 | 0.7 | 0.7 | 1.09 | 1.0 | 1.6 | 1.37 | 0.7 | 2.74 |
| 0.64 | 0.5 | 2.6 | 2.3 | 1.1 | 1.2 | 0.9 | 1.6 | 2.6 | 1.8 | 1.3 | 2.8 |
| 0.22 | 0.12 | 0.45 | 0.12 | 0.43 | 0.38 | 0.36 | 0.59 | 0.9 | 0.6 | 0.4 | 0.28 |
| 0.18 | 0.14 | 0.27 | 0.18 | 0.45 | 0.54 | 0.27 | 0.63 | 1.6 | 0.35 | 0.63 | 0.3 |
| NA | NA | NA | NA | NA | NA | NA | NA | NA | NA | NA | NA |
| 0.47 | 0.56 | 1.1 | 0.47 | 1.1 | 1.7 | 0.6 | 1.5 | 1.9 | 2.6 | 1.4 | 1.6 |
| 0.48 | 0.58 | 1.1 | 0.48 | 1.2 | 1.8 | 0.7 | 1.6 | 2.0 | 2.7 | 1.5 | 1.7 |
| 0.32 | 0.23 | 1.1 | 0.41 | NA | NA | NA | NA | NA | 1.0 | NA | NA |
| 0.53 | 0.26 | 2.2 | 0.18 | 1.8 | 1.7 | 1.5 | 2.4 | 2.9 | 2.7 | 1.8 | 6.5 |
| 0.67 | 0.33 | 2.6 | 0.26 | 1.63 | 1.7 | 0.96 | 2.25 | 3.2 | 3.35 | 1.7 | 6.9 |
| 0.75 | 0.68 | 3.0 | 0.35 | 1.8 | 1.9 | 1.1 | 2.6 | 3.5 | 3.7 | 1.9 | 6.3 |
| 0.62 | 0.4 | 2.26 | 0.41 | 1.03 | 1.33 | 0.72 | 1.74 | 2.57 | 0.92 | 1.33 | NA |
| 0.28 | 0.2 | 0.23 | 0.17 | 0.36 | 0.45 | 0.18 | 0.54 | 1.1 | 0.33 | 0.54 | 0.3 |
| – | – | – | – | – | – | – | – | – | – | – | – |
| – | – | – | – | – | – | – | – | – | – | – | – |
| – | – | – | – | – | – | – | – | – | – | – | – |

| Ingredients | Dry Matter % | Crude Protein % | Crude Fat % | Crude Fibre % | MJ DE/kg | Calcium % | Total Phos. % | Ash % |
|---|---|---|---|---|---|---|---|---|
| Molasses, Citrus | 67.7 | 5.7 | 0.2 | – | 9.97 | 1.2 | 0.12 | 5.4 |
| Molasses, Starch, Corn | 73.0 | 0.05 | – | – | NA | 0.1 | 0.6 | 8.0 |
| Molasses, Wood | 66.0 | 0.7 | 0.3 | 0.7 | 10.07 | 0.52 | 0.05 | 4.0 |
| Oats, Grain | 90.0 | 11.0 | 4.0 | 10.5 | 11.75 | 0.1 | 0.35 | 4.0 |
| Oats, Grain, Pacific Coast | 90.0 | 9.8 | 4.5 | 10.5 | 12.64 | 0.09 | 0.33 | 4.0 |
| Oat Groats (Dehulled Oats) | 92.2 | 16.0 | 6.0 | 2.6 | 15.01 | 0.07 | 0.45 | 2.2 |
| Oat Hulls | 93.0 | 5.0 | 2.0 | 30.0 | 3.30 | 0.16 | 0.19 | 10.0 |
| Pea Seed, Cull | 91.0 | 22.0 | 1.0 | 6.0 | 14.09 | 0.17 | 0.32 | 2.8 |
| Peanut Meal (Solvent) | 91.5 | 48.0 | 1.5 | 6.8 | 10.72 | 0.29 | 0.65 | 7.2 |
| Peanut Meal and Hulls (Mech Extd) | 91.8 | 45.0 | 5.0 | 12.0 | 14.09 | 0.15 | 0.55 | 5.8 |
| Peanut Meal and Hulls (Solvent) | 92.3 | 47.0 | 1.0 | 13.0 | 12.86 | 0.20 | 0.60 | 4.8 |
| Poultry By-Product Meal | 94.0 | 58.0 | 14.0 | 2.5 | 12.07 | 4.0 | 2.4 | 16.0 |
| Poultry Manure, Dried (Cage) | 88.6 | 28.7 | 1.7 | 14.9 | NA | 7.8 | 2.2 | 26.5 |
| Poultry Manure, Dried (Floor) | 84.5 | 25.3 | 2.3 | 18.6 | NA | 2.5 | 1.6 | 14.1 |
| Rapeseed Oil Meal (Expeller) | 94.0 | 36.0 | 6.7 | 12.2 | 11.76 | 0.71 | 1.0 | 6.8 |
| Rapeseed Oil Meal (Solvent) | 92.0 | 36.0 | 2.6 | 13.2 | 11.89 | 0.66 | 0.93 | 7.2 |
| Rapeseed Meal (PrePress Solvent) | 91.2 | 38.0 | 3.8 | 11.1 | 11.89 | 0.68 | 1.17 | 7.2 |
| Rice Bran (Solvent) | 91.0 | 13.5 | 0.6 | 13.0 | 9.69 | 0.1 | 1.7 | 11.0 |
| Rice Polishings | 89.8 | 11.0 | 12.0 | 4.0 | 13.21 | 0.04 | 1.4 | 11.0 |
| Rice, Grain, Rough | 89.0 | 7.3 | 1.7 | 10.0 | 10.39 | 0.04 | 0.26 | 4.5 |
| Rye, Grain | 88.6 | 12.6 | 1.85 | 2.8 | 11.94 | 0.08 | 0.3 | 1.45 |
| Safflower Seed Meal (Expeller) | 91.0 | 20.0 | 6.6 | 32.2 | 10.72 | 0.23 | 0.61 | 3.7 |
| Safflower Seed Meal (Solvent) | 90.0 | 22.0 | 0.5 | 37.0 | 10.68 | 0.34 | 0.84 | 5.0 |
| Safflower Seed Meal (Solvent) | 90.8 | 42.0 | 1.3 | 15.1 | NA | 0.4 | 1.25 | 7.8 |
| Sesame Meal (Expeller) | 93.6 | 42.0 | 7.0 | 6.5 | 11.28 | 2.0 | 1.3 | 12.0 |
| Skim Milk, Dried | 91.6 | 33.0 | 0.5 | 0.0 | 14.80 | 1.25 | 1.0 | 8.0 |
| Sorghum, Gluten Feed | 88.0 | 24.0 | 3.2 | 9.0 | 14.01 | 0.15 | 0.65 | 8.0 |
| Sorghum Gluten Meal | 90.0 | 42.0 | 4.3 | 3.5 | 13.60 | 0.04 | 0.3 | 1.8 |
| Sorghum, Milo, Grain | 88.8 | 11.0 | 2.8 | 2.0 | 14.22 | 0.04 | 0.29 | 1.7 |
| Soybeans, Full-Fat Cooked | 90.0 | 38.0 | 18.0 | 5.0 | 15.59 | 0.25 | 0.59 | 4.6 |
| Soybean Meal (Expeller) | 89.0 | 42.0 | 3.5 | 6.5 | 13.17 | 0.2 | 0.6 | 6.0 |
| Soybean Meal (Solvent) | 89.6 | 44.0 | 0.5 | 7.0 | 12.44 | 0.25 | 0.6 | 6.0 |
| Soybean Meal Dehulled (Solvent) | 89.3 | 47.5 | 0.5 | 3.0 | 12.69 | 0.2 | 0.65 | 6.0 |
| Sunflower Meal (Expeller) | 93.0 | 41.0 | 7.6 | 13.0 | 11.96 | 0.43 | 1.0 | 6.8 |
| Sunflower Meal (Solvent) | 93.0 | 42.0 | 2.3 | 13.0 | 11.47 | 0.4 | 1.0 | 7.7 |
| Sunflower Meal Partially Dehulled, (Solvent) | 92.0 | 34.0 | 0.5 | 21.0 | 10.12 | 0.3 | 1.25 | 7.1 |
| Tankage, Meat Meal | 93.7 | 60.0 | 9.0 | 2.0 | 9.03 | 6.0 | 3.0 | 21.0 |
| Tomato, Pulp, Dried | 93.0 | 21.0 | 10.0 | 25.0 | NA | 0.4 | 0.57 | 6.0 |

| AMINO ACIDS | | | | | | | | | | | |
|---|---|---|---|---|---|---|---|---|---|---|---|
| Methionine % | Cystine % | Lysine % | Tryptophane % | Threonine % | Isoleucine % | Histidine % | Valine % | Leucine % | Arginine % | Phenylalanine % | Glycine % |
| – | – | – | – | – | – | – | – | – | – | – | – |
| – | – | – | – | – | – | – | – | – | – | – | – |
| – | – | – | – | – | – | – | – | – | – | – | – |
| 0.2 | 0.21 | 0.4 | 0.18 | 0.28 | 0.53 | 0.18 | 0.62 | 0.9 | 0.8 | 0.62 | 0.54 |
| 0.14 | 0.18 | 0.38 | 0.12 | 0.28 | 0.37 | 0.15 | 0.48 | 0.7 | 0.6 | 0.42 | 0.4 |
| 0.2 | 0.26 | 0.45 | 0.18 | 0.5 | 0.5 | 0.25 | 0.65 | 1.0 | 0.9 | 0.65 | 0.6 |
| 0.1 | – | 0.2 | 0.1 | 0.2 | 0.2 | 0.1 | 0.1 | NA | 0.15 | 0.2 | – |
| 0.2 | 0.3 | 1.2 | 0.2 | NA | NA | NA | NA | NA | 2.1 | NA | NA |
| 0.42 | 0.73 | 1.77 | 0.5 | 1.16 | 1.76 | 0.95 | 1.88 | 2.7 | 4.55 | 2.04 | 2.35 |
| 0.41 | 0.68 | 1.55 | 0.46 | 1.4 | 1.8 | 1.1 | 2.6 | 3.6 | 4.7 | 2.6 | 2.3 |
| 0.43 | 0.7 | 1.6 | 0.48 | 1.5 | 2.0 | 1.2 | 2.8 | 3.7 | 4.9 | 2.7 | 2.4 |
| 1.04 | 1.0 | 2.57 | 0.55 | 2.03 | 2.33 | 1.61 | 2.65 | 4.4 | 3.84 | 1.79 | 2.93 |
| 0.12 | 0.15 | 0.39 | 0.53 | 0.35 | 0.36 | 0.23 | 0.46 | 0.8 | 0.38 | 0.35 | 1.33 |
| 0.13 | 0.14 | 0.49 | NA | 0.52 | 0.58 | 0.2 | 0.74 | 0.7 | 0.43 | 0.49 | 2.55 |
| 0.68 | 0.4 | 1.69 | 0.36 | 1.49 | 1.34 | 0.89 | 1.71 | 2.4 | 1.88 | 1.35 | 1.7 |
| 0.67 | 0.54 | 2.12 | 0.46 | 1.6 | 1.41 | 0.95 | 1.81 | 2.6 | 2.04 | 1.41 | 1.85 |
| 0.7 | 0.47 | 2.3 | 0.44 | 1.71 | 1.51 | 1.1 | 1.94 | 2.6 | 2.3 | 1.5 | 1.9 |
| 0.17 | 0.1 | 0.5 | 0.1 | 0.4 | 0.39 | 0.25 | 0.6 | 1.2 | 0.45 | 0.41 | 1.0 |
| 0.18 | 0.1 | 0.49 | 0.14 | 0.34 | 0.33 | 0.19 | 0.68 | 1.1 | 0.59 | 0.35 | 0.68 |
| 0.14 | 0.08 | 0.24 | 0.12 | 0.27 | 0.33 | 0.16 | 0.46 | 0.5 | 0.59 | 0.34 | 0.59 |
| 0.16 | 0.2 | 0.4 | 0.14 | 0.36 | 0.53 | 0.27 | 0.62 | 0.7 | 0.5 | 0.62 | NA |
| 0.4 | 0.5 | 0.7 | 0.3 | 0.47 | 0.28 | 0.48 | 1.0 | 1.1 | 1.2 | 1.0 | 1.1 |
| 0.33 | 0.35 | 0.7 | 0.26 | 0.5 | 0.27 | 0.5 | 1.0 | 1.2 | 1.9 | 1.0 | 1.1 |
| 0.69 | 0.7 | 1.3 | 0.6 | 1.35 | 1.7 | 1.0 | 2.3 | 2.5 | 3.7 | 1.85 | 2.4 |
| 1.48 | 0.6 | 1.37 | 0.82 | 1.71 | 2.28 | 1.16 | 2.53 | 3.3 | 5.06 | 2.32 | 4.43 |
| 0.98 | 0.42 | 2.6 | 0.45 | 1.75 | 2.1 | 0.84 | 2.38 | 3.3 | 1.1 | 1.58 | 0.2 |
| 0.4 | 0.45 | 0.9 | 0.2 | 0.8 | 1.0 | 0.8 | 1.3 | 2.5 | 0.8 | 1.0 | NA |
| 0.75 | 0.8 | 0.8 | 0.4 | 1.4 | 2.3 | 1.4 | 2.5 | 7.4 | 1.4 | 2.6 | NA |
| 0.1 | 0.2 | 0.27 | 0.09 | 0.27 | 0.6 | 0.27 | 0.53 | 1.4 | 0.4 | 0.45 | 0.3 |
| 0.54 | 0.55 | 2.40 | 0.52 | 1.69 | 2.18 | 1.01 | 2.02 | 2.8 | 2.80 | 2.10 | 2.00 |
| 0.6 | 0.62 | 2.7 | 0.65 | 1.7 | 2.8 | 1.1 | 2.2 | 3.8 | 3.2 | 2.1 | 2.3 |
| 0.65 | 0.67 | 2.9 | 0.7 | 1.7 | 2.5 | 1.1 | 2.4 | 3.4 | 3.4 | 2.2 | 2.4 |
| 0.75 | 0.74 | 3.2 | 0.6 | 2.0 | 2.6 | 1.3 | 2.7 | 3.8 | 3.8 | 2.7 | 2.3 |
| 1.6 | 0.8 | 2.0 | 0.6 | 1.6 | 2.4 | 1.1 | 2.4 | 2.5 | 4.2 | 2.4 | 2.9 |
| 1.5 | 0.7 | 1.7 | 0.5 | 1.5 | 2.1 | 1.0 | 2.3 | 2.6 | 3.5 | 2.2 | 2.7 |
| 0.64 | 0.55 | 1.42 | 0.35 | 1.48 | 1.39 | 1.51 | 1.64 | 2.58 | 2.8 | 1.61 | 2.22 |
| 0.8 | 0.5 | 3.8 | 0.65 | 2.4 | 1.9 | 1.9 | 4.2 | 5.1 | 3.6 | 2.7 | 5.1 |
| 0.1 | – | 1.6 | 0.2 | 0.7 | 0.7 | 0.4 | 1.0 | 1.7 | 1.2 | 0.9 | – |

| Ingredients | Dry Matter % | Crude Protein % | Crude Fat % | Crude Fibre % | MJ DE/kg | Calcium % | Total Phos. % | Ash % |
|---|---|---|---|---|---|---|---|---|
| Wheat, Hard, Grain | 88.0 | 13.5 | 1.9 | 3.0 | 14.18 | 0.05 | 0.41 | 2.0 |
| Wheat, Soft, Grain | 86.0 | 10.8 | 1.7 | 2.8 | 15.05 | 0.05 | 0.3 | 2.0 |
| Wheat Bran | 89.0 | 14.8 | 4.0 | 10.0 | 10.22 | 0.14 | 1.17 | 6.4 |
| Wheat Shorts | 89.0 | 16.8 | 4.2 | 8.2 | 12.82 | 0.11 | 0.76 | 8.2 |
| Wheat Germ Meal | 88.0 | 25.0 | 7.0 | 3.5 | 10.57 | 0.01 | 1.0 | 5.3 |
| Wheat Middlings | 89.0 | 17.7 | 3.6 | 7.0 | 8.81 | 0.15 | 0.91 | 5.5 |
| Wheat Grain Screenings #1 | 89.0 | 14.8 | 2.6 | 6.2 | 10.57 | 0.18 | 0.43 | 2.1 |
| Wheat Grain Screenings #2 | 91.5 | 12.5 | 3.9 | 7.6 | 9.25 | 0.13 | 0.32 | 4.3 |
| Wheat Refuse Screenings | 91.0 | 12.4 | 4.5 | 13.4 | 6.74 | 0.23 | 0.29 | 10.3 |
| Whey Low Lactose, Dried | 94.0 | 17.0 | 1.0 | 0.0 | 12.11 | 1.5 | 1.2 | 19.0 |
| Whey, Dried | 94.0 | 12.0 | 0.7 | 0.0 | 14.05 | 0.87 | 0.79 | 9.7 |
| Yeast Culture | 93.0 | 14.0 | 3.5 | 6.0 | 13.63 | 0.28 | 0.71 | 4.0 |
| Yeast, Torula Dried | 93.2 | 48.5 | 2.0 | 2.7 | 10.66 | 0.5 | 1.6 | 8.0 |

| | | | | | AMINO ACIDS | | | | | | | |
|---|---|---|---|---|---|---|---|---|---|---|---|
| Methi-onine % | Cystine % | Lysine % | Trypto-phane % | Threo-nine % | Iso-leucine % | Histi-dine % | Valine % | Leucine % | Arginine % | Phenyl-alanine % | Glycine % |
| 0.25 | 0.3 | 0.4 | 0.18 | 0.35 | 0.69 | 0.17 | 0.69 | 1.0 | 0.6 | 0.78 | 0.6 |
| 0.14 | 0.2 | 0.3 | 0.12 | 0.28 | 0.43 | 0.20 | 0.48 | 0.6 | 0.4 | 0.49 | 0.5 |
| 0.2 | 0.3 | 0.6 | 0.3 | 0.48 | 0.6 | 0.3 | 0.7 | 0.9 | 1.07 | 0.57 | 0.9 |
| 0.18 | 0.25 | 0.7 | 0.23 | 0.5 | 0.7 | 0.32 | 0.77 | 1.0 | 0.95 | 0.7 | 0.98 |
| 0.42 | 0.46 | 1.37 | 0.3 | 0.94 | 0.79 | 0.62 | 1.12 | 1.1 | 1.83 | 0.93 | 1.38 |
| 0.12 | 0.19 | 0.6 | 0.2 | 0.5 | 0.7 | 0.4 | 0.8 | 1.1 | 1.0 | 0.5 | 0.35 |
| 0.17 | 0.2 | 0.4 | 0.1 | 0.3 | 0.47 | 0.2 | 0.54 | 0.8 | 0.6 | 0.7 | 0.54 |
| 0.12 | 0.1 | 0.48 | 0.1 | 0.3 | 0.42 | 0.26 | 0.53 | 0.6 | 0.82 | 0.4 | 0.46 |
| 0.15 | NA | 0.3 | NA | 0.4 | 0.4 | 0.2 | 0.58 | 1.0 | 0.6 | 0.5 | 0.54 |
| 0.57 | 0.57 | 1.47 | 0.36 | 0.86 | 1.07 | 0.33 | 0.94 | 1.7 | 0.59 | 0.72 | 1.04 |
| 0.2 | 0.3 | 1.1 | 0.2 | 0.8 | 0.9 | 0.2 | 0.7 | 1.2 | 0.4 | 0.4 | NA |
| 0.34 | 0.25 | 0.65 | 0.13 | 0.6 | 0.71 | 0.45 | 0.81 | NA | 0.85 | 0.67 | 0.7 |
| 0.8 | 0.6 | 3.8 | 0.5 | 2.6 | 2.9 | 1.4 | 2.9 | 3.5 | 2.6 | 3.0 | 2.7 |

# APPENDIX 2

## Glossary of terms (adapted from ARC, 1981)

**Absorption**   The process of uptake of a nutrient from the lumen of the gastro-intestinal tract by the outermost cells of the walls of the tract.

**Ad libitum feeding**   The system in which the feed supply is unrestricted at all times. The feed is usually given dry. Synonymous with self-feeding.

**Allowance**   The amount of a nutrient which is given in the diet to meet under practical conditions the estimated daily **Requirement** of the animal. A margin of safety is included to allow for factors which cannot readily be quantitatively defined.

**Apparent digestibility**   The amount of a nutrient ingested over a period of time minus the amount of that nutrient voided in the faeces over that time, including any endogenous component of faecal loss, expressed as a decimal of nutrient ingested:

$$\frac{\text{Apparent digestibility}}{\text{of a nutrient}} = \frac{\text{Amount ingested} - \text{Amount in faeces}}{\text{Amount ingested}}$$

**Available amino acids**   The proportion of the total dietary amino acids that is not combined with compounds which interfere with its digestion, absorption or utilisation by the animal, i.e. that amino acid that can be digested, absorbed and utilised by the animal consuming it, for the purpose of maintenance or growth of new tissue.

**Calorie (cal.)**   The amount of heat required to raise the temperature of 1 g water from $14.5°$ to $15.5°C$. Now obsolete and superseded herein by the joule (J); 4.184 joules are equivalent to 1 cal. See **Joule (J)**.

**Cold carcass weight**   The weight of the cold eviscerated carcass from which the head, backbone, feet and kidneys have not been removed.

**Critical temperature**   Environmental temperature below which extra heat is required to maintain body temperature, heat loss is increased and less energy is available for growth purposes. The zone of thermoneutrality is the range of environmental temperature over which heat loss or heat production is minimal and independent of environmental temperature. The lower end of this zone is termed the lower critical temperature and the upper end the upper critical temperature.

**Digestion**   Process by which macromolecules in feedstuffs are hydrolysed in the digestive tract before absoprtion through the intestinal wall.

**Digestible energy (DE)**   The gross energy (or heat of combustion) of a feed minus the gross energy of the corresponding faeces, expressed as MJ or kJ/kg total feed. Usually DE = 0.75 to 0.80 **GE**.

**Dressing percentage**   The weight of the cold eviscerated carcass, including head, backbone, feet and kidneys, expressed as a percentage of the liveweight shortly before slaughter. Synonymous with killing-out percentage. (Note: dressing percentage is sometimes defined as the percentage of the eviscerated carcass put into bacon-curing tanks after trimming, which includes removal of the head, feet and kidneys. This definition has not been used herein.)

**Empty body weight**   The weight of the entire animal less the weight of the **contents** of the whole digestive tract.

**Endogenous loss (urinary and faecal)**   That amount of a nutrient which originates from the tissues of the animal and is excreted in the urine or faeces, or in both. It may consist in part of the **Obligatory loss** of the nutrient and in part of an excess of the nutrient that has been absorbed but not utilised.

**Essential amino acids**  Those amino acids which are not synthesized in the tissues of the animal, or otherwise made available to the animal in amounts sufficient to meet the requirements of the animal and which must therefore be present in the feed.

**Ether extract**  The group of chemical substances that are soluble in, and extracted by, ether. Whether diethyl ether or 40:60 petroleum ether is used should always be specified. Not necessarily synonymous with **Lipid** (see **Lipids**).

**Eye muscle (M. longissimus dorsi)**  Linear and area measurements of the cross section of the eye muscle are normally measured at the point where the carcass is cut at right angles to the backbone at the level of the posterior edge of the head of the last complete rib.

**Fat**  Used to describe the fatty **tissues** of the body in contrast to fat in the strictly chemical sense (see **Lipids**). Normally contains 0.80 to 0.90 **Lipid** in a 90-kg liveweight pig. Feeds such as tallow are strictly neither fat nor lipid as herein defined but by convention are termed fats.

**Fat deposition**  Lipid laid down by the animal; it has an average **Gross energy** of 39.6 MJ/kg.

**Gross energy (GE)**  The heat of combustion of unit weight of material (feed, excreta, etc.) as determined with a bomb calorimeter.

**Ideal protein**  The composition of dietary protein in terms of the proportions of amino acids when the addition of any one amino acid does not increase nitrogen retention in an animal capable of responding.

**Joule (J)**  SI (Systeme Internationale d'Unites) unit of energy. 4.184 J = 1 calorie.

**Kilojoule (kJ)**  $10^3$ joules.

**Lean tissue**  The skeletal muscle of the carcass, excluding that of the head, hocks and *m. panniculus*, with all visible subcutaneous and intermuscular fatty tissue removed by dissection.

**Lipids**  The group of chemical substances that are soluble in, and extracted by, chloroform: methanol. Not necessarily synonymous with **Ether extract** since some lipids are not extractable with ether.

**Maintenance**  At the maintenance level of feeding, the requirements of the animal for nutrients for the continuity of vital processes within the body, including the replacement of obligatory losses in faeces and urine and from the skin, are just met so that the net gain or loss of nutrients and other tissue substances by the animal as a whole is zero.

**Megajoule (MJ)**  $10^6$ joules.

**Metabolic faecal nitrogen (MFN)**  The nitrogen, other than the undigested feed nitrogen, which is excreted in the faeces, including **Obligatory faecal nitrogen losses**. It can arise from the unabsorbed constituents of the digestive juices, from cellular debris and mucus derived from the gastic and intestinal mucosa, from microorganisms and from nitrogenous compounds excreted into the gut.

**Metabolisable energy (ME)**  The digestible energy (DE) of a unit weight of feed less the heats of combustion of the corresponding urine and gaseous products of digestion. With pigs the gaseous products are usually considered to be insignificant ($<0.006$ gross energy intake) and are ignored. At the maintenance level of feeding, ME, by definition, equals the daily heat production. Often taken that ME = 0.96 **DE**.

**Muscle**  Used here to describe all muscle tissues of the body. Normally contains on average $0.19-0.23$ crude protein, $0.03-0.06$ lipids and $0.72-0.76$ moisture in a 90-kg liveweight pig.

**Net energy (NE)**  The energy value of product formed, or of body substance saved at or below maintenance, per unit weight of feed consumed. It is ME less the **Heat**

**increment**. NE value of a feed is not identical in pigs and ruminants, nor is it equal for maintenance and production. Thus it must be defined according to the type of animal and the physiological processes for which the feed is being used.

**Nitrogen retention (NR)**   The net gain of nitrogen (N) by the animal. NR = N in feed − (N in faeces + N in urine) − loss of ammonia in the air (usually 0.03−0.05 of N in feed). **Protein retention** is usually taken as being N retention × 6.25.

**Obligatory loss (urinary and faecal)**   That amount of a nutrient that has undergone metabolic change in the animal body and which is unavoidably excreted in the urine or faeces, or in both, irrespective of the presence or absence of that nutrient in the diet. The actual magnitude of the **Obligatory loss** of a given nutrient may be affected by the level of its intake and that of other nutrients in the diet.

**Protein (crude)**   Estimated protein content derived from chemically determined total nitrogen content. Since many proteins of animal origin have historically been found to contain c. 16% nitrogen by weight, **crude protein** is usually defined as total nitrogen × 6.25. For milk protein, however, the factor generally adopted is 6.38, while for dissected pig lean a different factor (of the order of 5.2) appears to be appropriate.

**Protein (true)**   That material consisting of 51 or more amino acids combined together through peptide bonds.

**Protein deposition**   Protein laid down by the animal; it has an average **Gross energy** of 23.7 MJ/kg.

**Protein-sparing effect**   Sparing the oxidation of protein to provide energy.

**Requirement**   The **Requirement** for any given nutrient is the amount of that nutrient which must be supplied in the diet to meet the **Requirement (Net)**.

**Requirement (Net)**   The quantity of a nutrient that should be absorbed by a normal healthy animal given a completely adequate diet in an environment compatible with good health in order to meet its needs for maintenance, including the replacement of obligatory losses, and for a stated rate of production or for reproduction.

**Total digestible nutrients (TDN)**   The sum of the amounts by weight in 1 kg feed of: (1) apparently digestible crude protein, (2) apparently digestible nitrogen-free extractives, (3) apparently digestible crude fibre and (4) 2.25 × the apparently digestible ether extract, expressed as a decimal. (1 kg of TDN is often taken as providing 18.4 MJ of **apparently digestible energy**.)

**True digestibility (TD)**   That proportion of a nutrient that has been ingested (in the feed) and absorbed, without reference to its subsequent fate, expressed as a decimal of nutrient ingested:

$$TD = \frac{\text{Amount ingested} - (\text{Amount in faeces} - \text{Endogenous faecal loss})}{\text{Amount ingested}}$$

# Index

# Index

# FARMING PRESS BOOKS & VIDEOS

Below is a sample of the wide range of agricultural and
veterinary books and videos we publish.
For more information or for a free illustrated catalogue
of all our publications please contact:

**Farming Press Books & Videos
Miller Freeman Professional Ltd
Wharfedale Road, Ipswich IP1 4LG, United Kingdom
Telephone (01473) 241122    Fax (01473) 240501**

## Stockmanship

*English, Burgess, Segundo, Dunne*

Gives a full account of the factors
influencing the quality of stockmanship
on the farrm.

## Pig Diseases

*David Taylor*

A new edition of this detailed technical
reference book about pig diseases for
the veterinary surgeon and pig unit
manager.

## Housing the Pig

*Gerry Brent*

Management standards and layouts for
all classes of stock, integrated systems
and ancillary services.

## Outdoor Pig Production

*Keith Thornton*

How to plan, set up and run a unit.

## Practical Outdoor Pig Production (video)

*Keith Thornton*

Film of three different units shows the
main factors to be considered when
setting up or running an outdoor pig
enterprise.

## Pigman's Handbook

Gerry Brent

Describes in detail the best routines for
the day-to-day running of a pig farm.

## Economics of Pig Production

*Bob Ridgeon*

A detailed survey of pig production
as monitored by the Cambridge Pig
Management Scheme over the period
1946–91.

Farming Press Books & Videos is a division of Miller Freeman Professional Ltd
which provides a wide range of media services in agriculture and allied businesses.
Among the magazines published by the group are *Arable Farming*, *Dairy Farmer*,
*Farming News*, *Pig Farming* and *What's New in Farming*. For a specimen copy of
any of these please contact the address above.